QA

E26
1979

Second Edition

MINICOMPUTER SYSTEMS

Organization, Programming, and Applications (PDP-11)

Richard H. Eckhouse, Jr.

*Research and Development Group,
Digital Equipment Corporation,
Maynard, Massachusetts*

L. Robert Morris

*Department of Systems Engineering
and Computing Science,
Carleton University,
Ottawa, Ontario*

PRENTICE-HALL, INC. ENGLEWOOD CLIFFS, NEW JERSEY 07632

Library of Congress Cataloging in Publication Data

ECKHOUSE, RICHARD H
  Minicomputer systems.

  Bibliography: p.
  Includes index.
    1. PDP-11 (Computer)–Programming.   2. Minicomputers
  Programming.   I. Morris, L. Robert, joint author.
  II. Title.
  QA76.8.P2E26 1979   001.6′4′04   79-267
  ISBN 0-13-583914-9

© 1979 by Prentice-Hall, Inc., Englewood Cliffs, N.J.   07632

Editorial/production supervision
    by Marianne Thomma Baltzell
Cover design by Suzanne Behnke
Cover art by Beverly Pope
Cover concept by Bob Morris
Manufacturing buyer: Gordon Osbourne

Printed in the United States of America

10 9 8 7 6 5

PRENTICE-HALL INTERNATIONAL, INC., *London*
PRENTICE-HALL OF AUSTRALIA PTY. LIMITED, *Sydney*
PRENTICE-HALL OF CANADA, LTD., *Toronto*
PRENTICE-HALL OF INDIA PRIVATE LIMITED, *New Delhi*
PRENTICE-HALL OF JAPAN, INC., *Tokyo*
PRENTICE-HALL OF SOUTHEAST ASIA PTE. LTD., *Singapore*
WHITEHALL BOOKS LIMITED, *Wellington, New Zealand*

Contents

PREFACE   xiii

ACKNOWLEDGEMENTS   xix

1 INTRODUCTION   1

    1.1 The Computer Challenge   *2*
    1.2 Computer Applications   *2*
    1.3 Computer Capabilities and Limitations   *4*
    1.4 Computer Architecture, Organization, and Implementation   *4*

2 COMPUTER STRUCTURES: HARDWARE AND SOFTWARE   7

    2.1 Computer Hardware: Basic Elements   *7*
        2.1.1 Arithmetic and Logical Unit   *8*
        2.1.2 Control Unit   *8*
        2.1.3 Memory Unit   *9*
        2.1.4 Input and Output Units   *9*
        2.1.5 Memory Organization   *10*
    2.2 Computer Software: Introduction to Programming   *11*
        2.2.1 Programming Phases   *11*
        2.2.2 Program Definition and Documentation   *12*
        2.2.3 Program Coding   *17*
        2.2.4 The Stored Program Concept   *18*
        2.2.5 Types of Instructions   *18*

iii

2.3 Architectures for Operand Addressing   *19*
    2.3.1 Three-Plus-One and Three-Address Machines   19
    2.3.2 Two-Address Machines   21
    2.3.3 One-Address Machines   22
    2.3.4 General Register Machines   23
    2.3.5 Zero-Address Machines   24
2.4 Address Specification and Manipulation   *26*
    2.4.1 Basic Address Specification   26
    2.4.2 Address Modification   28
    2.4.3 General-Purpose Registers   30
    2.4.4 Immediate Mode   31
    2.4.5 Autoindexing   32
    2.4.6 Deferred Addressing   33
2.5 The Stages of Processing Instructions in a Computer   *35*
    2.5.1 Instruction, Operand, and Execution Phases   35
2.6 The Symbolic Assembler: a Programming Aid   *37*
    2.6.1 The Assembly Process   38
    2.6.2 Location Counter   38
    2.6.3 Symbolic Addresses   39
    2.6.4 Symbolic Programming Syntax   40
    2.6.5 Control Statements   41
Exercises   *42*
References   *44*

3   THE PDP-11   45

3.1 PDP-11 Machine Structure   *46*
    3.1.1 The UNIBUS Concept   46
    3.1.2 Arithmetic and Logical Unit   47
    3.1.3 Fast Arithmetic Processing   47
    3.1.4 Control Unit   48
    3.1.5 Random Access Memory and the Input/Output Page   50
3.2 Data Representation   *51*
    3.2.1 Number Systems   51
    3.2.2 Representation of Numbers in a Computer   53
    3.2.3 Negative Numbers   53
    3.2.4 Fixed-Point (Integer) Numbers   54
    3.3.5 Floating-Point Numbers   55
    3.2.6 Alphanumeric Characters   58
3.3 PDP-11 Instruction Formats and Address Modes   *58*
    3.3.1 Operate Instructions 59
    3.3.2 Single-Operand Instructions   60
    3.3.3 Double-Operand Instructions   66
    3.3.4 Conditional Branches   67
    3.3.5 Use of the PC as a General Purpose Register   69
3.4 The MACRO-11 Assembler   *76*
    3.4.1 Sample Programs 77

3.5 PDP-11 Machine and Memory Hierarchies   *80*
    3.5.1 The Family Concept   80
    3.5.2 Technological Implementations   80
    3.5.3 Compatibility   81
    3.5.4 Instruction Processing Phases   82
    3.5.5 Program Execution Speeds:
      UNIBUS, FASTBUS, and Cache Memories   84
    3.5.6 Memory Extensions: Memory Management and Protection   86
Exercises   *88*
References   *91*

4 PROGRAMMING TECHNIQUES AND PROGRAM STRUCTURES   92

4.1 The Jump Instruction   *92*
    4.1.1 Jump Table Problem   93
4.2 Subroutines   *94*
    4.2.1 The Stack   95
    4.2.2 Subroutine Calls and Returns   96
    4.2.3 Argument Transmission   98
    4.2.4 Subroutine Register Usage   101
4.3 Position-Independent Programming   *102*
    4.3.1 Position-Independent Address Modes   102
    4.3.2 Absolute Modes   104
    4.3.3 Writing Automatic PIC   105
    4.3.4 Writing Nonautomatic PIC   105
4.4 Advanced Subroutine Concepts   *107*
    4.4.1 Reentrancy   107
    4.4.2 Recursion   109
    4.4.3 Coroutines   110
4.5 Macros and Macro Assemblers   *112*
    4.5.1 Location and Created Symbols   113
    4.5.2 Nesting of Macros   114
    4.5.3 Macro Calls Within Macro Definitions   115
    4.5.4 Recursive Calls and Conditional Assembly   116
    4.5.5 Repeat Blocks, Concatenation, and Numeric Arguments   118
    4.5.6 Power of the Macro Assembler:
      VAX-11 Address Modes on the PDP-11   119
Exercises   *123*
References   *127*

5 DATA MANIPULATION AND DATA STRUCTURES   128

5.1 Byte Handling and Character Codes   *128*
5.2 Fixed-point Arithmetic   *129*
    5.2.1 Carry and Overflow   129
    5.2.2 Multiple Precision Addition/Subtraction   131
    5.2.3 Shifting   134

     5.2.4 Multiplication 136
     5.2.5 Division 141
     5.2.6 Expanded Set of Branch Instructions 143
   5.3 Logical Operations *145*
   5.4 Floating-point Arithmetic *146*
     5.4.1 Multiplication/Division 146
     5.4.2 Addition/Subtraction 147
     5.4.3 The Floating Instruction Set (FIS) 147
     5.4.4 The Floating-Point Processor (FPP):
      Architecture and Instruction Set 150
   5.5 Internal and External Data Forms *153*
   5.6 Introduction to Data Structures *154*
     5.6.1 Arrays 155
     5.6.2 Stack, Deques and Queues 160
     5.6.3 Lists 166
     5.6.4 Case Study: the Assembly Process 171
     5.6.5 Data Structures in Practice 177
   Exercises *178*
   References *179*

**6 PDP-11 MICROMACHINE ARCHITECTURE
AND MICROPROGRAMMING 180**

   6.1 Boolean Algebra, Logical Functions,
     Digital Computer Elements 180
     6.1.1 Simple Logical Circuits 181
     6.1.2 Computer Elements 186
   6.2 Introduction to Microprogrammed Machines *190*
     6.2.1 Architecture vs. Organization 191
     6.2.2 Simple Hypothetical Computers and the PDP-11/60 191
   6.3 The PDP-11/60 Datapaths *192*
     6.3.1 Arithmetic and Logical Unit 192
     6.3.2 A and B Scratchpads 193
     6.3.3 C Scratchpad 197
     6.3.4 ALU Input/Output Elements 197
   6.4 The Microcycle *198*
     6.4.1 The Multiple Operation Microinstruction 198
   6.5 Shift Tree and Shift Register: Structure and Use *200*
     6.5.1 Shift Tree 200
     6.5.2 Shift Register 201
     6.5.3 Shifting Summary: Shift Tree vs. Shift Register 202
   6.6 Datapath Input/Output *202*
   6.7 The Residual Control Concept *202*
   6.8 Microinstruction Sequencing and Branch Microtests (BUTS) *203*
     6.8.1 Microbranching 203
     6.8.2 Normal BUT's 204
     6.8.3 Active BUT's: the Counter 204

6.9 Parallelism in Microcoding: the MUL Instruction   *205*
      6.9.1 MUL via D Register Shift Register, and Shift Tree   205
      6.9.2 MUL via D Register and Shift Tree   207
6.10 Implementation of the PDP-11 Instruction Set on the PDP-11/60   *207*
      6.10.1 I-phase   207
      6.10.2 O-phase   208
      6.10.3 E-phase   209
6.11 Concluding Remarks   *209*
    Exercises   *209*
    References   *210*

7   INPUT/OUTPUT PROGRAMMING   211

7.1 Basic Input/Output Programming and Operations   *212*
      7.1.1 Device Registers   213
7.2 Basic Device Fundamentals   *213*
      7.2.1 Terminal Keyboard/Reader   213
      7.2.2 Terminal Printer/Punch   215
      7.2.3 Simple Programming Example   216
      7.2.4 An Octal Dump Program   217
      7.2.5 High-speed Reader/Punch   221
7.3 The Initial Load Problem   *223*
      7.3.1 Software Bootstraps   223
7.4 Tape and Disk Storage Units   *226*
      7.4.1 DECtape Operation   226
      7.4.2 DECtape Programming Examples   230
      7.4.3 Disk Operation   233
      7.4.4 Programming a DECdisk   234
7.5 Interrupts   *236*
      7.5.1 Interrupt Linkages   237
      7.5.2 Machine State During Interrupt   237
      7.5.3 Stacking of Interrupts   238
      7.5.4 Priority Interrupts   238
      7.5.5 Automatic Priority Interrupts   239
      7.5.6 Reader Interrupt Service   240
      7.5.7 Priority Levels and Masking Interrupts   241
      7.5.8 Absolute vs. Relative Mode for
          Interrupt Vector and Device Addressing   248
7.6 Records and Buffering   *248*
      7.6.1 Overlap of Computation and I/O Processing   249
7.7 Input/Output Programming Systems   *250*
      7.7.1 Example of RT-11 IOPS   251
      7.7.2 IOPS Linkage Problem   252
      7.7.3 Other Interrupts and Traps   253
      7.7.4 System Handling of a Trap Instruction   254
      7.7.5 Coroutine Example Using RT-11 System Macros   254
7.8 Memory Management and the PSW   *255*
      7.8.1 PSW Extensions   256
      7.8.2 Memory Management and Processor Modes   256

Exercises   *259*
References   *260*

8 SYSTEM DEVELOPMENT SOFTWARE   261

8.1 Editor   *261*
    8.1.1 Use of the RT-11 Editor   264
    8.1.2 Window Editors   264
8.2 The Loader   *266*
    8.2.1 Relocation of Programs   267
    8.2.2 Linking and Loading   269
8.3 Debugging Techniques   *272*
    8.3.1 Example of a Debugging Session   274
8.4 Applications Software and Operating Environments   *275*
Exercises   *276*
References   *276*

**9 ADVANCED PROGRAMMING TECHNIQUES FOR
ALGORITHM IMPLEMENTATION   277**

9.1 Program Analysis Programs   *278*
    9.1.1 Activity and Instruction Analysis   278
    9.1.2 A Rudimentary Instruction Trace Program   278
9.2 Time/Space Tradeoffs in Scientific Programming   *279*
    9.2.1 Data-Dependent and Data-Independent Algorithms   280
9.3 Algorithm Structures for Arithmetic Data Processing   *283*
    9.3.1 Autocorrelation   283
    9.3.2 The Discrete Fourier Transform (DFT)   285
    *9.3.3 The Fast Fourier Transform (FFT):
           Derivation and Implementation   286*
9.4 Automatic Generation of Time-Efficient Digital Signal Processing Software   *290*
    9.4.1 Software Generation   291
9.5 Program Structures for Computational Kernel Implementation   *291*
    9.5.1 In-line Code   292
    9.5.2 Subroutines   293
    9.5.3 Threaded Code   293
    9.5.4 Knotted Code   295
    9.5.5 Autocorrelation Results: Time, Space and Hardware   296
9.6 The Fast Fourier Transform: A Time-Efficient EIS Implementation   *298*
    9.6.1 Butterfly Modules   299
    9.6.2 FFT Results: Time, Space and Hardware   305
9.7 Alternative Forms for High Level Language Output Code   *306*
    9.7.1 Threaded Code   306
    9.7.2 In-line Code (EIS/FIS)   308
    9.7.3 In-line Optimized Code (EIS/FPP)   310
    9.7.4 In-line Optimized Code (VAX-11, FIV Plus)   312
    9.7.5 High Level vs. Assembler Programming   314

References   *315*

10   REAL-TIME INTERACTIVE COMPUTING   316

10.1 Analog/digital Converters: Structure and Programming   *316*
    10.1.1 Digital-to-Analog (D/A) Converters   317
    10.1.2 Analog-to-Digital (A/D) Converters   318
    10.1.3 Sampling Requirements: Bits/Sample and Sampling Rate   319
    10.1.4 Programming the A/D, D/A and Real-Time Clock   320
10.2 Interactive Graphics Processors   *324*
    10.2.1 The Refreshed Tube Display Processor Unit (DPU)   325
    10.2.2 VT-11 Graphics Processor Instruction and Data Word Formats   326
    10.2.3 Dynamic Display File Manipulation   331
    10.2.4 Graphics Subroutines via CPU/DPU Cooperation   332
    10.2.5 Light Pen Interaction   333
10.3 On-line Digital Signal Processing via CPU, DPU, and A/D Interaction   *335*
    10.3.1 Spectral Analysis via the Fast Fourier Transform   335
    10.3.2 PDP-11/VT-11 Digital Oscilloscope:
        a Modular Approach to Software Construction   337
10.4 Fast Digital Speech Spectrogram Production and Display   *347*
    10.4.1 Display of Grey Scale Pictures on the VT-11   348
    10.4.2 A Fast Software-Based Speech Spectrogram Package
        for the PDP-11/VT-11   349
10.5 Speech Analysis/Synthesis   *351*
    10.5.1 Speech Analysis   351
    10.5.2 Automatic Translation of English Text to Phonemes
        via Letter-to-Sound Rules   353
    10.5.3 Real-Time Software Speech Synthesis   358
10.6 Computer Music Synthesis   *362*
    10.6.1 Wavetable Manipulation for Four-Part Harmony   362
    10.6.2 Chord Organ Software for 'Take Me Out to the Ballgame'   363
10.7 Speed Enhancement of Applications Software via
    Microprogramming   *366*
    10.7.1 Review: The Stages of Processing Instructions in a Computer   367
    10.7.2 The Microprogrammer's Resources and Objectives   367
    10.7.3 I- and O-Cycle Manipulation   368
    10.7.4 Recoding of Fundamental Operations for E-Cycle Reduction   370
    10.7.5 Alternative Algorithm Selection   371
    10.7.6 Summary   373
    References   *374*

11   OPERATING SYSTEMS   375

11.1 Very Basic Computer Systems   *376*
11.2 Components of a Disk Operating System   *377*
    11.2.1 Files — Organization and Access   377
    11.2.2 Directories   380
    11.2.3 Multilevel Directories   381
    11.2.4 Problems of Control   382
    11.2.5 File Management Utility   383
    11.2.6 Device Independence   385
    11.2.7 The Monitor   385

11.3 Use of Operating Systems   390
11.4 Batch and Time-Sharing Systems   391
11.5 Real-Time Control Systems 393
        11.5.1 Real-Time Programming   393
11.6 Data-Base Systems   394
        11.6.1 Effective Data Management   394
        11.6.2 Storage, Manipulation, and Access of Data   395
11.7 Computer Communication Systems   395
        11.7.1 Communications Software   397
        References   397

12 A MULTIPROGRAMMING APPLICATIONS ENVIRONMENT   398

12.1 Overall View of MMS   399
12.2 Structure of the Queues, Tables, and PSECT's   399
        12.2.1 CPU Queue   400
        12.2.2 CPU Queue Table   400
        12.2.3 PSECT Table   402
        12.2.4 PSECT Vector   403
12.3 MMS Supervisor   404
        12.3.1 Schedule Routine   405
        12.3.2 Register Save Routine   405
        12.3.3 Insert Routine   405
        12.3.4 Dispatch Routine   406
        12.3.5 Unchain Routine   406
12.4 Writing Programs to Run Under MMS   407
12.5 Expanded System   408
12.6 Listing of MMS   409
        Exercises   415

APPENDICES 417

A. PRIMER OF NUMBER SYSTEMS   417

A.1 Binary Number Systems   418
        A.1.1 Positional Coefficient   418
        A.1.2 Counting in Binary Numbers   419
        A.1.3 Arrangement of Values   420
        A.1.4 Significant Digits   420
        A.1.5 Conversion of Decimal to Binary   421
A.2 Grouped-Bit Number Systems   422
        A.2.1 Octal   422
        A.2.2 Hexadecimal   423
        A.2.3 Octal-to-Decimal Conversion   424
        A.2.4 Decimal-to-Octal Conversion   424
A.3 Arithmetic Operations with Binary and Octal Numbers   426
        A.3.1 Binary Addition   426
        A.3.2 Octal Addition   427

A.4 Negative Numbers and Subtraction *427*
    A.4.1 Binary Subtraction (direct) 427
    A.4.2 Two's-Complement Arithmetic 428
    A.4.3 One's-Complement Arithmetic 430
    A.4.4 Octal Subtraction 430
  Exercises *431*

B. PRIMER OF LOGIC OPERATIONS 434

B.1 The AND Operation *434*
B.2 The OR Operation *435*
B.3 The Exclusive-OR Operation *435*
B.4 Boolean Algebra *436*
  Exercises *439*

C. ASCII AND RADIX-50 CHARACTER SETS 440

C.1 ASCII Character Set *440*
C.2 Radix-50 Character Set *443*

D. INSTRUCTION REPERTOIRE OF THE PDP-11 445

E. THE OPERATOR'S CONSOLE 451

E.1 Console Elements *452*
    E.1.1 Indicator Lights 452
    E.1.2 Register Displays 453
    E.1.3 Switch Register 453
    E.1.4 Console Switches 453
E.2 Operating the Console Switches *454*

F. EIS AUTOGEN FFT THREAD GENERATOR 456

G. THE INTERACTIVE GRAPHICS 'TOWERS OF HANOI' PROGRAM 461

H. RADIX-4 FPP AUTOGEN FFT 466

H.1 Introduction *466*
H.2 Program Generation *467*
H.3 Test Program *472*
H.4 Radix-4 Butterfly FPP Modules *473*

BIBLIOGRAPHY 477

INDEX 484

Preface

There is a certain fascination one feels when using a small, stand-alone computer. The fascination has to do with being in complete control of an entire computing system, knowing that there is nothing one cannot do, nothing one cannot try. Our computer pioneers, having developed and used the first machines, must have felt this way, and this fascination still prevails among today's systems programmers.

Some might argue that the feeling described is nostalgic and not pertinent in today's world of closed shop computer operations. They would point out that the average computer user is quite satisfied programming in a high-level language. They would go on to describe these users as being primarily concerned with computer programming and very happy to ignore most aspects of computer hardware, software, and system design.

This book is not meant for the users just described, but rather for those whose fascination with computers has led them to want to understand the magic which surrounds the devices they have used. Such computer users (systems programmers, system designers, computer scientists, electrical engineers, application specialists) want to know something about minicomputer organization and assembly language programming, and it is with them in mind that this book was fashioned.

Thus, *MINICOMPUTER SYSTEMS* is an introduction to the *organization*, *programming*, and *applications* of small computer systems. As in the first edition, the central theme is the fundamental ideas of computer *architecture* and *structure*, both hardware and software, and the utilization of these concepts in *production of programs* for *data acquisition* and *data manipulation*. In this Second Edition, these basic topics have been amplified in several areas, and extended to examine the interaction of algorithms, programs, and data structures to yield efficient software. New, related topics include consideration of the stages of processing computer instructions (with reference to the implementation and operation of micropro-grammed machines), extended computation with fixed- and floating-point num-bers, and the concept of memory hierarchies and machine families. The role of assemblers, editors, linking loaders, and other systems software as aids in efficient production of modular code is stressed. Several aspects of hardware/software cooperation in input/output programs are considered, including interrupts and direct memory access. Finally, the role and function of operating systems is explained, complete with fully documented software for a modest multiprogram-ming system.

An important new feature of this expanded edition is that these concepts are reinforced and clarified by numerous example programs involving *hardware* (ana-log/digital converters, interactive graphics processors) and *algorithms* (autocorrela-tion, the fast Fourier transform) employed in *scientific data processing*. Included are a highly modular digital oscilloscope software package, programs for real-time speech and music synthesis, and a discussion of software performance enhance-ment via microprogramming. While these additions may be more than necessary for some, their introduction continues in the spirit of the first edition; namely, to introduce the reader to many new ideas and concepts which can be best explained at the assembly language level. Our philosophy is simple: familiarity will eventu-ally lead to understanding.

The motivation in developing the First Edition of this book came as a consequence of having taught computer organization and assembly language programming to diverse groups of students using widely different computers. In all cases it was deemed important to bring out the fundamental concepts in computer hardware and software, especially as these ideas affect the larger issue of computer systems and their organization. Having attempted various means for accomplish-ing these objectives, it was generally found that the use of a real computer to illustrate the concepts presented was far preferable to the use of a simulated machine.

Being widely available at relatively low cost, the minicomputer seemed to be the best choice for a real computer. Having features previously found only in larger systems (e.g., overlapped operations, interrupts, multiple registers, built-in multiply/divide, etc.), these small computers have gained widespread popularity and are to be found as an integral part of many systems. Thus these machines are well suited for a book such as this, covering the area of computer organization and assembly language programming.

It is assumed that readers of this book will have completed a basic course in a procedure-oriented language. Because of the prevalent use and the common knowledge of FORTRAN, that language was chosen to illustrate many of the examples. Actually, the choice of a higher-level language (FORTRAN) to illustrate the same ideas in a lower-level (MACRO-11) language serves to do more than merely exemplify one by the other. Programming fundamentals and techniques are largely independent of language implementation, and as a result, a variety of languages at various levels may be effectively used to illustrate new ideas. For the reader of this book, the result is that one can quite naturally develop the fundamental concepts of digital computers and programming while learning some of the details of PDP-11 programming.

The course in machine and assembly language programming is unique. It is often the only time that a real architecture can be presented and experimented with. Subsequent courses often teach or use logical (rather than physical) machines running under an operating system which effectively masks the structure and thus behavior of the basic computer. At the physical level, the student is presented with the fundamental features that must be manipulated to create sophisticated logical computers. It is our goal then, to give as much insight and breadth as we can.

The original choice of the PDP-11 as the real machine was prompted by several reasons. These included its early popularity and the large number of features available on the machine, especially the rich instruction set, the great flexibility in address formation via registers, and the ease of input/output device manipulation. The subsequent growth and development of the PDP-11 family in number of models, diversity of peripheral devices available, and in multiplicity of existing software systems is probably unique in the computer world. Furthermore, the virtues of the PDP-11 architecture have been confirmed not only by the machine's popularity among users, but also in architectural evaluation studies. Finally, many of the PDP-11's features have been "emulated" in processors developed by other manufacturers, and Digital Equipment Corporation (DEC) has itself extended the '11 architecture upwards in the VAX-11, some features of which are described in this edition.

In summary, we have attempted to present a concept or an idea and then illustrate its implementation on the PDP-11, not vice versa. Since we don't intend for this book to be a complete treatment of such topics as data stuctures or machine architecture, we will often develop a principle only for the sake of illustrating a programming concept. It is hoped that people without a computer or with a different type of computer might be able to understand the concepts presented and be able to relate them to their own experience. At this point, we will outline the features of this book on a chapter-by-chapter basis.

Chapter 1 is a brief introduction to the impact and challenges of the computer revolution.

Chapter 2 opens with a discussion of computer fundamentals quite independent of any specific machine. Subjects in this section of the text include computing machines and computer organization. Software topics include programming fundamentals, such as flowcharting and program coding, symbolic coding, and instruction types. Then, architectures for operand addressing and techniques for address specification and manipulation common to most digital computers are introduced. The basics of instruction processing in a computer are outlined, as is the function of the symbolic assembler, a program which is also a programming aid.

Chapter 3 discusses the organization and structure of the PDP-11. Included are data representation, instruction formats, and address modes. Simple examples illustrate how basic operations are performed on that computer. Then, extended attributes of assemblers (e.g., directives) are introduced in the MACRO-11 context. The family concept of machine architecture is then discussed, including the interrelationship between program execution efficiency and memory organization. The idea of memory extension and management, and program protection is then explained.

Chapter 4 deals with more advanced programming techniques and program structures. Specifically, program organization concepts fundamental to modular programming, including subroutines, coroutines, and macros, are explained and illustrated. These ideas are extended to include position-independent code, reentrancy, and recursion. Again, numerous examples are employed so as to enhance understanding.

Chapter 5 is an introduction to data manipulation and data structures. Techniques for byte handling and logical operations are introduced, along with basic algorithms for integer multiply/divide and multiple precision arithmetic, and for floating-point arithmetic. The use of PDP-11 architectural enhancements for extended arithmetic operations is illustrated with a number of examples, some of which are further utilized in later chapters. The relationship between internal and external data forms is explained. Algorithms often imply a data structure to be used in mechanizing the algorithm. Thus, the chapter includes an extensive section describing techniques for representation, storage, and manipulation of data structures such as arrays, stacks, queues, deques and lists. Included are more advanced ideas such as hashing and packing. Numerous examples are given to illustrate the interaction between computer architecture, especially addressing techniques, and software implementations of data structure protocols. The symbolic assembler is also used as a vehicle for demonstrating the concepts discussed.

Chapter 6 is concerned with the description of computer architecture and organization at the micromachine level. The very fundamental building blocks of computers are described, showing how simple registers and arithmetic units can be constructed and interconnected. Then, the idea of controlling such elements by a program is introduced, using the very concrete example of the PDP-11/60 datapaths. The basic resources available at the '11/60 micromachine level are described in some detail. Next, it is shown how these elements can be controlled by a microprogram to implement both existing and new PDP-11 machine language instructions, and for control of the sequencing of PDP-11 instructions. The PDP-11/60 is a real machine, and was designed with the idea of user microprogramming in mind. Thus its microstructure is simple enough to be understandable yet powerful enough to implement and demonstrate such ideas as parallel processing. Although this chapter is optional in the sense that only one subsequent chapter makes brief use of the concepts developed herein, the reader will find the ideas interesting and of use in reinforcing other concepts such as assembler level macros. Similarly, it is not imperative to have access to an '11/60 in order to appreciate the concepts introduced.

Being able to program a computer is of little value if there is no way of providing it with data and then obtaining results. Thus, *Chapter 7* discusses I/O programming and covers the subject from the basics to interrupt-driven devices. Also included in the chapter is a description of the system software that is usually provided by the computer manufacturer to facilitate effective utilization of the I/O devices and to assist the programmer in writing programs which require input, output, or both. Again, examples from a real system (RT-11 in this case) are both useful, relatively simple, and reasonably representative of other systems. This last section leads quite nicely to the subject of the next chapter, system software.

The attributes and operation of a macro assembler have already been discussed in some detail in Chapters 2, 3, and 4. *Chapter 8* presents a brief description of some other system software resources to be found on most small computers. Topics discussed include the functions of an editor (including the special attributes of video terminal-based "window" editors), the linking and loading process, and the facility of an on-line, dynamic debugging package.

At this point, the text breaks into two parallel and more or less independent paths. Both are designed with the same goals; first, to introduce further topics of interest to the minicomputer user, and second, to reinforce and illustrate at a more advanced level many of the topics covered in earlier chapters.

Chapter 9 explains the interaction between algorithms, computer architectures and computer programs, drawing sample algorithms and programs from the area of scientific data processing. Two useful and relatively simple-to-program algorithms, autocorrelation and the discrete Fourier transform (computed via the fast Fourier transform or FFT technique), are introduced. Then, alternative program structures are examined for efficiency in time and space. A relatively fast FFT program, using the PDP-11 Extended Instruction Set (EIS), is listed and explained. Finally, an FFT program which uses an alternative algorithm and another PDP-11 architectural enhancement, the floating-point processor (FPP), is compared to the EIS FFT. It is not necessary to fully understand the physical significance and applications of the algorithms (as opposed to how they are implemented) in order to appreciate the contents of Chapter 9. However, *Chapter 10* is used to illuminate the meaning and utility of the DFT/FFT in particular, and at the same time enhance understanding of concepts such as modular programming, interrupt handling, parallel processing, and microprogramming capabilities. The structure and programming of analog/digital converters and real-time clocks is described, and the use of digital/analog converters to draw pictures is demonstrated. Then, it is shown how autonomous refreshed graphics processors can create more complex pictures, while relieving the host processor of any large computational burden. Graphics processor/central processor cooperation is demonstrated using the graphics subpicture construct and light pen interaction. A technique for displaying grey scale pictures is used to introduce some aspects of speech, and computer speech processing. It is shown how sophisticated string manipulation techniques, implemented as system subroutines on the PDP-11 and as single instructions on some recent machines (e.g., VAX-11), can be used to translate English text into commands which cause readily available and inexpensive speech synthesizers to speak the text. Finally, short program examples show that computers can create high quality real-time speech and music through software alone.

The second parallel path describes features of operating systems and systems software in more detail. Having dealt with computer organization, assembly language programming, hardware features, and system software, *Chapters 11* and *12* serve to further summarize and unify the ideas and concepts presented. First, in *Chapter 11*, it is explained why an operating system is desirable. Second, a general-purpose system is conceived by considering what is needed and how it can be provided. Finally, having gained some insight into an operating system, the reader is then told about some other application areas which have been served by small computer system operating environments. Second, the last chapter, *Chapter 12*, is devoted to the description of a modest multiprogramming system. This system is simple to understand and yet embodies most of the ideas and concepts found in larger real-time operating systems supported by most small machine manufacturers. The system represents an applications environment, and the reader can learn, through the detailed analysis of its overall organization, how the basic system can be expanded for a particular application.

In order to help him remember what to do when, and also in order to clarify what has been presented, the reader is provided with many examples, successively more difficult problems, and references for further study. The examples and problems are drawn from many sources, including the classroom projects which were developed in the course of preparing this book. Since some subjects may need further explanation, there are several appendices devoted to such topics as number systems, introductory concepts in logical operations, the operator's console, etc. A unique feature of this book is that many software modules listed, and some which are only briefly described, have been made available in machine readable form from the Digital Equipment Computer User's Society (DECUS) library.

It is our intention that this introductory text serve as an educational stepping stone to more advanced topics in computer science. As a consequence, we have attempted to provide the reader with the necessary (and sufficient) skills required to further his understanding of computer systems. It is not our goal to teach the reader how to program and run a PDP-11 computer, although we expect that he will have acquired a good working knowledge of that machine. Rather, we do expect that as a result of using this text, the reader will become aware that he is learning something about the basic ideas of computer elements and the principles of computer systems organization.

Richard H. Eckhouse, Jr.

L. Robert Morris

ACKNOWLEDGEMENTS

The *first edition* of this book could not have been produced without the myriad of people who helped make it possible. I have chosen to single out Professors Bob Taylor and John Greaves, and students Elliot Soloway, Al Klein, Ed Machado, and Steve Beckhardt for their helpful comments, Lynn Gilbert, Kathy Browne, and Mary Ann Rosenthal for their excellent typing assistance, and Judy Eckhouse for her continuing support. Special thanks go to Digital Equipment Corporation, especially Gordon Bell, whose continued help made this book possible.

R. H. E., Jr.

Many people contributed to the production of this *second edition*, either directly or indirectly. The Department of Systems Engineering and Computing Science at Carleton University provided the physical and human environment which made much of the work developed for Chapters 9 and 10 possible. Professor David Coll, in particular, supported and encouraged such activities, while David Sword ensured that the equipment recovered from its periodic indispositions. Diane Dodds typed the first manuscript version accurately and efficiently.

Professor Bill Bezanson (Carleton), Dave Cuddy (Bell-Northern Research), Simon Steely (DEC), and Professor Jim McClellan (MIT) are among the many proof readers of the first version of this edition. Their comments and suggestions were incorporated into the text.

During my sabbatical leave at Digital Equipment Corporation, made possible with the help of Jim Bell and Gordon Bell, I was influenced by a number of colleagues. In particular, Craig Mudge facilitated and cooperated in the 11/60 microprogramming experiments reported in Chapter 10 while Trudi Jackson provided invaluable microcoding assistance. Bill Strecker, Mary Payne, and Rich Grove provided stimulating discussion in a number of areas.

Finally, this edition would not have been possible at all without the continuing support and encouragement of my wife Joanne and sons Andrew, James and David.

L. R. M.

1

Introduction

During the past 25 years the computer revolution has dramatically changed our world, and it promises to bring about even greater changes in the years ahead.

The general-purpose digital computers being built today are much faster, smaller, and more reliable than earlier computers and can be produced at lower cost. New technologies, different architectures, and faster memories are having a great impact on the computer. But even more significant breakthroughs have come in the many new ways in which we have learned to use computers.

The first big electronic computers were usually employed as supercalculators to solve complex mathematical problems that had been impossible to attack before. In recent years, computer programmers have begun using computers for nonnumerical applications, such as control systems, communications, artificial intelligence, pattern recognition, and data handling and processing. In these operations, the computer system processes vast quantities of data at high speed.

More recently, the advent of the microcomputer has both accelerated and expanded the impact of the computer revolution. Economies associated with the computer-on-a-chip have resulted in the availability of microcomputer systems with the functionality and performance of minicomputer systems costing two orders of magnitude more only a decade ago. Microprocessors have appeared as amazingly economical and impressively intelligent controllers in household appliances, games, toys, cameras, automobiles, and other consumer items. Thus the role and importance of the computer programmer has vastly expanded in breadth as well as depth.

1.1 THE COMPUTER CHALLENGE

It has been said that a computer can be programmed to do any problem that can be defined. The key word here is "defined," which means that the solution of the problem can be broken down into a series of steps that can be written as a sequence of computer instructions. The definition of some problems, such as the translating of natural languages, has turned out to be very difficult. A few years ago it was thought that computer programs could be written to translate French into English, for example. As a matter of fact, it is quite easy to translate a list of French words into English words with similar meanings. However, it is very difficult to translate sentences precisely because of the many shades of meaning associated with individual words and word combinations. For this reason, it is not practical to try to communicate with a computer using a conventional spoken language.

Although natural languages are impractical for computer use, programming languages such as BASIC and FORTRAN, with their precisely defined structure and syntax, greatly simplify communication with a computer. Programming languages are problem-oriented and contain familiar words and expressions; thus, by using a programming language it is possible to learn to write programs after a relatively short training period. Since most computer manufacturers have adopted standard programming languages and implemented the use of these languages on their computers, a given program can be executed on a large number of computers. Computer programmers often use FORTRAN for scientific and engineering problems and BASIC for shorter numerical calculations. Computer languages have been developed for programmed control of machine tools, computer typesetting, music composition, data acquisition, computer-aided instruction, and many other applications. It is likely that there will be many more new programming languages in the future. Each new language development will enable the user to more easily apply the power of the computer to his particular problem or task.

Who can be a programmer? In the early days of computer programming, most programmers were mathematicians. However, as this text illustrates, most programming requires only an elementary ability to handle arithmetic and logical operations. Perhaps the most basic requirement for programming is the ability to reason logically.

The rapid expansion of the computer field in the last decade has made the resources of the computer available to hundreds of thousands of people and has provided many new career opportunities.

1.2 COMPUTER APPLICATIONS

A computer, like any other machine, is used because it does certain tasks better and more efficiently than humans. Specifically, it can receive more information and process it faster than a human. Often, this speed means that weeks or months of pencil-and-paper work can be replaced by a method requiring only minutes of computer time. Therefore, computers are used when the time saved by using a computer offsets its cost. Further, because of its capacity to handle large volumes of data in a very short time, a computer may be the only means of resolving problems when time is limited. Because of the advantages of great speed and large capacity, computers are being used extensively in business, industry, and research. Most computer applications can be classified as either business (or data base related) uses, which usually rely upon the computer's capacity to store and quickly retrieve large amounts of information, or scientific uses, which require accuracy and speed in performing mathematical calculations. Both of these are performed on general-purpose computers. We shall now describe a few examples of computer applications.

Design problems: The computer is a very useful calculating tool for the design engineer. The wing design of a supersonic aircraft, for example, depends upon many factors. The designer describes each of these factors in the form of mathematical equations specified in a programming language. The computer can then be used to solve these equations for abitrary input data.

Scientific and laboratory experiments: In scientific and laboratory experiments, computers are used to evaluate, store and process information from numerous types of electronic sensing devices. Computers are particularly useful in such systems as telemetry, where signals must be quickly recorded or be lost. Such applications require rapid and accurate processing for both fixed conditions and dynamic situations.

Process control: The computer is a useful tool for manufacturing and inspecting products automatically. A computer may be programmed to run and control milling machines, turret lathes, and many other machine tools with more rapid and accurate response than is possible for humans. It can be programmed to use special sensors to inspect a part as it is being made and adjust the machine tool as needed. If an incoming part is defective, the computer may be programmed to reject it and start the next part.

Training by simulation: It is often expensive, dangerous, and impractical to train a large group of men under actual conditions to fly a commercial airplane, control a satellite, or operate a space vehicle. A computer can simulate all these conditions for a trainee, who can receive many hours of on-the-job training without risk to himself, others, or the expensive equipment involved.

Applications such as these often require the processing of both analog and digital information. Analog information consists of continuous physical quantities that can be easily generated and controlled, such as electrical voltages or shaft rotations. Digital information, however, consists of discrete numerical values, which represent the variables of a problem. Normally, analog values are converted to equivalent digital values for arithmetic calculations to be used in arithmetic computation to solve problems. Hybrid computers combine the analog and digital characteristics in one computer system.

1.3 COMPUTER CAPABILITIES AND LIMITATIONS

A computer is a machine and, like all machines, must be directed and controlled to perform a task. Until a program is prepared and stored in the computer's memory, the computer "knows" absolutely nothing, not even how to accept data. No matter how good a computer may be, it must be "told" what to do. The utility of a computer cannot be fully realized, therefore, until the capabilities (and the limitations) of the computer are recognized:

1. *Repetitive operation:* a computer can perform similar operations thousands of times, without becoming bored, tired, or careless.

2. *Speed:* a computer processes information at extremely rapid rates. For example, modern computers can solve certain classes of problems millions of times faster than a skilled mathematician.

3. *Flexibility:* general-purpose computers may be programmed to solve many types of problems.

4. *Accuracy:* computers may be programmed to calculate answers with a desired level of accuracy as specified by the programmer.

5. *Intuition:* a computer has no intuition. A man may suddenly find the answers to a problem without working out the details, but a computer can only proceed as ordered.

1.4 COMPUTER ARCHITECTURE, ORGANIZATION, AND IMPLEMENTATION

In examining any computer system, there are three levels at which it is useful to consider the candidate machine. The most familiar level is that of computer architecture.

The *architecture* of a computer is often defined as the set of resources seen by the programmer. This includes, for example, the *instruction set*, the *general registers*, the *processor status words*, and the *address space*.

At the *organizational level*, one views the computer system beneath the visible architectural level to find out how processors, memories, input/output devices and so on are organized into the functioning machine. In particular, one needs to consider the micromachine, which contains many of the elements that play a part in creation of the computer architecture. For example, is the micromachine microprogrammed? One can also show how different computers with the same architecture can be organized so as to give the user a choice in processing speeds and/or memory sizes.

Finally, at the *implementation* level, we view the computer system as a

4

collection of wires, cables, semiconductor chips, and discrete components. We are concerned with the choice of semiconductor technology, clock phases, and signalling levels between different elements, and other "electrical" parameters. At this level we must surely consider ourselves "computer designers".

Chapter 2 is devoted to a brief description of the architecture and general organization of the digital computer, the manner in which it handles data, and the nature of computer programs. Included is an introduction to the basic structure of computing hardware and software, together with a description of the fundamental arithmetic and logical operations of the computer. Alternative architectures for operand addressing, and various techniques for address specification and manipulation are discussed. This information provides a necessary background for all who desire a basic appreciation of computers and their uses, and it is a prerequisite to the study of machine- and assembly-language programming. For pedagogical reasons, the material is presented without tying it specifically to the PDP-11. Instead, a PDP-11-*like* machine is discussed without all of the trappings of the real machine.

In Chapter 3, the specific architecture of the PDP-11 is examined in detail, together with a discussion of *organizational* features of different PDP-11 family members. Instruction and data formats specific to this family of machines are considered in detail so that the reader can write real programs for real machines. Later, in Chapter 6, one PDP-11 (the 11/60) will be described in some detail, including the micromachine organization and microprogramming.

Fig. 1-1   PDP-11/60 minicomputer system.

While this book illustrates the functionality of one particular family of mini/ microcomputers, the PDP-11, a great deal of effort has gone into the presentation so as to make it more widely applicable. Some concepts, such as basic arithmetic instructions (e.g., ADD, SUBTRACT, and so on) are similar in intent for all computers. On the other hand, addressing modes are sometimes computer specific. However, in both cases the goal of the text is to generalize from the specific so that familiarity with one architecture allows a rapid transition to a different one.

Finally, the architecture of the PDP-11 has been recognized as being both *powerful* and *bit-efficient* in a variety of computing applications, primarily because of the flexiblity of address formation via registers. This recognition has occurred both in independent competitive architectural studies and in the widespread user acceptance of the machine. Statistically, then, the minicomputer user is very likely to encounter either a PDP-11 or machine with some '11-like features (e.g., M6800, MC68000, Z8000). Thus, given that it is useful to study a real machine, the PDP-11 family is a most satisfactory choice.

In Fig. 1-1, a typical PDP-11 minicomputer system is shown, together with some peripheral devices commonly found on such systems. The computer is a PDP-11/60. Bulk data storage is via floppy disk drives (upper left within the computer cabinet), small sized removable disk packs (the drive is upper right in computer cabinet), or medium size disk packs (drives in left background). The system console terminal is a 30 character-per-second teleprinter, while a refreshed graphics processor provides "soft copy" and high-speed display of both text and graphical images. Included are analog and digital interfaces, providing both serial and parallel input/output to the computer, thus enabling real-time interaction and data processing.

2

Computer Structures:
Hardware and Software

2.1 COMPUTER HARDWARE: BASIC ELEMENTS

From an elementary standpoint, almost every general-purpose digital computer can be described as having the same basic structure. This structure is shown in Fig. 2-1.

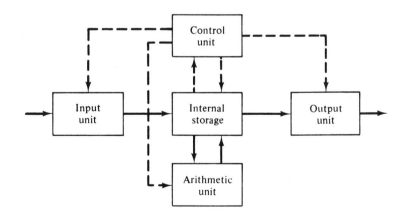

Fig. 2-1 General Organization of a Computer

If a machine is to be called a computer, it must have the capability of performing some types of arithmetic and logical operations. The element of a digital computer that meets this requirement is called the *arithmetic and logical unit*, or *ALU*. For the arithmetic unit to be able to do its required task, it must be told what to do; thus, a *control* unit is necessary.

Since mathematical operations are performed by the arithmetic unit, it may be necessary to store an intermediate result while the unit is computing another part of the problem. This stored partial answer can then be used to solve other parts of the problem. It is also helpful for the control unit and arithmetic unit to have information immediately available for their use and for the use of other units within the computer. This requirement is met by the portion of the computer designated as the *memory* or *main storage* unit.

The prime purpose of a digital computer is to serve society in some manner. To do this there must be a method of communicating with the computer and a means of receiving the results of the computer's calculations. The portions of the computer that carry out these functions are the *input* and *output* (*I/O*) units.

2.1.1 Arithmetic and Logical Unit

The *arithmetic and logical unit* (*ALU*) of a digital computer performs the actual work of computation and calculation. It carries out its job by the use of logic circuits. Switches and relays were used previously, and were once acceptable as far as their ability to perform computations was concerned. Modern computers make use of smaller, faster, and tremendously cost effective integrated circuits which often contain thousands of transistors. In fact, entire computers can now be implemented on a single chip of semiconductor material.

2.1.2 Control Unit

The *control unit* of a digital computer is an administrative section. It oversees information entering the machine and decides how and when to perform operations. It tells the arithmetic unit what to do and where to get the necessary information. It knows when the arithmetic unit has completed a calculation, and it tells the arithmetic unit what to do with the results and what to do next.

The control unit itself decides what to tell the arithmetic unit to do by interpreting a set of *instructions*. Instructions contain information such as what to do (*operation code*) and where the data are located (*operand address*). The set of instructions for the control unit is called a *program* and is stored in the computer memory.

Having just performed the operation specified by the current instruction, the control unit must fetch the next instruction to be executed. The location in memory where this instruction resides may be specified in one of two ways. First, the last instruction may specify the location. Second, and more commonly, a special *program counter* may specify the location in memory of the next instruction to be executed.

Instructions are executed one at a time by the control unit in a sequence specified either as a part of the instructions themselves or by the program counter. More sophisticated computers allow current instruction execution to be overlapped with the fetch of the next instruction, but this capability is generally transparent to the programmer.

2.1.3 Memory Unit

The *memory unit*, sometimes called the *main storage unit*, contains information for the control unit (instructions) and for the arithmetic unit (data). That instructions and data may be intermixed in the same memory is fundamental to the concept of a stored program computer. The computer will interpret any memory location pointed to by the program counter as an instruction if the data stored there has the required value.

Internal storage units, such as magnetic cores and semiconductor memories, are referred to as *primary storage*; external storage units, such as magnetic tapes and disks, are referred to as *secondary storage*. The requirements of the internal storage units, that is size or speed of operation, may vary greatly from computer to computer.

Memory is divided into sections called *locations* that can hold an element of data, an instruction, or part of an instruction. Storage systems in which each location can be specified and reached as rapidly as any other are referred to as *random-access*. Another type of storage, *sequential* storage, often involves spatial contact of a sensing device with the medium at the position where the desired data is stored. A magnetic tape, for example, must be reeled past a pickup head until the desired data is located and, only then, can the data be read.

2.1.4 Input and Output Units

Input devices are used to supply both the data needed by the computer and the instructions to tell the computer how to operate on the data. Input capabilities vary greatly from machine to machine. A keyboard may be sufficient for a small computer. Computers that require faster input may use punched cards for data input. Input may also be supplied via punched paper tape, magnetic tape, or disks, three forms common in small computer systems. Additional input devices of interest, especially in real-time environments, are analog-to-digital converters (A/D's), serial or parallel data streams from other devices (or other computers), and highly interactive devices such as the graphic display processor with its associated light pen, acoustic tablet, or joystick.

Output devices accept or record the results of the computer operations. These results may be recorded in a permanent form (e.g., as a "hard copy" printout on the teleprinter) or as "soft copy" on a video terminal, for example. Alternatively, the computer may be used to initiate a physical action (e.g., to adjust a pressure-value setting). Many of the media used for input, such as paper tape, punched cards, and magnetic tape, can also be used for "hard copy" output.

2.1.5 Memory Organization

The memory of a computer is the repository of both instructions and data, which we shall refer to as the *information units to be processed.* Each information unit resides in a distinct position or location in memory. That is, an information unit has a numbered value or address associated with it and by which it may be referenced uniquely. Such a memory location is characterized by two things:

1. An *address*, which has a numerical value associated with its relative position in memory.

2. The *contents*, which is a number that is physically stored at the particular location within memory.

It is important to understand the difference between the *address* (name) and the *contents* (information) of a memory location.

The information unit may be one binary digit, (a *bit*), a collection of bits (a *nibble*, *character* or *byte*) or an even larger unit called a *word*. Early computers were limited by economical considerations as to the size of the instruction set and hence the number of data types which could be *directly* manipulated by the instructions. Thus, when such computers were designed, the information unit sizes were fixed, based on the type of application for which the computer was designed. For example, byte machines are particularly useful for administrative data processing, where the information to be processed includes names and English words as well as numbers. On the other hand, word machines are required for scientific calculations, where large quantities of numbers are manipulated and accurate numerical results are desired.

The key difference among bit, byte, and word machines is the size of the *smallest* addressable information unit. For a bit machine, it is one binary digit (i.e., a unit of information capable of representing either 0 or a 1). For a character or byte machine, it is one character from the character set of that machine (i.e., a letter of the alphabet, a digit, or a special character). For a word machine, it is a numerical value from the range of permissible values that may be represented on a particular machine.

Words can often be subdivided into a fixed number of characters or digits. However, in a true word machine, we may reference only the collection, not the individual characters. Thus the subdivision is one of convenience in that it allows us to think of the word as "representing" the characters or digits. The representation is accomplished by "coding" the letters into unique combinations of binary digits.

The PDP-11, for example, is a byte machine in that it addresses information units using a byte address; however, it was designed so as to easily manipulate 8-bit bytes, or 16-bit words (composed of two adjacent bytes), with less complete capabilities for computation involving 32-bit longwords (two adjacent words), or

64-bit quadwords (two adjacent longwords). The advent of large scale integration (LSI), wherein tens of thousands of logical, arithmetic, and storage devices can be economically created on a tiny semiconductor chip, has now made commonplace computers with instruction sets capable of directly accessing and flexibly manipulating a number of different data types and sizes.

2.2 COMPUTER SOFTWARE: INTRODUCTION TO PROGRAMMING

Using the basic hardware elements described above, the modern digital computer is capable of accepting and storing information, performing calculations, making decisions based on the results, arriving at a final solution to a given problem, and communicating the results to the outside world. The computer cannot, however, perform these tasks without direction. Each step the computer is to perform must first be worked out by the computer user. He must write the *program*, a list of instructions for the computer to follow to arrive at a solution for a given problem. This list of instructions, the computer *program*, is based on a computational method, called an *algorithm*, used to solve the problem. The list of instructions is placed in the computer memory so that the computer can process the problem.

2.2.1 Programming Phases

In order to solve a problem successfully with a computer, the programmer proceeds through six programming phases:

1. Definition of the problem to be solved.

2. Determination of the most feasible solution method or algorithm.

3. Specification of the input data and output results.

4. Design and analysis of the solution — flowcharting, program documentation, and so on.

5. Coding the solution in the programming language, entering and running the program.

6. Program checkout.

The *definition of the problem* is not always obvious. A great amount of time and energy can be wasted if the problem is not adequately defined. When the problem is to sum four numbers, little clarification is necessary. However, when the problem is to monitor and control a performance test for semiconductors, a precise definition of the problem is necessary before its solution can be attempted. The question that must be answered in this phase is: *What precisely is the program to accomplish?*

Determining the method to be followed is the second important phase in solving a problem with a computer. There are sometimes an infinite number of methods to solve a problem, and the selection of one method over another is often influenced by the computer system to be used. Having decided upon a method based on the definition of the problem and the capabilities of the computer system, the programmer must develop the method into a workable solution.

Somewhere between the process of determining the method and designing the solution to a computer problem, the programmer must *consider* and *specify* the *type and amount of information or data* that is involved. Because the data may have some implicit structure, the programmer must consider the data very carefully when designing his program solution.

The programmer *must design and analyze the solution* by identifying the necessary steps to solve the problems and arranging them in a logical order, thus implementing the method. Flowcharting is a graphical means of representing the logical steps of the solution. The flowcharting technique is effective in providing an overview of the logical flow of a solution, thereby enabling further analysis and evaluation of alternative approaches.

Having designed the problem solution, the programmer begins *coding the solution in the programming language.* This phase is commonly called "programming" but is actually coding, and is only one part of the programming process. When the program has been coded and the program instructions have been stored in the computer memory, the problem can be solved by the computer. At this point, however, the programming process is rarely complete. There are very few programs written that function initially as expected. Whenever the program does not work properly, the programmer is forced to begin the sixth step of programming, that of checking out or *debugging* the program.

The *program checkout* phase requires the programmer to retrace the flow of the instructions methodically, step by step, to find any program errors that may exist. The programmer cannot tell a computer: "You know what I mean ", as he might say in daily life. The computer does not know what is meant until it is told, and once given a set of instructions, the computer follows them precisely. If needed instructions are left out or if coding is done incorrectly, the results may be surprising. These flaws, or "bugs" as they are often called, must be found and corrected. There are many approaches to finding bugs in a program; whatever the approach chosen, to be successful it must be organized and painstakingly methodical. Several techniques for debugging programs will be described later.

2.2.2 Program Definition and Documentation

A simple problem to add three numbers together is solved in a few easily determined steps. A programmer could sit at his desk and write out three or four instructions for the computer to solve the problem. However, he probably could have added the same three numbers with paper and pencil or pocket calculator in much less time than it took him to write the program. Thus the problems which the programmer is usually asked to solve are much more complex than the addition of three numbers, because the main value of the computer is in the solution of problems that are inconvenient or time-consuming by non-computer-based techniques.

Flowcharting: When a complex problem is to be solved by a computer, the program involves many steps, and writing it often becomes long and confusing. A problem solving description that is defined via conventional languages and mathematical equations is extremely hard to follow, and coding computer instructions from such a document would be equally difficult. A technique called *flowcharting* is used to simplify the writing of programs. A *flowchart* is a graphical representation of a given problem, indicating the logical sequence of operations that the computer is to perform. Having a diagram of the logical flow of a program is a tremendous advantage to the programmer when he is determining the method to be used for solving a problem, as well as when he writes the coded program instructions. In addition, the flowchart is often a valuable aid when the programmer checks the written program for errors.

The flowchart is basically a collection of symbols and lines. The symbols indicate what is to be done and the lines indicate the sequence of the operations represented by the symbols. The symbols are of various shapes which represent the different actions to be performed in the program. Figure 2-2 describes the various flowchart symbols as defined by ANSI/ISO symbol conventions.

Terminal

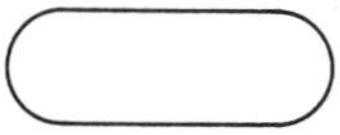

The oval symbol represents a terminal point in a program. It can be used to indicate a start, stop, or interrupt of program flow. The appropriate word is included with the symbol.

Processing

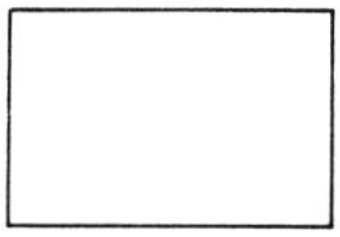

The rectangular symbol represents a processing function. The process could be an instruction or a group of instructions to carry out a given task. A brief description of the task to be performed is included within the symbol.

Fig. 2-2 Flowchart symbols.

Decision

A diamond is used to indicate a point where a choice is made on the flow of the program from the point. A test condition is included within the symbol and the possible results of the test are used to label the respective flows from the symbol.

Connector

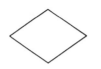

A small circle around a unique identifier terminates a line of flow and serves to connect it to another identical circle from which flow is to resume. Connectors thus allow flowcharts to be continued on different pages to link up independently constructed flowcharts, and to eliminate the crossing of flow lines.

Fig. 2-2 Flowchart symbols (continued).

Next, two examples of flowcharts are given. In example 1, three numbers are added together. In example 2, three numbers are arranged in increasing order of magnitude.

Example 1: Straight-Line Programming

Example 1 is an illustration of straight-line (or *in-line*) programming. As Fig. 2-3 shows, there is a straight-line progression through the processing steps with no change in course. The value of the expression A + B + C is in location D when the program stops.

Example 2: Program Branching

Example 2 is designed to arrange three numbers in increasing order of magnitude (Fig. 2-4). The program must branch to interchange numbers that are out of order. (Branching, a common feature of programming, is described in detail later in this chapter.) Note that the arithmetic operations of subtraction are done in an accumulator or AC, a storage unit or register often associated with the ALU. The AC must be cleared initially.

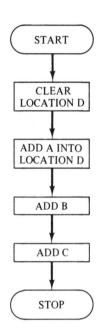

Fig. 2-3 Adding three numbers

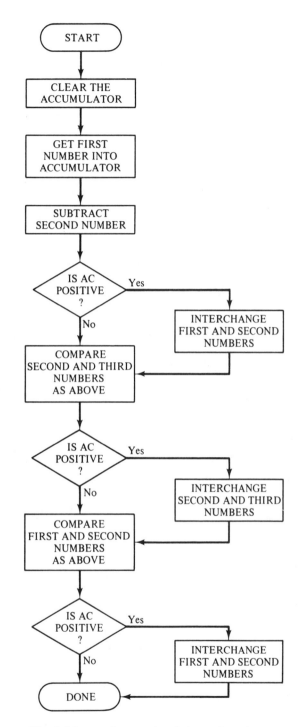

Fig. 2-4 Arrange three numbers in increasing order.

Additional Methods for Documentation: Because programs are very seldom written, used, and then forgotten, it is important that they be well documented. It is the documentation that assists the next person who needs to use, modify, or correct those programs which live on long after the programmer who created them. A complete and accurate flowchart is a common form of documentation. However, the flowchart often fails to show the intent of the programmer or the logic flow of the program. Equally important are the steps that must be performed to execute the program, the format of the input data items, the constraints of the algorithm being used, and the interdependencies that may exist among program units.

In many cases, English sentences serve as the best means for program documentation. For example, it is often desirable to include heading and dates as part of the source program. In addition, embedded comments logically block out the operations being performed so that the unfamiliar reader may learn the purpose or intent of the code without actually having to read it. On a larger scale, user's manuals serve to guide the non-programmer through the external program details so that he does not have to concern himself with why or how a program works.

An alternative to English sentences that is quite popular is the decision table. A decision table is a graphical representation that shows how a set of conditions relates to a set of actions for a set of rules. Taking advantage of the maxim that a picture is worth a thousand words, the decision table is a compact method for representing the rules of an algorithm without regard to any particular computer or computer language.

Figure 2-5 is an example of a decision table used to classify an animal according to the number of legs it has, the length of its neck, and the size of its nose, so that it can be fed appropriately. Although this is a trivial example, it is important to note that decision tables are extremely useful for describing complex decision processes by programmers and non-programmers alike. Decision tables are easily constructed and modified, easily understood, and very compact in their representation of information.

<table>
<tr><td rowspan="4">Condition</td><td>Characteristic</td><td colspan="3">Rule</td></tr>
<tr><td>Number of legs</td><td>4</td><td>4</td><td>2</td></tr>
<tr><td>Length of neck</td><td>$> 4'$</td><td>$< 4'$</td><td>$< 4'$</td></tr>
<tr><td>Small nose</td><td>Yes</td><td>No</td><td>Yes</td></tr>
<tr><td rowspan="3">Action</td><td>Animal is giraffe
feed it</td><td>Hay</td><td></td><td></td></tr>
<tr><td>Animal is elephant
feed it</td><td></td><td>Peanuts</td><td></td></tr>
<tr><td>Animal is human
feed it</td><td></td><td></td><td>Martini</td></tr>
</table>

Fig. 2-5 Decision table.

Decision tables, however, have two disadvantages associated with their use in writing programs. First, the translation from decision table to computer programming language is a complex task. Consequently, decision-table languages have been written that do not place this burden on the programmer, but perform it for him. Second, decision tables are too powerful and hence very cumbersome when representing simple choice situations. Simple binary or tertiary flowchart decision boxes are preferable in that case. Because this text concentrates on an understanding of computers at a lower level than is found in a text that introduces programming in a higher-level language (e.g., FORTRAN), the disadvantages associated with decision tables generally preclude their use.

2.2.3 Program Coding

Binary numbers are the only language that the computer is able to understand. (For a review of information on binary numbers, refer to Appendix A.) Numbers are stored in binary, and all arithmetic operations are in binary. What is more important to the programmer, however, is that for the computer to understand an instruction, it must be represented in binary. The computer cannot understand instructions that use English-language words. All instructions must ultimately be in the form of binary numbers (binary code).

Each computer uses a specific set of binary codes that it "understands" as instructions. In other words, the computer is designed and built to react to these binary numbers in a certain manner. These instructions have the same appearance as any other binary number; the computer can interpret the same binary configuration of 0's and 1's as data or as an instruction. The programmer tells the computer whether to interpret the binary configuration as an instruction or as data by the way in which the configuration is encountered in the program. Programmers seldom use the binary number system in actual practice. Instead, they substitute the octal (or hexadecimal) number system because it is easier for them to think in octal, the programs are more readable, and there is no loss of significance in doing so.

Coding a program in octal numbers, although an improvement upon binary coding, is nevertheless relatively inconvenient. The programmer must learn a complete set of octal numbers which have no logical connection with the operations they represent. The coding is difficult for the programmer when he is writing the program, and this difficulty is compounded when he is trying to debug or correct a program. There is no easy way to remember the correspondence between an octal number and a computer operation.

To simplify the process of writing or reading a program, each instruction is often represented by a simple two- to five-letter mnemonic symbol. These mnemonic symbols are considerably easier to relate to a computer operation because the letters often suggest the definition of the instruction. The programmer is now able to write a program in a language of letters and octal numbers that suggests the meaning of each instruction.

2.2.4 The Stored Program Concept

The utilization of memory for holding both data and instructions is referred to as the *stored program concept*. Although it seems quite natural to use memory in this fashion, historically, the first machines did not allow sharing memory, and it was not until the late 1940s that the idea was incorporated into computer systems by John von Neumann.

The impact of von Neumann's contribution was that it became possible to treat instructions as data, allowing arithmetic operations to be performed on the instructions. Even more importantly, it allowed for the rapid change in the order of instruction execution for both conditional and unconditional transfers. Thus the work of von Neumann is held as a major theoretical advance in computer design, and his name has been associated with the *stored program* or *von Neumann* concept.

2.2.5 Types of Instructions

There are four basic types of instructions which a computer understands. These instructions are arithmetic/logical, program control, internal data transmission, and input/output instructions.

Using *arithmetic/logical instructions*, a computer may add, subtract, multiply, divide, or perform logical operations. Some computers, such as the PDP-11/05, can only directly add and subtract, performing multiplication and division by repetitive addition or subtraction. Others, such as the IBM 1620, cannot even add, but have to look up arithmetic results from add and multiply tables stored in memory.

The second type of instruction, *program control*, directs the computer as to the order in which it is to add or subtract or perform any operation. In other words, you may instruct a computer to skip around from place to place or jump over a sequence of instructions as a result of arithmetic operations, because of some internal conditions, or simply because that is the way your program is written.

The third type of instruction, *internal data transmission*, allows for the movement of whole words or bytes as part of the internal data transmission required in most programs. In addition, this class of instructions includes the shift operations for manipulating the bits in a word.

The fourth and last type of instruction is an *input* or *output* instruction. The input codes direct the control unit to transmit information available at some input device external to the system to specified locations in memory where it can be stored internally to the system. The output codes direct the transmission of information in the reverse direction. Additionally, control and status information may be passed to, or collected from, a device so as to determine its condition or change its state.

2.3 ARCHITECTURES FOR OPERAND ADDRESSING

Two of the basic units in Fig. 2-1, the arithmetic and logical unit (ALU), and control unit, together form the *central processing unit* (CPU) of the computer. The job of the CPU is to fetch from memory, and decode, the next instruction to be executed; to fetch the operands necessary to carry out the instruction; and, finally, to execute the instruction. To perform these tasks, the CPU must be presented with instruction words that specify:

1. The operation to be performed, as specified by an *operation code* (e.g., ADD, SUBtract, MULtiply, etc.).

2. The addresses of the operands and resultants.

3. The address of the next instruction to be executed.

Since most arithmetic operations require two operands and a resultant, each instruction word would apparently require four addresses to be specified in addition to the operation code. In this section, alternative instruction formats (and hence machine architectures), all of which effectively satisfy the above constraints are described. Then, in Section 2.4, a number of different techniques for explicit specification of each address required are explored. Note that we will generally use the "*", "/", and "**" symbols to designate multiplication, division, and exponentiation, respectively.

2.3.1 Three-Plus-One and Three-Address Machines

Computers that utilize the instruction format shown in Fig. 2-6 are referred to as three-plus-one (3 + 1) address machines.

Operation code	Operand address 1	Operand address 2	Resultant address 3	Next instruction address

Fig. 2-6 Three-plus-one instruction format.

Instructions for such a machine could be written symbolically as

```
ADD   X,Y,Z,W
---   -------
 |       |
symbolic op-code    symbolic names for memory locations
```

meaning "add the contents of memory location X to the contents of memory location Y and place the results in memory location Z, taking the next instruction from memory location W." Adopting the convention that "(X)" means "the contents of memory location X," the words become unnecessary and the meaning of the symbolic ADD instruction may be expressed as

$$(Z) \leftarrow (X) + (Y) \quad \& \quad (W)$$

where the arrow ($\leftarrow$) is read as "becomes", "gets", or "is set equal to", and "&" is read as "and take the next instruction from the contents of". This form, which is used to describe the ADD instruction, is referred to as *infix notation*, where the operation to be performed is embedded between the operands to be operated on.

Let us now consider a sequence of computer instructions to calculate the FORTRAN expression:

$$A = (B*C) - (D*E)$$

where the instructions are to reside in consecutive memory locations I1: through I4:. Expressing this sequence of operations in both symbolic and infix notation we have

```
        Symbolic Format              Infix Notation
        ---------------              --------------
    I1: MUL B,C,T1,I2        I1: (T1) ← (B)*(C)   & (I2)
    I2: MUL D,E,T2,I3        I2: (T2) ← (D)*(E)   & (I3)
    I3: SUB T2,T1,A,I4       I3: (A)  ← (T1)-(T2) & (I4)
    I4: next instruction     I4: next instruction
```

where memory locations T1 and T2 represent temporary locations used to hold the intermediate arithmetic results. In the following sections we shall describe instructions using both the symbolic format and infix notation.

On closer examination, the instructions for this $3+1$ address machine reveal two important things. First, although the example presented utilized consecutive memory locations for holding instruction words, there is no requirement within the structure of the machine for this to be so. Second, since there are three explicit addresses in each instruction, there is no need to have internal computer hardware for holding the results of an arithmetic operation. Thus each operation is complete in itself and is performed in one instruction cycle.

It seems worthwhile to question why sequential ordering of instructions into consecutive memory locations is not a requirement. Since most programs are written in a sequential fashion, it seems quite normal to expect a computer to execute the instructions sequentially, from one location to another. The answer, as it turns out, is really part of the historical development of computer memories. Before the era of magnetic core and semiconductor memories, where each memory location could be accessed randomly without any difference in access time, memories were definitely not random access, being made from mercury delay lines or magnetic drums. On these types of devices, the next sequential location was not, in general, as accessible as one somewhere else. As a result, a strictly sequential program would have executed more slowly than one that could minimize access time by specifying the next instruction location as the one most readily available (and not necessarily the next consecutive location). (A classical example of such a machine was the IBM 650, although it used 1 + 1 addressing rather than 3 + 1.)

But, since random access memories do exist on most machines, the next instruction address is really not needed. Instead, a "pointer" called a *program counter* (*PC*) is maintained; it acts like a sliding arrow that always points to the next instruction to be executed. In reality, the PC is a hardware register that holds the address of the current instruction being executed and is updated to point to the next instruction before execution of the current one has been completed. [The CDC-6600 and the VAX-11 are examples of computers that use a PC (program counter/register) and execute three-address arithmetic instructions.]

Since an important cost factor in most machines is the memory, and the cost of memory is a function of the number of bits per word, it is clear that removing the next address field from each word and substituting one hardware register will effect a significant increase in cost effectiveness, resulting in, simply, a three-address machine. We may carry the savings further by removing one operand address field, resulting in an even more cost effective machine, a *two-address machine*.

2.3.2 Two-Address Machines

The loss of the third operand address is not as drastic a move as it might seem. Often there is no need to place the resultant of an arithmetic operation in a different location. Instead, it is just as convenient to use the address of the second operand as both the address of an operand and the address of the result. For example, let us consider the problem of adding the contents of location A to location B, and placing the result in C. In the case of the three-address machine it would be necessary to write an instruction such as

```
ADD     A,B,C            i.e.,   (C) ← (A) + (B)
```

By restricting the address of the result to be that of the second operand, one operand address specification per instruction is saved. For the two address machine, this instruction would require the following sequence:

```
MOV     A,C              i.e., (C) ← (A)
ADD     B,C              i.e., (C) ← (C) + (B)
```

The "MOV" instruction moves operands from one memory location (the *source*) to another (the *destination*). Note that the contents of location C are destroyed by being overwritten. Similarly, the previous sequence of A = (B*C) - (D*E) would be written:

```
MUL     B,C          (C) ← (B)*(C)
MUL     D,E          (E) ← (D)*(E)
SUB     E,C          (C) ← (C)-(E)
MOV     C,A          (A) ← (C)
```

Since, as specified above, the result of arithmetic operations overwrites the second operand, the initial contents of locations C and E are gone. Subsequent computations could not use these values. This is one of the consequences of using two-address arithmetic instructions.

Both large and small computers have been designed to use two-address arithmetic. The PDP-11, VAX-11, MC68000, Z8000, IBM 1620, UNIVAC 1105, and the IBM System/370 are all machines that exhibit this architectural feature.

2.3.3 One-Address Machines

To reduce costs even further, we may remove another operand field from the instruction word. As a result, the remaining address field must act as either a source or a destination address, and since most arithmetic operators must have two operands, it will be necessary to provide an implicit (part of the internal hardware) source/sink for the *one-address machine*. This implicit operand is called an *accumulator* and serves much the same purpose as the accumulator found in a desk calculator.

The arithmetic operations of the one-address machine will utilize the accumulator by adding to, subtracting from, and so on, the accumulator, since its use will be implicit in the execution of the instruction. In order to be able to initialize and save the values held in the accumulator, new instructions must be added to the one-address machine to *load the accumulator* (LAC) and *deposit the accumulator* (DAC) from or to memory.

A demonstration of the coding for the one-address machine is given below. Assuming the previously considered arithmetic calculation,

$$A = (B*C) - (D*E)$$

the code for the one-address machine might be

```
LAC     D          (ACC) ← (D)
MUL     E          (ACC) ← (ACC)*(E)
DAC     T1         (T1)  ← (ACC)
LAC     B          (ACC) ← (B)
MUL     C          (ACC) ← (ACC)*(C)
SUB     T1         (ACC) ← (ACC)-(T1)
DAC     A          (A)   ← (ACC)
```

where T1 stands for a temporary location as before and ACC stands for the accumulator. The observant reader will note that if the second multiplication had not been performed first, an extra temporary location would have been needed along with extra DAC's and LAC's.

By far the most popular addressing scheme implemented has been the one-address architecture. The PDP-8, PDP-15, IBM 1130, IBM 7090, CDC 3600, and others are all examples of computers that utilize single-address instructions and accumulators.

2.3.4 General Register Machines

Once we have accepted the idea of a computer with an accumulator, it is easy enough to expand the concept to a machine with many accumulators. These accumulators serve as useful places to hold intermediate results once generated, so that the need for temporary memory locations diminishes. As we shall see, these accumulators can be *directly* addressed and their contents are *immediately* available to the ALU; they thus exhibit a speed advantage relative to main memory.

For example, on a two-accumulator machine with instructions "load accumulator 1" (LA1), "deposit accumulator 2" (DA2), "multiply contents of accumulator 1 by contents of specified memory location, leaving the results in accumulator 1" (MP1), and so on, the coding sequence for the FORTRAN expression A = (B*C) - (D*E) might be

```
LA1    D        (ACC1)  ←  (D)
MP1    E        (ACC1)  ←  (ACC1)*(E)
LA2    B        (ACC2)  ←  (B)
MP2    C        (ACC2)  ←  (ACC2)*(C)
SB2    ACC1     (ACC2)  ←  (ACC2)-(ACC1)
DA2    A        (A)     ←  (ACC2)
```

Multiple accumulator machines are often referred to as *general register* computers. These computers utilize the registers not only to act as accumulators, but also to perform *indexing* on data items in an array, *looping* through a sequence of instructions a given number of times, and *pointing* to a particular place in memory. Thus we say that the registers may be used as accumulators, index registers, counters, and pointers.

Although the concept of general register computers has been developed from that of one-address machines, this should not be taken to imply that only such machines embody the idea. Rather, general register machines may be two- or three-address machines with the contents of general register(s) serving in place of a memory location as a given operand. For example, the PDP-11 (a two-address machine) can specify an ADD instruction to "add memory-to-register", "add register-to-memory", "add register-to-register", or "add memory-to-memory" as follows:

```
"Add-memory-to-register":    ADD A,Reg      (Reg)   ←  (Reg)+(A)
"Add-register-to-memory":    ADD Reg,A      (A)     ←  (A)+(Reg)
"Add register-to-register":  ADD Reg1,Reg2  (Reg2)  ←  (Reg2)+(Reg1)
"Add memory-to-memory":      ADD A,B        (B)     ←  (B)+(A)
```

where "A" and "B" represent memory locations and "Reg" stands for any of the eight general-purpose registers.

2.3.5 Zero-Address Machines

At this point we may ask ourselves whether we can conceive of a machine with no addresses at all. The answer is yes, but a qualified yes. What is necessary is a mechanism that implicitly maintains the operands required for the standard arithmetic operations. This mechanism is called a *stack*.

A stack can be thought of as an ordered collection of memory locations (or registers, like the accumulator) with a top or first element, a second element, and so on. However, only the top element has to be accessible to perform all necessary stack/arithmetic operations.

Fetching the operands necessary for some arithmetic operations requires that a *POP* operation be performed on the stack. This operation takes the top element off the stack and effectively moves every element up (toward the top of the stack) one position. Thus the second element becomes the first, the third the second, and so on. A complementary operation is *PUSH*, which places a new element on the stack, effectively moving all old elements down one position. Figure 2-7 shows examples of PUSH and POP acting on an initially empty stack.

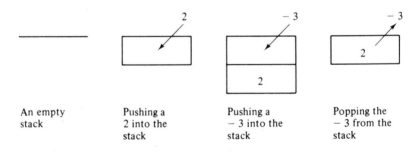

An empty stack   Pushing a 2 into the stack   Pushing a −3 into the stack   Popping the −3 from the stack

Fig. 2-7 Effective operation of PUSH and POP operations.

Arithmetic operations such as ADD can now be described as "PUSH first operand onto stack, PUSH second operand, POP operands into adder, and PUSH resultant back onto stack." While it may first appear that pushing and popping require all data in the stack to be moved, such is not the case. Rather, a stack may be implemented as a collection of contiguous memory elements with a pointer to the top of the stack (called *stack pointer* or SP). POP then means "copy the contents of the element pointed to by the SP and then increment the SP to point to the new top-of-stack element." PUSH is correspondingly defined.

Thus, the add may be described as follows:

```
ALU ← (SP),  SP  ← SP+1    i.e., ALU ← operand 1, increment SP
ALU ← (SP),  SP  ← SP+1    i.e., ALU ← operand 2, increment SP
ADD                        i.e., zero address ADD instruction
SP  ← SP-1, (SP) ← result  i.e., top-of-stack ← sum from ALU
```

Here SP is the address of the top of stack and (SP) is the memory element at that address, i.e., the top-of-stack or TOS. The first two elements on the stack are replaced by the single resultant. Such an add operation is shown in Fig. 2-8.

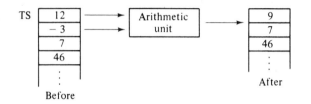

Fig. 2-8 Arithmetic stack operation

How would we direct such a machine to evaluate the arithmetic expression

$$A = (B * C) - (D * E) \quad ?$$

A possible code sequence might be

```
PUSH D
PUSH E
MUL
PUSH B
PUSH C
MUL
SUB
POP  A
```

It is obvious that this is not truly a zero-address machine, since PUSH and POP require one operand. (After all, they are nothing more than the LAC and DAC instructions of the one-address machine) Thus a zero-address machine does not have only zero-address instructions as part of the total instruction set, and so we are required to qualify our meaning of zero-address machines. A case in point is the Burroughs 5500. This is a stack machine which includes both the zero-address arithmetic instructions and instructions of the one-address load-and-store type. Other examples are the PDP-11/40 and '11/03 (also known as the LSI-11), which optionally contain a floating instruction set (FIS) with four zero address

instructions for adding, subtracting, multiplying, or dividing operands on a specified stack.

2.4 ADDRESS SPECIFICATION AND MANIPULATION

Given that various machine architectures require explicit specification of one
or more operand addresses, a number of questions arise. In particular, how do we
specify operand addresses and how can we manipulate the address specifications
associated with algorithms which are evaluated by computers? In order to facilitate
answering such questions, using simple examples as illustrations, we introduce a
short instruction set for a machine of the two address type:

```
Operation          Symbolic Form    Meaning
---------          -------------    -------
Move               MOV A,B          (B) ← (A)
Add                ADD A,B          (B) ← (B)+(A)
Subtract           SUB A,B          (B) ← (B)-(A)
Compare            CMP A,B          evaluate (A)-(B)
Branch (= 0)       BEQ X                      | = 0 |
Branch (≠ 0)       BNE X            IF LAST   | ≠ 0 | Then
Branch (≥ 0)       BPL X            OPERATION | ≥ 0 | (PC) ← X
Branch (< 0)       BMI X                      | < 0 |
Branch always      BR X             (PC) ← X
Halt               HALT             machine stops
```

The reader should note that although these instructions are indentical in form
to those found on the PDP-11, they may differ significantly in *internal representation* and *action* compared to their PDP-11 counterparts. These differences will be
clarified when the PDP-11 is discussed in Chapter 3.

The concept of a symbolic address, to be considered in detail in Section 2.6.3,
will be introduced informally to facilitate examples. The notation "X:" will specify
a symbolic address, that of the instruction or datum which follows on the same
line, and hence is pointed to or referenced by, the symbolic address "X". In
Section 2.3.1, for example, we implicitly allocated symbolic addresses I1, I2, I3,
and I4 to a sequence of four contiguous memory locations. In practice, only those
memory locations which are to be referenced by instructions need be given
symbolic addresses. Also, as we shall observe in the following examples, only the
first item in a block of contiguous data need generally be assigned a symbolic
address. Finally, so as to facilitate better understanding of the program examples,
comments are appended to selected instruction lines by preceding them with a ";".

2.4.1 Basic Address Specification

Historically, software breeds hardware. That is, the need for certain modes of
address specification, as observed by programmers, has given rise to such address
specification techniques implemented via more efficient "hardware" in later

machines. We will therefore provide motivation for the address specification techniques to be discussed by starting with a high level language example of a simple algorithm. One of the most common array manipulation problems is to sum elements in an integer array. The following FORTRAN program fragment illustrates a typical high level language approach to the problem:

```
          .
          .
          .
       ISUM = 0
       DO 10 I = 1,50
   10  ISUM = ISUM + K(I)
          .
          .
          .
```

The problem could be implemented on our two address machine, in assembler language, as follows:

```
             .
             .
             .
       MOV   ZERO,ISUM          ;INITIALIZE SUM
       ADD   K,ISUM             ;ADD FIRST K VALUE
       ADD   K+1,ISUM           ;ADD SECOND K VALUE
       ADD   K+2,ISUM           ;ADD THIRD K VALUE
             .
             .
             .
       ADD   K+49,ISUM          ;NOTE: DECIMAL 49
             .
             .
             .
ZERO:  0
ISUM:  0
K:     (ARRAY OF 50 ELEMENTS STARTS HERE)
```

The solution assumes that the array K occupies consecutive words in memory, and the programmer has chosen to code the problem as a linear sequence of steps. For example, the "accumulate" portion of the program could reside in consecutive memory locations beginning at 1000, with the array K stored in locations 2000 and up, and ISUM stored in location 3000. Further, assume that an ADD operation has a numeric value of 10. Then having loaded memory with the linear instruction sequence specified above, the memory contents would appear as:

Location	Contents
1000	10 2000 3000
1001	10 2001 3000
1002	10 2002 3000
.	. . .

In this hypothetical machine, *both* operand addresses are specified within the same memory word containing the operation code.

This example also illustrates what has been referred to as the programmer's "plus or minus one syndrome." This problem is exemplified by the question "How many numbers are there between 19 and 27, inclusive?", and by the usual and inaccurate answer, "8". Clearly, the computer programmer must remember to account for both end points. In the problem being considered, there can arise a similar confusion: What is the actual address of the last element of the 50-word array, K + 49, or K + 50? The answer assumed in the preceding program is correct, but it requires us to remember that when the first symbolic address is K + 0, the last address is "1 less" than the number of elements. A more space efficient (but probably less time efficient) solution involves address modification.

2.4.2 Address Modification

As any good FORTRAN programmer knows, the use of a *program loop*, in which a set of instructions is performed repeatedly, is common programming practice. Looping is one of the most powerful constructs or tools at the programmer's disposal. It enables him to perform similar operations many times using the same instructions many times. Looping also makes a program more flexible because it is relatively easy to change the number of loops required for differing conditions by resetting a counter. It is good to remember that looping is little more than a jump to an earlier part of the program; however, the jump is usually dependent upon changing program conditions.

For the program at hand, the changing program conditions are program addresses. Each ADD instruction is similar to the last except that its operand value (array address) is 1 greater than its predecessor. Consequently, if we are to remake the linear program into a looping program, the address portion of the ADD instruction must be modified each time the program executes the instructions in the loop.

Earlier, the von Neumann concept was discussed. One of the consequences of this concept was that a computer cannot distinguish between a number and an instruction. As applied to the problem at hand, it means that programs can operate on other programs, including themselves, so as to produce new programs. In particular, instructions in a program can be used to modify the operand or address portion of memory reference instructions.

Let us apply such address modification to the array problem on our hypothetical two address computer. The only difference in each instruction of the accumulate sequence is the first address. It is conceivable to take the contents of location 1001, add 1 to the *first address* and produce as a result the contents of location 1002, e.g.,

```
      contents of location 1001 i.e.,   10 2001 3000
                                              +1
  =   contents of location 1002 i.e.,   10 2002 3000
```

A flowchart showing the desired structure is shown in Fig. 2-9a.

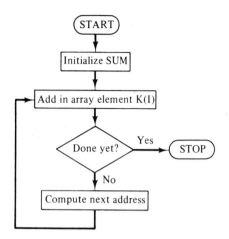

Fig. 2-9a Summing up the elements of the array K.

The resultant program segment is

```
            .
            .
            .
START:  MOV     ZERO,ISUM       ;INITIALIZE SUM
FIXUP:  ADD     K,ISUM          ;ADD ELEMENT OF ARRAY K
        CMP     FIXUP,LIMIT     ;DONE YET?
        BEQ     STOP            ;YES
        ADD     CONS,FIXUP      ;MODIFY ADDRESS
        BR      FIXUP           ;LOOP
STOP:   HALT
ZERO:   0                       ;CONSTANT ZERO
ISUM:   0                       ;RESULTANT SUM
CONS:   (A CONSTANT)            ;A SUITABLE VALUE SO AS TO
                                ;INCREMENT THE SOURCE OPERAND
                                ;ADDRESS OF "ADD K,ISUM" BY 1
LIMIT:  ADD     K+49,ISUM       ;SYMBOLIC REPRESENTATION OF "ADD"
                                ;INSTRUCTION AFTER FINAL LOOP
K:      (ARRAY OF 50 ELEMENTS STARTS HERE)
```

Fig. 2-9b Self modifying program

The reader can note several interesting points in this example. First, the instruction with label FIXUP is modified by adding a constant to the first operand address of this instruction. This generates a new operand address within the instruction so that the next time it is executed, the next element of the array K is added to ISUM. Second, the word labeled LIMIT contains a value that represents an instruction that will look like the instruction at FIXUP when it has been modified to add in the last element in the array K. Thus the CMP instruction is actually comparing two instruction values which are, in fact, represented by two numerical values. Third, although the program is self-modifying, it is not completely self-initializing. At the completion of its execution, the program will have modified the first operand address of the FIXUP instruction so that if the program is restarted, the results generated will be incorrect.

The use of address and instruction modification, although useful, should be discouraged. Some reasons for not using this technique are:

1. Such programs are often very difficult to debug.

2. Modern computing systems require treating instructions as pure, unmodified code because such programs may be protected, shared, handled more efficiently, and so on.

In order to avoid using instruction modification, we shall need to take advantage of other features to be found on our hypothetical computer.

2.4.3 General-Purpose Registers

Computer instruction sets are often more than sufficient in that they include "extra" instructions that duplicate the effect achieveable via other instructions in the same set. Nonetheless, these instructions do make programming easier, and often increase machine resource utilization through both time and space efficiency. Similarly, by developing effective strategies for easily manipulating elements of a simple data structure (e.g., the elements of a one-dimensional array or *vector*), the machine designer can significantly reduce the cost of programming and increase the speed of execution of programs. In particular, the availability of several *general-purpose registers* can assist the programmer in time-efficient operand addressing. The previous example for summing the 50 elements in the array K is a prime candidate for using general-purpose registers for operand addressing. Actually, the registers may be used both as address pointers, or more commonly, *index registers*, and as data accumulators.

When the general registers are used in index mode the final or *effective address* (EA) of the source and destination operands is calculated as the value of the operand or index word (X) plus the contents of the specified index register (R). The index word may be considered to be a signed number. As a result, the effective address for an indexed instruction is of the form

$$X + (R) = EA$$

where X may be a positive or negative value. For example, an indexed ADD instruction may be written symbolically as

```
ADD    X(R),ISUM
```

Assume that our hypothetical machine has two general-purpose registers, called R0 and R1. Each register is capable of holding either an address or a data word, and either may be used for indexing. Usually the general registers are hardware registers, within the processor, which operate at high transfer rates and thus provide speed advantages when used for operating on frequently accessed variables. In our machine the registers may be used in all instructions as both accumulators and index registers.

Using the general registers for indexing and accumulation, the example program can be rewritten (Fig. 2-10). Although this code sequence is longer than the earlier, self-modifying program, it does not modify the instructions and is self-initializing (i.e., R0 starts at zero each time it is executed).

The program as shown uses R0 as an accumulating register and R1 as an index register. After clearing both, it adds in elements of the array K by forming the effective address of the first operand from the contents of R1 and the base address K. Consequently, the effective addresses will be K, K + 1, K + 2, ..., K + 49. The CMP instruction limits the looping since it compares the contents of R1 to the decimal value 49. As long as R1 < 50, the contents of R1 will be incremented by 1 and the loop repeated. When the value of R1 reaches 50, the program stops. The careful reader will note that by using indexed addressing, the values being compared are no longer addresses but numerical offsets to a base address.

```
        .
        .
        MOV     ZERO,R0         ;SUM IN REGISTER 0
        MOV     ZERO,R1         ;COUNT IN REGISTER 1
LOOP:   ADD     K(R1),R0        ;ADD IN ELEMENT OF ARRAY K
        CMP     R1,D49          ;DONE?
        BPL     STOP            ;YES!
        ADD     ONE,R1          ;NO, GENERATE NEXT INDEX
        BR      LOOP            ;CONTINUE LOOP
        .
        .
STOP:   HALT                    ;STOP HERE
ZERO:   0                       ;CONSTANT ZERO
ONE:    1                       ;CONSTANT ONE
D49:    49                      ;CONSTANT 49
K:      (ARRAY OF 50 ELEMENTS)
```

Fig. 2-10 Indexed addressing

2.4.4 Immediate Mode

Before continuing the discussion of addressing techniques for more effectively using our computer, a slight digression seems worthwhile. This concerns the use of symbolic names to refer to frequently used constants in the program. For example, an instruction utilizing the constant 2 might be of the form,

```
        ADD     TWO,N
```

where the required constant is stored in a memory location with symbolic address "TWO". A more convenient way to specify that 2 is to be added to N, and one that does not require an explicitly addressed word to hold the constant, would be to include the constant as part of the instruction. This change introduces a new type of addressing, referred to as *immediate mode* addressing. For example, to add 2 to N, one could write

```
              ADD       #2,N
```

where the immediate mode is specified by preceding the number (or symbol) by a " # " sign. Thus, instead of specifying the operand *address* as part of the instruction, the *operand* itself is included in the instruction.

If " # " is read as "the value of", then $\#n$ (n a constant) is that constant, and $\#X$ ("X" a symbolic address) means the address pointed to by "X". It should be noted that immediate values, being limited by the size of the address field they replace, can be no larger than the largest address which the instruction can reference.

The immediate mode of addressing may be further illustrated by going back to the array problem. This problem may be reprogrammed as follows:

```
        .
        .
        .
        MOV     #0,R0         ;R0 ← 0
        MOV     #49,R1        ;R1 ← 49
LOOP:   ADD     K(R1),R0      ;ADD IN ELEMENT OF ARRAY K
        SUB     #1,R1         ;R1 ← R1 -1
        BPL     LOOP          ;LOOP WHILE R1 ≥ 0
        .
        .
```

The total number of statements has been decreased. However, the decrease in the number of instructions in the loop is a result of a new programming technique and not the result of immediate mode addressing. This technique recognizes the fact that the SUB instruction informs the control unit about the results of the last arithmetic operation just as the CMP instruction does. Thus by adding up the numbers in reverse order (last to first) and by allowing R1 to count down rather than up, it is unnecessary to use a CMP instruction. Instead, the program may simply test R1 after each subtraction, continuing to loop as long as R1 is non-negative.

2.4.5 Autoindexing

Indexing occurs so often in computer programs that some machines have built-in hardware to index automatically by automatically incrementing or decrementing an index register during use.

The *autoincrement* and *autodecrement* addressing modes on our machine provide for the automatic stepping of an index register value through the sequential elements of a table of values or operands. This mode assumes the contents of the selected general register to be the address of, or pointer to, the operand. Thus the pointer is stepped through a series of addresses so that it always points to the next sequential element of a table.

In autodecrement mode, written as -(R), the contents of the register are decremented *before* being used as the address of the operand. In autoincrement mode, written as (R)+, the contents of the register are incremented immediately *after* being used as the address of the operand.

Turning our attention once again to the array problem, the program to solve the problem may now be written as

```
        .
        .
        MOV     #0,R0           ;R0 ← 0
        MOV     #K,R1           ;R1 ← START ADDRESS OF ARRAY K
LOOP:   ADD     (R1)+,R0        ;R0 ← R0 + NEXT ELEMENT OF K
        CMP     #K+49,R1        ;DONE?
        BPL     LOOP            ;NO!
        .
        .
```

which is one of the shortest possible programs.

2.4.6 Deferred Addressing

An alternative to indexed addressing is *indirect addressing*, and while some computers have one mode of addressing or the other, our hypothetical machine has both. This *deferred* mode of addressing may be used in conjunction with the other modes of addressing, such as register, indexed, or autoincrement, providing for very sophisticated addressing techniques.

Indirect addressing may be used in many ways. For example, it can assist the programmer in passing parameters to subroutines (as an alternative to utilizing index registers), for creating linked data structures, and so on. All these capabilities occur because indirect addressing specifies the "address of the address of the operand" rather than "the address of the operand".

Assembler syntax for indicating deferred addressing is "@" [or "( )" when this is not ambiguous] associated with the operand. As an example, the following program segment could be used to clear the contents of location HERE:

```
        MOV     #0,@INDR        ;CLEAR OPERAND SPECIFIED BY
                                ;      CONTENTS OF "INDR"
                .
INDR:   HERE                    ;CONTAINS ADDRESS OF "HERE"
                .
HERE:   77                      ;"77" OVERWRITTEN BY "0"
```

The operation of clearing a memory location may be applied to clearing an array of memory locations. The logical flow of operations to be performed is shown by the flowchart and accompanying program segment shown in Fig. 2-11. In this example the MOV instruction is used to initialize R1 to the first address of the array A (i.e., since the first operand is #A, the address of A is placed in R1), so that the contents of R1 may be indirectly referenced.

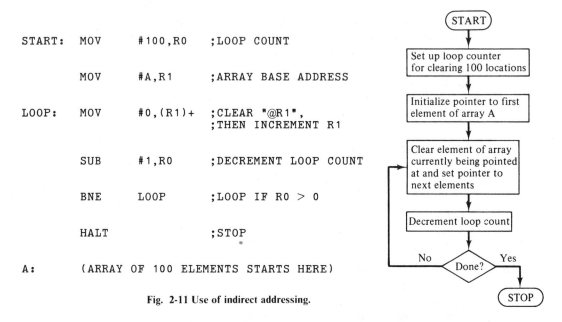

```
START:   MOV      #100,R0    ;LOOP COUNT

         MOV      #A,R1      ;ARRAY BASE ADDRESS

LOOP:    MOV      #0,(R1)+   ;CLEAR "@R1",
                            ;THEN INCREMENT R1

         SUB      #1,R0      ;DECREMENT LOOP COUNT

         BNE      LOOP       ;LOOP IF R0 > 0

         HALT                ;STOP

A:       (ARRAY OF 100 ELEMENTS STARTS HERE)
```

Fig. 2-11 Use of indirect addressing.

Both examples just presented illustrated single-level indirect addressing. It is possible for a computer to utilize multilevel indirect addressing if the location indirectly addressed is itself the address of another location to be indirectly referenced. Multilevel indirectness requires that each location referenced have a bit which specifies whether this location is an address to be used directly or indirectly.

The choice of multilevel versus single-level indirectness is one based on user convenience and cost. On a short-word-length machine typified by today's smallest and cheapest microcomputers, where every bit must be utilized efficiently, multilevel indirect addressing is often not provided. The reason is one of economics in that as many bits as possible in the instruction word are used for directly addressing memory and, as a consequence, the indirect bit becomes a part of the instruction word rather than a part of the operand address.

Another point to be considered is that a computer which has both indexing and indirect addressing must specify which mode of addressing is performed first. Although it may seem that it does not really matter, there are reasons for performing indexing before indirectness, or vice versa.

In a computer that has a short word length, where it is not possible to address all of memory directly, indirect addressing is performed first. The reason is that the word used as an indirect address is generally larger than the address field of the instruction and can, therefore, address all of memory before being indexed. On the other hand, if all of memory can be referenced by an instruction, as on a long-

or variable-instruction-length computer, it is more convenient to index first in order to facilitate such things as subroutine parameter passing.

2.5 THE STAGES OF PROCESSING INSTRUCTIONS IN A COMPUTER

Our attention has been focused on operand addressing. In the larger view, we need to be concerned with how a computer deals with a complete instruction. As shown in Fig. 2-12, each instruction has several stages of interpretation.

2.5.1 Instruction, Operand, and Execution Phases

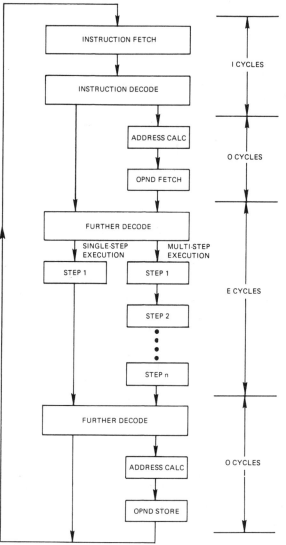

The instruction is first fetched from memory and decoded (Instruction or *I-phase*). Next, the operand address(es) are computed and the operands are fetched from memory (Operand or *O-phase*). The complexity of the *O*-phase processing obviously depends upon the address modes used. During the execution or *E-phase*, the specified operation is performed on the operand(s). The complexity of the *E*-phase varies significantly among different instructions. For example, a MOV instruction requires no arithmetic operations and involves two operands. A "MULtiply" involves a number of operations and two operands. Additional *O*-phase processing may be necessary if the result is to be stored in memory.

The complexity of the stages required for a computer to process an instruction, and hence the instruction execution time, depends on a number of factors. "MUL", for example, generally effects fixed-point multiplication via repeated addition and shifting, and thus requires many *E*-cycles. However, it is certainly preferable that these *E*-cycles be performed in a single instruction as opposed to the series of machine language add-and-shifts required when "MUL" is not available. Similarly, although multi-level indirection requires many *O*-cycles, such addressing modes are usually more time efficient than the multiple instructions necesary when such modes do not exist.

Fig. 2-12 The stages of processing instructions in a computer

What resources are available to aid a computer in instruction processing? If we examine the internal structure of the basic building blocks of a computer (Fig. 2-1), we find (Fig. 2-13) that in addition to the program counter, a number of registers generally invisible to the programmer are present:

1. The *instruction register* (IR) contains a copy of the instruction being executed.

2. The *memory address register* (MAR) is used to address memory.

3. The *memory data register* (MDR) is used as a buffer for holding data transferred between memory and CPU.

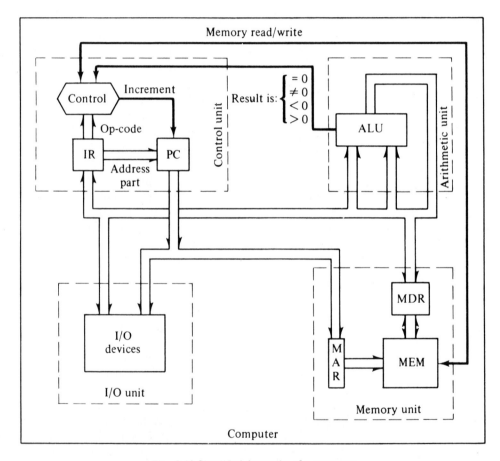

Fig. 2-13 Simplified datapaths of a computer.

For example, execution of an "ADD X,Y" instruction could proceed as follows:

```
I-phase
-------
1. (MAR)  ← (PC)                    ;ADDRESS OF INSTRUCTION INTO MAR
2. (MDR)  ← ((MAR))                 ;FETCH INSTRUCTION
3. (PC)   ← (PC) + 1                ;INCREMENT PC
4. (IR)   ← (MDR)                   ;COPY INSTRUCTION INTO IR
5. DECODE INSTRUCTION


O-phase
-------
1. (MAR)  ← (IR address opnd1)      ;COMPUTE ADDRESS OF OPERAND1
2. (MDR)  ← ((MAR))                 ;FETCH OPERAND1
3. (Rx)   ← (MDR)                   ;ROUTE OPERAND1 TO ALU RIGHT PORT
4. (MAR)  ← (IR address opnd2)      ;COMPUTE ADDRESS OF OPERAND2
5. (MDR)  ← ((MAR))                 ;FETCH OPERAND2
6. (Ry)   ← (MDR)                   ;ROUTE OPERAND2 TO ALU LEFT PORT


E-phase
-------
1. (MDR)  ← (Rx) + (Ry)             ;ADD


O-phase
-------
1. ((MAR)) ← (MDR)                  ;STORE RESULT
```

Here, *Rx* and *Ry* are the ALU input ports. In Section 3.5.4 we will examine the operations required for the *I-*, *O-*, and *E*-cycles of PDP-11 instructions in particular. Then, in Chapter 6, we will show how the inner architectural components of a specific PDP-11, the 11/60, is used to implement the PDP-11 instruction set.

2.6 THE SYMBOLIC ASSEMBLER: A PROGRAMMING AID

Coding a machine language program numerically is a difficult task. It requires the programmer to remember both the machine language operations codes and the addresses of the instruction operands. As we have seen in the examples of the previous few sections, by using mnemonic or memory assisting names for both *op-codes* and *operands*, it is much easier to program and to read programs already written. This is so not only because the mnemonics are descriptive of the operation to be performed but also because the names of the operands can be chosen so as to suggest their use (e.g., SUMX, ABS, COUNT, etc.) in much the way that variable names are chosen in higher-level languages. The *symbolic assembler* thus is an important programming aid.

2.6.1 The Asssembly Process

The clerical task of translating symbolic code to machine language is called the *assembly process*. Fortunately, this process is easily automated and may be done by the computer itself. A symbolic assembler is a translation program in the same sense that a FORTRAN compiler is. Both transform a program written in one language (the *source language*) into another language (the *object language*, Fig. 2-14). One difference between an assembler and a compiler is found in the complexity of the source language. Assemblers usually perform a one-to-one transliteration of the symbolic source statements into machine language or code. Compilers operate on higher-level language statements, often producing many machine language statements from just one source statement. Another difference is that the object language of compilers is often a symbolic language (e.g., assembly language) which must then undergo further stages of translation.

Fig. 2-14 Translation of a program.

In order to assemble a symbolic program, the assembly process requires three things:

1. Keeping track of instructions and where they are to reside in memory.

2. Keeping track of the symbols used and their values.

3. A translation technique for converting the op-codes and symbols into their machine language equivalents.

These requirements are facilitated by maintaining both a *location counter* and a *symbol table* within the assembler.

2.6.2 Location Counter

Most symbolic programs are written with the implicit idea that successive instructions will be stored in successive memory locations. If the programmer assigned an absolute location to the first instruction, the assembler could be told to assign the next instructions to the following locations in order.

If we consider the assembler as a computing machine, then the *location counter* (*LC*) acts for the assembler as the *program counter* (*PC*) acts for the computer. The job of the LC is to keep track of where the next instruction or operand is to be placed in memory. As each symbolic instruction is translated, the value of the LC is updated to reflect the fact that the current location has been utilized.

2.6.3 Symbolic Addresses

The programmer does not know (or need to know) at the outset which absolute memory locations he will use to hold initial values or constants, to store results in, or to branch to when such an action is appropriate. Therefore, he may arbitrarily assign symbolic names to the locations to which he must refer, and then allow the assembler the job of assigning numerical values to these symbolic names or addresses. As each of these symbolic locations is encountered by the assembler, the symbol is taken to be the *label* for, or pointer to, the location which the symbol represents, and the current value of the location counter is assigned to the symbol. In order to remember the values of all such symbols encountered, the assembler maintains a *symbol table* in which it records the numerical value of all encountered symbol labels. The recognition of symbols as labels is often facilitated by placing a special terminating character after the string of characters. As seen in previous examples, the special character used here is a colon (e.g., "A:").

In summary, the task of an assembly language programmer is to write in a symbolic language a *source program* (input) from which a machine language or *object program* (output) is to be produced. By using symbolic names and labels, the programmer is able to write a program that is relatively independent of all absolute memory references. Actually, the symbolic locations themselves are independent of location and the programmer is thus free to insert or delete such instructions at will.

In general, the assembler will accept the symbolic instructions and produce machine language statements on a one-for-one basis. Thus, symbolic programming may be defined as a method wherein names, instructions, and symbols are used to write programs. The process of programming in assembly language is one of using declarative, imperative, and control statements for the purpose of specifying both what is to be produced and how it is to be produced.

The three basic types of assembly language statements are described as follows:

1. **Declarative:** used to control assignment of storage for various names, input/output, and working areas. These are not really instructions but rather reservations of space, definition of symbols, and assignments of contents to locations.

2. **Imperative:** these are the actual machine instructions as they appear in their symbolic form.

3. **Control:** instructions directed to the assembler to allow the programmer to have some control over portions of the assembly process.

2.6.4 Symbolic Programming Syntax

Assembly language programming is similar to programming in any computer language. There are rigid rules that must be followed if the sentences (e.g., source statements) in the language are to be recognized by the assembler. Since both assemblers and compilers are language translators, it should not be surprising to find the rules for constructing sentences in assembly language similar to those found in FORTRAN.

Identifiers or *symbols* used in assembly language programs are made up of any sequence of letters (A, B, C, ..., Z) and digits, with the first character of the symbol a letter. In general, the mnemonic codes for the instructions defined for any given computer are symbols for which the assembler retains their numerical equivalents in a permanent symbol table. *User-defined* symbols usually have a fixed maximum length, or else only the first few characters are considered and any additional characters are ignored. Examples of user-defined symbols include NUM, START, and ONE, which have been used in previous example programs.

Any sequence of digits forms a *number*. For programmer convenience, most assemblers will accept numbers that are in different bases, such as octal and decimal. However, if the assembler expects values in one base, say octal, it is necessary to indicate that a different base is being used by a assembler control instruction, or pseudo-op, such as .BASE or by following the number with an identifying radix character such as a decimal point (e.g., 98. to specfy decimal 98 to a nominally octal assembler). Regardless of the base, each number and symbol written in the program must represent a binary value in order to be interpreted by the assembler.

Often there will be special characters in the assembler's character set to facilitate the recognition of labels, pseudo-ops, decimal values, comments, and so on. These characters include

$$. \quad \$ \quad : \quad = \quad \% \quad \# \quad @ \quad (\quad) \quad ; \quad " \quad ' \quad + \quad - \quad \& \quad !$$

plus the nonprinting space character, which does not have a graphic symbol but does affect the assembly process. These special characters are used to specify operations to be performed by the assembler upon the symbols or numbers appearing in programs. For example, the use of the colon after a label symbol has already been demonstrated.

Statement format up until now has been defined mainly by example. However, an assembler does have an assembly language format. For us, a symbolic line of code is composed of up to four fields, each field being either identified by its order of appearance or the special character used to terminate the last field. These fields are

LABEL   OPERATOR   OPERAND   COMMENT

The label and comment fields are optional. The operator and operand fields are interdependent; either may be omitted, depending on the contents of the other. An operand is that part of a statement which is operated on by the operator. Operands may be symbols, expressions, or numbers. When multiple operands appear within a statement, each must be separated from the next by a special character, usually a comma. In addition, comments must generally be preceded by a special character. For our purposes, a semicolon is used.

Rather than dictate a rigid format, an assembler that uses special characters to delimit fields allows for a *free-format layout* of assembler code. The statement format is thus controlled by the programmer, who may freely insert spaces. These spaces have no effect on the assembly process of the source program unless they are embedded within a symbol, number, or character string (to be discussed later); or are used as the operator field terminator. Thus they may be used to provide a neat, readable program. As an example, consider the statement:

```
LABEL:MOV(R0)+,TAG;POP VALUE OFF A STACK
```

which, using formating characters, may be written as

```
LABEL:    MOV     (R0)+,TAG      ;POP VALUE OFF A STACK
```

which is much easier to read.

2.6.5 Control Statements

The purpose of the control statement is to direct the assembler to perform certain processing options. The control statement is not a true machine language instruction, even though it is in a form similiar to an op-code (i.e., with a command, optional label and/or operands). Thus it is referred to as a *pseudo-op*, and generally flagged as such by preceding it with a special character such as a period.

The most common pseudo-op is the .END statement of the form

```
.END label
```

It acts as a control statement for the assembler, informing it that this line is the last to be translated, and that, once translated, the program is to begin at the instruction whose symbolic address is that of the .END operand. It is obviously equivalent to the END statement found in all FORTRAN programs. Other pseudo-ops are listed below:

```
Pseudo-op Format  Meaning
----------------  -------
```

	Pseudo-op Format	Meaning
label:	.WORD value	Place "value" in a word with symbolic address "label"
label:	.BLKW value	Reserves contiguous block of "value" words starting at symbolic address "label".
	.TITLE title	Gives a title to a program.

EXERCISES

1. Rewrite the flowchart of Fig. 2-3 for a two-address computer.

2. Construct a flowchart to sum up all the positive values in the array K of 50 elements. Place the sum in symbolic location SUM.

3. Assembly languages often have what appear to be arbitrary restrictions. However, these restrictions make sense to the programmer who writes the assembler program for an assembly language in that they eliminate ambiguities, facilitate memory assignment, and so on. Below are listed some of these restrictions. In each case, give an explanation, from the point of view of the person writing a two-pass assembly, why they exist.

   a. Symbols must begin with a letter.

   b. Symbols cannot contain special characters (+, -, comma) or blanks.

   c. A symbol may not appear in the location field more than once in a program.

4. Write a program to add together all the *positive* numbers found in locations 3001, 3002, 3003, ... The number of numbers, N, is stored in location 3000 and $0 \leq N \leq 99$. If $N = 0$, the results should be zero. The sum of the numbers should be stored in location 2777.

5. Write a program to perform the equivalent FORTRAN program sequence for the integer arrays A, B, and C:

```
          DO 10 I=1,1000
   10     C(I)= A(I)+B(I)
```

6. Write a program to sort N numbers in place. Show that your program will work for all values of N such as $0 \leq N \leq 99$. Your solution should make use of index registers and should not result in a self-modifying program.

7. Suppose that a computer has 4096 words of memory addressed from location 0 to 4095, and one index register R. If the effective address for an indexed instruction that references X is EA $= X + (R)$, then if $(R) = 0$ and the desired EA $= 4095$, what is the value of X?

8. Given the same computer as for Exercise 7 but that this time $(R) = 4095$ and the desired EA $= 0$, what is the value of X?

9. Rewrite the program segment in Section 2.4.5 so that it uses autodecrementing rather than autoincrementing.

10. In a computer with both indexing and indirect addressing, it is important to know which is done first when an indexed indirect instruction is encountered. Explain why the order is so important by considering machines that will handle both short (say 12 bits) and long (say 36 bits) instruction words.

11. In a machine that has both immediate and indirect addressing, what is the meaning of an indirect-immediate reference?

12. Given one level of indirectness *or* index registers, which do you think is preferable and why?

13. Assume that we have a fixed-word-length, signed-magnitude, decimal, two-address machine with full addressing mode capabilities for both instruction addresses (i.e., immediate, direct, and indirect). The symbolic instruction format is such that either address expression can be followed by a $ symbol to indicate immediate addressing, a # symbol to indicate indirect addressing, or neither symbol to indicate direct addressing. Also assume that * stands for the location counter and is the address of the instruction currently being assembled. Among the instruction set for this machine are the following operations and their interpretations:

```
ADD  A1,A2    (A1) ← (A1) + (A2)
SUB  A1,A2    (A1) ← (A1) - (A2)
BGT  A1,A2    if (A1) > (A2) skip next instruction
BZE  A1,A2    if (A1) = 0 jump to A2
```

where A1 and A2 are address expressions and include any addressing mode symbols that may be present. Assume, further, the following initial conditions for address symbols:

Symbol	Memory Location	Contents
A	0	2
B	1	1
	2	0
	3	-1
	4	3
C	5	4
D	6	5

State, for each of the following, the effect of executing the instruction or sequence of instructions; that is, what, if anything, has changed in memory?

(For example, executing ADD A,B changes the contents of memory location 0 to 3.) Assume that the initial conditions apply for each question.

```
a.    SUB  A,A

b.    ADD  B,5$

c.    SUB  B+2,C#

d.    BGT  A$,B#
      ADD  A#,B+3#

e.    BZE  2#,*+2
      SUB  D#,B+1$
```

REFERENCES

The purpose of this chapter was to develop programming concepts and fundamentals without unnecessarily tying them down to a particular computer. This approach has been taken by Abrams and Stein (1973), Walker (1972), Flores (1966), and Mauer (1968). Although still general in tone, books by Stone (1975), Gear (1974), and Katzan (1971) have tied their presentations to particular machines. Hopefully, the intent and style of presentation of this makes it possible to take a particular user's reference manual and relate the characteristics of a given computer to the topics being presented. Chapter 3, in fact, does this for the PDP-11; for those readers who are interested in this machine, the *PDP-11 Processor Handbook* can be used to reinforce the concepts being discussed. More advanced ideas on computer architecture are discussed in Stone (1975), Tannenbaum (1976), and Hayes (1978).

3

The PDP-11

The PDP-11 family consists of high-speed, general-purpose digital computers that operate primarily on either 8- or 16-bit binary numbers. The instruction set includes zero-, one-, and two-address instructions which utilize a set of eight general purpose registers to specify operands in a variety of modes. This flexibility generally enables the programmer to select instruction/address combinations which are appropriate for the problem being solved and thus produce programs which are both *space* and *time* efficient. That is, whatever the algorithm, the programmer can generally create code which is relatively *compact* (compared to programs realizing the same algorithm on other architectures) and relatively *fast* (compared to programs running on other machines implemented with the same technology as the relevant PDP-11).

The PDP-11's are parallel machines using two's-complement arithmetic for integer (fixed-point) arithmetic. The PDP-11/60 also includes an instruction set and associated registers for manipulating 32- or 64-bit floating-point numbers. The PDP-11/34 and 11/60 contain *memory management* to allow for primary memory sizes greater than the 64 Kbytes directly accessible by a 16-bit address. Both of these facilities are provided for optionally on most other PDP-11's.

The PDP-11 processor consists essentially of the five basic computer units that were discussed in Chapter 1. The components of the five units and their interrelationships are shown in Fig. 3-1.

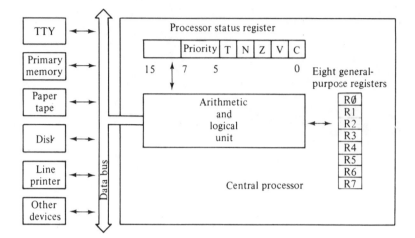

Fig. 3-1 PDP-11 system block diagram.

3.1 PDP-11 MACHINE STRUCTURE

Since the five functional units shown in Fig. 2-1 are not clearly delineated in Fig. 3-1, it is instructive to discuss the block structure of this machine in detail.

3.1.1 The UNIBUS Concept

Typical input and output units are shown in Fig. 3-1. The connection between the central processing unit (CPU) and the input and output devices is through the *data bus*. This common bus represents a collection of wires that carry information signals (e.g., *address*, *data*, and *control* signals) between the devices connected to it. Because the bus is capable of carrying many signals simultaneously (such as all 16 bits of a memory word), it is represented by a wide line in Fig. 3-1.

The common data bus of Fig. 3-1 can be likened to a common highway for computer data flow. Any input or output device, or the CPU, may place information onto the highway, and conversely, any of them may take information from it. The common bus thus provides an efficient and effective means for passing information between the functional units connected to it.

The data bus of the PDP-11, more properly referred to as the UNIBUS, allows all input and output units to connect to and communicate with each other, as well as the central processor and the memory. Since all system elements communicate with each other in identical fashion via the UNIBUS, the input and output units have the same easy access with each other as the processor and memory have with them. And, since the UNIBUS is capable of accepting any number of external devices, new options (e.g., expanded memory or additional input and output devices) can be simply plugged in as they become available.

With bidirectional and asynchronous communications on the UNIBUS, devices can send, receive, and exchange data independently without central processor intervention. For example, a cathode ray tube (CRT) display can refresh itself from memory while the central processor unit (CPU) attends to other tasks. Because it is asynchronous, the UNIBUS is compatible with devices operating over a wide range of speeds.

Device communications on the UNIBUS are interlocked. For each command issued by a "master" device, a response signal is received from a "slave," completing the data transfer. Device-to-device communication is completely independent of physical bus length and the response times of master and slave devices.

Many of the same devices connected to the UNIBUS may act as both an input and an output unit. The disk, for example, can be used to input information via the UNIBUS to the computer. Alternatively, the same device can accept processed information and store it as output. Thus the two units of input and output are very often joined and referred to as input/output (I/O). Chapter 7 describes the methods for transmitting data as either input or output, but for the present the reader can assume that the computer is able to accept information from devices such as those shown in the block diagram and to return output information to the devices. The PDP-11 console allows the programmer direct access to primary memory and the program counter by setting a series of switches, or in some machines, via a keyboard or terminal console (Appendix E).

3.1.2 Arithmetic and Logical Unit

Central to the PDP-11 block diagram is the arithmetic unit. This unit accepts data from the UNIBUS, from the eight general-purpose (*gp*) registers, or from the six floating-point (*fp*) registers, when available. It may transmit processed information to these units as well as to the status register. Since the PDP-11 uses a two-address instruction format for many of its arithmetic operations, there is no single register designated as accumulator in this machine. Instead, results may be stored either in the memory unit or in the *gp* or *fp* registers.

3.1.3 Fast Arithmetic Processing

Although extended fixed-point arithmetic operations (e.g., multiply, divide, and multiple shifts) may be programmed via the basic fixed-point and logical instructions available on all PDP-11's, optional facilities are needed for high-speed applications. An Extended Arithmetic Element (EAE) is available as a UNIBUS peripheral for effecting high-speed fixed-point multiply and divide, multiple shifts, and normalization. Some PDP-11's possess an Extended Instruction Set (EIS) which enables efficient fixed-point multiply, divide, and multiple arithmetic shifts using the general register set, thus obviating the need for an EAE. Time-efficient floating-point number manipulation may be effected via a Floating Instruction Set (FIS), which uses one or more stacks for accumulators, or via a Floating-Point

Processor (FPP) with its own instruction set and associated floating-point accumulators for fast 32- or 64-bit floating-point arithmetic.

The EIS is standard on the PDP-11/34, 45, 50, 55, 60 and 70, and optional on the LSI-ll (ll/03), and 11/40. The FIS is optional for the 11/03 and 11/40. High speed FPP hardware is optional on the 11/34, 45, 50, 55, 60 and 70. When installed on the 11/60, the FPP hardware intercepts the standard FPP "software" and executes the required instructions at very high speeds.

3.1.4 Control Unit

Although the control unit is not explicitly shown in Fig. 3-1, its presence is implicitly indicated by the status registers, the eight general-purpose registers, and the UNIBUS. For example, general register 7 acts as the PDP-11's program counter, while the N, Z, V, and C bits in the status register maintain the state of the machine by monitoring the results of previous instructions.

The program counter is used by the PDP-11 control unit to record the locations in memory (addresses) of the instructions to be executed. The PC always contains the address of the next word of the instruction being executed or the address of the next instruction to be executed. Thus, whenever the processor uses the program counter to acquire a word from memory, the PC is always incremented by 2 since, as we shall see, word addresses are always even. When an instruction is encountered, causing transfer of control to another portion of the stored program, the PC is set to the appropriate address. The PC must be initially set to specify the starting address of a program, but further actions are controlled by program instructions.

The use of a general register as the program counter is unique on the PDP-11. The flexibility in doing so leads to some interesting techniques for specifying relative and immediate addressing. The characteristics of using the program counter for operand addressing are discussed in greater detail later in this chapter and in Chapter 6.

The processor status register (PS) of the PDP-11 contains information about the results of the last operation performed. The register is subdivided into one-bit indicators called *condition codes* (CC), which are set according to the final value produced by an arithmetic operation (e.g., TST, ADD, SUB, and CMP), or data word manipulation (e.g., MOV). These indicators are therefore "remembered" until another operation manipulates them. Examining these bits, we find that the Z-bit indicates that the last result was zero and the N-bit indicates that the last result was negative. The C- and V-bits have to do with results that generate carries and overflow, and we shall postpone their discussion, along with that of the T-bit and the meaning of priority, until Chapters 4, 7, and 9.

It is important to stress the interrelation between the condition codes and the instruction set, since the former are so important to the operation of the latter. For example, in Chapter 2 the technique of counting down while looping through a sequence of instructions can be implemented as follows on a PDP-11:

```
              MOV      #100,R0        ;NUMBER OF TIMES THROUGH LOOP
              MOV      #A,R1          ;ADDRESS OF A(1)
     LOOP:    MOV      #0,(R1)+       ;CLEAR ARRAY LOCATION
              SUB      #1,R0          ;DECREMENT R0, SET Z BIT IF ZERO
              BNE      LOOP           ;LOOP UNTIL Z = 0
```

This strategy makes it unnecessary to compare the loop count to zero, thus saving an instruction. In fact, since this loop termination construct occurs so often, most PDP-11 family members include a subtract/conditional branch instruction of the form

```
              SOB      Rn,LOOP
```

where LOOP is the address (occurring *before* the SOB) to which transfer is to be made if Rn, decremented by the instruction, is *not* zero.

Since the condition codes are not reset by a branch instruction (or a SOB), multiple-way branches are possible using only one compare instruction. Thus if X is a value between 1 and 3 inclusive, a three-way branch based on the value of X could be easily coded:

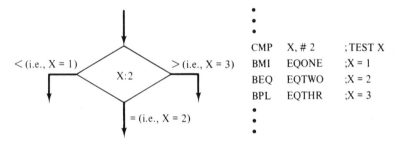

Not all the PDP-11 instructions affect the condition bits in the same manner, however. Whereas the CMP instruction sets all the bits (N, Z, V, and C) conditionally, the MOV instruction only sets the N- and Z-bits conditionally, while setting the V-bit unconditionally to 0 and not affecting the C-bit at all. Appendix D, a brief summary of the complete instruction set for the PDP-11, describes the operation of each instruction, including the effect on the four condition codes N, Z, V, and C. As can be seen from the summary, some apparently equivalent instructions, such as ADD #1,VALUE, and INC VALUE (see Section 3.3.2 for a description of the single-operand instructions), do not affect the carry bit identically. Consequently, the knowledgeable programmer needs to pay particular attention to both the instruction set and the condition codes each instruction affects.

Another area of concern between the condition codes and the instruction set is in the handling of conditional branches. There are two categories, simple and signed, for the conditional branches in which individual condition code bits and combinations of them are tested to decide whether or not the branch is to be taken. The conditional instructions BEQ, BNE, BMI, and BPL, discussed in Chapter 2, are all examples of simple conditional branches that test a single bit (N or Z). The more complex signed conditional branches will not be discussed until Chapter 4, since it is not until then that the concepts of carry and overflow are discussed. These topics are necessary for a complete understanding of this set of branches.

3.1.5 Random Access Memory and the Input/Output Page

The PDP-11 basic memory address space is 65,536 bytes (64 K, where K "means" 1024) or 32 Kwords. The upper 4 Kwords are designated as the *input/output (I/O) page* or block. The memory can be viewed as a series of locations, with a number (address) assigned to each location. Locations in the I/O page are each associated with control and buffer registers of peripheral devices. As we shall see, this allows such devices to be controlled without the need for special I/O instructions.

Because PDP-11 memories and instructions are designed to accommodate both 16-bit words and 8-bit half-words, called *bytes*, the total number of addresses does not correspond to the number of words. Every word contains 2 bytes, so a 4096-word block contains 8192 byte locations. Consecutive words are therefore found in *even-numbered addresses*. Looking back at the hypothetical machine of Chapter 2, we can now see one important difference between it and the PDP-11 — that word addresses will always be *even* values. Thus consecutive instructions will fall into consecutive *even* addresses, and word operand addressing depends on *even-numbered* values being used as address pointers.

A PDP-11 word is divided into a high byte and a low byte as follows:

Because low bytes are stored at even-numbered memory locations and high bytes at odd-numbered memory locations, the address of any word is identical to the address of the low byte of that word. Thus it is convenient for the programmer to view the PDP-11 memory as shown in Fig. 3-2.

Certain memory locations have been reserved for system use. These locations typically include addresses from 0 to 777(8) and, as noted previously, the top 4096 word addresses (from 160000(8) up). The use of these locations is described in Chapter 7. Note that where ambiguity is possible, either the "( )" construct or subscripts will be used to denote the arithmetic base.

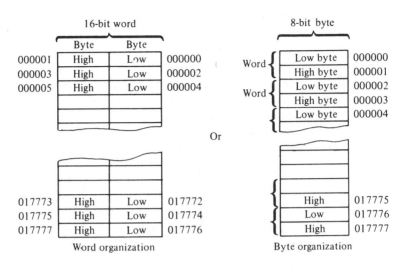

Fig. 3-2 PDP-11 Word and Byte Numbering.

3.2 DATA REPRESENTATION

Data stored with the PDP-11 is interpreted as one of three basic types:

1. Fixed-point numbers (integers)

2. Floating-point numbers

3. Alphanumeric characters

Before attempting to explain each type, we will briefly review the concept of number systems. Appendix A provides the necessary background for understanding these concepts.

3.2.1 Number Systems

It is important to realize that all data stored in the computer memory are indistinguishable in that all are, simply, binary numbers. Only by interpreting the data as a representation of something useful are we able to use the data meaningfully as information.

In the *decimal* numbering system (base 10), the value of a numeral depends upon the numeral's position in a number; for example,

$$347 = 3 * 100 = 300$$
$$+ 4 * 10 = 40$$
$$+ 7 * 1 = 7$$
$$---$$
$$347$$

The value of each position in a number is known as its *position coefficient*. Each must be multiplied by a power of the radix called the *digit-position weighting value*, *weighting value*, or simply the *weight*.

Utilizing the positional coefficients and weighting values, it is possible to express any weighted number system in the following generalized form:

$$X = x_n w_n + x_{n-1} w_{n-1} + \ldots + x_1 w_1 + x_0 w_0 + x_{-m} w_{-m}$$

where

$$w_i = r^i \text{ (i.e., } r^i = \text{weighting values and } r = \text{radix or base)}$$

and

$$0 \le x_i \le r-1 \text{ (i.e., } x_i = \text{positional coefficients).}$$

This formalism makes it clear that the largest value of a positional coefficient is always 1 less than the base value. For base 2 this means that the largest coefficient is 1; for base 10 it is a 9. Although this may seem intuitively obvious, it is not an uncommon mistake for the novice programmer (and even some old-timers) to write illegal numbers while coding programs (e.g., 10853 in base 8 or 102 in base 2).

Examples of writing the full formal expressions for weighted number systems are

$$132 = 1*10^2 + 3*10^1 + 2*10^0$$

$$= 1*2^7 + 0*2^6 + 0*2^5 + 0*2^4 + 0*2^3 + 1*2^2 + 0*2^1 + 0*2^0$$

$$= 2*8^2 + 0*8^1 + 4*8^0$$

$$= 8*16^1 + 4*16^0$$

In other words,

$$132_{10} = 10000100_2 = 204_8 = 84_{16}$$

It is interesting to note that although all examples have assumed a positive radix, negative radices are also possible. For example, assuming a radix of –3, the value 132. may be expressed as

$$132_{10} = 2*(-3)^4 +1*(-3)^3 +0*(-3)^2 +1*(-3)^1 +0*(-3)^0$$

$$= 21010_{-3}$$

It is even possible to conceive of nonweighted number systems (and such systems do exist, such as "Excess-3" and "2 out of 5"), but the discussion of such systems is beyond the scope of this book.

3.2.2 Representation of Numbers in a Computer

Because of the inherent binary nature of computer components, modern digital computers are all based on the binary number system. However, no matter how convenient the binary system may be for computers, it is exceedingly cumbersome for human beings. Consequently, most computer programmers use base 8 or base 16 arithmetic instead, and leave it up to the various system components (assemblers, compilers, loaders, etc.) to convert such numbers to their binary equivalents. Modern assemblers also permit decimal numbers, both integer and floating-point, to be input directly, a useful convenience for most applications programs.

Base 8 or *octal* and base 16 or *hexadecimal* representations of binary numbers are not only convenient but also easily derived. The conversion simply requires the programmer to separate the binary number into 3-bit (octal) or 4-bit (hexadecimal) groups, starting from the least significant digit (LSD) and replacing each binary group with its equivalent. Thus, for the binary number 010011100001,

$$010\ 011\ 100\ 001_2 = 2341_8$$
$$|$$
$$LSD$$

and

$$0100\ 1110\ 0001_2 = 4E1_{16}$$

This process is so naturally performed that most programmers can mentally convert visual representations of binary numbers (computer displays) to their octal (or hexadecimal) representation without consciously thinking about it. Special pocket calculators (e.g., the TI Programmer) are available which operate in both octal and hexadecimal for use as an aid in debugging programs.

3.2.3 Negative Numbers

For any base, there are three common ways to represent negative numbers. For example, negative binary numbers can be represented in *sign-magnitude, one's complement*, or *two's-complement* form. One might ask, therefore, which form a computer would use in performing arithmetic calculations.

In Appendix A, where the various representations of negative numbers are considered, sign-magnitude form is rejected in favor of complement form because it is more complex to add or subtract numbers using sign-magnitude arithmetic. Thus the choice of form for negative binary numbers is really between one's- and two's-complement representations. In reality, this choice boils down even further to the preference of the computer designer and the computer programmer.

Generation of one's-complement numbers is easier than generation of the two's-complement form. In addition, from the computer hardware point of view, it is more "uniform" to build a one's- than a two's-complement adder. On the other hand, the one's-complement notation allows for two representations of zero (e.g., both a positive and a negative zero):

```
000 000       zero
111 111       minus zero in one's complement
```

whereas only one zero exists in the two's-complement form:

```
                000 000       zero
                111 111       one's complement
                    +1        plus one
                -------
discarded 1) 000 000       two's complement of zero
```

Mathematically speaking, it is not nice to have two representations for zero. As a result, most machines today use two's complement notation to represent negative numbers.

3.2.4 Fixed-point (Integer) Numbers

Integers are represented in the PDP-11 as *bytes*, *words*, or *longwords*. The size, type, and range are shown below:

```
Type       Size       Signed      ← RANGE →    Unsigned
----       ----       ------      -----        --------
Byte        8 bits    -128 to +127             0 to 255
Word       16 bits    -32768 to +32767         0 to 65535
Longword   32 bits    -2**31 to +2**31-1       0 to 2**32-1
```

As we shall see, the PDP-11 has a complete set of instructions for addition, subtraction, multiplication, division, complementing and shifting of *words*. All of these operations treat the words as two's complement (signed) numbers. *Bytes* may only be added, subtracted, multiplied or divided via word instructions but may be manipulated directly for other arithmetic operations. *Longwords* appear as the product in word multiplication and as the dividend in division; they may be arithmetically shifted directly and added or subtracted via sequences involving word addition/subtraction. A complete set of conditional signed branches enables program control based on results of arithmetic operations. Note that because the most significant bit of a two's complement number always indicates the sign, this bit may be used for branch tests.

Additionally, instructions and branch tests are available which treat integers as unsigned quantities. These are useful for address manipulation.

3.2.5 Floating-Point Numbers

Integers are useful for data representation and problem solution in many areas, but they often lack the *dynamic range* necessary for correct solution of a wide range of scientific applications. That is, although the integers may represent the data with sufficient *precision*, the *magnitude* of the data or intermediate results may exceed the range defined by the width of the dataword. A *floating-point* number, like an integer, is a sequence of contiguous bits in memory. However the bits are interpreted as having two distinct parts, the *fraction* and the *exponent*. That is, the floating-point number may be stored in a computer word as

s	exponent	s	fraction

and is interpreted as ± .*nnnnnnnn* * 2**(±*mmmmmmmm*), where the "*n*" are bits in the fraction and the "*m*" are bits in the exponent. Note that we have arbitrarily allocated two sign bits so as to enable positive and negative exponents and fractions. It is more common, however, to assign only one sign bit to a word. Thus a different representation is used. This representation assigns the MSB as the sign of the fraction and divides the range of possible exponential values into two halves, one for the negative exponents and one for positive exponents. We illustrate this technique as follows.

Suppose that the value 46.5 is to be represented as a floating-point value in a 16-bit word-length machine. The bit assignments in the word are given as follows:

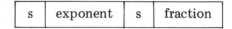

With the use of the base conversion techniques presented in Appendix A, the integer and fractional parts of the decimal number 46.5 are converted to octal and recombined to form the octal number 56.4. Expressing this octal value in binary, we obtain the result

$$46.5 = 56.4 = .564*(8**2) = .101110100*(2**6)$$

In order to express this binary result in floating-point format, it is necessary to divide the range of exponential values into two parts:

```
1111
  .              positive exponents
1000             zero exponent
  .              negative exponents
0000
```

A zero exponent is actually represented as 2**4 or 16, thereby attaching the name *excess-16 form* to this technique.

The value of 46.5 now becomes a fraction of .101110100 and an exponent of 10000 + 110 = 10110, and the number is represented as

```
0  10110  1011101000
```

The actual permissible values of floating-point numbers can be seen to range from a largest positive value of 0.1777(8)*2**15 (about 32,000) to a smallest positive value of 0.1000(8)*2**(−16) (about 0.00001), with a corresponding range for negative values. The difference, then, between integer and floating-point values is that, although the total range from largest positive value to largest negative value remains the same, floating-point values allow for representation of fractional numbers. However, the cost of using floating-point numbers can be measured by the loss of bits used to represent the fraction (only 10 rather than 16 in this case). Thus, given the same word size for representing both integer and floating-point numbers, the precision is less for floating-point.

When manipulating floating-point numbers it is often necessary to "align" the exponents before performing floating-point addition or subtraction. Thus, just as a human adds,

```
15.75*10**2  =  157.5*10
42.5 *10**1  =   42.5*10
                --------
                200.0*10  =  20.0*10**2
```

it is also necessary for the computer to scale the exponents in the floating-point numbers so that normal fixed-point arithmetic may be used to add or subtract values.

A problem arises when two values of nearly equal magnitude are subtracted. For example,

```
 46.75  =  0  10110  1011101100
-46.50  =  0  10110  1011101000
-----      ------------------
  .25   =  0  10110  0000000100
```

The result generated is said to be *unnormalized*. The *normalized* form is that form in which the first bit of the fraction is set. In the example above, this form is obtained by multiplying the fraction by an appropriate power-of-two and subtracting this power-of-two from the exponent:

$$.25 = 0\ 01111\ 1000000000 = 2**(-1)*0.5$$

Normalized numbers are used for two reasons. First, they allow the largest possible number of bits to be used for representing the fraction, and, second, they simplify the process of performing floating-point operations.

There are two exceptions to the form of a normalized number. First, the value zero is usually stored as an all-zero quantity. Second, powers of two are stored with a sign bit of 1 and a fractional part of 10000.... (i.e., an **MSB** = 1). Thus, for a 16-bit floating-point representation, the values $-(2**-1)$, $-(2**2)$, $-(2**0)$ and $-(2**-3)$ would be stored as

$$
\begin{array}{rl}
-1/2 =\ & 1\ 10000\ 1000000000 \\
-4\quad =\ & 1\ 10011\ 1000000000 \\
-1\quad =\ & 1\ 10001\ 1000000000 \\
-1/8 =\ & 1\ 01110\ 1000000000
\end{array}
$$

In the PDP-11, single precision floating-point numbers are actually stored within *two* contiguous 16-bit words so as to provide more precision and dynamic range than 16-bit integers, as well as allowing for fractional representation. Bit 15 of the high word designates the *sign* of the number while an 8-bit excess-128 *exponent* separates the high part of the *fraction* from its *sign*. The low part of the fraction is stored in the second 16-bit word:

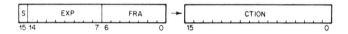

We may state all of this a little more formally; for all 32-bit single-precision floating-point numbers stored within the PDP-11:

1. The mantissa is expressed as a normalized 24-bit positive fraction fr, $0.5 \le fr < 1$, with binary point positioned to the left of the most significant bit. *Since this bit must be 1, it is not stored.* This effectively enables fr to be stored in 23 bits.

2. The exponent is stored as a biased 8-bit positive integer e. That is, when 128 is subtracted from e, the result represents the power of 2 by which the mantissa is multiplied to obtain the true value of the floating-point number.

3. The sign of the number is positive when s, the sign bit, is 0, and negative when $s = 1$.

Thus the number represented by the 32-bit word is

$$X = (1-2*s) * fr * 2**(e-128)$$

where $2**(-128) = 2.939*10**(-39) \le |X| \le 2**(127) = 1.701*10**38$.

The bits devoted to the fraction assure about seven decimal digits of precision; a second 32-bit word can be appended to the fraction to yield about sixteen decimal digits of accuracy in double-precision floating-point numbers. Note that if $e = 0$, the number X is assumed to be 0.0 regardless of s or fr.

The use of the FIS and FPP in manipulation of floating-point numbers will be examined in Section 5.4.

3.2.6 Alphanumeric Characters

Alphanumeric characters are represented in computers as *bytes* which contain a unique value for each character. In the PDP-11, the code used is ASCII (Appendix C). Here, the numerals 0-9 are coded as 60-71, the upper case characters as 101-132, and lower case letters as 140-172, all octal. Two ASCII characters are stored per word. Thus, for example, the character string AB is stored as

```
            high-order byte      low-order byte

B's value = 1     0     2 | 1     0     1     = A's value

            0 1/00 0/01 0/ 01/ 000/ 001

            0     4     1     1     0     1
```

That is, "AB" = 041101 .

3.3 PDP-11 INSTRUCTION FORMATS AND ADDRESS MODES

Data stored in memory must be accessed and manipulated. This data handling is defined by a PDP-11 instruction, which usually specifies

1. The function to be performed (i.e., the operation code).

2. A general-purpose register to be used when locating the source and/or destination operand.

3. An addressing mode (to specify how the selected register(s) is/are to be used).

The size of each field is very important in that it determines many of the external machine characteristics (e.g., how many registers, how much memory may be referenced directly, how many distinct op-codes will exist).

Of particular importance to the PDP-11 programmer is the instruction format and addressing techniques used by this computer. Unlike some older architectures where the programmer may only address some small portion of memory such as 256 (an 8-bit address field) or 4096 (a 12-bit address field) words, the PDP-11 allows the programmer to use a full 16-bit address. In addition, addressing may be immediate, direct, indirect, indexed, or autoindexed in conjunction with the eight general-purpose registers. The result is a very general (and initially overwhelming) addressing structure which includes *relative addressing* (i.e., addresses that are determined in relation to the current value of the program counter) that can be utilized for writing programs that are not dependent on where they reside in memory (this topic will be discussed further in Chapter 4).

Since a large portion of the data handled by a computer is usually structured (in character strings, in arrays, in lists, etc.), the computer must be designed to handle such data efficiently and flexibly. One of the functions of the general-purpose registers is to assist the programmer by functioning

1. As accumulators in which the data to be manipulated reside.

2. As pointers to the data rather than as data accumulators.

3. As indices that describe the relative location of data items in a table or a list.

The use of the registers for both data manipulation and address calculation leads to a variable-length instruction format for the PDP-11. For example, if registers alone are used to specify the data source and/or sink, only one memory word is needed to hold the instruction (op-code plus source and/or destination operand specification). However, when registers are used as pointers to memory, as indices, as part of memory referencing instructions, and so on, two or three memory words may be needed to hold the basic instruction parts [op-code, mode(s), register(s) used, and full address specification]. These additional words are used to address all 32,768 words (i.e., $2{**}15$ words) or 65,536 bytes (i.e., $2{**}16$ bytes).

Since instructions may be one, two, or three words long, the PDP-11 is described as a *variable-instruction-length processor*. The format of its instructions determines how the programmer is to specify the addressing mode. The PDP-11 has four main instruction formats; operate, single-operand, double-operand, and branches.

3.3.1 Operate Instructions

The format for the operate instructions is

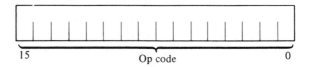

All bits of the instruction word are part of the op-code, and all instructions in the group are one word long. HALT, having octal code 000000, is the first instruction in this group. Some other operate instructions are WAIT, RESET, IOT, RTI, and EMT. These will be examined later.

3.3.2 Single-Operand Instructions

The instruction format for the first word of all single-operand instructions (such as clear, increment, test) is

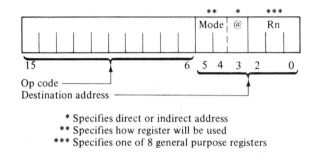

* Specifies direct or indirect address
** Specifies how register will be used
*** Specifies one of 8 general purpose registers

Bits 15 through 6 specify the operation code that defines the type of instruction to be executed. Bits 5 through 0 form a 6-bit field called the *destination address field*. This consists of two subfields:

1. **Register Specification:** Bits 0-2 specify which of the eight general-purpose registers is to be referenced by this instruction word.

2. **Address Mode Specification:** Bits 4-5 specify how the selected register will be used. Bit 3 indicates direct or deferred (indirect) addressing.

Thus, the destination address may be specified in one of eight ways with reference to one of eight registers. Specifically, a 16-bit address is effectively defined by reference to a register and directions on how to interpret the contents of that register. In some cases, a 16-bit memory word is used in conjunction with the register contents in specifying the address. It follows that, depending on the address mode specified, these instructions may be *one* or *two* words in length. The second word is generated by the assembler and contains a 16-bit address or data constant which is used to form the effective operand address for the specified instruction. Table 3-1 is a subset of the single-operand instructions to be found in the PDP-11.

Table 3-1 Single-operand instructions.

```
                Symbolic
Operation       Form     Meaning
---------       -------- --------
Clear           CLR      (DST) ← 0
Complement      COM      (DST) ← ~(DST) i.e., logical complement
Increment       INC      (DST) ← (DST) + 1
Decrement       DEC      (DST) ← (DST) - 1
Negate          NEG      (DST) ← -(DST) i.e., arithmetic complement
Test            TST      Check (DST), Set Condition Codes
Jump            JMP      (PC) ← DST
Swap Bytes      SWAB     (DST)[15:8] ← (DST)[7:0]
                           and, simultaneously,
                         (DST)[7:0]  ← (DST)[15:8]
```

The notation [m:n] specifies that that bits m to n, inclusive, of the operand are to be manipulated.

In the following sections, we will use various instructions to demonstrate the operation of each address mode. As before "( )" means *contents of,* and contents of registers or memory locations which were altered by the instruction are *emphasized.* Instructions are assumed to occupy location 1000(8) and consecutive locations as required. Most of these instructions have corresponding versions which operate on bytes.

Direct Addressing (Modes 0,2,4,6): Examples of Single-Operand Instructions

Register Mode (Mode 0): The single-word instruction "INC R3" has octal code 005203 and binary representation

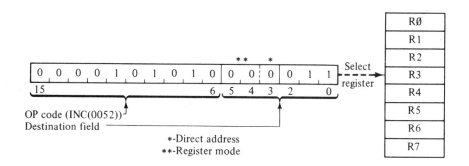

This is called *register mode;* the register contains the operand. If in this example register R3 contained a 5, then the before and after values of R3 can be depicted as

```
BEFORE                              AFTER
======                              =====
address space    register           address space    register
(001000)=005203  (R3)=000005        (001000)=005203  (R3)=000006
```

Autoincrement/Autodecrement Modes (Modes 2,4): Here, the register contains the address of the operand (i.e., the register acts as a pointer). The register can be automatically incremented (*autoincrement mode*) or decremented (*autodecrement mode*) In either case the contents of the register is stepped to address the next higher or lower location. Two single-operand, single-word examples are as shown in Table 3-2. The reader will note that autodecrementing is performed *before* using the register as a pointer, whereas autoincrementing is performed *after* pointer use. The byte operand versions of these instructions, denoted by an op-code mnemonic suffix "B" and an instruction MSB of 1 rather than 0, increment or decrement the relevant register by one rather than two.

Table 3-2 Autoincrement (Mode 2)/ Autodecrement (Mode 4)

Symbolic	Instruction Octal Code	Description
Autoincrement		
NEG (R5)+	005425	Use contents of R5 as the address of operand. Replace the selected operand with its 2's complement, and then increment the contents of R5 by 2 for the word operand.

BEFORE		AFTER	
address space	register	address space	register
(001000)=005425	(R5)=030000	(001000)=005425	(R5)=030002
.		.	
(030000)=000001		(030000)=177777	

Symbolic	Instruction Octal Code	Description
Autodecrement		
COM -(R3)	005143	The contents of R3 are decremented by 2 (for the word operand) and used as the address of operand. The operand is replaced by its logical or one's complement.

BEFORE		AFTER	
address space	register	address space	register
(001000)=005143	(R3)=001776	(001000)=005143	(R3)=001774
.		.	
(001774)=000000		(001774)=177777	

Index Mode (Mode 6): The final example of direct register usage demonstrates indexing. In *index mode*, the contents of the selected register and an index word following the instruction word are summed to form the address of the operand.

Since a 16-bit index word is needed to form the effective address, *two* words are necessary to specify this form of a single-operand instruction; see Table 3-3.

Table 3-3 Index Mode (Mode 6)

Symbolic	Instruction Octal Code	Description
CLR 200(R4)	005064 000200	The address of the operand is determined by adding 200 to the contents of R4. The location so specified is cleared.

BEFORE		AFTER	
======		======	
address space	register	address space	register
(001000)=005064	(R4)=002000	(001000)=005064	(R4)=002000
(001002)=000200		(001002)=000200	
.		.	
.		.	
(002200)=123456		(002200)=000000	

Table 3-4 Summary of basic direct addressing modes.

Binary Code	Name	Assembler Syntax	Function
000	Register	Rn	Register contains operand.
010	Autoincrement	(Rn)+	Register contains address of operand, then is incremented.
100	Autodecrement	-(Rn)	Register is decremented and then contains address of operand.
110	Index	X(Rn)	Value of X (assembled into location following instruction) is added to the contents of Rn to produce the operand address.

Indirect (Deferred) Addressing (Modes 1,3,5,7):

When bit 3 of the instruction is set, indirect addressing is specified and the four basic modes become deferred modes. In the *register deferred mode*, the contents of the selected register are taken as the address of the operand. The *autoincrement/autodecrement deferred* modes use the register contents (before incrementing, after decrementing) as the address of the address of the operand. (Note that because PDP-11 memory addresses are 16 bits, the register increment or decrement is *always* by two when a block of *addresses* is being stepped through via modes 3 or 5, irregardless of whether these addresses point to word or byte operands.) Finally, the *index deferred mode* uses the sum of a register and the word following the instruction to point to the address of the address of the operand.

To indicate deferred addressing, assembler syntax calls for prefacing the register operand(s) by an "@" sign or for parenthesizing the register when this is not ambiguous. Tables 3-5, 3-6, 3-7, and 3-8 illustrate the four deferred modes. The reader should note from these and the previous examples, that indexed, autoincrement, and autodecrement addressing are characterized by *implicit* deferred addressing, so that the addition of *explicit* deferral leads to *two* levels of deferral.

Table 3-5 Register deferred mode (Mode 1)

```
----------------------------------------------------------------
                      Instruction
Symbolic              Octal Code              Description
----------------------------------------------------------------
INC @R5               005215           Increment the location pointed
or INC (R5)                            to by R5.
----------------------------------------------------------------
BEFORE                                 AFTER
======                                 =====
address space   register               address space   register
(001000)=005215 (R5)=001700            (001000)=005215 (R5)=001700
              .                                      .
              .                                      .
(001700)=000100                        (001700)=000101
----------------------------------------------------------------
```

Table 3-6 Autoincrement deferred mode (Mode 3)

```
----------------------------------------------------------------
                      Instruction
Symbolic              Octal Code              Description
----------------------------------------------------------------
NEG @(R2)+            005432           The contents of R2 are used as
                                       the address of the  address of
                                       the operand, which is replaced
                                       by its  2's  complement.  Then
                                       the  contents of R2 are incre-
                                       mented by 2.
----------------------------------------------------------------
BEFORE                                 AFTER
======                                 ======
address space   register               address space   register
(001000)=005432 (R2)=010300            (001000)=005432 (R2)=010302
              .                                      .
              .                                      .
(001010)=000001                        (001010)=177777
              .                                      .
              .                                      .
(010300)=001010                        (010300)=001010
----------------------------------------------------------------
```

Table 3-7 Autodecrement deferred mode (Mode 5)

```
-------------------------------------------------------------
               Instruction
Symbolic       Octal Code              Description
-------------------------------------------------------------
COM @-(R0)       005150         The contents of R0  are decre-
                                mented  by  2 and then used as
                                the  address of the address of
                                the operand.  The  operand  is
                                one's complemented.
-------------------------------------------------------------
BEFORE                          AFTER
======                          =====
address space  register         address space  register
(001000)=005150 (R0)=010776     (001000)=005150 (R0)=010774
       .                               .
       .                               .
(010100)=000000                 (010100)=177777
       .                               .
       .                               .
(010774)=010100                 (010774)=010100
-------------------------------------------------------------
```

Table 3-8 Index deferred mode (Mode 7)

```
-------------------------------------------------------------
               Instruction
Symbolic       Octal Code              Description
-------------------------------------------------------------
CLR @1000(R2)    005072         The contents of R2 and the index
                 001000         word  are  summed  to  yield the
                                address of  the  address  of the
                                operand. The operand is cleared.
-------------------------------------------------------------
BEFORE                          AFTER
======                          =====
address space  register         address space  register
(001000)=005072 (R2)=000100     (001000)=005072 (R2)=000100
(001002)=001000                 (001002)=001000
       .                               .
       .                               .
(001050)=007777                 (001050)=000000
       .                               .
       .                               .
(001100)=001050                 (001100)=001050
-------------------------------------------------------------
```

Table 3-9 summarizes the same four basic modes, this time with indirect addressing.

Table 3-9 Deferred Modes

Binary Code	Name	Assembler Syntax	Function
001	Register Deferred	@Rn or (Rn)	Register contains address of the operand.
011	Autoincrement Deferred	@(Rn)+	Register is used as a pointer to a word containing the address of the operand. The register is then incremented by 2, even for byte instructions.
101	Autodecrement Deferred	@-(Rn)	Register is decremented by 2, even for byte instructions, and then used as a pointer to a word containing the operand address.
111	Index Deferred	@X(Rn)	Value X (stored in a word after the instruction) and the contents of Rn are added, and the sum is used as a pointer to a word which contains the operand address. Neither X nor Rn is modified.

For either direct or deferred addressing, the mode bits determine the actual number of words in the instructions (e.g., one or two). Only when indexing is performed is the actual instruction two words long.

3.3.3 Double-Operand Instructions

Operations that imply two operands (such as add, subtract, move, and compare) are handled by instructions that specify two addresses. The first operand is called the *source operand*, the second the *destination operand*. Bit assignments in the source and destination address fields may specify different modes and different registers. The instruction format for the double operand instruction is as follows:

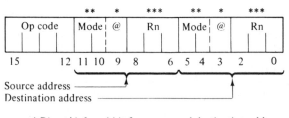

* Direct/deferred bit for source and destination address
** Specifies how selected registers are to be used
*** Specifies a general register

The source address field is used to select the source or first operand. The destination field is used similarly, and locates the second operand *and* the result. For example, the instruction "ADD A,B" adds the contents (source operand) of location A to the contents (destination operand) of location B. After execution, B will contain the result of the addition and the contents of A will be unchanged. Table 3-10 is a subset of the PDP-11 double-operand instructions:

Table 3-10 Double Operand Instructions

```
                    Symbolic
Operation           Form          Meaning
---------           --------      -------------------------------
Move                MOV           (DST) ← (SRC)
Add                 ADD           (DST) ← (DST) + (SRC)
Sub                 SUB           (DST) ← (DST) - (SRC)
Compare             CMP           Calculates (SRC) - (DST),
                                     then modifies condition codes.
Bit set             BIS           (DST) ← (SRC) V (DST)
                                     Inclusive OR of operands.
Bit clear           BIC           (DST) ← ~(SRC)∧(DST)
                                     Clear each bit in destination
                                     corresponding to a set bit in source.
Bit test            BIT           Performs logical AND of operands,
                                     modifies condition codes.
```

Example of Double-Operand Instructions

Since the meaning of the mode bits is the same for the double-operand group as for the single-operand group, instructions are also of variable length, being one, two, or three words long. Similarly, the calculation of the *effective address* of the operands is the same as for the single-operand group. For example, a two-word ADD instruction with one operand being indexed and the other register deferred would be as shown in Table 3-11. (See next page.)

3.3.4 Conditional Branches

The branch instructions (BEQ,BNE,BPL,BMI, and BR) as specified in Section 2.4 are one-word instructions with the format shown below:

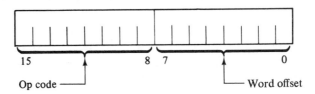

The high byte contains the op-code and the low byte contains an 8-bit signed word offset (7 bits plus sign), which effectively specifies the branch target address, relative to the PC.

Table 3-11 Double Operand Instruction Example

```
------------------------------------------------------------------------
                         Instruction
Symbolic                 Octal Code              Description
------------------------------------------------------------------------
ADD 30(R2),(R1)+         066221          The contents of R2 and  the  index
                         000030          word  are  summed  to  produce  the
                                         address  of the source operand, the
                                         contents  of  which are added to the
                                         operand addressed by R1. R1 is  then
                                         incremented by 2.
------------------------------------------------------------------------
BEFORE                                   AFTER
======                                   =====
address space     register              address space     register
(001000)=066221   (R1)=001500           (001000)=066221   (R1)=001502
(001002)=000030                         (001002)=000030
        .                                       .
        .                                       .
        .                                       .
(001130)=000001   (R2)=001100           (001130)=000001   (R2)=001100
                                                .
        .                                       .
        .                                       .
(001500)=000025                         (001500)=000026
------------------------------------------------------------------------
```

Branch instructions can cause a backwards branch of up to 128 words, or a forward branch of up to 127 words. Calculation of the correct value to store in the low byte of the instruction is not simple, but is performed with ease by the assembler. The assembler "knows" that, at *execution time*, the CPU calculates the branch target address as follows:

1. Extend the sign of the offset through bits 8-15.

2. Multiply the result by 2. This computes the requisite byte offset using the 8-bit word offset contained in the lower byte of the instruction.

3. Add the result to the PC to form the final branch address.

Thus, the *assembler* must perform the reverse operation to form the word offset from the specified target address (denoted as T). It is important to remember that when the offset is added to the PC at instruction execution time, the PC is pointing to the word following the branch instruction; hence the factor −2 in the calculation. That is, since PC = X + 2, where "X" is the symbolic address of the branch instruction itself, then

```
word offset = (T-X-2)/2 (truncated to 8 bits).
```

Again, the 8-bit offset allows branching in the backward direction by 200(8)

words (400(8) bytes) from the current PC, and in the forward direction by 177(8) words (376(8) bytes) from the current PC.

An illustration of relative branching can be found in the following program segment:

```
000100   005203   HERE:   INC R3
                            .
                            .
000150   000753           BR HERE
```

The offset is calculated by the assembler as follows, using 16-bit arithmetic:

```
branch target address   =            100
current location        =            150
                                   ------
difference (100-150)    =         177730
less 2                  =         177726
halved                  =         177753
truncated to 8 bits     =            353
```

and the branch instruction becomes

```
000400 + 353 = 000753.
```

When truncating a 16-bit word into an 8-bit byte, one has to be careful, since the octal representation does not correspond to byte boundaries. In the preceding example the 16-bit quantity 177753 would appear in binary as

The value of the high byte is 377; the value of the low byte is 353. Thus the reader is cautioned against simply dividing a 16-bit value into two parts (e.g., 177 and 753 for the given value), because the result generated is not correct.

3.3.5 Use of the PC as a General-Purpose Register

Although register 7 is a general-purpose register, it doubles in function as the PC for the PDP-11. Whenever the processor uses the PC to acquire a word from memory (e.g., when fetching an instruction), the PC is automatically incremented by 2 to contain the address of the next word of the instruction being executed or the address of the next instruction to be executed. (When the program uses the PC to access byte data, the PC is still incremented by 2.)

The PC responds to all the standard PDP-11 addressing modes. However, there are four of these modes with which the PC can provide advantages for handling *position-independent code* (see Chapter 4) and unstructured data. When referencing the PC, these modes are termed *immediate, absolute* (or immediate deferred), *relative*, and *relative deferred*. They are summarized in Table 3-12.

Table 3-12 Summary of PC Modes

Binary Code	Name	Assembler Syntax	Function
010	Immediate	#n	Operand follows instruction.
011	Absolute	@#n	Absolute address of operand follows instruction.
110	Relative	A	Address of operand, relative to the instruction, follows the instruction.
111	Relative Deferred	@A	Address of location containing address of operand, relative to the instruction, follows the instruction.

The reader should remember that the special-effect modes are executed exactly the same as the modes described earlier; they are special only in that the general register selected is R7, the program counter.

Note that in the *immediate mode* example (Table 3-13), just before the ADD instruction is fetched and executed, the PC points to the first word of that instruction. The processor fetches this word and increments the PC by 2 so as to point to the second word of the instruction. The source operand specification is mode 2, register 7 (autoincrement of PC); thus the PC is now used as a pointer to fetch the operand (the second word of the instruction) *before* being incremented by 2 to point to the next instruction.

Table 3-13 Immediate addressing mode (Mode 2, Register 7)

Symbolic	Instruction Octal Code	Description
ADD #10,R0	062700 000010	The constant "10", located in the second word of the instruction, is added to R0.

BEFORE		AFTER	
======		=====	
address space	register	address space	register
(001000)=062700	(R0)=000020	(001000)=062700	(R0)=000030
(001002)=000010	(PC)=001000	(001002)=000010	(PC)=001004

The *absolute addressing mode* (Table 3-14) is the equivalent of immediate deferred, i.e., autoincrement deferred using the PC. The contents of the second word of the instruction are taken as the address of the operand. Thus, execution of the instruction proceeds exactly as in the immediate mode in that

1. the PC is incremented by 2 so as to point to the immediate data as a part of *the instruction fetch cycle* and,

2. the PC is again incremented by 2 so as to point to the next instruction *as a result of the autoincrement mode.*

The sole difference is that the deferral causes the immediate data to be treated as the absolute address of the operand rather than as the operand itself.

Table 3-14 Absolute addressing mode (Mode 3, Register 7)

```
---------------------------------------------------------------------
                    Instruction
Symbolic            Octal Code              Description
---------------------------------------------------------------------
CLR @#1100          005037          Clear location 1100.
                    001100
---------------------------------------------------------------------
BEFORE                              AFTER
======                             =====
address space       register       address space       register
(001000)=005037     (PC)=001000    (001000)=005037     (PC)=001004
(001002)=001100                    (001002)=001100
        .                                  .
        .                                  .
(001100)=012345                    (001100)=000000
---------------------------------------------------------------------
```

Note that in both the immediate and absolute mode examples, "n" is a constant, so that #n is that constant itself. If "n" is a symbolic name, then #n is the *value* of that name as determined by the assembler. When the symbolic name is a *label*, the value assigned is that of the location counter when the label is encountered during assembly. For example, MOV #X,Rn can be used to load the *address* of X into Rn, while MOV @#X,Rn loads the *contents* of the location which has label X into Rn. An alternative technique for specifying the *contents* of a symbolic address as the operand is to use the relative mode.

The *relative mode* (Table 3-15) is assembled as index mode using R7. The base of the address calculation, which is stored in the second or third word of the instruction, is not the address of the operand, but the number which when added to the PC becomes the address of the operand.

Table 3-15 Relative addressing mode (Mode 6, Register 7)

```
------------------------------------------------------------------------
                   Instruction
Symbolic           Octal Code              Description
------------------------------------------------------------------------
INC A              005267          Contents of the  memory  location
                   000074          immediately following instruction
                                   word  are added  to PC to produce
                                   address of A.   Increment contents
                                   of A by 1.
------------------------------------------------------------------------
BEFORE                             AFTER
======                             =====
address space       register      address space      register
(001000)=005267                   (001000)=005267
(001002)=000074    (PC)=001000    (001002)=000074    (PC)=001004
      .                                 .
      .                                 .
(001100)=001200                   (001100)=001201

Note: 1004+74=1100
------------------------------------------------------------------------
```

The *relative deferred mode* (Table 3-16) is similar to the relative mode, except that the second word of the instruction, when added to the PC, specifies the address of the address of the operand rather than the address of the operand.

Table 3-16 Relative deferred addressing mode (Mode 7, Register 7)

```
------------------------------------------------------------------------
                   Instruction
Symbolic           Octal Code              Description
------------------------------------------------------------------------
CLR @A             005077          Add second word  of  instruction to
                   000020          PC to produce address  of  A, which
                                   contains address of operand.  Clear
                                   operand.
------------------------------------------------------------------------
BEFORE                             AFTER
======                             =====
address space       register      address space      register
(001000)=005077                   (001000)=005077
(001002)=000020    (PC)=001000    (001002)=000020    (PC)=001004
      .                                 .
      .                                 .
(001024)=010100                   (001024)=010100
      .                                 .
      .                                 .
(010100)=135531                   (010100)=000000

Note: 1004+20=1024
------------------------------------------------------------------------
```

One point is worth special mention and concerns absolute/relative addressing. This is that *relative mode* is the normal mode for symbolic memory addresses on the PDP-11. This follows because every single- and double-operand instruction *must* reference a general register. As a result, when the programmer writes (for example)

```
HERE:   MOV X,R3
```

the *base* of the address calculation to be effected at execution time is not the address of the operand "X". Rather, it is the number which when added to the PC becomes the address of the operand. Thus the base, which is stored in the second word of the instruction, is X – PC, where X = actual address. The operation can be illustrated as follows:

If the statement MOV X,R3 is assembled at location 20, and the symbolic variable X is stored in location 100, the assembled code will be

```
(20)= 016703
(22)= 000054
```

At execution time, the processor fetches the MOV instruction and adds 2 to the PC so that it points to location 22. The source operand specification is mode 6, register 7. Thus, the processor fetches the word pointed to by the PC and adds 2 to the PC. The PC now points to location 24. To calculate the address of the source operand, the base is added to the designated register, the PC in this case.

That is,

```
base + R7 = 54 + 24 = 100, the operand address.
```

Since the assembler considers "HERE" as the address of the first word of the instruction, an equivalent statement would be

```
HERE:   MOV X-HERE-4(PC),R3
```

Fortunately, the assembler recognizes that a symbolic address must be assembled as explained above. The reader should satisfy himself that, for example, the instruction

```
HERE:   ADD  X,Y
```

is equivalent to, and thus *assembled identically* to

```
HERE:   ADD X-HERE-4(PC),Y-HERE-6(PC)
```

This mode is called relative because the operand address is calculated relative to the current PC. The base is the distance (in bytes) between the operand and the current PC. If the operator and its operand are moved in memory so that the distance between the operator and data remains constant, the instruction will operate correctly. (By definition, branch instructions are also relative address instructions and can, therefore, be used in a position-independent fashion.)

Because the operand address is relative to the current PC, it is not a simple task to initialize instruction operands. Thus on machines such as the PDP-11 where the normal addressing mode is relative, self-modifying programs are much more difficult to write in self-initializing form and are therefore to be avoided. The value of using such relatively addressed operands will be found in Chapter 4, which includes a discussion of position-independent programming.

The following flow diagrams demonstrate graphically the action of the address modes discussed:

General Register Addressing Modes:

Mode 0, Register: OPR R [R contains operand.]

Mode 1, Register Deferred: OPR (R) or @R [R contains operand address.]

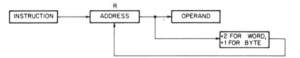

Mode 2, Autoincrement: OPR (R)+ [R contains operand address, then increment R.]

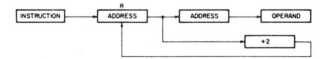

Mode 3, Autoincrement Deferred: OPR @(R)+ [R contains address of address of operand, then increment R by 2.]

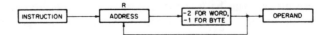

Mode 4, Autodecrement: OPR -(R) [Decrement R, then R contains operand address.]

Mode 5, Autodecrement Deferred: OPR @-(R) [Decrement R by 2, then R contains address of address of operand.]

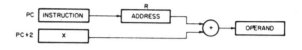

Mode 6, Index: OPR X(R) [R plus X, the second word of instruction, is operand address.]

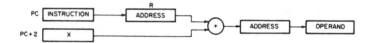

Mode 7, Index Deferred: OPR @X(R) [R plus X, the second word of the instruction, is address of address of operand.]

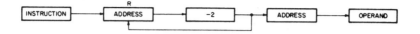

Program Counter Addressing Modes:

Mode 2, Register 7; Immediate: OPR #n [Operand is second word of instruction.]

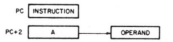

Mode 3, Register 7; Absolute: OPR @#A [Address of operand A is second word of instruction.]

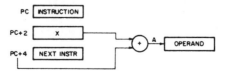

Mode 6, Register 7; Relative: OPR A [Updated PC, PC+4, plus second word of instruction, X, is address of operand A.]

Mode 7, Register 7; Relative Deferred: OPR @A [Updated PC, PC+4, plus second word of instruction, X, is address of A, which contains address of operand.]

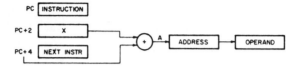

3.4 THE MACRO-11 ASSEMBLER

Having learned about the varied forms of addressing on the PDP-11, the reader can appreciate why machine language programming in octal was not discussed in Chapter 2. However, it is instructive now to present a symbolic program complete with its octal code. But first we must consider a few characteristics of MACRO-11 which extend the general assembler concepts presented in Section 2.6.

In MACRO-11 the period (.) is the symbol for the assembler location counter (LC). When used in the operand field of an instruction, it represents the address of the first word of the instruction. When used in the operand field of an assembler directive, it represents the address of the current byte or word. For example,

```
A:      MOV     #.,R0   ;"." REFERS TO LOCATION A; I.E, THE
                        ; ADDRESS OF THE  "MOV" INSTRUCTION
```

Note that if " # " is read as *the value of*, and ".'' means *here*, then " #." means *the value of this location* or, simply, *this adddress.*

At the beginning of each assembly pass (see Section 5.6.4), the assembler sets the location counter to zero. Normally, consecutive memory locations are assigned to each byte/word of object code generated. However, the location where the object code is stored may be changed by a direct assignment altering the location counter.

A *direct assignment statement* associates a symbol with a value. When a direct assignment statement defines a symbol for the first time, that symbol is entered into the assembler's symbol table and the specified value is associated with it. A symbol may be redefined by assigning a new value to a previously defined symbol. The newly assigned value will replace the previous value assigned to the symbol. The general format for a direct assignment is

```
symbol = expression
```

One use for direct assignment is to assign the location counter an initial value (e.g, . = 1000). Another use is in equating commonly used values or expressions to symbolic names thus increasing the information content (and hence, the clarity) of the program.

The decimal point, or period, is interpreted by the assembler in several ways. Used by itself it represents the value of the LC. As such it may be used both to initialize the LC (e.g., . = 1000) and to act as an operand of an instruction. For example, the instruction BR .-4 causes the computer to execute the instruction two words (or four half-words) preceding this instruction.

A common mistake would be to write BR .-2 in order to jump back two instructions. The error occurs because (1) the PDP-11 is both half-word and word addressable, and (2) PDP-11 instructions occupy one, two, or three PDP-11 words. Thus the use of ".." for calculating branch addresses is a tricky business until the novice programmer is sure just how many words (or bytes) are to be skipped. Consequently, the use of *explicit* labels is encouraged very strongly

The second use of the period can be found in its association with *assembler directives* or pseudo-ops, which direct the assembly process and may generate data. Examples of pseudo-ops (previously discussed) are the .END directive and the .WORD directive.

The .WORD assembler directive may have one or more operands. Each operand is stored in a word of the object program. If there is more than one operand, they are stored in successive words. The operands may be any legally formed expressions. *An operator field left blank will be interpreted as the .WORD directive if the operand field contains one or more expressions.* For example,

```
FIVE:   5
SIX:    .WORD   6
SEV:    .WORD   7,8.
```

will assign the constants 5, 6, 7, and 8 to consecutive memory word locations. A third use of the "." has just been demonstrated. MACRO-11 assumes all numbers to be octal unless informed otherwise. The "." may be used as a decimal point to perform this function.

These characters and conventions will be used throughout the remainder of this text to code programs in MACRO-11. Thus all examples given are real PDP-11 programs (or program segments) and may be assembled and executed on PDP-11 computers.

3.4.1 Sample Programs

Let us consider the array problem of Chapter 2 as flowcharted in Fig. 2-9a. Since we had not concerned ourselves with the real PDP-11 and its variable-length instructions, it was easy to assume that each instruction required one word and that consecutive instructions occupied consecutive memory locations. As the contents of this chapter have demonstrated, that assumption was *false* and an actual assembly listing for the program appears as shown in Fig. 3-3. This listing shows two subtle changes over the program written for the hypothetical computer of

Chapter 2. First, the instruction with label FIXUP is now modified by adding two to the second word of this three-word instruction (one word each is occupied by the op-code, and the source and destination operand relative offsets). The constant "two" must be added to the second word, since this word contains the relative base address of the array K.

```
--------------------------------------------------------------------------
 Program Program
 Address Contents Label  Op-code Operand(s)          Comments
--------------------------------------------------------------------------
1          000000         .ASECT                     ;ASSEMBLE ABSOLUTE CODE
2          001000         .=1000                     ;STARTING ADDRESS = 1000
3  001000  016767 START:  MOV     ZERO,ISUM          ;INITIALIZE SUM
           000032
           000032
4  001006  066767 FIXUP:  ADD     K,ISUM             ;ADD IN ELEMENT OF ARRAY K
           000034
           000024
5  001014  026767         CMP     FIXUP+2,LIMIT      ;DONE YET
           177770
           000022
6  001022  001404         BEQ     STOP               ;YES
7  001024  066767         ADD     CONS,FIXUP+2       ;MODIFY ADDRESS
           000012
           177756
8  001032  000765         BR      FIXUP              ;LOOP
9  001034  000000 STOP:   HALT                       ;STOP HERE
10 01036   000000 ZERO:   .WORD   0                  ;CONSTANT ZERO
11 01040   000000 ISUM:   .WORD   0                  ;RESULTANT ZERO
12 01042   000002 CONS:   .WORD   2                  ;CONSTANT TO GENERATE
                                                     ;NEXT ADDRESS
13 01044   000176 LIMIT:  K-FIXUP-4+98.              ;LAST RELATIVE ADDRESS
                                                     ; GENERATED
14 01046          K:      .BLKW   50.                ;RESERVE 50 LOCATIONS
                                                     ; FOR ARRAY K
15         001000'        .END    START
--------------------------------------------------------------------------
SYMBOL TABLE

CONS    001042          FIXUP   001006          ISUM    001040
K       001046          LIMIT   001044          START   001000
STOP    001034          ZERO    001036
--------------------------------------------------------------------------
```

Fig. 3-3 PDP-11 program for adding numbers using instruction modification.

Second, the word labeled LIMIT contains a value that represents the address of the last element in the array K. This value is K-FIXUP-4+98., where K-FIXUP-4 represents the relative address generated for the initial instruction and the decimal 98 is "1 less" than the number of elements (i.e., it is given by $2*[N-1]$). Note then that the CMP instruction is actually comparing two address values that are, in fact, represented by two numerical values.

The reader is once again reminded that self-modifying programs, although useful, are not considered good programming practice. In this particular example, the program, once self-modified, cannot be rerun without resetting the second word of the instruction labeled FIXUP. And since relative addressing is used to specify the address of K, the initializing statement

```
MOV     #K,FIXUP+2
```

will not reestablish the instruction offset word to its initial value.

The value of recoding this example was to show how real PDP-11 programs are assembled and what their object code looks like. Carrying this point one step further, a simpler version of the array problem is coded as shown in Fig. 3-4. Note that for the sake of brevity, the size of the array has been limited to 10 elements. This program also illustrates the use of an "equate" statement to assign a value to a symbol. Here, for example, "%0" (the assembler's notation for a register) is assigned to the symbol "R0".

```
----------------------------------------------------------------------------
 Program Program
 Address Contents Label Op code Operand(s)            Comments
----------------------------------------------------------------------------
1                        ;THIS IS A PROGRAM TO SUM THE ELEMENTS OF THE ARRAY "K".
2                        ;THE SUM IS LEFT IN R0.
3          000000        .ASECT
4          000000        R0=%0                        ;DEFINE REGISTER 0 AS SYMBOL R0
5          000001        R1=%1                        ;DEFINE REGISTER 1 AS SYMBOL R1
6          001000        .=1000                       ;DEFINE STARTING ADDRESS
7  001000  005000 START: CLR      R0                  ;INITIALIZE SUM
8  001002  012701        MOV      #K,R1               ;ADDRESS OF K MOVED INTO R1
           001020
9  001006         LOOP:
10 01006   062100        ADD      (R1)+,R0  ;ADD IN VALUE
11 01010   022701        CMP      #K+18.,R1 ;DONE?
           001042
12 01014   100374        BPL      LOOP       ;NO, CONTINUE
13 01016   000000        HALT
14 01020   000001 K:     1,2,3,4,5,6,7,8.,9.,10.  ;NOTE THAT ".WORD"
   01022   000002                                 ;IS IMPLIED
   01024   000003
   01026   000004
   01030   000005
   01032   000006
   01034   000007
   01036   000010
   01040   000011
   01042   000012
15         001000'       .END     START
----------------------------------------------------------------------------
SYMBOL TABLE

K          001020        LOOP     001006           R0      =%000000
R1       =%000001        START    001000
----------------------------------------------------------------------------
```

Fig. 3-4 PDP-11 program for summing array elements using autoincrement.

3.5 PDP-11 MACHINE AND MEMORY HIERARCHIES

During the last few years the cost of computer hardware systems has decreased radically. In particular, the CPU-on-a-chip has given rise to single board computer systems containing a full complement of memory (either read/write memory, RAM, and/or read only memory, ROM), and both serial and parallel I/O interfaces at a price which, a decade ago, might suffice to purchase only a single serial or parallel interface alone Nevertheless, labor intensive software development costs have continued to escalate. Although portability may be achieved through use of high level languages, maximal efficiency is only achieved in programs which fully exploit the particular architecture involved.

3.5.1 The Family Concept

The idea of production of a "family" of CPU's of varying capabilities, with each family member possessing a common architecture but a different implementation, is not new. The goal of course, is software compatibility across all CPU's at the *machine language level.* The benefits of this strategy are numerous. System software evolution continues and such software may generally be retrofitted to early family members at any time. Architectural shortcomings or ambiguities are recognized and rectified. Existing software may often be accelerated in performance simply by retiring one CPU for another version utilizing newer technology. Alternatively, newer memory technology (e.g., "denser" solid state memory, cache "add-ons", or "solid state disks") may enhance software performance on the same CPU. New system peripherals are developed to enhance the utility of existing CPU's. And, finally, the huge user base of the common architecture gives rise to an enormous number of useful programs, many of which are available at nominal cost from a central distribution point (e.g., the Digital Equipment Computer User's Society — *DECUS* — for the PDP-11).

3.5.2 Technological Implementations

The family concept has possibly seen its most widespread realization in the DEC PDP-11. Since introduction of the PDP-11 in 1970, about 10 different implementations have appeared. These different models can be grouped into four different chronological "streams":

1. *Constant Price, Increasing Performance:* 11/20 (1970), 11/40 (1972), 11/60 (1977).

2. *Decreasing Price, Constant Performance:* Series (i): 11/20 (1970), 11/05, 10 (1973), 11/04 (1975), 11/03 (1975), PDT-11's (1978); Series (ii): 11/40 (1972), 11/34 (1976), 11/23,24 (1979).

3. *Increasing Price, Substantially Increasing Performance:* 11/20 (1970), 11/45, 55 (1972, 1976), 11/70 (1974), VAX-11/780 (1977).

By "price" we imply minimum system cost, and "performance" includes functionality which includes both speed and reliability considerations. Performance enhancement may be achieved either by increasing CPU execution speeds, by extending the architecture (e.g., floating-point processor) or by enhancing memory performance (e.g., cache memory). For the PDP-11 family the the relevant enhancements were:

1. *Extended Arithmetic Element (EAE):* A fixed-point multiply/divide/shift UNIBUS peripheral.

2. *Extended Instruction Set (EIS):* A fixed-point multiply/divide/shift CPU architectural enhancement using the general purpose registers.

3. *Floating-Point Processor (FPP):* A floating-point arithmetic instruction set with 6 associated registers.

4. *FASTBUS and Associated High-speed Memory:* A high speed bus connecting the CPU to one port of dual port bipolar memory, the second port on the UNIBUS.

5. *Floating Instruction Set (FIS):* A stack oriented (i.e., zero address) floating-point instruction set.

6. *Cache Memory:* High speed bipolar memory interposed between CPU and main memory, and associated controllers.

7. *Memory Management:* A mapping/protection unit which extends the physical address space.

8. *MASSBUS:* A bus designed for high speed I/O.

3.5.3 Compatibility

Since PDP-11's are architecturally upward compatible, both hardware and software are portable. The UNIBUS ensures that peripheral devices may be moved from one machine to another. The hardware capabilities of the various PDP-11's are summarized in the following table:

PDP-11 Family Computers

Feature	11/03	11/04	11/05,10	11/34	11/35,40	11/60	11/45,70
gp registers	8	8	8	8/9	8/9	8/9	16
Memory Management	No	No	No	Yes	Yes(O)	Yes	Yes(O)
Automatic Priority Interrupts	Single-line, Multi-level	Multi-line, Multi-level	Multi-line, Multi-level	Multi-line, Multi-level	Multi-line, Multi-level	Multi-line, Multi-level	Multi-line, Multi-level
Processor Modes	1	1	1	2	2	2	3
Extended Arithmetic	EIS(O) FIS(O)	EAE(O)	EAE(O)	EIS FPP(O)	EIS(O) FIS(O)	EIS FPP	EIS FPP(O)
Cache Memory	No	No	No	Yes(O)	Yes(OEM)	Yes	No(45) Yes(70)
User Micro-programmable	Yes(O)	No	No	No	Yes(OEM)	Yes(O)	No
Register-to-register Add	3.5 us	3.2 us	3.7 us	2.1 us	1.0 us	.34 us	.30 us

(O) means that the feature is a DEC option and (OEM) means that the option is available from another manufacturer. The register-to-register add time, in microseconds, is indicative of CPU performance. Note that the Fortran IV compilers allow the user to specify the hardware support available at compile time (FIV, version II) or link time (FIV, version I). In contrast, the Fortran IV PLUS compiler requires the FPP instruction set and its associated floating-point registers to be present.

3.5.4 Instruction Processing Phases

At this point, however, it will prove profitable to briefly describe the basic components which account for the total execution time of any particular PDP-11 instruction. To do this first requires a detailed examination of what constitutes the *I-*, *O-*, and *E*-phases (Section 2.5) of instruction processing on the PDP-11. We shall do this for a *double operand instruction* using the PC, MAR, and MDR registers which, as noted earlier, exist (in concept at least) in all computers. Later (Section 6.10), the instruction processing phases of the PDP-11/60 will be examined.

Instruction Fetch (I-phase): The PDP-11 *I*-phase differs from that described earlier only in that the PC is incremented by 2 after the instruction fetch:

```
1. (MAR)  ←  (PC)           ;ADDRESS OF INSTRUCTION INTO MAR
2. (MDR)  ←  ((MAR))        ;FETCH FIRST WORD OF INSTRUCTION
3. (PC)   ←  (PC) + 2       ;INCREMENT PC
4. (IR)   ←  (MDR)          ;COPY MDR INTO IR
```

Double operand instructions, for example, undergo *O*-phase processing for both source and destination operands. If Rs and Rd are internal registers which are loaded with source *operand* and destination *address*, respectively, then the *O*-phase can be described as follows:

O-phase: First, the source operand is fetched:

```
If  IR[11:10] = 0, then   (Rs)  ← (Rn), n = IR[8:6]      ;REGISTER MODE

If  IR[11:10] = 1, then   (MAR) ← (Rn), n = IR[8:6]      ;AUTOINCREMENT MODE
                          (MDR) ← ((MAR))                ;MEMORY FETCH
                          (Rs)  ← (MDR)
                          (Rn)  ← (Rn) + 2               ;INCREMENT Rn

If  IR[11:10] = 2, then   (Rn)  ← (Rn) - 2, n = IR[8:6]  ;AUTODECREMENT MODE
                          (MAR) ← (Rn)
                          (MDR) ← ((MAR))                ;MEMORY FETCH
                          (Rs)  ← (MDR)

If  IR[11:10] = 3, then   (MAR) ← (PC)                   ;INDEX MODE
                          (PC)  ← (PC) + 2               ;INCREMENT PC
                          (MDR) ← ((MAR))                ;FETCH INDEX WORD
                          (MAR) ← (MDR) + (Rn), n = IR[8:6] ;COMPUTE ADDRESS
                          (MDR) ← ((MAR))
                          (Rs)  ← (MDR)

If  IR[9] = 1,     then   (MAR) ← (Rs)                   ;DEFERRED ADDRESSING
                          (MDR) ← ((MAR))                ;FETCH SOURCE OPERAND
                          (Rs)  ← (MDR)
```

At this point, the source operand is in Rs and the destination operand *O*-phase occurs:

```
If IR[5:4] = 0,    then (Rd)  ← 777700 + n, n = IR[2:0] ;COMPUTE ADDRESS OF Rn

If IR[5:4] = 1,    then (Rd)  ← (Rn), n = IR[2:0]       ;AUTOINCREMENT MODE
                       (Rn)  ← (Rn) + 2

If IR[5:4] = 2,    then (Rn)  ← (Rn) - 2, n = IR[2:0]   ;AUTODECREMENT MODE
                       (Rd)  ← (Rn)

If IR[5:4] = 3,    then (MAR) ← (PC)                    ;INDEX MODE
                       (PC)  ← (PC) + 2                 ;INCREMENT PC
                       (MDR) ← ((MAR))                  ;FETCH INDEX WORD
                       (Rd)  ← (MDR) + (Rn), n = IR[2:0] ;COMPUTE ADDRESS

If   IR[3] = 1,    then (MAR) ← (Rd)                    ;INDIRECT ADDRESSING
                       (MDR) ← ((MAR))
                       (Rd)  ← (MDR)                    ;FINAL ADDRESS IN Rd
```

Execute Phase: IR[15:12] is used to determine which double operand instruction is to be executed, and execution proceeds using the contents of Rs as one operand and the contents of Rd as the address of the other. The result then overwrites the destination operand.

In summary, execution time of a double operand arithmetic instruction may be decomposed into:

1. Fetch Instruction

2. Fetch Source Operand

3. Fetch Destination Operand

4. Execute Instruction

5. Store result

Steps 1 and 4, 2, and 3 and 5 are generally lumped into components called, respectively, Fetch/Execute, Source address, and Destination address Time.

3.5.5 Program Execution Speeds: UNIBUS, FASTBUS, and Cache Memories

The instruction execution components are tabulated below for the ADD instruction on the PDP-11/45,55 for bipolar (Bp), metal-oxide semiconductor (MOS), and magnetic core (Cr) memories. Also noted are the number of memory cycles (MC) required for the relevant operation:

```
                   Fetch/Execute Time (usec)
                   -------------------------
        SRC  MODE 0          SRC  MODE 1-7        SRC  MODE 0-7
        DST  MODE 0          DST  MODE 0          DST  MODE 1-7

        Bp MOS  Cr  MC       Bp MOS  Cr   MC      Bp MOS   Cr   MC
        -- ---  --  --       -- ---  --   --      -- ---   --   --
ADD     .30 .51 .97  1       .45 .66 1.12  2      .75 1.17 1.8   2
```

```
                   SRC or DST Address Time (usec)
                   ------------------------------
        Mode         Bp          MOS          Cr          MC
        ----         --          ---          --          --
         0           0            0           0            0
         1          .30          .51         .89           1
         2          .30          .51         .89           1
         3          .75         1.17        1.92           2
         4          .45          .66        1.04           1
         5          .90         1.32        2.07           2
         6          .60         1.02        1.86           2
         7         1.05         1.68        2.89           3
```

Note that bipolar, MOS and core memories have cycles times of approximately 0.3, 0.51, and 0.97 *u*sec, respectively. As noted earlier, both MOS and bipolar memory are connected to the CPU over the FASTBUS while core memory is a UNIBUS peripheral. The following general observations can be made:

1. For both SRC and DST modes 0, total execution time is a single memory cycle.

2. When SRC mode is not zero, extra time is sometimes required to evaluate SRC address, and is always required to fetch the source operand.

3. When the DST mode is not zero, the destination operand address may need to be computed, the destination operand fetched, the ADD operation carried out, and the result stored at the destination address. For this example, total execution time is essentially proportional to the total number and speed of memory cycles required to fetch the instruction, fetch the memory contents (if any) necessary to form the effective address of source/destination operands, fetch source/destination operands, and store the result.

Thus an ADD R0,R1 instruction stored in bipolar memory requires 0.3 usec to execute, while an ADD @X(R5),@Y(R3) with instruction and operands stored in core would require 7.59 usec for execution. Conversely, ADD @X(R5),@Y(R3) requires 2.85 usec in bipolar while ADD R0,R1 executes in 0.97 usec in core. Obviously, for maximum execution speed, the 11/45 programmer must ensure that

1. General purpose registers be used as wisely as possible for intermediate data storage.

2. The most time critical program sections be resident in bipolar memory, less time critical sections in MOS, and the rest in core.

The *first* criterion is a function of the cleverness of the programmer in matching machine architectural features to algorithm structure. Techniques for such enhancement of program execution speeds, generally independent of PDP-11 implementation and memory speed, will be examined in detail in Chapter 9. The use of microprogramming for further execution acceleration is discussed in Chapter 10.

The *second* criterion effectively requires that the programmer use activity analysis techniques (Section 9.1) to find time critical code sections and then ensure that such programs are stored in the appropriate memory via directions to the linker. This technique is not appropriate except in single user situations. The alternative, using exclusively bipolar memory, is certainly not cost effective.

An alternative to establishing a hierarchy of memory of varying speed, where the most time critical program sections are stored in fastest memory and the least time critical sections in slowest memory, involves the cache memory.

A *cache memory* is a small, fast memory located between the CPU and the relatively slow primary memory (*Mp*) of a computer. The cache contains address/ data (*AD*) pairs consisting of an *Mp* address and a copy of the *Mp* location corresponding to that address. Whenever the CPU accesses *Mp*, the address is compared to the addresses stored in cache. If there is a match (*hit*), the CPU accesses the data portion of the matched *AD* pair from the cache. If there is no match (*miss*), the CPU accesses *Mp* and a new *AD* pair is stored in the cache, usually displacing another *AD* pair. In a 2 kilobyte cache (11/60, 70), for example, *AD* pairs are allocated cache addresses corresponding to the lower 11 bits of the *AD* pair *Mp* memory address. Thus, *AD* pairs from *Mp* locations 0, 2048, 4096, etc., will occupy cache location 0, displacing any *AD* pair previously stored there. In conventional programs, especially those containing loop structures, most memory accesses over short periods of time are to small groups of contiguous *Mp* locations. These *Mp AD* pairs will typically migrate to the cache so that a majority of CPU accesses (e.g., about 90%) will be cache hits as long as this small group of *Mp* locations is repetitively accessed. The merit of cache memory is that cache hits are accessed at cache memory access time, usually a small fraction of that of slower main memory.

In summary, cache systems automatically and dynamically transfer the most needed programs and data to a small but fast memory and thus provide effective cycle times which, for programs with high hit rates, approach that of the fast cache memory alone.

The 11/70 computer consists of an 11/45-like central processor with a cache memory interposed between the CPU and primary memory. In this machine, for example, when the CPU accesses *Mp*, a two word block (consisting of the addressed operand and the contents of either the preceding or following memory location) are transferred to the 1024 word cache so as to form two contiguous *AD* pairs; in the 11/60, block size is one word. On either computer, the *principle of program locality* ensures, transparent to the programmer, that the most often used code sections become resident in the fastest memory available. For example, in Section 9.5.5 we demonstrate that for programs which are not specifically constructed so as to deviate from the statistical principles of cache design (e.g., in-line code), the 11/70 indeed exhibits 95% of the 11/55 bipolar performance.

3.5.6 Memory Extensions: Memory Management and Protection

From the very beginning, the designers of the PDP-11 realized that a 16-bit minicomputer with an address space of 32,768 words (32K) was not sufficient. With time, programmers would discover that their programs needed more memory space, and/or they would find new ways to use the computer (such as multiprogramming) which would require separation (and protection) of programs co-resident in memory at the same time.

The addresses generated by the first PDP-11 processor, the 11/20, were actually 18-bit direct byte addresses. Although the 11/20 word length and operational logic was 16-bit, the UNIBUS addressing logic actually was 18-bits in length. Thus, while the 11/20 word could only contain address references up to 32K, the UNIBUS could reference addresses up to 128 Kwords. All of this was not generally known to the 11/20 programmer, although if he looked carefully, he would find that all of his I/O page addresses (addresses between 160000 and 177777) were actually converted to addresses in the range of 760000 and 777777. The extra two bits of address were "hard-wired" in for the 11/20 so that all references to the I/O page had the two high-order bits (16 and 17) always fixed as ones.

With the introduction of the 11/40 and 11/45, 18-bit addressing was made possible so that not only UNIBUS addresses but also CPU addresses could be modified into 18-bit quantities. Later on, with the 11/70, it became possible to have 22-bit address lengths. However, we shall not concern ourselves with this second extension because it is sufficiently like the addressing mechanism which we shall now explain.

An option on some PDP-11's, and a standard feature on others, the memory management facility is the unit which allows for the extended addressing capability. When the PDP-11 memory management unit is operating, the normal 16-bit direct byte address is no longer interpreted as a direct physical address (PA) but as a virtual address (VA), containing information to be used in constructing a new 18-bit physical address. The information contained in the VA is combined with relocation and description information contained in the Active Page Register (APR) to yield an 18-bit PA (Fig. 3-5).

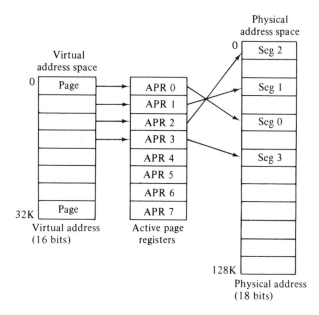

Fig. 3-5 Virtual address mapping into physical address.

The purpose of the APR's is to perform memory relocation and to provide extended memory addressing capability for systems with more than 28K of physical memory. There are two sets of these registers in the 11/34, 35, 40, 60 (more in the 11/45, 55, 70) which provide for memory management when operating in the kernel and user modes respectively. This allows the operating system to have one set of registers for its exclusive use, while users must share the other set. Indeed, one of the functions of a multiprogrammed operating system is the loading and reloading of the memory management registers as users are given the use of the processor for some "time slice" (see Chapter 11).

Each APR is actually a pair of 16-bit registers; a Page Address Register (PAR) and a Page Descriptor Register (PDR). The PAR contains the starting address where that page is found in memory. The PDR contains information relative to the size of the page, how the page can be expanded in size, and whether or not the page is accessible for reading, writing, or both.

The virtual address space the programmer uses is actually divided into eight 4 Kword pages. The first three bits of the 16-bit virtual address are used to select one of the APR's. The base address of that page, contained in the PAR, says where the page begins in the physical address space.

For example, if the virtual address of an instruction operand were 120000, then APR5 (using the first 3 bits or 101 of the VA) would be used. If APR5 contained starting address 3200, then the actual physical address would be 320000. But more on this later (Chapter 7).

EXERCISES

1. Assume that the instruction below begins in location 150 and show how MACRO-11 would assemble it. What change would occur in the assembled output if each of the constants in the instruction were preceded by a # sign? An "@#" sign pair?

```
MOV     100,200
```

2. What happens when each of the following PDP-11 code sequences is executed?

```
a)      MOV     -(R7),-(R7)

b) X:   MOV     (R7),@(R7)+
        BR      X
        HALT

c)      MOV     (R7),R0
        MOV     R0,(R7)
```

3. Play assembler for the following instruction pair:

```
        .=26
DO:     ADD     R1,R2
        .=100
        BMI     DO
```

4. Using the formats presented in this chapter to explain the different addressing modes, show how the instructions in Table 3-17 change the contents of certain memory locations (the BEFORE and AFTER address spaces). Assume that each instruction begins in location 1000 and that the initial contents of the registers and memory as given are the same for each.

Table 3-17

Instructions	Initial register and memory locations
a. CLR (R5)+	(R0) = 0, (R2) = 200, (R3) = 1000
b. ADD (R2)+,R4	(R4) = 400, (R5) = 30000
c. ADD -(R3),R0	(A) = 2000, (B) = 500
d. ADD 30(R2),20(R5)	(200) = 1000, (230) = 30000
e. DEC @(R2)+	(500) = 3000
f. ADD @1000(R2),R1	(776) = 100
g. MOV #10,R0	(1000) = 230
h. ADD @#1200,R5	(1200) = 30020
i. NEG A	(3000) = 123456
j. SWAB @B	(30020) = 1000

5. Rewrite the array problem, as given in Chapter 2, using the general registers for indexing through the array elements.

6. In most machines, instruction sets are often redundant. For example, CLR is not absolutely essential on the PDP-11 since it already has a MOV instruction. The ADD instruction on the PDP-11 is another candidate for removal provided that one can show how its function can be performed by an "ADD-equivalent" sequence of other PDP-11 instructions. Give such an equivalent.

7. Explain why the "forward reference" (.= A-6) in the program segment below would present problems to the MACRO-11 assembler.

```
        .=A-6
        .WORD   0
START:  MOV     #3,R0
A:      CMP     R0,R1
        .
        .
```

8. Do both the BR and JMP instructions use relative addressing through byte offsets? What, then, is the difference or similarity between the two instructions, and how would one be used where the other was not (could not be?)?

9. What are the contents of location A at the end of the following MACRO-11 program?

```
            .=200
            R1=%1
            R2=%2
START:      MOV     #230,R1
            MOV     2(R1),R2
            MOV     R1,B
            ADD     B,R2
            MOV     R2,A
            HALT
B:          .WORD   0
C:          .WORD   230,20,54
A:          .WORD   0
            .END    START
```

10. The program in Exercise 9 is to be assembled starting at location 400. The final contents of A, however, must remain the same as in Exercise 9. What, if any, changes are required? Explain.

11. Add together all the numbers found in locations 2004, 2006, ... that are within the range of MIN to MAX. The values for MIN and MAX are located in locations 2000 and 2002, and $0 \leq N \leq 99$. If $N = 0$, the result should be zero. The sum of the numbers should be stored in location 1776. Note that there is no range associated with MIN and MAX; the actual values may be anything (positive or negative) within the range of acceptable numbers on the PDP-11.

12. Write a program to find the mode (most frequent value) of a set of N numbers. The numbers will be sorted (all numbers of equal value stored in sequential memory locations) but not ordered in ascending or descending order. Show that your program will work for all values of N in the range $0 < N < 99$.

13. Explain, with reference to the general principles of operation of an assembler, why the following code segment will be assembled properly. Then, hand assemble the code. What undesirable characteristics does this code possess?

```
            .=1000
MOV:        MOV     SUB,ADD
SUB:        ADD     MOV,SUB
ADD:        SUB     ADD,MOV
```

14. It is desired to *increment* R4 by one and to *decrement* R5 by two. A conventional instruction sequence would be INC R4 followed by SUB #2,R5. Student *A* says that the single instruction

CMPB (R4)+,@-(R5) will also work. Student *B* claims that the sequence TSTB (R4)+ followed by TST -(R5) is also suitable. First, show that the techniques proposed by both students work. Then, *carefully* compare the three methods for *time* and *space* efficiency. Hint: Follow each code sequence through the various instruction processing phases (Section 3.5.4), allocating "suitable" relative times for performing each part of each instruction. Which technique is best from the point of view of good programming practice?

REFERENCES

Since this chapter served to introduce the PDP-11, further readings can be found in the various Digital Equipment Corp. manuals describing this computer. These manuals include the Processor Handbooks for the PDP-11/04, 34, 45, 55, 60 and for the PDP-11/70. The LSI-11, or PDP-11/03 is covered in the Microcomputer Handbook. The PDP-11 Software Systems Handbook describes the DEC software available for the PDP-11's. The final test, however, of how well the material has been understood is found in the writing and running of actual computer programs. For this, the real thing is needed — a PDP-11 computer.

The PDP-11 architecture has been examined in a number of studies, reported briefly by Burr (1977), and more comprehensively in a special issue of IEEE *Computer* (October, 1977). Mudge has outlined price/performance aspects of minicomputer design, with reference to the PDP-11/60 in particular, and Mudge *et. al.* (1978) discuss minicomputer evolution in general. Strecker (1976) reported on several aspects of cache memory design for the PDP-11 family.

4

Programming Techniques and Program Structures

Mastery of a basic instruction set is the first step in learning to program. The next step is to learn to use the instruction set to obtain correct results and to obtain them efficiently. This is best done by studying the following programming techniques. Examples, which should further familiarize the reader with the total instruction set and its use, are given to illustrate each technique.

4.1 THE JUMP INSTRUCTION

Although mentioned earlier, the JMP instruction has been overlooked somewhat up to now. The astute reader will, no doubt, recognize that the necessity of a jump instruction is dictated by the fact that the branch instructions, although relative, are incapable of branching more than 128 words in either a positive or a negative direction. Thus to branch from one end of memory to another, a jump instruction must be a part of the instruction set and must allow full-word addressing.

The jump instruction is indeed a part of the PDP-11 instruction set and belongs to the single-operand group. As a result, jumps may be relative, absolute, indirect, and indexed. This flexibility in determining the effective jump target address is quite useful in solving a particular class of problems that occur in programming. This class is best illustrated by example.

4.1.1 Jump Table Problem

A common type of problem is one in which the input data represent a code for an action to be performed. For each code, the program is to take a certain action by executing a specified block of code. Such a problem would be coded in FORTRAN as

```
      .
      .
      INDEX=..
      GO TO (10,100,37,1150,...,7), INDEX
      .
      .
```

In other words, the program will go to the statement labeled 10 for INDEX = 1, 100 for INDEX = 2, 37 for INDEX = 3, and so on.

The "computed GO TO" in FORTRAN must eventually be translated into machine language. One possibility in the language of the PDP-11 would be:

```
         .
         .
         MOV     INDEX,R1        ;R1 ← INDEX
         DEC     R1              ;0 ≤ INDEX < max
         ADD     R1,R1           ;R1 ← 2*R1
         JMP     @TABLE(R1)      ;DEFFERED JUMP
         .
TABLE:   .WORD L10,L100,L37,L1150,...,L7
         .
         .
```

The method used is called the *jump table method*, since it uses a table of addresses to jump to. The method works as follows:

1. Since the range of INDEX is 1 ≤ INDEX ≤ max, 1 is subtracted from the index so that its range is 0 ≤ INDEX < max .

2. The value of index is doubled to take care of the fact that entries in the table of possible jump destination addresses are 16-bit words and thus require 2 bytes per entry. The necessity of converting integer offsets to PDP-11 word offsets by decrementing and multiplying by 2 is somewhat commonplace in PDP-11 code.

3. The effective address of the JMP instruction will then be retrieved from a location given by the sum of (R1) + TABLE.

Although the jump instruction transfers control to the correct program label, it does not specify any way to come back. In the next section, where we shall consider subroutines, we shall see that a slight modification of the jump instruction allows for an orderly transfer of control, and a return, from one section of code to another.

4.2 SUBROUTINES

A good programming practice is program modularization. That is, large programs should generally be divided into *subprograms* which are developed and debugged individually. The subprograms, or subroutines, can then be invoked by a simple sequence of "calls" to each subroutine in turn. After execution, the subroutine "returns" control to the calling program. In particular, the first instruction following the "call" which invoked the subroutine will be executed. Subroutines may also call each other. Thus, routines may be shared among various programs, with a resultant saving of space. Additionally, the programmer need only code a frequently used program module once. Indeed, the concept of program modularity has given rise to large libraries of subroutines, both in high level languages and in assembler code for particular machines. This means that to solve complex problems whose *computational kernels* or *ck's* include fundamental arithmetic transformations (e.g., matrix manipulation, Fourier transforms, autocorrelation) the programmer may have efficient implementations of most required programs already available.

In order to share common subprograms, there must be a mechanism to

1. Allow the transfer of control from one routine to another

2. Pass values among the various routines.

The mechanism that accomplishes both these actions is called the *subroutine linkage* and is, in general, a combination of hardware features and software conventions. The hardware features on the PDP-11 which assist in subroutine linkage are the instructions JSR and RTS. These instructions have the following assembler syntax and instruction format:

JSR register, destination

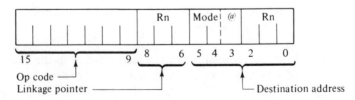

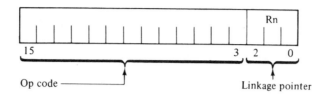

Before describing the detailed operation of JSR and RTS, the concept of stack must be re-introduced.

4.2.1 The Stack

A *stack* is an area of memory set aside by the programmer for temporary data storage. The stack uses the *last-in, first-out* or LIFO concept; that is, items are retrieved from a stack in the reverse order in which the items entered the stack. Thus the PDP-11 operand addressing features that facilitate stack manipulation are the autoincrement/autodecrement modes. They allow a program to dynamically establish, modify, or delete a stack or items on it. On the PDP-11, a stack starts at the highest location reserved for it and expands linearly downward towards lower addresses as items are added to the stack.

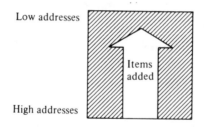

Fig. 4-1 Stack organization.

The programmer does not need to keep track of the actual locations his data are being "stacked into". This is done automatically via a *stack pointer*, a general register which always contains the memory address where the last item is stored on the stack. In the PDP-11, the programmer may establish a stack, or stacks, using any register(s) except for register 7 (R7, the PC) as a stack pointer. However, instructions associated with subroutine linkage (i.e., JSR, RTS) and interrupt service (Section 7.5) *automatically* use R6 as a stack pointer, referred to as the *system stack pointer*, or *SP*.

Stacks in the PDP-11 may be maintained in either full-word or byte units, except for the *SP* which must be maintained in full-word units only. Items are added to a stack ("pushed") using the autodecrement addressing mode [i.e., MOV ITEM,-(Rn)]; items are removed from the stack ("popped") using the autoincrement addressing mode [i.e., MOV (Rn)+,ITEM]. The use of these addressing modes now makes it clear why autodecrement decrements before reference, while autoincrement increments after reference. The reason is that the stack pointer points to the top element in the stack and must be advanced before a new element is stored; conversely, an element is removed before the stack pointer is moved. If Rn is other than R6, the SP, then "MOVB ITEM,-(Rn)" and "MOVB (Rn)+,ITEM" may be used to "push" and "pop" bytes.

Note that the stack pointer always points to the last used memory location, and that items are always pushed into the next lower memory location.

4.2.2 Subroutine Calls and Returns

When a jump-to-subroutine (JSR) is executed, the contents of the linkage register are saved on the R6 system stack as if a "MOV Rn,-(SP)" had been performed. Then the same register is loaded with the memory address following the JSR instruction (the contents of the current PC) and program execution resumes at the destination address specified. Specifically, when JSR Rn,DST is executed, the following sequence occurs following evaluation of the destination address:

```
(TMP)  ←  (Rd)     ;SAVE Rd, (DST ADDRESS, SEC. 3.5.4b)
-(SP)  ←  (Rn)     ;PUSH Rn ONTO STACK
(Rn)   ←  (PC)     ;LOAD Rn WITH RETURN ADDRESS
(PC)   ←  (TMP)    ;TRANSFER CONTROL TO SUBROUTINE
```

Here, TMP and Rd are internal processor registers. Figure 4-2 gives the "before" and after conditions when executing JSR R5,SUBR, where the first word of the JSR instruction occupies location 1000 and the symbolic address "SUBR" has value 1064:

```
          BEFORE                           AFTER
          ======                           =====
          (R5)=000132                      (R5)=001004
          (R6)=001776                      (R6)=001774
(PC)  =   (R7)=001000          (PC)  =     (R7)=001064

(001772)  = ??????                (001772)  = ??????
(001774)  = ??????                (001774)  = 000132    ←  SP
(001776)  = xxxxxx   ←  SP        (001776)  = xxxxxx
(002000)  = yyyyyy                (002000)  = yyyyyy
```

Fig. 4-2 JSR Instruction.

In order to return from a subroutine, the RTS Rn instruction is executed. It performs the inverse operation of the JSR, the unstacking and restoring of the saved register value, and the return of control to the instruction following the JSR instruction:

```
(PC) ← (Rn)      ;RESUME PROGRAM EXECUTION AT RETURN ADDRESS
(Rn) ← (SP)+     ;POP OLD Rn FROM STACK
```

The use of a stack mechanism for subroutine calls and returns is particularly advantageous for two reasons. First, many JSR instructions can be executed without the need to provide any saving procedure for the linkage information, since all linkage information is automatically pushed into the stack in sequential order. Returns can simply be made by automatically popping this information from the stack in opposite order by invoking RTS with the proper linkage register specified. Such linkage address bookkeeping is called automatic *nesting* of subroutine calls. This feature enables the programmer to construct fast, efficient linkages in an easy, flexible manner. It even permits a routine to be recalled or to call itself in those cases where this is meaningful (Sections 4.4.1 and 4.4.2). Other ramifications will appear after we examine the interrupt mechanism for the PDP-11 (Section 7.5).

The second advantage of the stack mechanism is found in its ease of use for saving and restoring registers. This case arises when a subroutine wants to use the general registers, but these registers were already in use by the calling program and must therefore be returned to it with their contents intact. The called subroutine (JSR PC,SUBR) could be written, then, as shown in Fig. 4-3.

```
SUBR:   MOV     R0,TEMP          ;SAVE R0
        MOV     R1,TEMP+2        ;SAVE R1
        MOV     R2,TEMP+4        ;SAVE R2
        MOV     R3,TEMP+6        ;SAVE R3
          .
          .
        MOV     TEMP+6,R3        ;RESTORE R3
        MOV     TEMP+4,R2        ;RESTORE R2
        MOV     TEMP+2,R1        ;RESTORE R1
        MOV     TEMP,R0          ;RESTORE R0
        RTS     PC               ;RETURN
TEMP:   .WORD   0,0,0,0,0,0      ;SAVE AREA
```

or using the stack as

```
SUBR:   MOV     R0,-(SP)         ;SAVE R0
        MOV     R1,-(SP)         ;SAVE R1
          .
          .
        MOV     (SP)+,R1         ;RESTORE R1
        MOV     (SP)+,R0         ;RESTORE R0
        RTS     PC
```

Fig. 4-3 Saving and restoring registers using the stack.

The second routine uses two fewer words per register save/restore and allows another routine to use the temporary stack storage at a later point rather than permanently tying some memory locations (TEMP) to a particular routine. This ability to share temporary storage in the form of a stack is a very economical way to save on memory usage, especially when the total amount of memory is limited. Also, as we shall see, the use of local temporary storage prevents the use of reentrancy.

The reader should note that the subroutine call JSR PC,SUBR is indeed a legitimate form for a subroutine call. The instruction does not utilize or stack any registers but the PC. That is, the return address is pushed onto the stack by the JSR and popped by the RTS. (It is instructive to trace the action of JSR PC,SUBR using the JSR protocol outlined above.) On the other hand, the instruction "JSR SP,SUBR", where SP = R6, is not normally considered a meaningful combination.

4.2.3 Argument Transmission

The JSR and RTS instructions handle the linkage problem for transferring control. What remains is the problem of passing arguments back and forth to the subroutine during its invocation. As it turns out, this is a fairly straightforward problem, and the real question becomes one of choosing one solution from the large number of techniques available for passing values.

A very simple-minded approach for argument transmission would be to agree ahead of time on the locations that might be used. For example, suppose that there exists a subroutine MULT which multiplies two 16-bit words together, producing a 32-bit result. The subroutine expects the multiplier and multiplicand to be placed in symbolic locations ARG1 and ARG2 respectively, and upon completion, the subroutine will leave the resultant in the same locations.

The subroutine linkage needed to set up, call, and save the generated results might look like:

```
        MOV     X,ARG1          ;MULTIPLIER
        MOV     Y,ARG2          ;MULTIPLICAND
        JSR     PC,MULT         ;CALL MULTIPLY
        MOV     ARG1,RSLT       ;SAVE HIGH ORDER WORD
        MOV     ARG2,RSLT+2     ;SAVE LOW ORDER WORD
```

As an alternative to this linkage, one could use the registers for the subroutine arguments and write:

```
        MOV     X,R1            ;MULTIPLIER
        MOV     Y,R2            ;MULTIPLICAND
        JSR     PC,MULT         ;CALL MULTIPLY
```

This last method, although acceptable, is somewhat restricted in that a maximum of six arguments could be transmitted, corresponding to the number of general registers available. As a result of this restriction, another alternative is used which makes use of the memory locations pointed to by the linkage register of the JSR instruction. Since this register points to the first word following the JSR instruction, it may be used as a pointer to the first word of a vector of arguments or argument addresses.

Considering the first case where the *arguments* follow the JSR instruction, the subroutine linkage would be of the form:

```
JSR     R0,MULT         ;CALL MULTIPLY
.WORD   XVALUE,YVALUE   ;ARGUMENTS
```

These arguments could be accessed using autoincrement mode:

```
MULT:   MOV     (R0)+,R1        ;GET MULTIPLIER
        MOV     (R0)+,R2        ;GET MULTIPLICAND
        .
        .
        RTS     R0
```

At the time of return, the value (address pointer) in R0 will have been incremented by 4 so that R0 contains the address of the next executable instruction following the JSR.

In the second case, where the *address of the arguments* follow the subroutine call, the linkage looks like

```
JSR     R0,MULT         ;CALL MULTIPLY
.WORD   XADDR,YADDR     ;ARGUMENT ADDRESSES
```

For this case, the values to be manipulated are fetched indirectly:

```
MULT:   MOV     @(R0)+,R1       ;FETCH MULTIPLIER
        MOV     @(R0)+,R2       ;FETCH MULTIPLICAND
        .
        .
        RTS     R0              ;RETURN
```

Another method of transmitting arguments is to transmit only the address of the first item by placing this address in a general-purpose register. It is not necessary to have the actual argument list in the same general area as the subroutine call. Thus a subroutine can be called to work on data located anywhere in memory. In fact, in many cases, the operations performed by the subroutine can be applied directly to the data located on or pointed to by a stack (Fig. 4-4) without ever actually needing to move these data into the subroutine area.

```
Item #1  ← R1 (points to item #1)
Item #2
```

Fig. 4-4 Transmitting stacks as arguments.

Calling program:

```
MOV     #POINTER,R1     ;SET UP POINTER
JSR     PC,SUBR         ;CALL SUBROUTINE
```

Subroutine:

```
      ADD       (R1)+,(R1)        ;ADD ITEM #1 TO ITEM #2
        .                         ;PLACE RESULT IN ITEM #2
        .                         ;R1 POINTS TO ITEM #2 NOW
or
      ADD       (R1),2(R1)        ;SAME EFFECT AS ABOVE,
        .                         ;BUT R1 STILL POINTS TO ITEM #1
```

Given these many ways to pass arguments to a subroutine, it is worthwhile to ask, why have so many been presented and what is the rationale for presenting them all? The answer is that each method was presented as being somewhat "better" than the last, in that

1. Fewer registers were used to transmit arguments.

2. The number of parameters passed could be quite large.

3. The linkage mechanism was simplified.

Point 3 requires some additional explanation. Since subroutines, like any other programs, may be written in *position-independent code* (Section 4.3)it is possible to write and assemble them independently from the main program that uses them. The problem is filling in the appropriate address for the JSR instruction.

Another point not to be overlooked in recapping argument passing is the significant difference in the methods used. The first techniques presented used the simple method of passing a value to the subroutine. The later techniques passed the address of the value. The difference in these two techniques, *call by value* and *call by address*, can be quite important, as illustrated by the following FORTRAN-like program example:

```
C       PROGRAM TRICKY           SUBROUTINE SWAP(X,Y)
        A=1.                     TEMP=X
        B=2.                     X=Y
        PRINT, A-B               Y=TEMP
        CALL SWAP(1.,2.)         RETURN
        A=1.                     END
        B=2.
        PRINT, A-B
        STOP
        END
```

If the real constants are passed by value, both print statements will print out a -1. This occurs because subroutine SWAP interchanges the values that it has received, not the actual contents of the arguments themselves.

However, if the real constants are passed in by address, the two print statements will produce -1. and 1., respectively. In this case the subroutine SWAP references real constants themselves, interchanging the actual argument values.

Higher-level languages, such as FORTRAN, can pass parameters both by value and by address. Often the normal mode is by address, but when the argument is an expression, the address represents the location of the evaluated expression. Therefore, if one wished to call SWAP effectively by value, it could be performed as

```
CALL SWAP(1.*1.,2.*1.)
```

causing the contents of the expressions, but not the contents themselves, to be switched.

These techniques for passing parameters are easy to understand at the assembly language level because the programmer can see exactly which method is being used. In higher-level languages, however, where the technique is not so transparent, interesting results can occur. Thus the knowledgeable higher-level language programmer must be aware of the techniques used if he is to avoid unusual or unexpected results.

4.2.4 Subroutine Register Usage

A subroutine, like any other program, will often use the registers during its execution. As a result, the contents of the registers at the time that the subroutine is invoked may not be the same as when the subroutine returns. The sharing of these common resources (e.g., the registers) therefore dictates that on entry to the subroutine the registers be saved and, on exit, restored.

The responsibility for performing the save and restore function falls either on the calling routine or the called routine. Although arguments exist for making the calling program save the registers (since it need save only the ones in current use), it is more common for the subroutine itself to save and restore all registers used. On the PDP-11 the save and restore routine is greatly simplified by the use of a stack, as was illustrated in Fig. 4-3.

As pointed out previously, stacks grow downward in memory and are traditionally defined to occupy the memory space immediately preceding the program(s) that use them. One of the first things that any program which uses a stack (in particular one that executes a JSR) must do is to set the stack pointer up. For example, if SP (i.e., R6) is to be used, the program should begin with

```
                                ;BEG IS THE FIRST INSTRUCTION
BEG:    MOV     #BEG,SP         ;SP ← ADDR OF BEG
                                ;FIRST ITEM PUSHED ONTO STACK
                                ;WILL RESIDE AT ADDR BEG-2
```

Unfortunately, this program cannot be automatically relocated anywhere in memory; it is position dependent. The question of *position independence* of PDP-11 code will now be considered.

4.3 POSITION-INDEPENDENT PROGRAMMING

As suggested earlier, it is inherent to the concept of modular programming that it is very desireable to have standard programs (e.g., scientific subroutines) which are available to many different users. Since it will not be known a priori where such programs are to be loaded, it is sometimes necessary to be able to load programs into different areas of memory and to run them there. There are several ways to do this:

1. Reassemble the program so as to start at the desired location.

2. Use a relocating loader which accepts specially coded binary output from a relocatable assembler.

3. Have the program relocate itself after it is loaded.

4. Write a program that is position-independent.

On small machines, reassembly is often performed. When the required memory is available, a relocating loader (usually called a *linking loader*) is preferable. It generally is not economical to have a program relocate itself, since hundreds or thousands of addresses may need adjustment. Writing position-independent code is usually not possible because of the structure of the addressing of the object machine. However, on the PDP-11 in particular, *position-independent code (PIC) is* possible.

PIC is achieved on the PDP-11 by using addressing modes which form an effective memory address relative to the program counter (PC). Thus, if an instruction and its target(s) are moved in such a way that the relative distance between them is not altered, the same offset relative to the PC can be used in all positions in memory. Thus PIC usually references locations relative to the current location. PIC programs may make absolute references as long as the locations referenced stay in the same place while the PIC program is relocated.

4.3.1 Position-Independent Address Modes

There are three position-independent modes or forms of instructions:

1. **Branches:** the conditional branches, as well as the unconditional branch, BR, are position-independent, since the branch address is computed as an offset to the PC.

2. **Relative memory references:** any relative memory reference of the form "CLR X" or "MOV X,Y" is position-independent because the assembler assembles it as an offset indexed by the PC. The offset is the difference

between the referenced location and the PC. For example, assume that the instruction CLR X is at address 100, with X stored 100 locations away, i.e., in location 200:

Address	Contents		Symbolic Instruction		Comments
000100	005067		CLR	X	;FIRST WORD
000102	000074				;OFFSET=200-104
000104	??????		next instruction		

The offset is added to the PC. The PC contains 104, which is the address of the next word following the offset (the second word of this two-word instruction). Note that although the form CLR X is position-independent, the form CLR @X is not. We may see this when we consider the following:

Address	Contents	Label	Symbolic Instruction		Comments
001000	005077	S:	CLR	@X	;CLEAR LOCATION A
001002	000774		.		
			.		
002000	003000	X:	.WORD	A	;POINTER TO A
			.		
003000	000001	A:	.WORD	1	

The contents of location X are used as the address of the operand, which is symbolically labeled A. The value stored at location X is the absolute address of the symbolic location A rather than the relative address or offset between location X and A. Thus, if all the code is relocated after assembly, the contents of location X must be altered to reflect the fact that location A now stands for a new absolute address. If A, however, was the name associated with a fixed, absolute location, statements S and X could be relocated. Thus the following code is position-independent:

Address	Contents	Label	Symbolic Instruction		Comments
	000036		A=36		
001000	005077	S:	CLR	@X	;CLEAR LOCATION A
	000774				
			.		
			.		
002000	000036	X:	.WORD	A	;POINTER TO A

3. **Immediate operands:** the assembler addressing form #X specifies immediate data; that is, the "value" of operand is assembled as part of the instruction.

Immediate data that are not addresses are position-independent, since they are constants. Consequently, SUB #2,HERE is position-independent (since #2 is not an address), while MOV #A,ADRPTR is position-dependent if A is a symbolic address. This is so even though the operand is fetched, in both cases, using the PC in the autoincrement mode.

4.3.2 Absolute Modes

Whenever a memory location or register is used as a pointer to data, the reference is absolute as opposed to relative. If the referenced data remain always fixed in memory (e.g., an absolute memory location) independent of the position of the PIC, the absolute modes must be used. (When PIC is *not* being written, references to fixed locations may be performed with either the absolute or relative forms.) Alternatively, if the data are relative to the position of the code, the absolute modes must not be used unless the pointers involved are modified. Restating this point in different words, if addressing is direct and relative, it is position-independent; if it is indirect and either relative or absolute, it is *not* position-independent. For example, the instruction

MOV @#X,HERE

i.e., "move the contents of the word pointed to by the PC (in this case, absolute location X) to the word indexed relative to the PC (symbolically called HERE)" contains one operand that is referenced indirectly (X) and one operand that is referenced relatively (HERE). This instruction can be moved anywhere in memory as long as absolute location X stays the same.

The absolute modes are:

@X	Location X is a pointer
@#X	The "immediate" word is a pointer
(R)	The register is a pointer
(R)+ and -(R)	The register is a pointer
@(R)+,@-(R)	The register points to a pointer
X(R)	The base, X, plus (R) is the address of the operand
@X(R)	The base plus (R) is a pointer

The nondeferred index modes require a little clarification. As described in Chapter 3, the form X(PC) is the normal mode in which to reference memory and is a relative mode. Index mode, using a register, is generally used in the absolute mode but may also be used in a relative mode and may be used conveniently in PIC. Basically, the register pointer points to a dynamic storage area, and the index mode is used to access data relative to the pointer. Once the pointer is set up, all data are referenced relative to the pointer.

4.3.3 Writing Automatic PIC

Automatic PIC is code that requires no alteration of addresses or pointers. Thus memory references are limited to relative modes unless the location referenced is fixed. In addition to the above rules, the following must be observed:

1. Start the program at location 0 to allow easy relocation using the absolute loader (see Chapter 7).

2. All location-setting statements must be of the form ".=.+X", ".=.-X", or ".= function of symbols *within the PIC*". For example, .=A+10, where A is a local label.

3. There must not be any absolute location-setting statements. This means that a block of PIC cannot set up specified core areas at load time with statements such as

   ```
   .=177404      ;SET LC TO 177404
   .WORD 5,-512. ;PRE-LOAD 177404, 177406
   ```

The absolute loader, when it is relocating PIC, relocates all data by the load bias (see Chapter 8). Thus the data for the absolute location would be relocated to some other place. Such areas must be loaded at execution time, as follows:

```
MOV    #5,@#177404    ;LOC 177404  ← 5
MOV    #-512.,@#177406 ;LOC 177406  ← -512.
```

4.3.4 Writing Nonautomatic PIC

Often it is not possible or economical to write totally automatic PIC. In these cases some relocation may be easily performed at execution time. Some of the required methods of solution are presented below. Basically, the methods operate by examining the PC to determine where the PIC is actually located. Then a relocation factor can be easily computed. In all examples it is assumed that the code is assembled starting at zero and has been relocated somewhere else by the absolute loader.

Setting Up Fixed Core Locations: Consider first the previous example to clear the contents of A indirectly. The pointer to A, contained in symbolic location X, must be changed if the code is to be relocated. The program segment in Fig. 4-5 recomputes the pointer value each time that it is executed. Thus the pointer value no longer depends on the value of the location counter at the time the program was assembled, but on the value of the PC where it is loaded.

```
000000 010700   S:      MOV     PC,R0           ;R0 ← ADDR OF S+2
000002 062700           ADD     #A-S-2,R0       ;ADD IN OFFSET
       001776
000006 010067           MOV     R0,X            ;MOVE POINTER TO X
       000766
000012 005077           CLR     @X              ;CLEAR VALUE
       000762                                   ;     INDIRECTLY
000016 000000           HALT
                        ;
                        ;
                        .=.+760
001000 002000   X:      .WORD   A               ;POINTER TO A
                        ;
                        ;
                        .=.+776
002000 000001   A:      .WORD   1               ;VALUE TO BE CLEARED
                        .END
```

Fig. 4-5 Non-automatic PIC.

Now if this program is loaded, for example, starting at location 4000, it should be clear that none of the program values is changed. This point could be shown pictorially by taking the Fig. 4-5 material, recopying it, but changing only the values in the leftmost column, the address column. Thus if one were to look in, say, location 4010, the contents would be 766 and the value found in location 5000 would be 2000 (i.e., neither value is changed).

Given that the program data have not changed, the question is: How does it work? The answer is that the offset $A-S-2$ is equivalent to $A-(S+2)$ and $S+2$ is the value of PC which is placed in R0 by the statement MOV PC,R0. At assembly time the offset value is $A-PCz$, where $PCz = S+2$, is the PC that was assumed for the program when assembled beginning at location zero.

Later, after the program has been relocated, the move instruction will no longer store PCz in R0, but a new value, PCn , which is the current value of PC for the executing program. However, the ADD instruction still adds in the immediate value $A-PCz$, producing the final result in R0:

$$PCn+(A-PCz) = A+(PCn-PCz)$$

which is the desired value, since it yields the new absolute location of A [e.g., the assembled value of A plus the relocation factor $(PCn-PCz)$].

Relocating Pointers: If pointers must be used, they may be relocated as we have just shown. For example, assume that a list of data is to be accessed with the instruction

```
        ADD     (R0)+,R1
```

The pointer to the list, list L, may be calculated at execution time as follows:

```
M:      MOV     PC,R0           ;GET CURRENT PC
        ADD     #L-M-2,R0       ;ADD OFFSET
```

Another variation is to gather all pointers into a table. The relocation factor may be calculated once and then applied to all pointers in the table in a loop. The program in Fig. 4-6 is an example of this technique. The reader should verify (Exercise 3 at the end of this chapter) that if this program is relocated so that it begins in location 10000, the values in the pointer table PTRTBL, will be 10000, 10020 and 10030.

```
000000 010700    X:      MOV     PC,R0           ;PC POINTS TO X+2
000002 062700            ADD     #X-X-2,R0       ;R0 ← RELOCATION FACTOR
       177776
;
000006 012701            MOV     #PTRTBL,R1      ;GET A POINTER
       000030
000012 060001            ADD     R0,R1           ; AND RELOCATE IT
;
000014 012702            MOV     #TBLLEN,R2      ;GET TABLE LENGTH
       000003
;
000020 060021    LOOP:   ADD     R0,(R1)+        ;RELOCATE AN ENTRY
000022 005302            DEC     R2              ;COUNT DOWN
000024 001375            BNE     LOOP            ;STOP WHEN DONE
000026 000000            HALT
       000003            TBLLEN=3
000030 000000    PTRTBL: .WORD   X,LOOP,PTRTBL
000032 000020
000034 000030
       000001            .END
```

Fig. 4-6 Relocating pointers.

Care must be exercised when restarting a program that relocates a table of pointers. The restart procedure must not include the relocating again (i.e., the table must be relocated exactly once after each load).

4.4 ADVANCED SUBROUTINE CONCEPTS

Further advantages of stack organization become apparent in complex situations which can arise in program systems that are engaged in the concurrent handling of several tasks. Such multitask program environments may range from relatively simple single-user applications which must manage an intermix of I/O service and background computation to large complex multi-programming systems that manage a very intricate mixture of system and user programs. In all these applications there is a need for flexibility and time/memory economy. The use of the stack provides this economy and flexibility by providing a method for allowing many tasks to use a single copy of the same routine and a simple, unambiguous method for keeping track of complex program linkages.

4.4.1 Reentrancy

The ability to share a single copy of a given program among users or tasks is called *reentrancy*. Reentrant program routines differ from ordinary subroutines in that it is unnecessary for reentrant routines to finish processing a given task before they can be used by another task. Multiple tasks can be in various stages of completion in the same routine at any time. Thus the situation shown in Fig. 4-7 may occur.

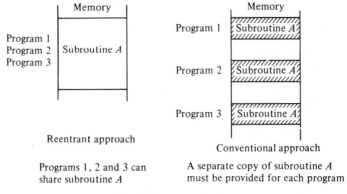

Fig. 4-7 Reentrant routines.

The chief programming distinction between a nonshareable routine and a reentrant routine is that the reentrant routine is composed solely of *pure code*; that is, it contains only instructions and constants. There can be no data areas within the routine that are read or written into. Thus a section of program code is reentrant (shareable) if and only if it is non-self-modifying; that is, no information within it is subject to modification. The philosophy behind pure code is actually not limited to reentrant routines. Any non-modifying program segment that has no temporary storage or data associated with it will be

1. Simpler to debug.

2. Read-only protectable (i.e., it can be kept in read-only memory).

3. Interruptable and restartable, besides being reentrant.

Using reentrant routines, control of a given routine may be shared as illustrated in Fig. 4-8.

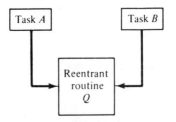

Fig. 4-8 Reentrant routine sharing.

1. Task A has requested processing by reentrant routine Q.

2. Task A temporarily relinquishes control of reentrant routine Q (i.e., is interrupted) before it finishes processing.

3. Task B starts processing the same copy of reentrant routine Q.

4. Task B relinquishes control of reentrant routine Q at some point in its processing.

5. Task A regains control of reentrant routine Q and resumes processing from where it stopped.

The use of reentrant programming allows many tasks to share frequently used routines such as device service routines and ASCII-Binary conversion routines. In fact, in a multiuser system it is possible, for instance, to construct a reentrant FORTRAN compiler that can be used as a single copy by many user programs.

4.4.2 Recursion

It is often meaningful for a program segment to call itself. The ability to nest subroutine calls to the same subroutine is called *self-reentrancy* or *recursion*. Recursion is of great use to the mathematical analyst, as it often permits the evaluation of fairly complex algorithms using comparatively straightforward and compact code. This technique often permits very significant memory and speed economies in the linguistic operations of compilers and other higher-level software programs, as we shall illustrate.

A classical example of the technique of recursion can be found in computing N factorial ($N!$). Although

$$N! = N * (N-1) * (N-2) * \ldots * 1$$

it is also true that

$$N! = N * (N-1)!$$

and

$$0! = 1.$$

Written in "pseudo-FORTRAN," a function for calculation of $N!$ would look like:

```
      INTEGER FUNCTION FACT(N)
      IF (N.NE.0) GO TO 1
      FACT = 1
      RETURN
1     FACT = N * FACT(N-1)
      RETURN
      END
```

This code is pseudo-FORTRAN because it cannot actually be translated by most FORTRAN compilers; the problem is that the recursive call requires a stack capable of maintaining both the current values of FACT and the return pointers either to the function itself or its calling program. However, the function may be coded in PDP-11 assembly language in a simple fashion by taking advantage of its stack mechanism. Assuming that the value of N is pushed onto the stack and that the value of $N!$ is to be left on the stack, the function FACTOR could be coded recursively as shown in Fig. 4-9.

```
FACT:    MOV    N,-(SP)        ;INITIAL VALUE ON STACK
         JSR    PC,FACTOR      ;CALCULATE N!
         MOV    (SP)+,NFACT    ;GET ANSWER
         RTS    PC             ;RETURN TO CALLING PROGRAM
         ;
FACTOR:  MOV    2(SP),R1       ;R1 ← N. ("2" INDEXES AROUND
                               ;        RETURN ADDRESS ON STACK)
         BEQ    ZERO           ;N = 0?
         DEC    R1             ;NO. R1 ← N-1
         MOV    R1,-(SP)       ;PUSH R1 = N-1 ONTO STACK
         JSR    PC,FACTOR      ;RECURSIVE CALL
RET:     MOV    (SP)+,R1       ;POP (N-1)! INTO R1
         MUL    2(SP),R1       ;R1 ← (N-1)!*N
         MOV    R1,2(SP)       ;N! = (N-1)!*N REPLACES N
         RTS    PC
ZERO:    MOV    #1,2(SP)       ;0! = 1
         RTS    PC
```

Fig. 4-9 Recursive coding of factorial function.

The program of Fig. 4-9 calls itself recursively by executing the JSR PC,FACTOR instruction. Each time it does so, it places both the decremented value of N and the return address (label RET) in the stack.

The multiply instruction (MUL) uses the value of R1 to perform a multiplication of R1 by the value of an internal number (initially 1), which represents the partial product. This partial product is also stored on the stack.

Upon completing the multiplication, the program encounters the RTS instruction again. Either the stack contains the return address of the calling program for FACTOR, or else another address-data pair of words generated by a recursive call on FACTOR. In the latter case, R1 is again loaded with an N value that is to be multiplied by the partial product being held on the stack, and the above process is again repeated. Otherwise, the return to the calling program is performed, with $N!$ saved on the stack.

4.4.3 Coroutines

In some situations it happens that several program segments or routines are highly interactive. Control is passed back and forth between the routines, and each goes through a period of suspension before being resumed. Because the routines maintain a symmetric relationship to each other, they are called *coroutines*.

Basically, the coroutine idea is an extension of the subroutine concept. The difference between them is that a subroutine is subordinate to the calling program while the coroutine is not. Consequently, passing control is different for the two concepts.

When the calling program makes a call to a subroutine, it suspends itself and transfers control to the subroutine. The subroutine is entered at its beginning, performs its function, and terminates by passing control back to the calling program, which is thereupon resumed.

In passing control from one coroutine to another, execution begins in the newly activated routine where it last left off, not at the entrance to the routine. The flow of control passes back and forth between coroutines, and each time a coroutine gains control, its computational progress is advanced until it passes control on to another coroutine.

The PDP-11, with its hardware stack feature, can be easily programmed to implement a coroutine relationship between two interacting routines. Using a special case of the JSR instruction [i.e., JSR PC,@(R6)+], which exchanges the top element of the register 6 processor stack and the contents of the program counter (PC), the two routines may be permitted to swap program control and resume operation where they stopped, when recalled. This control swapping is illustrated in Fig. 4-10. Note that the stack must first be intialized with MOV #PC2,-(R6).

The power of a coroutine structure is to be found in modern operating systems, a topic beyond the scope of this book. However, in Chapter 7 we demonstrate the use of coroutines for the double buffering of I/O while overlapping with computation. The example presented in that chapter is elegant in its seeming simplicity, and yet it represents one of the most basic I/O operations to be performed in most operating systems.

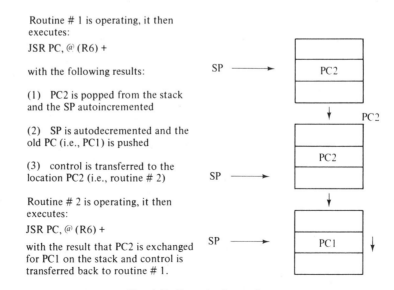

Routine # 1 is operating, it then executes:

JSR PC, @ (R6) +

with the following results:

(1)   PC2 is popped from the stack and the SP autoincremented

(2)   SP is autodecremented and the old PC (i.e., PC1) is pushed

(3)   control is transferred to the location PC2 (i.e., routine # 2)

Routine # 2 is operating, it then executes:

JSR PC, @ (R6) +

with the result that PC2 is exchanged for PC1 on the stack and control is transferred back to routine # 1.

Fig. 4-10 Coroutine interaction.

The reader will find it instructive to trace the operation of JSR PC,@(R6)+ using the JSR protocol defined in Section 4.2.2.

4.5 MACROS AND MACRO ASSEMBLERS

There is another technique besides the subroutine for invoking the *same* code sequence at *different* points in a program. This is the *macro*. Discussion of the macro, however, also demands introduction of the concept of *macro assembler*.

The reader has already read how a basic symbolic assembler makes machine language programming easier, faster, and more efficient. In addition, the reader has been presented with the need for and advantage of pseudo-operation instructions for directing the actions of the assembler. Now we shall discuss the advanced features of a macro instruction generator, which is a part of an expanded or macro assembler. Note that the keyword is "expanded," since the macro assembler contains all the features normally found in a symbolic assembler plus those necessary to handle macro instruction generation.

One of the features of a macro-instruction generator is that it permits easy handling of repetitive instruction sequences utilizing the simple technique of parameterization. The generator allows the programmer to create new language elements in order to be able to adapt the assembler to his specific programming applications. In addition, macros may be called inside macros, nested to multiple levels, and redefined within the program.

At this point it might be well to define just what a macro is rather than only what it can do. Very specifically, a macro is an *open routine* which is defined in a formal sequence of coded instructions and, when called or evoked, results in the replacement of the macro call by the actual body of code that it represents. The use of a macro statement does not result in saving memory locations but rather in saving programmer time. (Sometimes, the macro is also useful for economically trading memory for execution speed.)

When a program is being written, it often happens that certain coding sequences are repeated several times, with only the arguments changed. It would be convenient if the entire repeated sequence could be generated by a single statement. To accomplish this it is first necessary to define the coding sequence with dummy parameters as a macro instruction, referring to the macro name along with a list of real arguments that will replace the dummy parameters and generate the desired sequence.

Macros must be defined before they may be used. The way to define a macro is to bound the sequence of symbolic instructions with the pseudo-ops .MACRO and .ENDM. For example,

```
.MACRO   MAC          ;MACRO NAME
LINE1
LINE2                  ;MACRO BODY
LINE3
.ENDM                  ;TERMINATE MACRO
```

With each macro call (macro order), the macro body is substituted in place of the macro name:

```
Macro                           Macro
Processor Input                 Processor Output
---------------                 ----------------
ADD     A,B                     ADD     A,B
MOV     B,A                     MOV     B,A
MAC                             LINE1
                                LINE2
                                LINE3
MOV     C,B                     MOV     C,B
```

This replacement process occurs essentially before assembly and can be conceived of as a character-string substitution.

Since the programmer may wish to use the same macro but on different data, macro calls include argument transmission. Thus, if a programmer desires to define a macro instruction "add byte" (ADDB), the following macro definition would suffice:

```
.MACRO  ADDB X,Y
MOV     R0,-(SP)    ;SAVE R0
MOV     R1,-(SP)    ;SAVE R1
MOVB    X,R0        ;R0 ← BYTE 1, SIGN EXT. TO HIGH BYTE
MOVB    Y,R1        ;R1 ← BYTE 2, SIGN EXT. TO HIGH BYTE
ADD     R0,R1       ;RESULT
MOVB    R1,Y        ;RESULT INTO Y
MOV     (SP)+,R1    ;RESTORE R1
MOV     (SP)+,R0    ;RESTORE R0
.ENDM
```

The reader should note that, while the add byte is correctly performed, the condition codes will not be set as they would for the ADD instruction.

4.5.1 Location and Created Symbols

A problem which often occurs when using macros has to do with labels. For example, a macro to implement a *block move* of data might look like

```
.MACRO  BLKMOV X,Y,N
MOV     #X,R0          ;X IS STARTING ADDRESS OF ARRAY 1
MOV     #Y,R1          ;Y IS STARTING ADDRESS OF ARRAY 2
MOV     N,R2           ;NUMBER OF POINTS IN EACH ARRAY
LOOP:
MOV     (R0)+,(R1)+    ;MOVE DATA
SOB     R2,LOOP
.ENDM
```

Unfortunately, each time BLKMOV is called, the label LOOP will be redefined, resulting in an error.

There are, fortunately, two ways out of this dilemma:

1. Parameterize the label, leaving its definition up to the programmer; for example,

```
        .MACRO BLKMOV X,Y,N,L
            .
L:
            .
```

2. Allow the programmer to inform the assembler that certain symbols are known only to the macro and should be replaced by the macro assembler with a created symbol, which will be unique for each call of the macro:

```
        .MACRO BLKMOV X,Y,N,?L
            .
L:
            .
```

which generates the following code when called:

```
BLKMOV A,B,NPTS          MOV     #A,R0
                         MOV     #B,R1
                         MOV     NPTS,R2
                64$:     MOV     (R0)+,(R1)+
                         SOB     R2,64$

BLKMOV C,D,NPTS          MOV     #C,R0
                         MOV     #D,R1
                         MOV     NPTS,R2
                65$:     MOV     (R0)+,(R1)+
                         SOB     R2,65$
```

Created symbols are always local symbols between 64$ and 127$. The local symbols are created by the macro assembler in numerical order and are generated only when there is no real argument being substituted in place of the dummy argument in the macro definition. If a real argument is specified in the macro call, the generation of a local symbol is inhibited and normal replacement is performed.

4.5.2 Nesting of Macros

Macros may be nested; that is, macros may be defined within other macros. For ease of discussion, levels are assigned to nested macros. The outermost macros (those defined directly) are called *first-level macros*. Macros defined within first-level macros are called *second-level macros*; and so on. For example,

```
.MACRO LEVEL1 A,B        ;START LEVEL 1 DEFINITION
ADD    A,B
.MACRO LEVEL2 C,D        ;START LEVEL 2 DEFINITION
SUB    C,D
.MACRO LEVEL3 E,F        ;START LEVEL 3 DEFINITION
ADD    E,F
ADD    F,F
.ENDM                    ;END LEVEL 3 DEFINITION
CLR    C
.ENDM                    ;END LEVEL 2 DEFINITION
CLR    A
.ENDM                    ;END LEVEL 1 DEFINITION
```

At the beginning of the macro processing only first-level macros are defined and may be called in the normal manner. Second- and higher-level macros will not yet become defined. Thereafter, the level of definition is irrelevant and macros at either level may be called in the normal manner. Of course, higher-level macros will not be defined until the lower-level macros containing them have been called. Using the last example, the following would occur:

```
        Call    Expansion       Comments
        ----    ---------       --------
LEVEL1  X,Y     ADD     X,Y     Causes LEVEL2 to
                CLR     X       be defined.

LEVEL2  I,J     SUB     I,J     Causes LEVEL3 to
                CLR     I       be defined.

LEVEL3  Y,I     ADD     Y,I
                ADD     I,I
```

If a call to LEVEL3 were made before LEVEL2 defined it, an error would result, since the code expansion would be undefined.

4.5.3 Macro Calls Within Macro Definitions

The body of a macro definition may contain calls for other macros which have not yet been defined. However, the embedded calls must be defined before a call is issued to the macro which contains the embedded call.

As an example, we consider the macro called SWITCH, which transfers the contents of buffer A to buffer B and vice versa:

```
.MACRO SWITCH A,B,TEMP,N
SAV012
COPY   A,TEMP,N
COPY   B,A,N
COPY   TEMP,B,N
UNS012
.ENDM
```

```
        .MACRO  COPY FROM,TO,COUNT,?L
        MOV     #FROM,R1
        MOV     #TO,R2
        MOV     COUNT,R0
L:      MOV     (R1)+,(R2)+
        SOB     R0,L
        .ENDM

        .MACRO  SAVO12
        MOV     R0,-(SP)
        MOV     R1,-(SP)
        MOV     R2,-(SP)
        .ENDM

        .MACRO  UNSO12
        MOV     (SP)+,R2
        MOV     (SP)+,R1
        MOV     (SP)+,R0
        .ENDM
```

The reader should expand out the preceding example as an exercise.

4.5.4 Recursive Calls and Conditional Assembly

Although it is legal for a macro definition to contain an embedded call to itself, care must be taken to ensure that the recursive macro expansion will eventually terminate. Somehow the assembler must be told that a condition has been detected and that the recursive definition may now stop. The technique used to accomplish this is the conditional assembly statement, although such statements may be used for things other than recursive macro definitions.

Conditional assembly directives are most often used to assemble certain parts of a source program on an optional basis. The instruction is of the form

```
    .IF   cond,argument(s)
```

where "cond" represents a conditional that

1. Tests the value of an argument expression; or

2. Tests the assembly environment; or

3. Determines the attributes of a single symbol or address expression; or

4. Tests the value of character strings.

If the condition is satisfied, that part of the source program starting with the statement immediately following the conditional statement, and including the statements up to the .ENDC (end conditional) assembly directive, are assembled. However, if the condition is not satisfied, the code is not assembled.

Conditional statements may be nested. For each .IF statement there must be a termination .ENDC statement. If the outermost .IF is not satisfied, the entire group is not assembled. If the first .IF is satisfied, the following code is assembled. However, if an inner .IF is encountered, its condition is tested, and the code given in Table 4-1 is assembled only if the second .IF is satisfied. Logically, nested .IF statements are like AND circuits. If the first, second, and third are satisfied, the code that follows the third nested .IF statement is assembled.

Table 4-1   Conditional assembly directives.

Type	Pseudo-op	Condition
Comparand	.IF EQ	argument = 0
	.IF NE	argument ≠ 0
	.IF GT	argument > 0
	.IF GE	argument ≥ 0
	.IF LT	argumeny < 0
	.IF LE	argument ≤ 0
Environment	.IF B	Is macro-type argument blank (i.e., missing)?
	.IF NB	Is macro-type argument not blank (i.e., present)?
Attribute	.IF DF	Is argument symbol defined?
	.IF NDF	Is argument symbol undefined?
Character String	.IF IDN	Are two macro-type arguments identical?
	.IF DIF	Are two macro-type arguments different?

Note that a macro-type argument is one enclosed in angle brackets (i.e., $<A,B,C>$). Such arguments allow expressions to be treated as single terms. Examples using conditionals are:

1. The conditional assembly code may be used to terminate macro recursion.

```
A=0
.MACRO SUM X,Y
ADD    X,Y
A=A+1
.IF    NE,A-3
SUM    X,Y
.ENDC
.ENDM
```

2. The code generator *should* put out a SOB Rn,LOOP instruction if the relative distance for the backwards branch is 128 bytes or less, a DEC Rn/BNE LOOP if the relative distance is greater than 128 bytes and not more than 256 bytes, and DEC Rn/BEQ .+6/JMP LOOP if the branch is greater than 256 bytes. (Under what conditions will the macro fail?)

```
        .MACRO  SOBC     R0,LOOP
        SIZE=.-LOOP
;SOB?
        .IF     GT,126.-SIZE
        SOB     R0,LOOP
        .ENDC
;DEC & BRANCH?
        .IF     LT,124.-SIZE
        .IF     GE,252.-SIZE
        DEC     R0
        BNE     LOOP
        .ENDC
        .ENDC
;DEC & JUMP?
        .IF     LT,252.-SIZE
        DEC     R0
        BEQ     .+6
        JMP     LOOP
        .ENDC
;
        .ENDM
```

4.5.5 Repeat Blocks, Concatenation, and Numeric Arguments

Occasionally it is useful to duplicate a block of code a number of times in line with other source codes. This is performed by creating a repeat block of the form

```
.REPT     EXPR
code to be repeated
.ENDR
```

where EXPR is any legal expression controlling the number of times the block of code is assembled. For example, suppose it is desired to generate a fast, fixed-size block move instruction. We note that the SOB entails a significant portion of the overhead of the the macro as previously specified. Thus, trading memory for speed:

```
.MACRO BLKMVF X,Y
MOV     #X,R0         ;X IS FIRST ADDRESS OF ARRAY 1
MOV     #Y,R1         ;Y IS FIRST ADDRESS OF ARRAY 2
.REPT   100.
MOV     (R0)+,(R1)+
.ENDR
.ENDM
```

The repeat pseudo-op can also be usefully combined with two other macro features. The first is concatenation. This feature allows the apostrophe or single quote (') character to operate as a legal separating character such that when the ' precedes and/or follows a dummy argument, the ' is removed and substitution of the real argument occurs at that point.

The second feature is the capability of passing a symbolic argument as a numeric string. Such an argument is preceded by the unary operator backslash (\ )

and is treated as a number. Combining these features, we get the following
interesting example:

```
.MACRO   INC A,B
CNT      A,\B
B=B+1
.ENDM

       .MACRO  CNT A,B
A'B:    .WORD B
       .ENDM
```

This macro pair, when called by

```
C=0
.REPT   5
INC     X,C
.ENDR
```

results in the following macro expansion:

```
X0:     .WORD   0
X1:     .WORD   1
X2:     .WORD   2
X3:     .WORD   3
X4:     .WORD   4
```

The two macros are necessary because the dummy value of B cannot be
updated in the CNT macro. This is because the characters representing the number
internally are inserted in the macro expansion. Thus in the CNT macro, the
number passed is treated as a string argument. It is important to note that when a
macro uses the same name as a standard assembly language op-code, the standard
is superceeded. Thus INC in the above macro now takes on a new meaning.

4.5.6 Power of the Macro Assembler: VAX-11 Address Modes on the PDP-11

Macro assemblers, which possess the features of nested definitions, conditional
code generation, and recursive calls, provide a capability more powerful than a
subroutine facility. The reason is that the macro assembler allows code generation
at translation time so that the actual program generated fits the applications for
which it was intended. Thus, unlike the subroutine, it does not require extensive
testing of conditions that *may occur* at execution time because the code was
generated to handle only those cases that *were known to occur.*

An interesting example of code generation at translation time is implemention
of the VAX-11 true indexing mode on the PDP-11. In VAX-11, all basic PDP-11
address modes (excepting mode 5) are present. The operand address represented
by these modes (except register mode, of course) can be augmented by adding a

constant equal to the contents of a second register multiplied by the given operand size. Operand size for bytes, words, longwords or single precision floating-point, and quadwords or double-precision floating-point is 1, 2, 4, and 8 bytes, respectively; operand size is specified by the instruction, as in MOV and MOVB on the PDP-11. Indexing is specified by following the normal address specification with the indexing register in "[ ]". For example, in the execution of

INCW @(R2)+ [R5]

an address is fetched from the location pointed to by R2, R2 is incremented by two (word instruction as per W suffix) and twice the contents of R5 added to compute the effective operand address. R5 is *not* modified. In general, the PC or a register involved in autoincrement/decrement should not also be specified as the indexing register. The value of true indexing will become apparent when data structures are studied in the next chapter.

The following translator, written in MACRO-11, implements VAX indexing modes for a number of PDP-11 single operand instructions. It is intended to demonstrate the power of a macro-assembler and will not, of course, duplicate the execution efficiency of VAX's indexing modes. Since "[" and "]" are not recognized delimiters in MACRO-11, "<" and ">" are used instead. The key to the VAX macro is the .NTYPE SYM,*arg* command, which determines the PDP-11 6-bit address specification of *arg* (assumed a valid PDP-11 address specification) and places it in SYM. Thus, the mode and register of *arg* can be extracted by use of the logical "and" MACRO-11 operator, &. ".IRPC c,*arg*" repeats the defined block of code with *c* in turn equal to each character in *arg*.

It is suggested that the reader trace through the macro in order to confirm his understanding of the numerous MACRO-11 capabilities demonstrated. Similarly, he should examine the output code to convince himself that the required VAX-like address modes are indeed implemented. Note that, to conserve memory, the output code generated by this macro makes use of self-modifying code. As suggested earlier, this practice is to be avoided except in those single-user situations where time and/or space efficiency is indeed of prime importance.

```
7     ;MACRO GENERATES UP TO 3 INSTRUCTIONS: A1, A2, AND A3
8     ;
9              .MACRO   VAX    A,SYM1,A1,A2,A3
10             .IRPC    XX,A
11             .IF      EQ,RN&70-XX'0
12             .IRPC    X,01234567
13             .IF      EQ,SYM1&07-X
14     A1
15     A2
16     A3
17             .ENDC
18             .ENDM
19             .ENDC
20             .ENDM
21             .ENDM
22     ;
```

```
23              ;Decode and implement "OPW DST <Rm>" instruction in PDP-11 code,
24              ; where OP is CLR, COM, INC, DEC, NEG or TST.  DST references Rn.
25              ;
26                  .IRP OP, <CLR,COM,INC,DEC,NEG,TST>
27                      .MACRO  OP'W  DST, INDEX, ?L
28              ;
29                  .NTYPE RN, DST    ;RN ← 6-bit value =  MODE, REGISTER of DST
30                  .NTYPE RM, INDEX  ;RM ← 6-bit value =  MODE, REGISTER of INDEX
31              ;......................................................................
32              ;a) MODE 4? Generate "Pre-decrement Rn" instruction.
33              ;
34                  VAX 4,RN,<    TST -(R'X)>
35              ;......................................................................
36              ;b) MODE 1,2,3,4, or 5? Generate "Compute 2*Rm in offset" instrs.
37              ;
38                  VAX 12345,RM,<    MOV R'X,L+2>,<    ASL L+2>
39              ;
40              ;c) MODE 6? Generate "Compute offset, add offset to base" instrs.
41              ;
42                  VAX 6,RM,<    MOV R'X,T1>,<    ASL T1>,<    ADD T1,L+2>
43              ;......................................................................
44              ;d) MODE 1,2, or 4? Generate OP 0(Rn). "0" will receive 2*Rm.
45              ;
46                  VAX 124,RN,<L: OP 0(R'X)>
47              ;
48              ;e) MODE 3? Generate OP @#0. "0" contains PDP-11 address + 2*Rm.
49              ;
50                  VAX 3,RN,<    ADD (R'X)+,L+2>,<L: OP @#0>
51              ;
52              ;f) MODE 5? Generate OP @#0. "0" contains PDP-11 address + 2*Rm.
53              ;
54                  VAX 5,RN,<    ADD -(R'X),L+2>,<L: OP @#0>
55              ;
56              ;g) MODE 6? Generate OP DST. Offset will have 2*Rm added in,
57              ;            and old offset will later be restored by subtraction.
58              ;
59                  VAX 6,RN,<L: OP DST>,<    SUB T1,L+2>
60              ;......................................................................
61              ;h) MODE 2? Generate "Post increment Rn" instruction.
62              ;
63                  VAX 2,RN,<    TST (R'X)+>
64              ;......................................................................
65                      .ENDM                        ;END FOR "OP'W" MACRO DEFINITION
66              .ENDM                                 ;END FOR INITIAL .IRP OP, <...>
67                                                    ;
68                                                    ;*******************************
69 000000                                  CLRW    (R1) <R4>
   000000   010467   000006                   MOV R4,64$+2
   000004   006367   000002                   ASL 64$+2
   000010   005061   000000               64$: CLR 0(R1)
70                                                    ;*******************************
71 000014                                  COMW    (R2)+ <R5>
   000014   010567   000006                   MOV R5,65$+2
   000020   006367   000002                   ASL 65$+2
   000024   005162   000000               65$: COM 0(R2)
   000030   005722                            TST (R2)+
```

```
72                                           ;******************************
73  000032                                   TSTW    @(R4)+ <R5>
    000032  010567  000012                           MOV R5,66$+2
    000036  006367  000006                           ASL 66$+2
    000042  062467  000002                           ADD (R4)+,66$+2
    000046  005737  000000                   66$: TST @#0
74                                           ;******************************
75  000052                                   INCW    -(R3) <R4>
    000052  005743                                   TST -(R3)
    000054  010467  000006                           MOV R4,67$+2
    000060  006367  000002                           ASL 67$+2
    000064  005263  000000                   67$: INC 0(R3)
76                                           ;******************************
77  000070                                   NEGW    @-(R0) <R2>
    000070  010267  000012                           MOV R2,68$+2
    000074  006367  000006                           ASL 68$+2
    000100  064067  000002                           ADD -(R0),68$+2
    000104  005437  000000                   68$: NEG @#0
78                                           ;******************************
79  000110                                   CLRW    A <R4>
    000110  010467  000056                           MOV R4,T1
    000114  006367  000052                           ASL T1
    000120  066767  000046  000002                   ADD T1,69$+2
    000126  005067  000036                   69$: CLR A
    000132  166767  000034  177770                   SUB T1,69$+2
80                                           ;******************************
81  000140                                   DECW    A(R4) <R0>
    000140  010067  000026                           MOV R0,T1
    000144  006367  000022                           ASL T1
    000150  066767  000016  000002                   ADD T1,70$+2
    000156  005364  000170'                  70$: DEC A(R4)
    000162  166767  000004  177770                   SUB T1,70$+2
82                                           ;******************************
83  000170  000052                           A:      52
84  000172  000000                           T1:     0
85          000001'                                  .END
```

Another example of the use of such macro assemblers can be found in system generators. System generators are parameterized macro programs that allow the user to define his particular operation environment as arguments to the program. The program may then be assembled, and will produce machine language programs tailored to the particular installation. Such programs do not test to see how much memory or what options are available; instead, such information is already embedded in the operating environment code. As a result, instructions for testing memory size, or whether or not a printer is available, need never be executed.

Finally, a powerful use of macros can be found in totally parameterized macro programs. The instructions in such programs are either macro calls or macro definitions based entirely on previously defined macros. Thus the macro programmer need never know what the actual machine instructions are or what they are capable of doing. Indeed, the programmer need not know anything at all about the host computer, since the macro expansion is based on character strings and does not depend on the generated result.

A classic example of the use of such a macro-generation scheme can be found in the implementation of SNOBOL4 by its designers and users. This language is written as a macro-generation implementation and only requires that each macro be defined for the host computer. Once each macro is defined, the macros, along with the SNOBOL4 system, may be assembled into a running SNOBOL4 interpretor.

EXERCISES

1. Write a subroutine to multiply two signed integer values to produce a double-length integer result. The subroutine linkage will be of the form

```
MOV     #MIER,R0      ;MULTIPLIER ADDRESS IN R0
MOV     #MAND,R1      ;MAND ADDRESS IN R1
JSR     PC,MULT       ;CALL MULTIPLY
```

2. Write the multiply subroutine in PIC form so that it may be called by

```
JSR     R5,MULT
.WORD   M1-ADDRESS,M2-ADDRESS
```

3. Verify that the program of Section 4.3.4b does indeed perform the required relocation of all pointers in the pointer table.

4. Write a PIC program that clears all the memory below where the program is loaded (e.g., if the program is loaded in location 10000 and higher, it should clear locations 0-7777).

5. Write a mainline program to call the subroutine of Exercise 4 and execute it.

6. A main program fragment and subroutine are as follows:

```
        .=1000                          .=2000
BEGIN:  MOV     #BEGIN,SP     SUB:      MOV     (R0)+,R1
        MOV     #1,R0                   DEC     R1
        JSR     R0,SUB                  TST     R1
        .WORD   3                       BEQ     RETURN
                                        JSR     R0,SUB
                                        .WORD   1
                              RETURN:   RTS     R0
```

   a. Show the value of the stack pointer and the values in the processor stack before execution of the program. (Note: In this and in all succeeding parts, indicate that quantity is unknown by filling the symbol "?".)

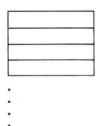

b. Show the value of the stack pointer and the values in the processor stack just after execution of the MOV #1.R0 instruction in the main program.

c. Show the value of the stack pointer and the values in the processor stack *after each stack operation* (i.e., push-down or a pop-up). Also indicate the address of each stack location used. Several blanks have been included below for your use; you may or may not need to use them all. Work from the left of the page.

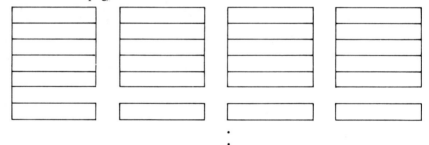

d. Show the value of the stack pointer and the values in the processor stack upon completion of the execution of the main program fragment.

7. The following program is a recursive subroutine for manipulating a data structure called a *binary rooted tree*. Binary trees consist of *nodes* and *branches*, with each branch connecting two nodes. Although such structures will not be studied in this book, the program is of interest for a number of reasons, the most important of which is to demonstrate the value and power of recursive subroutines. Any binary rooted tree consists of a root, a left subtree of that root, and a right subtree of that root. *Each subtree is a tree itself.* Hence, the recursion.

```
        .MCALL .EXIT .TTYOUT    ;RT-11 SYSTEM MACROS
TRAVRS:
        MOV     #TRAVRS,SP      ;INITIALIZE THE STACK
        MOV     ROOT,R1         ;ROOT CONTAINS ADDRESS OF ROOT NODE
        JSR     R5,GO
        .EXIT                   ;BACK TO RT-11 MONITOR
GO:
        TST     R1              ;ZERO MEANS NO SUCCESSOR
        BEQ     RETURN
        ;
        .TTYOUT 2(R1)           ;OUTPUT  2(R1) ON TERMINAL (SEC. 7.7)
        ;
        MOV     R1,-(SP)        ;SAVE POINTER
        MOV     (R1),R1         ;ADDRESS OF LEFT SUCCESSOR
        JSR     R5,GO
        ;
        MOV     (SP)+,R1        ;RECOVER POINTER
        MOV     4(R1),R1        ;ADDRESS OF RIGHT SUCCESSOR
        JSR     R5,GO
RETURN:
        RTS     R5
        ;
        .MACRO NODE LEFT,NAME,RIGHT
NAME:   .WORD   LEFT            ;LEFT SUCCESSOR IDENTITY
        .ASCII  /NAME/          ;CONTENTS OF THIS NODE
        .BYTE   0
        .WORD   RIGHT           ;RIGHT SUCCESSOR IDENTITY
        .ENDM
        ;
ROOT:   .WORD   A               ;ROOT OF THE TREE
        NODE    B,A,C
        NODE    D,B,0
        NODE    E,C,F
        NODE    0,D,0
        NODE    0,E,G
        NODE    H,F,J
        NODE    0,G,0
        NODE    0,H,0
        NODE    0,J,0
        ;
        .END    TRAVRS
```

a) Starting at the top of a page, draw a "dot" to represent the tree root "A".
   Then moving downwards, draw in left and right branches which join each
   node to its successor. For example, the first two branches look like:

b) The manipulation performed by the subroutine is to "traverse" the tree. In
   traversing the tree, each node is "visited" once and, for example, the
   contents of the node printed out. Three basic algorithms exist for tree
   traversal:

   i) ***Inorder:*** Visit the nodes in an order such that, for any node V in the
      tree, all the nodes in the left subtree are visited *before* V and all the
      nodes in the right subtree are visited *after* V. More succinctly,
      At a given root,

```
1. Traverse the left subtree in inorder.
2. Visit the root.
3. Traverse the right subtree in inorder.
```

   The two other algorithms are:

   ii) ***Preorder:***
   At a given root,

```
1. Visit the root.
2. Traverse the left subtree in preorder.
3. Traverse the right subtree in preorder.
```

   iii) ***Postorder:***
   At a given root,

```
1. Traverse the left subtree in postorder.
2. Traverse the right subtree in postorder.
3. Visit the root.
```

c) Trace the program through. Which algorithm does it implement? Can you
   change the program to implement each of the other two algorithms? Note
   that the operation of the system macros .TTYOUT and .EXIT will be
   explained in Chapter 7.

8. Expand the macro call

   SWITCH BUF1,BUF2,SPARE,10

for the macro definition given in Section 4.5.3.

9. Rewrite the macro definitions for SWITCH so that the intermediate storage array TEMP need only be one word long.

10. Define the macro BSS X which is to reserve a block of storage locations X bytes long.

11. Develop a macro that can perform multiplication through recursive calls to the macro body, which performs shifting and adding.

REFERENCES

Since position-independent coding is not very different from coding using a base register, the reader interested in this subject can read further in Stone (1975), Gear (1974), Abrams and Stein (1973), and Mauer (1968). These books also cover the subjects of subroutines and subroutine linkages. However, one should read Wegner (1968) and Ralston (1971) for coverage of the topics call-by-value, call-by-name, and call-by-address. The tiny book by Barron (1968) is a classic on the basic techniques of recursion. The flavor of his approach is exemplified by the very first paragraph of the book: "It has been remarked that 'if computers had existed in the Middle Ages, programmers would have been burned at the stake by other programmers for heresy' ... (and that) one of the main heresies would have been a belief (or disbelief) in recursion." The general problem of assembling code for machines with span dependent instructions, raised by the SOBC macro of Section 4.5.4, has been considered in detail by Szymanski (1978).

5

Data Manipulation
and
Data Structures

Up to this point, the reader's interest in computer-based manipulation of information has been centered on instruction and data formats, and on programming techniques and program structures for accessing *primitive* data elements (bits, bytes, words), and for operating upon them using comparatively *simple* arithmetic and logical functions (e.g., add, OR). In this chapter, that interest is explicitly directed towards the details involved in more complex arithmetic and logical operations, and in representation and manipulation of highly structured data.

5.1 BYTE HANDLING AND CHARACTER CODES

The PDP-11 processor includes a full complement of instructions to manipulate byte operands. Since all PDP-11 addressing is byte-oriented, byte manipulation is straightforward and enables the PDP-11 to perform as either a word or a byte processor. With the exception of ADD and SUB, all single- and double-operand instructions may become byte instructions by simply attaching a "B" to their mnemonic operation code (e.g., MOVB, DECB).

The value of a byte-addressable computer lies in its ability to manipulate a quantity that represents a character. The 8-bit bytes in the PDP-11 are able to represent 256 different character codes, of which the 7-bit ASCII code is a subset. This subset (see Appendix C) forms the alphanumeric character set for the PDP-11 and allows for full character manipulation within it.

When one manipulates characters or bytes through byte operations, two things occur. First, byte operations in register mode access the low-order byte of the specified register. Second, byte instructions using autoincrement or autodecrement direct addressing cause the specified register to be modified by 1 to point to the adjacent byte of data. As a result, a no-operation type of instruction to add 4 to a register might be

```
CMP      (R0)+,(R0)+
```

while the same instruction in byte mode,

```
CMPB     (R0)+,(R0)+
```

will only add 2 to the register.

To assist the programmer in byte and character manipulation, the MACRO-11 assembler includes the .BYTE pseudo-op which stores 8-bit values in successive byte locations. In addition, the .ASCII pseudo-op is useful for assembling a string of ASCII characters into their byte representations while the .EVEN pseudo-op is used to force the current location counter to an even or word boundary value if it is odd.

When a character is preceded by an apostrophe, its value is that of the ASCII character it represents. When it is preceded by a quotation mark, two ASCII characters are assigned the ASCII values of each of the characters to be used. Each value is stored in an 8-bit byte, and the bytes are combined to form a word. For example, "AB will store the ASCII value of A in the low-order (even) byte and the value of B in the high-order (odd) byte. Thus, to place the character representation of A in R0, the code would be

```
MOVB     #'A,R0
```

while to place the character string AB in R0, the code is

```
MOV      #"AB,R0
```

(Note carefully the use of the # sign; without it the character representation is used as an address !)

5.2 FIXED-POINT ARITHMETIC

Addition and subtraction using single words have been considered up to this point. However, fixed-point arithmetic is more generally concerned with multiple word (i.e., extended precision) arithmetic. Such arithmetic requires additional computer instructions to enable consideration of the *carry* and *overflow* bits. Further, the availability of *shift* instructions facilitates multiply and divide operations.

5.2.1 Carry and Overflow

In Chapter 3, where a discussion of binary and octal arithmetic was presented, one subject was intentionally left out, namely the problems of arithmetically manipulating large numbers which could conceivably exceed the arithmetic capability of the computer. For example, suppose that there exists a 4-bit two's complement computer that can add or subtract. The range of numbers representable on such a machine is from $+7$ to -8, as shown in Table 5-1.

Table 5-1 Four-bit two's complement values.

Binary Value	Decimal Value
0111	+7
0110	+6
0101	+5
0100	+4
0011	+3
0010	+2
0001	+1
0000	0
1111	−1
1110	−2
1101	−3
1100	−4
1011	−5
1010	−6
1001	−7
1000	−8

To add the decimal values 3 and 4, the binary arithmetic would look as follows:

```
3        0011
4        0100
--       ----
7        0111
```

On the other hand, adding 3 and 5 results in -8

```
3        0011
5        0101
--       ----
8        1000  =  -8
```

The problem is that there is a *carry* into the sign position of the number, producing an incorrect result. The computer arithmetic is said to have generated an *overflow* condition in that the arithmetic results have spilled over into the *most significant bit* (MSB) position or sign position. However, because both the words *carry* and *overflow* have been used to describe the same phenomena, there tends to be some confusion over the exact meaning of the overflow and carry conditions that may be generated on two's-complement machines.

As the reader will soon see, the meaning of the carry and overflow conditions is truly different. In order to demonstrate their meaning and difference, an exact and consistent definition of their generation will be given. The definition for an ADD operation is as follows:

1. CARRY: defined to be the carry out of the MSB position of the word.

2. OVERFLOW: defined to have occurred whenever both operands are of the same sign and the result generated is of an opposite sign.

The difference between CARRY and OVERFLOW is that CARRY is useful for *multiple-precision arithmetic*, while OVERFLOW is useful for determining whether or not the arithmetically generated results are correct.

To show the meaning of overflow and carry, examples using a 4-bit machine are presented in Table 5-2. Only for those cases where the overflow bit is set (i.e., when overflow occurs) are the results incorrect; the carry bit appears to have no significance at all.

Table 5-2   Setting of V- and C-bits for addition of 4-bit numbers

Decimal	Binary	Carry from MSB	Unlike Signs	V	C	Results
1	0001					
+2	0010	no	no	0	0	correct
–	----					
3	0011					
5	0101					
+6	0110	no	yes	1	0	incorrect
–	----					
11	1011					
−6	1010					
+7	0111	yes	no	0	1	correct
–	----					
1	0001					
−6	1010					
−6	1010	yes	yes	1	1	incorrect
––	----					
−12	0100					

5.2.2 Multiple Precision Addition/Subtraction

The meaning of the carry bit becomes clear when double-precision arithmetic is performed. For this case, the two 4-bit words of the previous example are taken to represent an 8-bit double-precision value. The range of possible values for double-precision is $-128 \leq$ value < 128, since there are seven bits plus sign used to represent each unique value.

To perform double-precision arithmetic, the following algorithm is used:

1. Perform addition on the least significant 4-bits (*low-order word*).

2. Perform addition on the most significant 4-bits (*high-order word*), adding in the carry bit if set.

3. The overflow last recorded (due to step 2) shows if the result is correct.

Table 5-3 Examples of double-precision addition.

		First-half Add		Second-half Add		
Decimal	Binary	V	C	V	C	Results
49	0011 0001					
+50	0011 0010	0	0	0	0	correct
---	---------					
99	0110 0011					
53	0011 0101					
+70	0100 0110	1	0	0	0	correct
---	---------					
123	0111 1011					
60	0011 1100					
+70	0100 0110	0	1	1	0	incorrect
---	---------					
130	1000 0010					
26	0001 1010					
+26	0001 1010	1	1	0	0	correct
---	---------					
52	0011 0100					
−70	1011 1010					
−70	1011 1010	1	1	1	1	incorrect
---	---------					
−140	0111 0100					
−70	1011 1010					
80	0101 0000	0	0	0	1	correct
---	---------					
10	0000 1010					

The examples of Table 5-3 serve to make the significance of the carry bit clear — it propagates the carry from the addition of the least significant word into the addition of the most significant word. Additionally, the overflow bit should be ignored, except for the last addition, since in double-precision arithmetic there is no sign bit associated with the least significant word   Overflow into this bit position is therefore normal when performing double-precision arithmetic.

Double- and multiple-precision arithmetic is common on minicomputers, where the range of possible values is small due to the small word size. As a result, special instructions are included to add or subtract the carry bits. On the PDP-11 these instructions are as follows:

Operation	Symbolic Form	Meaning
Add Carry	ADC X	(X) ← (X) + (C)
Subtract Carry	SBC X	(X) ← (X) − (C)

Here, (C) = value of C condition code bit. If the C and V are to be useful to the programmer, they must be set as part of the result of an arithmetic operation such as ADD, SUB, COM, or NEG, as indeed they are on the PDP-11. Thus not only are the N and Z condition bits affected by the result of an arithmetic operation, but so are the C and V condition bits. For example, if one were to add two numbers,

```
          ADD     A,B
          .
A:        .WORD   121354
B:        .WORD   134201
```

the erroneous result placed in B would be 055555, and the processor status word would be set to 000003 (see Fig. 3-1). Additionally, some instructions, such as MOV, clear the overflow or V-bit while setting the N- and Z-bits and not affecting the C-bit at all. And since it may be necessary to set and clear any or all of the condition code bits directly, the following instructions are included in the PDP-11 instruction set:

```
Operation          Symbolic Form          Meaning
---------          -------------          -------
Clear C bit        CLC                    (C) ← 0
Clear V bit        CLV                    (V) ← 0
Clear Z bit        CLZ                    (Z) ← 0
Clear N bit        CLN                    (N) ← 0
Set C bit          SEC                    (C) ← 1
Set V bit          SEV                    (V) ← 1
Set Z bit          SEZ                    (Z) ← 1
Set N bit          SEN                    (N) ← 1
```

The format of these instructions is as follows:

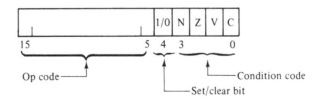

Selectable combinations of these bits may be cleared or set together. This is accomplished by "ORing" the op-codes together to form a combination (e.g., CLC!CLV, where ! is taken to mean "OR" by the assembler).

Taking advantage of the setting and clearing of the V- and C-bits by the ADD and NEG instructions, a double-precision add would be performed as

```
     ADD     A0,B0        ;ADD LOW-ORDER WORDS
     ADC     B1           ;ADD CARRY INTO HIGH-ORDER WORD
     ADD     A1,B1        ;ADD HIGH-ORDER WORDS
```

and a double-precision complement as

```
NEG     A1              ;2'S COMPLEMENT HIGH-ORDER WORD
NEG     A0              ;2'S COMPLEMENT LOW-ORDER WORD
SBC     A1              ;PROPAGATE CARRY
```

(The NEG instruction sets the carry to a 1 if the two's-complemented result is nonzero; otherwise it sets it to a zero.) The use of double- and multiple-precision arithmetic can be found in multiplying two single-precision values together, forming a double-precision result, and as part of floating-point arithmetic, to be discussed in Section 5.2.4.

5.2.3 Shifting

Although the word and byte instructions are useful for manipulating data at the word or byte level, it is still often necessary to manipulate bits within a word or a byte. The shift and rotate instructions, along with the logical operations (Section 5.3), provide this capability in the PDP-11.

The shift and rotate instructions belong to the single-operand group. The shift instructions perform one-bit arithmetic shifts either left or right, with the C-bit used as a register extender. Thus, for a left shift, the MSB is shifted into the C-bit, while all other bits are shifted left one position and the LSB is filled with a zero. The right shift is very much like the left shift except that the MSB is filled with a replication of the sign bit rather than a zero, and the LSB is shifted into the C-bit. In this way right shifts do not cause the sign to be changed if the number is negative, and right and left shifting may be thought of as a scaling of data by a factor of 2.

The arithmetic shift instructions can be shown pictorially as:

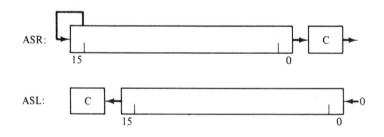

As expected, the N, Z, and C condition bits are set according to the result generated. The V-bit is set as the exclusive-OR of the N- and the C-bits to indicate arithmetic overflow when the result is of a different sign than the operand.

The rotate instructions operate on their operands and the C-bit as if they formed a 17-bit "circular buffer". Thus on a rotate left, the MSB is shifted into the C-bit, the C-bit shifts into the LSB, and all other bits are shifted left one position.

A rotate right is the inverse operation. Together, these instructions facilitate sequential bit testing and detailed bit manipulation.

The pictorial representation of the rotate instructions looks as follows:

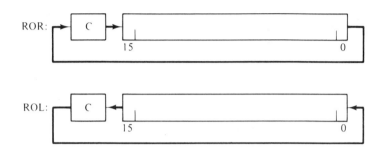

The setting of the condition codes for the rotate instructions follows the same rules as for the arithmetic shifts.

The four instructions are written as

Operation	Symbolic Form	Meaning
Arithmetic shift right	ASR X	$(C) \leftarrow (X[0])$ $(X[14:0]) \leftarrow (X[15:1])$ $(X[15]) \leftarrow (X[15])$
Arithmetic shift left	ASL X	$(C) \leftarrow (X[15])$ $(X[15:1]) \leftarrow (X[14:0])$ $(X[0]) \leftarrow 0$
Rotate right	ROR X	$(X[14:0]) \leftarrow (X[15:1])$ $(X[15]) \leftarrow (C)$ $(C) \leftarrow (\text{old } X[0])$
Rotate left	ROL X	$(X[15:1]) \leftarrow (X[14:0])$ $(X[0]) \leftarrow (C)$ $(C) \leftarrow (\text{old } X([15])$

Multiple shifts and rotates are available in the Extended Instruction Set (EIS) via the ASH and ASHC instructions. ASH SRC,Rn effects a left shift up to 31 bits or a right shift up to 32 bits, on Rn, according to the value of SRC. *Positive* SRC gives *left* shift, *negative* SRC *right* shift. On left shift, 0's enter the low bit of Rn; on right shift the sign bit of Rn is extended. ASHC SRC,Rn shifts the 32-bit longword in Rn, Rn + 1 (n even) as specified by SRC as per ASH. If n is odd, Rn *only* is rotated right up to 16 bits if a right shift is specifed. Thus ASHC is like a double length ASR or ASH, where the amount of shift can be specified as an operand.

5.2.4 Multiplication

Multiplication of unsigned numbers can be carried out by the shift and add technique:

```
e.g.,   118(10)=   001 110 110 (2)
         11(10)=   000 001 011 (2)
                   ------------
                     1 110 110
                    11 101 10
                   000 000 0
                 1 110 110
                   ------------
                10 100 010 010 (2)  =  1298 (10)
```

This can be programmed as follows:

```
        CLR  R0          ;CLEAR ACCUMULATOR
        MOV  MIER,R1     ;GET MULTIPLIER
        MOV  MAND,R2     ;GET MULTIPLICAND
        MOV  #16.,R3     ;SET LOOP COUNT

        ROR  R1          ;SHIFT LOW BIT OF MULTIPLIER INTO C
LOOP:   BCC  NADD        ;NO ADD IF LOW BIT OF MULTIPLIER ZERO
        ADD  R2,R0       ;ADD MULTIPLICAND TO PARIAL PRODUCT
NADD:   CLC              ;CLEAR CARRY AS PARTIAL PRODUCT UNSIGNED
        ROR  R0          ;SHIFT HIGH WORD OF PARTIAL PRODUCT RIGHT
        ROR  R1          ;SHIFT LOW  WORD OF PARTIAL PRODUCT RIGHT
        SOB  R3,LOOP     ;LOOP. SOB DOES NOT ALTER C BIT
```

The 32-bit product resides in R0, R1. In general, however, 2's complement negative numbers cannot be multiplied in this manner. Instead, Booth's algorithm, which allows for positive and negative numbers is used. Although the algorithm is difficult to derive, a simple example demonstrates its basis.

We begin by assuming that the multiplier is -41. As a 16-bit 2's complement number, it looks like

```
1 111 111 111 010 111(2)  =   177727(8)  =  -41(10)
```

Now, representing the muliplier as a sum and difference of integers which can be written in binary as strings of 1's (i.e., $2**n-1$), we can express the binary representation of -41 as

```
    1 111 111 111 111 111    -    111 111
  +               11 111    -      1 111
  +                                  111
```

Writing $(2**n-1)$ as $(2**n)-(1)$, we get

```
  (10 000 000 000 000 000-1)-  (1 000 000-1)
  +                (100 000-1)-  (10 000-1)
  +                              (1 000-1)
```

Then, collecting all the 1's, we then obtain

```
10 000 000 000 000 000     -     1 000 000
+              100 000     -        10 000
+                1 000     -             1

=     2**16   -2**6 +2**5 -2**4 +2**3 -2**0
```

Disregarding $2**16$ and noting that $2**5 = 2*2**4$, then

```
1 111 111 111 010 111      = -2**6 +2**4 +2**3 -2**0
```

Thus, $(1\ 111\ 111\ 111\ 010\ 111)*m = -(2**6)*m + (2**4)*m + (2**3)*m - m$, where m is the multiplicand. Thus, for $m = 75$, $-41*75 = -3075 = -64*75 + 16*75 + 8*75 - 75$.

In general, an operation — addition or subtraction — is necessary only when a transition from 0 to 1 or 1 to 0 occurs in the multiplier. *Booth's modified algorithm* utilizes this fact and enables mechanization of the generation of such sequences. Assume a 16-bit 2's complement multiplier mr with least significant bit (LSB) $y(0)$ and MSB $y(15)$. Then for $i = 0, 2, 4, ..., 14$, examine $y(i-1)$, $y(i)$, and $y(i+1)$. On the basis of each result, using Table 5-4, shift the partial product right (R), with sign bit extension, and then add (A) or subtract (S) the multiplicand to/from the partial product. Note: $y(-1) = 0$.

Table 5-4 Decoding of multiplier for Booth's modified algorithm

y(i+1)	y(i)	y(i-1)	Partial product shift(s), (R), multiplier add/subtract, (A or S)
0	0	0	R,R
0	0	1	A,R,R
0	1	0	A,R,R
0	1	1	R,A,R
1	0	0	R,S,R
1	0	1	S,R,R
1	1	0	S,R,R
1	1	1	R,R

Applying this, right-to-left, with $mr = -41$,

```
1 111 111 111 010 111.0 (2)  = -41(10)
                  -- -           → S,R,R
               - --              → R,A,R
              ---                → A,R,R
           -- -                  → S,R,R
         - --                    → R,R
       ---                       → R,R
     -- -                        → R,R
   - --                          → R,R
```

Thus the sequence generated is S, R, R, R, A, R, A, R, R, S, R, R, R, R, R, R, R, R, R, R. Using the fact that a run of r R's is equivalent to a multiplication by $2**(-r)$, we may write $-41*m$ as

$$[[[[-m]*2**(-3) +m]*2**(-1) +m]*2**(-2) -m]*2**(-10)$$

$$= -m*2**(-16) +m*2**(-13) +m*2**(-12) -m*2**(-10)$$

However, the result must be multiplied by $2**16$ to compensate for the right shifting. That is $-41*m = -(2**6)*m +(2**4)*m +(2**3)*m -(2**0)*m$, as derived earlier.

Booth's modified algorithm can be implemented efficiently using a jump table as follows. Initially, the multiplier, *mr*, multiplied by two (so that the least significant bit, *y(-1)* above, $= 0$) is contained in a 17-bit "register" comprising C and R1, and the initial zero partial product is in R0. *R0* concatenated with *C* and *R1* will be interpreted as a 33-bit "register". At each step, this register can be shifted right *twice* via two ROR, ASR sequences with the multiplicand, *m*, added to (or subtracted from) the 16 MSB's of this register when appropriate.

Since the ASL R4 (required for indexing into TABLE) and the ADD/SUB instructions both conditionally alter the carry bit, the *first* ROR R1 must precede the relevant ASL or ADD/SUB so that the bit of the partial product residing in C is saved in bit 15 of R1. Since the *second* ASR R0 is always the final instruction of each module invoked using the JUMP table, this ASR is moved to the main program at label JMPRET.

Note that a computed JSR could replace the JMP, but the latter is more efficient, particularly in the return. A final ROR R1, at label FIN, is necessary to compensate for the ROL R1 used to compute $2*mr$ initially.

```
MULT:
        MOV   MIER,R1      ;R1 ← MULTIPLIER
        MOV   MAND,R2      ;R2 ← MULTIPLICAND
        MOV   #8.,R3       ;LOOP 8 TIMES
        ;
                          ;R0,C,R1 FORM 33-BIT SHIFT REGISTER
        CLC               ;CLEAR CARRY
        ROL   R1           ;2*MULTIPLIER IN C,R1.
        CLR   R0           ;ZERO PARTIAL PRODUCT HIGH WORD
        ;
;       *** INNER LOOP, EXECUTED 8 TIMES ********************************
LOOP:
        MOV   R1,R4        ;DUPLICATE R1
ROR1:   ROR   R1           ;SHIFT R1 RIGHT, SAVING CARRY IN BIT 15 OF R1
        ;
        BIC   #17770,R4    ;MASK OUT UPPER 13 BITS OF MR FOR BYTE OFFSET
        ASL   R4           ;FORM WORD OFFSET
        JMP   @TABLE(R4)   ;JUMP TO CORRECT MODULE
        ;
JMPRET: ASR   R0           ;FINAL "ASR" OF EACH SEQUENCE DONE HERE
        SOB   R3,LOOP      ;CARRY NOT AFFECTED BY 'SOB'
;       *** END OF INNER LOOP ******************************************
        ;
FIN:    ROR   R1           ;COMPENSATE FOR INITIAL 'ROL R1'
        MOV   R0,HIGANS    ;32-BIT PRODUCT
        MOV   R1,LOWANS    ; STORED
        RTS   PC           ;RETURN
```

```
TABLE:                          ;JUMP TABLE
        RR
        ARR
        ARR
        RAR
        RSR
        SRR
        SRR
        RR
        ;
RR:     ASR  R0                 ;1'ST 'ROR' AT "ROR1" IN MAIN, 1'ST 'ASR' HERE
        ROR  R1                 ;2'ND 'ROR' HERE,2'ND 'ASR' AT "JMPRET" IN MAIN
        BR   JMPRET
        ;
ARR:    ADD R2,R0               ;ADD MULTIPLICAND TO PARTIAL PRODUCT
        ASR  R0
        ROR  R1
        BR   JMPRET
        ;
RAR:    ASR  R0
        ROR  R1
        ADD R2,R0               ;ADD MULTIPLICAND TO PARTIAL PRODUCT
        BR   JMPRET
        ;
RSR:    ASR  R0
        ROR  R1
        SUB  R2,R0              ;SUBTRACT MULTIPLICAND FROM PARTIAL PRODUCT
        BR   JMPRET
        ;
SRR:    SUB  R2,R0              ;SUBTRACT MULTIPLICAND FROM PARTIAL PRODUCT
        ASR  R0
        ROR  R1
        BR   JMPRET
```

In both this and the preceding algorithm the magnitude of m must be less than $(2**15-1)/1.5$ to prevent temporary overflow. Although the average number of 0's (or 1's) in an n-bit word is $n/2$, it can be shown that the average number of transitions from 1 to 0 (or vice versa) is $n/3$. Although this program executes slower than one based on a conventional multiply, it has been introduced for a number of reasons. First, implementation of the algorithm is an interesting demonstration of the jump table, and second, in Section 10.7.4 it will be shown how application of Booth's algorithm at the microcode level may result in substantial speed enhancement of fixed-point multiply. Finally, Booth's algorithm has been the basis for achieving very high speed multiplication in several recent hardware multiplier "chips".

The *Extended Instruction Set* (EIS) includes a 2's complement multiply instruction with syntax

```
MUL SRC,Rn
```

The SRC operand may be specified via any of the 8 PDP-11 address modes. If Rn specifies R0, R2, or R4, the 32-bit product is stored in (R0,R1), (R2,R3) or (R4,R5), respectively; if "Rn" specifies R1, R3 or R5, only the low 16 bits of the product are stored in R1, R3 or R5, respectively. The latter technique is useful for index calculation, while the 16x16 bit multiply, 32-bit result is useful in digital signal processing (DSP) applications. For example, suppose the real and imaginary components of a sequence of complex numbers are stored in the even and odd positions of an array. Then the sum of the squares of the components may be efficiently calculated and stored into the original array as follows:

```
          MOV     #A,R0           ;ADDRESS OF 1'ST ELEMENT OF ARRAY
          MOV     R0,R1           ;DUPLICATE
          MOV     #n,-(SP)        ;NUMBER OF COMPLEX DATA POINTS
          ;
LOOP:     MOV     (R0)+,R2        ;Re[A(  )]
          MUL     R2,R2           ;Re[A(  )]**2
          MOV     (R0)+,R4        ;Im[A(  )]
          MUL     R4,R4           ;Im[A(  )]**2
          ADD     R5,R3           ;32-BIT ADDITION
          ADC     R2
          ADD     R4,R2           ;Re[A(  )]**2 + Im[A(  )]**2
          MOV     R2,(R1)+        ;STORE HIGH WORD
          MOV     R3,(R1)+        ;STORE LOW WORD
          DEC     (SP)
          BNE     LOOP
          ;
          TST     (SP)+           ;POP COUNT
```

Note that since "MUL SRC,Rn", n even, computes Rn, Rn+1 ← Rn*SRC, the above technique for squaring numbers is valid and time efficient.

In DSP applications, "integer" data from an analog-to-digital (A/D) converter are often multiplied by fractional numbers such as sines and cosines. The fractions may be multiplied by some integer power of 2 such that the integer part of the result is less than $2**15-1$, and greater than $2**14$, and stored as an integer table. For example, suppose that

$$x(i) \leftarrow x(i)*[0.54-0.46*\cos(2\pi[i-1]/N)], \quad i = 1, 2, \ldots, N$$

is to be calculated, where the *x(i)* are 2's complement data points. A FORTRAN program is used to compute

$$NW(I)=(2.**15-1.)*(0.54-0.46*\cos(2.*PI*XI/XN))$$

where XI = I-1 and XN = N, so that $|NW(I)| \leq 2**15-1$. Then, if *x(i)* is computed as

```
          MOV     #X,R0           ;I/O ARRAY STARTING ADDRESS
          MOV     #NW,R1          ;WEIGHTING ARRAY STARTING ADDRESS
          MOV     #n,R2           ;n = NUMBER OF POINTS IN ARRAYS
          ;
LOOP:     MOV     (R0),R4         ;R4    ← x(i)
          MUL     (R1)+,R4        ;R4,R5 ← x(i)*NW(I)
          MOV     R4,(R0)+        ;HIGH WORD = PRODUCT/2**16
          SOB     R2,LOOP         ;DECREMENT R2, BRANCH IF NOT ZERO
```

the results can be interpreted as

```
x(i)  ←  [x(i)*|(2.**15-1.)*[0.54-0.46*cos(2π[i-1]/N)]|]/[2.**16]
      = 0.5*x(i)*[0.54-0.46*cos(2π[i-1]/N)],
```

since the 16-bit high word of the product is effectively the 32-bit product divided by $2**16$. This interpretation is quite useful and time efficient in DSP computation, particularly the fast Fourier transform (FFT, Section 9.8).

5.2.5 Division

Division is more complicated than multiplication for several reasons:

1. Division produces two results, a quotient and a remainder. The quotient of two integers is rarely an integer, and the correct quotient is dependent on a correct remainder.

2. The maximum value that can result from a division is infinite. Some quotients cannot be expressed in the number of bits available, and overflow may therefore occur.

The quotient in a division is the number of times that the divisor can be subtracted from the dividend without the dividend changing sign. Thus repeated subtraction and sign checking can effect division; when the dividend changes sign, reduce the subtract count by one, and add the divisor to the dividend. The dividend is now the remainder, and the subtract count is the quotient.

A faster technique is the non-restoring algorithm: *subtract* a power-of-two multiple of the divisor from the dividend. If the sign of the result (the remainder) is unchanged, add the same power of two to the quotient. If the sign of the result changes, however, do not increase the quotient. This is repeated for successively smaller powers of two, until the zeroth power is reached.

When the remainder sign does change, the algorithm becomes: *add* the relevent power-of-two multiple of the divisor to the remainder, until sign change again occurs, and only then add the power of two to the quotient. An example will illustrate:

```
              Compute 17/5 = 3, + 2 remainder

                                         Q = 0
              17 - 5 * 8 = -23;          Q = Q + 0 = 0
             -23 + 5 * 4 =  -3;          Q = Q + 0 = 0
              -3 + 5 * 2 =  +7;          Q = Q + 2 = 2
               7 - 5 * 1 =  +2;          Q = Q + 1 = 3
```

The following program implements the non-restoring algorithm for positive 16-bit integers:

```
ONE=%0
DIVS=%1
;NON-RESTORING DIVISION PROGRAM
;DIVIDEND, DIVISOR ASSUMED 16-BIT POSITIVE INTEGERS PASSED VIA R5
DIVNRS:
        MOV     #1,R0           ;USED FOR QUOTIENT BIT SETTING
        CLR     @10.(R5)        ;OVERFLOW FLAG INITIALLY CLEARED
        CLR     R2              ;CLEAR REMAINDER
        MOV     @2(R5),R3       ;DIVIDEND IN R3
        BEQ     ZERO            ;ZERO DIVIDEND?
        MOV     #16.,R4         ;LOOP COUNT
        MOV     @4(R5),DIVS     ;DIVISOR  IN R1
        BEQ     OVFL            ;DIVISOR = 0, NO GO!
POSSTP:
        ASL     R3              ;LEFT SHIFT R2,R3
        ROL     R2
        SUB     DIVS,R2         ;SUBTRACT DIVISOR FROM REMAINDER
        BMI     NEG             ;BRANCH IF SIGN CHANGE
        BIS     ONE,R3          ;NO, SET QUOTIENT BIT
        SOB     R4,POSSTP       ;AND AROUND AGAIN
        BR      FIN
NEGSTP:
        ASL     R3              ;LEFT SHIFT R2,R3
        ROL     R2
        ADD     DIVS,R2         ;ADD DIVISOR TO REMAINDER
        BMI     NEG             ;DO AGAIN IF SIGN STILL NEGATIVE
        BIS     ONE,R3          ;NO, SET QUOTIENT BIT
        SOB     R4,POSSTP       ; AND BACK TO SUBTRACTING DIVISOR
        BR      FIN
NEG:
        SOB     R4,NEGSTP
FIN:
        TST     R2              ;REMAINDER NEGATIVE
        BGE     OK              ;NO
        ADD     DIVS,R2         ;YES, ADD DIVISOR TO REMAINDER
OK:     MOV     R2,@6(R5)       ;REMAINDER
        MOV     R3,@8.(R5)      ;QUOTIENT
        RTS     PC
OVFL:
        INC     @10.(R5)        ;SET OVERFLOW FLAG FOR ERROR
        RTS     PC
ZERO:
        MOV     @4(R5),@6(R5)   ;REMAINDER IS DIVISOR IF DIVIDEND ZERO
        CLR     @8.(R5)         ;QUOTIENT IS ZERO
        RTS     PC
        .END
```

The EIS divide instruction syntax is

```
DIV   SRC,Rn
```

where Rn must be R0, R2, or R4. The 32-bit longword dividend in Rn, Rn + 1 is divided by SRC with the quotient left in Rn and remainder in Rn + 1. A division of one 16-bit number by another is therefore programmed as

```
MOV     DIVDND,R3       ;16-BIT DIVIDEND
SXT     R2              ;SIGN EXTEND TO FORM 32-BIT DIVIDEND
DIV     DIVSOR,R2       ;DIVIDE
MOV     R2,QUOT         ;QUOTIENT
MOV     R3,REM          ;REMAINDER
```

In Section 9.2.1, an example of chained 32-bit MUL/DIV is shown.

5.2.6 Expanded Set of Branch Instructions

The carry and overflow bits are also use in more complex conditional branches as well as for multiple precision arithmetic and shifting. While some of the conditional branches consider numbers absolutely (e.g., BEQ and BNE), others interpret the data as having a sign bit, bit 15 (e.g., BPL and BMI). It may have occurred to the reader that other branch instructions, such as branch less than (BLT), branch less than or equal (BLE), branch greater than (BGT), and branch greater than or equal (BGE), would be quite useful to have. They do exist, but each of these branches uses the C- and V- as well as the N- and Z-bits, and up until now, it would not have been clear why.

The *unsigned* conditional branches (BHI, BLOS, BHIS, and BLO) operate on all 16-bit numbers by treating the arithmetic sequence as

```
highest value    177777
                 177776
                    .
                    .
                    .
                 000001
lowest value     000000
```

On the other hand, the sequence of arithmetic values in signed, 16-bit, two's-complement arithmetic is

```
largest positive value    077777
                          077776
                             .
                             .
                             .
                          000001
smallest positive value   000000
                          ------
smallest negative value   177777
                          177776
                             .
                             .
                             .
largest negative value    100000
```

The difference between the two sequences is obvious; however, it is not clear why there should be a difference in conditional branches. A simple example will make the point clear.

Suppose that we wish to test the results of an instruction in which the operands are considered to be 16-bit signed (two's-complement) values. Then if we were to compare a negative source (-32767) to a position destination (32767), by calculating (SRC)-(DST), the setting of the condition bits would be

```
  -32767.        100001        100001     with Z = 0
-  32767.  →  - 077777  →  + 100001          N = 0
 --------     --------      --------          C = 0
      2.       000002      1)000002           V = 1
```

The condition bits C and V are set according to the definition for a SUB operation:

1. CARRY: defined to be the borrow into the MSB position of the word.

2. OVERFLOW: defined to have occurred whenever the operands were of opposite signs and the result generated is of the same sign as the subtrahend (i.e., the source operand for a SUB operation and the destination operand for a CMP operation).

Then the instruction pair

```
CMP     #-77777,#77777
BMI     LESS
```

would not result in a branch (since N = 0). On the other hand, the pair

```
CMP     #-77777,#77777
BLT     LESS
```

would. The reason for the difference in these two branches lies in the specification of which condition bits are to be tested. Simple branches simply test the sign bit; more complex branches test the sign, overflow, and carry bits which will be set as a result of the arithmetic compare. Using "$\veebar$" for *exclusive* OR, and "$\vee$" for *inclusive* OR, these instructions are:

Operation	Symbolic Form	Meaning: Branch if
Branch less than	BLT X	$N \veebar V = 1$
Branch less than or equal	BLE X	$Z \vee (N \veebar V) = 1$
Branch greater than	BGT X	$Z \vee (N \veebar V) = 0$
Branch greater than or equal	BGE X	$N \veebar V = 0$

In addition to the branches already discussed, there are several *unsigned* and simple conditional branches which are usefully introduced here:

Operation	Symbolic Form	Meaning: Branch if
Branch if higher	BHI X	$C = 0$ and $Z = 0$
Branch if lower or same	BLOS X	$C \vee Z = 1$
Branch if higher or same	BHIS X or BCC X	$C = 0$
Branch if lower	BLO X or BCS X	$C = 1$
Branch if overflow clear	BVC X	$V = 0$
Branch if overflow set	BVS X	$V = 1$

Using the first four instructions, the programmer can test all two's-complement arithmetic results. Using the last six, he can test both unsigned arithmetic results and individual condition bits. For example, CMP X,Y *clears* C if the computation of X - Y generates a carry and *sets* C otherwise. If Y = X - K, where X, Y, and K are *unsigned* binary numbers, then, using "~" as the one's complement operator,

```
X - Y   =         X + ~(X - K)       + 1
        =         X + ~(X + ~K + 1) + 1
        =         (X + 1) + ~(X + 1) + K
        =         177777 + K
```

If K > 0, (i.e., X > Y), a carry *is* generated so that C = 0 and both BHI and BHIS operate correctly. Since PDP-11 addresses are *unsigned binary numbers*, address comparison is possible using CMP and the unsigned branches.

5.3 LOGICAL OPERATIONS

The logical operations belong to the double-operand group and (as noted in Section 3.3.3) include BIS, BIC, and BIT for the setting, clearing, and testing of bits within a word. They are defined as follows, with "~" logical inversion, or NOT, and "∧" for logical AND:

```
Operation        Symbolic Form   Meaning
---------        -------------   -------
Bit set          BIS X,Y         (Y) ← (X) V (Y) (inclusive OR)
Bit clear        BIC X,Y         (Y) ← ~(X) ∧ (Y)
Bit test         BIT X,Y         compute (X) ∧ (Y), set condition codes
Exclusive or     XOR Rn,Y        (Y) ← (Rn) ∀ (Y)
```

XOR is not available on the 11/04, 05, or 10. Since each of these instructions is performed in the central processor, each one affects the setting of the condition codes in the processor status register in the following manner:

1. The N- and Z-bits are set conditionally.

2. The V-bit is cleared.

3. The C-bit is not affected.

Within the PDP-11, all input/output (I/O) devices have particular words set aside in memory as control and status registers. These registers have unique memory addresses and thus may be tested and set using the logical operations. For example, to test bits 15 and 7 in a status register (e.g., STAT), one could write

```
   .
BIT     #100200,STAT    ;TEST BITS 15 AND 7
BMI     BIT15           ;BIT 15 IS SET
BNE     BIT7            ;BIT 7 IS SET
   .
```

If the BMI instruction is removed, the BNE becomes a test for both bits 15 and 7.

5.4 FLOATING-POINT ARITHMETIC

Floating-point arithmetic involves manipulation of signs, exponents, and fractions of floating-point operands. Fixed-point multiplication of *n* bit operands, if implemented in "software" consists essentially of an inner loop of *n* shifts and conditional additions. However, both floating-point multiplication and addition entail relatively complex algorithms.

5.4.1 Multiplication/Division

The product of two floating-point numbers

$$X_1 = s_1 * f_1 * 2^{**}(e_1)$$

and

$$X_2 = s_2 * f_2 * 2^{**}(e_2)$$

is

$$P = (s_1 * s_2) * (f_1 * f_2) * 2^{**}(e_1 + e_2)$$

$$= s_p * f_p * 2^{**}(e_p)$$

The resultant sign can be computed via an exclusive OR of the signs. Since the fractions are normalized, their product may require a single bit shift for renormalization: `i.e.,`

$$0.5 \leq f_1 < 1 \ , \ 0.5 \leq f_2 < 1 \ \text{so that} \ 0.25 \leq f_p < 1.$$

Thus, if the resultant fraction is less than 0.5, it is multiplied by 2 and the exponent decremented by unity. Floating-point multiplication is therefore dominated by the *product computation*; for single precision floating-point numbers on the PDP-11, a 24x24 bit fixed-point (unsigned) multiplication must be carried out. Assuming that either hardware (e.g., EIS) or software is available for 16x16 bit fixed-point multiplication, the required 24x24 bit product can be computed as follows:

$$f_1 * f_2 = (f_1' + f_1'' * 2^{-16}) * (f_2' + f_2'' * 2^{-16})$$

$$= f_1' * f_2' + (f_1' * f_2'' + f_2' * f_1'') * 2^{-16}$$

where f' and f'' are unsigned 16- and 8-bit integers, respectively.
In floating-point division,

$$Q = X_1/X_2 = (s_1 * s_2)*(f_1/f_2)\, 2**(e_1 - e_2)$$

It is apparent that single bit renormalization may also be required.

5.4.2 Addition/Subtraction

Floating-point additions/subtractions are not generally dominated by the add/subtract operations Due to the implied normalization of operand mantissas or fractions, the operand with the smaller exponent must have its fraction shifted right, with each shift accompanied by an incrementing of the exponent, until both operands have *equal* exponents. Only then can the fractions be added/subtracted. Finally, the resultant fraction must be renormalized, and this normalization may be as many bits as the fraction length.

In summary, floating-point multiplication/division are dominated by the fraction *multiplication/division* while floating-point addition and subtraction are dominated by the fraction pre- and post-operation *normalization*.

The PDP-11 user generally need not be concerned with the details of how floating-point arithmetic operations are implemented when only fixed-point hardware (or software) is present, since both high level language and assembler programs can access readily available floating-point software packages. However, just as the power of various PDP-11 address modes in efficient manipulation of various data structures can best be maximized at the assembler level, the time-efficiency of PDP-11 floating-point "hardware" can be easily enhanced by the knowledgeable programmer.

5.4.3 The Floating Instruction Set (FIS)

The FIS, optional on the PDP-11/35, 40, and LSI-11 (PDP-11/03), consists of four zero-address floating-point instructions: FADD, FSUB, FMUL and FDIV. These instructions effectively *pop* the two operands off the top of a referenced stack, compute the result, and *push* the result back onto the stack. Thus, to compute the floating-point operation, FLOP,

```
                    r = a "FLOP" b
```

where *a* is stored at A, A + 2, *b* at B, B + 2, and the result *r* at R, R + 2:

```
            MOV #C,Rn          ;INITIALIZE STACK
PUSH:       MOV A+2,-(Rn)      ;PUSH LOW  A
            MOV A  ,-(Rn)      ;PUSH HIGH A
            MOV B+2,-(Rn)      :PUSH LOW  B
            MOV B  ,-(Rn)      ;PUSH HIGH B, CONTENTS Rn=#C-8
OPR:        FLOP Rn
                               ;CONTENTS Rn=#C-4
POP:        MOV (Rn)+,R        ;POP HIGH R
            MOV (Rn)+,R+2      ;POP LOW  R,   CONTENTS Rn=#C
```

The result is $a+b$, $a-b$, $a*b$ or a/b as FLOP is FADD, FSUB, FMUL, or FDIV, respectively. A diagram best illustrates the stack manipulation involved in these instructions:

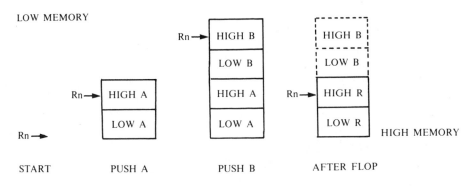

Note that B is still "unofficially" present on the stack; that is, it is invisible to the data structure. As shown in the first example, the user can take advantage of this to reduce data manipulation. However, the system stack must *not* be used since, unknown to the user, it may be manipulated by the machine (Chapter 7).

Factorial Calculation: Although factorial is meaningful only for integers, use of the FIS enables a 24-bit "integer" result. Here, "FACT" is invoked by JSR R5,FACT and computes *N!* iteratively, i.e., $N! = N(N-1)(N-2)$, ..., 1.

```
            JSR R5,FACT
            .WORD n            ;N INPUT, HIGH RESULT OUT
            .WORD 0            ;LOW RESULT OUT
                .
                .
FACT:
            MOV (R5),R2        ;R2 ← N, N > 1
            DEC R2             ;R2 ← N-1
            MOV ONE,RESULT     ;INITIALIZE RESULT
            MOV ONE+2,RESULT+2
            MOV ONE,X          ;INTIALIZE X
            MOV ONE+2,X+2
LOOP:
            MOV #ONE,R0        ;SET UP STACK
            FADD R0            ;X ←   X+1
            FMUL R0            ;RESULT ← RESULT*X
            SOB R2,LOOP
```

```
        ;
        MOV  (R0)+,(R5)+            ;RESULT FOLLOWS
        MOV  (R0)+,(R5)+            ;SUB CALL
        RTS R5
;
ONE:      .FLT2  1.
X:        .FLT2  1.
RESULT:   .FLT2  1.
```

.FLT2 is a pseudo-op which converts the argument to its equivalent 32-bit binary representation.

Polynomial Evaluation: The DEC VAX-11 continues the trend of implementation of certain very useful algorithms as single "hardware" instructions. For example the instruction POLY has the following syntax:

```
        POLY      X,#n,PTABLE
```

where X is the symbolic address of a floating-point number, n is an integer, and PTABLE is the symbolic address of a table containing $n+1$ floating-point numbers $C(n)$, $C(n-1)$, ..., $C(0)$. A FORTRAN implementation of POLY is as follows, assuming that a zero array index is permitted:

```
            R = C(N)
            DO 1 I =1,N
    1       R = R * X + C(N-I)
```

Thus, POLY effectively calculates

$$R = C(0) + X*C(1) + X^2*C(2) + ...+ X^{n-1}*C(n-1) + X^n * C(n)$$

POLY may be implemented as follows:

```
        JSR       R5,POLY
        .WORD     X
        .WORD     n
        .WORD     ENDTAB
                  .
                  .
PTABLE: C(0) (high word)
        C(0) (low word)
             .
             .
        C(n) (high word)
        C(n) (low word)
ENDTAB: .WORD     0
        .BLKW     9.
STACK:  .WORD     0
X:      .FLT2     x                    ;X
```

```
;
POLY:     MOV     (R5)+,R1        ;ADDRESS OF X HIGH
          MOV     (R1)+,R0        ;X HIGH
          MOV     (R1)+,R1        ;X LOW
          MOV     (R5)+,R2        ; n = ORDER OF POLYNOMIAL
          MOV     (R5)+,R3        ;ENDTAB = TABLE END+2
          MOV     #STACK,R4       ;SET UP USER STACK
;
          MOV     -(R3),-(R4)     ;C(n) LOW  = R LOW
          MOV     -(R3),-(R4)     ;C(n) HIGH = R HIGH
;
LOOP:     MOV     R1,-(R4)        ;X LOW
          MOV     R0,-(R4)        ;X HIGH
          FMUL    R4              ;R ← R * X
          MOV     -(R3),-(R4)     ;C(n-I) LOW
          MOV     -(R3),-(R4)     ;C(n-I) HIGH
          FADD    R4              ;R ← R + C(n-I)
          SOB     R2,LOOP
;
          MOV     (R4)+,R0        ;R HIGH
          MOV     (R4)+,R1        ;R LOW
          RTS     R5
```

POLY is especially useful for trigonometric polynomial evaluation.

5.4.4 The Floating-point Processor (FPP): Architecture and Instruction Set

The FPP is implemented in microcode on the PDP-11/60, and is available as a hardware accelerator on the '11/34, 45, 55, 60, and 70. It includes six 64-bit accumulators (AC0-AC5) and a powerful instruction set for manipulation of single- and double-precision floating-point numbers, and for conversion of these numbers to or from integer words or longwords. The FPP structure, and FPP/CPU relationship is shown in Fig. 5-1. FPP instructions are divided into single- and double-operand groups:

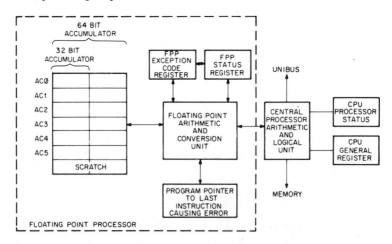

Fig. 5-1 Floating-point Processor (FPP) and CPU

Double Operand FPP Instructions: These instructions have the following format:

			FPP Op code	ACO-3	FSRC or FDST	
					Mode	Register
1	1	1				

```
15  14  13  12  11  10   9   8   7   6   5   4   3   2   1   0
```

Either the floating-point SRC *or* DST operand is specified using the familiar PDP-11 addressing modes *excepting* that

1. In mode 0, the register bits specify one of AC0-AC5.

2. In modes 2 and 4, increment or decrement is by *4* or *8*, depending on whether the FPP is in single- or double-precision mode, respectively.

The other operand is limited to one of AC0-AC3. Hence, memory operands may *not* interact directly with AC4-AC5.

FPP mode is determined by a bit in the FPP status register, which is accessible to the user. In contrast to PDP-11 integer instructions, which are word or byte by virtue of the instruction MSB, FPP instructions operate on single- or double-precision floating-point numbers as determined by a FPP status register bit.

Double operand FPP instructions are subdivided into the *load* and *store* classes, and are specified as either single- or double-precision by the last letter of the op-code mnemonic:

FPP Load Class Instructions:

```
Symbolic Code      Meaning
-------------      -------
LDF,LDD            (AC) ← (FSRC)
ADDF,ADDD          (AC) ← (AC) + (FSRC)
SUBF,SUBD          (AC) ← (AC) - (FSRC)
MULF,MULD          (AC) ← (AC) * (FSRC)
DIVF,DIVD          (AC) ← (AC) / (FSRC)
CMPF,CMPD          Compute (FSRC) - (AC),
                     set FPP Condition Codes
MODF,MODD          Compute PROD = (FSRC) * (ACi) ,
                     then  (ACi V 1) ← N = INT(PROD)
                     and   (ACi)     ← g = PROD - N .
                   Thus, if i = 1 or 3,
                     only g retained in (ACi).
```

FPP Store Class Instructions:

```
Symbolic Code      Meaning
-------------      -------
STF,STD            (FDST) ← (AC)
```

Other load and store class instructions enable loads or stores to be effected with simultaneous conversion *from* any floating-point mode *to* the other floating-point mode, or *to* any of the two integer modes, or visa versa. Instructions are also available for manipulation of the sign and exponent, setting the FPP floating- and (conversion) integer-mode, and for manipulating the FPP status register.

Besides the versatilty suggested by its diversified instruction set, and the ability to operate, to some extent, in parallel with the CPU on the 11/55, 70, and 60 (accelerator only), the FPP's accumulators make the CPU/FPP into a general register, floating-point machine with all the advantages of general register machines noted earlier. Some examples follow:

FPP POLY Subroutine:

```
           JSR      R5,POLYX
           .WORD    XX
           .WORD    n
           .WORD    ENDTAB
                      .
PTABLE:    C(0) (high word)
           C(0) (low word)

             .

           C(n) (high word)
           C(n) (low word)
ENDTAB:    .WORD    0
XX:        .FLT2    x                 ;X
X=%0                                  ;DEFINE X AND R AS FP REGISTERS
R=%1
POLYX:     SETF                       ;SINGLE PRECISION MODE
           LDF      @(R5)+,X          ;X
           MOV      (R5)+,R2          ;n = ORDER OF POLYNOMIAL
           MOV      (R5)+,R3          ;ENDTAB = TABLE END+2
                                      ;NOTE: AUTODECREMENT IS BY 4
           LDF      -(R3),R           ;R ← C(n)
LOOP:
           MULF     X,R               ;R ← R * X
           ADDF     -(R3),R           ;R ← R + C(n-I)
           SOB      R2,LOOP
;
           STF      R,ANS             ;ANSWER INTO MEMORY
           RTS      R5
ANS:       .FLT2    0
```

Use of the floating-point accumulators as temporaries halves the amount of memory data traffic per iteration compared to that of the FIS implementation.

Complex Multiplication: A complex multiplication usually requires four real multiplications and two real additions. That is, $(a+j\ b) * (c-j\ d) = (ac+bd) + j(bc-ad)$. If c and d are constants, a precalculated table of $c-d$, $c+d$, and d may be stored and the complex multiplication effected efficiently using three real multiplications and three real additions via the FPP registers:

```
SETF                         ;SINGLE PRECISION MODE
MOV      #AB,R0              ;POINTER TO a, b
MOV      #CD,R1              ;POINTER TO c - d, c + d, d
LDF      (R0)+,AC0           ;AC0 ← a
LDF      (R0)+,AC1           ;AC1 ← b
LDF      AC0,AC2             ;AC2 ← a
ADDF     AC1,AC2             ;AC2 ← a + b
MULF     (R1)+,AC0           ;AC0 ← a*(c - d)
MULF     (R1)+,AC1           ;AC1 ← b*(c + d)
MULF     (R1)+,AC2           ;AC2 ← d*(a + b)
ADDF     AC2,AC0             ;AC0 ← ac + bd
SUBF     AC2,AC1             ;AC1 ← bc - ad
```

In Chapter 9, an FPP fast Fourier transform is referenced which, since c and d are trigonometric values, uses this technique.

5.5 INTERNAL AND EXTERNAL DATA FORMS

At this point we have considered how fixed- and floating-point numbers are represented within the computer memory and how they are manipulated by the CPU in arithmetic operations. It is important to understand how such numbers enter and leave the computer system.

In FORTRAN, the conversion of data from an *external* form to an *internal* form is controlled by the FORMAT statement associated with a READ statement. The FORMAT associated with a WRITE statement assists in the reverse operation. Still, whether or not a programmer utilizes a high-level language (HLL), there remains the necessity for external/internal conversion.

The problem can be stated more precisely in terms of a typical I/O operation utilizing the terminal common to most minicomputers. If a user strikes the keys "3" and "5", for example, he may believe that he has stored the octal value "35" in some memory word. On closer examination, it becomes clear that he has only stored two bytes which have the values 63(8) and 65(8), respectively. Clearly what is necessary is to perform the conversion from the terminal-produced ASCII code to the internal value of 35(8). A subroutine to perform this conversion, assuming the ASCII character to be in R0 and the result in R1, might be

```
CONV:    BIC      #177770,R0         ;CLEAR ALL BUT LOWER 3 BITS
         ASH      #3,R1              ;PREVIOUS NUMBER * 8
         BIS      R0,R1              ;"OR" IN R0
         RTS      PC
```

R1 should be zeroed before the first character is converted.

Outputting to the terminal presents the inverse problem. In this case, the internal form must be converted to external ASCII. A subroutine to take a 16-bit word in R1 and store the six ASCII characters which represent the word into the buffer addressed by R2 could be written as:

```
OUT:    MOV     #5,R0               ;LOOP COUNT
LOOP:   MOV     R1,R3               ;COPY WORD
        BIC     #177770,R3          ;ONE OCTAL VALUE
        ADD     #'0,R3              ;CONVERT TO ASCII
        MOVB    R3,-(R2)            ;STORE IN BUFFER
        ASH     #-3,R1              ;SHIFT RIGHT THREE
        SOB     R0,LOOP             ;DECR R0, BRANCH IF NOT ZERO
;
        BIC     #177776,R1          ;GET LAST BIT
        ADD     #'0,R1              ;CONVERT TO ASCII
        MOVB    R1,-(R2)            ;STORE IN BUFFER
        RTS     PC                  ;DONE, RETURN
```

The use of " #'0" serves to add in the representation for ASCII zero, without requiring the programmer to know what it actually is.

In Chapter 7 we shall see how data is actually exchanged between the CPU and the outside world.

5.6 INTRODUCTION TO DATA STRUCTURES

Data structures are of concern to the computer programmer for two reasons: (1) they play a key role in algorithm and hence program design, and (2) they limit and guide the process of problem specification and program coding. Since data structures are a means for the representation of information, they have a form both inside and outside a computer. For example, a decimal number has both a mathematical representation such as $0.465 * 10**2$ and a computer floating-point form such as 0101101011101000. Indeed, the FORTRAN programmer spends a considerable amount of his time learning the various format specifications to be able to describe how the external-to-internal conversions (and vice versa) are to be performed by a running FORTRAN program.

A study of data structures is so fundamental a part of the study of algorithms and programming that all textbooks cover the subject implicitly if not explicitly. For example, the readers of this text have already considered the primitive data structures available to the PDP-11 programmer (bits, bytes, words, registers), and they have also delved into the representation and meaning of such data concepts as address, pointer, character, and stack. And in the more general context of information structures, the reader has been presented with the representations of computers and programs, including the transformation of symbolic information structures that constitute programs.

Now the reader's attention is focused on the construction and manipulation of somewhat more complex data structures; he should not be surprised to learn that the new data structures are based upon the more primitive ones already well understood. These new data types and structures (arrays, stacks, queues, circular buffers, lists, symbol tables, and so on) are nothing more than the combination of primitive data types to produce new aggregates of bits, bytes, words, and so on.

Good programming practice requires that the programmer carefully consider the form of his data so that he may create data structures that will be effectively and efficiently manipulated by his program. It is important that a new data structure be chosen carefully, since its use in a program may greatly affect the size and speed of execution of the program utilizing it. By considering some of the fundamental data structures that programmers use, the assembly language programmer will have a better understanding of what these data structures are and how they can be manipulated. A natural beginning is to start by considering a fundamental type, the *array*, with which every FORTRAN programmer is familiar.

5.6.1 Arrays

In its simplest form, the array is a *one-dimensional structure* that associates a collection of identical data types as members of a larger block identified by a single name. The array can be easily mapped from its external, conceptual representation into its internal form by assigning contiguous memory locations to elements of the array. The choice of contiguous locations is clearly one of efficiency, since it allows elements of the array to be accessed through indexed or autoincrement addressing, as was seen by the example of Chapter 2.

Multidimensional arrays are also data structures commonly used by the FORTRAN programmer. The elements of such arrays are stored by columns in ascending order of storage location. An example is shown in Fig. 5-2 for the three dimensional array A(3,2,2). As shown in the figure, multidimensional arrays can be considered simple extensions of one-dimensional arrays. However, simple indexing cannot be performed in order to access individual array elements.

Element	Position	Element	Position
A(1,1,1)	0	A(1,2,1)	3
A(2,1,1)	1	A(2,2,1)	4
A(3,1,1)	2	A(3,2,1)	5

Element	Position	Element	Position
A(1,1,2)	6	A(1,2,2)	9
A(2,1,2)	7	A(2,2,2)	10
A(3,1,2)	8	A(3,2,2)	11

Fig. 5-1 Mapping of array A(3,2,2).

To find the location of an element in a three-dimensional array, an *address equation* must be used which describes the mapping of the three-dimensional array into the one-dimensional computer memory. For an array with dimensions I, J, and K, the address of the particular element A(i,j,k) is given by the equation

```
address[A(i,j,k)] = address[A(1,1,1)] + (i-1) + I*(j-1) + I*J*(k-1)
```

This equation serves to transform the values given for the three indices into a *linear index* into the array storage area. Using the example shown in Fig. 5-2, the element A(2,1,2) is seen to be in relative position 7 with respect to the first element of the array, A(1,1,1).

In its most general form, the address equation for a multi-dimensional array A(I,J,K,...,M,N) is given by the rather complicated equation

```
address[A(i,j,k,..,m,n)] = address[A(1,1,1,..,1,1) +
                           (i-1) + I*(J*(..M*(n-1) + m-1)...j-1)
```

Although complicated, this equation serves to establish the fact that as the number of dimensions increases, so does the complexity of the address calculation. Even for a three-dimensional array, the equation results in a three-term multiplication which represents a time-consuming task for a small computer that lacks multiplication hardware.

Simplified Array Address Calculation: When calculating array element addresses, two points must be considered. First, as mentioned above, the fewer the multiplications, the better. Second, address calculations are dynamic in that languages such as FORTRAN delay the evaluation of the address polynomial until the array element is actually required. These considerations lead to the following, often-used technique. For each array defined as

```
        ARRAY(K1,K2,...,Kn)
```

where *n* specifies the dimensionality of the array, there is a corresponding *array descriptor block* (sometimes called a dope vector) which holds the information given in Fig. 5-3.

```
Word #     Contents
------     --------
  1        SIZE, N
  2        N*K1
  3        N*K1*K2
  n        N*K1*...*Kn-1
 n+1       address of first element of array
```

Fig. 5-3 Array descriptor block (ADB).

There, SIZE = $N*K1*K2*...*Kn$, with TYPE, the data type, and N, the number of words per element specified as

Array Description	Type	N
INTEGER	0	1
REAL	1	2
DOUBLE PRECISION	2	4
COMPLEX	3	4
.	.	.

The information in the array descriptor block is made available to a run-time subroutine which calculates the address of the first word (of a multiple-word) array element. Each call to this subroutine results in the evaluation of the *address polynomial* as follows:

```
Given ARRAY(K1,K2,...,Kn), then the address of
  element ARRAY(k1,k2,...,kn), where 1 ≤ kj ≤ Kj, j = 1,2,..,n
```

is

```
A = WD(n+1) + (k1-1)*N + (k2-1)*WD(2) + ... + (kn-1)*WD(n),
```

where WD(2), WD(3), .. stand for the contents of words 2, 3, ... of the array descriptor block for the given array.

Now what is the value of using this technique? The answer is that it buys the user several advantages. First, it transforms the address polynomial into a simpler sum-of-products equation. Second, the number of terms in the equation grows linearly with the number of dimensions in the array. Third, it allows the translator to evaluate or bind some of the multiplications (e.g., N*K1, N*K1*K2, ...) early and not make this part of the execution-time evaluation. Fourth, it presents a generalized data structure (the array descriptor block) which may be changed during execution time to allow the array to be dynamically allocated. Users of ALGOL recognize this last point as an important attribute of block-structured languages, which permit arrays to be variably dimensioned. In use, variably dimensioned and dynamically allocated arrays allow the programmer to make more effective use of the limited amounts of memory provided on small computers.

Example: Suppose that we wish to create an INTEGER array M(I,J,K) on the PDP-11, with I = 3, J = 5, and K = 7. In assembly language we would reserve room for the array and create the array descriptor block (shown in Fig. 5-3) as follows:

```
      .
      .
      .
      N=1               ;ARRAY TYPE IS INTEGER
      SIZE=N*3*5*7      ;SIZE OF ARRAY = N*I*J*K WORDS [n = 3]
M:    .BLKW SIZE        ;STORAGE RESERVATION FOR ARRAY
      .BYTE N,SIZE      ;ADB WD(1)
      3                 ;ADB WD(2) = I
      15.               ;ADB WD(3) = I*J
ADB:  M                 ;ABD WD(4), ADDRESS OF M(1,1,1)
      .
      .
```

Access to any element, say M(2,3,4), can be performed by a *calculate Array Element Address Subroutine*, AEAS, which has the calling sequence:

```
        JSR      R0,AEAS   ;CALL SUBROUTINE
        ADB                ;ADDRESS OF ADB WD(4)
        2                  ;FIRST SUBSCRIPT   = i
        3                  ;SECOND SUBSCRIPT  = j
        4                  ;THIRD SUBSCRIPT   = k
        0                  ;ARRAY ELEMENT ADDRESS WILL BE PUT HERE
NEXT:                      ;NEXT INSTRUCTION
```

A straightforward implementation of AEAS for N = 1 or 2 would have the logical flow of Fig. 5-4. However, by factoring "N" out of the address polynomial, we can easily provide for arrays of any type by simply altering the definition of "N" when the ADB is created. The subroutine to calculate the element address uses the register save (SAVE) and restore (REST) routines and is coded as shown in Fig. 5-5. Changing "N" to 2, for example, will reserve space for a real array, say XM(3,5,7), and JSR R0,AEAS will compute the address of element XM(2,3,4).

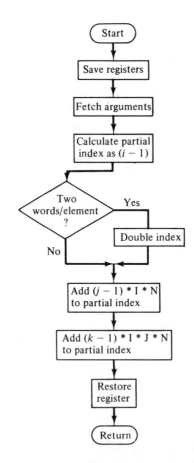

Fig. 5-4 Flow chart of array polynomial evaluation.

```
AEAS:   JSR     PC,SAVE         ;SAVE R1-R5
        CLR     R1              ;HOLDS RELATIVE DISPLACEMENT
        MOV     (R0)+,R2        ;ARRAY DESCRIPTOR BLOCK ADDRESS, ADB
;*******CALCULATE (i-1) + I*(j-1) + I*J*(k-1) *********************
        MOV     (R0)+,R3        ;FIRST SUBSCRIPT = i
        DEC     R3              ;   LESS ONE = i-1
        BLE     SKIP            ;IGNORE IF ≤ 0
        ADD     R3,R1           ;ADD TO RELATIVE DISP = i-1
SKIP:   MOV     (R0)+,R3        ;SECOND SUBSCRIPT = j
        DEC     R3              ;   LESS ONE = j-1
        BLE     SKIP1           ;IGNORE IF ≤ 0
        MOV     -4(R2),R4       ;WORD 2 OF ADB = I
AGAIN:  ADD     R4,R1           ;ADD IT IN
        SOB     R3,AGAIN        ;R1 ← (i-1) + I*(j-1)
SKIP1:  MOV     (R0)+,R3        ;THIRD SUBSCRIPT = k
        DEC     R3              ;   LESS ONE = k-1
        BLE     TEST            ;IGNORE IF ≤ 0
        MOV     -2(R2),R4       ;WORD 3 OF ADB = I*J
AGN1:   ADD     R4,R1           ;R1 ← (i-1) + I*(j-1) + I*J*(k-1)
        SOB     R3,AGN1         ;R1 ← (i-1) + I*(j-1) + I*J*(k-1)
;*******CONVERT TO BYTE INDEX ************************************
TEST:   ASL     R1              ;R1 ← 2*R1, TWO BYTES PER WORD
        CLR     R4              ;SET UP ACCUMULATOR
        MOV     -6(R2),R5       ;GET N, SIZE
        BIC     #177400,R5      ;N = LOW BYTE = WORDS/ELEMENT
SCALE:  ADD     R1,R4
        SOB     R5,SCALE        ;R4 ← [(i-1)+I*(j-1)+I*J*(k-1)]*2N
;*******TEST FOR ARRAY BOUNDARY *********************************
        MOV     -6(R2),R5       ;GET N, SIZE
        SWAB    R5              ;SIZE, N
        BIC     #177400,R5      ;SIZE = N*I*J*K
        ASL     R5              ;2*SIZE (2 BYTES/WORD)
        CMP     R5,R4           ;INDEX TOO GREAT?
        BLOS    YES             ;YES!
OK:     MOV     (R2),(R0)       ;NO, BASE ADDRESS OF ARRAY, M(1,1,1)
        ADD     R4,(R0)         ;ADD IN INDEX TO GET ADDRESS OF M(i,j,k)
YES:    TST     (R0)+           ;BUMP R0 BEFORE RTS R0
        JSR     PC,REST         ;RESTORE R1-R5
        RTS     R0              ;AND RETURN
```

Fig. 5-5 Array evaluation subroutine.

This subroutine thus calculates the actual byte address of an array element $M(i,j,k)$ by forming

$$M(i,j,k) = M(1,1,1) + [(i-1) + I*(j-1) + I*J*(k-1)]*2*N$$

word 4   word 2   word 3
of ADB   of ADB   of ABD

where

N = number of words per element = 1, 2, or 4
I,J,K = maximum values of i,j,k respectively.

Since some multiplications are required, the use of the left shift instruction or multiple additions avoids the necessity of calling on a separate multiply subroutine when MUL is not available.

Before returning to the caller, the subroutine checks to see if the relative address (or index) calculated is less that the given size of the array. If it is not, no array element address is returned. Otherwise the actual array address is returned.

5.6.2 Stacks, Deques, and Queues

Because stack hardware is part of the PDP-11, the reader is already familiar with *push-down stacks*, or, more simply, stacks. Seen in the context of this chapter on data structures, a stack is nothing more than a special form of a one-dimensional array. As a matter of fact, most FORTRAN programmers have probably implemented the traditional PUSH and POP operations on a stack by writing the FORTRAN instructions shown in Fig. 5-6. As implemented, elements are not physically pushed or popped from the stack. Instead, a pointer is moved so that it always points to the most accessible or top element in the stack.

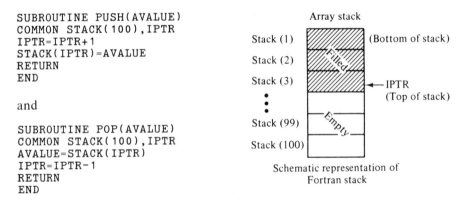

```
SUBROUTINE PUSH(AVALUE)
COMMON STACK(100),IPTR
IPTR=IPTR+1
STACK(IPTR)=AVALUE
RETURN
END
```

and

```
SUBROUTINE POP(AVALUE)
COMMON STACK(100),IPTR
AVALUE=STACK(IPTR)
IPTR=IPTR-1
RETURN
END
```

Fig. 5-6 FORTRAN PUSH and POP subroutines.

We have already seen how stacks may be used for saving and restoring registers, for implementing automatic nesting of subroutine calls, and for writing recursive procedures. Stacks are also commonly found in language translators, where they aid in the process of compilation of arithmetic expression and code generation, and in operating systems, where they serve to keep a list of items in an order consistent with the need to know "which occurred last."

The growth of information on a stack is usually defined as being unidirectional. However, if it is possible to allow growth in two directions, then the basic stack structure can be transformed into a *deque* or *double-ended queue*. On a computer such as the PDP-11, which implements stacks by use of register pointers, a deque can be considered a stack with two pointers, one growing upward in memory and one growing downward.

Deques have the additional property that when information is removed from a deque, it is erased at the source. Thus, unlike a move or copy operation, a fetch operation on a deque does not make a copy of what was on the deque but rather represents the more intuitive notion about fetching and removing an item from some storage place.

Deques can be implemented easily on the PDP-11 since it has both positive and negative autoindexing. However, because the autodecrementing and autoincrementing are done before and after the operand fetch, respectively, it is necessary to use the essentially null statements,

$$
\begin{array}{ll}
\text{TST} & \text{-(Rn)} \\
\text{TST} & \text{(Rn)+}
\end{array}
$$

to keep the stack pointers in correct position.

There are four basic deque operations — LSTORE (lower store), USTORE (upper store), LFETCH (lower fetch), and UFETCH (upper fetch) — and these are programmed as shown by the four routines in Fig. 5-7.

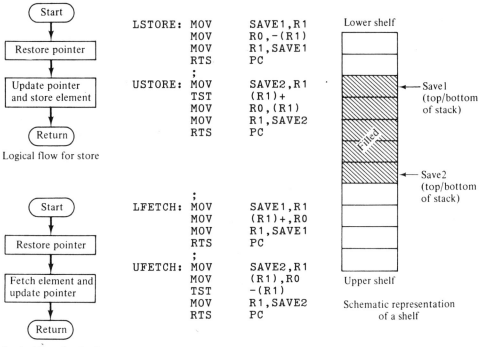

Fig. 5-7 Deque operations.

A call on a deque subroutine presumes that either the value to be stored is in R0, or else the value to be fetched will be left in R0. As programmed, the fetch operation does not actually destroy the fetched information, but rather, like the stack operation it is, simply moves a stack pointer. Only when a new store is performed on that end of the deque will the information be destroyed.

Deques are quite useful in applications where a program may need to add or delete items at either end of a stack. The need to do so arises when these items are added to or removed from the deques according to their order of importance. For example, a time-sharing system might service users in a round-robin fashion, taking each user to be served from one end of the deque and returning him to the other end upon completion of his service request. However, some users may demand immediate service, and they would have to be added to the serving end of the deque rather than the receiving end.

When deques are used so as to add on one end and to remove from the other, the characteristics of the deque are changed significantly. Each item on a deque becomes ordered with respect to its neighbors (the order being a function of when it was placed on the deque), and it is not possible to remove items out of order. The ordering is known as *first in, first out* (FIFO), and the data form taken by the deque is called a *single-ended queue*, or just *queue*. Like all other data structures discussed in this section, the queue is a special form of a one-dimensional array.

Although queues are not very complex data structures, one has to be careful about their implementation. For example, taking the simplistic approach of implementing a queue as a specialized form of a deque can clearly lead to disaster. Instead, it is generally necessary to make a queue of a fixed size and percolate all information through the queue. One question remains, however, and it is whether the items in the queue ought to actually percolate through the queue, or whether some pointers can be used to describe the percolation process.

Let us first consider items percolating through the queue. In FORTRAN, the queue and dequeue operations could be coded as shown in Fig. 5-8. The reader should note that the solution presented for implementing the queue not only moves all elements in the queue each time an add-to-queue is performed, but it also requires a pointer to keep track of where the queue ends in the 'static' array QUE.

Another approach to queue implementation can be found in the *circular buffer algorithm*. This technique allows the queue to be considered as if it were a cylindrical surface on which the highest addressed location is immediately followed by the lowest (such as the addresses on a disk). Logically the queue is pictured as shown in Fig. 5-9a, but physically the queue is actually as shown in Fig. 5-9b.

Two pointers associated with the queue, BEGIN and END, are used to indicate the limits of the queue, while two others, IN and OUT, are used to indicate where the next item is to be placed in the queue and where the last item was taken from it, respectively. When IN = OUT, the queue is empty.

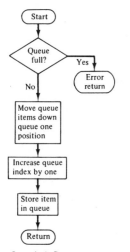

Queue logic flow

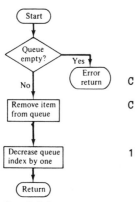

Deque logic flow

```
      SUBROUTINE QUEUE (X)
      COMMON QUE(100),IPTR
C     TEST IF QUEUE IS FULL
      IF (IPTR .EQ. 100) GO TO 20
C     NO, PERCOLATE QUEUE
      DO 10 I=1,IPTR
         K=IPTR+1-I
         QUE(K+1)=QUE(K)
10    CONTINUE
C     ENTER ELEMENT AND RETURN
      IPTR=IPTR+1
      QUE(1)=X
      RETURN
20    ERROR CONDITION
      ...
      END
```

```
      SUBROUTINE DEQUEUE (X)
      COMMON QUE(100),IPTR
C     TEST IF QUEUE IS EMPTY
      IF (IPTR .EQ. 0) GO TO 10
C     DEQUEUE ELEMENT AND RETURN
      X=QUE(IPTR)
      IPTR=IPTR-1
      RETURN
10    ERROR CONDITION
      ...
      END
```

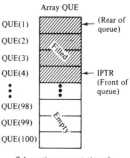

Schematic representation of
FORTRAN queue

Fig. 5-8 Queue manipulation routines.

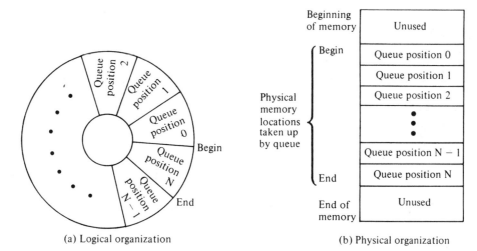

(a) Logical organization

(b) Physical organization

Fig. 5-9 Queue structure.

This is the status of the queue initially. As an element is added to the queue, IN is advanced; correspondingly, as an element is removed from the queue, OUT is advanced. Thus when IN > OUT, the area from OUT to IN - 1 contains queued elements. And when OUT > IN, the area from OUT to END contains the first part of the queue and the area from BEGIN to IN - 1 contains the balance.

Queue and dequeue routines using the circular buffer algorithms can be flowcharted and coded as shown in Figs. 5-10 and 5-11. These routines assume that R0 holds the item entered on or removed from the queue, and that the routines are called by the instruction JSR PC,QUEUE or JSR PC,DEQUE.

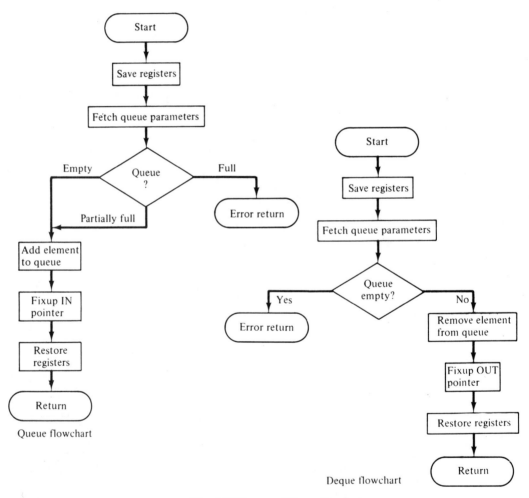

Fig. 5-10 Queue and Deque flowcharts.

```
QUE:      .BLKW 100.               ;QUEUE SIZE=100 WORDS
BEGIN:    0                        ;START OF QUEUE
END:      200                      ;QUEUE LIMIT
IN:       0                        ;IN POINTER
OUT:      0                        ;OUT POINTER
QUEUE:    JSR     PC,SAVE          ;SAVE REGISTERS
;
          MOV     IN,R1            ;FETCH IN
          MOV     OUT,R2           ;FETCH OUT
          MOV     END,R3           ;FETCH END
          CMP     R1,R2            ;TEST IN:OUT
          BEQ     OKAY             ;IN = OUT
          BLO     INV              ;OUT > IN
          SUB     R1,R3            ;END - IN
          ADD     R2,R3            ;END - IN + OUT
          BHI     OKAY             ;TESTS OKAY
INV:      SUB     R2,R3            ;END - OUT
          ADD     R1,R3            ;END - OUT + IN
          BLOS    ERROR1           ;QUEUE FULL
OKAY:     MOV     R0,QUE(R1)       ;PUT ELEMENT IN QUEUE
          TST     (R1)+            ;INCREMENT IN
          CMP     R1,END           ;AT END OF QUEUE?
          BLO     STORE            ;NO
          CLR     R1               ;RESET IN (WRAP-AROUND)
STORE:    MOV     R1,IN            ;SAVE NEW IN POINTER
          JSR     PC,REST          ;RESTORE REGISTERS
          RTS     PC               ;RETURN
ERROR1:   ...                      ;QUEUE FULL
          ...                      ;ERROR RETURN
DEQUE:    JSR     PC,SAVE          ;SAVE REGISTERS
          MOV     IN,R1            ;FETCH IN
          MOV     OUT,R2           ;FETCH OUT
          SUB     R2,R1            ;QUEUE EMPTY?
          BEQ     ERROR2           ;YES
          MOV     QUE(R2),R0       ;TAKE ELEMENT OFF QUEUE
          TST     (R2)+            ;INCREMENT OUT
          CMP     R2,END           ;AT END OF QUEUE?
          BLO     STR              ;NO
          CLR     R2               ;RESET OUT
STR:      MOV     R2,OUT           ;SAVE NEW OUT POINTER
          JSR     PC,REST          ;RESTORE REGISTERS
          RTS     PC               ;RETURN
ERROR2:   ...                      ;QUEUE EMPTY
          ...                      ;ERROR RETURN
```

Fig. 5-11 Queue and Deque routines.

Of the two routines, QUEUE is clearly the longer. The reason is simple; in testing for an empty queue, all one need do is check whether IN = OUT. However, when testing for full queue, two conditions may occur, as shown in Fig. 5-12. Either IN > OUT or OUT > IN.

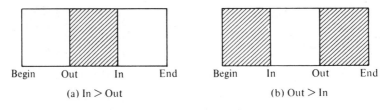

(a) In > Out   (b) Out > In

Note: Shaded area = current queue

Fig. 5-12 Possibilities for current filling of queue.

In the first case (Fig. 5-9a), as long as END - IN + OUT > 0, the queue is either empty or partially filled. In the second case (Fig. 5-9b), as long as END - OUT + IN > 0, the queue is only partially filled. The QUEUE routine must therefore determine which condition has occurred, and then test accordingly.

5.6.3 Lists

Another commonly used data structure is the *list*. In its simplest form, a list may be conceived of as a one-dimensional array that need not occupy a block of adjoining memory locations. Instead, elements may reside anywhere in memory and can be *linked* together, forming a *linked list* rather than a contiguous list. For example, a list structure representing this sentence might be

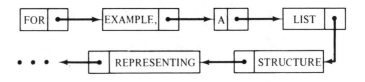

Except for the first and last elements, each element of a list has a *successor* and a *predecessor*. If the list is linked only to its successor, the list is called a *one-way list*. When doubly linked to both its successor and predecessor, such a list is called a *two-way list*.

Whether or not a list is one-way or two-way, there remains the problem of describing where a list begins, i.e., what the first element on the list is. This problem is resolved by using a special pointer, called the *head*, to point to the beginning of a list. As a matter of convenience, a second pointer, called the *tail*, is used to point to the end of a list. The tailpointer is not absolutely necessary because the link in the last element of a list is made to contain a special value, called *NIL*, which indicates that there is no successor element.

Lists are not constrained to one dimension, but like arrays may be multidimensional. An interesting two-dimensional list would be one that describes the FORTRAN expression

$$A = (B + C) * (D - E)$$

This expression can be represented by the following list structure:

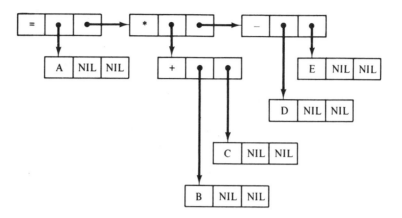

For each binary operator there are two links to the operands of the operator. In some cases the operands are simply variables; in others they are expressions. When traversing such a two-dimensional list, one has to have some way of recognizing the difference between list elements having the same physical representations. One method for doing so is to include descriptors, as part of the list structure, which characterize the list elements explicitly.

Whether one needs to manipulate one- or multi-dimensional lists, the basic list operations remain the same. These operations are: (1) create a list, (2) add an element to a list, (3) delete an element from a list, and (4) search for an element on a list. Thus when one is learning how these operations are performed, the simpler the list structure, the better.

Using the PDP-11 as the host machine, it will be easiest to consider a list element as a two-word pair. The first word will be the datum and the second will be the pointer to a successor list element. HEAD and TAIL will act as the special pointers to the beginning and end of the list. A NIL pointer will be represented by an all-zero value. Initially, then, an empty list will be indicated by

```
HEAD:   0
TAIL:   0
```

The function of a CREATE routine will be to zero out HEAD and TAIL:

```
CREATE: CLR     HEAD    ;NIL IN HEAD
        CLR     TAIL    ;NIL IN TAIL
        RTS     PC
```

The next routine, ADD, must take a new list element and put it on the list. Two arguments needed by ADD are (1) the relative position on the list where the new element is to be placed, and (2) the new word pair to be added. The relative position is programmer-dependent with the following interpretation: If the value given is negative, the new element is added to the end of the list; if it is positive, the new element is added after the element specified by the given relative position (a zero is interpreted to mean add to the beginning of the list).

Obtaining word pairs, however, is not programmer-dependent. Instead, it is the job of an "allocate" routine (see Exercise 11 at the end of this chapter), which is capable of managing the available memory locations (those not used by the programmer or the "system"). Each time the allocate routine is called, it returns with either an address of a word pair *or* a flag indicating that no more word pairs are available.

Assuming that the programmer has utilized allocate and wishes to ADD an element to a list, the calling sequence to ADD might be

```
JSR     R0,ADD              ;CALL ADD SUBROUTINE
(RELATIVE POSITION)         ;FIRST ARGUMENT
(WORD-PAIR ADDRESS)         ;SECOND ARGUMENT
```

and ADD would be as shown in Fig. 5-13.

```
ADD:    JSR     PC,SAVE         ;SAVE REGISTERS
        MOV     (R0)+,R1        ;RELATIVE POSITION
        MOV     (R0)+,R2        ;WORD-PAIR ADDRESS
        MOV     HEAD,R3         ;GET LIST POINTER
        TST     R1              ;NEGATIVE OR ZERO?
        BMI     END             ;ADD TO END
        BEQ     BEGIN           ;ADD TO BEGINNING
LOOP:   MOV     2(R3),R3        ;GET NEXT ELEMENT
        SOB     R1,LOOP         ;ADD HERE?
        MOV     R3,2(R2)        ;YES, SET UP LINK IN NEW ELEMENT
        MOV     R2,(R3)         ;AND OLD ELEMENT
RET:    JSR     PC,REST         ;RESTORE REGISTERS
        RTS     R0              ;RETURN
BEGIN:  MOV     R3,2(R2)        ;LINK UP NEW ELEMENT
        MOV     R2,HEAD         ;FIX UP HEAD
        BR      RET             ;DONE
END:    MOV     TAIL,R3         ;GET TAIL
        MOV     2(R2),2(R3)     ;LINK IN NEW ELEMENT
        MOV     R2,TAIL         ;FIX UP TAIL
        BR      RET             ;RETURN
```

Fig. 5-13 ADD-to-list element subroutine.

A picture of the ADD operation is shown in Fig. 5-14. The figures represent the list before and after the addition of an element to the middle of it.

Similar pictures could be drawn for adding an element to the beginning or end of the list. These pictures are left as reader exercises, as in the programming of the DELETE routine. The linkage to the DELETE routine would be

```
JSR      R0,DELETE          ;CALL DELETE SUBROUTINE
(RELATIVE POSITION)         ;FIRST ARGUMENT FOR DELETE
(WORD-PAIR ADDRESS)         ;SECOND ARGUMENT FOR DELETE
```

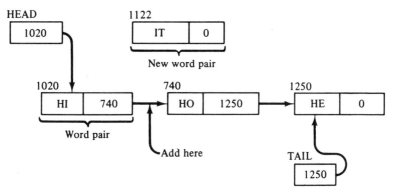

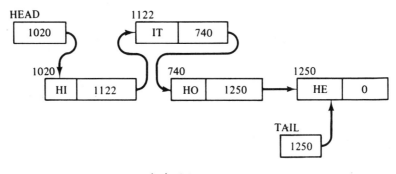

(b) After

Fig. 5-14 ADDing an element to a list.

Complementary to the ADD process, the DELETE process requires the user to call a "free" routine which can return a word pair to the pool of available memory locations. Should the programmer not do so, there will be a continually diminishing supply of word pairs available and an increasing supply of unallocated and unavailable word pairs. As a result, when allocate runs out of word pairs, either the list processing stops, or someone has to perform a *garbage collection*, somehow picking up the unallocated word pairs.

Although the problems of garbage collection are not trivial, a technique may be given for simple lists. A simple list is one that does not have a closed path or loop in it, such as the following list:

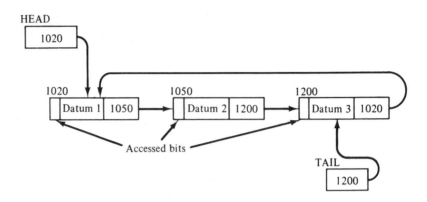

The garbage-collection technique to be used on simple lists requires that a bit, called the *accessed bit*, be reserved as part of each list element. Except during garbage collection, this bit is always 0. However, during garbage collection, every list is traversed, and as each element on the list is accessed, its accessed bit is set to 1. As a result of this operation, only those list elements that do not belong to any list will have an accessed bit of 0. These elements can be easily located (say by defining the accessed bit to the sign bit and testing for nonnegative elements) and can be added to the list of free elements to be used once again. Garbage collection is not complete, however, until all accessed bits are reset back to 0.

Returning to the last problem for searching a list, let us consider the SEARCH routine. This routine is called by

```
JSR      R0,SEARCH          ;CALL SEARCH
(DATUM)                     ;DATUM TO BE LOCATED
(WORD-PAIR ADDRESS)         ;VALUE TO BE RETURNED
```

and could be programmed as shown in Fig. 5-15.

```
SEARCH: JSR     PC,SAVE       ;SAVE REGISTERS
        MOV     (R0),R1       ;DATUM
        MOV     #1,R4         ;RELATIVE POSITION
        MOV     HEAD,R2       ;START OF LIST
        MOV     TAIL,R3       ;END OF LIST
LOOP:   CMP     R2,R3         ;EMPTY LIST OR NO MATCH
        BEQ     RET           ;NO HIT
        CMP     R1,(R2)       ;TEST FOR MATCH
        BEQ     FOUND         ;GOT A HIT
        MOV     2(R2),R2      ;NEXT ELEMENT
        INC     R4            ;ADD ONE TO RELATIVE POSITION
        BR      LOOP          ;AT END
FOUND:  MOV     R4,(R0)+      ;RETURN REL. POSITION
        MOV     R2,(R0)+      ;AND WORD-PAIR ADDRESS
RET:    JSR     PC,REST       ;RESTORE REGISTERS
        RTS     R0            ;RETURN
```

Fig. 5-15 Linked list search routine.

The SEARCH routine as written does a datum search, returning both the relative position and the word-pair address, if a match is found. Otherwise, no values are returned. Another form of the search routine might be to find the n'th item on a list. For this case, the call to search would include the relative position rather than the datum. The perceptive reader will have recognized that this search function is already performed by the ADD routine and that only small changes are necessary to that routine in order to add this new search capability.

The significant advantage of list structures lies in the flexibility of manipulation as has been demonstrated. Additionally, lists are often more convenient data structures for the representation of nonnumeric information in the areas of artificial intelligence, pattern recognition, theorem proving, syntactic analysis, operating systems, and so on. Thus an understanding of list structures is fundamental to an understanding of the topics in these areas.

5.6.4 Case Study: the Assembly Process

In a very meaningful sense, the assembly process is an example of the utilization of various data structures. The assembler accepts a program as data to be transformed into a machine language that can be executed on some computer. The transformation performed by the assembler is traditionally a two-step process whereby the program being assembled is passed through the assembler twice.

Figure 5-16 shows, in greatly simplified form, the basic operations of a *two-pass assembler*. At the heart of the assembly process, as seen in the figure, is the *symbol table*. The symbol table is also a data structure and provides a transformation between the symbols and the values they represent. Initially the symbol table may only include entries for each symbolic op-code, but as user-defined symbols are encountered during the assembly process, the symbol table is expanded to include these new entries.

Symbol Table: Because the symbol table is scanned frequently (either to enter a new symbol or to retrieve the value of a previously defined one), the construction of the symbol table must be considered carefully. For example, since op-codes will be referenced, in general, more frequently than user-defined symbols, and some op-codes may be used more often than others, ordering the symbols can certainly reduce the search time required to locate symbols in the table.

If the symbol table is structured as either a one-dimensional array or a simple linked list, a linear search of the table for a particular symbol will require scanning about half the table. By preordering the table, this scan can be reduced somewhat, but it will still be on the average, fairly long. Consequently, another technique is often used which restructures the symbol table so as to avoid a linear search with its attendantly longer search time.

The technique used is that of *hashing* or *randomizing* the symbol being searched for into a pointer, and using the pointer as the address of the symbol's entry in the symbol table. The hashing thus acts as a mapping function which is

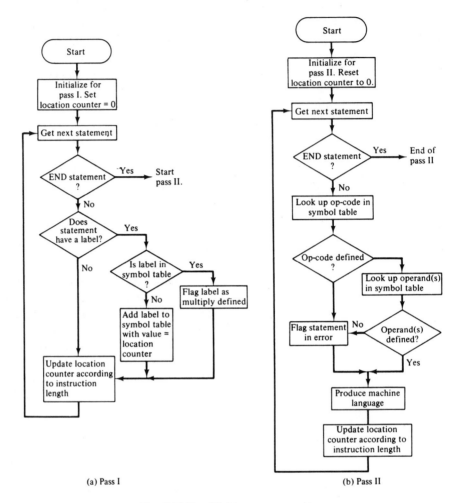

(a) Pass I   (b) Pass II

Fig. 5-16 Simplified two-pass assembler.

easily performed and which (one hopes) maps each symbol into a unique entry in the table. For example, given symbols each 6 bytes in length, a simple hashing function might be to exclusive-OR the 6 bytes together. The hashed result could then be used as an index into a symbol table in much the same way that an index is used to specify a particular array element.

In FORTRAN, the process might be coded as

```
HINDEX = HASH(SYMBOL)
SYMVAL = SYMTBL(HINDEX)
```

where HASH is the hashing function and SYMTBL is the symbol-table array. In assembly language for the PDP-11 the hashing function could be coded as

```
HASHER: MOV     #HINDEX,R0      ;R0 ← HINDEX ADDRESS
        CLRB    (R0)            ;HINDEX ← 0
        MOV     #SYMB,R1        ;R1 ← ADDRESS OF Bn, n = 0
HASH:   MOVB    (R1),R2         ;R2 ← Bn
        BICB    (R0),R2         ;R2 ← ~HINDEX ∧ Bn
        BICB    (R1)+,(R0)      ;HINDEX ← ~Bn ∧ HINDEX, n ← n+1
        BISB    R2,(R0)         ;HINDEX ← R2 V HINDEX
        CMP     R1,#SYMB+5      ;ALL SIX BYTES USED?
        BLOS    HASH            ;NO, REITERATE PROCESS
```

Not all PDP-11's have an exclusive-OR operation. For generality, then, the program makes use of the relationship

$$A \veebar B = (\sim A \wedge B) \vee (\sim B \wedge A)$$

where $\sim A \wedge B$ is equivalent to a BIC operation. As shown, the routine actually forms, from the 6-byte symbol consisting of B0, B1, B2, B3, B4, B5, the hashed result

$$HINDEX = ((((((0 \veebar B0) \veebar B1) \veebar B2) \veebar B3) \veebar B4) \veebar B5)$$

This hash value thus serves as an index into a symbol table consisting of 256 entries (e.g., 256 because HINDEX is a byte location capable of holding 256 bit combinations).

There are two apparent problems with this simple hashing technique; either the number of indices generated will be too small, or more than one symbol may map into the same hash index. Fortunately, both problems may be resolved using another simple technique. Instead of assuming the hashed symbol table to be a one-dimensional table, it is better to consider it two-dimensional such that for each prime entry or row (specified by the hash index) there are four columns in which to place the actual entry. Pictorially the situation looks as follows:

```
                                Column
-----------------------------------------------------------------------
Hindex  0                    1                    2                    3
-----------------------------------------------------------------------
0       entry                entry                entry                entry
             0,0                  0,1                  0,2                  0,3
1       entry                entry                entry                entry
             1,0                  1,1                  1,2                  1,3
.           .                    .                    .                    .
.           .                    .                    .                    .
.           .                    .                    .                    .
255     entry
             255,0
-----------------------------------------------------------------------
```

The two-dimensional scheme requires both that the hash index be computed and that a linear search be performed on each columnar entry until a match or an empty entry is found.

The two-dimensional approach has two drawbacks, however. First, since several entries may share the same hash index, the row entries must hold both the symbol itself and its value. Second, the approach must have allocated enough columns so that hashing conflicts may be uniquely resolved for a reasonable set of symbols. Should there be too few columns, and many symbols with the same hash index, the table will be sparsely filled; yet the assembler will be unable to add a new symbol to the table. Fortunately, this problem can be resolved by making each entry a list, adding list elements as needed.

As an alternative to using a two-dimensional table, there is the technique of adding a constant offset to the hash index each time a nonempty or non-match entry is found. This technique allows the table to be searched linearly after the hash index is computed, and attempts to fill the table to capacity. The algorithm for searching the table can be described as follows:

1. Calculate the hash index,

2. Test the entry for a match or an empty condition; if either, terminate search in success,

3. Add offset to hash index; check index to see if it points to an entry within the table; if it does not, go to step 5,

4. Check index to see if it is equal to the initial index (e.g., the index of the first entry in the table); if it is, terminate search in failure,

5. Subtract off table size from hash index; go to step 2.

As an example of such a search, consider a 16-element symbol table with an offset of 5 (offset must be relatively prime). Entries in the table have indices ranging from 0 to 15. If the hash index first computed was 2, the possible order of total entries searched would be

```
[2,7,12,1,6,11,0]
                   search terminates whenever hash index
                   computed = 0
```

Packed Entries in the Symbol Table: In almost all cases, one of the entries in the symbol table has to be the symbol itself. Since symbols may be several characters long, it is highly desirable to place as many characters in a word as possible. Having read about how a small computer, such as the PDP-11, packs 2 bytes or characters per word, the reader is probably convinced that the maximum number of characters per word is 2. Such is not the case.

Since the number of possible characters acceptable to a symbolic assembler is considerably less than 256 (i.e., $2**8$), being more probably 36-40 (i.e., the 26 letters of the alphabet plus the 10 numerals and a few special symbols), it is quite conceivable to be able to pack three characters into a 16-bit word by using the formula

$$((C(1) \ * \ 50_8) + C(2)) \ * \ 50_8 + C(3)$$

where the C's are the three characters in converted or *Radix-50* format. The relationship of Radix-50 format to ASCII is given by

Symbol	ASCII	Radix-50
Space	40	0
A-Z	101-132	1-32
$	44	33
.	56	34
Unused		35
0-9	60-71	36-47

Appendix C includes both the ASCII and Radix-50 octal codes. Using the tables, we can convert the six-character ASCII "SYMBOL",

	odd byte	even byte	
word1	131	123	
word2	102	115	= .ASCII /SYMBOL/
word3	114	117	

occupying three words, into the RADIX-50 format:

S = 073300	B = 006200
Y = 001750	O = 001130
M = 000015	L = 000014
------	------
075265	007344
word 1	word 2

which requires only two words and results in a significant saving in memory space.

There are two ways to write a Radix-50 format packing routine. One way would be to use a table of values for each character in each position as shown in Appendix C. A second would generate the final result by using the formula given earlier. A brief flowchart of this second method might be as shown in Fig. 5-17 and the program that utilizes this flowchart could be coded as shown in Fig. 5-18. The routine first extracts the RADIX-50 byte from the three-word pair. Next, the byte is shifted left three positions, effectively multiplying its value by 8. This partial result $C(1)*8$ is saved, and the byte is shifted twice more, resulting in a value of $C(1)*32$. When the partial result is added in, the new partial result is

$$C(1) \ * \ 32 + C(1) \ * \ 8 = C(1) \ * \ 40 = C(1) \ * \ 50_8$$

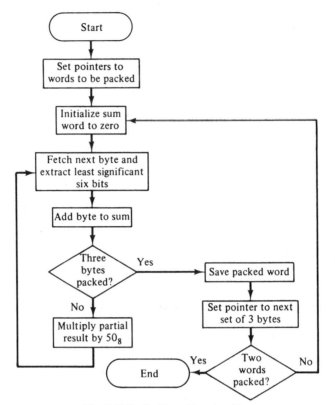

Fig. 5-17 Radix-50 packing algorithm.

```
PACKER: MOV     #SYMADR,R4        ;ADDRESS OF 1'st WORD TO BE PACKED
        MOV     #SYMADR+2,R5      ;ADDRESS OF 2'nd WORD TO BE PACKED
        MOV     R4,R1             ;INITIALIZE R1
;
PACK:   CLR     R3                ;SUM ← 0
PACK1:
        MOVB    (R1),R2           ;GET CHARACTER
        JSR     PC,CNVRT          ;CONVERT TO RADIX-50
        ADD     R2,R3             ;SUM ← SUM+TRANSLATED CHARACTER
        CLRB    (R1)+             ;CLEAR CHARACTER OUT
        CMP     R1,R5             ;IS R1 ≤ R5?
        BHI     PACK2             ;NOPE, TRIAD COMPLETED
        ASH     #3,R3             ;SHIFT SUM LEFT 3 BITS → C*8
        MOV     R3,-(SP)          ;SAVE PARTIAL RESULT
        ASH     #2,R3             ;SHIFT SUM LEFT 2 BITS → C*32
        ADD     (SP)+,R3          ;SUM ← SUM+PARTIAL RESULT = C*40
        BR      PACK1             ;PROCESS NEXT CHARACTER
PACK2:  MOV     R3,(R4)+          ;STORE RESULTANT TRIAD
        ADD     #3,R5             ;LAST WORD ADDRESS
        CMP     R5,#SYMADR+6      ;DONE?
        BLO     PACK              ;NOPE, REITERATE PACKING
```

Fig. 5-18 Radix-50 packing routine.

When the process is repeated for the second byte, the partial result is

$$((\ C(1) \ * \ 50_8 \ ) \ + \ C(2) \ ) \ * \ 50_8$$

to which $C(3)$ may be added, giving the resultant triad. The conversion from ASCII to Radix-50, and the unpacking routine, are left as exercises for the reader.

5.6.5 Data Structures in Practice

In almost every facit of computing, data structures play an important role in the specification, design, and implementation of complete software systems. From the simple variable types found in higher-level languages (e.g., queues, multilevel lists), there exists a need to be able to represent information in a form that is convenient for use by both the programmer and the computer system. An example will make this point clear.

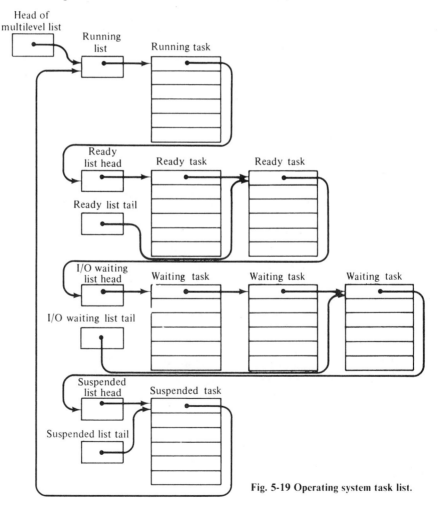

Fig. 5-19 Operating system task list.

Internal to any multiprogrammed computer system (see Chapter 11), there is a queue of the tasks to be performed. Each entry in the queue may consist of several consecutive words to hold such things as (1) the task name, (2) task status, (3) task starting/restarting address, and (4) task invocation information. If tasks are grouped according to their status (e.g., running, ready, waiting for I/O, suspended), a multilevel list structure exists as shown in Fig. 5-19.

The multilevel list actually combines the features found not only in lists, but also tables, dequeues, queues, and stacks. For example, each task is described by a table and belongs to one of the four queues (e.g., running, ready, waiting, suspended). Since each queue has both a head and a tail pointer, task tables can be added and removed from either end; that is, the queue can be treated as a deque. But the deque can be used as a stack if items are added and removed from one end only, as might be the case when one program interrupts another and interrupted programs are stacked to await execution at a later time. Finally, the basic structure of the data form is that of a list, and it is the list structure which allows us to restructure the data so conveniently into what suits us.

EXERCISES

1. What are the differences in the definitions of overflow and carry when defined for subtraction?

2. Develop a table similar to Table 5-3 (i.e., use the same decimal values) for double-precision subtraction.

3. Represent 16,768 in both fixed-point and floating-point form for a 16-bit word computer with 10 bits for the fraction and 5 for the exponent.

4. Using a 16-bit word as defined above, show how a negative floating-point value can be formed directly without using the technique of complementation of the positive value.

5. Using the PDP-11 instruction set, write a subprogram to form the exclusive-OR of two values X and Y; that is, write a subprogram equivalent of the XOR present on some of the newer '11's.

6. Given a string of ASCII characters stored in a byte stack pointed to by R0, write a subroutine to search for a "?" in the string. The search should be terminated when either a "?" character or a zero byte is found.

7. Write a program to translate the condition code instructions mnemonics (CLC, CLV, etc.) to their op-code equivalents. The instructions should be stored in arbitrary order in a table called INST, and their op-code equivalents should be placed in a table called OPS.

8. How must the *calculate array element address subroutine* be modified so as to correctly process all the array types given in the table in Section 5.6.1?

9. Implement the FORTRAN QUEUE and DEQUE routines in MACRO-11 assembly language. How do these routines compare to the routines coded using the circular buffer algorithm?

10. Write the DELETE routine as described in Section 5.6.3.

11. Write the ALLOCATE and FREE routines described in Section 5.6.3.

12. Given a list of two-letter words, develop a sorting program to place the list in alphabetical order.

13. Rewrite ADD so that it may be called to perform a relative position search function.

14. Show how a list structure can be used to implement a queue.

15. What is a suitable offset for a 32-element symbol table using the hashing technique to search the table? Give a set of possible indices searched if the hash index first computed was 5.

16. Write an unpack routine for words in Radix-50 format.

REFERENCES

There are several good texts devoted to data structures, including Berztiss (1971), Brillinger and Cohen (1972), Flores (1970), Johnson (1970), Lewis and Smith (1977), and Maurer (1977). Of course, Knuth's book (1968) remains a classic and is one of the few texts that discusses data structures in the context of machine and assembly language programming. Stone (1975) also covers data structures, but most of his examples are in ALGOL. Since the trend is toward higher-level languages for creating and manipulating data structures, many indirect references to this subject can be found in the language manuals describing SNOBOL, LISP, COMIT, COBOL, PL/1, PASCAL and so on. Booth's modified algorithm is proved formally by Rubinfeld (1975).

6

PDP-11
Micromachine Architecture
and Microprogramming

Although we have described the use of computer hardware elements such as the arithmetic and logical unit from the programmer's viewpoint, it is of interest to examine these components "microscopically". In fact, it is fruitful to extend this discussion so as to try to understand how a PDP-11 is implemented at the hardware level. Although each '11 is implemented in a different way, most recent implementations have sufficient commonality that it is possible to study this area realistically and usefully by describing the microstructure of a single machine, the PDP-11/60. The 11/60 is a microprogrammed machine and is user microprogrammable. That is, *each* PDP-11 instruction as implemented on the PDP-11/60 is effectively implemented by execution of *many* "micro" instructions which are unique to the PDP-11/60. Additionally, the user may define new instructions which become unique to his machine. Because the 11/60 was designed with user microprogramming in mind, it would be expected that its internal architecture (as seen by the microprogrammer) is *simple* enough to be "understandable" yet *powerful* enough to make the microprogrammer's investment profitable. This is indeed the case.

In order to establish a foundation for a discussion of the 11/60 microstructure we must first describe the very basic elements or building blocks of all digital computers.

6.1 BOOLEAN ALGEBRA, LOGICAL FUNCTIONS, AND DIGITAL COMPUTER ELEMENTS

Although originally conceived as a means for dealing with certain classes of problems in symbolic logic, Boolean algebra is best known to computer programmers as a means for expressing logical relationships. Using the basic operations AND, OR, and NOT, the FORTRAN programmer is able to develop complex logical expressions that can be used both in logical assignment statements such as

```
LOGIC = 5 .LT. NUM .AND. .NOT. X
```

and in logical IF statements such as

```
IF (X . NE . Y) GO TO 10
```

On the other hand, one of the first uses of Boolean algebra as applied to computers was in the understanding of switching circuits. Using the postulates and theorems of Boolean algebra, one can express algebraically the way computer circuits operate. Consequently, using only simple building blocks, complex circuits can be easily described, manipulated, and possibly simplified.

Although it is currently possible to build a "computer on a chip," it is still worthwhile to consider the nature of simple logical circuits and computer elements. By doing so, some of the "magic" behind the operation of a computer is removed, and the user of the machine gains an appreciation for what is going on inside.

6.1.1 Simple Logical Circuits

In the description of simple logical circuits, the basic logical functions OR($\vee$), AND($\wedge$), XOR($\veebar$), and NOT($\sim$), which are presented in Appendix B, can be represented graphically (as shown in Fig. 6-1) by the logic circuit symbols used in schematic drawings. The use of the small circle at the input (or output) to a logic circuit symbol indicates that input (or output) is complemented.

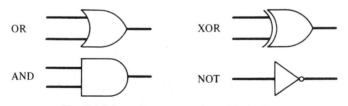

Fig. 6-1 Schematic representations of logic elements.

For example, the graphic representation of F = A + ~B is shown in Fig. 6-2:

Fig. 6-2 Symbolic representation of F = A + ~B.

To define the operation of a simple logical circuit it is necessary to define the meaning of both its inputs and its outputs. As described in Appendix B, there are two possible input/output states, conveniently referred to as 0 and 1: the state 0, which indicates that a relatively low electrical signal is present, and the state 1, which indicates that a relatively high signal is present. Graphically, these two states are shown in Fig. 6-3.

Fig. 6-3 Possible input/output states of a logic circuit.

If the signals being input to a logical circuit change with time, so might the output signal coming from it. For example, the representation of the function F = A + ~B given in Fig. 6-2 with time-varying input signals is shown in Fig. 6-4. Figure 6-5 shows the corresponding output signal.

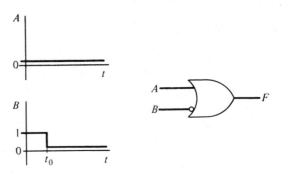

Fig. 6-4 Logic circuit with its inputs.

The output signal shown can be justified as follows: Since the function F is 1 only when A is 1 or B is 0, and since A is always 0, then only when B becomes 0 at time $t0$ does F become 1. The reader may infer from this description that changes in the state of the input signal causing changes in the state of the output signal are instantaneous; that is, there is no delay in the logical circuit itself. This is not what

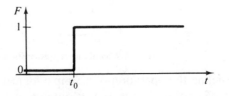

Fig. 6-5 Output signal for the circuit of Fig. 6-4.

actually happens, but it is convenient and perfectly acceptable for us to regard such delays as relatively negligible for our purposes.

Although it is possible with current technology to fabricate very complicated computer circuits (and even whole computers) in one tiny package called a chip, it is very instructive to consider how computer circuits may be constructed from the simple logical building blocks described so far. However, in order to use the building blocks to build computer circuits, one additional building block will be needed. This is a delay box:

Signals entering the delay box emerge only after a delay of n units of time.

The delay building block, when connected on itself as shown in Fig. 6-6, forms a simple storage device. Given an initial 1 signal, the device will continue to produce a 1 as an output signal. The device works because the input signal is replicated at the output after being delayed one unit of time. Thus if the input signal is maintained high for at least one time unit, and then goes low, the output signal will go high; this signal can be fed back (through an OR circuit) to maintain the output signal. This circuit has a *feedback* loop which utilizes the output signal for its input so that once initiated it stores or "remembers" what has occurred without requiring the continued presence of the input signal.

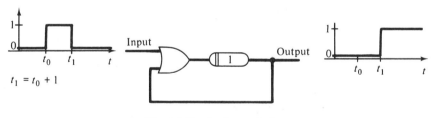

Fig. 6-6 Simple storage device.

The presence of an input signal serves to turn this storage device on, for example, to remember that a 1 signal once occurred. By adding another logic element in the feedback loop, it is possible to turn the storage device off. The circuit of Fig. 6-7 accomplishes just that, with the two input lines now labeled "set 1" and "set 0". As long as there is no set 0 signal, the AND element will pass the output signal through to the OR element. However, as soon as the set 0 signal becomes a 1, the output will no longer be passed through. A graph of the possible states for given set signals is shown in Fig. 6-8. As before, the width of the set 0 and set 1 signals (often called pulses) are one time unit (e.g., $t1 - t0 = t3 - t2 = 1$).

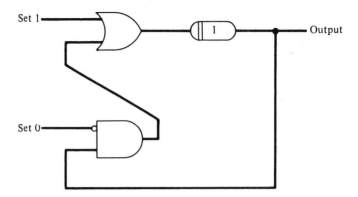

Fig. 6-7 Setable storage device.

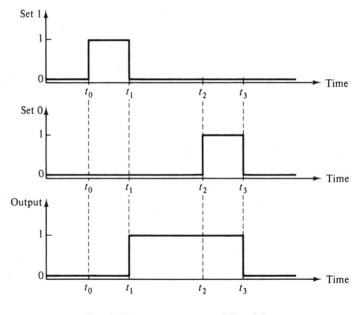

Fig. 6-8 Input/output states of Fig. 6-6.

Being able to set the circuit to 1 or 0 (called *set* and *reset*, for obvious reasons) is not enough. What is needed is the capability to reset it if it is set, or set it if it is not, without knowing or caring what the original state might have been. To obtain this new capability, an exclusive-OR building block is added between the AND and OR blocks. This block acts as a "set/reset" line, since if a 1 is flowing through the circuit and a 1 is placed on the set/reset line, the output of the exclusive-OR will be 0 (i.e., the device is reset to 0); or if a 0 is flowing through the circuit and a 1 is presented to set/reset, the output of the exclusive-OR will be a 1 (i.e., the device is set to 1). This circuit is shown in Fig. 6-9.

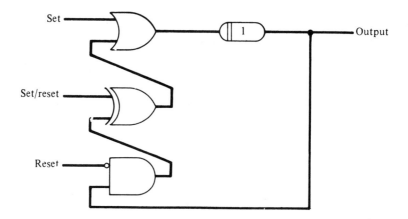

Fig. 6-9 Switchable storage device.

Another name for the set/reset line is *trigger*, since the input signal to this line causes the circuit to be changed or triggered from one state to another. Adding one more refinement to the circuit, a NOT block, results in the circuit shown in Fig. 6-10.

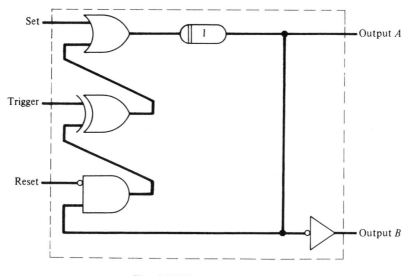

Fig. 6-10 Flip-flop.

The circuit of Fig. 6-10 has two outputs, labelled A and B. When output A is a 1 (e.g., the circuit is set), output B will be a 0. Alternatively, if the circuit is not set, output A will be a 0 and B will be a 1. A simple rotation of the figure, while painting out all the components inside the dashed lines (e.g., making it a black box), makes the circuit look as follows:

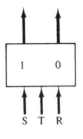

This is called a *flip-flop* or *RST flip-flop* and forms one of the most common circuit components in all computers.

6.1.2 Computer Elements

By connecting *n* flip-flops together and treating the collection as an *ordered unit*, it is possible to build a *register* capable of holding *n* bits of information. Operations may be performed on the register such as to "clear" it:

(where the clear line serves to reset each flip-flop to the 0 state) and to transfer the contents from one register to another:

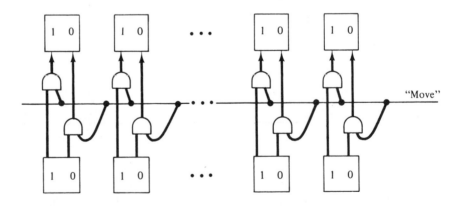

Next, these registers may be combined with "adder circuits" in order to perform computer addition. An adder circuit in its simplest form must be capable of adding two inputs to produce a sum and a possible carry. Expressed in truth-table form:

186

Inputs		Outputs	
A	B	Sum	Carry
-	-	---	-----
0	0	0	0
0	1	1	0
1	0	1	0
1	1	0	1

The logical equations for this binary arithmetic can be deduced as follows: The sum is 1 when A is 0 and B is 1, or when A is 1 and B is 0. The carry is 1 when both A and B are 1. Expressing this as a logical equation,

$$S = (\sim A \wedge B) \vee (A \wedge \sim B) = A \veebar B$$

$$C = A \wedge B$$

Since these equations require only the AND, OR, and NOT building blocks already discussed, it is a simple matter to interconnect them to produce the adder circuit shown in Fig. 6-11. This adder suffers from one serious defect — it can perform only 1-bit arithmetic. To correct this deficiency it is necessary to use *n* of them to perform *n*-bit arithmetic, as shown in Fig. 6-12.

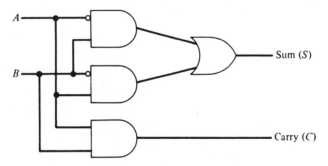

Fig. 6-11 Simple 1-bit adder.

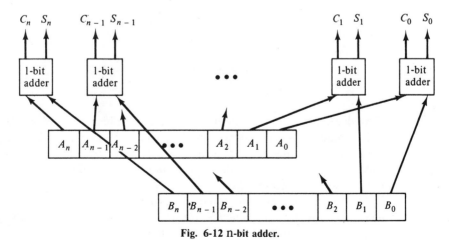

Fig. 6-12 n-bit adder.

However, what happens with the carries remains unclear. Obviously the carry from the preceding adder must participate in the adder to its left. Each adder thus must look as shown in Fig. 6-13. Such an adder is called a *full-adder*, in contrast to the

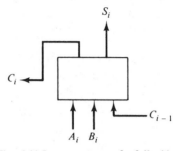

Fig. 6-13 Inputs/outputs of a full-adder.

half-adder, which does not account for the carry from the previous bit position. Another reason for these names is that a full-adder may be constructed from two half-adders, as shown in Fig. 6-14. (The development of the full-adder is left as an exercise for the reader.)

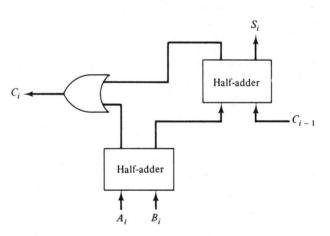

Fig. 6-14 Full-adder made up of two half-adders.

As developed, the full-adder is still a 1-bit adder. To add two *n*-bit numbers together requires *n* full-adders, or the switching of a single full-adder so that each of the bit pairs is added one at a time, in sequence. When the numbers are added a bit at a time, the circuit is called a *serial adder*; when all bits are added at once the circuit is called a *parallel* adder.

Most computer systems today have parallel adders and parallel data paths which allow for the simultaneous transfer of all bits within a computer word. For example, the sequence of operations for an "add" might be:

1. Move operand A (in register A) to the adders together with operand B (in register B), causing A and B to be added together.

2. Clear register B.

3. Move the resultant from the adders to the B register.

A computer circuit to perform these operations is shown in Fig. 6-15. The figure illustrates an interesting point: that there are two flows of information within a computer circuit. The first flow represents the *data flow* and is illustrated by the double lines in the picture.

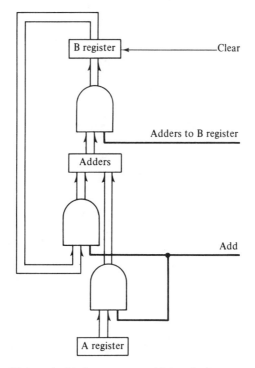

(Note: a double line means an *n*-bit transfer.)

Fig. 6-15 ADD circuit for (B) ← (A) + (B).

The second flow consists of the *control signals* which clear a register, cause an add to be performed, or set some data into a register. Although in both cases the actual flow is nothing more than electrical signals, the difference between them lies in their use. At the heart of a computer is the control unit, which is able to direct the sequence of operations to be performed. The control flow directs the operations performed on the data flow, causing (one hopes) meaningful results to be generated. For results to be generated correctly, the control signals must occur in the correct order. It is obvious that, in Fig. 6-15, the "Adders to B register" must occur after the "Add" signal has occurred and the adder has had time to perform its operation. We call this ordering the *clocking* of the control signals.

For the control unit to know what to do, control signals must be passed to it jointly from the instruction to be executed and from the results of the last calculation. The steps that the control unit performs are called *microinstructions*, and usually several microinstructions will be executed by the control unit to execute one machine instruction. Thus, in the same way that macro's are composed of a number of machine language instructions which are invoked by a single macro "call", machine language instructions are really composed of a sequence of microinstructions. Relative to the *microprogrammer*, then, the machine language programmer can be thought of as a *macroprogrammer*.

6.2 INTRODUCTION TO MICROPROGRAMMED MACHINES

As suggested earlier, simple circuits may be combined to form elements which, when appropriately connected, constitute a *datapath*, the nucleus of any computer. The datapath components can be classified as *combinational units* (e.g., adders, decoders), *sequential units* (such as counters), and *interconnections*. For convenience, we now repeat Fig. 2-13, expanding the simple computer structure of Fig. 2-1 so as to view the datapath components in some detail.

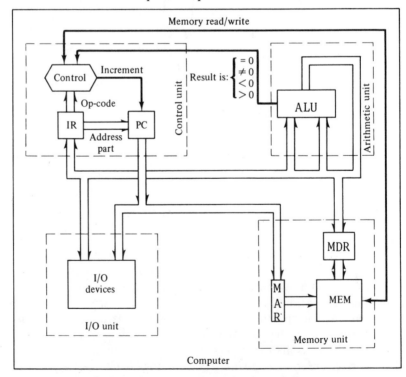

Fig. 6-16 Control and datapaths for a simple computer.

Again, registers which are invisible to the machine language programmer ("macroprogrammer") but play such an important part in instruction sequencing (e.g., IR, MAR, MDR, as per Section 2.5) are now visualized.

In a *microprogrammed computer*, the sequence of transfers from one register to another (possibly involving arithmetic or logical operations) which constitute the nucleus of each computer *macroinstruction* (i.e., machine language instruction) is controlled by *microinstructions*. In fact, the entire conduct of the machine is under *microprogram* control. As we shall see, microinstructions and machine language instructions are similar in form yet different with regard to control function.

6.2.1 Architecture vs. Organization

Most programs which run on a PDP-11/34, for example, can also be executed on a PDP-11/60 since the *architecture* of both machines is identical. As suggested earlier, architecture in this context means that set of a computer's resources which are visible to the macroprogrammer, including the instruction set, general purpose registers, processor status word, and memory management registers. However, the *organization* of the two machines differs in that the datapaths, and hence the microinstructions which control the datapaths to implement any particular PDP-11 instruction, are unique to each machine.

6.2.2 Simple Hypothetical Computers and the PDP-11/60

In texts at this level it is usual to introduce a "simple hypothetical computer", describe its organization at the microlevel, and then show how the machine can be microprogrammed to implement simple machine level instructions. Although this path is advantagous because of the inherent simplicity of the hypothetical computer, the strategy has at least two disadvantages. First, there is little motivation to study a machine that will never be used and which may bear only a superficial resemblance to any particular existing computer. Second, the simplicity necessary in a machine to be discussed down to the gate level prevents the more powerful and interesting aspects of microprogramming from being realistically demonstrated.

We have chosen an alternative technique. A subset of the micromachine structure of a real computer, the PDP-11/60, will be described noting

1. the resources available in the inner machine, especially those elements not "seen" by the machine level programmer,

2. the paths and programmable "switches" available for dynamically routing data among those resources and between the inner machine and main storage, and,

3. the timing operations and constraints necessary to insure that desired operations occur in correct sequence.

The PDP-11/60 is a real machine, and besides being a microprogrammed machine, it was designed with the idea of user microprogramming in mind. Thus its micromachine structure is indeed *simple* enough to be *understandable*, yet sufficiently *complex* to implement and to demonstrate such *powerful* ideas as parallel processing. Thus, it can serve as a vehicle to illustrate the general goals and utility of microprogramming: base machine instruction set implementation, execution efficiency enhancement, and emulation of other instruction sets. The 11/60 datapaths will be described in enough detail to demonstrate *realistically* all of these applications. The reader is cautioned, however, that *any* attempts at 11/60 microprogramming must be preceded by a thorough reading of the relevant literature.

In summary, the reader will find the next few sections *challenging* (in that the descriptions of the resources are relatively brief) and *rewarding*. The reward consists of an overview of the internal structure and operation of a powerful, *real*, minicomputer and an appreciation of the techniques used to cause the micromachine to implement and execute non-trivial PDP-11 instructions. In Chapter 10, these ideas will be extended to show how user microprogramming can be employed to enhance basic CPU performance.

6.3 THE PDP-11/60 DATAPATHS

The 11/60 datapath consists of a number of elements which provide resources available only at the microlevel. Control of datapath elements is via the 48-bit 11/60 microword shown in Fig. 6-17b. Each datapath element X will be described as to its function, input/output, and control by the relevant microword field, *X*. *In some cases*, we will also specify the *mnemonic* which a microassembler could recognize (in the same way that an ordinary assembler recognizes operation codes and address modes) so as to supply the correct value for the relevant microfield. Thus, in the next few sections we will describe the "tool kit" available to the microprogrammer. These tools are more complex, and hence more powerful, than those available to the macroprogrammer. Later, we will illustrate how these resources are used to implement and augment the PDP-11 instruction set.

The reader should examine Fig. 6-17a to locate the position and data routes available to each element as it is described.

6.3.1 Arithmetic and Logical Unit

The nucleus of the datapaths is the *arithmetic and logical unit*, or *ALU*. Each of the two ports of the ALU may receive *input* from a number of registers:

1. The A bus port from XMUX or CMUX (i.e., X or C multiplexer, each a single 16-bit register), or from one of sixteen 16-bit registers in either of two A bus scratch pads, ASP LO or ASP HI. The input register to be selected is determined by a *multiplexer*, a device which routes one of its *n* inputs to its output.

2. The B bus port, from one of sixteen 16-bit registers in the C scratch pad (CSP) or either of the two B scratch pads, BSP HI or BSP LO.

The ALU provides the basic integer arithmetic and logical operation capability which is the foundation of all computations performed by the central processor. As shown in Table 6-1, the 4-bit *ALU* control field (bits 44-47 of the microword) selects the function to be performed on the inputs from each of two 16-bit buses, A and B, along with the source of the carry in (CIN) to the ALU. "Op" is the ALU output. On output, PS(C) is the carry bit of the inner machine ALU whereas D(C) is the C-bit of the PDP-11, located in the PSW.

Table 6-1 PDP-11/60 ALU functions vs. ALU Code

ALU/Mnemonic	Definition	CIN Source	Comments
0 NOT-A	Op ← ~A	1	1's complement
1 A-PLUS-B-PLUS-PS(C)	Op ← A+B+PS(C)	PS(C)	Used for ADC
2 NOT-A-AND-B	Op ← ~A∧B	PS(C)	Used for BIC
3 ZERO	Op ← 0	PS(C)	Generate 0
4 A-PLUS-B-PLUS-D(C)	Op ← A+ B+D(C)	D(C)	Used for FPP
5 A-PLUS-~B-PLUS-D(C)	Op ← A+~B+D(C)	D(C)	Used for FPP
6 A-XOR-B	Op ← A ⊻ B	D(C)	Exclusive Or
7 A-AND-~B	Op ← A∧~B	D(C)	Reversed BIC
10 DIVIDE	Op ← A-B, D(C)=1	0	Conditional add/sub,
	Op ← A+B, D(C)=0	0	used in DIV
11 A-PLUS-B	Op ← A + B	0	Add
12 B	Op ← B	0	Select B
13 A-AND-B	Op ← A∧B	0	Logical AND
14 A-PLUS-B-PLUS-1	Op ← A + B + 1	1	
15 A-MINUS-B	Op ← A - B	1	Subtract
16 A-IOR-B	Op ← A ∨ B	1	Inclusive OR
17 A	Op ← A	1	Select A

6.3.2 A and B Scratchpads

Each of the two scratchpads (A and B) provides thirty-two 16-bit registers for primary data storage within the datapath. Each scratchpad is divided into 2 sections, HI and LO. Since registers other than those in the A and B scratchpads can be gated onto the A and B buses, respectively, the scratchpads must first be *selected* or *enabled* before their contents can appear on the relevant bus. The 2-bit A enable and B enable (*AEN, BEN*) microfields serve this function.

If *direct address selection* is in effect, as specified by the 2-bit A Select and B select (*ASEL,BSEL*) fields (see below), the 5-bit register address within the A or B scratchpads is determined by a 3-bit Register Immediate Field (*RIF*) in conjunction with the *ASEL/BSEL* and the *AEN/BEN* microfields. The use of the *BEN*, *BSEL*, and *RIF* microfields to specify locations in BSP is shown in Fig. 6-18. *AEN* and *ASEL* similarly select locations in ASP. Note, however, that the existence of only *one RIF* field limits the way in which ASP and BSP locations can be addressed.

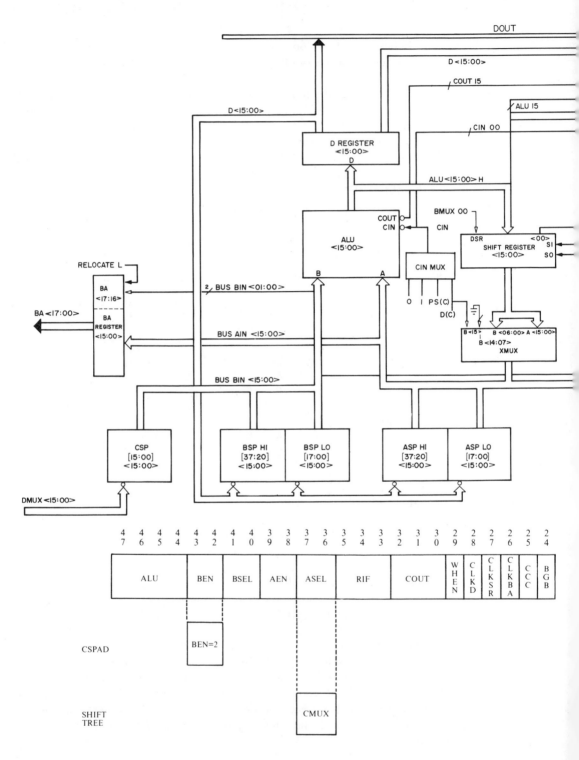

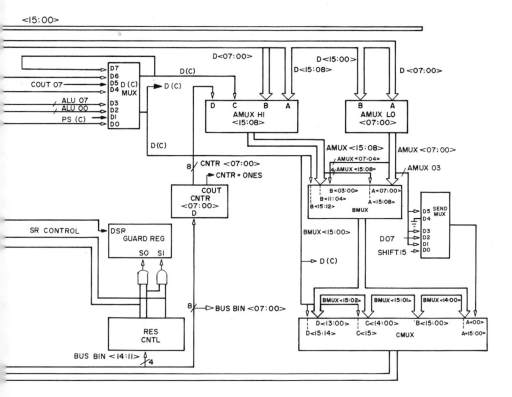

Fig. 6-17a Simplified datapaths of PDP-11/60.

$<m{:}n>$ specifies bit positions m to n, inclusive, within a word.
$[m{:}n]$ specifies the word position in the scratchpad.

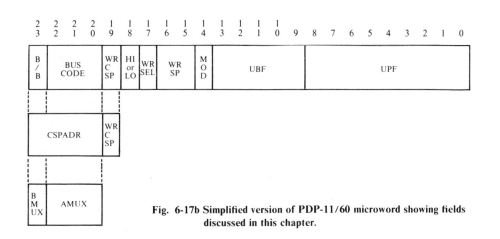

Fig. 6-17b Simplified version of PDP-11/60 microword showing fields discussed in this chapter.

Alternatively, *ASEL* or *BSEL* can specify that either the 3-bit source *or* destination field of the current PDP-11 instruction (i.e., macroinstruction) — contained within the instruction register or IR — be used instead of the *RIF* microfield in scratchpad address specification. The IR is *not* shown in Fig. 6-17.

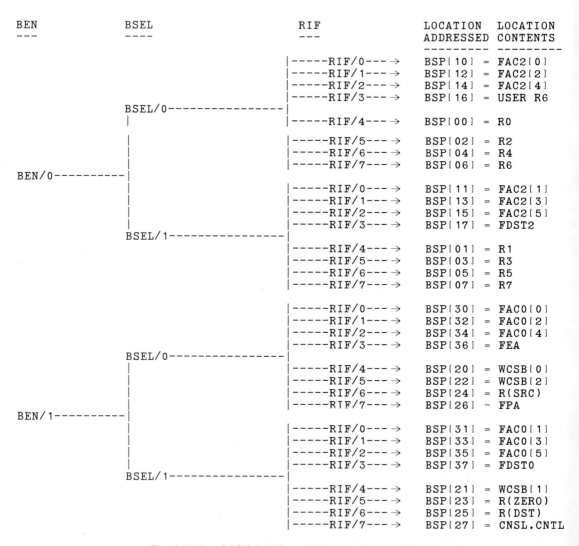

BEN	BSEL	RIF	LOCATION ADDRESSED	LOCATION CONTENTS
		|-----RIF/0---→	BSP[10]	= FAC2[0]
		|-----RIF/1---→	BSP[12]	= FAC2[2]
		|-----RIF/2---→	BSP[14]	= FAC2[4]
		|-----RIF/3---→	BSP[16]	= USER R6
	BSEL/0----------------|			
	|	|-----RIF/4---→	BSP[00]	= R0
	|	|-----RIF/5---→	BSP[02]	= R2
	|	|-----RIF/6---→	BSP[04]	= R4
	|	|-----RIF/7---→	BSP[06]	= R6
BEN/0----------|			
	|	|-----RIF/0---→	BSP[11]	= FAC2[1]
	|	|-----RIF/1---→	BSP[13]	= FAC2[3]
	|	|-----RIF/2---→	BSP[15]	= FAC2[5]
	|	|-----RIF/3---→	BSP[17]	= FDST2
	BSEL/1----------------|			
		|-----RIF/4---→	BSP[01]	= R1
		|-----RIF/5---→	BSP[03]	= R3
		|-----RIF/6---→	BSP[05]	= R5
		|-----RIF/7---→	BSP[07]	= R7
		|-----RIF/0---→	BSP[30]	= FAC0[0]
		|-----RIF/1---→	BSP[32]	= FAC0[2]
		|-----RIF/2---→	BSP[34]	= FAC0[4]
		|-----RIF/3---→	BSP[36]	= FEA
	BSEL/0----------------|			
	|	|-----RIF/4---→	BSP[20]	= WCSB[0]
	|	|-----RIF/5---→	BSP[22]	= WCSB[2]
	|	|-----RIF/6---→	BSP[24]	= R(SRC)
	|	|-----RIF/7---→	BSP[26]	- FPA
BEN/1----------|			
	|	|-----RIF/0---→	BSP[31]	= FAC0[1]
	|	|-----RIF/1---→	BSP[33]	= FAC0[3]
	|	|-----RIF/2---→	BSP[35]	= FAC0[5]
	|	|-----RIF/3---→	BSP[37]	= FDST0
	BSEL/1----------------|			
		|-----RIF/4---→	BSP[21]	= WCSB[1]
		|-----RIF/5---→	BSP[23]	= R(ZERO)
		|-----RIF/6---→	BSP[25]	= R(DST)
		|-----RIF/7---→	BSP[27]	= CNSL.CNTL

Fig. 6-18 Use of BEN, BSEL, and RIF microfields in BSP addressing.

For efficient implementation of the PDP-11 address modes it is necessary that the general register contents be duplicated. They thus appear in the first 8 locations of both the A and B scratchpads. FAC$i[j]$, $i = 0,1,2,3$ and $j = 0,1,...,5$ are the six 64-bit floating-point accumulators for the microcoded FPP instruction set ("warm" FPP). FAC1$[j]$ and FAC3$[j]$ are in the positions of ASP HI and ASP LO, respectively, corresponding to those locations shown for FAC0$[j]$ and FAC2$[j]$ of BSP HI and BSP LO. When the hardware FPP accelerator ("hot" FPP) is present, a bit is set in the WHAMI (What am I?) register in the ASP, and the twenty-four 16-bit registers for the warm FPP are available for the user. Bits in the WHAMI describe the 11/60 hardware options status (e.g., cache on/off, hot FPP on/off, etc.) so that cache and hot FPP can be turned off if faults occur, with loss of speed but not functionality.

6.3.3 C Scratchpad

A third potential source of data for the B bus is the 16-word C scratchpad (CSP), selected when $BEN = 2$. The CSP is the datapath window to main memory (via CSP[15], the memory data register or MDR) and is also used for error logging. The constants 0, 1, and 2, (used by the PDP-11 for zeroing data locations, and for manipulating register contents in the autoincrement/decrement modes) are "permanently" stored in CSP 16, 17 and 14, respectively. When $BEN = 3$, use of $BSEL = 0, 1, 2,$ or 3 can also select CSP[17], CSP[16], CSP[15], or CSP[14], respectively.

6.3.4 ALU Input/Output Elements

1. **D Register:** The ALU output is stored into the 16-bit D register if and only if so specified by the single bit *CLKD* microfield at a time determined by another single bit microfield, the *WHEN* field (Section 6.4). The D register holds the ALU output for future use.

2. **CIN,D(C):** As noted earlier, the source of the ALU carry in, CIN, is either the constants 0 or 1, the carry bit of the PSW, D (C), or the last ALU carry out, PS(C). If and when D is clocked, then either of ALU output bits 0, 7, or 15 *or* the output of the CIN selector *or* the word or byte carries of the current ALU operation *or* PS(C) *or* the *previous* D(C) becomes the *present* D(C). It is the 3-bit *COUT* microfield which selects which one of the 8 noted inputs is to become D(C) if and when D is clocked.

3. **Shift Register and X Multiplexer:** The Shift Register (SR) is a 16-bit register which may be loaded from the ALU. The X multiplexer (XMUX) is a selector, or multiplexer, which routes *either* the contents of the SR *or* a special word (i.e., bits 0 to 6 = bits 0 to 6 of SR, bits 7 to 14 = 0, and bit 15 = D(C)) onto the A bus. The 1-bit *XMUX* microfield actually overlaps the *ASEL* field rather than appearing as a separate field. Thus, when $AEN = 2$ or 3, *ASEL* functions as per Section 6.3.2. When $AEN = 0$, the lower bit of

ASEL becomes *XMUX*. The SR can effect either right or left 1-bit shifts of 16-bit numbers. However, in conjunction with the D register, the SR may be used to implement shifts of 32-bit numbers (Section 6.5.2).

4. **The Shift Tree:** The Shift Tree (ST) is a combinational unit made up of three multiplexers, AMUX, BMUX, and CMUX. The ST operates on the D register output to provide a number of operations on 16-bit numbers. Among these are single bit left shift, *n* bit signed or unsigned right shift ($0 < n < 15$), or byte swap. AMUX, BMUX, and CMUX are controlled by microfields of bit width 3 (*AMUX*), 1 (*BMUX*), and 2 (*CMUX*), respectively. Note that *AMUX* and *BMUX* overlap the CSP selector bits, *CSPADRS*. Thus, when the ST is in use, only the four base constant locations of CSP can be accessed, using the *BEN* = 3 option.

The detailed structure and use of both the Shift Tree and the Shift Register will be discussed in Sections 6.5.1 and 6.5.2, respectively.

6.4 THE MICROCYCLE

Electrical signals require a finite time to propagate through wires, and both active and passive electronic components require finite times before the input signals produce the required output. Thus, each 11/60 microcycle of 170 nanoseconds (1 nsec = 10**-9 seconds) is divided into four time segments marked by four "pulses", P1, P2, P3, and *u*P3 (micro P3). A microcycle is formally the interval between two consecutive trailing edges of *u*P3.

6.4.1 The Multiple Operation Microinstruction

More than one operation may occur during a single microcycle. The restrictions on when any given operation may occur must be obeyed in constructing microprograms. For example:

1. The ALU result may be clocked or loaded into D either at P2 or P3, as specified by *WHEN* = 0 (mnemonic P2-T) or 1 (P3-T), respectively, provided that *CLKD* = 1. As noted earlier, the D(C) selected by *COUT* is clocked at the same time as D. Similarly, if *CLKSR* = 1, the SR is clocked at the same time as D. When clocked, the SR will *either* right shift one, left shift one, *or* be loaded with the ALU output contents, depending on the state of a 2-bit field within the RES register (Section 6.7).

2. The output of D may be written back into selected locations of ASP, BSP, and/or CSP during the same microcycle if, and only if, D is clocked at P2. Which locations are written into is determined by the microword scratchpad write fields, as noted below. The usual mnemonics are noted in parentheses.

```
MOD   = 0, enable write to ASP and/or BSP (CLKSP)
      = 1, disable write to ASP and/or BSP (NOCLK)

WRSP  = 0, no write (NOP)
      = 1, write to ASP, if enabled as per MOD (WR-A)
      = 2, write to BSP, if enabled as per MOD (WR-B)
      = 3, write to ASP & BSP, if enabled as per MOD (WR-A-AND-B)

WRSEL = 0, use ASP read address as write address (A-ADDR)
      = 1, use BSP read address as write address (B-ADDR)

HI/LO = 0, write LO section of selected scratchpads (LO)
      = 1, write HI section of selected scratchpads (HI)

WRCSP = 0, do not write to CSP (NO)
      = 1, write to CSP (YES)
```

Note that the scratchpad rewrite as specified above, if enabled, occurs at P3; thus the need to clock D at P2.

At this point a single example will illustrate the multiple events which occur during a microcycle, and thus the power afforded the microprogrammer. Multiple lines of code which assign field values to the *same* microinstruction are terminated by a comma:

Macroinstruction :

```
        ADD Rn,Rm      (assumed resident in IR)
```

Microinstruction :

```
            ALU/A-PLUS-B,
            BEN/BSPLO, BSEL/SF,
            AEN/ASPLO, ASEL/DF,
            CLKD/YES, WHEN/P2-T,
            MOD/CLKSP,
            HILO/LO,
            WRSP/WR-A-AND-B,
            WRSEL/A-ADDR
```

That is, set the ALU to ADD, use the macroinstruction SRC field (SF) to select the BSP operand and the macroinstruction DST field (DF) to select the ASP operand, both from the *low* areas of the scratchpads. Clock the result into D at P2. Enable writeback to the *low* areas of both ASP *and* BSP, and use the ASP operand address as the write address for *both* scratchpads. For correct operation, this microinstruction requires that the macroinstruction "ADD Rn,Rm" be present in the IR, having been fetched earlier. Also, the symbolic field definition mnemonics following the / 's must have been defined meaningfully, i.e., so as to set the required bits in the relevant positions of the microword. Finally, by simply specifying B-ADDR for *WRSEL* instead of A-ADDR, a reverse ADD instruction, ADR Rn,Rm, would be created such that Rn ← Rn + Rm.

3. Since the shift tree *output* (i.e., CMUX) may be selected as the A bus *input*, data residing in the D register at the end of one microcycle may, in the *next* microcycle: (a) first, be operated upon by the shift tree and the result passed into the ALU A bus port; (b) then, an ALU operation may be invoked involving selected B bus data and the result of (a); (c) next, the ALU result clocked into D at P2; and, finally, (d) the D register written into one or both scratchpads at P3.

6.5 SHIFT TREE AND SHIFT REGISTER: STRUCTURE AND USE

6.5.1 Shift Tree

As noted earlier, the shift tree consists of three multiplexers, AMUX, BMUX, and CMUX:

1. AMUX: AMUX is split into two bytes, AMUX LO and AMUX HI, each of which receives *both* the low byte and high byte of the D register [D(LO) and D(HI)]. The AMUX input also receives the output of an 8-bit counter register (CNTR) and D(C) replicated 8 times. With 1 bit of the *AMUX* field controlling AMUX LO and 2 bits of *AMUX* controlling AMUX HI, the following 8 possibilities exist for AMUX out:

AMUX HI Out	AMUX LO Out	Interpretation	Mnemonic/AMUX	
D(HI)	D(LO)	D unchanged	DIRECT	0
D(LO)	D(LO)	D(LO) duplicated	DLO#DLO	1
D(C) replicated	D(LO)	D(LO) sign extended if D(C)=ALU 07	SIGNEXT	2
COUNTER	D(LO)	Counter introduced into datapath	COUNTR	3
D(HI)	D(HI)	D(HI) duplicated	DHI#DHI	4
D(LO)	D(HI)	Byte swap	SWAB	5
D(C)	D(HI)	Right shift 8 of D(HI)	RIGHT-8	6
COUNTER	D(HI)	Counter introduced into datapath	COUNTR#DHI	7

2. BMUX: The output of AMUX can either be passed directly through BMUX (DIRECT, *BMUX* = 0) or can be right shifted 4, with replication of D(C) in the high 4 bits (RIGHT-4, *BMUX* = 1).

3. CMUX: The 2-bit *CMUX* field produces one of four outputs:

CMUX Out	Interpretation	Mnemonic/CMUX	
BMUX left one, SENDMUX enters low bit	Arithmetic left shift by 1	LEFT-1	0
BMUX	BMUX unchanged	DIRECT	1
BMUX right one with D(C) into high bit	BMUX right shifted by 1	RIGHT-1	2
BMUX right two with D(C) into high bits	BMUX right shifted by 2	RIGHT-2	3

Thus, correct selection of D(C) and the appropriate choice of right shifts (0 or 8, *plus* 0 or 4, *plus* -1 or 0 or 1 or 2) can effect a signed (arithmetic) or unsigned (logical) right shift of 0 to 14 bits in a single microcycle, with a 16-bit result routed onto the A bus.

For example, the following *single* microinstruction takes the contents of the D register, arithmetically shifts it right 11 places (8 + 4 - 1 = 11), subtracts the contents of R0 from the result, and places the final result in the D register:

Microinstruction :

```
ALU/A-MINUS-B,COUT/ALU15,
BEN/BSPL0,BSEL/IMMED0,RIF/4,
AEN/CMUX,AMUX/RIGHT-8,BMUX/RIGHT-4,ASEL/LEFT-1,
CLKD/YES,WHEN/P2-T
```

Among other useful operations possible via the shift tree are byte swap and sign extension of the low byte of D; the former is a PDP-11 macroinstruction and the latter must be effected when a PDP-11 MOVB destination is a *gp* register.

6.5.2 Shift Register

The 16-bit shift register (SR) is effectively extended by a 4-bit GUARD register (GD). GD can be enabled to clock when SR is clocked (Section 6.7).

On a right shift, the contents of SR are shifted right one, with the low bit of BMUX entering the high bit of SR, and the low bit of SR entering the high bit of GD if GD is enabled for clocking.

On a left shift, the contents of SR are shifted left one, with the high bit of SR entering SENDMUX and the high bit of GD *or* D(C) shifted into the low bit of SR.

Two of the *RES* bits (Section 6.7) determine the action of SR when clocked: i.e., no shift, shift left, shift right, or accept ALU output. The D and SR combination can therefore be used to effect shifts of 32-bit numbers. For example, when AMUX transmits D directly through BMUX ($AMUX = 0$, $BMUX = 0$), and CMUX effects a left shift of 1 ($CMUX = 0$), then D can receive D left shifted 1, with the high order bit of SR entering SENDMUX (if SR is clocked) and thus the low order bit of D. If the high order word of a 32-bit number was previously placed in D, and the low order word in SR, and if *RES* specifies a left shift of SR, then a single bit left shift of the 32-bit D, SR occurs. Similarly, if $AMUX = 0$, $BMUX = 0$ and $CMUX = 1$ (right shift), the low bit of BMUX (i.e., the low bit of D) enters the high bit of SR as SR is right shifted one, and a single right shift of the 32-bit D, SR occurs. This shift can be arithmetic or logical depending on D(C) selection.

In Section 6.9 we will show how the D and SR combination is used to implement a 16x16 bit MULtiply instruction yielding a 32-bit result.

6.5.3 Shifting Summary: Shift Tree vs. Shift Register

The ST can effect multiple right shifts of D in a single microcycle, with low order bits falling off so as to produce a 16-bit result. Alternatively, it can shift D one bit left. The D, SR combination can effect single bit left or right shifts of a 32-bit longword in a single microcycle.

6.6 DATAPATH INPUT/OUTPUT

The data path components described so far perform arithmetic/logical operations on data located in the A, B, or C scratchpads, or in the D or SR registers. How does data enter the datapaths from main memory? How does the microprogram access main memory data? Where are MAR and MDR, described in Sections 2.5.1 and 3.5.4?

These questions are answered as follows: If the *CLKBA* microfield is set to 1, then a 16-bit *virtual* address of requested data will be loaded into the BA register from the specified A bus source at P1. If a DATA-in is then initiated, the data at the address pointed to by the BA contents, generally found in main memory or cache, will be written into the CSP at P3 of the *following* microcycle (if the *WRCSP* field is unity). By convention, appropriate microfields are set up such that CSP[15] is selected as the MDR to receive the incoming data. Note that if the data requested is not in the cache (i.e., it's in main memory) a "pulse suppress" signal is automatically generated which prevents any clock pulses until the UNIBUS fetch cycle is complete. Incoming data can simultaneously be loaded into the IR by setting appropriate microfield bits.

Similarly, when data is to be output to memory (from the D register), cache update begins at P3 of the same microcycle as CLK BA, and P3 of the following microcycle is suppressed until memory update is complete.

Thus, the BA register is the 11/60 MAR, while CSP[15] serves as the MDR.

6.7 THE RESIDUAL CONTROL CONCEPT

Certain information remains static, or unchanged, across a sequence of microcycles. For example, during a multiple right shift of a 32-bit number, as implemented by the SR and ST in conjunction with D, the SR remains in the right shift mode and D(C) is *always* selected as either 0 (logical shift) or the ALU sign bit (arithmetic shift). Thus, the SR control field is in a "residual control register" (RES) whose contents are altered only when the action of the SR and GD registers in future microcycles is to change from that of previous microcycles. In summary, signals which, statistically, need be changed relatively infrequently are controlled "indirectly" via registers rather than by microfield bits.

6.8 MICROINSTRUCTION SEQUENCING AND BRANCH MICROTESTS (BUTS)

PDP-11 instructions are, in the absence of branches, executed sequentially. In contrast, each PDP-11/60 *microinstruction* contains the address of the next microinstruction to be executed in the 9-bit micropointer field (*UPF*). At execution time, the contents of *UPF* are subject to modification for branch purposes. Since the 11/60 can effect overlapped fetch (i.e., the fetch of the next microinstruction may begin during the execution of the current microinstruction, Section 6.10) errors are conceivable unless special programming techniques are used when results of the current microinstruction may dictate that a branch occur.

6.8.1 Microbranching

The 5-bit microbranch field (*UBF*) provides control signals for a branch multiplexer (BUTMUX) whose *output* is OR'ed with *UPF* to form the next microaddress (NUA). Input to the BUTMUX are various machine states. Thus, for example, when BUTMUX output is all 0's, NUA = *UPF*. The logical OR operation implies that, since 1's in *UPF* will always appear as 1's in NUA, the choice of the target microaddress affects the extent to which that target address may be altered by the BUTMUX output (Fig. 6-19).

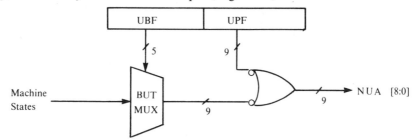

Fig. 6-19 Formation of Next Micro Address (NUA) by UBF, BUTMUX, and UPF.

A different branch microtest (BUT) is associated with each of the 32 possible values of *UBF*. Some BUT's (active BUT's) cause changes to certain machine states as well as effecting NUA alteration. NUA formation for the next microinstruction occurs at the start of the current microinstruction; fetch of the next microinstruction begins well before the end of the current microinstruction. This implies that the conditions required for a BUT to effect a conditional branch (i.e., to affect formation of NUA) must be set up in the microcycle *previous* to that in which NUA is formed. Thus test conditions "settle" in microcycle 1, the conditions are tested and NUA formed via a BUT code in microcycle 2, and the microinstruction executed during microcycle 3 will be that dictated by the resultant conditional microbranch.

6.8.2 Normal BUT's

Normal BUTS select certain fields to provide potential *n*-way branches. Again, since a 1 in the *UPF* will not be affected by an OR with any other field, the microprogrammer can decrease branch possibilities by selection of the intial target microaddress. Some of the normal BUTS are:

1. [*UBF* = 0] BUT(CASE) provides a potential 16-way branch using the 4 LSB's of SR as BUTMUX output.

2. [*UBF* = 1] BUT(DOP), used to decode double operand PDP-11 instructions, provides a potential 16-way branch using the 4 MSB's of the IR as BUTMUX output.

3. [*UBF* = 3] BUT(SOP), used to decode single operand PDP-11 instructions, provides a potential 16-way branch using bits 6 through 9 of the IR as BUTMUX output.

4. [*UBF* = 12] BUT(GUARD), used in checking shift operations, provides a potential 4-way branch using bits 2 and 3 of the GUARD register as BUTMUX output.

Other normal BUT's are available, and some will be examined in later examples.

6.8.3 Active BUT's: the Counter

Active BUT's also cause ORing of the BUTMUX output with *UPF*, for potential *n*-way branches; however, these BUT's also cause some change in machine state. The most interesting BUT, for our purposes, is BUT(COUNT).

The presence of the counter in the PDP-11/60 datapaths enables the microprogrammer to effectively augment any microinstruction with a SOB-like action. That is, an 8-bit negative number is loaded into the counter; then, every time BUT(COUNT) is specified, the counter is tested, then incremented. A test result of all 1's causes a 1 to be OR'ed with the LSB of *UPF*, with a possible 2-way microbranch. As we shall see, this enables the powerful and time efficient construct of a single microinstruction branching onto itself. This has applications in effecting multiplication and variable multi-bit shifting of a 32-bit word.

6.9 PARALLELISM IN MICROCODING: THE MUL INSTRUCTION

As we have noted earlier (Section 5.2.4), signed numbers cannot be multiplied directly by a simple shift/add algorithm. Thus, we shall first consider inplementation of the computational kernel of the MUL instruction via the D and SR registers.

6.9.1 MUL via D Register, Shift Register, and Shift Tree

Let us assume that the *unsigned* magnitudes of the multiplicand (MAND) and multiplier (MIER) have been stored in R(T), a temporary register, and in the SR, respectively. Further, we shall also assume that the counter has been loaded with −16 and RES with the code for SR right shift when clocked. Figure 6-20 shows the microinstruction flow during the 16-step inner loop. In each step of this inner loop sequence, the *current* microinstruction effects the shift or shift/add as determined by the test carried out by the bit test of the *previous* microinstruction.

Hence, each inner loop microinstruction effectively carries out a conditional 16-bit add, a 1-bit right shift of a 32-bit integer, a test for a 1 or 0 in the low bit of the 32-bit integer and a conditional branch based on the result, and an increment of an 8-bit counter with a conditional branch based on that result The parallelism inherent in microprogrammed control of the powerful micromachine is therefore vividly demonstrated.

The sequencing of the microinstructions of Fig. 6-20 may be explained as follows:

1. The first microinstruction zeros the D register and does a conditional branch to one of the next pair by testing the low bit of the MIER, which has been loaded into SR. *Go to 2.*

2. The next *pair* of microinstructions, the first of the inner loop, implement D ← D + R(T) or D ← D + 0. The pair member executed depends upon the low bit of the MIER as detected in the first microinstruction. The SR is also shifted one right with zero entering the high bit of SR. If the incremented COUNT < 377 − which must be the case − a conditional branch to one of the next pair of microinstructions is executed based upon the low bit of SR, i.e., the 2'nd LSB of the MIER. *Go to 3.*

3. The *second pair* of microinstructions implement D ← D/2 + R(T) or D ← D/2 + 0. The pair member executed depends upon the low bit of the SR as detected in the previous microinstruction. The SR is also shifted one right with the bit which "fell off" D entering the high bit of SR. A conditional branch on the low bit of the MIER is then implemented, with control transferred to one of the *second* pair of microinstructions (incremented COUNT < 377) (*Go to 3.*) or to one of the *third* pair of microinstructions (incremented COUNT = 377) (*Go to 4.*). *One* or the *other* of this second pair is executed during each of the 15 cycles required for the counter to reach 377.

```
                  ALU/GENERATE ZERO,           ;ALU OUTPUT = 0
                  CLKD/YES,                     ;D ← 0
                  WHEN/P2-T,                    ; AT P2-T
                  BEN/BASCON, BSEL/MD,          ;MD ← 0
                  COUT/ALU00,                   ;COUT ← ALU0 = 0
                  UBF/CASE                      ;BRANCH ON LOW BIT OF SR
SR0=0                    V                 SR0=1
 . . . . . . . . . . . . . . . . . . . . - . - . . . . .
 .                                        .
 V                                        V
ALU/A-PLUS-B,                            ALU/A-PLUS-B,
BEN/BASCON,                              BEN/BSPHI,
BSEL/ZERO,                               BSEL/3,RIF/6,
AEN/CMUX,                                AEN/CMUX,
AMUX/DIRECT,                             AMUX/DIRECT,
BMUX/DIRECT,                             BMUX/DIRECT,
ASEL/DIRECT,                             ASEL/DIRECT,
COUT/COUT15,                             COUT/COUT15,
CLKD/YES,WHEN/P3-T,                      CLKD/YES,WHEN/P3-T,
CLKSR/YES,                               CLKSR/YES,
UBF/SR[1:0]#COUNT-IS-377                 UBF/SR[1:0]#COUNT-IS-377
            .                                         |
            V                                         V
   .-.-.-.-.-.-.-.-.-.-.-.-.-.-.-.-.-.-.-.-.-         |
   .                                         |        |
   V                                         V        V
. . . . . . .>  SR0=0  ← - - - - - - - - - .  . . . . . . . . . .> SR0=1  ← - - - - - - - -
.                             | .                                                          |
.    ALU/A-PLUS-B,            | .   ALU/A-PLUS-B,                                           |
.    BEN/BASCON,              | .   BEN/BSPHI,                                              |
.    BSEL/ZERO,               | .   BSEL/3,RIF/6,                                           |
.    AEN/CMUX,                | .   AEN/CMUX,                                               |
.    AMUX/DIRECT,             | .   AMUX/DIRECT,                                            |
.    BMUX/DIRECT,             | .   BMUX/DIRECT,                                            |
.    ASEL/RIGHT-1,            | .   ASEL/RIGHT-1,                                           |
.    COUT/COUT15,             | .   COUT/COUT15,                                            |
.    CLKD/YES,WHEN/P3-T,      | .   CLKD/YES,WHEN/P3-T,                                     |
.    CLKSR/YES,           - - ← -   CLKSR/YES,                                              |
.    UBF/SR[1:0]#COUNT-IS-377 .  |  UBF/SR[1:0]#COUNT-IS-377                                |
.                             .  |            |                                            |
.                             V  .  |          V                                           |
. . . . . .<. . . . . . . . . . . . . .>. . . . .   - - - - - - ← - - - - - - - - - - →- - - - - - - - - -
.                    . COUNT-IS-377            |  COUNT-IS-377
.                    .                         |
V                    V                         V
.-.-.-.-.-.-.-.-.-.-.-.-.-.-.-.-.-.-.-.-.-.`.-         |
.                                                      |
V  SR0=0                                 V  SR0=1
```

Fig. 6-20 Microinstructions for inner loop of MUL instruction.

206

4. The *third pair* of microinstructions (not shown), are similar to the second pair. They implement $D \leftarrow D/2 + R(T)$ or $D \leftarrow D/2 + 0$. The pair member executed depends upon the low bit of the SR as detected in the previous microinstruction. The SR is also shifted one right with the bit which "fell off" D entering the high bit of SR. This pair implements the final shift/ conditional add of the MUL inner loop. Control is transferred to the next microinstruction in the MUL sequence, that is, the first of the final phase.

Thus we have seen that the parallelism inherent in the datapaths of a machine like the 11/60 enables powerful code to be written, but that care must be taken to ensure correctness.

6.9.2 MUL via D Register and Shift Tree

In Section 6.5.1 we noted that the contents of the D register could be shifted right up to 14 places, a number in the B scratch pad added to or subtracted from the result, *and* the final 16-bit result put back in D in a single microcycle. This means that, using Booth's algorithm as per Section 5.2.4, a 16-bit multiply can be effected in an average of 5.33 microcyles if a custom microsubroutine is written for each desired multiplier. This precludes use of the technique in general but suggests that in cases when only a few different multipliers are needed *and* these multipliers do not change with time (or change infrequently) that the technique is indeed useful. In fact, many digital signal processing algorithms satisfy these requirements and, in Section 10.7, application of microprogramming to DSP software will be discussed.

6.10 IMPLEMENTATION OF THE PDP-11 INSTRUCTION SET ON THE PDP-11/60

We have already see how the *E*-phase of some PDP-11 instructions can be implemented using the 11/60 datapaths. What about the *I*- and *O*-phases?

6.10.1 I-phase

The *first* microinstruction of the *I*-phase is FET01:

```
ALU/A-PLUS-B,                         ;SELECT ALU ADD
AEN/ASPLO,ASEL/1,RIF/7,               ;SELECT R7 ON "A" BUS
BEN/BASCON,BSEL/TWO,                  ;SELECT CONSTANT "2" IN CSP
CLKBA/YES,                            ;BA ← R7 AT P1 (DEFAULT)
CLKD/YES,WHEN/P2-T,                   ;D   ← R7 + 2 AT P2-T
MOD/CLKSP,WRSP/A AND B,               ;WRITE D INTO ASP AND BSP
HILO/LO,WRSEL/USE A ADDRESS,          ;LOW SECTION, USING ASP ADDR
                                            ;DONE AT P3 (DEFAULT)
BGB/YES,BUSBOX/YES,                   ;INITIATE A DATA-IN CYCLE TO READ
BUSCODE/DATI-CLKIR                    ;DATA ADDRESSED BY BA INTO IR, MDR
```

That is, the copy of the PC in the ASP is clocked into the BA register at P1; the constant "2" from the CSP is added to the PC by the ALU and the result (i.e., updated PC) clocked into D at P2-T and rewritten in both scratch pads at P3, using the A bus address; and a DATA-in cyle is initiated with the data addressed by the BA (old PC) to be read into the IR *and* MDR. Thus, in the 11/60, the *I*-phase described in Section 3.5.4 is initiated in a *single* microinstruction.

The data is actually received in the IR and MDR during the *second* microcycle, a "null" microinstruction, FET02. The microcycle is automatically extended if the data is not in the cache.

The *third* microinstruction, FET03, is a BUT(INSTR1) which performs a hardware decode and approximately 75-way branch to a microaddress which depends on the instruction to be executed. FET03 also updates the PC (PC ← PC+2), initiates a DATA-in to the MDR, and checks to see if the word being fetched is the next *instruction*, as opposed to a *data word* for the current instruction (e.g., MODE 6, 7). If an instruction fetch is underway, the DATA-in is changed to a DATA-in, CLK-IR so that the data being fetched will be loaded into the IR as well as the MDR. Thus, for certain machine language PDP-11 instructions, FET01 of the *next* instruction is done at the same time as FET03 of the *current* instruction, performing instruction overlap and saving time. In the next section, we will assume that a mode 6, register 7, SRC operand has been specified (Relative Mode) so that an offset word rather than a new instruction is on its way to the MDR.

6.10.2 O-phase

In order to calculate the effective address of the operand, the offset word and the current PC are added. The result is then placed in the BA register and a *DATA-in* is issued to initiate operand fetch:

```
I1:     ALU/A-PLUS-B,                    ;ALU FUNCTION ADD
        AEN/ASPLO,ASEL/1,RIF/7,          ;SELECT PC ON "A" BUS
        BEN/BASCON,BSEL/MD,              ;SELECT MDR ON "B" BUS
        CLKSR/YES,WHEN/P2-T              ;SR ← PC + MDR

I2:     AEN/XMUX,ASEL/SR,                ;SELECT SR ON "A" BUS
        CLKBA/YES,                       ;BA ← SR
        BGB/YES,BUSBOX/BUS,BUSCODE/DATAI ;ISSUE DATA-IN REQUEST

I3:     BEN/BASCON,BSEL/MD,              ;SELECT MDR ON "B" BUS
        WRSCP/YES                        ;MD ← SRC OPERAND
```

Thus a relative mode SRC operand fetch has required four microinstructions (FET03 and I1-I3) involving two reads from "memory", offset and operand. These are in addition to the two microinstructions involved in the *I*-phase, FET0 and FET02.

6.10.3 E-phase

The SRC operand is now in MDR, and the execute phase must occur. It should be obvious to the reader, at this point, that the *E*-phase operation can range from a single cycle (for those instructions whose operation can be carried out directly by the ALU) to many cycles (for multi-phase operations, such as MUL, DIV, ASH/ASHC, and "warm" floating-point instructions).

6.11 CONCLUDING REMARKS

We have examined many of the resources available at the 11/60 micromachine level, and shown some examples of how these "tools" are used to implement various operations, including fragments of PDP-11 instructions. We have *not* explored the microsubroutine capability of the 11/60 or the sophistication of the many BUT's.

It should be clear, however, that microprograms are more complex than macro- or machine language programs. This is primarily because the microprogrammer must keep track of multiple events occurring during a single microinstruction, and, for maximum speed, he must incorporate overlap between adjacent microinstructions. In Chapter 10, the use of microprogramming for speed enhancement will be demonstrated. Another application of microprogramming is in computer emulation. Given the proper microprogram, the 11/60 may be made to appear to a macroprogram to be *any desired machine*. For, example, a PDP-11/60 has been microprogrammed to emulate a PDP-8

EXERCISES

1. Suppose that the signals shown here are inputs to the circuits of Fig. 6-10. What are the outputs A and B for that circuit? Note: Each pulse of unit width.

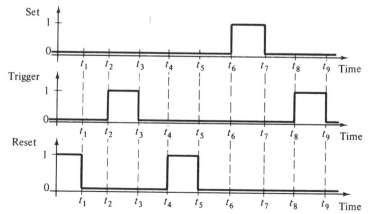

2. Develop a truth table for a full-adder. Write the logical equations using the truth table.

3. Using the simple computer of Fig. 6-16, develop a microsequence·for a one-address instruction to load the accumulator from memory (LDA) of the form

4. Compare and contrast the microsequences in control memory to the instruction sequences in the main memory. What differences, if any, are there between micro-programming and programming?

5. In the VAX-11/780, about half the microcode which defines the VAX instruction set is resident in a read-only memory (ROM) while the other half is read into a *writeable control store* (WCS) from a floppy disc every time the machine is turned on. What are the advantages to this scheme? Why would it not be useful to read in *all* the microcode using this technique?

6. Explain the utility of the 11/60 *next microaddress* (NUA) specification technique with respect to correction of microcode errors.

REFERENCES

For a different approach to the understanding of computer fundamentals, readers may wish to peruse through the earlier books by Gear (1974), Stone (1975), and Abrams and Stein (1973). Specified books on logical design [Phister (1959)], computer architecture [Foster (1970)], microprogramming [Husson (1970)], and system principles [Hellerman (1967)] may also be consulted, if the reader wishes a thorough in-depth treatment. The microprogramming sections are based upon Jackson's 11/60 Microprogramming Specification (1977), which is much more detailed than the overview presented here.

7

Input/Output Programming

Being able to program a computer to do calculations is of little use if there is no way of inputting data to the machine and getting the results of the computation from the machine. A programmer must, therefore, be provided with the means to transfer information between the computer and the peripheral devices that supply input or that serve as a means of output.

In order to perform an I/O function, the programmer must specify what the data are, where they are to go or come from, and how the I/O device is to be controlled. Depending on the computer being utilized, the I/O function may require the CPU to wait until the I/O operation is complete, or the I/O function may allow the CPU to go on and process other functions while the operation is being performed. When the I/O function holds up the CPU, we say that the I/O operation is *interlocked* with the CPU. When both can be performed simultaneously, we say that I/O is *concurrent* with computation.

Concurrent operation is becoming the standard mode for most minicomputer systems. This mode takes several forms. In one form, the concurrent I/O function can operate on data words one at a time. During the operation, the data word is held temporarily in a special register, such as the accumulator.

In another form, the I/O function operates directly between memory and the I/O unit. This mode of operation requires a separate path [called a *direct memory access* (DMA) path] between the memory and the I/O unit. The DMA allows the I/O function to be performed with a minimum of dependency on the part of the CPU.

A third mode of operation allows a large block of I/O information to be passed between an I/O unit and the memory. As support for such *block transfers,* special registers are provided for holding a count of the number of words yet to be transferred, the current I/O unit and memory address of the data word being transferred, and the data. Once initiated by an I/O instruction, block transfers run concurrently and independently of the CPU until they are completed (i.e., the word count goes to zero or an addressing error occurs).

Whenever there is a DMA path as well as a CPU path to memory, conflicts may arise. Because the I/O requests for memory are time dependent, occur infrequently, and are of short duration, the I/O request is given preference over the CPU request. Such preferential treatment is called *cycle stealing* in that the I/O unit is granted memory cycles at the expense of the CPU.

It should be fairly obvious from this brief introduction that with the various possibilities, I/O programming is very machine dependent. The complexity of the I/O system determines the corresponding complexity of the I/O programming. On the PDP-11, the programming of I/O devices is extremely simple, and no new I/O instructions are necessary for dealing with input/output operations.

The key to the simplicity of I/O programming is the UNIBUS, described in Chapter 3. The UNIBUS permits a unified addressing structure in which control, status, and data registers for *peripheral devices* are *directly* addressed as memory locations. Therefore, all operations on these registers, such as transferring information into or out of them or manipulating data with them, are performed by normal memory reference instructions.

7.1 BASIC INPUT/OUTPUT PROGRAMMING AND OPERATIONS

The use of memory reference instructions on peripheral device registers greatly increases the flexibility of I/O programming. For example, information in a device register can be compared directly with a value and a branch made on the result:

```
CMPB    @#TKB,#'Y       ;IS CHARACTER = Y?
BEQ     YES             ;BRANCH IF SO
```

In this case the program looks for a "Y" in the keyboard data buffer (TKB) and branches if it finds it. There is no need to transfer the information into an intermediate register for comparison.

When the character is of interest and is to be saved, a memory reference instruction can transfer the character into a user buffer in memory or to another peripheral device. The instruction

```
MOVB    @#PRB,LOC       ;SAVE CHARACTER IN MEMORY "LOC"
```

transfers a character from the paper tape reader buffer (PRB) into a user-defined location.

Another aspect of I/O programming is that arithmetic operations may be performed on a peripheral device register that is used for both input and output.

Thus there is no need to funnel all data transfers, arithmetic operations, and comparison through other words or general-purpose registers. Instead, the peripheral device register can itself be treated as an accumulator.

7.1.1 Device Registers

All peripheral devices are specified by a set of registers that are addressed as memory and manipulated as flexibly as an accumulator. For each device, there are two types of associated registers:

1. Control and status registers.

2. Data registers.

Each peripheral has one or more control and status registers (CSR's) that contain all the information necessary to communicate with that device. The general form shown in the table which follows does not necessarily apply to every device, but is presented as a guide. Many devices require less than 16 status bits. Other devices will require more than 16 bits and therefore will require additional status and control registers. The bits in the control and status registers are *generally* assigned as shown below.

Each device has at least one buffer register, besides the CSR registers, for temporarily storing data to be transferred into or out of the computer. The number and type of data registers is a function of the device. The paper tape reader and punch use single 8-bit data buffer registers. A disk would use 16-bit data registers and some devices may use two 16-bit registers for data buffers.

7.2 BASIC DEVICE FUNDAMENTALS

The most basic peripheral devices commonly attached to a PDP-11 are the terminal (e.g., a DECwriter or ASR-33 Teletype), a high speed paper tape reader/punch (e.g., DEC PC-11) and a mass storage magnetic medium device (e.g., RK05, RK06/7, or RL01 DECpack disc drive; RX01 floppy disc drive; or DECtape). Note that the ASR-33 contains a keyboard/tape reader and a printer/tape punch. The ASR-33 operation will be described but the keyboard/printer operation subset is valid for any terminal connected to the computer console device interface.

7.2.1 Terminal Keyboard/Reader

The terminal control contains an 8-bit buffer (TKB) which assembles and holds the code for the last character struck on the keyboard or read from the tape. Upon program command, the contents of the TKB may be transferred in parallel to a memory location or a general register.

General Bit Assignments for Peripheral Devices

Bit	Name	Description
15-12	Errors	Generally, there is an individual bit associated with a specific error. When more bits are required for errors, they can be obtained by expanding the error section in the word or by using another status word. Generally, bit 15 is the inclusive OR of all other error bits (if there is more than one). All errors are generally indicated by individual status bits.
11	Busy	Indicates that device is in midst of operation.
10-8	Unit select	Some peripheral systems have more than one device per controller. For example, a disk system can have multiple drives and an analog-to-digital converter can have multiple channels.
7	Done or Ready	The register can contain a DONE bit, a READY bit, or a DONE-BUSY pair of bits, depending on the device. These bits are set and cleared by the hardware, but may be interrogated by the program to determine the availability of the device. The position of the DONE bit is significant. A byte test of the register low byte will clear the N bit if bit 7 is low and raise the N bit if bit 7 is high.
6	Interrupt Enable	If bit 6 is set, an interrupt will occur as a result of function completed or error condition.
5-4	Memory Extension	Will allow devices to use full 18 bits to specify address on UNIBUS.
3-1	Device Function	Specify operations that a device is to perform. For example, a paper tape read function could be "read a character" or a disk operation could be "read a block of words from memory and write them onto the disk".
0	Enable	When set, this bit enables the device to perform its designated function.

When a terminal key is struck, the corresponding character is assembled into TKB and, when this is completed, the DONE bit is set. Alternatively, on the ASR-33 Teletype, a character is read from the low-speed reader by setting the teletype reader enable bit, (RDR ENB), to a 1. This sets the busy bit (BUSY) to a 1. When a teletype character starts to enter, the control deenergizes a relay in the teletype unit to release the tape feed latch. When released, the latch mechanism stops tape motion only when a complete character has been sensed and before sensing of the next character is started. When the character is available in the buffer (TKB), the busy bit (BUSY) is cleared and the done flag (DONE) is set. The ASR-33 TKB must be read within 18 milliseconds of DONE to ensure that there is no loss of information.

Terminal Keyboard/Reader (ASR-33 only) Status Register (TKS)

Bit	Name	Description
15-12		Not used.
11	Busy	Indicates that the terminal control is receiving a start bit or information bits. Read only.
10-8		Not used.
7	Done	Set when character available in buffer. Cleared when data buffer is referenced (e.g., data is picked up). Causes interrupt when bit 6 is set. Read only.
6	Reader Interrupt Enable	Enables interrupt to occur when bit 7 is set.
5-1		Not used.
0	Paper Tape Reader Enable	Enables ASR-33 paper tape reader to read one character. Write only. Cleared during read operation.

Note: Bits 11, 7, 6, and 0 are also cleared by the INIT pulse, issued when the machine is started up or when a "RESET" instruction is issued by the programmer.

Terminal Keyboard/Reader Buffer (TKB)

Bit	Name	Description
15-8		Not used
7-0	Data	Holds character read. Read only.

Any reference to TKB (as a word or byte) or TKB + 1 clears DONE. The "unused" and "write only" bits are always read as zeros. Loading "unused" or "read only" bits has no effect on the bit position. The mnemonic "INIT" refers to the initialization signal issued by ON, POWER UP, console START, or RESET.

7.2.2 Terminal Printer/Punch

On program command, a character is sent in parallel from a memory location (or a general register) to the TPB for transmission to the teleprinter/punch unit. This transfer of information from the TPB into the teleprinter/punch unit is accomplished at the normal Teletype rate and requires 100 milliseconds for completion. The READY flag in the teleprinter/punch indicates that the TPB is ready to receive a new character. A maintenance mode is provided which connects the TPB output to the TKB input so that the teletypewriter operation may be verified.

Terminal Printer/Punch (ASR-33 only) Status Register (TPS)

Bit	Name	Description
15-8		Not used.
7	Ready	Printer/punch available. Set by INIT, cleared when buffer is written into, set when printing/punching is complete. Causes interrupt if bit 6 = 1. Read only.
6	Interrupt Enable	Enables interrupt when bit 7 is set.
5-3		Not used.
2		Maintenance function.
1-0		Not used.

Terminal Printer/Punch Buffer Register (TPB)

Bit	Name	Description
15-8		Not used.
7-0	Data	Holds character to be printed or punched. Write only.

Any instruction that could modify TPB as a byte or word clears READY and initiates punching.

The four addressable registers associated with the terminal may be read or written into using any PDP-11 instruction that refers to their address. The normal address assignments for these registers are as follows:

Register	Address
TKS	177560
TKB	177562
TPS	177564
TPB	177566

When using MACRO-11, a direct assignment is made (e.g., TKB = 177562) so that the device registers may be referenced symbolically.

7.2.3 Simple Programming Example

Since the teletype keyboard is treated as a separate unit from the printer, it is necessary to write a simple program to "echo" back to the printer a character typed on the keyboard. A sample program is as follows:

```
           TKS=177560                ;DEFINE
           TKB=TKS+2                 ;STATUS
           TPS=TKS+4                 ;AND BUFFER
           TPB=TKS+6                 ;REGISTERS
ECHO:      INC    @#TKS             ;SET PAPER TAPE READER TO READ
LOOP1:     TSTB   @#TKS             ;IS CHARACTER IN BUFFER YET?
           BPL    LOOP1             ;BRANCH IF NOT
LOOP2:     TSTB   @#TPS             ;IS PRINTER FREE?
           BPL    LOOP2             ;BRANCH IF NOT
           MOVB   @#TKB,@#TPB       ;READER BUFFER TO PRINTER
           BR     ECHO              ;LOOP AGAIN
```

The value of making the DONE bit line up with the byte boundary is clearly demonstrated in this example. Had it not been set up as the sign bit of the byte, it would have been necessary to set up a mask word and do a bit test followed by a branch on zero. Since this alternative, although possible, is not as "neat" (time *and* space efficient) as the TSTB, it illustrates once again the value of properly designing a computer at both the hardware and software levels.

The setting of the reader enable bit in this program is superfluous. However, by including the instruction to do so the program is generalized in that input is allowed to come from either the keyboard or the reader. Likewise, output can go to either the printer or the punch. All that is necessary is for the user to place a paper tape in the reader and set it to "start," or to turn on the punch, and these paper tape devices become operative (in parallel) with their counterpart (e.g., the keyboard or the printer). Consequently, this one program allows for any legitimate combination of Teletype devices to be connected together.

7.2.4 An Octal Dump Program

A programming tool frequently used by assembly language programmers is the memory dump program. This program aids the user who is developing or debugging programs by providing him with an octal copy of a program or portion of a program that resides in the computer's memory.

The program shown is a memory-to-teletypewriter octal dump routine and illustrates basic I/O programming utilizing the teleprinter. It also illustrates the use of position-independent coding. The need for PIC is dictated, of course, by the necessity of being able to load the dump routine anywhere in memory.

The program begins by typing an "A" character and waiting for the user to type in an octal starting location (up to five digits). The return key causes the program to respond with a line feed and an "N" character, signifying a program request for number of words to be dumped. The second return begins the dump, which in this example is the first 16 words of the EDUMP program itself:

```
A1000
N20

001000   010706   005746   005037   177560   005037   177564   112700   000015
001020   004767   000140   112700   000012   004767   000130   112700   000101
```

A flowchart of this program is shown in Fig. 7-1, and the actual program looks as shown in Fig. 7-2.

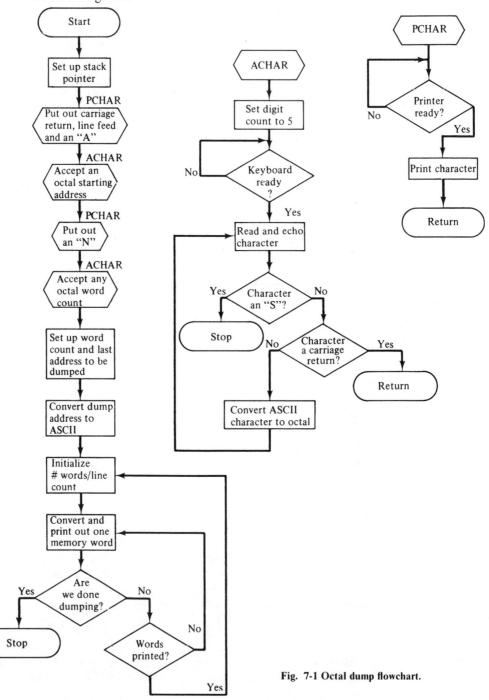

Fig. 7-1 Octal dump flowchart.

```
;                  EDUMP - AN OCTAL DUMP PROGRAM WRITTEN IN PIC
;
; INPUTS ARE N -- THE NUMBER OF WORDS,  AND A -- THE STARTING ADDRESS
;
; OUTPUT IS THE STARTING MEMORY ADDRESS
;     AND THE CONTENTS OF UP TO 8 WORDS OF MEMORY, PER LINE OF OUTPUT
;
            TKS=177560
            TKB=TKS+2
            TPS=TKS+4
            TPB=TKS+6
;
            CR=15
            LF=12
;
CORE:   MOV     PC,SP               ;SET UP STACK POINTER USING
        TST     -(SP)               ; POSITION INDEPENDENT CODE (PIC)
        CLR     @#TKS               ;INITIALIZE KEYBOARD STATUS REGISTER
        CLR     @#TPS               ;INITIALIZE PRINTER STATUS REGISTER
        MOVB    #CR,R0              ;PRINT INITIAL CARRIAGE
        JSR     PC,PCHAR            ;RETURN AND
        MOVB    #LF,R0              ;LINE FEED USING
        JSR     PC,PCHAR            ;PUT CHARACTER SUBROUTINE
ADDR:   MOVB    #'A,R0              ;PRINT AN "A"
        JSR     PC,PCHAR
        JSR     PC,ACHAR            ;ACCEPT UP TO 5 OCTAL DIGITS AS ADDRESS
        MOV     R5,R1               ;R1 CONTAINS START ADDRESS
        MOVB    #'N,R0              ;PRINT AN N FOR NUMBER OF WORDS
        JSR     PC,PCHAR
        JSR     PC,ACHAR            ;ACCEPT ≤ 5 OCTAL DIGITS
        MOV     R5,R2               ;FORM WORD COUNT NUMBER
        ADD     R5,R2               ;TO BE DUMPED
        ADD     R1,R2               ;FORM ENDING ADDRESS
        TST     -(R2)               ;LESS TWO
LOOP1:  MOV     PC,R4               ;SET UP RELATIVE ADDRESS
        ADD     #BUF-LOOP1-2+6,R4        ;OUTPUT BUFFER START ADDRESS
        MOV     #CR,R0              ;RESET PRINTER
        JSR     PC,PCHAR            ;CARRIAGE
        MOV     #LF,R0              ;FOR DUMP
        JSR     PC,PCHAR            ;INFORMATION
ARND:   MOV     R1,R0               ;CONVERT THE DUMP ADDRESS
        JSR     PC,CNVRT2           ;TO ASCII CHARACTERS
        MOV     #8.,R3              ;NUMBER OF WORDS DUMPED PER LINE
OCTAL:  MOV     PC,R4               ;SET UP RELATIVE ADDRESS OF
        ADD     #BUF-OCTAL-2+6,R4        ;BUFFER
        JSR     PC,CNVRT1           ;PRINT ONE WORD
        TST     (R1)+               ;NEXT ADDRESS TO BE DUMPED
        CMP     R2,R1               ;ARE WE DONE?
        BLO     FUDG                ;YES, PRINT A CR,LF
        SOB     R3,OCTAL            ;8 WORDS PRINTED? NO, GO BACK.
        BR      LOOP1               ;OTHERWISE START A NEW LINE
STOP:   HALT                        ;RESTING PLACE
;
;       THE PCHAR SUBROUTINE PUTS OUT ONE ASCII
;       CHARACTER WHICH IT FINDS IN R0
;
PCHAR:  TSTB    @#TPS               ;DEVICE BUSY?
        BPL     PCHAR               ;IF YES, KEEP TESTING
        MOVB    R0,@#TPB            ;PRINT A CHARACTER
        RTS     PC                  ;AND RETURN
```

```
;
;           THE ACHAR SUBROUTINE ACCEPTS AN ASCII STRING AND CONVERTS IT
;           TO A 16-BIT WORD WHICH IS LEFT IN R5
;
ACHAR:  MOV     #5,CNT              ;MAX NUMBER OF ASCII DIGITS
        CLR     R5                  ;OCTAL NUMBER IN INTERNAL FORM
AGAIN:  TSTB    @#TKS               ;DEVICE BUSY
        BPL     AGAIN               ;IF SO WAIT
        MOVB    @#TKB,R0            ;READ A CHARACTER
        JSR     PC,PCHAR            ;AND ECHO IT
        CMPB    R0,#123             ;TEST FOR AN "S" = 123 (8)
        BEQ     STOP                ;FIND IT--THEN HALT
        CMPB    R0,#215             ;FIND A CR
        BEQ     L1                  ;IF FOUND THEN NUMBER IN R5
        ASH     #3,R5               ;SET UP R5 FOR NEXT DIGITS CONVERTED
        DIC     #177770,R0          ;ONLY NEED LOWER THREE BITS
        BIS     R0,R5               ;OR'ED INTO NUMBER FIELD
        DEC     CNT                 ;DECREMENT CHARACTER COUNT
        BNE     AGAIN               ;GOT 5 CHARACTERS? NO-GO BACK
        MOV     #CR,R0              ;IF YES THEN
        JSR     PC,PCHAR            ;   SEND A CR
L1:     MOV     #LF,R0              ;      AND A LF
        JSR     PC,PCHAR
        RTS     PC                  ;AND RETURN WITH VALUE IN R5
;
;           THE CNVRT SUBROUTINE CONVERTS A 16-BIT
;           WORD TO SIX OCTAL ASCII CHARACTERS
;
CNVRT1: MOV     (R1),R0             ;R0 CONTAINS OCTAL WORD TO BE CONVERTED
CNVRT2: MOV     #5,FIVE             ;ENTER HERE TO CONVERT THE CHARACTERS
L2:     MOVB    R0,R5               ;OCTAL BYTE ADDRESS OF LINE DUMPED
        BICB    #370,R5             ;STRIP OFF LOW ORDER THREE BITS
        ADD     #'0,R5              ;ADD IN ASCII ZERO
        MOVB    R5,-(R4)            ;TO OUTPUT BUFFER IN REVERSE ORDER
        ASH     #-3,R0              ;SHIFT OVER FOR NEXT THREE BITS
        DEC     FIVE                ;COUNT OCTAL CHARACTERS
        BNE     L2                  ;HAVE WE DONE 5? NO, GO BACK
        MOVB    R0,R5               ;YES, SQUEEZE OUT LAST BIT
        BICB    #376,R5
        ADD     #'0,R5              ;ADD IN ASCII BASE
        MOVB    R5,-(R4)            ;STORE IT AWAY
DUMP:   TSTB    @#TPS               ;NOW DUMP THAT WORD
        BPL     DUMP                ;WAIT UNTIL FREE
        MOVB    (R4)+,@#TPB         ;MOVE IT TO TELEPRINTER
COMP:   MOV     PC,R0               ;CALCULATE LAST BYTE ADDRESS
        ADD     #BUF-COMP-2+7,R0;   OF BUFFER
        CMP     R0,R4               ;ARE WE DONE?
        BHIS    DUMP                ;NO, PRINT ANOTHER CHARACTER
        RTS     PC                  ;YES, RETURN
FUDG:   MOVB    #CR,R0              ;PUT OUT THE CR
        JSR     PC,PCHAR
        MOVB    #LF,R0              ;AND LF COMBINATION
        JSR     PC,PCHAR
        JSR     PC,PCHAR
        JMP     ADDR                ;RETURN
;
;           CONSTANTS AND DATA BUFFERS
;
FIVE:   .WORD   0
BUF:    .BLKB   6                   ;SPACE FOR 6 ASCII CHARACTERS
        .ASCII  /  /                ;TWO SPACES WILL FOLLOW CHARACTERS
CNT:    .WORD   0
        .END CORE
```

Fig. 7-2 Octal dump program using PIC.

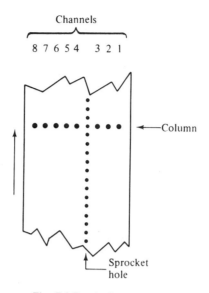

Channels

8 7 6 5 4   3 2 1

←—Column

↑

Sprocket hole

Fig. 7-3 Punched paper tape.

7.2.5 High-Speed Reader/Punch

The high-speed reader/punch consists of two units for reading and punching eight-hole perforated paper tape at, respectively, 300 characters per second and 60 characters per second. Each unit has its own status and buffer registers capable of controlling the transfer of one byte to or from the unit.

Data are recorded (punched) on paper tape by groups of holes arranged in a definite format along the length of the tape. The tape is divided into channels, which run the length of the tape, and into columns, which extend across the width of the tape as shown in Fig. 7-3.

The status register for the paper tape reader (below) is almost identical in format to the status register for the teletypewriter keyboard/reader. The difference is found in the error bit, which is set by an "out of tape" or "off-line" condition.

The paper tape punch unit behaves much like the teletypewriter keyboard/ punch, only at a higher speed. It, too, like the paper tape reader, has an error bit which is set when the punch is "out of tape" or is "off-line".

7.3 THE INITIAL LOAD PROBLEM

When a computer is first received by the customer, its memory is usually in an unloaded state. With the exception of the hardware bootstrap option (discussed later), which may have been purchased with the system, the computer "knows" nothing, not even how to accept input. The problem is that in order to load

Paper Tape Reader Status Register (PRS)

Bit	Name	Description
15	Error	Indicates one of three possible error conditions: no tape in reader, reader is off line, or reader has no power. Disables bit 0; causes interrupt if bit 6 set.
14-12		Not used.
11	Busy	Indicates that a character is in the process of being read. Cleared by INIT, set by RDR ENB, cleared when character is available in buffer. Read only.
10-8		Not used.
7	Done	Set when character available in buffer, cleared by referencing reader buffer(PRB), or by setting RDR ENA or by INIT. Causes interrupt when set if bit 6 = 1. Read only.
6	Reader	Enables interrupt on done or error when set. Cleared by INIT.
5-1		Not used.
0	Reader Enable	Enables reader to fetch one character. Clears done, sets busy, clears reader buffer (PRB). Operation of this bit is disabled if bit 15 (error) = 1; will cause immediate interrupt if set under this condition if bit 6 = 1. Write only.

Paper Tape Punch Status (PPS)

Bit	Name	Description
15	Error	Indicates one of two error conditions in punch; no tape in punch, or no power to punch. Causes interrupt if bit 6 = 1.
14-8		Not used.
7	Ready	Ready to punch character. Set by INIT, cleared by loading data buffer, set when punching complete. Causes interrupt when set if bit 6 = 1. Read only.
6	Punch Interrupt Enable	Enables interrupt when "ready" or "error" bits are set. Cleared by INIT.
5-0		Not used.

Paper Tape Reader Buffer (PRB)

Bit	Name	Description
15-8		Not used.
7-0	Data	Holds character to be read by user program.

Paper Tape Punch Buffer Register (PPB)

Bit	Name	Description
15-8		Not used.
7-0	Data	Write only. Any instruction that could modify bits 7-0 of PPB clears "ready" and initiates punching. An immediate interrupt will occur when punching is initiated if bits 15 and 6 of PRS are 1.

memory with a user program, there must already be instructions in memory for loading the user program. This seeming contradiction is often compared to lifting oneself up by one's bootstraps, and therefore gains the name of the *bootstrap* or *initial load problem.*

One possible solution to this apparent dilemma is to require the CPU to have some form of *deposit* mechanism which allows the user to deposit machine language instructions in specified memory locations. This mechanism includes a way of specifying both the data to be deposited and the address in memory of where it is to go. Early computers used switches and lights as the "console" input/output device; keypads and octal/hexadecimal displays are more common in current computers. Some larger minicomputers use a microcomputer/terminal as the console device (e.g., VAX-11/780).

Although current disk-based operating systems allow bootstrapping via a short read-only-memory (ROM) based program (which reads block zero of the system device into low memory, and then starts executing the program just read in), it is instructive to examine a paper tape bootstrap system, still of interest to the computer hobbyist, or for loading diagnostics when the system device fails.

7.3.1 Software Bootstraps

The *software bootstrap* for the PDP-11 is a sequence of instructions for loading user programs. The bootstrap utilizes a special paper tape format and self-modification in order to work. The bootstrap loader source program is shown in

Fig. 7-4. The starting address in the example denotes that the loader is to be loaded into the high locations of memory (a 16K system). It is entered by hand, using the deposit switch, into the last 14 memory words of the computer.

```
       077400                  LOAD=77400        ;DATA MAY BE LOADED NO LOWER THAN THIS
       077744                  .=77744           ;START ADDRESS OF THE BOOTSTRAP LOADER
077744 016701 START:  MOV      DEVICE,R1         ;PICK UP DEVICE ADDRESS
       000026
077750 012702 LOOP:   MOV      #LOOP-LOAD+2,R2   ;PICK UP ADDRESS DISPLACEMENT
       000352
077754 005211 ENABLE: INC      @R1               ;ENABLE THE PAPER TAPE READER
077756 105711 WAIT:   TSTB     @R1               ;WAIT UNTIL FRAME
077760 100376         BPL      WAIT              ;IS AVAILABLE
077762 116162         MOVB     2(R1),LOAD(R2)    ;STORE FRAME READ FROM TAPE
       000002
       077400
077770 005267         INC      LOOP+2            ;INCREMENT LOAD ADDRESS
                                                 ;DISPLACEMENT
       177756
077774 000765 BRNCH:  BR       LOOP              ;GO BACK AND READ MORE DATA
077776 000000 DEVICE: 0                          ;ADDR OF INPUT DEVICE
                                                 ;PUT HERE BY OPERATOR USING
                                                 ;CONSOLE DEPOSIT SWITCH
       000001                  .END
```

Fig. 7-4 Software bootstrap.

In operation, the bootstrap actually loads the data read into successive bytes located *above* the LOAD address. A sample tape input to load data starting at location 77600 and ending at 77742 would be

```
351     ─
351     │
351     │
 .      │
 .      │  ←     leader
 .      │
351     ─
177     │  ←     lower byte of starting displacement-1
 .      ─
 .      │  ←     data to be loaded
 .      ─
301     ─
035     │  ←     byte equivalent to MOV DEVICE,R1
026     │
000     ─
302     ─
025     │  ←     byte equivalent of MOV #LOOP-LOAD+2,R2
373     ─
XXX     │  ←     effective offset address between 77600 and
                 77742 where loaded program is to start execution
```

The necessity for the special leader is dictated by the need to be able to load an all-zero byte or blank tape. The bootstrap loader starts by loading the device status register address into R1 and 352(8) into R2. The next instruction indicates a read operation on the device and the following two instructions form a loop to wait for the read operation to be completed. When the data byte is ready, it is transferred to a location determined by the sum of the index word (77400) and the contents of R2, via MOVB 2(R1),LOAD(R2).

Because R2 is initially 352(8), the first data byte is moved to location 77752, incremented (INC LOOP+2), and the program branches to label LOOP. The incremented data thus becomes the immediate data to be loaded into R2 when MOV #LOOP-LOAD+2,R2 is next executed.

The leader code, plus the increment, is equal in value to the data placed in R2 during the initial pass (i.e., 352); therefore, leader code has no effect on the loader program. Each time leader code is read, the processor executes the same loop and the program remains unmodified. The first code other than leader code, however, replaces the data to be loaded into R2 with some other value which acts as a pointer to the program starting location (loading address); that is, LOAD+(R2) = 77400+(177+1) = 77600. Subsequent bytes are read *not* into the location of the immediate data but into consecutive memory locations, 77600, 77601, 77602, ..., 77742. The program will thus be read in byte by byte.

As we have seen, the INC instruction which operates on the data for R2 puts data bytes into sequential locations and requires that the value of the leader code and the offset be 1 less than the desired value in R2.

The boot overlay code will eventually overwrite the first two instructions of the loader, because the last data byte is placed in the memory location immediately preceding the loader. The first instruction (MOV DEVICE,R1) is unchanged by this action, but the second instruction is changed so as to place the next byte read, a jump offset, into the lower byte of the branch instruction. That is, the MOV loads R2 with 374 (i.e., the input byte, 373, incremented) so that the MOVB destination is now 77400+374 = 77774, the lower byte of BR LOOP. By overwriting the offset of this branch instruction with XXX, the loader can branch to the start of the loaded program or to any point within the program.

Thus, the self-modification scheme used not only loads the data but also initializes the bootstrap code and forces a jump to an address 77XXX within the program just loaded.

The key requirement for a deposited bootstrap loader is that it be short in length. Clearly, as the bootstrap program becomes longer, its usefulness decreases as frustration to deposit it in memory increases. Therefore, another technique is used to bootstrap in user programs.

As noted earlier, an alternative technique is to add a hardware bootstrap loader to the CPU so that the hardware can perform the initial program load (IPL). The IPL is activated by pushing a "load" button on the CPU, causing a predefined instruction sequence to be executed. This instruction sequence includes both the command sequence for the input device and the specific memory locations into which information is to be placed.

The form that the hardware bootstrap mechanism takes varies from machine to machine. Examples include either reading a data record into memory and executing the first (or last) instruction word read in, or executing an instruction sequence held in read-only-memory (the PDP-11 uses a ROM) or on an alterable "dead-start" panel. Regardless of the method, the result is usually the same, the loading into memory of a short program sequence called the *absolute loader*.

The *absolute loader* is a systems program for reading input records that contain machine language instructions bound to absolute memory locations. Unlike the bootstrap loader, the absolute loader is capable of reading large amounts of information into various segments of memory. The format of the information is such that each record contains

1. A word count of the number of words in the record.

2. A load address where the first and subsequent words in the record are to be loaded.

3. The words to be loaded.

4. A transfer address for the absolute loader.

Both the absolute and bootstrap loaders are systems programs. Systems programs are those programs which of themselves do not produce useful results but rather aid the programmer in accomplishing his desired objective. Systems programs are written by systems programmers whose job is the support of the users of the system. Systems programs include such things as MACRO-11 and LINK. Chapter 8 is devoted entirely to discussing some of the multitude of systems programs available to PDP-11 users.

7.4 TAPE AND DISK STORAGE UNITS

Many large-capacity storage devices may be connected to a small computer such as the PDP-11. Two such devices commonly found on this computer are the DECtape (capacity 147,968 words) and the RK05 DECdisk (capacity 1,228,800 words). Disks, in particular, are undergoing rapid evolution and capacities now range from 256 Kbytes (RX01 floppy drive) to 176 Mbytes (RP07 drive). Since these bulk storage devices require more elaborate programming and control, it is instructive to examine their characteristics and operation.

The two devices to be examined in greater detail are the DECtape and the RK05. These devices were chosen because they are representative of other more contemporary devices, such as the TU58 and RP07, and because programming of them is more straightforward.

7.4.1 DECtape Operation

DECtapes consist of 10 tracks arranged in the format shown in Fig. 7-5. On a tape the first five tracks include the timing and mark tracks, plus three data tracks. The other five tracks are identical counterparts and serve to increase system reliability through redundant recording. The timing and mark channels are recorded prior to all normal data reading and writing on the information channels. Information read from the mark channel is used during the reading and writing of data to indicate the beginning and ending of data blocks and to determine the functions to be performed by the system in each control mode. The data in one bit position of each track are referred to as a line or a character. Since six lines or characters make up a word, the tape can record 18-bit data words. Normally, the 2 extra bits are ignored.

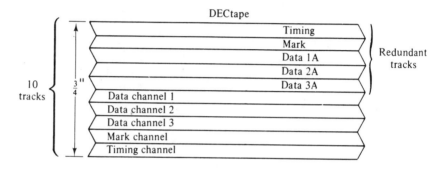

Fig. 7-5 DECtape format.

A reel of DECtape is divided into three major areas: end zones, extension zones, and the information zones. The information area consists of blocks of data, containing 256 data words per block. Altogether there are 578 blocks of information (see Fig. 7-6).

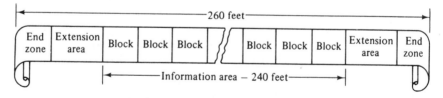

Fig. 7-6 DECtape block arrangement.

The blocks permit digital data to be partitioned into groups of words that are interrelated, at the same time reducing the amount of storage area that would be needed for addressing individual words. A simple example of such a group of words is a program. A program can be stored and retrieved from magnetic tape in a single block format because it is not necessary to be able to retrieve only a single word from the program. It is necessary, however, to be able to retrieve different programs that may not be related in any way. Thus each program can be stored in a different block on the tape.

Since DECtape is a fixed address system, the programmer need not know accurately where the tape has stopped. To locate a specific point on the tape he must only start the tape motion in the search mode. The address of the block currently passing over the head is read into the DECtape controller and loaded into an interface register. Simultaneously, a flag is set and a program interrupt can occur. The program can then compare the block number found with the desired block address and tape motion continued or reversed accordingly.

All DECtape operations are handled by the controller through programmed instructions. The controller selects the transport, controls tape motion and direction, selects a read or write operation, and buffers data transferred.

The controller can select any one of eight commands that control operation of the DECtape system. When the system is operated on-line, these commands are used for reading or writing data on the tape and for controlling tape motion. The desired command is selected by the program, which sets or clears bits 3, 2, and 1 in the command register (TCCM) to specify an octal code representing the desired command.

The commands are as follows:

Code	Mnemonic	Function
0	SAT	Stops all tape motion.
1	RNUM	Finds the mark track code that identifies the block number on the tape in the selected tape unit. Block number found is available in the data register (TCDT).
2	RDATA	Assembles one word of data at a time, transfers it directly to memory. Transfers continue until word count overflow, at which time data is read to the end of the current block and parity is checked.
3	RALL	Reads information on the tape that is not read by the RDATA function.
4	SST	Stops all tape motion on selected transport only.
5	WRTM	Writes timing and mark track information on blank DECtape. Used for formatting new tape.
6	WDATA	Writes data into the three data tracks. 16 bits of data are transferred directly from memory.
7	WALL	Writes information on tape areas not accessible to WDATA function.

All software control of the DECtape system is performed by means of five device registers. They can be read or loaded using any PDP-11 instruction that refers to their address.

Register	Address
Control and Status Register (TCST)	177340
Command Register (TCCM)	177342
Word Count Register (TCWC)	177344
Bus Address Register (TCBA)	177346
Data Register (TCDT)	177350

The bit utilization for each of these registers is shown in Fig. 7-7.

Control and status register (TCST):

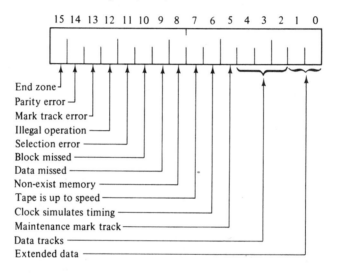

Command register (TCCM):

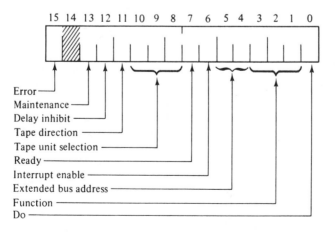

Fig. 7-7 DECtape control and status registers.

Word count register (TCWC):

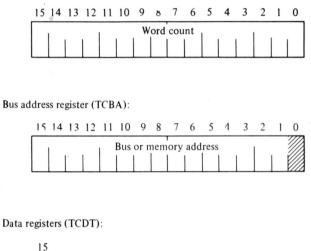

```
15  14  13  12  11  10   9   8   7   6   5   4   3   2   1   0
                            Word count
```

Bus address register (TCBA):

```
15  14  13  12  11  10   9   8   7   6   5   4   3   2   1   0
                      Bus or memory address
```

Data registers (TCDT):

```
15
                            Data word
```

Fig. 7-7 DECtape control and status registers (cont.).

7.4.2 DECtape Programming Examples

Because DECtapes are organized like disks, they are programmed in much the same fashion. Thus, before one can write in a specified block, the block must be located. A typical method to locate a block is to initiate tape motion and then search for the desired block in either the forward or reverse direction. The search consists of examining each block number as it is read and comparing it to the block number being sought. As soon as a match occurs, reading or writing to the located block may begin.

Although this procedure is relatively simple, several DECtape characteristics must be taken into consideration. First, before DECtapes can be read or written, they must be "up to speed". Thus it takes some time and hence some tape passed over the tape heads before the first block number will actually be read. Second, while waiting for a block number to read after start-up the tape may be repositioned in the end zone. This error condition requires the tape motion to be reversed so that the tape may be searched in the opposite direction. Third, and finally, having found the desired block, reading or writing must be initiated shortly thereafter, or else the transfer will be unsuccessful and a tape error condition raised.

With these points in mind, it is possible to flowchart and code the search procedure as shown in Fig. 7-8. The routine to find a specified block (1) expects

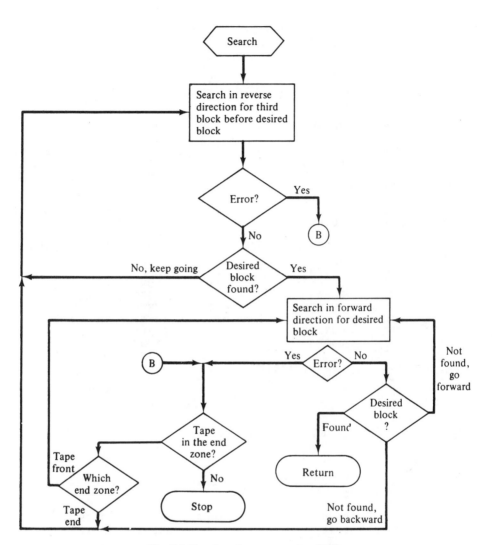

Fig. 7-8 Flowchart for programming DECtape.

the block number wanted to be legitimate and in R0, and (2) finds the block while searching in the forward direction; see Fig. 7-9.

When a specified block has been searched for and found, the next thing to do is to transfer information from or to it. The routine shown in Fig. 7-10 uses the SEARCH subroutine to read 100 words from block 50 on DECtape unit 0. The program calls SEARCH, sets up the word count and buffer address, and then waits for the read to be completed. The reader should note that although blocks contain 256 data words, any number of words (up to 256) may be specified in the transfer operation.

```
;DECTAPE SEARCH ROUTINE
;R0 CONTAINS DESIRED BLOCK NUMBER
;BLOCK FOUND IN FORWARD DIRECTION
;
        TCST=177340             ;CONTROL/STATUS REGISTER
        TCCM=TCST+2             ;COMMAND REGISTER
        TCDT=TCST+10            ;DATA REGISTER
;
SEARCH: MOV     R0,BWANT        ;SAVE BLOCK NUMBER
        SUB     #3,BWANT        ;OFFSET TO DESIRED BLOCK
        MOV     #4003,@#TCCM    ;READ BLOCK NUMBERS IN REVERSE DIR.
LOOP1:  BIT     #100200,@#TCCM  ;CHECK READY AND ERROR BITS
        BEQ     LOOP1           ;WAIT FOR READY
        BMI     ERROR           ;FOUND AN ERROR?
        SUB     @#TCDT,BWANT    ;CHECK BLOCK FOUND
        BLT     SEARCH          ;KEEP SEARCHING BACKWARDS
FORWRD: MOV     R0,BWANT        ;SAVE BLOCK NUMBER
        MOV     #3,@#TCCM       ;READ BLOCK NUMBERS IN FORWARD DIR.
LOOP2:  BIT     #100200,@#TCCM  ;CHECK READY AND ERROR BITS
        BEQ     LOOP2           ;WAIT FOR READY
        BMI     ERROR           ;HAVE AN ERROR?
        SUB     @#TCDT,BWANT    ;CHECK BLOCK FOUND
        BGT     FORWRD          ;BLOCK NUMBER TOO SMALL
        BLT     SEARCH          ;BLOCK NUMBER TOO BIG
        RTS     PC              ;RETURN WHEN BLOCK FOUND
ERROR:  TST     @#TCST          ;END ZONE ERROR?
        BMI     LOOP3           ;IF SO BRANCH
        HALT                    ;OTHERWISE HALT ON ERROR
LOOP3:  BIT     #4000,@#TCCM    ;TEST DIRECTION
        BNE     FORWRD          ;IF REVERSE, SEARCH FORWARD
        BR      SEARCH          ;IF FORWARD, SEARCH REVERSE
BWANT:  0                       ;BLOCK NUMBER
```

Fig. 7-9 DECtape search routine.

```
;ROUTINE TO READ 100 WORDS FROM
;BLOCK 50, DECTAPE UNIT 0
        TCCM=177342            ;COMMAND REGISTER
        TCWC=TCCM+2            ;WORD COUNT REGISTER
        TCBA=TCCM+4           ;BUS ADDRESS REGISTER
;
START:  MOV     #START,SP       ;INITIALIZE STACK
        MOV     #50,R0          ;BLOCK 50 TO BE
        JSR     PC,SEARCH       ;    SEARCHED FOR
        MOV     #-100.,@#TCWC   ;COMPLEMENT OF WORD COUNT
        MOV     #BUFFER,@#TCBA  ;BUFFER ADDRESS
        MOV     #5,@#TCCM       ;READ DATA FORWARD DIRECTION
LOOP:   BIT     #100200,@#TCCM  ;CHECK ERROR AND READY
        BEQ     LOOP            ;WAIT FOR READY AND NO ERROR
        BMI     ERR             ;BRANCH ON ERROR
        .
        .
ERR:    HALT                    ;HALT ON ERROR
BUFFER: .BLKW   100.            ;SAVE ROOM FOR BUFFER
```

Fig. 7-10 DECtape read routine.

232

7.4.3 Disk Operation

Generally, all disk devices are organized around flat magnetic surfaces, called *platters*, which look like pancakes. The surface is divided into concentric rings called *tracks*, with each track subdivided into *sectors*. The sector is the smallest addressable unit and generally is capable of storing many computer words (e.g., 256 words per sector). Figure 7-11 shows such a disk organization.

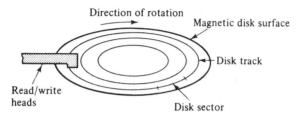

Fig. 7-11 Disk organization.

Because of the differing requirements for disk storage, many storage alternatives are available to the small computer user. The choice of disk systems spans the range from small amounts of storage and fast access to large amounts of storage and medium-speed access devices. For example, *fixed-head* disk systems have a read head for every track and are thus suited for swapping-type devices (e.g., those where the contents of memory and disk must be rapidly exchanged) and scientific applications where fast access and fast transfer are important.

If the disk platter can be removed from the disk drive mechanism, and another platter used in its place, the removable surface becomes a *disk pack*. Disk packs may consist of one or more platters, with multiple surfaces being stacked vertically on the same shaft, as shown in Fig. 7-12. By logically grouping all the tracks at the same radius on each surface into a *cylinder*, more information is accessible as a unit, thereby effectively increasing the density of the system.

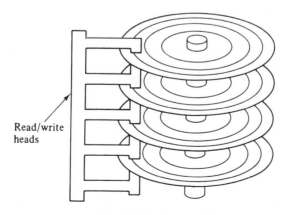

Fig. 7-12 Multisurface disk pack.

Moving-head systems have a single read/write head for all tracks on a given surface. Thus, disk transfers are often dominated by the mechanical seek time associated with the physical positioning of the head assembly over the appropriate track. In addition, there is a small electronic switching time required to select the appropriate head. The fixed-head system thus requires less time before the accessing of data, but there is a greater cost associated with it because more read/write heads are needed (i.e., one head per track). Such systems are ideal for large storage requirements where fast access times are less vital. Cost-effectiveness considerations often dictate interchangeable disk packs, possible only in moving head designs.

Since disk pack devices are manipulated in a similar fashion to simpler one-surface devices, it is sufficient to consider only the programming of devices typified by Fig. 7-11.

Regardless of the type of system, fixed or moving head, there is another delay associated with the disk called *latency*. This is the time it takes for a sector to pass under the read/write head after the appropriate head has been selected. Another name for latency is *rotational delay*, and in a sense it corresponds to the latency of a tape unit while waiting for a particular tape block to come under the tape unit's read/write heads.

Latency time can be reduced by speeding up the rotation of the disk. This also has the effect of passing more information by the read/write head in a given amount of time, thereby increasing the number of characters per second, or *transfer rate* of the device itself. Alternatively, the transfer rate may be increased by just putting more information on a track (e.g., increasing the *density* of information). All these factors, then, density, transfer rate, latency, seek time, fixed/moving head, number of disk surfaces, and so on, must be considered when selecting the appropriate disk system for a particular problem.

7.4.4 Programming a DECdisk

For simplicity, we shall consider an RK05 moving-head DECpack which has 256 words per sector, 12 sectors per track, and 200 usable tracks per surface, providing a total capacity of 1,228,800 words per disk cartridge. Software control of this DECpack system is performed by means of eight device registers. Like the registers of other I/O devices, these registers can be read or loaded using any PDP-11 instruction that refers to their address:

```
Register                                    Address
--------                                    -------
Drive Status Register (RKDS)                177400
Error Register (RKER)                       177402
Control Status Register (RKCS)              177404
Word Count Register (RKWC)                  177406
Current Bus Address Register (RKBA)         177410
Disk Address Register (RKDA)                177412
Data Buffer Register (RKDB)                 177416
```

The bit utilizations for a subset of these registers are shown in Fig. 7-13.

Control Status Register (RKCS) 777 404

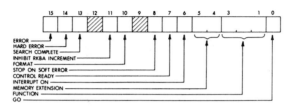

Disk Address Register (RKDA) 777 412

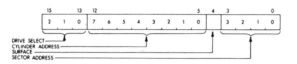

Fig. 7-13 RK05 registers.

RKWC must be loaded with the 2's complement of the number of words to be transferred, while RKBA is loaded with the memory address to/from which transfer will be made. RKBA is incremented after each transfer. Although there are more registers associated with the disk than with the tape unit, programming is easier because the search for a particular sector does not require us to start, stop or reverse the direction of the disk. Instead, the disk rotates at a constant speed, and all that is necessary is for us to set up the sector address, word count, any buffer address and then wait for the transfer to occur. This sequence of operations can be programmed as shown in Fig. 7-14.

```
;PROGRAM TO READ 512. WORDS FROM
;DISK UNIT 0, CYLINDER 4, SURFACE 1, SECTOR 7 TO MEMORY
          RKCS=177404             ;DISK CONTROL/STATUS REGISTER
          RKWC=RKCS+2             ;DISK WORD COUNT REGISTER
          RKBA=RKCS+4             ;CURRENT BUS ADDRESS REGISTER
;         RKDA=RKCS+6             ;DISK ADDRESS REGISTER
START:    MOV    #227,@#RKDA      ;DRIVE, CYLINDER, SURFACE, SECTOR
          MOV    #-512.,@#RKWC    ;WORD COUNT
          MOV    #BUFFER,@#RKBA   ;BUFFER ADDRESS
          MOV    #5,@#RKCS        ;INITIATE READ
BUSY:     TSTB   @#RKCS           ;CONTROLLER BUSY?
          BPL    BUSY             ;YES
          TST    @#RKCS           ;ANY ERRORS?
          BMI    RKERR            ;IF NEGATIVE, YES
           .
           .
RKERR:                            ;CHECK ERRORS
           .
           .
BUFFER:   .BLKW 512.
```

Fig. 7-14 Disk read program.

As in the tape operation, any number of words (limited by memory) may be transferred, since the disk address register is incremented automatically after each sector is transfered. This process continues both across cylinders, surfaces, and even across disk units. Alternatively, if only a portion of the sector (less than 256 words) is desired, the word count register is set accordingly, and only that number of words is transferred to the buffer area.

It is instructive to examine the RK05 bootstrap program, designed to read in the first sector of a system disk into memory:

```
012700          MOV     #177406,R0      ;R0 ← ADDRESS OF WORD COUNT REG.
177406
012710          MOV     #177400,(R0)    ;MOVE -256. TO WORD COUNT REGISTER
177400
012740          MOV     #5,-(R0)        ;MOVE 5. TO CSR REGISTER. (READ!)
000005
105710    T:    TSTB    (R0)            ;TEST FOR READ COMPLETION
100376          BPL     T               ;WAIT FOR IT
005007          CLR     R7              ;GO TO LOCATION 0 TO EXECUTE
                                        ;    256 WORD PROGRAM JUST READ IN
```

The bootstrap is predicated on the console RESET being issued before starting the bootstrap program. This action zeros all peripheral registers, including both RKBA and RKDA, so that words are read into memory, starting at location 0, from RK05 drive 0, starting at cylinder 0, surface 0, and sector 0. In this way, the size of the bootstrap program is reduced considerably. The final instruction, CLR R7, transfers control to memory location 0, the starting address of the 256 word program just read in from disk.

7.5 INTERRUPTS

The running time of programs using input and output routines is primarily made up of the time spent waiting for an I/O device to accept or transmit information. Specifically, this time is spent in testing or "polling" the status register of a device and waiting in a loop for a done condition:

```
TEST:     TSTB    @#TKS           ;TEST CSR
          BPL     TEST            ;WAIT FOR DONE
```

Such waiting loops waste a large amount of computer time. In those cases where the computer can be doing something else rather than waiting, the loops may be eliminated and useful routines included to take advantage of the waiting time. This sharing of a computer between two routines or tasks is accomplished through a program interrupt facility, which is standard on all PDP-11 series computers.

The value of an interrupt facility lies in the ability of the processor to respond automatically to conditions outside the system, or in the processor itself. Unusual conditions occurring at unknown times (such as I/O completion) can generate an interrupt and force the computer to execute an *interrupt service routine* (ISR) in response to the interrupting action. Thus the user need not poll or test for the occurrence of an event after the execution of each instruction, but he may write ISR's which are to be executed when such events do occur.

Basically, an interrupt is a subroutine jump invoked or "forced" by the hardware, as opposed to one entered via an explicit "jump to subroutine" software instruction. The interrupt occurs after the execution of an instruction (and before the *I*-fetch of the next instruction) and must inform the system of the cause of the interrupt. For example, when an interrupt occurs on some machines, an interrupt bit is set in an interrupt status register, indicating what condition raised the interrupt. At the same time, the CPU takes the address of the next instruction from a fixed interrupt location (possibly memory location zero) and begins execution of the interrupt analysis routine at that location.

7.5.1 Interrupt Linkages

Like subroutines, interrupts have linkage information so that a return to the interrupted program can be made. More information is actually necessary for an interrupt transfer than a subroutine transfer because of the random nature of interrupts. The complete machine state of the program immediately prior to the occurrence of the interrupt must be preserved in order to return to the program without any noticeable effects (i.e., was the previous operation zero or negative?). In this way the interrupt will be "invisible" to the interrupted program, since no information, only time, will be lost between the time the running program is interrupted and the time its execution is resumed.

7.5.2 Machine State During Interrupt

The complete machine state of the program immediately prior to the occurrence of the interrupt is generally held in a *processor status word* (*PSW*). On computers with sufficiently long memory words, the PSW includes both the condition codes and the program counter. On minicomputers such as the PDP-11, it is necessary to subdivide the PSW into two or more words in order to maintain the *processor status* (PS) and the program counter (PC).

Using one or several words, the technique for handling the interrupt is to replace the current PSW with the interrupt PSW, saving the current PSW somewhere in memory. Diagrammatically this process is depicted in Fig. 7-15. The figure shows that two memory locations are required for the interrupt process, plus a register to hold the current PSW.

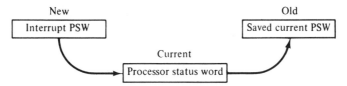

Fig. 7-15 Swapping processor status.

7.5.3 Stacking of Interrupts

One problem with this scheme is that all interrupts use the same swapping technique. Thus, should a second interrupt occur during the execution of the routine to service the first interrupt, the old PSW for the first interrupt will be overwritten and lost. To prevent this, it is necessary to disable further interrupts while the interrupt is being serviced. By allocating a bit in the PSW for interrupts enabled/disabled, it is a simple matter to have this bit on in the old PSW and off in the new PSW. Thus when the current PSW becomes the new PSW, interrupts are disabled. When a *return from interrupt* (RTI) occurs, the current PSW becomes the old or saved PSW and interrupts are once more enabled.

During the time in which interrupts are disabled, it is conceivable that other I/O conditions which would ordinarily cause an interrupt may occur. Instead of being allowed to cause an interrupt, these conditions are noted and held in the *interrupt status register*. Consequently, when interrupts are enabled, they can cause an interrupt; this guarantees their eventual service.

The interrupt status register serves many purposes. First, it indicates which device has raised an interrupt condition. Second, it saves interruptable conditions during the time that interrupts are disabled. And third, it allows the programmer flexibility in deciding what device to service next after an interrupt has been raised. In particular, this flexibility allows the programmer to decide on the relative priorities of the various interrupts. In this way, under programmer control, when several interrupts occur simultaneously, the most critical interrupt may be serviced first.

Allowing' the programmer to assign the priorities can lead to problems, however. For example, if a high-priority interrupt is raised when interrupts are disabled, there is no way the interrupt can be serviced until the interrupt analysis program is once again executed. Thus it becomes necessary to reenable the interrupt mechanism during interrupt processing. To do so requires stacking the interrupt return information (the old PSW) and setting the interrupt enable bit. However, one problem connected with the priority of interrupting devices still remains.

7.5.4 Priority Interrupts

Once the interrupt enable bit is set, any device may interrupt. The program to analyze interrupts must therefore examine all the bits in the interrupt status register to choose the highest-priority interrupt to process. Clearly, all that is needed is to allow only higher-priority routines to cause new interrupts, since interrupts at the same or lower levels can wait to be serviced. Thus for programmer convenience, the priority can be built into the hardware and a *priority interrupt* scheme can assign devices to groups within a given priority level. Part of the PSW is used to hold the current priority level, and the loading of the PSW determines the value of the priority level.

Typical PSW and interrupt status register words are shown in Fig. 7-16. These words could serve as the basis for a sophisticated interrupt scheme except for one thing. Although only higher-level priority interrupts are allowed to cause an interrupt, it still is the programmer's job to determine who caused the interrupt. A better scheme would be to let each priority group take its PSW from a different memory location. Thus when an interrupt occurred, it would be known a priori that only certain devices could have caused the interrupt.

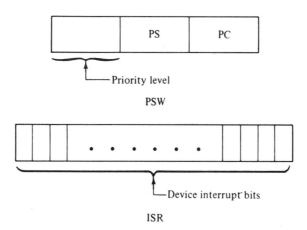

Fig. 7-16 Processor and interrupt status words.

7.5.5 Automatic Priority Interrupts

Carrying this idea to its logical conclusion, it should be possible for each device to have its own PSW. Thus, given 100 devices, there will be 100 new PSWs (and 100 old PSWs) pointing to 100 potentially different interrupt service routines (ISR's). Since each interrupt is uniquely identified, there is no need to have an interrupt status register, and hence no interrupt analysis routine is needed. The resultant savings in time and program space is absorbed, however, by the large number of PSW words that must be reserved in memory.

A modified version of this *automatic priority interrupt* scheme can be found in the PDP-11. This computer uses two words, the processor status word and the program counter, to hold all the machine state information. Upon interrupt, the contents of the PC and the PS are automatically pushed onto the system stack maintained by the SP (register 6). The effect is the same as if

```
MOV     PS,-(SP)        ;PUSH PROCESSOR STATUS
MOV     PC,-(SP)        ;AND PROGRAM COUNTER
```

had been executed.

The new contents of the PC and the PS are loaded from two preassigned consecutive memory locations called an *interrupt vector*. The actual locations are chosen by the device interface designer and are located in low memory addresses. The first word contains the interrupt service routine address (the address of the new program sequence), and the second word contains the new PS, which will determine the machine status and priority level. The contents of these vectors are determined by the programmer and may be set under program control.

After the ISR has been completed, an RTI (return from interrupt) is performed. The two top words of the stack are automatically "popped" and placed in the PC and PS, respectively, thus resuming the interrupted program. Because the interrupt mechanism utilizes the stack automatically, interrupts may be nested in much the same manner that subroutines are nested. In fact, it is possible to nest any arbitrary mixture of subroutines and interrupts without confusion. By using the RTI and RTS instructions, respectively, the proper returns are automatic.

7.5.6 Reader Interrupt Service

An example of an interrupt operation for the PDP-11 can be found in the routine to read a block of characters from the paper tape reader to a buffer as shown in Fig. 7-17. This code is written in a PIC format and includes setting up the interrupt vector (memory location 70) for the paper tape reader. There are two separate routines. The first, beginning at label INIT, initializes the word count for the interrupt service routine, then calculates the relocation factor from the offset PRSER-X-2 as follows:

If PCz is the PC that was assumed for the program when loaded at zero, and if PCn is the current PC, the calculation is

$$\text{PRSER} - \text{X} - 2 + \text{PCn} = \text{PRSER} - \text{PCz} + \text{PCn}$$
$$= \text{PRSER} + (\text{PCn} - \text{PCz})$$

since $(\text{X} + 2) = \text{PCz}$. As a result, the relocation factor, PCn – PCz, is added to the assembled value of PRSER to produce the relocated value of PRSER. The relocated value of BUFADR is computed in a similar fashion.

Then, it establishes the priority level for the reader and sets it to interrupt after a character has been read. This frees up the CPU so that other code may be executed while the buffer is being filled.

The second routine, the paper tape interrupt service routine, PRSER, is activated each time a character is received. Once activated, the routine stores the character in the buffer, updates the buffer pointer and word count, and re-enables the device if more characters are to be read. Since it is conceivable that there are less than 100 characters to be read, or a paper tape read error could occur, either of which is an error condition, a *function complete* code can be returned to indicate what has happened. In Fig. 7-18, CRCNT is used to pass back a –1 to the initiating routine to signify an error condition. The logical flow, then, of these two routines looks as shown in Fig. 7-17, and the code is as given in Fig. 7-18.

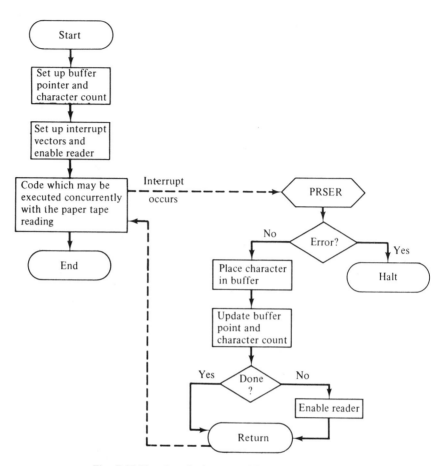

Fig. 7-17 Flowchart for interrupt driven paper tape read.

7.5.7 Priority Levels and Masking Interrupts

Within a group, any number of devices may cause an interrupt at a given priority level. Since it is conceivable that at any given time a programmer may wish to ignore some of the devices, the hardware usually includes a mechanism to mask interrupts from selected devices.

The PDP-11 uses a simple mechanism to mask device interrupts, by allowing the programmer to clear the interrupt enable bit in the device control and status register. Actually, the interrupt bit is automatically cleared each time the system is initialized (by pushing the START key or executing the RESET instruction) and must be set under program control. However, once set, the bit stays set until cleared.

Another approach to this program is to use a *mask register*. This register contains a bit for each interruptable group (or bit in the interrupt status register, if one exists), and the hardware uses the mask bits by ANDing them to the interrupt bits. Only if the result is a 1 is the interrupt allowed to occur. In effect, the mask

```
;INTERRUPT DRIVEN ROUTINE TO INPUT CHARS FROM PAPER TAPE READER
            PRS=177550                 ;DEFINE DEVICE
            PRB=PRS+2                  ;REGISTERS
;
INIT:   MOV     PC,SP                  ;INITIALIZE STACK
        TST     -(SP)                  ;TO POINT TO INIT
        MOV     #100.,CRCNT            ;SET UP CHARACTER COUNT
;
X:      MOV     PC,R0                  ;R0 ← ADDR(X+2)
        ADD     #PRSER-X-2,R0          ;ADD OFFSET TO GET ISR ADDRESS
;
Y:      MOV     PC,PTR
        ADD     #BUFADR-Y-2,PTR        ;SET UP BUFFER ADDRESS POINTER
;
        MOV     R0,@#70                ;SET UP ISR VECTOR ADDRESS
        MOV     #200,@#72              ; STATUS TO PRIORITY 4
;
        MOV     #101,@#PRS             ;SET INTR ENB AND RDR ENB
        .
        .                     CODE WHICH MAY BE EXECUTED WHILE
        .                     BUFFER IS BEING FILLED
        .
BUFADR: .BLKB 100.                     ;100 CHARACTER BUFFER
PRSER:  TST     @#PRS                  ;TEST FOR ERROR
        BMI     ERROR                  ;DO ERROR THING
        MOVB    @#PRB,@PTR             ;STORE CHARACTER IN BUFFER
        INC     PTR                    ;BUMP POINTER
        DEC     CRCNT                  ;DECREMENT CHARACTER COUNT
        BEQ     DONE                   ;BRANCH WHEN INPUT DONE
        INC     @#PRS                  ;START UP READER AGAIN
DONE:   RTI                            ;RETURN
ERROR:  MOV     #-1,CRCNT              ;RETURN ERROR CODE
        RTI                            ;RETURN
PTR:    0                              ;BUFFER POINTER
CRCNT:  0                              ;CHARACTER COUNTER
        .END    INIT                   ;END OF ASSEMBLY
```

Fig. 7-18 Interrupt driven paper tape routine (PIC).

disarms certain specified interrupts. Still, the mask only disarms interrupts within a group and does not set up any priorities between interrupts or groups.

The need for priorities is demonstrated by the following example program. This program utilizes the teleprinter and the 60-cycle clock on the PDP-11. After being loaded and started, the program types out

WHAT TIME IS IT?

to which the user responds with a four-digit number. Thereafter, the program, utilizing clock interrupts every 1/60 of a second, keeps track of the time, responding with

AT THE BELL THE TIME WILL BE: XX:XX:XX

every time a keyboard character is struck.

Two devices (keyboard and clock) are interrupt-driven. While the keyboard ISR is effecting the time printout via polled use of the printer, the clock can be interrupting to tick off another 1/60 of a second. However, the priority of the clock must be greater than that of the keyboard *and* the printout ISR if ticks are not to be lost. (That this loss of ticks can actually occur can be demonstrated by changing the priority levels set near label NOFIX in the program).

Thus, priority level is not simply a function of the device. Although each group or device has its own priority level, the running ISR program also has a *CPU priority level.* Each device that causes an interrupt to occur can raise, lower, or maintain the current priority level of the running program. As a result, if an interrupt occurs at level 7, say, and the interrupt routine does not set the new level at 7, it is quite possible for the higher-level interrupt service routine to be constantly interrupted by lower-level devices. With this in mind, it can be seen that the processor priority level as maintained in the PS word acts as an I/O device interrupt mask. Note that any program running with CPU priority "n" requires a device priority *greater than* "n" to interrupt it.

The various vector addresses and priority levels for the teletypewriter, high-speed reader/punch, and clock on the PDP-11 are as follows:

Device	Vector Address	Priority
Terminal keyboard	60/62	4
Terminal printer	64/66	4
High-speed reader	70/72	4
High-speed punch	74/76	4
Line clock	100/102	6

The example in Figs. 7-19 and 7-20 demonstrates the use of priority levels. In addition, it uses recursive programming, and it freely intermixes subroutine stacking with interrupt processing. It is therefore far from a trivial example of the power and flexibility of an interrupt facility on a small computer. A logical flow is included (Fig. 7-19) because it provides an overall picture of what the program does. Of particular interest is the clock interrupt routine, which calls on the clock increment subroutine in a recursive fashion.

To understand how the increment clock routine works, it is necessary to examine the stack after each call. Just after the line following LKINT is executed, the symbolic contents of the stack (and R0) will be

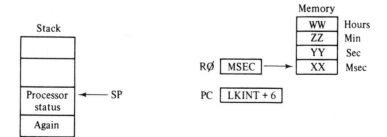

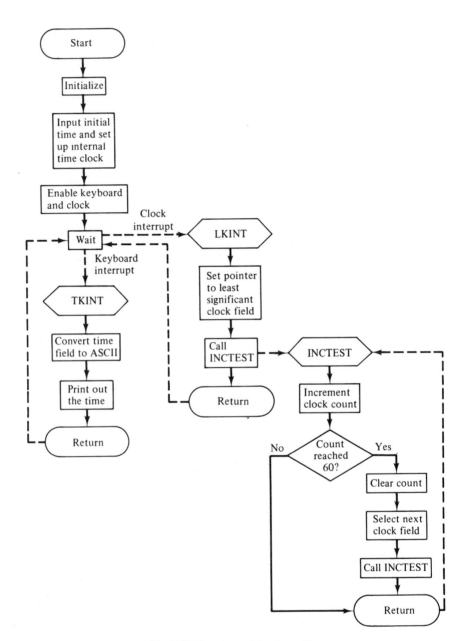

Fig. 7-19 Flowchart of the time teller.

```
                TKCSR=177560
                TKDBR=177562
                TPCSR=177564
                TPDBR=177566
                LKCSR=177546
                ;
BEGIN:   MOV     #BEGIN,SP           ;INITIALIZE SP
         CLR     TKCSR               ;INITIALIZE KEYBOARD CSR
         CLR     TPCSR               ;INITIALIZE PRINTER CSR
;
         MOV     #M1,R2              ;ASK FOR
         MOV     #EM1,R3             ;THE TIME
         JSR     PC,DPR1             ;PRINT IT OUT
         MOV     #TIME,R2            ;ADDR OF TIME FIELD  .
         MOV     #4,R1               ;COUNT FOUR CHARACTERS
         MOV     R2,R3               ;PRINT ADDRESSES
NEXTD:   INC     TKCSR               ;READ THE TIME
TST1:    TSTB    TKCSR               ;TEST FOR A CHARACTER
         BPL     TST1                ;WAIT
         MOVB    TKDBR,(R2)          ;PUT IT IN TIME FIELD
         JSR     PC,DPR1             ;PRINT IT
         TSTB    (R3)+               ;NEXT BYTE
         SOB     R1,NEXTD            ;DECREASE COUNT, KEEP GOING
         MOVB    TIME+1,HOURS        ;LSD OF HOURS
         BIC     #177700,HOURS       ;CLEAR PARITY
         SUB     #60,HOURS           ;CONVERT TO OCTAL ('0' = 60 (8))
         BIC     #177700,TIME        ;CLEAR PARITY
NEXT:    CMPB    TIME,#61            ;ANY TENS?
         BLT     AROUND              ;NO
         ADD     #10.,HOURS          ;INCREASE VALUE BY 10.
         SUB     #1,TIME             ;DEC TENS COUNT
         BR      NEXT                ;ANYMORE?
AROUND:  MOVB    TIME+3,MIN          ;GET MINUTES LSD
         BIC     #177700,MIN         ;CLEAR PARITY
         SUB     #60,MIN             ;CONVERT TO OCTAL ('0' = 60 (8))
         MOVB    TIME+2,R0           ;MUST CORRECT TENS
         BIC     #177700,R0          ;REMOVE PARITY
         MOV     #10.,R1             ;ADD 10 DECIMAL
         SUB     #61,R0              ;TEST FOR A ONE ('1' = 61 (8))
         BMI     NOFIX               ;NO TENS
         BEQ     ADD                 ;ONE TEN
MORE:    ADD     #10.,R1             ;TRY AGAIN
         SOB     R0,MORE             ;COUNT THE TENS, MORE?
ADD:     ADD     R1,MIN              ;ADD IN # OF TENS
;
NOFIX:   MOV     #200,@#62           ;LEVEL 4 PRIORITY
         MOV     #TKINT,@#60         ;FOR THE TTY KBD ISR
         MOV     #340,@#102          ;LEVEL 7 PRIORITY
         MOV     #LKINT,@#100        ;FOR THE CLOCK ISR
         MOV     #101,TKCSR          ;INIT KBD
         MOV     #100,LKCSR          ;AND CLOCK
AGAIN:   WAIT                        ;NOTHING TO DO
         BR      AGAIN               ;HANG IN THERE
; CLOCK INTERRUPT SERVICE ROUTINE ******** CPU PRIORITY 7 ********
LKINT:   MOV     R0,R5               ;SAVE R0
         MOV     #MSEC,R0            ;ADDRESS OF LS FIELD
         JSR     PC,INCTEST          ;RECURSIVE CALL
         MOV     R5,R0               ;RESTORE R0
         RTI                         ;CLOCK UPDATED
```

```
INCTEST:INC      (R0)              ;ADD ONE
        CMP      (R0),#60.         ;REACHED LIMIT?
        BNE      RETURN            ;NO
        CLR      (R0)              ;RESET FIELD
        TST      -(R0)             ;ADDR OF NEXT FIELD
        JSR      PC,INCTEST        ;CALL ME AGAIN
RETURN: RTS      PC                ;RETURN HOME
; TTY INTERRUPT SERVICE ROUTINE ********** CPU PRIORITY 4 ******
TKINT:  MOV      #M2,R2            ;PRINT OUT
        MOV      #EM2,R3           ;THE TIME
        JSR      PC,DPR1           ;MESSAGE
        MOV      #3,R3             ;NUMBER OF FIELDS
        MOV      #OUT,R2           ;OUTPUT AREA
        MOV      #HOURS,R4         ;FIRST FIELD ADDR
CNVRT:  CLR      R0                ;INITIALIZE
        MOV      (R4)+,R1          ;FIRST VALUE
LOOP:   CMP      R1,#10.           ;ANY TENS?
        BLT      ADDUP             ;NO
        INC      R0                ;YES, COUNT
        SUB      #10.,R1           ;DEC TENS
        BR       LOOP              ;DO IT AGAIN
ADDUP:  ADD      #60,R0            ;TENS IN ASCII
        MOVB     R0,(R2)+          ;STORE IT
        ADD      #60,R1            ;UNITS IN ASCII
        MOVB     R1,(R2)+          ;STORE IT
        TSTB     (R2)+             ;SKIP :
        SOB      R3,CNVRT          ;LOOP COUNT, DO IT THREE TIMES
        MOV      #OUT,R2           ;READY
        MOV      #BELL,R3          ;TO PRINT
        MOV      #101,TKCSR        ;RDR ENB
        TST      TKDBR             ;CLEAR DONE BIT
        JSR      PC,DPR1           ;YES
        RTI                        ;DONE AT LAST
; MESSAGE PRINTER *********************************************
DPR1:   CMP      R2,R3             ;ARE WE DONE?
        BHI      DPR2              ;YES
TST2:   TSTB     TPCSR             ;READY TO PRINT?
        BPL      TST2              ;NO
        MOVB     (R2)+,TPDBR       ;PUT IN BUFFER
        BR       DPR1              ;NEXT CHARACTER
DPR2:   RTS      PC                ;RETURN
; DATA ******************************************************
M1:     .BYTE    15,12             ;CR AND LF
        .ASCII   /WHAT TIME IS IT?/
EM1:    .BYTE    '
        .EVEN
TIME:   .BYTE    0,0,0,0           ;FOUR CHAR TIME
OUT:    .BYTE    0,0,':,0,0,':,0,0
BELL:   .BYTE    7                 ;STRIKE THE GONG
        .EVEN
HOURS:  .WORD    0
MIN:    .WORD    0
SEC:    .WORD    0
MSEC:   .WORD    0
M2:     .BYTE    15,12
        .ASCII   /AT THE BELL THE TIME WILL BE:/
EM2:    .BYTE    '
        .END     BEGIN
```

Fig. 7-20 Time teller routine (NON PIC).

Now, when the subroutine INCTEST is called, the picture changes to

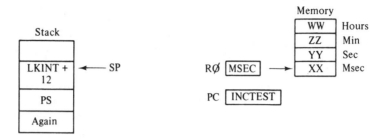

If the value in location MSEC is less than 59, it will be incremented by 1, a return made from the subroutine (e.g., the stack is popped) followed by a return from the interrupt routine (popping off the PC and PS from the stack); and the program will once again wait for an interrupt.

Suppose, however, that the value in location MSEC equals 59. In this case the increment subroutine will now set MSEC = 0, advance the pointer in R0 to point to the location SEC, and call the subroutine INCTEST recursively. At this point the picture looks as follows:

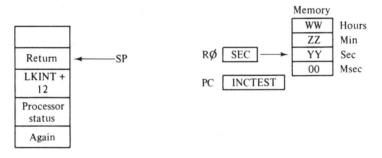

Again the value at the location pointed to by R0 is checked to see if it is 59. If it is, it is zeroed, R0 is advanced to point to the next most significant field, and the routine INCTEST is once again called recursively.

Alternatively, if the value pointed to by R0 is less than 59, we have the case discussed previously, where the value pointed to by R0 is incremented and a subroutine return is made. Since the return causes the instruction following the subroutine call to be executed and this instruction is a return from subroutine, the stack is popped twice (or more) until the return from interrupt occurs, at which point the program waits for a new interrupt to occur. The actual unwinding of the recursive calls becomes quite simple, since it only serves to restore the stack.

If the priority level of the keyboard ISR is changed to 6 or higher (e.g., MOV #300,@#62 at label NOFIX) then the clock will no longer be able to increment the time while the keyboard ISR is effecting time printout. Thus the importance of correct CPU priorities relative to device priorities.

7.5.8 Absolute vs. Relative Mode for Interrupt Vector and Device Addressing

The astute reader will have noted that some programs in this Chapter use the absolute mode for addressing of device registers and interrupt vectors, while others use relative addressing. Clearly, the need for absolute addressing in PIC programs (e.g., Figs. 7-2, 7-18) is obvious. However, it is not so clear which addressing mode is to be preferred in non-PIC programs (e.g., Fig. 7-20).

If the absolute mode is used for symbolic addressing of interrupt vectors and device registers, and the relative mode is used for direct, symbolic addressing of local, memory-based variables, then such operand specifications are *automatically* position independent. In this sense, the absolute mode is "natural" (and thus preferred) for symbolic specification of fixed addresses. Moreover, although use of sensible mnemonics for symbolic addressing of device registers is useful for enhancing clarity with respect to the intended action of the code, use of absolute mode leaves no doubt that a fixed location is being addressed. Further, because the absolute mode generates absolute addresses in an assembler listing, instructions can be visually checked for correct register or vector value without cross referencing either the assignment statement which established a value for the symbol or the symbol table. And, finally, when debugging is being carried out via an interactive, Dynamic Debugging Program (DDP, Section 8.3), with the help of an assembler listing and a linking loader "load map" (Section 8.2), then the use of absolute mode eases the task of altering references to fixed locations; an absolute address rather than a PC offset is altered when a change is made.

Thus, although relative symbolic addressing of fixed locations is *satisfactory* when a linking loader is used, absolute addressing is *preferable* from the point of view of good programming practice.

7.6 RECORDS AND BUFFERING

Although basic I/O units (teleprinter and paper tape reader/punch) operate on characters, characters per se are not exactly what the programmer wishes to input or output. Rather, I/O programming is concerned with strings of characters such as 10-digit numbers, people's names, octal representations of memory words, or lines of assembly code. In other words, the I/O consists of *records* made up of characters that have a logical connection.

Since the I/O device does not perform I/O in a record fashion, it is generally the programmer's responsibility to group characters on input and degroup them on output. *Buffers*, which are contiguous chunks of memory, act as repositories for the data records and allow the program to stream data to or from an I/O unit at a rate consistent with the I/O device. Buffers are of particular use between two I/O devices with dissimilar I/O rates. For example, if the high-speed paper tape reader is six times faster than the high-speed paper tape punch, a buffer can be used to allow simultaneous input and output, provided, of course, that a buffer terminates input and an empty buffer terminates output.

The overlap of input and output on the high-speed reader punch is shown in Fig. 7-21. Each device is running in interrupt mode at its maximum rate. Because the reader has a higher I/O transfer rate, it will finish first, followed by the punch routine emptying the buffer, and then by termination of the program.

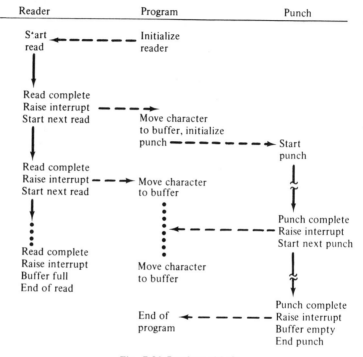

Fig. 7-21 Overlapped I/O.

7.6.1 Overlap of Computation and I/O Processing

Another use of records and buffers can be found in the overlap of computation and I/O processing. For this situation double buffering is used, so that while one buffer is being filled (or emptied), a second buffer is available to the running program. Actually, the number of buffers may be more than two, depending upon their rate of utilization by the program and the I/O device, and upon the size of the buffers. In a *balanced system*, the buffer size and number are adjusted so that computation and I/O processing are 100 percent overlapped. When the computation is less than 100 percent, the system is said to be *I/O bound*. Correspondingly, when the system is *computation bound*, the I/O utilization is less than 100 percent.

Whether a system is one way or another depends on many things, including the computer configuration, economic considerations, system load, and so on.

These considerations fall into the province of the systems programmer, who is concerned with operating systems design and performance.

7.7 INPUT/OUTPUT PROGRAMMING SYSTEMS

In order to facilitate effective utilization of I/O devices and to assist the user in writing his I/O code, most computer manufacturers provide their computer users with an *input/output programming system* (IOPS). Such a system

1. Frees the programmer from the details of dealing directly with I/O devices.

2. Provides better I/O organization and service.

3. Facilitates I/O programming through simple assembly language macros.

4. Provides conformity across various operating environments.

In addition, the programmer can use an I/O programming system to allow

1. Asynchronous I/O service.

2. Concurrent (overlapped) I/O operation.

3. Device-independent programming.

4. Blocking and buffering.

I/O programming system macros for DEC's RT-11 operating system generally fall into three categories. The first includes the *data transfer commands* such as READ and WRITE. The second category includes the *initialization commands* to OPEN and CLOSE a file and obtain the status. Finally, the third category includes the control commands such as WAIT and RESTART.

7.7.1 Example of RT-11 IOPS

An example of the use of an IOPS (under RT-11) to provide a simple input-process-output sequence would include:

1. The specification of the necessary buffers and control blocks.

2. The fetching of the necessary I/O handlers.

3. The read into the buffer and a wait for completion.

4. A check to see if the read was successfully completed.

5. The processing of the data just read.

6. A write from the buffer.

The sequence, greatly abbreviated, using the RT-11 programmed requests is as follows:

```
START:   .FETCH  #HNDLSP,#PRNAME                   ;GET PAPER TAPE HANDLER
                 .

         .READW  #AREA,#CHN0,#BUFF,#WDCT,#BLK  ;READ DATA AND WAIT
         BCS     RDERR                             ;CARRY SET IF ERROR
                 .

         PROCESS BUFFER
                 .

         .WRITW  #AREA,#CHN1,#BUFF,#WDCT,#BLK  ;WRITE DATA AND WAIT
         BCS     WDERR                             ;CARRY SET IF ERROR
                 .

PRNAME:  .RAD50  /PR/                              ;NO FILE NAME NEEDED
         .WORD   0                                 ;USE "0"
AREA:    .BLKW   10                                ;PROGRAM REQUEST BLOCK
BUFF:    .BLKW   80.                               ;DATA BUFFER
CHN0=0                                             ;CHANNEL 0
CHN1=1                                             ;CHANNEL 1
WDCT=80.                                           ;NUMBER OF DATA WORDS
BLK=0.                                             ;BLOCK TO BE READ/WRITE
HNDLSP=.                                           ;HANDER GOES HERE
```

This example shows some of the unique features and requirements of RT-11. First, the I/O device driver must be fetched and stored with the user's program. Second, some requests must include an "area" in which the macro arguments are placed. This area is pointed to by R0, and for the .READW looks like:

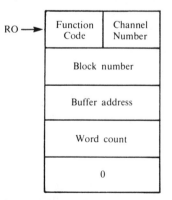

This area serves to describe the function to be performed, what logical channel it is to be performed on, which logical block to start at, where the buffer is, and how many blocks to read or write.

The reader may ask "Why not place all of this on the stack?". This could have been done, but the RT designers settled on the protocol shown here.

Note the use of the carry bit to signify an error, and hence the BCS instruction. Further processing is needed to determine which error has indeed occured. Finally, the "W" apppended to READ and WRITE means "wait". Other forms of READ/WRITE are available which do not wait, and may or may not signify when the function is complete. These are used when overlapped I/O is desired.

The following program illustrates the use of simple system macros for input/output from the system console:

```
SYSTST: .PRINT   #MESS1              ;PRINT MESSAGE #1
        MOV      #BUFF,R1            ;SET POINTER TO INPUT BUFFER
        CLR      R2                  ;RESET CHARACTER COUNTER
LOOP1:  .TTYIN   (R1)               ;GET CHARACTER
        INC      R2                  ;INCREMENT COUNTER
        CMPB     #12,(R1)+           ;END OF INPUT? (LINE FEED?)
        BNE      LOOP1               ;NO!
        MOV      #BUFF,R1            ;YES, RESET BUFFER POINTER
        .PRINT   #MESS2              ;OUTPUT RESPONSE
LOOP2:  .TTYOUT  (R1)+              ;OUTPUT NAME
        SOB      R2,LOOP2
        .EXIT
MESS1:  .ASCII   /WHAT IS YOUR NAME?/<200>
MESS2:  .ASCII   /HELLO THERE, /<200>
BUFF:   .BLKB    80.
        .END     SYSTST
```

The use of the <200> in MESS1 and MESS2 serves to terminate the message without a <CR> and <LF>. It also illustrates the use of < > to enclose an expression to be used as a single term. Finally, the < > construct serves to specify to the assembler the octal codes for non-printing characters such as tab, <CR> and <LF>.

The macros serve as a linkage to the RT-11 system. Each macro instruction results in a service call to the operating system with the particulars of what's to be done carried in the request area.

7.7.2 IOPS Linkage Problem

In a large computer system the expansion of a macro into a service routine linkage requires both a macro assembler and a linking loader. Since it is possible that neither of these exist as part of the basic software supplied with some small computer system (although they may be available as part of advanced software systems), it may become the programmer's responsibility to expand the macros into assembly language statements and to link up the program with the IOPS. Even with complete operating systems, such as RT-11, which do include a macro assembler and a linking loader, there may still exist the problem of linking up the program with IOPS. The reason this occurs is that the device drivers are generally not loaded with the small, resident operating system. Only at program execution time is the driver loaded and the connection made with the program request macro.

Thus, the technique most often used to link programs with an IOPS is through interrupt-producing machine instructions called *service calls* (SVC) or *emulator traps* (EMT). These program-initiated interrupts are handled like I/O interrupts, and result in the replacement of the current PSW by a new PSW pointing to the I/O programming system. Such SVC's or EMT's have all the advantages of subroutine calls, including arguments passing (the old PC in the PSW points to the first word in the argument list); they also facilitate the functioning of the I/O programming system in that

1. It need not save the processor state (except for the registers it uses).

2. It can operate at any priority level it wishes to.

3. It provides a direct linkage between the user program and IOPS through a fixed memory location.

The last point is clearly the most important. The trap instruction effectively eliminates the need for a linking loader, since all IOPS calls will be through EMT's, which do not require direct linkage to IOPS. Instead, IOPS need only preload its trap vector so that all EMT's will cause a transfer of control to IOPS, at which point the reason for the IOPS call can be determined. In this regard an emulator trap is analogous to the single-level interrupt system already discussed.

7.7.3 Other Interrupts and Traps

It is worthwhile to digress for a moment and point out that interrupts and traps are not associated only with I/O instructions. Indeed, interrupts may be used to

1. Indicate program faults, such as addressing errors, illegal instruction errors, and abnormal arithmetic results (e.g., after divide by zero).

2. Handle machine errors, including memory parity checks and automatically detected hardware malfunctions.

3. Flag external conditions, such as power failure and console key interruptions.

Additionally, since these interrupts cause a change in the current PSW, it is possible to utilize an interrupt-generating condition to change the *protection state* of the system (see Section 7.8).

For example, if I/O instructions are illegal in the protected or user state, they will cause an interrupt to be raised whenever the computer attempts to execute them. However, should the system be in the unprotected or monitor state, no interrupt will occur. Consequently, all I/O requests must be handled by an I/O programming system, which is activated by an SVC or EMT instruction that results in a change of state from protected to unprotected mode.

The monitor and user modes permit a structured environment by providing for two distinct states of system operation. Depending upon the state, full or limited memory addressing and instruction execution capabilities are permitted. By making the system state a bit in the PSW, a change of state can occur automatically, thus guaranteeing that all system capabilities may be made available to the interrupt service routine. In Chapter 11, where more advanced operating systems (such as multiprogrammed and time-sharing systems) are discussed, this concept of system state will be discussed more fully.

7.7.4 System Handling of a Trap Instruction

Turning back to the use of an I/O programming system, it would be well to examine how such a system might be used on the PDP-11. To do so we shall consider how the .READW macro is expanded. Assuming the same form of the instruction as before,

```
.READW   #AREA,#CHN0,#BUFF,#WDCT,#BLK
```

the macro expansion results in:

```
MOV      #AREA,R0
MOVB     #8.,1(R0)
MOVB     #CHN0,(R0)
MOV      #BLK,2(R0)
MOV      #BUFF,4(R0)
MOV      #WDCT,6(R0)
MOV      #0,8.(R0)
```

which results in the intialization of the program request area, as described previously. An EMT is then performed, transferring control to the RT monitor and thus effecting the I/O request.

7.7.5 Coroutine Example Utilizing RT-11 System Macros

In Chapter 4 it was mentioned that coroutines were used for I/O processing and represented one of the basic operations to be performed by modern operating systems. The example that follows demonstrates the use of coroutines in a double-buffer I/O overlapped with computation, performing as follows:

```
Write 01                              Write 02
Read I1         concurrently          Read I2   concurrently
Process I2                            Process I1
```

Here, O1 and O2 designate output buffers 1 and 2, and I1 and I2 are input buffers

1 and 2. The reader should recall that the JSR PC,@(SP)+ always performs a jump to the address specified on top of the stack and replaces that address with the new return address. Thus each time the JSR at B is executed, it jumps to a different location; initially to A and thereafter to the location following the JSR executed prior to the one at B. All other JSR's jump to B+2 (Fig. 7-22). It is assumed here that data processing time exceeds data read/write time.

This code, although deceptively short, is a powerful and elegant solution for the programming of double-buffer I/O overlapped with computation. It clearly demonstrates the power and capability of the small computer, on which may be developed time-sharing real-time, and communications-based systems.

```
BEGIN:                                      ;INITIALIZATION
           .
        .READW  #AREA1,#CHN1,#I1,....,   ;READ INTO I1 TO START PROCESS,
           .                             ;        WAIT FOR READ COMPLETE
        MOV     #A,-(SP)                 ;INITIALIZE STACK FOR FIRST JSR
;
B:      JSR     PC,@(SP)+                ;DO I/O FOR 01 AND I1, OR 02 AND I2
           .
        PERFORM PROCESSING: I1 → 01 OR I2 → 02
           .
        BR      B                        ;MORE I/O
;
;I/O CO-ROUTINES FOLLOW
;
A:      .READ   #AREA1,#CHN1,#I2,...     ;INTITIATE READ INTO I2
           .
        SET PARAMETERS TO PROCESS I1 TO GET 01
           .
        JSR     PC,@(SP)+                ;GO TO B+2
;
        .WRITE  #AREA2,#CHN2,#01,...     ;INITIATE WRITE FROM 01
        .READ   #AREA1,#CHN1,#I1,...     ;INITIATE READ INTO I1
           .
        SET PARAMETERS TO PROCESS I2 TO GET 02
           .
        JSR     PC,@(SP)+                ;GO TO B+2
;
        .WRITE  #AREA2,#CHN2,#02,...     ;INITIATE WRITE FROM 02
;
        BR      A                        ;GO TO A
        .END    BEGIN
```

Fig. 7-22 Coroutine example: RT system macros for overlapped I/O and processing.

7.8 MEMORY MANAGEMENT AND THE PSW

Earlier, we discussed the use of memory management, a feature which provides extended addressing capability for systems with more than 28K of physical memory. The memory management unit has capabilities beyond that of memory extension. Specifically, in cooperation with bits of the *Processor Status Word* and some special instructions, memory management can provide up to three modes of operation for the CPU, *kernel, user,* and *supervisor,* with a separate stack pointer for each mode. The latter mode is implemented only on the 11/45, 55, and 70.

7.8.1 PSW Extensions

As we have seen, the low byte of the PSW contains the condition codes (N, Z, V, and C) and the current CPU priority; it also contains the T-bit, to be discussed later (Section 9.1).

The PSW high byte contains the *Current* and *Previous* mode bit fields, [14:15] and [12:13], respectively. In addition, bit 11, when set, causes an 11/45, 55, or 70 to switch to a second set of registers (R0-R5 only). Since DEC software never uses these extra *gp* registers, the user can "permanently" utilize them for memory pointers in a *single,* very high rate, interrupt service routine. If bit 11 is set in the ISR vector, the routine automatically uses this second register set and there is no need to save/unsave registers. With an interrupt rate of 10 kHz or more, possible in real-time data analysis, the time saved by using this technique in an ISR which requires R0-R5 for efficient execution can approximate the entire CPU power of an 11/34 !

7.8.2 Memory Management and Processor Modes

At this point we shall show how the memory management computes physical addresses. Since some programs may not require the full 4K page, the page length field in the *Page Descriptor Register* (PDR) allows for variable size pages of from 1 to 128 blocks of 32 words. The starting address of each page is then an integral multiple of 32 words, with a maximum size of 4096 words. Pages may be located anywhere in memory (as was shown in Fig. 3-5).

The formation of the physical address is illustrated in Fig. 7-23.

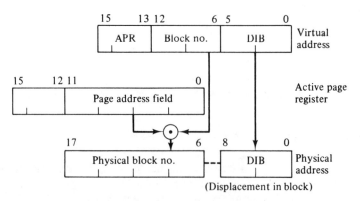

Fig. 7-23 Construction of a physical address.

The logical sequence involved in constructing a Physical Address is as follows:

1. Select a set of active page registers depending on the current mode as specified in the PSW.

2. The active page field of the virtual address is used to select an active page register (APR0-APR7).

3. The page address field of the selected active page register contains the starting address of the currently active page as a block number in physical memory.

4. The block number from the virtual address is added to the block number from the page address field to yield the number of the block in physical memory that will contain the physical address being constructed.

5. The displacement in block from the displacement field of the virtual address is joined to the physical block number to yield a true 18-bit physical address.

Several points may now be made. First, although the programs appear to the processor to be in a contiguous address space, the 32K physical address space is actually scattered through several separate areas of physical memory.

Second, pages may be relocated to higher or lower physical addresses with respect to their virtual address ranges. Third, all of the pages shown start on a 32-word boundary. Fourth, each page is relocated independently. There is no reason why two or more pages could not be relocated to the same physical memory space. Using more than one page address register in the set to access the same space would be one way of providing different memory access rights to the same data, depending upon which part of the program was referencing the data.

To assist the programmer in using memory management, there are several new instructions. These instructions provide communication between the user and kernel by allowing data to be moved from or to the previous data space. Thus, should the operating system need to access some data in the users space, it could execute a MFPD (Move From Previous Data space) instruction which would fetch the data using the APR's for that previous (user) mode.

An example will demonstrate the use of memory management. Suppose that memory is arranged as shown in Fig. 7-24 where the first three pages of physical memory contain the operating system, the next two contain the first 8K for program one, the next page contains program two, and the last physical page holds the remaining part of program one. (We assume all programs need one or more 4K pages for the sake of simplicity.)

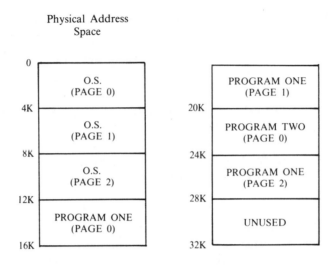

Physical Address
Space

Fig. 7-24 Layout of memory.

To set up the operating system it is necessary to load the PAR and PDR registers with the relocation values and control information, and then turn on memory management. The instruction sequence would look like:

```
KPAR0=772340          ;KERNEL MEMORY MANAGEMENT REGISTER
KPAR1=772342          ;LOCATED IN THE I/O PAGE
KPAR3=772344          ;GIVING THE RELOCATION VALUE 100
KPDR0=772300          ;KERNEL PAGE DESCRIPTOR REGISTER
        .
        .
UPAR0=777640          ;USER PAR
        .
        .
UPDR3=777606          ;USER PDR
        .
SR0=777572            ;MEMORY MANAGEMENT CONTROL REGISTER
  .
        .
MOV     #0,@#KPAR0     ;PAGE ZERO STARTS AT PHYSICAL ADDRS ZERO
MOV     #200,@#KPAR1   ;PAGE ONE FOLLOWS AT PHYSICAL ADDRS 20000
MOV     #400,@#KPAR2   ;AND SO ON

MOV     #77406,@#KPDR0 ;4K PAGES TO BE READ/WRITE
MOV     #77406,@#KPDR1 ;
MOV     #77406,@#KPDR2 ;

MOV     #1,@#SR0       ;TURN ON MEMORY MANAGEMENT
        .
        .
```

258

The operating system will now give control to the user:

```
;
        MOV     #600,@#UPAR0    ;PAGE ZERO STARTS AT 60000
        MOV     #1000,@#UPAR1   ;NEXT PAGE IS CONTIGUOUS
        MOV     #1400,@#UPAR2   ;BUT LAST PAGE IS NOT
;
        MOV     #77406,@#UPDR0  ;4K PAGES TO BE READ/WRITE
        MOV     #77406,@#UPDR1  ;
        MOV     #77406,@#UPDR2  ;
;
        MOV     #140000,-(SP)   ;PUSH USER MODE INTO STACK
        CLR     -(SP)           ;START AT VIRTUAL ADDRESS ZERO
        RTI                     ;POP STACK AND RETURN
```

The program segment thus initializes the memory management registers so that there is 12K of operating system space, where the virtual addresses and the physical addresses are the same. At some later point, it sets up the memory management registers for the first program so that while its virtual addresses are from 0-12K, its physical addresses are not contiguous but distributed from 12-20K, and 24-28K.

To start the user, a processor status word and a program counter value are pushed onto the stack. Then, using an RTI instruction, these two words are restored, thereby setting the PSW to user mode and starting the user program at virtual address zero.

In fact, this program segment will not actually run successfully. The astute reader will have noticed that the operating system did not initialize an APR for the I/O page in which the memory management registers reside. Thus, having turned on memory management by setting SR0, only virtual addresses between 0-12K can be reached by the kernel. I/O page addresses will cause a memory management fault when the operating system attempts to set up the registers for program one. Still, the flavor of memory management is captured by this example.

EXERCISES

1. Write a program to type out the message "HELLO?" on the teleprinter.

2. Write a format subroutine for the teleprinter to tab-space the teleprinter carriage. The subroutine is entered with the number of spaces to be tabbed in register R0.

3. Write a program to read columns from the low-speed paper tape reader, punching out each column on the high-speed paper tape punch as three octal digits.

4. Write a subroutine that accepts one to six octal digits from the teleprinter and forms a 16-bit word in R0. As each character is typed, it should be echoed back to the teleprinter. Assume that the line is terminated with a carriage return and that your routine will insert a line feed.

5. Rewrite Exercise 3 to utilize interrupts.

6. Write an interrupt structured program to read 400 characters simultaneously from the high-speed reader, while punching and printing the first 100 characters read. Be careful to terminate the reading while allowing the slower printing and punching devices to complete.

7. Devise a scheme for measuring execution time used by a program. This scheme should be accurate to within 16.6 milliseconds.

8. Code Exercise 3 utilizing RT-11 system macros.

9. Can Exercise 6 be coded using RT-11 system macros?

10. Code the coroutine double-buffer example on page 200 so that it can duplicate a paper tape from the low-speed reader to the high-speed punch.

REFERENCES

I/O programming is very special in the sense that each computer type has its own I/O instructions and hence I/O idiosyncracies. Books by Flores (1969), Hellerman (1967), and Foster (1970) discuss I/O from the conceptual level, making it more universal in flavor. Others, like this book, treat I/O as it is embodied in a particular machine. For the PDP-11 the best source is the Peripherals Handbook, which covers not only I/O devices but also UNIBUS extensions, communication interfaces, and data and control options.

8

System Development Software

A comprehensive package of system software accompanies each computer in use today, from the small minicomputer to the large number cruncher. These packages include programs and routines plus associated documentation which allow the programmer to write, edit, assemble, compile, debug, and run his programs, making the full data-processing capability of the computer immediately available.

System software represents the on-going process and continual efforts of system programmers to make the utilization of computers easier, more comprehensible, and less time-consuming than was possible before. Most systems are modular and open-ended, permitting the user to construct specified systems tailored to his particular environment. As such, they act as the buffers or interfaces between the user's needs and the hardware's capability.

The reader has been introduced previously to three software systems: the assembler (including the macro capability), the I/O programming system, and the memory dump routine. Now our attention is directed to some other software systems that assist in the creation and execution of programs — the editor, and the loader. In addition, since no nontrivial program or system is ever fully debugged or tested, it is worthwhile to conclude our investigation of system software with an examination of testing and debugging techniques.

8.1 EDITOR

The text editor is a powerful context-editing program used to create and modify symbolic source programs and other text material. By means of commands issued from the terminal, the editor can be used to create and delete characters, a line, or groups of lines which it maintains in its internal buffer. Because the editor is on-line in most systems, response to commands is immediate and dynamic.

A good editor is both productive and cost-effective. In use it turns the teleprinter into a very sophisticated typewriter that assists the programmer in the normal "cut and paste" operation of putting a program together. As a result, the editor must not only allow for the insertion and deletion of characters and lines, but it must also be capable of locating symbols, making corrections, and reading or writing blocks of data.

Most editors have similar attributes but we will describe some specific commands (and associated syntax) of the RT-11 editor in particular. Associated with the internal buffer of the RT-11 editor is a "current location pointer" that refers to the character in the buffer considered to be the current character. The current character is defined as the character that is being created or edited by the user; that is, the current position of the editor within the text buffer.

Some editors operate only on lines, some only on characters; others operate on both. If the editor recognizes entire lines, it does so by defining a line to end with an especially significant character, such as a carriage return. In this way the editor may assume that each line begins with the character after the terminating carriage return in the last line and ends with the terminating carriage return for the current line.

Typical editor commands (i.e., RT-11) include the following:

1. INSERT: to enter a new string of characters. *Example*: Itext$ inserts "text" after the pointer. Note that the escape key, ESC, echoed as "$", terminates each command.

2. DELETE: to delete a string of characters. *Example*: nD$ will delete the next "n" characters after the pointer ["n" positive] or preceding the pointer ["n" negative].

3. CHANGE: to replace one string of characters with another. *Example*: nCtext$ replaces the "n" characters following ["n" positive] or preceding the pointer ["n" negative] with "text".

4. KILL: to erase a specified number of lines from the current text buffer. *Example*: nK$ deletes lines beginning at the pointer and ending at the n'th line ["n" positive], or lines beginning with the –n'th line and ending at the pointer ["n" negative].

5. GET or FIND: to find the first or n'th occurrence of a character string. *Example*: nGtext$ positions the pointer after the n'th occurence of the string "text".

6. LIST: to print a string of characters. *Example*: nL$ prints all characters beginning at the pointer and ending with the n'th line.

7. VERIFY: to print out a string after it has been changed, or located. *Example*: V$.

8. READ: to fill the editor's internal buffer by reading a block of text from some peripheral device. *Example*: ERfile$R$ intitiates reading the first block of "file" from the system device.

9. WRITE: to empty the internal buffer onto a peripheral device. *Example*: EWfile$W$ intitiates writing the current block of text to the "file" on the system device.

10. EXIT: to close the current file being edited. *Example*: EX$ closes the file being edited.

In addition, there are commands that have to do with the character or line pointer. Various editor requests are provided for moving the current location pointer. These requests include

1. BEGIN: to position the pointer at the beginning of the buffer.

2. JUMP: to move the pointer over a specified number of characters in the text buffer.

3. ADVANCE: to move the pointer a specified number of lines forward or backward.

All commands must be terminated by a second ESC ($). This indicates that multiple commands may be concatenated and processing deferred until the terminating ESC is typed.

A particularly powerful attribute of editors is a Macro capability. Suppose the user wants to find *all* occurrences of one string (say, "Morse") and change it to another (e.g., "Morris"). Using the RT-11 Editor, for example, he would first clear the macro buffer (M//$$), enter the macro (M/FMorse$-5CMorris$/$$), proceed to the top of his buffer (B$$) and then type "9999EM", i.e., execute the macro 9999 times. The editor would scan the entire file, since "F", for FIND, in the macro brings in new pages, replacing the first string with the second in all cases.

The sophistication of the editor depends greatly on its operating environment. Some computer systems allow for maximum editor flexibility, including full or abbreviated commands, concatenation of command strings, file manipulating requests, and sophisticated text editing. Other computers may have very terse, one-letter commands, limited internal buffers, and rigid command formats. Nonetheless, even small computer editors allow sufficient flexibility for creating and modifying source programs.

8.1.1 Use of the RT-11 Editor

The RT-11 editor possesses many sophisticated attributes, including the macro capability and the ability to "save" and "unsave" character strings in an internal buffer. Requests are entered while the editor is in command mode (each line begins with the editor typing out an *).

A subset of editor commands may be used to write the trivial program given in Fig. 8-1. In the example, the editor is assumed to be running and all nonprinting characters are not shown (e.g., carriage return, tab, line feed). Additionally, the right-hand comments have been added for the sake of readability:

```
*I      .TITLE START          USER PLACES EDITOR
        R0=%0                 IN INPUT MODE AND TYPES
        R1=%1                 LINES OF INPUT
        MOV     #1,R0
        CLR     R1
        CMP     R0,R1
        .END    START
$$                            TWO "ESC", ECHOED AS "$",
                              TERMINATE INPUT, RETURN TO COMMAND MODE
*B$$                          GO TO TOP OF BUFFER
*3A$L$$
        MOV     #1,R0         ADVANCE 3 LINES AND PRINT CURRENT LINE
*ISTART:$0A$L$$               ADD A LABEL, REPOSITION POINTER TO START
                              OF LINE, AND LIST THE LINE
START:  MOV     #1,R0
*GR0$-C0$0A$L$$               FIND "R0", CHANGE IT TO "R0",
                              REPOSITON POINTER TO START OF LINE, LIST
START:  MOV     #1,R0
*EWDK1:FILE.MAC$EX$$          WRITE THIS OUT AS "FILE.MAC" TO DK1
.                             NOW BACK TO MONITOR
```

Fig. 8-1 Example of an RT-11 Edit session.

Again note that a single "ESC", echoed by "$", terminates each command and a second "ESC" cause the preceding command string to be executed. Although far from exhaustive, this short example demonstrates the use of the editor for the RT-11 software system.

8.1.2 Window Editors

The advent of video terminals and refreshed tube interactive display processors (Section 10.2) has given rise to a number of *window editors*. A limitation of conventional "typewriter-based" editors is the ability to "see", and correct, only a single line of text at a time. Since programs are structured and have line-to-line and other local correlation, the programmer should ideally be able to see and correct *blocks* of code. This ability also greatly facilitates editing program areas containing branch structures. A window editor allows the user to see a block of code at a single instant, typically at least 24 lines of 80 characters each. A blinking cursor clearly indicates the position in the users's text which will receive new characters and the window will "immediately" and unambiguously display any characters entered.

On systems running RT-11 and having VT-11 or VS-60 graphics processors, a special window version of EDIT is available. Users see a 20 line area of his current text buffer, with a blinking cursor indicating the pointer position. A separate area displays commands. In *immediate mode*, entered via two ESC sequences, the user may easily move the cursor positon and enter text at the cursor position.

On systems running RT-11 or RSX-11M with VT-52 or VT-100 video terminals, another editor, TECO, with an associated VT-52 edit MACRO implements a window editor which is, in some repects, superior to the RT/VT editor. This editor makes use of a special keypad on these terminals and shows the user a 24 line window into the current segment (i.e., "page") of his text file. The editor is always in an "accept text" mode as far as the main keyboard is concerned, and the keypad at the console right is always in an "accept command" mode, with the keys interpreted as shown in Fig. 8-2. Note that CTRL, BACKSP, and DELETE are single keys and not keystroke sequences. This editor facilitates extremely time-effective editing.

```
    VT-52   Keypad layout                          Other keys
---------------------------------------
| "BLUE"  | "RED"   | "GREY"  | "^"     |       CTRL/C  Exit from macro
| Save    | TECO    | Unsave  | Up in   |       CTRL/D  Kill rest of line*
| text*   | command | text    | column* |       CTRL/K  Kill line*
|---------|---------|---------|---------|       CTRL/U  Kill start of line
| "7"     | "8"     | "9"     | "v"     |       CTRL/Z  Exit from macro
| Open    | New     | Quote   | Down in |       BACKSP  Go to end of line*
|new line*| page*   | next*   | column* |       DELETE  Delete previous*
|---------|---------|---------|---------|       2 ESC's Repeat TECO command
| "4"     | "5"     | "6"     | ">"     |
| Up      | Delete* | Delete  | Cursor  |       Arguments
| line*   |character| last    | right*  |
|---------|---------|---------|---------|       All starred (*) commands
| "1"     | "2"     | "3"     | "<"     |       optionally take an argument
| Top     | Bottom  | Start   | Cursor  |       entered as <ESC><digits>.
| of page*| of page | of line | left*   |
|---------|---------|---------|---------|
|        "0"        | "."     | "ENTER" |
|     Down line*    | Search* | Search  |
|                   |         |argument*|
---------------------------------------
```

Fig. 8-2 TECO VT-52 window editor keypad controls

The cursor, at all times visible in a 24 line window into the text buffer, may be moved to the beginning of either the previous line ("4" key on keypad, i.e., [4KP]) or the next line [0KP], or to the top [1KP] or bottom [2KP] of the current page. Or, the cursor may be moved left [<KP] or right [>KP] on the current *line*, or up

[^KP] or down [vKP] in the current *column.* [8KP] brings the next page into the buffer, with the top 24 lines displayed in the window; the current page is automatically written into the output file. Any "*" tagged key repeats that command *n* times when preceded by ESC*n*.

In particular, it is especially easy to search repeatedly for different occurrences of the same string: the user presses "ENTER" and the word "Search:" appears. The user types the desired string and then presses the "." key of the keypad [.KP]. The cursor *and* window will be moved to the first occurrence of the string. Subsequent [.KP]'s will locate successive occurrences of the string while ESC*n* [.KP] will move the cursor to the *n*'th occurrence of the string. [6KP] deletes the string just found, if so desired. The search string remains saved until overwritten. Also, for example, ESC*n* [BLUE KP] will save a copy of the next *n* lines of text, [6KP] then will delete those lines — if so desired —, and each [GREY KP] will unsave the saved lines at the current cursor position. The saved text copy remains in an internal buffer until a new save occurs, and thus may be unsaved repeatedly if desired.

8.2 THE LOADER

The initial load problem was discussed in Chapter 7 in connection with the bootstrap loader. The bootstrap loader, although sufficient for loading short programs, was not general or flexible enough for loading long programs. Instead, that task falls on the *absolute loader.*

The absolute loader is a system program which enables the programmer to load his programs into any available memory locations, in any order. It is used to load programs that are in absolute binary (i.e., fixed to absolute memory locations) or position independent format. Having completed its task, the absolute loader will either halt or transfer control to the start of the newly loaded program.

The absolute loader is usually loaded by the bootstrap into the uppermost area of available memory. In this way it may be preserved across user or system program loads so that it can be available without reloading. Of course, when writing programs, the user must be aware of what memory locations the absolute loader (and the bootstrap if it resides in memory) occupies so that it will not be altered by his program(s).

An absolute program as seen by the absolute loader consists of one or more blocks of data. Each block may include

1. A start-of-block indicator.

2. A record count of the number of bytes, words, and so on, to be loaded.

3. A load address.

4. The information to be loaded.

5. A block checksum.

Although the first and last items are not absolutely necessary, they occur frequently in block requirements for small computer loaders.

The start-of-block indicator is used to indicate that a load block follows. In this way non-loader data may be mixed with loader information. For example, a small computer with only a Teletype as a system I/O device may put both the assembly listing and the binary loader tape out to the Teletype punch, and leave it up to the loader to separate the two.

The block checksum is used as error indicator for the loader. As each load record (usually a byte) is generated by the absolute assembler it is added (logically) to the checksum, which eventually becomes part of the load block. During normal program loading, the checksum is again computed, and if this new value does not agree with the block checksum of the block data (e.g., due to faulty read), a load error is indicated and the loader halts. Thus the block checksum serves to guarantee that the load operation has been performed correctly.

The rest of the loader block fields are used as shown by the flowchart in Fig. 8-3. Note that the last load address may or may not be used as a transfer address upon completion of the load process. This decision depends on whether the assembly program terminated with a

> `.END     LABEL`

or simply an ".END". One way of indicating this difference, which is used by the absolute loader for the PDP-11, is to make the load address even or odd, depending on its being a transfer address or not.

As an alternative to taking the load address from the load block, it may be possible to indicate the load address by use of the computer console switches. This capability allows PIC programs to be loaded in memory locations different from the relative load addresses given in the load blocks. PIC programs are thereby relocated into new memory positions by the simple process of making the actual load address for each block be the sum of the two addresses provided.

8.2.1 Relocation of Programs

Relocation of PIC programs by the absolute loader turns out to be not only useful but also necessary. For example, it allows the user to control the loading of the dump routine so that it may be placed in a location of memory that does not overlap the area to be dumped. More generally, such relocation of PIC programs makes it possible for the user to write separate PIC segments, which may be combined in memory to form one large program.

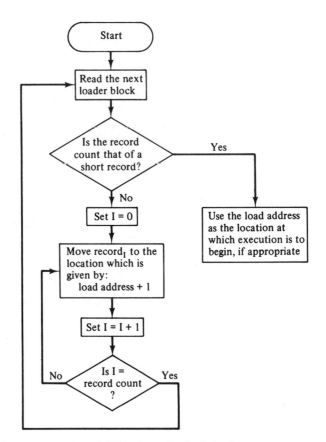

Fig. 8-3 Flowchart of a simple loader.

However, making the programmer write all his relocatable programs in PIC format is unduly restrictive. Instead, it seems much more sensible to leave the mechanical process of relocation up to the computer since it can easily handle the problem. Consequently, the programmer is encouraged to write all his programs so as to be relocatable by a linking loader.

As the FORTRAN programmer knows, each FORTRAN program and subprogram requires a separate compilation by the FORTRAN translator. The following are advantages of this requirement:

1. Errors discovered in one FORTRAN program (or subprogram) require only that that program and not all others be recompiled.

2. Absolute addresses need not be assigned at translation time. Thus programs are prevented from arbitrarily overlaying each other. This flexibility also allows subroutines to change size without influencing the placement of other routines or affecting their operation.

3. Separate translations allow the same symbols to be used in different source programs.

4. Once translated, subroutines may be placed for general use in a library for future use without retranslation.

Fortunately, these advantages apply to assembly language programming as well, provided that a *relocatable assembler* and a *linker/loader* are available as system programs, as is the case with RT-11, for example.

Up to now we have not really considered how subroutines are linked and loaded with their calling routines. By default, the absolute assembler would be used to assemble all programs and subprograms together, determining which portions of memory each routine is to occupy, and maintaining the subroutine entry addresses in the assembler's symbol table. However, should we have decided to assemble each routine separately, we would have been faced with the tasks of keeping track of what memory is to be allocated to which routine and what addresses need to be adjusted (e.g., the address portion of the

```
JSR    REG,SUBR
```

instruction must be modified to point to the entry point of the subroutine).

The relocatable assembler and linker/loader mechanize this process for us in the following way. First, the assembler produces object code as if it were to be loaded starting at location zero. Second, the assembler flags each relative address and data word so that the linker/loader will know what parts of the program will be affected by relocation. Third, the assembler allows the programmer to declare certain symbols global symbols. A global symbol is either defined in a program (as a label or by direct assignment) or it is assumed to be defined in some other separately assembled program. In the first case the global is called an *entry symbol*; in the second case it is called an *external symbol*.

8.2.2 Linking and Loading

At the start of the linking and loading process, the linker/loader receives the following information from the relocatable assembler:

1. Object code.

2. Relocation information about the individual fields in the object code.

3. Relative assembly address of the first instruction or datum in the load module.

4. Global entry point and external reference symbols.

5. Length of the load module.

This information assists the linker/loader in developing a load map detailing what programs have been loaded, how long they are, where they reside in memory, and what other programs they require. The linker/loader will attempt to load programs until all programs are loaded and no new ones are required, or programs are found to be missing. To assist in this process, the assembler has pseudo-ops ".GLOBL" and ".CSECT". The former makes a symbol known globally among all the load modules and the latter makes the name of the load module known globally, besides defining some of the characteristics of a load module. (Conversely, the .ASECT declares an absolute section where all subsequent addresses assembled are considered to be fixed.)

Some programs may be part of a user or system library. Such libraries include already translated user routines and intrinsic functions such as SIN, COS, TAN, EXP, LOG, and so on. These programs must be located by the linker/loader through a *directory* which describes the routine, its entry points (some routines such as SIN and COS may share common code), what other routines this routine may need, the length of the routine, and where the routine is to be found. A typical load map and directory are shown in Fig. 8-4.

```
RT-11 LINK      V04-04A      LOAD MAP
NINEMA.SAV                   06-AUG-78

SECTION ADDR     SIZE     ENTRY   ADDR     ENTRY   ADDR     ENTRY    ADDR

. ABS. 000000   001000   $USRSW  000000   $RF1C1  000000   .V011S   000001
                         $NLCHN  000006   $HRDWR  000006   $WASIZ   000075
                         $LRECL  000210   $TRACE  004737
.$$$$. 001000   002170
XX     003170   000050
       003240   002514
       005754   013534   COEFF9  005754
       021510   001306   REALMA  021510
       023016   000016   ABS     023016
                           .
                           .
       024742   000132   SQRT    024742
                           .
                           .
       025074   000026   DIF$PS  025074   DIF$MS  025100   DIF$IS   025112
                         DIF$SS  025116   $DVR    025116
       032076   000340   EXP     032076
       032536   000354   COS     032536   SIN     032572
       033112   000102   AINT    033112   $INTR   033130
                           .
       033734   000036   DII$PS  033734   DII$MS  033742   DII$IS   033746

TRANSFER ADDRESS = 003240
HIGH LIMIT = 033772
```

Fig. 8-4 Portion of RT-11 Linker load map and directory.

Note that all the sections which have a name (i.e., are declared as a .CSECT) in their respective modules are shown along with their base load address, size, and symbolic entry point and actual memory address. All symbols declared as globals within a module appear with both symbolic and actual memory location. The last two lines specify the starting address of the load module and the last memory location occupied.

The actual process of linking and loading is generally handled by one of two possible techniques. The first is called the *transfer vector method* and utilizes a technique similar to the jump table example presented in Chapter 4. By making each external routine call result in a transfer into a jump table, the loader can eventually fill in the address where the called routine has been loaded. Figure 8-5 shows how the assembler code for the PDP-11 could be used to produce relocatable code that includes a jump table to the called routines MULT and DIVD. After loading, these table entries will contain jump addresses to the actual starting locations for MULT and DIVD.

Assembler Code		Relocatable Output			Program in Memory		
					(with MULT at 200, DIVD at 300)		
		0	MULT: 0		100	.WORD	200
.GLOBL	MULT,DIVD	2	DIVD: 0		102	.WORD	300
ADD	A,B	4	ADD	50,52	104	ADD	150,152
JSR	PC,@MULT	12	JSR	PC,@0	112	JSR	PC,@100
SUB	B,C	16	SUB	52,54	116	SUB	152,154
JSR	PC,@DIVD	24	JSR	PC,@2	124	JSR	PC,@102
JSR	PC,@MULT	30	JSR	PC,@0	130	JSR	PC,@100
.			.			.	
.			.			.	

Fig. 8-5 Loading process using the transfer vector technique.

The second method is the linking loader method and it attempts to avoid the one level of indirectness of the transfer vector technique. It therefore creates a linked list of all calls to the external routine and preserves this list until such time as the relative load address of the external routine is known. At that time, the linking loader traverses the linked list, building up direct calls to the external routine(s).

Figure 8-6 shows the same PDP-11 code being linked and loaded as in Fig. 8-5, except that the linking loader technique is used in the figure. The relocatable output of the assembler includes a linked list of all references to the same external routine, with the list terminating in a null [shown by a dash (-) in the figure]. The basic difference between these two techniques is that the transfer vector method resolves links during loading, while the linking loader does it before loading. The output of the linker part of the linking loader is, therefore, one complete load module, which is loaded by the relocatable loader part.

```
Assembler Code            Relocatable Output      Program in Memory
--------------            ------------------      -----------------
                                                  (with MULT at 200, DIVD at 300)
                          MULT  L24
      .GLOBL MULT,DIVD    DIVD  L20
ADD    A,B                0   ADD    50,52   100  ADD    150,152
JSR    PC,MULT            6   JSR    PC,-    106  JSR    PC,200
SUB    B,C               12   SUB    52,54   112  SUB    152,154
JSR    PC,DIVD           20   JSR    PC,-    120  JSR    PC,300
JSR    PC,MULT           24   JSR    PC,L6   124  JSR    PC,200
  .                             .                   .
  .                             .                   .
```

Fig. 8-6 Loading process using linking loader technique.

In either case, the results are the same:

1. Object modules are relocated and assigned absolute addresses.

2. Different modules are linked together and global symbols are correlated between those modules which define them and those which use them.

3. A load map is produced, displaying the assigned absolute addresses.

thus allowing the programmer to assemble his program and subprograms separately.

8.3 DEBUGGING TECHNIQUES

One of the maxims of programming seems to be that no program of any degree of complexity will run correctly the first time it is executed. The problem is that a symbolic program can be assembled correctly and still contain logical errors, that is, errors that cause the program to do something other than what is intended. Although the assembler can check for and detect syntactic errors, it cannot detect logical errors. Consequently, logical errors are usually detected only when the program is run on a computer.

Determining whether or not a program has a logical error is sometimes difficult in itself. A computer is generally used to solve the kinds of problems that require involved calculations, which preclude knowing much about the answers generated. As a result, only when answers are grossly incorrect is the programmer sure that a logical error exists. When seemingly small errors or results that cannot be measured against known values appear, the programmer is faced with the difficult task of deciding whether or not his program is indeed incorrect. And given a large, complicated program, the programmer may not be able to test all conceivable cases that could be generated, thus causing him to accept on faith that his program does work, until proved wrong!

Assuming that a logical error is known to exist, the problem becomes that of determining its cause. Several techniques for this are available:

1. Taking a memory dump of all locations that affect the results.

2. Using the console switches and lights to monitor program execution.

3. Tracing the program as it is executed.

4. Producing intermediate output as the results are generated.

Taking a memory dump, although often helpful, is both static and after the fact. By the time the dump is taken, the error may have caused all pertinent information, including the cause of the error itself, to be altered or eliminated.

Alternatively, the programmer, having the machine to himself, may use the console switches to examine specific locations while stepping through the program instruction by instruction. Besides the difficulty in both interpreting binary console displays and translating them into symbolic expressions related to the user's program listing, this technique is extremely time-consuming and very tiring. A better technique would be to place a halt in the program just before the section of code which is to be checked so that the magnitude of the operation may be reduced. Of course, this requires the programmer to know where to place the halt.

A better technique would be to let the computer print out the program instructions and results as they are being interpreted by some trace program. This, too, is a time-consuming process, but only on the part of the computer, since the programmer need not be present while the trace is being run. Some computers, the PDP-11 for example, even have a T-bit in the processor status word to assist in tracing instructions. This bit, when set, causes a processor trap at the end of each instruction execution, greatly facilitating the tracing process (Section 9.1).

If computer time is a matter of concern, the programmer is faced with having to trace only selected variables or locations. Either a trace routine is used, or the programmer himself generates intermediate output which indicates that a certain variable has changed value or a specific location has been branched to or referenced.

The programmer can, of course, while sitting at his desk using the program assembly listing, mentally execute his program. This method is frequently used with very short programs, but only with very short ones. Human memory cannot retain every step and instruction in even a fairly short program; it cannot match a computer memory.

What is needed to debug a user program conveniently and accurately is a service program that will assume the tasks the programmer would have to perform if he used the console switches, took a memory dump, and/or selectively traced his program. Such a facility is known as *dynamic debugging program* (DDP).

On a small computer, the DDP takes the form of a conversational system program. It provides the user with a convenient means for debugging and closely monitoring the operation of his program. In fact, the DDP acts both as a program supervisor and as a binary editor.

Through commands issued to the DDP via the terminal, the user is able to: (1) start a program, (2) suspend its execution at predetermined points, (3) examine and modify the contents of memory words and registers, and (4) make additions and corrections to the running program using either symbolic or octal code. Commands are of the following forms:

1. OPEN: to examine and/or modify contents.

2. CLOSE: to go on to another OPEN or DDP operation.

3. MODE: to establish the type of input or output modes of operation.

4. BREAKPOINT: to suspend the execution of the program at a predetermined point.

5. SEARCH: to search for a particular occurrence of a bit pattern (e.g., an address, a constant, or an instruction).

6. LIMIT: to establish the limits (memory addresses) of the search.

7. BEGIN: to start execution of the user program at a specified location.

8. PROCEED: to continue execution after a breakpoint interruption.

Like all other system programs discussed in this chapter, the sophistication of the dynamic debugging program depends on its operating environment.

8.3.1 Example of a Debugging Session

ODT-11 (On-Line Debugging Technique) for the PDP-11 is typical of a small-computer dynamic debugging program. Like the PDP-11 editor, ODT has a command mode that is indicated by an asterisk being printed out by the system. Basic commands include

1. n/: opens word n.

2. cr: a carriage return to close an open location.

3. n;G: begins execution at location n.

4. n;B: sets a breakpoint at location n. ⋅

5. ;P: proceeds from a breakpoint.

6. $n/: opens register n.

Given the following trivial assembly language program

```
        .=1000
START:  MOV     #1,R0
        CLR     R1
        CMP     R0,R1
        HALT
        .END
```

(no label follows .END since ODT will begin execution of the program), then using ODT-11, the following dialogue may occur (comments have been added for readability):

```
*1004/005001              EXAMINE THE CLR INSTRUCTION

*$1/000000  123456        CHANGE THE CONTENTS OF R1
*1004;B                   PLACE BREAKPOINTS AT
*1010;B                   LOCATIONS 1004 AND 1010

*1000;G                   BEGIN EXECUTION AT START

B0;001004                 BREAKPOINT OCCURS

*$0/000001                CHECK R0
*$1/123456                AND R1
*;P                       THEN PROCEED

B1;001010                 NEXT BREAKPOINT

*$1/000000                CHECK R1

*$0/000001                AND R0 AGAIN
```

Although this example is rather brief, it does give the reader some idea of what a dynamic debugging program does. When faced with a typical small computer, with its often-limited number of display lights and means for examining memory or processor registers, the programmer quickly seizes the opportunity to use a DDP rather than probe memory and measure program progress through the console.

8.4 APPLICATIONS SOFTWARE AND OPERATING ENVIRONMENTS

Having dealt with computers, including their organization and programming, we should now be interested in applying computers for solution of non-trivial problems. The operating environment in which the programs which implement the solutions are edited, assembled/compiled, linked/loaded, and run is also of interest.

In the next chapter we will discuss, and illustrate, advanced programming techniques for applications software. These examples serve first as concrete (and, hopefully, useful) implementations of algorithms which are have widespread applications in the computing community (e.g., the fast Fourier transform). Second, the programs illustrate useful examples of *efficient* application of several PDP-11 architectural features, including the more powerful addressing modes and the hardware fixed-point/floating-point instruction sets (EIS/FIS/FPP).

In Chapter 10, real-time interactive computing is discussed. Again, useful applications provide a vehicle for graphic illustration and reinforcement of several concepts presented earlier (e.g., interrupt-driven computing, direct memory access, and microprogramming). Additionally, several hardware peripherals frequently found in real-time environments (e.g., analog/digital converters and graphics processors) are described from a hardware/software viewpoint. Examples are given of computer-based software/hardware speech and music synthesis. Of particular interest is a program which utilizes the powerful and efficient RT-11 string manipulation program modules to analyze English input text and produce parameters to drive a commercial speech sythesizer.

The last two chapters are devoted to an in depth discussion of the internals of *operating systems* and *multiprogramming/timesharing systems*.

EXERCISES

1. What are the differences between an editor used for program creation and one used for manuscript creation? What types of commands might you find in one or the other?

2. Using the PDP-11 program editor as an example, list its good and bad features. Then give a suggested remedy for each of its bad features.

3. Write a program to implement the absolute loader functions as flowcharted in Fig. 8-3.

4. What features are missing from ODT-11 as described in the text? Describe a method for implementing them.

REFERENCES

One of the best references for text editing can be found in the survey article by Van Dam and Rice (1971). Of course, for a particular system, one should read the appropriate manual, such as the PDP-11 Edit-11 Text Editor. Similarly, the manuals for the various PDP-11 operating systems describe operation of the system programs in detail. RT-11 V02C, V03 TECO is available as DECUS 11-288, while RSX-11M video TECO is DECUS 11-333; TECO documentation is DECUS 11-350.

9

Advanced Programming Techniques for Algorithm Implementation

The concept of program modularity together with the common use of high level languages such as FORTRAN has yielded a number of easily accessible libraries of subroutines for scientific computing. Nevertheless, for maximum performance, the user may want to program time-critical applications in assembly language. Only in this way can the architecture of the machine be exploited to yield a maximally time efficient implementation of any particular algorithm. In this chapter, therefore, we will examine time/space tradeoffs in assembly language programming of applications software. The algorithms presented are in the area of *digital signal processing*, a field where speed is often of paramount importance. However, in addition to the practical utility of the programs presented, they have been chosen to further illustrate advanced applications of various elements of the PDP-11 architecture. Included are use of the Extended Instruction Set (EIS) and Floating-point Processor (FPP), multiple precision fixed-point addition/subtraction, alternative subprogram constructs and argument passing techniques, and efficient application of the autoincrement/autodecrement addressing modes for data manipulation.

For completeness, in the concluding section of this chapter the use of high level programming languages is approached from one specific point of view: the *time* and *space* characteristics of the output code generated by four *different* FORTRAN compilers for the *same* input program are examined. In this way, the interaction among compilers, algorithms, and computer architectures is clarified.

Later, in Chapter 10, some of the program modules developed herein are incorporated into useful software systems and a further step, that of microcoding some extremely time-critical code sections, is examined.

9.1 PROGRAM ANALYSIS PROGRAMS

An ancient programmer's maxim suggests that 80 per cent of program run time is spent executing 20 per cent of the program code. While the percentages may vary, it is certainly true that various code segments are generally of very unequal importance in determining overall program efficiency. It is assumed that when an appropriate high level language is available, and a complicated software system is to be implemented, the programmer (or programming team) will first create a working modular system using that language. Then, the process of converting time-critical subprograms to assembly language can proceed. At each stage the system can be retested to ensure that it continues to function properly. Modern disk-based linking loaders or task builders make such a process viable and cost efficient.

9.1.1 Activity and Instruction Analysis

How does the programmer decide which modules are "time-critical"? The knowledgeable programmer can sometimes answer this question by visual examination of the software system control program. Alternatively, straightforward use of system timing programs may provide the required data. However, more accurate statistics can be gathered through use of *program analysis programs*. The PDP-11 enables construction of such programs using the T bit trap. When the T bit of the PSW is set, a trap via location 14 follows execution of *every* instruction. The trap service routine (executed with the T bit off, of course) can gather information about the program. Simply, after each T bit trap, the address of the next instruction in the *traced program* is found on the stack. This means that the trap service routine can create a histogram of *memory address* vs. *number of times pointed to by PC* and/or can build a table showing the number of times each different PDP-11 instruction type was executed during the chosen code segment. In fact, a program can be written so as to completely analyze each instruction executed and, via incorporation of data from the relevant PDP-11 Processor Handbook, compute any desired statistics regarding the code executed.

9.1.2 A Rudimentary Instruction Trace Program

Instruction tracing requires a collection of subroutines for data gathering. Typically, the user program will first load the T bit trap vector (CALL SETUP). Then "CALL TRCON" starts the trace while "CALL TRCOFF" stops the trace and calls a statistics printing program:

```
SETUP:  MOV     #TRACE,@#14     ;T BIT TRAP SERVICE ROUTINE (TSR)
        MOV     #340,@#16       ;PRIORITY 7, T BIT NOT SET
        RTS     PC
```

```
;
TRCON:  MOV     (SP),-(SP)      ;DUPLICATE RETURN ADDRESS
        MOV     #360,2(SP)      ;PSW WITH T BIT SET
        RTT                     ;RETURN TO TRACED PROGRAM WITH T BIT SET
;
TRCOFF: CLR     -(SP)           ;PSW WITH T BIT CLEARED
        MOV     #STATS,-(SP)    ;ADDRESS OF STATISTICS PRINTOUT PROGRAM
        RTT
;
TRACE:  MOV     R0,-(SP)        ;T BIT NOW CLEARED
        MOV     R1,-(SP)
        .       .
        MOV     R5,-(SP)        ;SAVE REGISTERS OF TRACED PROGRAM
        MOV     @14(SP),R0      ;GET NEXT INSTRUCTION OF TRACED PROGRAM
                                ;  USING ADDRESS ON STACK
        MOV     #OPTBLE,R1      ;OP CODE DECODE TABLE
SEARCH: CMP     R0,(R1)+        ;FOUND OPCODE?
        BHI     SEARCH          ;NO
        SUB     #OPTBLE+2,R1
        ASL     R1              ;CONVERT TO DISPLACEMENT
        INC     ICOUNT(R1)      ;INCREMENT TABLE OF
                                ;INSTRUCTION TYPE VS. # OF TIMES EXECUTED
;
        .       .               ;GATHER OTHER DESIRED STATISTICS
;
        MOV     (SP)+,R5        ;RESTORE REGISTERS OF TRACED PROGRAM
        .
        MOV     (SP)+,R0
        RTT                     ;BACK TO TRACED PROGRAM, T BIT SET
;
ICOUNT: .REPT   110.
        .WORD   0
        .ENDR                   ;SPACE FOR INSTRUCION COUNTS
;
OPTBLE: .WORD   0               ;HALT
        .WORD   1               ;WAIT
        .WORD   2               ;RTI
        .WORD   3               ;BPT
        .WORD   4               ;IOT
                .
        .WORD   207             ;RTS
                .
        .WORD   17777           ;MOV
                .
        .WORD   177777          ;LDC
        .END
```

It is left as an exercise for interested readers to complete the OPTBLE, develop a statistics printout program, and to enhance the program so as to gather other useful data, such as frequency of various SRC and DST modes.

9.2 TIME/SPACE TRADEOFFS IN SCIENTIFIC PROGRAMMING

The scientific programmer has a comparatively simple goal when coding any specific algorithm; implement the algorithm correctly with results computed to a specified degree of accuracy. Beyond this criterion is the question of time and space efficiency. In the role of a special purpose component within an original equipment manufacturer (OEM) system, the mini- or microcomputer is subject to cost considerations which often dictate that program space efficiency is of paramount importance. However, the "end-user" or laboratory minicomputer systems we are most concerned with present ample opportunities for program tuning so as to achieve minimal execution times. That is, current technology (circa 1979) makes a 32 Kword PDP-11 system "standard" because the memory component cost is less than that of the 4K of memory included in a PDP-11 system circa 1971. In fact, single modules containing 128 Kwords of semiconductor memory are available at a cost less than that of 4K of core memory only five years ago! The time conscious user will often employ a relatively small, fast operating system (e.g., RT-11) and thus have sufficient free memory so that possible time/space tradeoffs are indeed of interest.

In this chapter, we will examine techniques which often enable the PDP-11 to achieve program execution times nearly an order of magnitude faster than that of "conventional" programs. The algorithms used as examples are drawn from the area of *digital signal processing* and speech processing in particular. For example, time-efficient modules will be developed for high-speed, fixed-point fast Fourier transforms (FFT's) and autocorrelation.

9.2.1 Data-Dependent and Data-Independent Algorithms

Consider the Newton-Raphson algorithm for finding a root r of the function $f(x)$ such that $f(r) = 0$.

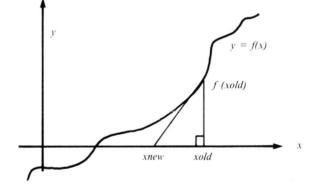

Fig. 9-1 Geometrical derivation of Newton-Raphson algorithm.

Using Fig. 9-1, we find

```
f'(xold) = f(xold)/(xold - xnew)
```
or
```
        xnew = xold  - f(xold )/f'(xold)
```

If *xold* is considered a "first guess", then *xnew* may be used as a "better guess" for a second iteration.

For example, the square root of a positive integer C may be found by computing *x* such that

```
f(x) = x*x  - C = 0
```

Using $f'(x) = 2*x$, we may write

```
xnew = xold - (xold*xold - C)/2*xold
```

If we ignore the real possibility of divergence (discussed at length in standard texts on numerical analysis) and assume convergence, then the algorithm might be programmed in FORTRAN as follows:

```
        XOLD=25.
        EPS=0.00001
1       XNEW=XOLD-F(XOLD)/FP(XOLD)
        DELTA=ABS(XNEW-XOLD)
        IF(DELTA.LT.EPS) GO TO 2
        XOLD=XNEW
        GO TO 1
2       X=XNEW
            .
            .
C       EXAMPLE: FIND SQUARE ROOT OF 1000.
        FUNCTION F(X)
        F=X*X-1000.
        RETURN
        END
C
        FUNCTION FP(X)
        FP=2.*X
        RETURN
        END
```

A possible assembly language implementation for finding the 16-bit integer square root *x* of a 32-bit integer *C*, invoked by JSR PC,NEWTON, is:

```
;          ASSUME  C in R2,R3
;
NEWTON:  MOV  #077777,R4    ;R4     ← X1'= 2**15-1
         BR   FIRST
;
ITER:    SUB  R0,R4         ;R4     ← X1'= X1-(X1**2-C)/(2*X1)
;
FIRST:   MOV  R4,R0         ;R0     ← X1 = X1'
         MUL  R0,R0         ;R0,R1  ← X1*X1
         SUB  R3,R1
         SBC  R0
         SUB  R2,R0         ;R0,R1  ← (X1*X1-C)
         DIV  R4,R0         ;R0     ← (X1*X1-C)/X1
         ASR  R0            ;R0     ← (X1*X1-C)/(2*X1)
         BNE  ITER
         DEC  R4            ;ASSUME R0 WAS 1 BEFORE DIVISION
         RTS  PC
```

It is clear that the number of iterations in the above program is dependent on C. That is, the course of computation is *non-deterministic* and *data-dependent*. Many scientific algorithms are in this class. Other examples are matrix inversion using pivotal condensation, numerical sorting, and floating-point addition via fixed-point operations. This subroutine also clearly illustrates the use of chained 32-bit MUL and DIV instructions.

Other algorithms have control flows which are *data-independent*. For example, in summing n integers, $a(i)$, the course of the algorithm is independent of the values of the data points $a(i)$ and dependent only on n. Consider the following implementation, invoked by JSR PC,SUM.

```
SUM:    MOV   #A,R0          ;STARTING ADDRESS OF ARRAY
        MOV   #99.,R1        ;R1 ← n-1
        MOV   (R0)+,R2       ;R2 ← a(1)
LOOP:   ADD   (R0)+,R2       ;R2 ← R2 + a(i)
        SOB   R1,LOOP        ;R1 ← R1 - 1, BRANCH IF NOT ZERO
        RTS   PC
A:      .BLKW 100.           ;ARRAY OF 100 INTEGERS
```

If we compute the timing for this program on, for example, a PDP-11/55 with bipolar memory, we find that the time for data-dependent computation — the 0.75 $u$sec per loop for the ADD instruction — only slightly exceeds that for the data-independent computation, the 0.6 $u$sec per loop for the SOB. Assuming that a requirement exists for a time efficient routine which accumulates a fixed number of data points, then the following in-line code routine could be used:

```
SUM:    MOV   #A,R0          ;STARTING ADDRESS OF ARRAY
        MOV   (R0)+,R2       ;R2 ← a(1)
        .REPT 99.            ;GENERATE 99 "ADD (R0)+,R2" INSTRUCTIONS
        ADD   (R0)+,R2       ;R2 ← R2 + a(i)
        .ENDR
        RTS   PC
A:      .BLKW 100.           ;ARRAY OF 100 INTEGERS
```

In the PDP-11/05,10, where the SOB must be programmed as DEC Rn, then BNE LOOP, this results in a speedup of about 2.3 at the expense of the memory occupied by the "in-line" code.

In this example, of course, both the data-dependent operation or *computational kernel* (ck) and the control flow are trivial. Where this technique will obviously be of most value is in data-independent algorithms with relatively simple ck's and relatively complex control flows. In recent years, a number of *digital signal processing* (DSP) algorithms have been developed which effectively exchange algorithmic complexity for a reduction in data-dependent operations. These algorithms are thus amenable to efficient implementation via techniques such as *in-line* code. The conventional limitations on production and use of such code are first, the cost of manually coding extremely long programs correctly, and second, the lengths of the programs themselves. We shall first demonstrate that correct in-line code can be efficiently produced. In the preceding example, the

REPT directive achieved this goal. Then, we shall show that other, more space efficient techniques (which also eliminate data-independent computation for loop control and data access) are possible. First, however, two important algorithms will be described with respect to structure, application, and programming.

9.3 ALGORITHM STRUCTURES FOR ARITHMETIC DATA PROCESSING

Digital signal processing (DSP) involves representing signals by sequences of numbers, and the processing of these sequences so as to either estimate parameters associated with the sequences or to transform the sequences into another form. The rapid growth of interest in DSP has been prompted by comparatively recent theoretical and technological innovations. In particular, the *fast Fourier transform algorithm* (FFT) and the evolution of integrated circuit technology over the last decade were instrumental in, on the one hand, prompting further interest in DSP algorithms and applications, and on the other, making economical minicomputers available for implementation, testing and further development of such algorithms. In this section, we will describe from an algorithmic and programming viewpoint, two widely used DSP "transforms", the *discrete Fourier transform* (DFT) and *autocorrelation*. In Chapter 10, we will discuss acquisition of digital signals and transformation of these signals using modular systems which may contain a number of DSP transformations as components.

9.3.1 Autocorrelation

The autocorrelation of a number sequence $f(n)$, $n = 1, 2, ..., N$ is defined as

$$r(k) = \sum_{n=1}^{N} f(n)*f(n+k), \quad k=0, 1, ..., p$$

where $f(n) = 0$, $n > N$. A characteristic of autocorrelation is that $r(0) \geq r(k)$. Autocorrelation has numerous uses, including extraction of periodic signals from noise, and estimation of parameters for speech analysis/synthesis. Implementing autocorrelation is quite straightforward, as shown in Fig. 9-2. Here, the data are 16-bit words and the results are 32-bit longwords. For convenience (and brevity), we will use a MACRO, ADD32, for the three instruction sequence "ADD R5,R3", "ADC R2", and "ADD R4,R2" which implements the 32-bit addition following each multiplication.

```
AUTO:
        MOV   #R,OUT      ;POINTER TO OUTPUT ARRAY
        MOV   #F,R0       ;START OF ARRAY DATA
        MOV   N,R1        ;NUMBER OF POINTS
        CLR   R2          ;R2,R3 ← 0
        CLR   R3
;
```

```
LOOP1:
        MOV   (R0)+,R4        ;R4     ← f(n)
        MUL   R4,R4           ;R4,R5 ← f(n)*f(n)
        ADD32                 ;R2,R3 ← R2,R3 + R4,R5
        SOB   R1,LOOP1
;
        MOV   R2,@OUT         ;OUTPUT 32-BIT r(0)
        ADD   #2,OUT
        MOV   R3,@OUT
        ADD   #2,OUT
;
        MOV   #2,KK
LOOP2:
        MOV   KK,R4           ;R4 ← KK
        DEC   R4              ;R4 ← K = KK-1
        MOV   N,R1            ;R1 ← N
        SUB   R4,R1           ;R1 ← N-K = LOOP COUNT
        ASL   R4              ;R4 ← 2*K = OFFSET
        MOV   R4,OFFSET       ;UPDATE OFFSET OF f(n) FROM f(n+k)
        MOV   #F,R0           ;R0 ← DATA STARTING ADDRESS
        CLR   R2             ;R2,R3 ← 0
        CLR   R3
;
LOOP3:
        MOV   0(R0),R4        ;R4     ← f(n+k)
        OFFSET =.-2
        MUL   (R0)+,R4        ;R4,R5 ← f(n+k)*f(n)
        ADD32                 ;R2,R3 ← R2,R3 + R4,R5
        SOB   R1,LOOP3
;
        MOV   R2,@OUT         ;OUTPUT 32-BIT r(k)
        ADD   #2,OUT
        MOV   R3,@OUT
        ADD   #2,OUT
;
        INC   KK             ;KK ← KK+1
        CMP   KK,PP1         ;FINISHED?
        BLE   LOOP2          ;NO
        RTS   PC
;
F:      .BLKW  n             ;INPUT DATA ARAY
OUT:    .WORD  R             ;POINTER TO OUTPUT ARRAY
R:      .BLKW  2*(p+1)       ;OUTPUT DATA ARRAY
PP1:    .WORD  p+1           ;p+1
KK:     .WORD  0
N:      .WORD  n             ;NUMBER OF DATA POINTS
```

Fig. 9-2 Conventional autocorrelation implementation.

Note that this program is not reentrant. In particular, in order to index efficiently, the byte offset of $f(n+k)$ from $f(n)$ is changed in the outer loop. For $N \gg p$, this algorithm requires approximately $(p+1)*N**2$ operations, where an operation is a 16x16 bit multiplication followed by a 32-bit addition.

Since fixed-point multiplication is significantly slower than fixed-point addition, it would be profitable to decrease the number of multiplications if possible. In fact, for $0 < p < N/2$, approximately half the multiplications can be replaced by additions. Letting $N = 8$, then for $k = 1$,

```
r(1)  =  f(1)*f(2)+f(2)*f(3)+f(3)*f(4)+f(4)*f(5)
         +f(5)*f(6)+f(6)*f(7)+f(7)*f(8)

      =  f(2)*[f(1)+f(3)]+f(4)*[f(3)+f(5)]
         +f(6)*[f(5)+f(7)]+f(7)*f(8)
```

This grouping of terms, the Pfiefer/Blankinship (PB) algorithm, can be generalized as follows:

```
         q-1   k
r(k)  =   Σ    Σ     f(m) * [f(m-k)+f(m+k)],  k = 0, 1, ..., p
         j=0  i=1
```

where $q = \lceil N/2\ k \rceil$, $m = 2\ jk + i + k$, $f(n) = 0$ for $n < 0$ or $n > N$, and $p < N/2$.

An extra level of looping has been introduced so that, if programmed conventionally, indexing overhead outweighs the savings introduced by conversion of half the multiplications into additions. Since the control and indexing are independent of the data values, for a given N and p, a customized program can be created with all indexing and control effectively precomputed. Techniques for automatically generating such programs will be examined in Section 9.4; different program structures, all of which accommodate this technique, are discussed in Section 9.5.

9.3.2 The Discrete Fourier Transform (DFT)

Given an array of N complex data points, $x(n)$, then the discrete Fourier transform (DFT) of the array is defined as

```
          N-1
X(k)  =    Σ    x(n)*exp(-j 2πnk/N),  k = 0, 1, ..., N-1
          n=0
```

where $j = (-1)**0.5$ and $\exp(jZ) = \cos(Z) + j \sin(Z)$. Conversely, given the sequence $X(k)$, then

```
                 N-1
x(n)  =(1/N)      Σ    X(k)*exp(j 2πnk/N),  n = 0, 1, ..., N-1
                 k=0
```

An important property of the DFT is that $x(n) = x(n+N)$ and $X(k) = X(k+N)$; that is, both $x(n)$ and $X(k)$ are periodic, with period N. This follows directly since $\exp(j2\pi p) = 1$, p an integer.

The DFT has numerous applications in spectral analysis and estimation and, via the use of the fast Fourier transform (FFT), in convolution and correlation. Convolution enables the response of a linear, time-invariant system to an arbitrary input to be calculated. Since convolution of sequences corresponds to multiplication of their DFT's, an important property of the DFT is that it can indirectly effect convolution. In fact, the computational economics of the FFT implementation of the DFT are such that this latter technique is often to be preferred.

9.3.3 The Fast Fourier Transform (FFT): Derivation and Implementation

Since N complex samples $x(n)$ result in N complex DFT coefficients $X(k)$, N**2 operations are apparently required to compute all $X(k)$. An operation is defined here as a complex multiplication followed by a complex addition. It is possible to substantially reduce this computation using the Cooley-Tukey fast Fourier transform (FFT) algorithm if N = 2**M, M an integer. First, we decompose $x(n)$ into its even and odd numbered points, and evaluate $X(k)$ as the sum of the DFT's of these two subsequences.
That is, with

$$W_N = \exp(-j2\pi/N),$$

$$X(k) = \sum_{r=0}^{(N/2)-1} x(2r)\, W_N^{2rk} + \sum_{r=0}^{(N/2)-1} x(2r+1)\, W_N^{(2r+1)k}$$

$$= \sum_{r=0}^{(N/2)-1} x(2r)\, (W_N^2)^{rk} + W_N^k \sum_{r=0}^{(N/2)-1} x(2r+1)(W_N^2)^{rk}$$

But

$$W_N^2 = \exp(-2j\, 2\pi/N) = \exp(-j\, 2\pi/[N/2]) = W_{N/2}$$

Thus

$$X(k) = \sum_{r=0}^{(N/2)-1} x(2r)\, W_{N/2}^{rk} + W_N^k \sum_{r=0}^{(N/2)-1} x(2r+1)\, W_{N/2}^{rk}$$

$$= G(k) + W_N^k\, H(k) \qquad ,$$

where $G(k)$ is the N/2-point DFT of the even-numbered $x(n)$ subsequence and $H(k)$ is the N/2-point DFT of the odd-numbered point $x(n)$ subsequence. Since

G(k) and *H(k)* are periodic in N/2, only two N/2-point DFT's need be computed, requiring 2(N∗N/4) complex operations. The two N/2-point DFT's are then combined to form the N-point DFT using N complex operations. Thus, a total of N + (N∗N)/2 operations would be necessary. However, using similar arguments, each N/2-point DFT can be computed using two N/4-point DFT's and N/2 complex "combination" operations, requiring a total of 2[2(N∗N/16) + N/2], or N∗N/4 + N operations instead of N∗N/2 operations. An N-point DFT would then require N + N + N∗N/4 complex operations. However, because N = 2∗∗M, this decomposition can be carried out M times. Thus, an N-point DFT requires only a total of MN complex operations rather than N∗∗2. For example, when M = 10, only 10,240 rather than 1,048,576 operations are required!

A flow graph for M = 3 or N = 8, is shown in Fig. 9-3.

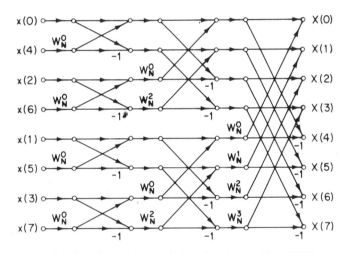

Fig. 9-3 Flow diagram for 8 point fast Fourier transform (FFT).

Examination of this figure reveals a number of interesting properties of the FFT algorithm. First, if the index *n* of each input point *x(n)* is represented as an M-bit binary number, it is apparent that the input array must initially be "shuffled" into *bit reversed* order before the FFT is implemented:

INDEX	BIT REVERSED INDEX	OPERATION
0 0 0 = 0	0 0 0 = 0	X(0) = x(0)
0 0 1 = 1	1 0 0 = 4	X(1) = x(4)
0 1 0 = 2	0 1 0 = 2	X(2) = x(2)
0 1 1 = 3	1 1 0 = 6	X(3) = x(6)
1 0 0 = 4	0 0 1 = 1	X(4) = x(1)
1 0 1 = 5	1 0 1 = 5	X(5) = x(5)
1 1 0 = 6	0 1 1 = 3	X(6) = x(3)
1 1 1 = 7	1 1 1 = 7	X(7) = x(7)

Second, M stages are required. In the i'th stage, $i = 1, 2, ..., M$, N/2 computations of the form

$$X_i(p) = X_{i-1}(p) + W_N^r * X_{i-1}(q)$$

$$X_i(q) = X_{i-1}(p) + W_N^{r+N/2} * X_{i-1}(q)$$

are carried out, where p and q are the indices of the *butterfly* pair. For $i = 1$, the *input X*'s are the x's shuffled as per above. Since

$$W_N^{N/2} = \exp(-j\pi) = -1,$$

these reduce to

$$X_i(p) = X_{i-1}(p) + W_N^r * X_{i-1}(q)$$

$$X_i(q) = X_{i-1}(p) - W_N^r * X_{i-1}(q)$$

This effectively halves the number of multiplications required. At each point, two complex points are operated upon to produce two results which effectively replace the two input points. That is,

$$X_i(p) \text{ and } X_i(q)$$

can be stored in the same location as

$$X_{i-1}(p) \text{ and } X_{i-1}(q)$$

Thus, the FFT can be done in-place; the bit-reversed input array is progressively replaced with the output array. This particular version is the decimation in time (DIT) Cooley-Tukey FFT algorithm. Other decompositions are possible, such as decimation in frequency. Figure 9-4a shows a FORTRAN implementation of the DIT FFT algorithm, while Fig. 9-4b lists a test program which calls the FFT program.

It is assumed that the real and imaginary parts of the input array are stored in odd and even positions of the array XX, equivalenced to the complex array X for convenience. The bit reversal phase occurs first. Note that a significant amount of data-independent integer computation/testing occurs for both indexing and loop control. It is obvious that, if a transform of any particular power of 2 is to be performed a substantial number of times, a table could be computed and stored, thus decreasing run-time computation during the bit reversal phase.

```
          SUBROUTINE FFT(X,M)
          COMPLEX X(1024),U,W,T
          N=2**M
          PI=3.14159265
C         BIT REVERSAL, OR "SHUFFLING"
          NV2=N/2
          NM1=N-1
          J=1
          DO 30 I=1,NM1
          IF(I.GE.J) GO TO 25
          T=X(J)
          X(J)=X(I)
          X(I)=T
   25     K=NV2
   26     IF(K.GE.J) GO TO 30
          J=J-K
          K=K/2
          GO TO 26
   30     J=J+K
C         "M" STAGES FOR 2**M POINTS
          DO 20 L=1,M
                  LE=2**L
                  LE1=LE/2
                  U=(1.0,0.0)
                  W=CMPLX(COS(PI/FLOAT(LE1)),SIN(PI/FLOAT(LE1)))
                  DO 20 J=1,LE1
                          DO 10 I=J,N,LE
                          IP=I+LE1
C                         ----THE "BUTTERFLY"---
                          T=X(IP)*U
                          X(IP)=X(I)-T
   10                     X(I) =X(I)+T
C                         ---END OF BUTTERFLY---
   20             U=U*W
          RETURN
          END
```

Fig. 9-4a Fortran FFT Program.

```
C         FFT TEST PROGRAM
          DIMENSION XX(2048)
          COMPLEX X(1024)
          EQUIVALENCE (X,XX)
          PI=3.1415926
          M=10
          N=2**M
          XN=N
          DO 1 J=1,N
          XJ=J-1
          XX(2*J-1)=COS(2.*PI*XJ/XN)
    1     XX(2*J)=0.0
          CALL FFT(X,M)
          DO 2 J=1,N
          WRITE(7,3) XX(2*J-1),XX(2*J)
    3     FORMAT(1X,2(E14.6,3X))
    2     CONTINUE
          STOP
          END
```

Fig. 9-4b Test program for FFT. Computes DFT of 1024 point complex signal
$$x(n) = COS (2*PI* [n - 1] /N), n = 1,2, ..., N.$$

The computational kernel (ck) of the FFT, the butterfly, occurs at the center of a triply nested loop. This again incurrs significant data-independent, algorithm-dependent, computation for indexing and loop control. Further, special cases of $\exp(j\theta)$ are not specially treated. That is, when $\theta = 0$, $\pi/2$, π, or $3\pi/2$, zero multiplications are required, and when $|\sin\theta| = |\cos\theta| = 0.7071$, two, rather than four, multiplications suffice. Finally, required sine and cosine values are computed "recursively" using

```
cos (kθ) = cos ([k-1]θ) cos (θ) - sin ([k-1]θ) sin (θ)
```

and

```
sin (kθ) = cos ([k-1]θ) sin (θ) + sin ([k-1]θ) cos (θ)
```

It is therefore obvious that a number of steps could be taken to reduce run-time computation for a given size transform. A table of precomputed cos/sin values could be prepared, and special butterfly ck's could be written for those cases noted above. This latter step would normally entail additional run-time computation for butterfly selection so that less data-dependent computation is somewhat offset by more data-independent computation.

In summary, it would be profitable, for a given size transform, to "unroll" all loops so that data access information, optimum butterfly modules, and trig coefficients (if any) required for each butterfly would appear at the appropriate point in an "in-line" program. Such a program would consist of mostly data-dependent computation (carried out with a time optimum butterfly in each case), and thus be relatively time-efficient.

9.4 AUTOMATIC GENERATION OF TIME-EFFICIENT DIGITAL SIGNAL PROCESSING SOFTWARE

For both the PB autocorrelation algorithm, and the fast Fourier transform, programs with properly written in-line code can be relatively time-efficient. In fact, in the last decade a number of other new algorithms have been developed in which a reduction in data-dependent operations (or an exchange of less costly operations for more time consuming operations) is achieved at the expense of relatively increased algorithm complexity. All of these algorithms are amenable to speed enhancement through in-line code-based techniques.

The conventional limitations on production and use of such code are first, the cost of manually coding long programs correctly, and second, the length of the programs themselves. In the following sections it is demonstrated that the cost of producing programs which automatically generate correct in-line code is comparable to that of producing conventional programs, and that other program structures which incorporate the properties noted earlier are available when in-line code is prohibitive due to memory considerations.

9.4.1 Software Generation

The technique for generating correct in-line code is simple. An existing high-level language signal processing program which employs looping structures and involves arithmetic/logical computation to select data or effect loop control (and thus, program sequencing) is modified to produce another related high-level language program which, at run time, *auto*matically *gen*erates (*autogen*) an in-line program. The generated program is most often assembly language but may be a high-level language for some applications. The modifications to the original program consist mainly of replacing the signal processing computational kernel with one or more "write" statements. As suggested earlier, the code thus generated can effectively incorporate (and thus eliminate) most explicit deterministic run-time calculations. The generated program will then consist of a time-optimized linear instruction sequence, with the optimization occurring at program generation time rather than at run time.

A valuable attribute of this technique is that future changes in the algorithm can first be implemented and tested by modification of the original high-level language program. The results of the modifications can then be rapidly propagated into fast operational code by simply changing the generator program to reflect the altered "original" program, and then automatically regenerating a new time efficient in-line program.

The technique is best illustrated by examples. Since the autocorrelation *ck* is trivial, it will be used to examine various software structures for the autogen technique.

9.5 PROGRAM STRUCTURES FOR COMPUTATIONAL KERNEL IMPLEMENTATION

A number of program structures satisfy the requirements of autogen code. Among these are in-line code, subroutines, threaded code, and "knotted code". The autocorrelation algorithm will provide a vehicle for illustration of the time/space tradeoffs inherent in these structures. The kernel will be implemented for N = 8, and k = 1 with an example for each program structure.

That is,

$$r(1) = \sum_{i=0}^{3} [f(2i+1) + f(2i+3)]*f(2i+2)$$

is computed with $f(n) = 0$, $n > 8$. The ADD32 MACRO introduced in Section 9.3.1 will again be used to accumulate the 32-bit $r(1)$ in R2, R3.

9.5.1 In-Line code

In-line code can obviously incorporate the properties noted above:

```
; IN-LINE CODE COMPUTATIONAL KERNEL EXPANSION *******************
;
F:    .BLKW 8.
START:
        CLR R2              ;R2,R3  ←  0
        CLR R3
;
        MOV F+ 0 ,R4        ;R4     ←  f(1)
        ADD F+ 4 ,R4        ;R4     ←  f(1)+f(3)
        MUL F+ 2 ,R4        ;R4,R5  ←  [f(1)+f(3)]*f(2)
        ADD32              ;R2,R3  ←  R2,R3 + R4,R5
;
        MOV F+ 4 ,R4        ;R4     ←  f(3)
        ADD F+ 8.,R4        ;R4     ←  f(3)+f(5)
        MUL F+ 6 ,R4        ;R4,R5  ←  [f(3)+f(5)]*f(4)
        ADD32              ;R2,R3  ←  R2,R3 + R4,R5
;
        MOV F+ 8.,R4        ;R4     ←  f(5)
        ADD F+12.,R4        ;R4     ←  f(5)+f(7)
        MUL F+10.,R4        ;R4,R5  ←  [f(5)+f(7)]*f(6)
        ADD32              ;R2,R3  ←  R2,R3 + R4,R5
;
        MOV F+12.,R4        ;R4     ←  f(7)
        MUL F+14.,R4        ;R4,R5  ←  f(7)*f(8) as m+k > N
        ADD32              ;R2,R3  ←  R2,R3 + R4,R5
                .
```

Note that the above program could have been easily generated by another program. In DECUS 11-296, a FORTRAN program capable of generating a custom program with the above structure, for arbitrary N and $p < N/2$, is available. When this generator program is compiled and run, a complete in-line PDP-11 assembly language program is created. When assembled, the resultant program computes a p lag autocorrelation of N input points and requires approximately $N(5+4.5p)$ memory locations. With $N = 256$ and $p = 14$, for example, the program occupies 17,000 words of memory and computes the 32-bit integer autocorrelation $r(k)$ in 14.1 msec on a PDP 11/45 with 300 ns bipolar memory. All returned $r(k)$ are scaled by the same power of 2 and only 16 bits retained so that $2**14 \leq r(0) < 2**15$.

Although this structure is optimal in terms of minimizing execution time for a given non-cache PDP-11 CPU, the program storage requirements increase by the ck size linearly as each ck is invoked. For larger ck's, FFT butterflies for example, it is clear that in-line code may be prohibitive in the amount of storage required, especially as the number of data points increases.

9.5.2 Subroutines

In-line subroutine calls, with precomputed arguments, also can incorporate the desired properties of autogen software:

```
; IN-LINE SUBROUTINE CALLS WITH PRECOMPUTED ARGUMENTS***********
;MAIN PROGRAM
F:          .BLKW 8.
START:
            CLR R2              ;R2,R3 ← 0
            CLR R3
;
            JSR R0,CORR0
            F+ 0,F+ 4,F+ 2  ;ADDRESS BLOCK
            JSR R0,CORR0
            F+ 4,F+ 8.,F+ 6 ;ADDRESS BLOCK
            JSR R0,CORR0
            F+ 8.,F+12.,F+10. ;ADDRESS BLOCK
            JSR R0,CORR1
            F+12.,F+14.        ;ADDRESS BLOCK
            .
            .
            .
;SUBROUTINES
CORR0:
            MOV @(R0)+,R4    ;R4      ← f(m-k)
            ADD @(R0)+,R4    ;R4      ← f(m-k)+f(m+k)
            MUL @(R0)+,R4    ;R4,R5 ← [f(m-k)+f(m+k)]*f(m)
            ADD32            ;R2,R3 ← R2,R3 + R4,R5
            RTS R0
;
CORR1:
            MOV @(R0)+,R4    ;R4      ← f(m-k)
            MUL @(R0)+,R4    ;R4,R5 ← f(m-k)*f(m) as m+k > N
            ADD32            ;R2,R3 ← R2,R3 + R4,R5
            RTS R0
```

This construct makes use of an *argument address block* following each subroutine call, with the autoincrement deferred mode used to insure that the data points will be accessed correctly and that the RTS will be performed properly.

The main program would be automatically generated, while the subroutines are hand coded. Note that in this case, program size increases linearly only by the subroutine call/return program overhead plus the number of passed parameters, irrespective of subroutine size. A time penalty occurs, of course, in executing the subroutine call/return sequence.

9.5.3 Threaded Code

Threaded code enables economical invocation of a sequence of program modules without the need to return to a main program. A single precomputed *thread*, consisting of a data array, contains addresses of the requisite modules and the parameters to be used in the modules, intermixed in correct order of usage.

Threaded code is of particular interest on the PDP-11 since it is output by some of
the FORTRAN IV compilers. An example will best illustrate the concept:

```
;  THREADED CODE***********************************************
F:        .BLKW 8.
L:                                    ;THREAD
          CORR0,F+ 0 ,F+ 4 ,F+ 2
          CORR0,F+ 4 ,F+ 8.,F +6
          CORR0,F+ 8.,F+12.,F+10.
          CORR1,F+12.,F+14.
          NEXT
;
START:
          CLR R2            ;R2,R3 ← 0
          CLR R3
          MOV #L,R0         ;STARTING ADDRESS OF THREAD
          JMP @(R0)+
CORR0:
          MOV @(R0)+,R4     ;R4      ← f(m-k)
          ADD @(R0)+,R4     ;R4      ← f(m-k)+f(m+k)
          MUL @(R0)+,R4     ;R4,R5 ← [f(m-k)+f(m+k)]*f(m)
          ADD32             ;R2,R3 ← R2,R3 + R4,R5       .
          JMP @(R0)+
CORR1:
          MOV @(R0)+,R4     ;R4      ← f(m-k)
          MUL @(R0)+,R4     ;R4,R5 ← f(m-k)*f(m) as m+k > N
          ADD32             ;R2,R3 ← R2,R3 + R4,R5
          JMP @(R0)+
NEXT:
          .
```

The (automatically generated) thread, the array "L", effectively contains precomputed addresses of *subroutines* and *data* to be used during the entire course of the
program. More important, once the required computational kernels have been
written, a new autocorrelation program for arbitrary N and *p* can be created
simply by generating a new thread; program, data points, and thread occupy non-
overlapping memory spaces.

In comparing threaded code and subroutines for the specific PDP-11 example
it can also be noted that the subroutine call occupies 2 words of storage while the
"indirect jump/increment register" instruction requires only a single word for
address specification. Finally, execution of the latter instruction requires less than
half the time required by the subroutine call/return sequence.

Examination of autogen program space requirements for the three PDP-11
examples is instructive:

```
              Algorithm:  N point by p lag autocorrelation
         ----------------------------------------------------
      Technique                       Approximate Storage (words)
      ---------                       ---------------------------
      1. In-line ck expansion               9(Np/2)
      2. In-line subroutine calls           5(Np/2)
      3. Threaded code                      4(Np/2)
```

We emphasize that for algorithms such as the FFT, where the *ck*'s are substantially larger than those of autocorrelation, the storage requirement for (1) above is unacceptable while those for (2) and (3) are entirely realistic. Also, while the autocorrelation algorithm requires only three *ck*'s, other digital signal processing programs in general require more. For example, to minimize data-dependent computation, including multiplications, both radix-2 and radix-4 FFT's require 5 different *ck*'s each.

9.5.4 Knotted Code

We make a transition from threaded code to another form (which obviates the need to repeatedly call the same subroutine) by making two observations. First, threaded code has the freedom to execute any two subprograms in sequence. Second, digital signal processing algorithms generally execute each *ck* a number of times before moving to another; this does not, of course, preclude returning to the same *ck* later in the program. Thus we will further reduce the storage requirement by allowing for "knots" in the thread.

In effect, we will allow loops. However, we need not waste run time overhead in decrementing a counter because the number of times each program module must be invoked before moving on to the next is precomputed and thus implicit in the thread. A solution is the "precomputed loop". Simply, the precomputed loop involves effectively inserting a thread element ordinarily not permissible and a test for the presence of that element at the end of each *ck*. Since 0 is generally not allowed as a FORTRAN array subscript, and since computer system software most often uses lower memory (thus making use of memory location 0 for user arrays unlikely), 0 will indicate knot termination. Because a "zero test/branch" instruction is both commonplace and time efficient, the time/space tradeoff proves very worthwhile.

Here, the address of *f(m)* is passed via the thread into R1; note that ND = −MD = −2*k as each 16-bit data word requires 2 bytes.

```
; Knotted Code**********************************************************
F:    .BLKW 8.
L:                        ;THREAD
        CORR0,F+2
              F+6
              F+10.,0
        CORR1,F+14.,0
        NEXT
ND=2
MD=-2
START:
        CLR R2           ;R2,R3 ← 0
        CLR R3
        MOV #L,R0        ;STARTING ADDRESS OF THREAD
        JMP @(R0)+
```

```
;
CORR0:
        MOV (R0)+,R1        ;FETCH POINTER TO f(m)
        MOV MD(R1),R4       ;R4     ← f(m-k)
        ADD ND(R1),R4       ;R4     ← f(m-k)+f(m+k)
        MUL (R1),R4         ;R4,R5  ← [f(m-k)+f(m+k)]*f(m)
        ADD32              ;R2,R3  ← R2,R3 + R4,R5
        MOV (R0)+,R1        ;FETCH POINTER TO f(m).
        BNE CORR0+2         ;POINTER NON-ZERO, BACK AGAIN
        JMP @(R0)+          ;ON TO NEXT ck
;
CORR1:
        MOV (R0)+,R1        ;FETCH POINTER TO f(m)
        MOV MD(R1),R4       ;R4     ← f(m-k)
        MUL (R1),R4         ;R4,R5  ← f(m-k)*f(m) as m+k > N
        ADD32              ;R2,R3  ← R2,R3 + R4,R5
        MOV (R0)+,R1        ;FETCH POINTER TO f(m).
        BNE CORR1+2         ;POINTER NON-ZERO, BACK AGAIN
        JMP @(R0)+          ;ON TO NEXT ck
NEXT:   .
```

The variables ND and MD are constant within the two inner loops. Thus a reduction in operand pointers per *ck* from 3 to 1 has occurred.

Also, if each *ck* is (realistically) executed a number of times $n \gg 1$ per "call", then the threaded code storage requirements are further reduced, by 1 address pointer per *ck*, in knotted code. Finally, the "test/branch" instruction requires only half the execution time of the "indirect jump/increment register" so that both time and space are conserved by knotted code in comparison to threaded code. Note especially that there is zero incremental run time overhead in fetching the thread element which may indicate knot termination, except when the element does indeed indicate termination. At all other times the word fetched is a data pointer which is required for use in the *ck*. A knotted-code autocorrelation generator program is included in DECUS 11-296: a knotted code EIS FFT program will be described in Section 9.6.

In summary, exploitation of both internal *ck* structure and the knotted code technique has reduced generated program size by a further factor of 75% to a final figure of $(Np)/2$. Thus, knotted code requires nearly an order of magnitude less program space than in-line code and, on an 11/55, executes only 15% slower than the in-line version. Examination of the radix-2 and radix-4 FFT similarly reveals that pointer structures are such that knotted code can be used with a variety of *ck*'s to effect the same function, but with one *ck* program structure offering a minimization in thread and hence program length.

9.5.5 Autocorrelation Results: Time, Space and Hardware

Table 9-1 summarizes the time/space trade-offs of in-line code, subroutines, threaded code, and knotted code, assuming $N \gg p$.

Table 9-1 Incremental Space/Time Overhead in Autocorrelation ck Invokation

Incremental Invokation Overhead	In-line	Subroutines	Threaded	Knotted
Code	Space for ck	Space for JSR Rn,SUB + parameters passed	Space for SUB address + parameters passed	Space for parameters passed only
Time	0	Execution: JSR Rn,SUB +RTS Rn	Execution: JMP @(Rn)+	Execution: BNE only

Knotted code is obviously superior to threaded code insofar as storage space required for the thread is concerned ($Np/2$ vs. $2Np$ words). Comparison of the two *ck*'s also makes it clear that knotted code will execute faster than threaded code due to the substantially fewer address pointers fetched.

Observed execution times, in msec, and program sizes, in words, are as follows ($N = 128, p = 12$):

	PDP 11/55	PDP 11/70	PDP 11/60	Program Size (Words)
Conventional	9.69	9.72	17.35	80
In-line	5.25	9.42	18.03	7552
Knotted	6.70	7.05	11.35	768

From these results, the reader can note that in-line code is clearly inappropriate for a cache machine.

A program analysis program of the type outlined at the beginning of this chapter was applied to the three programs timed above. The program was parameterized for the PDP-11/55. Results are as follows, with estimated *time* in msec followed by *number of times instruction executed* in parentheses:

	Conventional	Program Structure In-line, PB Algorithm	Knotted, PB Algorithm
MUL	5.94 (1617)	3.49 (893)	3.25 (893)
MOV	1.66 (1701)	0.89 (949)	1.46 (1738)
ADD	1.31 (3237)	1.43 (2510)	1.50 (2510)
SOB	1.13 (1615)	....	0.09 (130)
ADC	0.64 (1600)	0.36 (888)	0.36 (888)
BNE	....	....	0.54 (766)
	10.68	6.17	7.20

Note that the timings are somewhat greater than the observed run times. It is normal for CPU's to have 10% speed variations from "theoretical" estimates. However, it is apparent that the goal of halving MUL time at the expense of increased ADD time has been achieved. In applications such as speech analysis/

synthesis, autocorrelation can constitute by far the greatest relative time component of the many algorithms applied to each speech segment analyzed. Thus, the savings realized here are significant. In Section 10.7, further speed enhancements possible through microprogramming the ck's will be explored.

9.6 THE FAST FOURIER TRANSFORM: A TIME-EFFICIENT EIS IMPLEMENTATION

Examination of the Fortran FFT program of Fig. 9-4a reveals that only 6 lines of source code operate on the data; 3 lines effect bit reversal and 3 lines implement the FFT ck or butterfly. This means that most of the code is involved with integer arithmetic for data access and loop control. Since this arithmetic is both algorithm-dependent and data-independent, results of such computation at any step of the algorithm (for a given N) are the same every time the program is run. Thus, when a fixed-size FFT is to be invoked repeatedly (see Chapter 10, for example) it would be productive to "unwind" the FFT program and produce a custom, in-line program having precomputed indices and trigonometric constants available at each point in the algorithm. Since there are no loops, no arithmetic operations for loop control are necessary. Further, when $W = \pm 1 + j\,0$, $0 \pm j\,1$, or $0.707 \pm j\,0.707$, special butterfly modules can be introduced to eliminate multiplications or reduce the number required in that butterfly. And, note that

$$(a + j\ b)*(\cos\theta + j\ \sin\theta)$$
$$= \quad (a\ \cos\theta - b\ \sin\theta) + j\ (a\ \sin\theta + b\ \cos\theta)$$

can be computed as

$$\text{temp} \quad = \quad (a + b)\ \cos\theta$$
$$a\ \sin\theta + b\ \cos\theta \quad = \quad \text{temp} + a\ (\sin\theta - \cos\theta)$$
$$a\ \cos\theta - b\ \sin\theta \quad = \quad \text{temp} - b\ (\sin\theta + \cos\theta).$$

This requires only 3 multiplications and 3 additions if precomputed values of $(\sin\theta + \cos\theta)$, $(\sin\theta - \cos\theta)$, and $\cos\theta$ are available at each step. Due to register requirements, a 3 multiply, 4 add algorithm is used in the EIS FFT. The ck implemented is a fixed-point version of that shown in Fig. 9-5. This is the butterfly of Fig. 9-4a with the real array A replacing the complex array X. That is, $A(2*i-1) + j\ A(2*i) = X(i)$, and $UR + jUI = U = \cos\theta + j\ \sin\theta$.

```
TR=A(2*IP  )*UR
TX=A(2*IP-1)*UI
TI=TX+TR
TR=TX-TR+(A(2*IP-1)+A(2*IP))*(UR-UI)
A(2*IP  )=A(2*I  )-TI
A(2*I   )=A(2*I  )+TI
A(2*IP-1)=A(2*I-1)-TR
A(2*I-1 )=A(2*I-1)+TR
```

Fig. 9-5 FFT butterfly (computational kernel).

In the EIS implementation, precomputed values of scaled UR, UI, and (UR−UI) are made available at each step as are indices for access of data. Although in-line code was feasible (and profitable) for the PB algorithm (on non-cache machines), such is not the case for the FFT with its relatively large *ck*'s. Thus, in the EIS FFT, knotted code is used. The resultant program consists of 4 distinct segments:

1. FFT butterfly routines

2. data array

3. trigonometric coefficient array (contains precomputed, scaled values of UR, UI, and (UR−UI))

4. driver array, or *thread* (contains precomputed parameters for accessing data and butterflies)

The latter 2 arrays are generated by a special program (see Appendix F) and are unique to each value of N. The butterfly modules are common to FFT's of all sizes.

9.6.1 Butterfly Modules

The 6 EIS butterfly routines listed below use ADD, SUB, MUL, ASR, and ASL to implement a time efficient radix-2 fixed-point FFT. The algorithm implemented is decimation-in-time, with a divide by 2 at each stage. Since there are M stages, and $N = 2**M$, the resultant coefficients are those of Fig. 9-5 divided by N.

An alternative fixed-point algorithm implements a divide by 2 only when overflow occurs. This algorithm is more time-consuming, and gives coefficients scaled by a data-dependent (and thus variable) factor. This is undesirable. In terms of accuracy, the algorithm used here suffices for most spectral analysis applications. The complex data points are assumed to be pairs of 16-bit, 2's complement numbers, each with magnitude less than $2**14$, contained in alternate locations of a 2N-point array. The following notes are of interest:

1. Given (A+B)/2, then (A−B)/2 = (A+B)/2 − B. An instruction sequence for efficiently computing (A±B)/2 is thus

```
MOV     A,Rn      ;Rn ← A
ADD     B,Rn      ;Rn ← A+B
ASR     Rn        ;Rn ← (A+B)/2
MOV     Rn,--     ;Store (A+B)/2
SUB     B,Rn      ;Rn ← (A+B)/2 - B = (A-B)/2
MOV     Rn,--     ;Store (A-B)/2
```

2. Also, as noted earlier, if $\cos\theta$ is stored as $C = (2.**15-1.)*\cos\theta$, then the 16 MSB of the 32-bit product $X*C$ is approximately $(X*\cos\theta)/2$. Hence if $B = X*\cos\theta$, $B/2$ directly results from the MULtiply of X and C. To efficiently compute $(A \pm X*\cos\theta)/2$,

```
MOV     A,R0        ;R0  ←  A
ASR     R0          ;R0  ←  A/2
MOV     R0,R1       ;R1  ←  A/2
MOV     C,R2        ;R2  ←  C = (2.**15-1)*cosθ
MUL     X,R2        ;R2  ←  X*cosθ/2
ADD     R2,R0       ;R0  ←  (A+X*cosθ)/2
SUB     R2,R1       ;R1  ←  (A-X*cosθ)/2
```

3. The corner address of each butterfly is passed via the thread, as is the address of the first of a triplet of sequential trig values. The address of the second data point within each butterfly is calculated by adding an offset, stored on the stack, to the first address. This offset is halved once per stage, or M times per FFT.

4. Autoincrement/decrement address modes are used to efficiently access the real and imaginary parts of the 2 complex data points which are manipulated by each butterfly.

5. Six different butterfly modules are used to minimize multiplications.

6. Knotted code effects looping within each butterfly. Thus, following the MOV (R5)+,Rn which accepts the precomputed butterfly corner address from the thread, a BNE checks for zero address. This initiates transition to a different butterfly via the JMP @(R5)+ immediately following the BNE.

7. Although the FFT is done "in-place", the bit reversal is carried out using a second array. This is done so that, for example, while the FFT output is being further processed, the input array can be filled via a DMA A/D converter.

8. A driver program FTMUF*m*, m = 3, 4, ..., 9, 0 for 8, 16, ..., 512, 1024 complex points, respectively, is generated by using FTMULF.BLD (Appendix F). FTMUF4 is listed below, with added comments. An example test program is shown in Fig. 9-6. For $m \neq 4$, the DIMENSIONing constants "32" become $2**(m+1)$ and the "N=16" statement becomes "N=$2**m$".

9. The output of the FFT appears in the second array ("Y") as follows ["$X(\ )+$" implies *positive* frequencies, "$X(\ )-$" implies negative frequencies]. For i = 1, 2, ..., N/2, array elements $2*i-1$ and $2*i$, respectively, contain *Re* $X(i-1)+$ and *Im* $X(i-1)+$. When i = (N/2+1), array element

```
C         16 POINT EIS FFT TEST PROGRAM
          INTEGER X(32),Y(32)
          COMMON /XX/X,Y
          N=16
          PI=3.1415926
          Z=2.**14-1.
          XN=N
          DO 1 J=1,N
          XJ=J-1
          X(2*J-1)=Z*COS(2.*PI*XJ/XN)
1         X(2*J)=0.0
          CALL FTMUF4
          DO 2 J=1,N
          WRITE(7,3) Y(2*J-1),Y(2*J)
3         FORMAT(1X,2(I7,2X))
2         CONTINUE
          STOP
          END
```

Fig. 9-6 EIS FFT test program.

2*i-1 contains 2*$Re\ X(i-1)+$ = 2*$Re\ X(i-1)$-, and array element 2*i contains zero. And, for i = (N/2+2), ..., N, array elements 2*i-1 and 2*i, respectively, contain $Re\ X(N+1-i)$- and $Im\ X(N+1-i)$-. Here, $X(k)$ = $X(k/NT\ Hz)$ where N data points were sampled, one every T seconds. For real signals, $Re\ X(k)+$ = $Re\ X(k)$- and $Im\ X(k)+$ = -$Im\ X(k)$-.

```
;OUTPUT OF FTMULF.BLD (APPENDIX F) FOR M=4

          .TITLE FTMUF4
          .GLOBL FTMUF4 BUTTOV BUTT BUT225 BUT270 BUT315
          .GLOBL LE1,BUT0,OFFSET
          .CSECT XX
          A=.
          B=.+  100
  FTMUF4:
          MOV #ARRAY,R5
          MOV LE1,-(R6)
          JMP @(R5)+
;THREAD
ARRAY:
    OFFSET,0
      BUT0,A+2,A+22,A+12,A+32,A+6,A+26,A+16,A+36,0
    OFFSET,0
      BUT0,A+2,A+12,A+6,A+16,0
      BUT270,A+42,A+52,A+46,A+56,0
    OFFSET,0
      BUT0,A+2,A+6,0
      BUT315,A+52,A+56,0
      BUT270,A+22,A+26,0
      BUT225,A+72,A+76,0
    OFFSET,0
```

```
        BUT0,A+2,0
        BUTTOV,A+46,COSTBL+12,0
        BUT315,A+26,0
        BUTTOV,A+66,COSTBL+26,0
        BUT270,A+12,0
        BUTT,A+56,COSTBL+42,0
        BUT225,A+36,0
        BUTT,A+76,COSTBL+56,0
     OFFSET,0
     BITREV
;BIT REVERSAL COMPUTATIONAL KERNEL
BITREV:
        MOV    #A,R1
        MOV    (R1)+,B+   0

                    .
                    .

        MOV    (R1)+,B+   76
        TST    (SP)+
        RTS    PC
;TRIG VALUE TABLE
COSTBL:
        37777,      0, 77777, 51635,147406, 73101, 55201,122577
        55202, 51635,104700, 30373, 77777,100002,      0, 42505
       104700,147406,      0,122577,122577,135274,147406,104700
LE1:    100
        .END
```

Fig. 9-7 Radix-2 16 point EIS FFT driver program.

```
;COMPUTATIONAL KERNELS (BUTTERFLYS) FOR RADIX-2 EIS FFT
;RE(I), IM(I), ARE RE[X(I)] = A(2*I-1), IM[X(I)] = A(2*I), ETC.
;WITH ALL DATA 16-BIT 2'S COMPLEMENT INTEGERS
        .TITLE   BUTMUF
        .GLOBL   BUT0,BUT225,BUT270,BUT315,BUTT,BUTTOV
        .GLOBL   OFFSET
;
;  COSINE = 1
;
BUT0:
        MOV     (R5)+,R1        ;SET UP 'I' POINTER
        MOV     R1,R2           ;DUPLICATE 'I'
        ADD     (R6),R2         ;'IP'='I'+OFFSET
        MOV     (R1),R3         ;R3    ← IM(I)
        MOV     -(R1),R4        ;R4    ← RE(I)
        ADD     (R2),R3         ;R3    ← IM(I)+IM(IP)
        ADD     -(R2),R4        ;R4    ← RE(I)+RE(IP)
        ASR     R3              ;DIV BY 2
        ASR     R4              ;DIV BY 2
        MOV     R4,(R1)+        ;RE(I)  ← (RE(I)+RE(IP))/2
        MOV     R3,(R1)         ;IM(I)  ← (IM(I)+IM(IP))/2
        SUB     (R2),R4         ;R4     ← (RE(I)-RE(IP))/2
        MOV     R4,(R2)+        ;RE(IP) ← (RE(I)-RE(IP))/2
        SUB     (R2),R3         ;R3     ← (IM(I)-IM(IP))/2
        MOV     R3,(R2)         ;IM(IP) ← (IM(I)-IM(IP))/2
        MOV     (R5)+,R1        ;SET UP 'I' POINTER
        BNE     BUT0+2          ;0 POINTER IS END
        JMP     @(R5)+          ;ON TO NEXT SUBROUTINE
```

Fig. 9-8 Radix-2 EIS FFT butterfly modules.   a) 0 multiply butterfly.

```
;
; COSINE = 0
;
BUT270:
        MOV     (R5)+,R1            ;SET UP 'I' POINTER
        MOV     R1,R2              ;DUPLICATE 'I'
        ADD     (R6),R2            ;'IP'= 'I'+OFFSET
        MOV     (R1),R3            ;R3    ← IM(I)
        MOV     -(R1),R4           ;R4    ← RE(I)
        ADD     (R2),R4            ;R4    ← RE(I)+IM(IP)
        SUB     -(R2),R3           ;R3    ← IM(I)-RE(IP)
        ASR     R3                 ;DIV BY 2
        ASR     R4                 ;DIV BY 2
        MOV     R4,(R1)+           ;RE(I)  ← (RE(I)+IM(IP))/2
        MOV     R3,(R1)            ;IM(I)  ← (IM(I)-RE(IP))/2
        ADD     (R2)+,R3           ;R3     ← (IM(I)+RE(IP))/2
        MOV     (R2),-(R2)         ;SAVE IM(IP)
        SUB     (R2),R4            ;R4     ← (RE(I)-IM(IP))/2
        MOV     R4,(R2)+           ;RE(IP) ← (RE(I)-IM(IP))/2
        MOV     R3,(R2)            ;IM(IP) ← (IM(I)+RE(IP))/2
        MOV     (R5)+,R1           ;SET UP 'I' POINTER
        BNE     BUT270+2           ;0 POINTER IS END OF LOOP
        JMP     @(R5)+             ;ON TO NEXT SUBROUTINE
```

Fig. 9-8 Radix-2 EIS FFT butterfly modules.   b) 0 multiply butterfly.

```
;
; COSINE OF 315 DEGREES
;
        COS=55201
        SIN=122577
BUT315:
        MOV     (R5)+,R4           ;SET UP 'IP' POINTER
        MOV     (R4),R0            ;R0 ← IM(IP)
        ADD     -(R4),R0           ;R0 ← RE(IP)+IM(IP)
        MUL     #COS,R0            ;R0 ← (RE(IP)+IM(IP))*COS/2
        MOV     (R4)+,R2           ;R2 ← RE(IP)
        SUB     (R4),R2            ;R2 ← (RE(IP)-IM(IP))
        MUL     #SIN,R2            ;R2 ← (RE(IP)-IM(IP))*SIN/2
        MOV     R4,R1              ;R1 ← 'IP'
        SUB     (R6),R1            ;'I'='IP'-OFFSET
        ASR     (R1)               ;IM(I)/2
        MOV     (R1),(R4)          ;DUPLICATE IM(I)/2
        SUB     R2,(R4)            ;IM(IP) ← (IM(I)/2-(R2))
        ADD     R2,(R1)            ;IM(I)  ← (IM(I)/2+(R2))
        ASR     -(R1)              ;RE(I)/2
        MOV     (R1),-(R4)         ;DUPLICATE RE(I)/2
        SUB     R0,(R4)            ;RE(IP) ← (RE(I)/2-(R0))
        ADD     R0,(R1)            ;RE(I)  ← (RE(I)/2+(R0))
        MOV     (R5)+,R4           ;SET UP 'IP' POINTER
        BNE     BUT315+2           ;0 POINTER IS END OF LOOP
        JMP     @(R5)+             ;ON TO NEXT SUBROUTINE
```

Fig. 9-8 Radix-2 EIS FFT butterfly modules.   c) 2 multiply butterfly.

```
;
; COSINE OF 225 DEGREES
;
            COS=122577                  ;-1/SQR(2)
            MCOS=-COS                   ;1/SQR(2)
BUT225:
            MOV     (R5)+,R4            ;SET UP 'IP' POINTER
            MOV     (R4),R0             ;R0 ← IM(IP)
            SUB     -(R4),R0            ;R0 ← IM(IP)-RE(IP)
            MUL     #MCOS,R0            ;R0 ← (IM(IP)-RE(IP))*MCOS/2
            MOV     (R4)+,R2            ;R2 ← RE(IP)
            ADD     (R4),R2             ;R2 ← RE(IP)+IM(IP)
            MUL     #COS,R2             ;R2 ← (RE(IP)+IM(IP))*COS/2
            MOV     R4,R1               ;R1 ← 'IP'
            SUB     (R6),R1             ;'I'='IP'-OFFSET
            ASR     (R1)                ;IM(I)/2
            MOV     (R1),(R4)           ;DUPLICATE IM(I)/2
            SUB     R2,(R4)             ;IM(IP) ← (IM(I)/2-(R2))
            ASR     -(R1)               ;RE(I)/2
            MOV     (R1),-(R4)          ;DUPLICATE RE(I)/2
            SUB     R0,(R4)             ;RE(IP) ← (RE(I)/2-(R0))
            ADD     R0,(R1)+            ;RE(I)  ← (RE(I)/2+(R0))
            ADD     R2,(R1)             ;IM(I)  ← (IM(I)/2+(R2))
            MOV     (R5)+,R4            ;SET UP 'IP' POINTER
            BNE     BUT225+2            ;0 POINTER IS END OF LOOP
            JMP     @(R5)+              ;ON TO NEXT SUBROUTINE
```

Fig. 9-8 Radix-2 EIS FFT butterfly modules. d) 2 multiply butterfly.

```
;
; COSINE OF AN ANGLE BETWEEN 270 AND 180 DEGR OTHER THAN 270,225
;
BUTT:
            MOV     (R5)+,R2            ;SET UP 'IP' POINTER
            MOV     (R5)+,R3            ;SET UP 'COS' POINTER
            MOV     R5,-(SP)            ;SAVE R5 ON STACK
            MOV     (R2),R4             ;R4 ← IM(IP)
            MUL     (R3),R4             ;R4 ← IM(IP)*COS/2
            MOV     -(R2),R0            ;R0 ← RE(IP)
            MUL     -(R3),R0            ;R0 ← RE(IP)*SIN/2
            MOV     R0,R1               ;R1 ← RE(IP)*SIN/2
            SUB     R4,R0               ;R0 ← RE(IP)*SIN/2-IM(IP)*COS/2
            ADD     R4,R1               ;R1 ← RE(IP)*SIN/2+IM(IP)*COS/2
            MOV     (R2)+,R4            ;R4 ← RE(IP)
            ADD     (R2),R4             ;R4 ← RE(IP)+IM(IP)
            MUL     -(R3),R4            ;R4 ← (RE(IP)+IM(IP))*(COS-SIN)/2
            ADD     R4,R0               ;R0 ← RE(IP)*COS/2-IM(IP)*SIN/2
            MOV     (SP)+,R5            ;RESTORE R5
            MOV     R2,R3               ;R3 ← 'IP'
            SUB     (R6),R3             ;'I'='IP'-OFFSET
            ASR     (R3)                ;IM(I)/2
            MOV     (R3),(R2)           ;DUPLICATE IM(I)/2
            ADD     R1,(R3)             ;IM(I)  ← (IM(I)/2+(R1))
            SUB     R1,(R2)             ;IM(IP) ← (IM(I)/2-(R1))
            ASR     -(R3)               ;RE(I)/2
            MOV     (R3),-(R2)          ;DUPLICATE RE(I)/2
            ADD     R0,(R3)             ;RE(I)  ← (RE(I)/2+(R0))
            SUB     R0,(R2)             ;RE(IP) ← (RE(I)/2-(R0))
            MOV     (R5)+,R2            ;SET UP 'IP' POINTER
            BNE     BUTT+2              ;0 POINTER IS END OF LOOP
            JMP     @(R5)+              ;ON TO NEXT SUBROUTINE
```

Fig. 9-8 Radix-2 EIS FFT butterfly modules. e) 3 multiply butterfly.

```
;
; COSINE OF AN ANGLE BETWEEN 0 AND -90 OTHER THAN 0,315,270
; SAME AS "BUTT" EXCEPT FOR 2 EXTRA SCALING INSTRUCTIONS
BUTTOV:
        MOV         (R5)+,R2            ;SET UP 'IP' POINTER
                        •
        MUL         -(R3),R4            ;R4 ← (RE(IP)+IM(IP))*(COS-SIN)/4
; 2 EXTRA INSTRUCTIONS
        ASL         R5
        ROL         R4                  ;[R4,R5] ← [R4,R5]*2
;
        ADD         R4,R0               ;R0 ← RE(IP)*COS/2-IM(IP)*SIN/2
                        •
        MOV         (R5)+,R2
        BNE         BUTTOV+2
        JMP         @(R5)+              ;ON TO NEXT SUBROUTINE
;
OFFSET: ASR         (R6)
        TST         (R5)+               ;BUMP OVER 0
        JMP         @(R5)+
;
        .END
```

Fig. 9-8 Radix-2 EIS FFT butterfly modules. f) 3 multiply butterfly.

9.6.2 FFT Results: Time, Space and Hardware

Execution time of the EIS autogen FFT is approximately $11k$MN $u$sec, where $k = 1$ for an 11/45, 55 with bipolar memory, 1.53 for an 11/45 with MOS, 2.77 for an 11/45 with core, 3.31 for an 11/34, 40, and 9.1 for an LSI-11/03. For example, a 1K complex FFT takes 118 msec on the 11/55. Memory requirements are approximately 0.75MN + 5.5N + 142 words for FTMUFm + BUTMUF, the butterfly routines. In Chapter 10, the EIS FFT will be used as part of a "digital oscilloscope" and a speech spectrogram or "voiceprint" system. For these applications, a technique is used wherein two N-point real FFT's can be computed using a single N-point complex FFT followed by a relatively simple "unscrambling" program.

In an N = 2**M point radix-2 FFT, N/2 butterflies are computed in each of M passes. Each butterfly accesses and manipulates a pair of complex data points. If sufficient *gp* registers are available for storage of intermediate results, then only 4 fetches and 4 stores — 8 data point memory references in total — are required per butterfly. In practice, this is possible in only one of the 6 EIS butterfly routines. The second register required for the 32-bit EIS MUL is essentially lost for efficient use as a temporary, and at least 2 *gp* registers are required for pointers. For a floating-point FFT, however, all *gp* registers are available for use as pointers and 6 *fp* registers are present for use as floating-point accumulators. This architecture suits an alternative FFT algorithm. In the radix-4 FFT, 4 complex data points are manipulated during each of N/4 butterflys performed in each of M stages, for an N = 4**M point DFT. Thus, only 1/4 the butterflies are required compared to a radix-2 FFT, with — given sufficient temporaries — only 1/2 the memory data accesses. Finally, at most, 3/4 the multiplications are required compared to an equal size radix-2 transform. The radix-4 butterflies and generator program are also available in DECUS 11-296, and in Appendix H.

Execution time for the FPP autogen FFT is approximately 16.4kMN *u*sec, where $k = 1$ for an 11/55 (FP 11-C), 1.34 for an 11/60 (FP 11-E), 3.9 for an 11/34 (FP 11-A), and 5.32 for an 11/60 (firmware FPP). For example, a 1K complex FFT takes 168 msec on an 11/55. Memory requirements are approximately 0.6MN + 5.2N + 445 words for an N = 4**M point transform.

9.7 ALTERNATIVE FORMS FOR HIGH LEVEL LANGUAGE OUTPUT CODE

A substantial portion of this text has been devoted to discussion and demonstration of assembler programming techniques which exploit various architectural features of the PDP-11 family, and the powerful address modes in particular. Assembler coding of applications programs *is* of value, especially when the algorithms implemented are of such universal importance that the software development costs are amortized over many runs by many users. Thus, for example, FORTRAN users may invoke efficient assembler library routines for computing trigonometric values, exponentials, and other common functions. Similarly, efficient assembler versions of more complex algorithms are available from libraries established by users of various computer families (e.g., DECUS). Nevertheless, software development cost factors dictate that the bulk of programming be carried out in high level languages. Given this, it is of interest to consider the various types of output code that can be produced by a high level language compiler. In particular, one might compare the time/space efficiency of the best object code generated for an arbitrary input program compared to a programmer-optimized assembler version.

One must first be able to judge the efficiency of *different* implementations of the *same* algorithm on a specific computer. Although relative execution speed of such programs on a given machine is often a realistic indicator of time efficiency, other time-independent measures are available. One such set of parameters is *program size* and, more importantly, the number of bits of *instructions* and *data* transferred between CPU, registers, and main memory during program execution. Indeed, time efficiency is often directly related to this latter measure.

We will briefly examine alternative forms for the output of four *different* FORTRAN compilers, three producing code for the PDP-11 and one for the VAX-11. The short, radix-2 FFT inner loop (butterfly) of Fig. 9-4a, converted to REAL arithmetic for clarity (Fig. 9-9), will be the common input to all compilers.

9.7.1 Threaded Code

We have seen (Section 9.5.3) that threaded code consists essentially of a driver array which contains a mixture of *module addresses* and *data addresses*. In the example shown there, different size autocorrelations could be implemented by

```
0035              DO 10  I = J,N,LE
0036              IP=I+LE1
0037              TR=A(2*IP  )*UR
0038              TX=A(2*IP-1)*UI
0039              TI=TX+TR
0040              TR=TX-TR+(A(2*IP-1)+A(2*IP))*(UR-UI)
0041              A(2*IP  )=A(2*I  )-TI
0042              A(2*I   )=A(2*I  )+TI
0043              A(2*IP-1)=A(2*I-1)-TR
0044     10       A(2*I-1 )=A(2*I-1)+TR
```

Fig. 9-9 REAL version of innner loop of radix-2 FFT (Fig. 9-4a).

computing a unique thread whose length and content are dependent on N and p; the *ck* modules are invariant. Suppose, however, that the MUL instruction is not available, as is the case for the PDP-11/05. A new set of *ck*'s could be written which might effect fixed-point multiplication by repeated add/shifts. These *ck*'s can be invoked by the *same* thread. Thus, threaded code enables the module *sequencing* and data *selection* information necessary to implement a given algorithm to be generated independently of the computational modules themselves. In this way, a thread can be generated (compiled) which can be executed on any PDP-11, with the computational modules reflecting the "hardware" present on the target machine (e.g., EAE, EIS, FIS, FPP) chosen at program link time.

In Fig. 9-10, a portion of the output code of the FORTRAN IV threaded code compiler is shown, for the input program segment of Fig. 9-9. Comments have been added for clarity.

Memory Address	Routine Pointer	Data 1 Pointer	Data 2 Pointer	Comments
;39				
000750	MOF$MM	000040	000044	;TI ← TX
000756	ADF$MM	000112	000044	;TI ← TI+TR=TX+TR
;40				
000764	MOF$MS	000112		;TOS ← TX
000770	SUF$MS	000040		;TOS ← TX-TR
000774	MOF$MS	000154		;TOS ← A(2*IP-1)
001000	ADF$MS	000150		;TOS ← A(2*IP-1)+A(2*IP)
001004	MOF$MS	000070		;TOS ← UR
001010	SUF$MS	000074		;TOS ← UR-UI
001014	MUF$SS			;TOS ← (A(2*IP-1)+A(2*IP))*(UR-UI)
001016	ADF$SS			;TOS ← TX-TR+(A(2*IP-1)+A(2*IP))*(UR-UI)
001020	MOF$SM	000040		;TR ← TOS

Fig. 9-10 Portion of PDP-11 threaded code compiler output, input code Fig. 9-9.

Note that the FORTRAN "virtual machine" is a zero address (stack) machine in that arithmetic instructions may operate on operands located on the "top-of-stack" (TOS). However, operations can also be effected between stack/memory, memory/stack, or memory/memory. The thread module pointers generated are appropriately tagged with SS, SM, MS, or MM, with zero, one, or two addresses inserted into the thread following the relevant module pointer. The operations carried out here are floating-point move (MOF), add (ADF), subtract (SUF), and multiply (MUF). Note that SS, MS, SM, and MM varieties of "sources" and "destinations" are present in the example. At link time, the routines are made available from a FORTRAN library, i.e., FORLIB.OBJ under RT-11, which is custom built to suit the arithmetic hardware present on the target machine. Thus the compiler output code can be moved from one model PDP-11 to another *without* recompiling.

Assuming that R4 is to be the thread pointer, the sequence above would be started by MOV #750,R4 followed by JMP @(R4)+. For example, the MUF$SS routines for FIS and FPP could be written:

```
        ;FIS VERSION                    ;FPP VERSION
MUF$SS: FMUL    SP             MUF$SS: LDF     (SP)+,F0
        JMP     @(R4)+                 MULF    (SP)+,F0
                                       STF     F0,-(SP)
                                       JMP     @(R4)+
```

Similarly, ADF$MM routines for FIS and FPP are:

```
        ;FIS VERSION                    ;FPP VERSION
ADF$MM: MOV     (R4)+,R1       ADF$MM: LDF     @(R4)+,F0
        MOV     2(R1),-(SP)            MOV     (R4)+,R0
        MOV     (R1),-(SP)             ADDF    (R0),F0
        MOV     (R4)+,R0               STF     F0,(R0)
        MOV     2(R0),-(SP)            JMP     @(R4)+
        MOV     (R0),-(SP)
        FADD    SP
        MOV     (SP)+,(R0)+
        MOV     (SP)+,(R0)
        JMP     @(R4)+
```

The FIS MUF$SS is more space efficient than the FPP MUF$$SS, whereas the opposite is the case for the ADF$MM modules.

9.7.2 In-line Code (EIS/FIS)

The versatility of the threaded code approach incurrs a number of penalties. Most important, the JMP @(R4)+ requires two memory cycles of overhead. Thus, in some cases (fixed-point addition, for example), the overhead of the "virtual machine" can far exceed the time required for the arithmetic operation itself. If a specific architecture is assumed, then the "hardware" independence disappears, but more efficient in-line code can be generated. Thus, in Fig. 9-11, the commented output for the complete FFT inner loop of Fig. 9-9 is shown for a FORTRAN compiler with both EIS and FIS assumed present (e.g., 11/03, 35, 40). Here, to conserve space, we have replaced some commonly appearing constructs with macros.

Note that in-line code is generated, with integer values (e.g., addresses) sometimes preserved in *gp* registers across a number of FORTRAN source statements. It is clear that, for floating-point arithmetic, the PDP-11 has become a true *zero address* computer, with operations sometimes chained on the stack (e.g., the FSUB, FMUL, FADD sequence of the code for statement 40). Thus, when the *sequence* of arithmetic operations is appropriate, the stack is used to advantage for temporary floating-point storage locations, thus eliminating costly stack/memory transfers.

```
        .MACRO  PUSH    X                  .MACRO  POP       X
        MOV     X+2,-(SP)                  MOV     (SP)+,X
        MOV     X  ,-(SP)                  MOV     (SP)+,X+2
        .ENDM                              .ENDM
;
        .MACRO  PUSHR   R0,X               .MACRO  POPR     R0,X
        MOV     A-2-X(R0),-(SP)            MOV     (SP)+,A-4-X(R0)
        MOV     A-4-X(R0),-(SP)            MOV     (SP)+,A-2-X(R0)
        .ENDM                              .ENDM
;
        .MACRO  INDEX   R0,X
        MOV     X,R0
        ASL     R0
        ASL     R0
        .ENDM
;
```

Address	Label	Instruction		Comments
`;35`				
000656	L$ENB:	MOV	J,R2	;R2 ← J
000662		MOV	R2,I	;I ← R2 = J
000666		MOV	N,R1	;R1 ← N
000672		SUB	R2,R1	;R1 ← R1-R2 = N-J
000674		SXT	R0	;R0 ← SIGN (N-J)
000676		MOV	LE,R3	;R3 ← LE
000702		DIV	R3,R0	;R0 ← (N-J)/LE
000704		INC	R0	;R0 ← R0+1
000706		MOV	R0,T$GAC	;T$GAC ← R0 = LOOP COUNT
000712		ASL	R2	;R2 ← 2*R2 = 2*J
000714		MOV	R2,T$MPB	;T$MPB ← R2 = 2*J
000720		ASL	R3	;R3 ← 2*R3 = 2*LE
000722		MOV	R3,T$ABC	;T$ABC ← 2*LE
`;36`				
000726	L$ONB:	MOV	LE1,R2	;R2 ← LE1
000732		MOV	I,R3	;R3 ← IP
000736		ADD	R2,R3	;R3 ← IP+LE1
000740		MOV	R3,IP	;IP ← IP+LE1
`;37`				
000744		ASL	R3	;R3 ← 2*IP
000746		INDEX	R1,R3	;R1 ← 4*(2*IP)
000754		MOV	A-4(R1),T$IDC	;TIDC,TIDC+2 ← A(2*IP)
000762		MOV	A-2(R1),T$IDC+2	
000770		PUSH	UR	;TOS ← UR
001000		PUSH	T$IDC	;TOS ← A(2*IP)
001010		FMUL	SP	;TOS ← UR*A(2*IP)
001012		POP	TR	;TR ← TOS = UR*A(2*IP)
`;38`				
001022		MOV	A-10(R1),T$CEC	;TCEC,TCEC+2 ← A(2*IP-1)
001030		MOV	A-6(R1),T$CEC+2	
001036		PUSH	UI	;TOS ← UI
001046		PUSH	T$CEC	;TOS ← A(2*IP-1)
001056		FMUL	SP	;TOS ← UI*A(2*IP-1)
001060		POP	TX	;TI ← TOS = UI*A(2*IP-1)

```
;39
 001070        PUSH      TR                    ;TOS  ←  TR
 001100        PUSH      TX                    ;TOS  ←  TX
 001110        FADD      SP                    ;TOS  ←  TR+TX
 001112        POP       TI                    ;TI   ←  TOS = TR+TX
;40
 001122        PUSH      TX                    ;TOS  ←  TX
 001132        PUSH      TR                    ;TOS  ←  TR
 001142        FSUB      SP                    ;TOS  ←  TX-TR
 001144        PUSH      T$CEC                 ;TOS  ←  A(2*IP-1)
 001154        PUSH      T$IDC                 ;TOS  ←  A(2*IP)
 001164        FADD      SP                    ;TOS  ←  A(2*IP-1)+A(2*IP)
 001166        PUSH      UR                    ;TOS  ←  UR
 001176        PUSH      UI                    ;TOS  ←  UI
 001206        FSUB      SP                    ;TOS  ←  UR-UI
 001210        FMUL      SP                    ;TOS  ←  (A(2*IP-1)+A(2*IP))*(UR-UI)
 001212        FADD      SP          ;TOS  ←  TX-TR + (A(2*IP-1)+A(2*IP))*(UR-UI)
 001214        POP       TR ;TR  ←  TOS =  TX-TR + (A(2*IP-1)+A(2*IP))*(UR-UI)
;41
 001224        INDEX     R0,T$MPB              ;R0   ←  4*(2*I)
 001234        PUSHR     R0,0                  ;TOS  ←  A(2*I)
 001244        PUSH      TI                    ;TOS  ←  TI
 001254        FSUB      SP                    ;TOS  ←  A(2*I)-TI
 001256        POPR      R1,0                  ;A(2*IP)  ←  TOS = A(2*I)-TI
;42
 001266        INDEX     R0,T$MPB              ;R0   ←  4*(2*I)
 001276        PUSH      TI                    ;TOS  ←  TI
 001306        PUSHR     R0,0                  ;TOS  ←  A(2*I)
 001316        FADD      SP                    ;TOS  ←  A(2*I)+TI
 001320        INDEX     R0,T$MPB              ;R0   ←  4*(2*I)
 001330        POPR      R0,0                  ;A(2*I)  ←  TOS  =  A(2*I)+TI
;43
 001340        INDEX     R0,T$MPB              ;R0   ←  4*(2*I)
 001350        PUSHR     R0,4                  ;TOS  ←  A(2*I-1)
 001360        PUSH      TR                    ;TOS  ←  TR
 001370        FSUB      SP                    ;TOS  ←  A(2*I-1)-TR
 001372        POPR      R1,4                  ;A(2*IP-1)  ←  TOS = A(2*I-1)-TR
;44
 001402        INDEX     R0,T$MPB              ;R0   ←  4*(2*I)
 001412        PUSH      TR                    ;TOS  ←  TR
 001422        PUSHR     R0,4                  ;TOS  ←  A(2*I-1)
 001432        FADD      SP                    ;TOS  ←  A(2*I-1)+TR
 001434        INDEX     R0,T$MPB              ;R0   ←  4*(2*I)
 001444        POPR      R0,4                  ;A(2*I-1)  ←  TOS = A(2*I-1)+TR
 001454        ADD       T$ABC,T$MPB           ;2*I  ←  2*I+2*LE
 001462        ADD       LE,I                  ;I  ←  I+LE
 001470        DEC       T$GAC                 ;DEC COUNT
 001474        BLE       .+6                   ;FINISHED?
 001476        JMP       L$ONB                 ;NO!
```

Fig. 9-11 PDP-11 FIV EIS/FIS output code for FFT inner loop.

9.7.3 In-line Optimized Code (EIS/FPP)

The four floating-point processor (FPP) registers directly accessible to memory, F0-F3, may be used for temporary storage as well as for memory/register or register/register floating-point operations (Section 5.4.4). Since the *fp* registers may be independently addressed, the sequence restrictions implied in using the stack for chained FIS operations are absent; this greatly enhances the temporary storage utility of these registers. The FORTRAN IV PLUS compiler assumes the presence of the EIS and FPP instructions and both *gp* and *fp* register sets. This restriction is accompanied by enhanced capability with respect to time and space optimization. *Both* register sets are used extensively as temporaries across blocks of code. Indeed, in Fig. 9-12, note the use of R1 and R2 for retention of the 2*IP and 2*I floating-point base addresses for the butterfly, with the "-1" of 2*IP-1 and 2*I-1 absorbed into the index word at compile time. Also note the extensive use of F0-F3 as temporaries, thus minimizing 32-bit operand load/store operations so as to enhance run time efficiency.

```
Address Label   Instruction             Comments
------- -----   -----------             --------
;35
000450  L$EBMB: MOV     J,R0            ;R0  ←  J
000454          MOV     N,R1            ;R1  ←  N
000460          SUB     R0,R1           ;R1  ←  N-J
000462          MOV     R1,R3           ;R3  ←  N-J
000464          SXT     R2              ;R2  ←  SIGN(N-J)
000466          DIV     LE,R2           ;R2  ←  (N-J)/LE
000472          MOV     R2,$TEMPS+4     ;TEMPS+4  ←  (N-J)/LE
000476          LDF     UR,F1           ;F1  ←  UR
000502          SUBF    UI,F1           ;F1  ←  UR-UI
000506          STF     F1,$TEMPS+6     ;$TEMPS+6,$TEMPS+10  ←  UR-UI
;36
000512  L$EBOD: MOV     R0,R1           ;R0  ←  J
000514          ADD     LE1,R1          ;R1  ←  J+LE1
000520          MOV     R1,IP           ;IP  ←  J+LE1
;37
000524          MOV     IP,R1           ;R1  ←  IP
000530          ASH     #3,R1           ;R1  ←  4*(2*IP)
000534          LDF     A-4(R1),F1      ;F1  ←  A(2*IP)
000540          LDF     F1,F2           ;F2  ←  A(2*IP)
000542          MULF    UR,F2           ;F2  ←  TR=A(2*IP)*UR
000546          LDF     F2,F0           ;F0  ←  TR=A(2*IP)*UR
;38
000550          LDF     A-10(R1),F2     ;F2  ←  A(2*IP-1)
000554          LDF     F2,F3           ;F3  ←  A(2*IP-1)
000556          MULF    UI,F3           ;F3  ←  A(2*IP-1)*UI
000562          STF     F3,TX           ;TX  ←  A(2*IP-1)*UI
;39
000566          LDF     TX,F3           ;F3  ←  TX
000572          ADDF    F0,F3           ;F3  ←  TX+TR
000574          STF     F3,TI           ;TI  ←  TX+TR
;40
000600          ADDF    F1,F2           ;F2  ←  A(2*IP-1)+A(2*IP)
000602          MULF    $TEMPS+6,F2     ;F2  ←  (A(2*IP-1)+A(2*IP))*(UR-UI)
000606          LDF     TX,F1           ;F1  ←  TX
000612          SUBF    F0,F1           ;F1  ←  TX-TR
000614          ADDF    F1,F2       ;F2  ←  TX-TR+(A(2*IP-1)+A(2*IP))*(UR-UI)
000616          LDF     F2,F0           ;F0  ←  TR
;41
000620          MOV     R0,R2           ;R2  ←  I
000622          ASH     #3,R2           ;R2  ←  4*(2*I)
000626          LDF     A-4(R2),F1      ;F1  ←  A(2*I)
000632          SUBF    TI,F1           ;F1  ←  A(2*I)-TI
000636          STF     F1,A-4(R1)      ;A(2*IP)  ←  A(2*I)-TI
```

```
;42
000642          LDF     A-4(R2),F1      ;F1 ← A(2*I)
000646          ADDF    TI,F1           ;F1 ← A(2*I)+TI
000652          STF     F1,A-4(R2)      ;A(2*I) ← A(2*I)+TI
;43
000656          LDF     A-10(R2),F1     ;F1 ← A(2*I-1)
000662          SUBF    F0,F1           ;F1 ← A(2*I-1)-TR
000664          STF     F1,A-10(R1)     ;A(2*IP-1) ← A(2*I-1)-TR
;44
000670          LDF     A-10(R2),F1     ;F1 ← A(2*I-1)
000674          ADDF    F0,F1           ;F1 ← A(2*I-1)+TR
000676          STF     F1,A-10(R2)     ;A(2*I-1) ← A(2*I-1)+TR
000702          ADD     LE,R0           ;R0 ← R0+LE = I+LE
000706          DEC     $TEMPS+4        ;DEC COUNT
000712          BGE     L$EBOD          ;LOOP
                                        ;END DO LOOP
```

Fig. 9-12 Output of PDP-11 FIV PLUS compiler for FFT butterfly.

Numerous optimizations are performed by *optimizing compilers*, such as FIV PLUS. These include elimination of redundant computations and removal of constant computations from the inside of loops. In *strength reduction*, some arithmetic operations may be replaced by others requiring less time. Thus a multiply-by-four becomes two ASL's while, as in Fig. 9-12, multiplication by a higher power-of-two is effected by ASH. Similarly, X**2 becomes X*X. The power of optimizing compilers is demonstrated by noting that many floating-point intensive programs executed on a high-speed machine (PDP-11/55, 70) exhibit a factor of three speedup when compiled in FIV PLUS as opposed to FIV threaded code.

9.7.4 In-line Optimized Code (VAX-11, FIV PLUS)

The power of machine architecture in enhancement of run time code efficiency and code storage requirements is demonstrated in the output of the VAX-11 FIV PLUS compiler (Fig. 9-13). The significant architectural features of interest are:

1. ***Three Operand Addressing:*** Instructions of the form "OP OPND1,OPND2,OPND3" (Section 2.3.1), wherein OPND3 ← OPND1 op OPND2, are implemented on the VAX-11 as an extension of the PDP-11 architecture. Such instructions enable elimination of some explicit operand load and store instructions (i.e., MOV and LDF/STF), along with the overhead of the relevant instruction fetch.

2. ***True Indexing:*** Here, the power of true indexing (see Section 4.5.6) is vividly demonstrated. Integers stored in registers specified by "[ ]" (e.g., 2*IP, 2*I in the example) are *transparently* "copied" and internally left shifted the number of bits necessary to directly access the operand specified by the instruction type (i.e., 0 bits for bytes, 1 bit for words, 2 bits for longwords or single precision floating-point, and 3 bits for quadwords or

312

double precision floating-point). The explicit, time consuming ASL's or ASH's of the PDP-11 code are gone. Thus, integer variables appearing in the high level language as indexing parameters can be *directly* used for operand access at the assembler level no matter what data type is being manipulated.

Both space and time efficiency are improved by these architectural enhancements. For example, FORTRAN programs executed on the VAX-11/780, a machine implemented in the same technology as the PDP-11/70, often exhibit improvements of two or more in speed of execution.

The reader should note the reduction in storage required for code generated, from FIV EIS/FIS (400 bytes) to FIV PLUS EIS/FPP (162 bytes) to FIV PLUS VAX-11 (106 bytes).

```
Hex
Address   Label   Instruction                           Comments
-------   -----   -----------                           --------
;35
  00E8   L$IBIC:MOVL    J(R11), R7                       ;R7 ← J
  00EC          SUBF3   R6, UR(R11), R5                  ;R5 ← UR-UI
;36
  00F1   L$IBHE:ADDL3   LE1(R11), R7, IP(R11)            ;IP ← I+LE1
;37
  00F7          MULL3   #2, IP(R11), R9                  ;R9 ← 2*IP
  00FC          MULF3   UR(R11), A-4[R9], R8             ;R8 ← TR=A(2*IP)*UR
;38
  0106          MULF3   R6, A-8[R9], TX(R11)             ;TX ← A(2*IP-1)*UI
;39
  0110          ADDF3   R8, TX(R11), TI(R11)             ;TI ← TX+TR
;40
  0116          ADDF3   A-4[R9], A-8[R9], R0             ;R0 ← A(2*IP-1)+A(2*IP)
  0124          MULF2   R5, R0                           ;R0 ← R0*(UR-UI)
  0127          SUBF3   R8, TX(R11), R1                  ;R1 ← TX-TR
  012C          ADDF3   R1, R0, R8   ;R8 ← TX-TR+(A(2*IP-1)+A(2*IP))*(UR-UI)
;41
  0130          MULL3   #2, R7, R10                      ;R10 ← 2*I
  0134          SUBF3   TI(R11), A-4[R10], A-4[R9] ;A(2*IP)   ← A(2*I)   -TI
;42
  0143          ADDF2   TI(R11), A-4[R10]                ;A(2*I)   ← A(2*I)   +TI
;43
  014C          SUBF3   R8, A-8[R10], A-8[R9]            ;A(2*IP-1) ← A(2*I-1)-TR
;44
  015A          ADDF2   R8, A-8[R10]                     ;A(2*I-1)  ← A(2*I-1)+TR
  0162          ACBL    N(R11), LE(R11), R7, L$IBHE ;R7 ← R7+LE,
                                                   ; BR TO L$IBHE IF LE N
```

Fig. 9-13 VAX-11 FIV PLUS compiler output for FFT inner loop.

The VAX-11 has sixteen 64-bit registers which may be used for pointers or as fixed- *or* floating-point accumulators; R14 and R15 are SP and PC, respectively. In this example, R11 contains the base address of a local storage area while R6 holds UI.

9.7.5 High Level vs. Assembler Programming

The radically decreasing costs and increasing density of semiconductor technology have given rise to computers with architectures which are optimized for both *time* and *space* efficiency. That is, *relatively* fewer bits are required for implementing a given algorithm (compared to programs for less powerful architectures) and the code execution is *relatively* fast (compared to alternative architectures implemented using the same technology). The time and space factors are related, as has been demonstrated via the VAX-11 example of the previous section. Thus, the performance gains in moving from FORTRAN (for example) to assembler are lessened by better optimizing compilers for target machines with more powerful architectures.

Nevertheless, in some cases, various addressing modes cannot be fully exploited from high level languages and time crucial, widely used algorithms *may* benefit from assembler coding. Thus, for example, the widely available Singleton mixed-radix FORTRAN program effects a 1024 point, complex, floating-point FFT in 1.12 seconds when compiled in FIV threaded code and run on a PDP-11/55. Using FIV PLUS, the execution time becomes 0.33 seconds. A transition has been made from the stack-oriented "virtual machine" (Section 9.7.1) to the in-line code of the "real" PDP-11 with its independently addressable floating-point accumulators. Then, application of the *autogen* technique (Section 9.4), to transform the program into a knotted code structure (Section 9.5.4), further reduces execution time to 0.25 seconds. Here, most data-independent, algorithm-dependent computation is carried out at thread generation time rather than at program execution time. Finally, *manually* coding the *ck*'s (i.e., radix-4 butterflies) in assembly language, as opposed to *compiling* them, yields an execution time of 0.16 seconds (DECUS 11-296). This time differential can be accounted for rather easily. In this case, the "human compiler" is able to match the algorithm *ck* structure to the machine architecture better than the compiler in at least two respects. First, the autoincrement/autodecrement modes enable more efficient data point access, eliminating the offset word fetches entailed in the mode 6 memory operand addressing utilized by the compiler. Second, the two *fp* accumulators not directly accessible from main memory (Section 5.4.4) can be used to advantage for temporary storage by the assembly language programmer, thus further reducing both instruction and data traffic amongst CPU, memory, and *fp* register/accumulators.

Again, as architectures become more powerful, the compiler/assembler code efficiency gap is reduced. Conversely, it should be noted that the relative computational power of competing architectures implemented in similar technology can only be completely realized or revealed by *mature* optimizing compilers which fully exploit the features of the machines. Since maturity implies a time factor, one expects to see a delay between the introduction of a new architecture and the full realization of its power. Thus the value of the *family concept* (Section 3.5.1) is fully recognized. That is, implementations of faster machines of the same architecture are accompanied by enhancement of optimization capabilities of existing compilers and introduction of compilers for evolving or new languages (e.g., PASCAL, C). Similary, extension of old architectures into new (e.g., PDP-11 to VAX-11) can be accomplished gracefully when the family relationships involve evolutionary rather than revolutionary changes.

REFERENCES

Knuth (Vol. 1, 1968, 1973), Aho *et. al.* (1974), and Baase (1978) are all invaluable references on design and analysis of computer algorithms in general. Wirth (1976) emphasizes interaction of algorithms and data structures. The standard texts on digital signal processing are Oppenheim and Schafer (1975) and Rabiner and Gold (1975); both, however, are at the graduate level. Fortunately, Steiglitz (1974) presents a very simple and clear introduction to the field, using many short FORTRAN programs to reinforce the concepts presented. Pfiefer and Blankinship (1973, 1974) almost simultaneously derived the muliplication-saving autocorrelation algorithm, while Bell (1975) formally introduced the threaded code concept. Morris (1977, 1978) outlined the *autogen* technique, and has made the autocorrelation, and fixed- and floating-point PDP-11 specific FFT software available in DECUS. T-Thong and Liu (1976) present an extensive error analysis of fixed-point FFT's, including the divide-by-two at each stage, truncation algorithm listed in this chapter. Brender (1978) describes the development and operation of the PDP-11 FORTRAN threaded code compiler, while Lowry (1969) shows how optimization techniques are applied in compilers. The bimonthly *IEEE Transactions on Acoustics, Speech, and Signal Processing* presents state-of-the-art results in the DSP area.

10
Real-time Interactive Computing

Despite the advent of the *computer society*, the image of a computer conveying its results to the world via reams of paper still persists. Similarly, although the video terminal is rapidly becoming more proliferate than the teletypewriter, computer data entry by keyboard is still the accepted norm. In this chapter we will examine some aspects of the world of *real-time interactive computing*. Here, computer *input* is via direct analog waveform (including speech and other biological signals) or from "indirect" analog sources including light pen, joy-stick, or writing tablet. Computer *output* is via analog waveforms (especially speech), pictures drawn on a cathode ray tube (CRT) or, in some cases, unconventional alphanumeric displays (light emitting diodes, plasma panels etc.). In most of these applications some form of computer/operator real-time interaction is implied. Here, the use of interrupts and the idea of event driven task initiation and execution achieve prime importance. Here too, the optimal usage of computer architectural features to achieve minimum program execution time often means the difference between true real-time computation and slower than real-time computation, the latter often being completely unacceptable.

Nature is analog and most computers are digital. Thus, the analog/digital interface is crucial in achieving the efficient man/machine interface requisite for interactive, real-time computing.

10.1 ANALOG/DIGITAL CONVERTERS: STRUCTURE AND PROGRAMMING

Analog-to-digital (A/D) and digital-to-analog (D/A) converters are related in structure. Specifically, an A/D converter can be constructed from a D/A converter using a few extra, but simple, components. Thus, an understanding of the D/A converter is crucial.

10.1.1 Digital-to-Analog (D/A) Converters

The role of a D/A is to convert numbers (generally composed of binary digits) into an analog voltage. A basic D/A converter consists of a voltage reference, a set of binary weighted precision resistors and set of digitally controlled switches (Fig. 10-1).

DIGITAL INPUT CODE

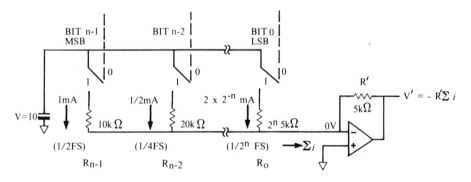

ALL 1's: $\Sigma i \big|_{max} = 2mA\ (1 - 2^{-n})$

FS = FULL SCALE OUTPUT

Fig. 10-1 Digital-to-analog (D/A) converter structure.

Ohm's law states that the current (I) through a resistor is directly proportional to the voltage (V) across the resistor and inversely proportional to its "resistance" (R). That is, I = V/R. In the D/A converter, a set of switched binary weighted resistors

$$R_0, R_1 = R_0/2, \ldots, R_{n-1} = R_{n-2}/2$$

produce currents

$$i, 2*i, 4*i, \ldots, [2**(n-1)]*i,$$

respectively, if the relevant bit of the binary word to be converted is 1; zero current is produced if the relevant bit is a zero. These currents are summed and applied to another resistor to produce the desired voltage.

Thus

$$I = (V/R_{n-1}) \sum_{j=n-1}^{0} [B_j / 2**(n-1-j)]$$

where

$$B_j = 0 \text{ or } 1, \text{ and } V' = -IR'$$

Note that this produces zero voltage out when the binary word is 0, and that, when the binary word is all 1's, $V' = (2V/Rn-1)*R'$ If the D/A converter switches were connected to a memory location being continuously incremented by a CPU, the observed voltage output would ideally be a staircase linearly increasing with time.

Other D/A codes are possible. For example, by adding an offset current equal and opposite to the current produced when the most significant bit (MSB) is set, 2's complement numbers may be directly converted to an analog voltage.

In practice, however, it is not possible to obtain inexpensive precision resistors with the dynamic range necessary for practical D/A converters (between 8 and 16 bits). "Quads" of binary weighted resistors are cascaded with voltage dividers which successively halve the output contribution of the quads as the LSB region is approached. State-of-the-art techniques enable 12-bit D/A's to be constructed on chips and be sold at a 1979 price of about $25.

Important parameters with respect to D/A converters are:

1. *Settling time:* Switches require a finite amount of time to operate, and the operational amplifier used to sum the currents from the individual resistors has a finite bandwith.

2. *Linearity:* When a binary number makes a transition from 00..01111...1 to 00..10000...0, all resistors making a contribution to the previous voltage output become inactive and a new resistor is the sole source of the current which produces the new analog voltage. It is obvious that resistor tolerances are critical so as to insure that the single resistor has the requisite value.

3. *Glitches:* In the previous example, if the "0 to 1" switch is very slow compared to all the "1 to 0" switches the voltage output will momentarily fall towards zero, and then rise towards the correct voltage. This will produce an undesired transient voltage spike or "glitch".

10.1.2 Analog-to-Digital (A/D) Converters

The task of converting rapidly changing analog voltages to binary numbers is more challenging than the digital-to-analog problem. Many solutions are possible, with the successive approximation technique being the most interesting and, perhaps, cost effective. The technique is similar to the weighing process using a balance employing binary-related weights (e.g., 1/2 lb., 1/4 lb., 1/8 lb., etc. are sufficient to achieve balance with an unknown weight up to 1 lb.). It is also analogous to the divide algorithm discussed earlier (Section 5.2.5).

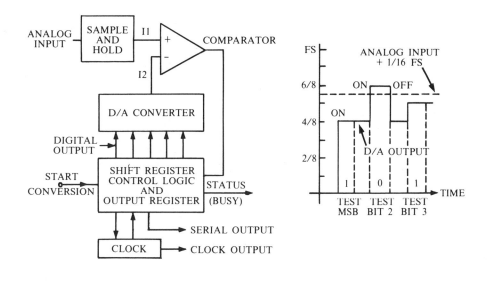

a. Block Diagram   *b. 3-Bit Weighing*

Fig. 10-2 Analog-to-digital converter

The analog signal to be converted is first "sampled and held" to achieve a time invariant value. It is then applied to one input (I1) of a comparator (Fig. 10-2), the other input (I2) being the output of a D/A converter. The comparator output is binary: "1" for I1 > I2, "0" for I2 > I1. If the resultant D/A voltage is less than that of the analog signal (i.e., I1 > I2), the MSB is set; otherwise, it is cleared. Successively lower bits are set (and perhaps cleared, according to comparator output) until the LSB has been tested. Then, the conversion is complete. In contrast to the D/A process, A/D conversion takes a variable amount of time; at worst, every bit must be switched on and off. Thus an A/D converter is more complex (and more costly) than a D/A converter. Indeed, to achieve fast A/D conversion requires a *very* fast D/A converter and a "sample-and-hold" circuit to precede the A/D itself.

10.1.3 Sampling Requirements: Bits/Sample and Sampling Rate

Two important parameters are associated with A/D sampling:

1. **Bits/Sample:** Since the output of a D/A converter consists of only a finite number of states, an arbitrary analog waveform can only, at best, be approximated by a D/A output. An n-bit D/A has about a $6n$ db signal-to-quantizing noise-ratio (SQNR), the "quantizing noise" being the error between the ideal output desired (e.g., a ramp), and the actual D/A output (e.g., a staircase). Quantizing noise is perceptually unobtrusive (i.e., nearly

absent) if at least 10 bits are used for speech output. Dynamic range considerations suggest that at least 12 bits be used in practice. Modern digital high fidelity systems, often experimentally simulated on minicomputer systems, use more expensive 16-bit D/A's to achieve SQNR's approaching the 100 db dynamic range of live music.

2. **Sampling Rate:** Nyquist's theorem dictates that to preserve an analog signal completely one need only sample it at twice the rate of the highest frequency present in the signal. This means that digital high fidelity systems require, minimally, 30,000 samples per second, while 6,000 samples per second suffice to preserve telephone quality speech. In practice, sampling is performed at more than twice the rate corresponding to the effective signal bandwidth since the filters used to preprocess signals are not ideal.

10.1.4 Programming the A/D, D/A and Real-time Clock

Programming of analog/digital converters for data input/output requires techniques which relate to the A/D and D/A internal operation. For example, a finite time is required between initiation of A/D operation and completion of sample conversion to digital form. Thus, interrupts are appropriate for invocation of sample aquisition software.

Although a number of different analog-digital converter modules are available for the PDP-11, the techniques for programming them are similar. Since the AR-11 module offered by DEC contains a programmable real-time clock and dual D/A converters in addition to a multiplexed A/D converter, we will discuss the AR-11 exclusively. However, the programs and techniques examined are compatible with the more recent DEC modules (AD/ADV11 A/D's, KW/KWV11 programmable clocks, and AA/AAV11 D/A's) and the LPS-11 system which preceded the AR-11. In most cases, the sole program change necessary is that the 9-bit bias used for AR-11 2's complement translation becomes an 11-bit bias for all other DEC modules. In practice, then, whether it is the AR-11 on the PDP-11, or some other module on a completely different machine, the programs developed will all exhibit the same basic structure. For convenience, in the discussion and program examples which follow, specific values are assumed for interrupt vectors and register addresses. The A/D status register of the AR-11 (address 170400) is shown in Fig. 10-3.

An A/D conversion can be initiated by setting bit 0 via program control. For repeated sampling, the A/D conversion is started by the internal clock (bit 5 set) or by an external signal (bit 4 set). Approximately 30 $u$sec after A/D start, "conversion complete" is indicated by the A/D done flag, bit 7, being set. Usually, bit 6 is set to enable a priority 6 interrupt via locations 340/342 when A/D is "done". The interrupt service routine (ISR) then moves the 10-bit data from the A/D buffer (at address 170402) to a memory storage buffer. Bit 13 selects either

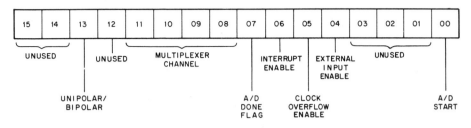

Fig. 10-3 AR-11 A/D Status register.

unipolar (0 to 5 volts) or bipolar (-2.5 to +2.5V) operation, while bits 8-11 select one of 16 A/D channels.

The programmable clock is often used in conjunction with the A/D converter. A basic clock tick rate (100 Hz, 1 KHz, 10 KHz, 100 KHz, or 1 MHz) is first selected by bits 1-3 of the Clock Status Register (Fig. 10-4), at address 170404.

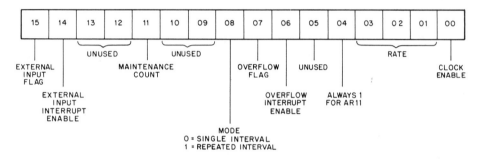

Fig. 10-4 AR-11 Clock status register.

The Clock Buffer Register (170406) is then loaded with an 8-bit number T equal to the 2's complement of the desired total clock ticks per clock overflow. If the repeat mode bit (bit 8) is set, and the clock is enabled by setting bit 0, the clock will *then* start. After every T ticks, the overflow flag will be raised (bit 7) and, if bit 6 is set, a level 6 interrupt via locations 344/346 will occur. T will be automatically reloaded into the clock's count register and the clock will continue ticking with overflow occurring every T ticks. When the clock is to be used for uniform interval timing, the clock ISR initiates the desired computation.

For the clock to initiate the A/D converter, the clock interrupt is disabled, and the clock overflow *and* interrupt enable bits are set in the A/D status register. The clock will then start the A/D after every T ticks, and the A/D done ISR will retrieve each time sample from the A/D buffer and change channels if so desired. In Section 10.3, a complete "digital oscilloscope" software system is described. The system displays a continually sampled signal and its discrete Fourier transform magnitude, and utilizes the A/D converter and clock in the mode just described.

The dual D/A converters of the AR-11 may be used individually to output waveforms for applications such as speech synthesis. In such applications, the number to be converted is simply moved to the X-D/A (170412) or Y-D/A (170414) buffer. Conversion of data from PDP-11 2's complement to the requisite binary offset format is accomplished by adding 512. to the data, which must have a magnitude less than 511. to be converted properly to an analog voltage. Synchronization may be achieved by using the clock ISR. The data is prepared and left in a memory buffer. The first instruction of the clock ISR is simply MOV BUFF,@#170412/4. All of this is illustrated in Section 10.4 in a speech synthesis software system.

The interrupt latency or delay of ISR initiation caused by completion of "long" instructions (e.g., DIV) may cause unacceptable jitter in the D/A transitions if the D/A's are to be updated at a rate comparable to that of the execution speed of the instruction in question. Conversely, certain relatively time consuming operations (e.g., the LSI-11 EIS/FIS instructions) are backed up in mid-instruction if an interrupt request is pending, and restarted following ISR completion. If interrupts occur too often, these instructions may never be completed!

The dual D/A's may also be used with the Display Status Register (170410) as an oscilloscope controller for plotting pictures. A limitation of this technique becomes immediately apparent. Lines with arbitrary slope cannot be drawn by simply updating the D/A converters with the binary numbers which are to be translated into the voltage coordinates of the new line end point. The oscilloscope beam will move from the old coordinates to the new coordinates but will not maintain the desired slope during the transition. Indeed, since two MOV's are required to update the X- and Y-D/A's, the beam will start moving along one axis before the other. Thus, excepting the special horizontal or vertical cases, straight lines must be composed of many short staircase segments. This is illustrated in the program of Fig. 10-5. Figure 10-6 shows the result when the X- and Y-D/A outputs, under control of this program, are applied to the horizontal and vertical inputs of an oscilloscope. A triangle is repeatedly drawn. The program returns to the RT-11 monitor when any terminal key is struck.

```
;ROUTINE TO DRAW A TRIANGLE ON AN OSCILLOSCOPE.
;THE THREE SIDES ARE SEGMENTS 0,1,AND 2. TYPE ANY CHARACTER TO STOP PROGRAM.
        KBS=177560
        KBB=177562
        CKSR=170404
        CKBR=170406
        XREG=170412
        YREG=170414
        LKSR=177546
;
START:  CLR @#LKSR       ;TURN OFF THE 60 HZ CLOCK TO PREVENT INTERFERENCE
        MOV #UPDATE,@#344 ;SET UP INT VECTOR ISR ADDRESS
        MOV #300,@#346   ;AND CPU PRIORITY
        BIC #100,@#KBS   ;DISABLE KEYBOARD INTERRUPT
        MOV #-1,@#CKBR   ;SET PROGRAMMABLE CLOCK FOR ONE TICK
        MOV #507,@#CKSR  ;REPEAT MODE, OVRFLOW INT ENABLE, 10 KHZ RATE ,GO!
```

```
;
AGAIN:    MOV #-764,X        ;INITIALIZE X
          MOV #-764,Y        ;AND Y
          CLR DOT            ;DOT 0
          CLR SEG            ;OF SEGMENT 0
STALL:    WAIT
SEG0:     TST SEG            ;IS IT SEGMENT 0?
          BGT SEG1           ;NO
          ADD TEN,X          ;YES, INCREMENT X
          ADD TEN,Y          ;AND Y
          CMP DOT,#31        ;END OF SEG 0?
          BLT STALL          ;NO
          CLR DOT            ;DOT 0
          INC SEG            ;OF NEXT SEGMENT
          BR STALL
;
SEG1:     CMP SEG,#1         ;IS IT SEGMENT 1?
          BGT SEG2           ;NO
          ADD TEN,X          ;YES, INCREMENT X
          SUB TEN,Y          ;AND DECREMENT Y
          CMP DOT,#31        ;END OF SEG 1?
          BLT STALL          ;NO
          CLR DOT            ;DOT 0
          INC SEG            ;OF NEXT SEGMENT
          BR STALL
;
SEG2:     SUB TEN,X
          CMP DOT,#62        ;END OF SEGMENT?
          BLT STALL          ;NO
          TSTB @#KBS         ;QUIT IF TTY KEY HIT
          BPL AGAIN          ;NOT YET.
;
          CLR @#XREG         ;CLEANUP BEFORE
          CLR @#YREG         ;LEAVING
          CLR @#CKSR         ;STOP CLOCK
          TSTB @#KBB         ;CLEAR KBS DONE FLAG
          BIS #100,@#KBS     ;RE-ENABLE KB INT
          .EXIT              ;BYE! (BACK TO RT-11)
;
UPDATE:   MOV X,@#XREG       ;BLAST OUT X
          MOV Y,@#YREG       ;AND Y
          INC DOT            ;NEXT DOT
          RTI                ;BACK AGAIN
;
SEG:      .WORD 0
DOT:      .WORD 0
X:        .WORD 0
Y:        .WORD 0
TEN:      .WORD 12
          .END START
```

Fig. 10-5 Program for point plotting with D/A converters.

Examination of the program reveals a further shortcoming of this technique, the inordinate CPU overhead required to manipulate the D/A's. Given the requirement for a large quantity of high quality graphic output, it would be profitable to have a separate processor which, when primed with appropriate information, could autonomously draw graphic entities such as lines and characters.

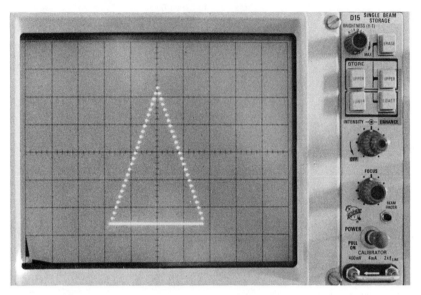

Fig. 10-6 "Output" of Fig. 10-5 when X-, Y-D/A's are input to oscilloscope.

10.2 INTERACTIVE GRAPHICS PROCESSORS

The DEC VT-11 is an autonomous *display processor unit* (DPU) which, as a UNIBUS peripheral, is capable of fetching and executing instructions residing in the *same* memory accessed by a PDP-11 CPU. The net result of the DPU instruction executions are pictures drawn on a CRT display. These pictures may be an end in themselves, or, more important perhaps, may serve as tools which aid operator interaction in tasks unrelated to pictures *per se*. The refreshed tube DPU is of interest not only for what it does, but also for how it accomplishes its tasks.

For example, the VT-11 utilizes the direct memory access (DMA) technique discussed previously with respect to I/O units. And, it makes substantial use of the residual concept discussed in conjunction with the PDP-11/60 micromachine. Finally, light pen interaction and picture subroutines are effected via intimate cooperation between the CPU and DPU. Thus, elementary ideas concerning multiprocessor systems are well illustrated via examination of the VT-11 DPU operation. Since the VT-11 is representative of the general class of DPU's available, it is profitable to discuss the VT-11 instruction set and operation in particular rather than that of some hypothetical DPU. Fortunately, the VS-60 DPU instruction set is a superset of that of the VT-11; all VT-11 programs will thus run on a VS-60.

10.2.1 The Refreshed Tube Display Processor Unit (DPU)

A refreshed tube graphics processor is somewhat like a conventional television set. That is, pictures are redrawn about 30 times a second, the minimum rate which will provide a flicker free appearance. This redrawing action provides the opportunity to animate the picture by changing it slightly each time around. In contrast to a television picture, which consists of about 525 horizontal lines which vary in intensity along each line, pictures created by the DPU consist of an arbitrary number of line segments, each of which may have different orientations and intensities, and other visible objects such as characters. Additionally, because the CRT beam repeatedly scans through each picture point, the user may easily interact with the picture.

In Fig. 10-7, the screen of a VT-11 is shown with an animated "Towers of Hanoi" program moving disks from peg-to-peg. The user can adjust the speed of disk movement via the light pen "potentiometer" in the upper right corner of the screen (See Appendix G).

Fig. 10-7 Animated Towers of Hanoi on VT-11 graphic processor

The DPU draws the picture by repeatedly scanning a *display file*, which consists of *instructions* and *data*. This display file is resident in the *same* memory as conventional PDP-11 instructions and data. Thus, display files can be loaded from a storage device in the same way as programs and, once in memory, can be manipulated by the CPU.

The instructions can cause the DPU to

1. Move the beam to any point in a 1024 x 1024 point coordinate system.

2. Draw a line as defined by signed x and y displacements relative to the current beam position.

3. Draw characters as defined by an ASCII string in a font determined by instructions in an internal read-only memory (ROM).

4. Plot either $f(x)$ vs x or $f(y)$ vs y with uniform x or y increments.

Each of the entities drawn may have 1 of 8 intensities, may blink (or not blink), and lines (vectors) may be drawn as one of 4 types (solid, dotted, dashed, or dotted-dashed). Additionally, any item may be "enabled" such that a light pen pointed at that item will cause the CPU to take specified action, possibly resulting in changes to the picture.

In order to gain an understanding of the VT-11 display processor, we will now examine its instruction set and data formats.

10.2.2 VT-11 Graphics Processor Instruction and Data Word Formats

All VT-11 DPU *instructions* have a MSB of "1":

The SET GRAPHICS MODE instruction

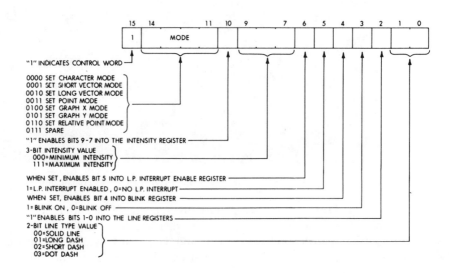

1. *determines* how following 16-bit data words will be interpreted by the DPU and/or

2. *sets* bits in registers which affect the attributes of entities being displayed (e.g., brightness, blink, line type) .

The DJMP instruction causes the display processor counter (DPC), normally incremented after each DPU memory access, to be loaded with the address following the DJMP instruction.

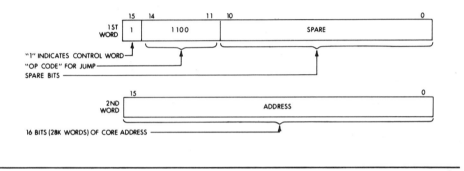

The LOAD STATUS REGISTER A instruction loads another register whose contents affect attributes of displayed items or alter the DPU action under certain conditions.

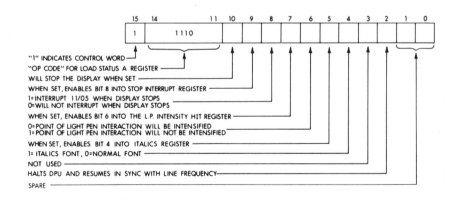

The LOAD STATUS REGISTER B instruction is used in conjunction with point plotting of uniformly spaced data via the GRAPH mode.

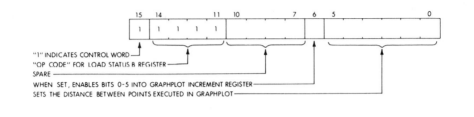

The VT-11 uses the residual concept. That is, the current mode is the mode set by the last "SET GRAPHIC MODE" instruction encountered. All *data* words subsequently encountered will be interpreted according to the current mode. All VT-11 data have "0" as MSB:

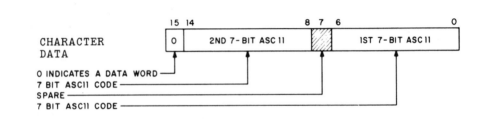

Each data word encountered by the DPU while in mode 0 will be interpreted as above, and 2 characters will be drawn. The lower left hand corner of character 1 will start at the current beam position and the beam will end up 1 raster unit to the right of the lower right hand corner of the 2'nd character, which is drawn to the right of the first character.

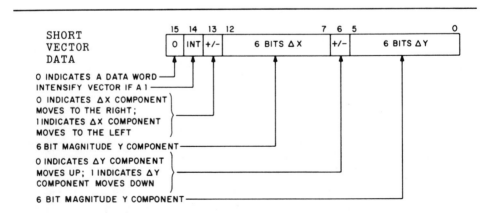

Here, the 6 bits specify the magnitude of the beam displacement from the current postion along the *x* and *y* axes, while bit 13 specifies the *x* direction (0 = right) and bit 6 specifies the *y* direction (0 = up). Thus, each data word encountered while in mode 1 will be interpreted as above, and a smooth visible (bit 14 = 1) or invisible vector will be drawn. Invisible vectors provide relative beam displacements.

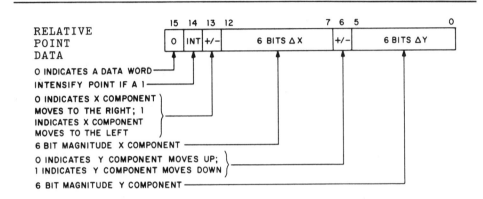

The beam is moved as per the SHORT VECTOR MODE, except that no visible line is drawn. When bit 14 = 1, a visible *dot* is placed at final beam position.

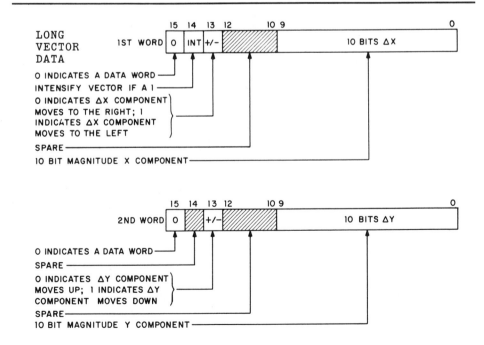

Here, each *pair* of data words encountered while in mode 2 is interpreted so as to draw a long relative vector. Direction bits and magnitudes are as per the SHORT VECTOR data. XX..X signifies unused bits.

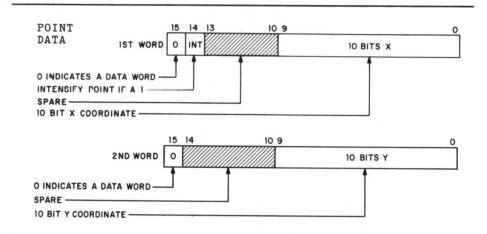

Each pair of data words encountered while in mode 3 is interpreted so as to move the invisible beam to the specified *x* and *y* coordinates. A *dot* is placed at the final position if the INT bit is "1".

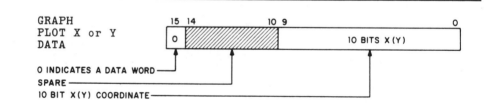

Each word encountered while in mode 4 or 5 is interpreted as *f(x)* or *f(y)*, respectively, and plotted as a dot. The *x* or *y* coordinate is incremented by the contents of the GRAPHPLOT INCREMENT register, previously loaded by a LOAD STATUS REGISTER B instruction. Thus, GRAPHPLOT enables plotting uniformly spaced data with only a single word per data point.

To summarize, SET GRAPHIC MODE instructions need be issued only when a *new* type of graphic entity is to be plotted. Again, note that the residual approach is used here. When any visible entity is being drawn, the intensity, blink, light pen enable, and (for lines only) the line type registers are examined and the sum of the parameters is reflected in the visible output. This means that only when a parameter is to be changed from its present value does a parameter command have to be issued. Finally, for simplicity, all coordinates will be given in decimal.

The following short program, when executed by the DPU, draws a square with sides 128 x 128 raster units in length, and with the bottom left hand corner at coordinates (320,320). The square has brightness level 4, solid lines, does not blink, and is not enabled for a light pen hit. Note that the mnemonics for correctly setting graphic modes, loading status registers, and defining data are available by using the RT-11 system macro ".GTDEF". The display file is defined by the programmer and loaded into memory at program load time. The only CPU action required is to start the DPU by MOVing the display file starting address to the Display Program Counter (DPC), at address 172000. The DPU then repeatedly scans and "executes" the display file, displaying the resultant picture. *The CPU is completely free for other applications.*

```
        START:   MOV      #A,@#DPC           ;LOAD DPC WITH STARTING ADDRESS
                                             ;OF DISPLAY FILE
        WAIT:    WAIT                        ;CPU NO LONGER NEEDED
                 BR       WAIT               ;BACK TO WAIT AFTER INTERRUPT
                                             ;E.G., LINE CLOCK
;DISPLAY FILE
117124  A:       POINT+LPOFF+INT4+BLKOFF+LINE0 ;POINT MODE, LIGHT PEN DISABLE
                                             ;INTENSITY 4, NO BLINK, SOLID LINES
000500  PX:      500                         ;MOVE BEAM TO X = 500(8) = 320.
000500  PY:      500                         ;AND            Y = 500(8) = 320.
110000           LONGV                       ;LONG VECTOR MODE
040200           200+INTX                    ;L1:DELTA X = 200,  INTENSIFY
000000           0                           ;   DELTA Y = 0
040000           0+INTX                      ;L2:DELTA X = 0  ,  INTENSIFY
000200           200                         ;   DELTA Y = 200
060200           200+INTX+MINUSX             ;L3:DELTA X =-200,  INTENSIFY
000000           0                           ;   DELTA Y = 0
040000           0+INTX                      ;L4:DELTA X = 0  ,  INTENSIFY
020200           200+MINUSY                  ;   DELTA Y =-200
160000           DJMP
??????  TARGET:  A                           ;ABSOLUTE ADDRESS OF "A"
                 .END START
```

Note that all instructions have MSB "1" while all data have MSB "0".

10.2.3 Dynamic Display File Manipulation

If we assume that the programmer wishes to cause the square to drift slowly across the screen, two courses of action are possible. First, the CPU can be used to increment the locations "PX" and "PY" at appropriate intervals while the DPU is continually scanning and re-executing the display file. Second, the CPU could create a second display file with the square shifted slightly. If "TARGET" is overwritten with the starting address of the new display file, the next DJMP executed in the old display file will invoke the new display file. The old display file, no longer being executed, can then be modified. The switching process is then repeated.

The latter technique, *double buffered display files*, is generally preferred, particularly when the display file may change structure between frames (e.g., in animations). The former technique is used in Section 10.2.5 for a light pen tracker demonstration program.

10.2.4 Graphics Subroutines via CPU/DPU Cooperation

By combining line segments, the user can draw objects of high complexity. Conversely, arbitrary pictures can be decomposed into sub units more complex than lines, and many of these "subpictures" are often identical. For example, a chessboard is composed of squares, and a front view of a mansion would probably entail repeated identical windows and pillars. It is economical to define the subpicture once, and after moving the beam to the required point on the screen, to invoke the subpicture. This is in fact how characters are drawn, with the definitions contained in a ROM. Sophisticated graphics processors (e.g., the VS-60) have true hardware "subroutine" capability analogous to CPU subroutines; that is, registers and return addresses can be saved on a stack. In the VT-11, subroutines require CPU cooperation.

The DSTOP instruction is used to stop the graphics processor momentarily. The DSTOP ISR loads the DPC with the address of the required subpicture display file (contained in the memory location following the DSTOP) and restarts the DPU. A display RTS (return from subpicture) is effected by a DSTOP followed by a zero. An example best illustrates the concept. Squares will be drawn on the screen with bottom left hand corner coordinates (100,100), (300,300), and (750,750).

```
;GRAPHICS SUBROUTINES VIA DSTOP
START:  MOV     #DSUB,@#320      ;ADDRESS OF DSTOP ISR
        MOV     #200,@#322      ;PRIORITY OF DSTOP ISR
        MOV     #STACK,R5       ;SET UP R5 STACK FOR ISR
;
        MOV     #A,@#DPC        ;START DISPLAY PROCESSOR
WAIT:   WAIT                    ;CPU ONLY REQUIRED DURING ISR
        BR      WAIT            ;AFTER DSTOP INTERRUPT, BACK TO WAIT
;
        .BLKW   10.             ;SPACE FOR R5 STACK
STACK:  .WORD   0
                                ;DISPLAY FILE
A:      POINT+LPOFF+INT4+LINE0,100.,100. ;SAME AS ORIGINAL
        DSTOP
        SQUARE                  ;ADDRESS OF SQUARE DISPLAY FILE SUBR
        POINT,300.,300.         ;MOVE BEAM TO (300,300)
        DSTOP
        SQUARE                  ;THE SQUARE AGAIN
        POINT,750.,750.         ;MOVE BEAM TO (750,750)
        DSTOP
        SQUARE                  ;AND AGAIN
        DJMP
        A                       ;END OF MAIN DISPLAY FILE
```

```
;
SQUARE: LONGV                           ;LONG VECTOR MODE
         .                              ;INSTRUCTIONS TO DRAW SQUARE
         .                              ;AS PREVIOUSLY
         DSTOP                          ;EFFECTS DISPLAY RTS

         0
;
DSUB:    TST     @DPC                   ;IF DPC POINTS TO "0", DISPLAY RTS
         BEQ     DRTS                   ;YES!
;
;NO, IMPLEMENT DISPLAY SUBROUTINE
;
         MOV     @#DPC,-(R5)            ;SAVE DPC CONTENTS OF HALTED DPU
         ADD     #2,(R5)               ;RETURN ADDR FROM SUBROUTINE = @#DPC+2
         MOV     @DPC,@#DPC            ;MOVING SUBROUTINE STARTING ADDRESS INTO
                                        ;      DPC RESTARTS DPU AT THAT ADDRESS
         RTI                            ;DPU DOING SUBROUTINE, RELEASE CPU
;
;YES, IMPLEMENT DISPLAY RETURN FROM SUBROUTINE
DRTS:    MOV     (R5)+,@#DPC           ;MOVING RETURN ADDRESS FROM SUBROUTINE
                                        ;INTO DPC RESTARTS DPU AT THAT ADDRESS
         RTI
;
         .END START
```

The appearance of the screen upon execution of the above program is shown in Fig. 10-8a. A subpicture can be invoked as many times as desired with a relatively small display file memory overhead. This overhead is *independent of the complexity of the subpicture.*

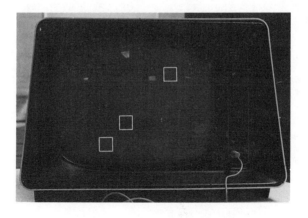

Fig. 10-8a Output of graphics subroutine program.

10.2.5 Light Pen Interaction

Light pen interaction often seems somewhat magical to the layman. However, it is quite simple when it is recalled that the beam repetitively drawing the picture is really only at a single point on the screen at any instant in time, and that it was caused to be at that point by a graphics instruction. A light pen contains a photodiode which detects light only in a small spectral range; it will therefore emit a pulse when, and only when, the beam position coincides with the position on the screen at which the light pen is pointed. If the pulse causes the DPU to stop momentarily, two sets of information are available which will enable the light pen ISR to interact with the picture. First, the halted DPC can be used to determine the instruction responsible for the picture entity which received a "light pen hit". Second, the DPU has two registers (at addresses 172004, 172006) which contain the "position" of the stopped beam. The ISR thus performs the appropriate action and then restarts the DPU. Again, a short example will illustrate the concept. A small square will follow the light pen across the screen (Fig. 10.8b):

```
;LIGHT PEN PROGRAM
START:  MOV     #LPSERV,@#324       ;LIGHT PEN ISR ADDR
        MOV     #340,@#326          ;PRIORITY OF LIGHT PEN ISR
        MOV     #A,@#DPC            ;START DISPLAY PROCESSOR
WAIT:   WAIT                        ;CPU NOW IDLE
        BR      WAIT
;
A:      POINT+LPON+INT4+BLKOFF+LINE0    ;AS BEFORE, BUT LIGHT PEN ENABLED
PX:     500.
PY:     380.
        LONGV                       ;DRAW A SQUARE, AS ABOVE
        200+INTX,0,0+INTX,200,200+INTX+MINUSX,0,0+INTX,200+MINUSY
        DJMP
        A
;DPU IS STOPPED WHEN LIGHT PEN HIT OCCURS
LPSERV: MOV     @#172004,R1         ;GET "X" DPU REGISTER CONTENTS
        BIC     #176000,R1          ;UPPER 6 BITS ARE UNDEFINED
        MOV     @#172006,R2         ;GET "Y" DPU REGISTER CONTENTS
        BIC     #176000,R2          ;UPPER 6 BITS ARE UNDEFINED
;
        MOV     PX,R3               ;GET X POS OF LOWER LEFT CORNER OF SQUARE
        MOV     PY,R4               ;GET Y POS OF LOWER LEFT CORNER OF SQUARE
;FIND OUT WHICH SIDE OF SQUARE HAD "HIT" BY SERIES OF COMPARISONS
        CMP     R1,R3
        BNE     N1
LEFT:   SUB     #2,PX               ;LEFT SIDE HIT, MOVE SQUARE LEFT
        BR      OUT
N1:     CMP     R2,R4
        BNE     N2
BOTTOM: SUB     #2,PY               ;BOTTOM HIT, MOVE SQUARE DOWN
        BR      OUT
N2:     ADD     #200,R4
        CMP     R2,R4
        BNE     RIGHT
TOP:    ADD     #2,PY               ;TOP HIT (BY DEFAULT), MOVE SQUARE UP
        BR      OUT
RIGHT:  ADD     #2,PX               ;RIGHT SIDE HIT, MOVE SQUARE RIGHT
OUT:    MOV     #1,@#DPC            ;LOADING DPC WITH "1" RESTARTS DPU
                                    ;              WHERE IT STOPPED
        RTI
        .END START
```

The reader should trace through the logic to satisfy himself that the square will follow the light pen across the screen. In practice, the square is made very small and, in fact, more sophisticated light pen trackers use shapes such as octagons (why?). Nevertheless, a program as simple as the above is the nucleus of such impressive graphics techniques as "rubber banding" (one end of a straight line follows the light pen) and "drawing" (the light pen leaves a trail behind it).

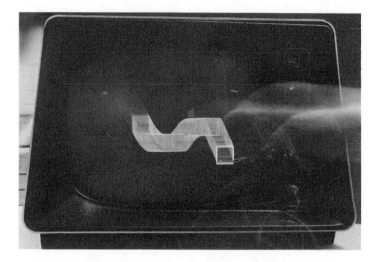

Fig. 10-8b Light pen follow (time exposure).

10.3 ON-LINE DIGITAL SIGNAL PROCESSING VIA CPU, DPU AND A/D INTERACTION

Graphical output is an invaluable tool for providing visual feedback concerning operation of arbitrary algorithms. In the following example, several digital signal processing modules are combined with a display routine to create a "digital oscilloscope". A *changing signal* and its *amplitude spectrum* are *continuously* displayed on the screen.

10.3.1 Spectral Analysis via the Fast Fourier Transform

We have already noted that a signal bandlimited to W Hz must be sampled $2W$ times per second to preserve it completely. Once the sampling rate has been selected, the signal must be sharply attenuated above W Hz so as to ensure that "aliasing" does not occur. Everyone has observed "aliasing" in western movies; as the stagecoach accelerates, the wagon wheels — their motion sampled at 24 pictures per second — seem to move faster, then stop, then move backwards. This "false" backwards motion is "aliasing".

If the *x(n)* input to a discrete Fourier transform (DFT) are samples of a *real* signal (sampling interval $=$ T sec), then the *X(k)* output from the DFT can be interpreted as follows:

X(k) is the output at time (N-1)T of a digital filter with frequency response

$$|H_k(f)| = |sin(\pi fTN)/sin[\pi(fT-k/N)]|$$

when the sampled signal *x(nT)* is input to that digital filter starting at time $t = 0$; i.e., $n = 0$. Thus the DFT can be viewed as a number of bandpass filters with center frequencies k/NT, and magnitude response $|sin\ x/x|$. *For example, for a real signal,*

$$x_p(n) = cos(2\pi\ pn/N),\ n = 0,\ldots,N-1$$

$$= 0.5 * [EXP(j\ 2\pi\ pn/N)+EXP(-j\ 2\pi\ pn/N)]\ ,\quad p < N/2,$$

$$X(k) = 0.5*[\ \sum_{n=0}^{N-1} EXP(-j\ 2\pi\ n[k-p]/N) + \sum_{n=0}^{N-1} EXP(-j\ 2\pi\ n[k+p]/N]$$

It can be shown that the first summation is equal to N for $k = p$, and zero otherwise; similarly, the second summation is equal to N for $k = N-p$ and zero otherwise. That is $X(k) = N/2$ if $k = p$ or $k = N-p$. Likewise, if

$$x_p(n) = sin(2\pi\ pn/N),$$

then $X(k) = -jN/2\ (k = p)$, or $jN/2\ (k = N-p)$. Finally, if

$$x_p(n) = a_p\ cos(2\pi\ pn/N) + b_p\ sin(2\pi\ pn/N)$$

$$= (a_p^2 +b_p^2)^{0.5}\ cos(2\pi\ pn/N - \theta),$$

$$\theta_p = tan^{-1}(b_p/a_p)$$

then

$$|X(k)| = N/2\ (a_p^2 +b_p^2)^{0.5}\ ,\quad k = p\ or\ k = N-p$$

and

$$\angle X(k) = tan^{-1}(Im[X(k)]/Re[X(k)])$$

$$= \theta_p\ ,\ k = p$$

$$= -\theta_p\ ,\ k = N-p.$$

It follows that periodic signals with period N samples are analyzed into a Fourier series by the DFT: the *X(k)* are the complex discrete Fourier series coefficients.

However, because $\exp(+j2\pi p) = \cos(2\pi p) + j \sin(2\pi p) = 1$, p an integer, it is easy to show that both DFT defining equations are periodic functions of N. That is, $x(n+N) = x(n)$ and $X(k+N) = X(k)$. This means that for an *arbitrary* sequence *x(n)*, the output of the DFT is the transform of a periodic sequence, one period of which is identical to *x(n)*. In other words, the DFT treats any sequence analyzed as though it were one period of a periodic sequence.

From a time/space point-of-view, it is profitable to use two special algorithms when dealing with spectral analysis of real signals:

a. *Two N-point real transforms from one N-point complex transform:* Place the N samples of one real sequence *x(n)* into the real part, and the N samples of the other real sequence *y(n)* into the imaginary part, of an N-point complex array *z(n)*. An N-point complex FFT is carried out to get *Z(k)*, $k = 0$, ..., N-1. Then the transforms of *x(n)* and *y(n)* — *X(k)* and *Y(k)* — can be recovered as follows:

$$X(k) = [Z^*(N-k) + Z(k)]/2$$

and

$$Y(k) = j [Z^*(N-k) - Z(k)]/2, \quad k = 0,1,\ldots,N/2-1.$$

"*" means complex conjugate and $Z(N) = Z(0)$.

b. *One 2N-point real transform from one N-point complex transform:* If the even samples of *c(n)*, $n = 0$, ... ,2N-1, become *x(n)* and the odd samples *y(n)* — as above — then first compute *X(k)* and *Y(k)* as per (1) and then

$$C(k) = [X(k) + Y(k)*W^{-k}]/2, \qquad k = 0,\ldots,N-1$$

where $W = \exp(j2\pi/2N)$.

10.3.2 PDP-11/VT-11 Digital Oscilloscope: a Modular Approach to Software Construction

The digital oscilloscope (Fig. 10-9) uses the concepts of *double buffering, high level control* and *modular software construction*. This is seen clearly by examination of the control program:

```
C           LINKING INSTRUCTIONS FOR MODULES:
C           SCOPET=SCOPET/F,TRIGGR,WINDOW,FTMUF7/C
C           BUTMUF,CTOR7S,DOUBLE,COMPU3,SCOPED
C
            INTEGER A(256),B(256),NTAB(256),N1(300),N2(300)
            COMMON /XX/A,B,NTAB
            PI=3.1415926
C           CREATE WINDOW TABLE
            DO 1 I=1,256
            XI=I-1
1           NTAB(I)=(2.**15-1.)*(0.54-0.46*COS(2.*PI*XI/256.))
C
            NFLAG=0
            NSMPL=260
            NTICK=125
C           START TO SAMPLE INTO BUFFER 1
            CALL TRIGGR(N1(1),NSMPL,NTICK)
C           WAIT, USER GIVES <CR>
            PAUSE
C
C           START TO SAMPLE INTO BUFFER 2
11          CALL TRIGGR(N2(1),NSMPL,NTICK)
C
C           PROCESS BUFFER 1
            CALL WINDOW(N1(1))
            CALL FTMUF7
            CALL CTOR7
            CALL DOUBLE
C
C           SWITCH TO DISPLAY FILE 1
            CALL SCOPE1(N1(1),NFLAG)
            NFLAG=1
C
C           START TO SAMPLE INTO BUFFER 1
            CALL TRIGGR(N1(1),NSMPL,NTICK)
C
C           PROCESS BUFFER 2
            CALL WINDOW(N2(1))
            CALL FTMUF7
            CALL CTOR7
            CALL DOUBLE
C
C           SWITCH TO DISPLAY FILE 2
            CALL SCOPE1(N2(1),NFLAG)
            GO TO 11
            END
```

That is, buffer 1 receives waveform samples on an interrupt basis while buffer 2 is processed by the CPU. Simultaneously, the results of the previous processing phase are displayed by the DMA graphics processor. Buffers are then switched and the sequence repeated. A photograph of the *digital oscilloscope* output is shown in Fig. 10-9.

We will examine the modules in sequence:

a) **Input waveform is bandlimited square wave multiplied by a WINDOW function.**

b) **Output are** $X(k)$, $k = 0, 1, ..., 127$; **the DFT coefficients of the waveform of a).**

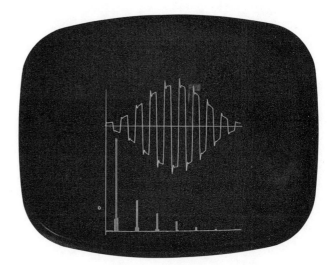

Fig. 10-9 Digital oscilloscope output.

TRIGGER: It is desirable to ensure a stable image of the sampled waveform by starting the sampling following a positive going zero crossing. That is, the previous sample was negative and the present sample is positive. Once this condition is detected, by ISR "SERV1", a switch to ISR "SERV2" is made and the processing on the previous buffer collected can proceed while the current buffer is being filled.

```
        .TITLE  TRIGGR
        .GLOBL  TRIGGR TYPE
FLG:    0
TYPE:   1
        ADVEC1=340                      ;A/D ISR VECTOR
        ADVEC2=342                      ;A/D ISR VECTOR
        ADSR=170400                     ;A/D STATUS REGISTER
        ADBR=170402                     ;A/D BUFFER
        CLKSR=170404                    ;CLOCK STATUS REGISTER
        CLKBR=170406                    ;CLOCK BUFFER
TRIGGR:
        MOV     2(R5),ADDR              ;ADDRESS OF OUTPUT SAMPLE BUFFER
        MOV     @4(R5),R0               ;NUMBER OF SAMPLES TO BE GATHERED
        MOV     @6(R5),R1               ;T = # OF USEC BETWEEN SAMPLES
        NEG     R1
        MOV     R1,@#CLKBR              ;-T INTO CLOCK BUFFER
        MOV     #SERV1,@#ADVEC1         ;SET UP A/D ISR VECTOR
        MOV     #340,@#ADVEC2           ;PRIORITY 7
        MOV     #140,@#ADSR             ;A/D STATUS: START ON CLOCK
                                        ;OVERFLOW, INTERRUPT WHEN DONE
        CLR     R1
        CLR     R2
        CLR     FLG                     ;BUFFER SWITCHING FLAG
        MOV     #423,@#CLKSR            ;CLOCK STATUS: REPEATED INTERVAL
                                        ;            1 USEC TICKS, GO!
        MOV     #256.,COUNT             ;256 SAMPLES GATHERED
```

```
WAITL:
        WAIT                            ;WAIT FOR A/D DONE INTERRUPT
        TST     FLG     ;STILL WAITING FOR POSITIVE GOING ZERO CROSSING?
        BEQ     WAITL                   ;YES!
        RTS     PC                      ;NO, RETURN TO MAIN
;ISR FOR POSITIVE GOING ZERO CROSSING DETECTION
SERV1:
        MOV     @#ADBR,R2               ;PICK UP A/D SAMPLE
        SUB     #1000,R2                ;CONVERT TO 2'S COMPLEMENT
        BLT     OUT                     ;IF SAMPLE < 0, RETURN TO WAIT
        TST     R1                      ;IF > 0, TEST PREVIOUS SAMPLE
        BGE     OUT                     ;IF IT WAS > 0, RETURN TO WAIT
        MOV     #1,FLG                  ;PRESENT > 0, PREVIOUS < 0! GO!
        MOV     #SERV2,@#ADVEC1         ;NEW ISR TO GATHER REST OF SAMPLES
        MOV     @#ADBR,@ADDR            ;SAMPLE INTO BUFFER
        ADD     #2,ADDR                 ;BUMP BUFFER POINTER
        DEC     COUNT                   ;DECREMENT SAMPLE COUNT
        RTI                             ;RTI
OUT:
        MOV     R2,R1                   ;SAVE THIS SAMPLE FOR NEXT TIME
        RTI
;ISR FOR BACKGROUND SAMPLE GATHERING.  NO REGISTERS USED.
SERV2:
        MOV     @#ADBR,@ADDR            ;SAMPLE INTO BUFFER
        ADD     #2,ADDR                 ;BUMP BUFFER POINTER
        DEC     COUNT                   ;DECREMENT SAMPLE COUNT
        BEQ     STOP                    ;ENOUGH SAMPLES?
        RTI                             ;NO.
STOP:   CLR     @#CLKSR                 ;YES. TURN OFF CLOCK, A/D
        RTI
COUNT:  0
ADDR:   0
        .END
```

WINDOW: The input samples must be first converted to 2's complement (SUB #1000,R4) and then multiplied by a positive "window function",

```
w(i) = (2.**15-1)*[0.54-0.46*cos(2π[i-1]/N)], i = 1, 2, ..., N
```

where N = 256 in the example. Application of a window provides "better" spectral estimates. Note that two versions of the windowed signal are saved: an unscaled version for display (MOV R4,(R0)+) and a scaled up version for input to the FFT (ASHC #3,R4, MOV R4,(R3)+).

```
        .TITLE  WINDOW
        .GLOBL  WINDOW,TYPE
        .CSECT  XX              ;LABELLED COMMON
        A=.
        B=.+512.
        TABLEN=.+512.
        .CSECT
WINDOW:
        MOV     2(R5),R0        ;GET THE ADDRESS OF ARGUMENT #1
        MOV     #A,R3           ;GET THE ADDRESS OF THE A ARRAY
```

```
;       NARROW BAND
NARROW:
        MOV     #TABLEN,R2      ;GET THE ADDRESS OF THE WINDOW TABLE
        MOV     #256.,R1        ;INITIALIZE THE LOOP COUNTER
;       DO THE WINDOWING USING A 256 POINT WINDOW (I.E., N = 256)
LOOPN:
        MOV     (R0),R4         ;GET SAMPLE
        SUB     #1000,R4        ;ELIMINATE BIAS OF AR-11 A/D
        MUL     (R2)+,R4        ;MULTIPLY BY WINDOW FUNCTION
        MOV     R4,(R0)+        ;BACK TO BUFFER FOR DISPLAY USE
        ASHC    #3,R4           ;SHIFT LEFT 3 PLACES
        MOV     R4,(R3)+        ;INTO ANOTHER BUFFER FOR FFT USE
        SOB     R1,LOOPN
;
        RTS     PC              ;RETURN
        .END
```

FTMUF7: FTMUF7 is the 128 point complex FFT of Section 9.6.

CTOR7/DOUBLE/COMPU3: CTOR7 computes $2*X(k)$, $2*Y(k)$ as per 10.3.1a and DOUBLE uses COMPU3 to compute $2*C(k)$ as per Section 10.3.1b. The factors of 2 are retained for convenience and speed. The reader should note the use of autoincrement/autodecrement modes in CTOR7 so as to produce extremely time and space efficient code. The address modes, data structure, and algorithm are perfectly matched.

```
        .TITLE CTOR7
        .GLOBL CTOR7
        .CSECT XX               ;LABELLED COMMON
        A=.
        B=.+512.
        .CSECT
CTOR7:
        MOV #B,R0               ;START OF B BUFFER (INPUT)
        MOV #B+ 508.,R1         ;"END" OF B BUFFER (INPUT)
        MOV #A,R2               ;START OF A BUFFER (INPUT/OUTPUT)
;SPECIAL CODE FOR POINTS 0,1
        ASL (R0)+               ; Re[X(0)]  ← 2*Re[Z(0)]
        MOV (R0),(R2)
        ASL (R2)+               ; Re[Y(0)]  ← 2*Im[Z(0)]
        CLR (R0)+               ; Im[X(0)]  ← 0
        CLR (R2)+               ; Im[Y(0)]  ← 0
        TST (R2)+               ; POINT TO Im[Y(1)]
        MOV (R1),(R2)
        SUB (R0),(R2)           ; Im[Y(1)]  ← Re[Z(N-1)]-Re[Z(1)]
        ADD (R1)+,(R0)+         ; Re[X(1)]  ← Re[Z(N-1)]+Re[Z(1)]
        MOV (R1),-(R2)
        ADD (R0),(R2)           ; Re[Y(1)]  ← Im[Z(1)]+Im[Z(N-1)]
        SUB (R1),(R0)+          ; Im[X(1)]  ← Im[Z(1)]-Im[Z(N-1)]
        MOV #B+510.,R1
        MOV #A+  4,R2
        MOV #   62.,R3
        MOV #    6,R4
```

```
;
LOOP:       SUB R4,R1                 ;BUMP POINTER
            ADD R4,R2                 ;BUMP POINTER
            MOV (R1),(R2)
            SUB (R0),(R2)             ; Im[Y(k)] ←  Re[Z(N-k)]-Re[Z(k)]
            ADD (R1)+,(R0)+           ; Re[X(k)] ←  Re[Z(N-k)]+Re[Z(k)]
            MOV (R1),-(R2)
            ADD (R0),(R2)             ; Re[Y(k)] ←  Im[Z(k)]+Im[Z(N-k)]
            SUB (R1),(R0)+            ; Im[X(k)] ←  Im[Z(k)]-Im[Z(N-k)]
            SOB R3,LOOP
;
            RTS PC
            .END
;
            .TITLE DOUBLE
            .GLOBL DOUBLE,COMPUT,TYPE,TABLE
            .CSECT XX                 ;LABELLED COMMON
            A=.
            B=.+  1000
            .CSECT
DOUBLE:
            TST TYPE
            BNE 1$
            RTS PC
  1$:
            ADD A,B
            ASR B
            ADD A+2,B+2
            ASR B+2
            MOV #      63.,R4
            MOV #A,R2
            MOV #TABLE+2,R3
            MOV #B,R5
            JSR PC,COMPUT
            NEG B+     402
;
            RTS PC
TABLE:
     .WORD       0, 77777,  1444, 77765,  3107, 77727,  4552, 77646
     .WORD    6213, 77541,  7653, 77410, 11307, 77234, 12741, 77034
     .WORD   14370, 76611, 16013, 76342, 17431, 76051, 21043, 75534
     .WORD   22447, 75174, 24046, 74611, 25436, 74203, 27020, 73553
     .WORD   30373, 73100, 31736, 72403, 33271, 71665, 34614, 71124
     .WORD   36126, 70341, 37426, 67536, 40715, 66711, 42172, 66043
     .WORD   43434, 65154, 44663, 64245, 46077, 63316, 47277, 62347
     .WORD   50463, 61361, 51632, 60353, 52764, 57326, 54102, 56263
     .WORD   55201, 55201, 56263, 54102, 57326, 52764, 60353, 51632
     .WORD   61361, 50463, 62347, 47277, 63316, 46077, 64245, 44663
     .WORD   65154, 43434, 66043, 42172, 66711, 40715, 67536, 37426
     .WORD   70341, 36126, 71124, 34614, 71665, 33271, 72403, 31736
     .WORD   73100, 30373, 73553, 27020, 74203, 25436, 74611, 24046
     .WORD   75174, 22447, 75534, 21043, 76051, 17431, 76342, 16013
     .WORD   76611, 14370, 77034, 12741, 77234, 11307, 77410,  7653
     .WORD   77541,  6213, 77646,  4552, 77727,  3107, 77765,  1444
            .END
;
```

```
        .TITLE   COMPU3
        .GLOBL   COMPUT
        .CSECT XX              ;LABELLED COMMON
        A=.
        B=.+1000
        .CSECT
COMPUT:
        MOV      R4,-(SP)      ;PUT COUNT ON STACK
LOOP:   ADD      #6,R2         ;R2 GETS R2-2 EACH PASS
        ADD      #4,R3         ;R3 OK
        ADD      #6,R5         ;R5 GETS R5-2 EACH PASS
        MOV      R5,-(SP)      ;SAVE R5 FOR LATER
        MOV      (R2),R0
        MUL      (R3),R0       ;R0 ← IM(A2)*COS/2
        MOV      -(R2),R4
        MUL      (R3),R4
        MOV      R4,R1         ;R1 ← RE(A2)*COS/2
        MOV      -(R3),R4
        MUL      (R2)+,R4      ;R4 ← RE(A2)*SIN/2
        SUB      R4,R0         ;R0 ← IM(A2)*COS/2-RE(A2)*SIN/2
        MOV      (R3)+,R4
        MUL      (R2),R4       ;R4 ← IM(A2)*SIN/2
        ADD      R1,R4         ;R4 ← RE(A2)*COS/2+IM(A2)*SIN/2
        MOV      (SP)+,R5      ;RESTORE R5
        ASR      (R5)          ;SCALE IM(A1)
        MOV      (R5),(R2)
        ADD      R0,(R5)       ;IM(A1) ← IM(A1)+R0
        SUB      R0,(R2)       ;IM(A2) ← IM(A1)-R0
        NEG      (R2)
        ASR      -(R5)         ;SCALE RE(A1)
        MOV      (R5),-(R2)
        ADD      R4,(R5)       ;RE(A1) ← RE(A1)+R4
        SUB      R4,(R2)       ;RE(A2) ← RE(A1)-R4
        DEC      (SP)
        BNE      LOOP
        TST      (SP)+         ;POP COUNTER OFF STACK
        RTS      PC
        .END
```

SCOPE1: SCOPE1 first computes $|C(k)|$, the magnitude of $C(k)$, by forming the sum of the squares of the real and imaginary parts of $C(k)$, and then uses the Newton-Raphson algorithm (program of Section 9.2) to extract the square root. The output of SCOPE1 is shown in Fig. 10-9 . The windowed time waveform is displayed by using line segments to connect the sample points while the spectral output consists of vertical lines. A double buffer is used here also. While one waveform and spectrum are being displayed, a second display file is being built for the other. The initial display file structure is as follows:

```
DISPST:                 .                   ;DISPLAY FILE FOR AXES, LABELLING
                        .
                        .
DIS1:                   DJMP
D1:                     END1                ;WAVEFORM/SPECTRUM DISPLAY FILE #1
                        .
                        .
                        .
END1:                   DJMP
                        DIS2
;
DIS2:                   DJMP
D2:                     END2
                        .                   ;WAVEFORM/SPECTRUM DISPLAY FILE #2
                        .
                        .
END2:                   DJMP
                        DISPST
```

The reader should satisfy himself that the instruction sequence

```
        MOV #END2,D2
        MOV #D1+2,D1
```

will *stop* display of buffer 2 and *start* display of buffer 1, while

```
        MOV #END1,D1
        MOV #D2+2,D2
```

will *stop* display of buffer 1 and *start* display of buffer 2.

The following program accepts the complex DFT output samples, computes the magnitude of each sample (i.e., square root of the sum of the squares of the real and imaginary components), then creates a display file for each of the input signal and the amplitude spectrum of that signal. Again, the windowed signal is displayed by interpolating the samples with straight lines ("connect the dots") while the spectrum consists of vertical lines of the requisite length.

```
.GLOBL SCOPE1 DIS1 D1 END1 DIS2 D2 END2
.CSECT XX                       ;LABELLED COMMON
A=.
B=.+1000
.CSECT
BLKOFF=20
POINT=    114000
LONGV=    110000
SHORTV=   104000
INT7=     3600
CHAR=     100000
LPON=     140
LPOFF=    100
LINE0=    4
DJMP=     160000
INTX=     40000
DNOP=     164000
MINUSX=   20000
DPC=      172000
```

```
SCOPE1:
        MOV     2(R5),ARG         ;ADDRESS OF TIME WAVEFORM BUFFER
        TST     @4(R5)            ;IS IT FIRST CALL?
        BNE     GO
;START DISPLAY AND INITIALIZE FLAG FIRST TIME AROUND
        MOV     #DISPST,@#DPC     ;YES,START DISPLAY
        MOV     #-1,FLAG          ;BUFFER FLAG
;
GO:     NEG     FLAG              ;FLAG WILL BE +1 ON FIRST CALL
        CLR     BUF1              ;D.C. OUTPUT = 0
        MOV     #B+4,R5           ;INPUT 1'ST HARMONIC ADDRESS
        MOV     #BUF1+2,OUTADD    ;OUTPUT 1'ST HARMONIC ADDRESS
        MOV     #64.,-(SP)        ;STORE COUNT ON STACK FOR EFFICIENCY
;
;CALCULATE POWER SPECTRUM/AMPLITUDE SPECTRUM
;A) FIRST HALF OF ARRAY
LOOPA:
        MOV     (R5)+,R0          ;REAL
        MUL     R0,R0             ;REAL*REAL
        MOV     (R5)+,R2          ;IMAG
        MUL     R2,R2             ;IMAG*IMAG
        ADD     R1,R3
        ADC     R2                ;SUM SQUARES "K" IN R2,R3
        ADD     R0,R2
        JSR     PC,NEWTON         ;GET SQUARE ROOT OF R2,R3 IN R4
        MOV     R4,@OUTADD        ;OUTPUT SQUARE ROOT
        ADD     #2,OUTADD         ;BUMP ARRAY ADDRESS
        DEC     (SP)              ;DECREMENT COUNTER
        BGT     LOOPA             ;BRANCH IF NON ZERO
;
        MOV     #63.,(SP)         ;RELOAD COUNTER
        MOV     #A+252.,R5
;B) SECOND HALF OF ARRAY, SAME STEPS AS FIRST
LOOPB:
        MOV     -(R5),R0          ;IMAG
        MUL     R0,R0             ;IMAG*IMAG
        MOV     -(R5),R2          ;REAL
        MUL     R2,R2             ;REAL*REAL
        ADD     R1,R3
        ADC     R2                ;SUM SQUARES "K" IN R2,R3
        ADD     R0,R2
        JSR     PC,NEWTON         ;GET SQUARE ROOT OF R2,R3 IN R4
        MOV     R4,@OUTADD        ;OUTPUT SQUARE ROOT
        ADD     #2,OUTADD         ;BUMP ARRAY ADDRESS
        DEC     (SP)              ;DECREMENT COUNTER
        BGT     LOOPB             ;BRANCH IF NON-ZERO
        TST     (SP)+             ;POP COUNT
;
        BR      OUTPUT
;
;USE NEWTON-RAPHSON ALGORITHM TO CALCULATE SQUARE ROOT
NEWTON:
        .....program of Section 9.2 .....
;
;START OBTAINING VALUES FOR SPECTRUM DISPLAY
OUTPUT:
        MOV     ARG,R2            ;INPUT BUFFER ADDRESS FOR TIME WAVEFORM
        MOV     #BUF1,R4          ;ADDRESS OF AMPLITUDE SPECTRUM ARRAY
;
        TST     FLAG              ;ALTERNATE BUFFER FLAG, CHANGED EACH PASS
        BMI     NEG
```

```
POS:
        CLR     TIMFL1-2            ;TIME WAVE =0 AT T=-1 FOR DELTA TO T=0
        MOV     #TIMFL1,R5         ;OUTPUT BUFFER FOR TIME WAVEFORM
                                   ;"CONNECT THE DOTS"
        MOV     #FFL1,R3           ;OUTPUT BUFFER FOR AMPLITUDE SPECTRUM
                                   ;"VERTICAL LINES"
        BR      LOOP3
;
NEG:
        CLR     TIMFL2-2           ;SAME AS ABOVE FOR ALTERNATE PASSES
        MOV     #TIMFL2,R5
        MOV     #FFL2,R3
LOOP3:
;
;SPECTRAL SAMPLE--VISIBLE VERTICAL LINE
        MOV     #INTX,(R3)+        ;INTENSIFY, DEL X = 0 FOR SPECTRAL SAMPLE
        ASR     (R4)
        ASR     (R4)
        MOV     (R4),(R3)+         ;DEL Y = SPECTRAL VALUE/4, ALWAYS POSITIVE
;
;INVISIBLE LINE FROM TOP OF PRESENT LINE TO BOTTOM OF NEXT LINE
        MOV     #6,(R3)+           ;DEL X =6 TO BASE OF NEXT SPECTRAL LINE
        MOV     (R4)+,(R3)         ;
        BIS     #MINUSX,(R3)+      ;DEL Y = -DEL Y TO BASE OF NEXT LINE
;
;DO 2 SIGNAL SAMPLES--CONNECT THE DOTS
        MOV     #2,COUNT
;
LOOP4:
        MOV     #INTX+3,(R5)+      ;INTENSIFY X, DEL X = 3 BETWEEN SAMPLES
        ASR     (R2)               ;YNEW=SIGNAL/2
        MOV     (R2),-(SP)         ;YNEW STORED TEMPORARILY
        SUB     R0,(R2)            ;DEL Y=YNEW-YOLD TO "CONNECT THE DOTS"
        MOV     (SP)+,R0           ;YOLD NEXT=YNEW PRESENT
;
        TST     (R2)               ;IS DEL Y NEGATIVE?
        BGE     XONT20
        NEG     (R2)               ;NEGATE IF NEGATIVE
        BIS     #MINUSX,(R2)
XONT20: MOV     (R2)+,(R5)+        ;DEL Y = MAG(YNEW-YOLD),
                                   ;    WITH CORRECT SIGN BIT
        DEC     COUNT
        BNE     LOOP4
;
        CMP     R4,#BUF1+254.      ;FINISHED?
        BLO     LOOP3              ;NO
;
        TST     FLAG
        BMI     NEG2
POS2:   MOV     #END2,D2           ;STOP DISPLAY FILE #2
        MOV     #D1+2,D1           ;START DISPLAY FILE #1
        RTS     PC
;
NEG2:   MOV     #END1,D1           ;STOP DISPLAY FILE #1
        MOV     #D2+2,D2           ;START DISPLAY FILE #2
        RTS     PC
;
```

346

```
COUNT:   0
OUTADD:  0
FLAG:    0
ARG:     0
TEMP:    0
N:       0
BUF1:    .BLKW    256.
;
;DISPLAY FILE WITH DOUBLE BUFFER
;
DISPST:  POINT!LINE0!LPOFF!INT7!BLKOFF,100.,0  ;BEAM TO (100,0)
         LONGV,0+INTX,767.          ;VERTICAL LINE 767 UNITS
         POINT,100.,576.            ;BEAM TO (100,576)
         LONGV,768.+INTX,0          ;HORIZONTAL LINE 768 UNITS, TIME AXIS
         POINT,100.,20.             ;BEAM TO (100,20)
         LONGV,768.+INTX,0          ;HORIZONTAL LINE 768 UNITS, FREQ AXIS
;
DIS1:    DJMP                       ;DISPLAY FILE 1
D1:      END1
         POINT,100.,576.            ;BEAM TO (100,576) [TIME WAVEFORM START]
         LONGV,MINUSX+3,0
TIMFL1:  .BLKW    508.              ;TIME WAVEFORM VECTORS GO HERE
         POINT,100.,20.             ;BEAM TO (100,20)  [SPECTRUM START]
         LONGV
FFL1:    .BLKW    508.              ;SPECTRUM VECTORS GO HERE
END1:    DJMP
         DIS2
;
DIS2:    DJMP                       ;DISPLAY FILE 2
D2:      END2
         POINT,100.,576.            ;BEAM TO (100,576) [TIME WAVEFORM START]
         LONGV,MINUSX+3,0
TIMFL2:  .BLKW    508.              ;TIME WAVEFORM VECTORS GO HERE
         POINT,100.,20.             ;BEAM TO (100,20)  [SPECTRUM START]
         LONGV
FFL2:    .BLKW    508.              ;SPECTRUM VECTORS GO HERE
END2:    DJMP
         DISPST
;
         .END
```

10.4 FAST DIGITAL SPEECH SPECTROGRAM PRODUCTION AND DISPLAY

The *digital oscilloscope* shows the spectrum of a signal at each point in time. Often it is useful to be able to see the history of the *change in spectrum with time*. This requires a three dimensional plot, *spectral amplitude* vs. *frequency* as a function of *time*. In the late 1940's an instrument called the *sound spectrograph* was invented for this purpose. This machine records a short segment of audio signal on a magnetic strip and then, in a two or three minute interval creates a spectrogram by a burning technique on a heat sensitive paper. Thus, areas of high spectral energy are *black* (i.e., burnt) while areas of low spectral energy remain *white*.

10.4.1 Display of Grey Scale Pictures on the VT-11

The problems of displaying a multi-valued function *f(x,y)* are such that refreshed graphics processors are inappropriate. Although, in principle, a P-point, 8-intensity-per-point spectral cross section could be displayed by using the CPU to produce a sequence of P "change intensity" ... "plot short vertical vector" commands to be executed by the DPU, a typical spectrogram requiring 256 spectral cross sections of 64 "points" (short vectors), each with one of eight intensities, would require about 32 Kwords of memory for the display file alone. Since "change intensity" and "plot short vector" commands typically require DPU/CRT execution times on the order of 5 and 10 *u*sec, respectively, such a display file would be scanned and executed less than 4 times a second, an unacceptable rate in terms of the flicker produced.

The solution devised is to create a band of pairs of vertical lines, each consisting of P sequential *short vertical vectors* (DVV, Fig. 10-10). In this example,

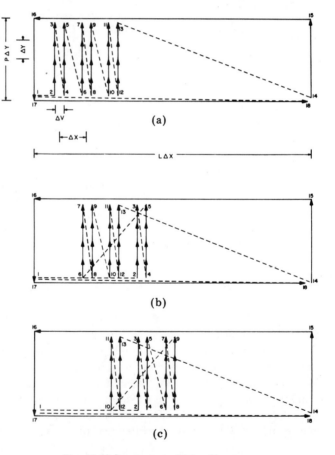

Fig. 10-10 Spectrogram display file sweep.

P = 4; ΔV is actually zero in the display so that each spectral value consists of 2 overlaid short vertical vectors (each of length ΔY) with 16 possible pair intensity values. In Fig. 10-10a, three DVV groups illuminate the first three spectral cross sections. The static display (including frame) requires zero CPU overhead. Solid lines are visible, dotted lines invisible. Vectors are drawn as per number sequence. Then, (Fig. 10-10b), the CPU alters the DPU "set point" instruction so as to move DVV group #1 to the right of DVV group #3 and decodes the stored spectral data so that DVV group #1 now illuminates spectral cross section #4. In Fig. 10-10c, the CPU alters the DPU "set point" instruction to move DVV group #2 to the right of DVV group #1 and decodes stored spectral data so that DVV group #2 now illuminates spectral cross section #5. The sequence continues with the left-most DVV group moved to the right of the right-most DVV group until the entire spectrogram has been swept. The process is then repeated.

The reader should note that two overwritten vectors of eight possible intensity levels each can produce an acceptable 16-level display if pairs of intensity levels are used as follows: (0,0), (0,1), (1,1), ..., (6,7), (7,7). Thus there are a total of $2*(M/2)*P$ short vectors in the display. The band is displayed by the DPU while the CPU dynamically decodes spectral information, and then updates and translates sequential vertical vector groups to effectively scan the L stored (encoded) spectral cross sections with a moving phosphor band. The encoded spectral point values are packed 4 to a 16-bit word. Decoding each spectral value consists of 4 right shifts with a "check carry bit" after each shift. A simple tree search then yields a correct pair of new "intensity" instructions which are over-written into the display file at the appropriate locations.

In order for this display to be effective, certain conditions must be satisfied which are dependent on the phosphor characteristics, the DPU instruction decode/ display time, and the ambient lighting. Specifically, a band of sufficient width such that each spectral point builds up to maximum fluorescence during a single spectrogram sweep must be repetitively swept across the screen fast enough such that the phosphorescent component of the entire spectrogram is physiologically acceptable under the existing lighting conditions.

10.4.2 A Fast Software-Based Speech Spectrogram Package for the PDP- 11/VT-11

The general techniques described above have been used in conjunction with the sampling and FFT modules already introduced to produce a modular package for very fast spectrogram production and display on a PDP-11/VT-11. Hardware requirements besides the VT-11 are an A/D converter with programmable clock (e.g., AR-11) and a PDP-11 CPU with EIS (i.e., MUL, etc). The complete software package is available as DECUS 11-361. In Fig. 10-11 we show two time exposure pictures illustrating the output of the software speech spectrograph. As suggested above, this approximates what is seen in a darkened room when directly viewing the screen. Processing time from speech input to spectrogram output is about 3 seconds on a PDP-11/55!

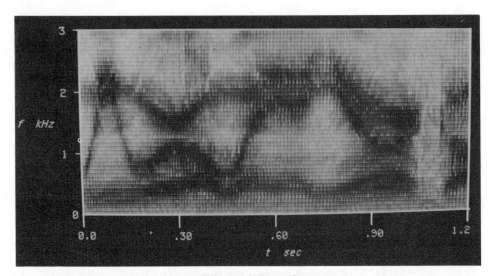

a)Wide-band: P = 48

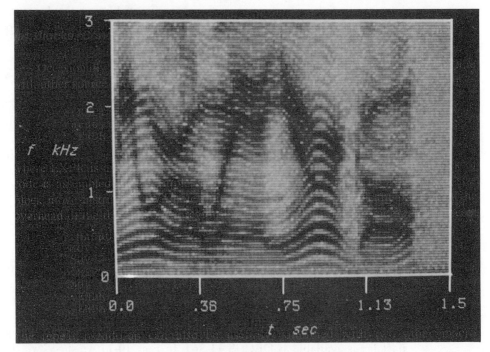

b)Narrow-band: P = 96

Fig. 10-11 Software produced speech spectrograms.

10.5 SPEECH ANALYSIS/SYNTHESIS

Talking computers are not yet commonplace but they are not now unusual. Machines which speak date back to 1791 and the acoustic apparatus of von Kempelen. Until very recently, most successful *speech synthesizers* were essentially electrical apparatus which simulated the acoustical properties of the human vocal system — vocal cords (glottis), vocal tract, mouth and nose — as schematically represented in Fig. 10-12.

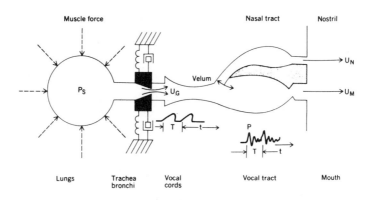

Fig. 10-12 Schematic diagram of the human vocal apparatus.

10.5.1 Speech Analysis

The *speech spectrogram* (Fig. 10-11) has been the source of much information concerning the nature of human speech. *Voiced sounds* (e.g., all vowels and voiced consonants) are produced when air from the lungs is passed via the trachea through the glottis which vibrates and thus modulates the air into "pulses". These pulses excite the vocal tract, whose shape may be varied by opening and closing the mouth and, most importantly, manipulating the tongue backwards and forwards or up and down. The resultant sounds are characterized by

1. A series of three primary time varying peaks or resonances, called *formants*. These formants are revealed as the dark bands (Fig. 10-11a) in a wideband spectrogram. Studies of the *same* voiced sounds as spoken by *different* speakers reveals that each vowel for example, can be "assigned" a set of "standard" formant frequencies. For example, a short sustained vowel with formants at 270, 2290 and 3010 Hz will generally be perceived as /i/ as in *feet* by an English speaking listener. In Fig. 10-13, the standard frequencies for some other vowels are listed.

2. A near-absence of energy *except* at those frequencies which are multiples of the fundamental frequency, F0, of the vocal cords vibration (about 100 Hz for a male speaker). Thus, in the narrow band spectrogram (Fig. 10-11b), we see energy concentrated in narrow horizontal bands whose vertical separation varies with time as the speaker varies his *pitch*. If pitch remains constant, the speech remains very intelligible but is monotone, and often described as "computer-like"!

In summary, *voiced speech* consists of a quasi-periodic time signal (with period 1/F0 sec.) whose spectral energy is concentrated in those harmonics of F0 nearest the *formant* frequencies for the particular sound being uttered.

```
Key Word     Formant Frequencies (Hz)
--------     ------------------------
it           390,1990,2550
bet          530,1840,2480
at           660,1720,2410
father       730,1090,2440
all          570,1090,2410
foot         440,1020,2240
boot         300, 870,2240
up           640,1190,2390
```

Fig. 10-13 Standard formant frequencies of American English vowels.

Nasals (*m, n, ing*) are like vowels except that the *velum* (Fig. 10-12) is lowered, introducing a second acoustic side path (the nose!) whose spectral effect is to suppress energy in a certain region. *Unvoiced* sounds (*s, f, th*, etc.) are produced by excitation of the vocal system caused by air turbulence at a constriction (e.g, teeth, tongue); thus the spectral line structure observed in voiced sounds is absent. In all, about 40 different sounds or *phonemes* are distinguishable in English.

A computer (or other machine) could be made to speak synthetically if

1. we could electrically (or digitally, as we shall see) effectively duplicate the actions of the human vocal tract and thus create a *speech sythesizer*

2. a set of commands could be derived to drive the synthesizer.

Speech synthesizers are now widely available. In fact, the Texas Instruments *Speak & Spell* electronic learning aid contains a true speech synthesizer which, with the aid of a microprocessor and specialized large scale integrated circuits, creates speech from stored parameters. Thus we shall briefly examine an algorithm (and resultant program) which accepts English text and derives a set of driver parameters for one synthesizer (the **VOTRAX**, available both in commerical and hobbyist versions). Then we will demonstrate how computers, the PDP-11 in particular, can effect real-time speech synthesis entirely via software techniques.

10.5.2 Automatic Translation of English Text to Phonemes via Letter-to-Sound Rules

Unrestricted text-to-speech translation can be effected using rules which take into account context. The algorithm to be described here is that of Elovitz *et. al.* (1976) at the Naval Research Labs (NRL), Washington. The program documented was derived from Crowley's Basic Plus IV version (1977) of the NRL SNOBOL version.

The NRL team developed a set of 330 rules which statistically were shown to produce correct pronunciation for about 90% of the words in an average sample of English text. The rules are defined in an easily machine and human readable ASCII table, and read into the system at startup. Thus, extra rules can easily be introduced to ensure correct pronunciation of any important application-specific jargon which is not dealt with properly by the basic rule set. The software system is particularly interesting as it is almost entirely couched in terms of the string manipulation primitives available as efficient RT-11 Syslib functions. The software runs in real time on an LSI-11, and is available as DECUS 11-375.

Each rule is of the form

$$A[B]C = D$$

That is, "the character string B, occurring with left context A and right context C, results in the pronunciation D". D, in this case, is one or more of the 64 VOTRAX input symbols. B is the character or character string to be translated. A and C are characters, character strings, or special symbols representing a class of character strings which denote categories of sounds such as vowels, voiced consonants, etc. Blanks denote beginnings and ends of words. The absence of A or C in a rule means that the corresponding context is irrelevant.

The special symbols used are:

Symbol	Meaning
#	1 or more vowels (A,E,I,O,U, or Y)
?	2 or more vowels
^	1 consonant (B,C,D,F,G,H,J,K,L,M,N,P,Q,R,S,T,V,W,X, or Z)
:	0 or more consonants
*	1 or more consonants
.	voiced consonant
$	consonant plus E or I
%	suffix (E, ER, ES, ED, ING, or ELY)
&	sibilant (S, C, G, Z, X, J, CH, or SH)
@	non-palatal (T, S, R, D, L, Z, N, J, TH, CH, or SH)
+	front vowel (E, I, or Y)

A typical rule is '[A]WA=[UH2]', which means *A* preceded by anything and followed by *WA* is pronounced "UH2" (i.e., as in "b*u*t"). This rule is followed in the table by '[AW]=[AW]', which means that the string *AW* is output as VOTRAX phoneme "AW" and thus pronounced as in "*aw*ful" whatever the context. Thus, *rule order* is important; both AWAY and AWFUL will be pronounced correctly because the algorithm ceases scanning when the first success is encountered. When the user introduces more rules, he must ensure that more specific rules precede more general rules.

The rules are grouped according to the starting letter of the B or "rule body" string. Text is scanned from left to right. The rule group pertinent to the single character pointed to at any given time is scanned. When a match is found (the last rule in the scanned group is always a default pronunciation for that letter) the equivalent sequence is output to the VOTRAX buffer, the pointer is bumped over the body characters bracketed (i.e., the rule body), and the scan is resumed using the rule group relevant to the new "pointer" character. Thus, ' LOCAL JUDGE ' is translated as shown below, with the pointer position denoted. Note that blanks within the ' ' construct are significant.

```
       Pointer Position        Rule Used      Corresponding VOTRAX Commands
       ----------------        ---------      -----------------------------
a)  LOCAL JUDGE              '[LO]C#'              LUH 01 U1
      ^
b)  LOCAL JUDGE              '[C]'                 K
       ^
c)  LOCAL JUDGE              '#:[AL] '             UH2 L
        ^
d)  LOCAL JUDGE              '[ ]'                 silence
          ^
e)  LOCAL JUDGE              '[J]'                 DJ
           ^
f)  LOCAL JUDGE              '[U]^'                UH
            ^
g)  LOCAL JUDGE              '[D]'                 D
             ^
h)  LOCAL JUDGE              '[G]+'                DJ
              ^
i)  LOCAL JUDGE              '#:[E] '              silence
               ^
```

Thus, for example, AL preceded by zero or more consonants and a vowel, and followed by a blank, is translated as UH2 L, whereas E preceded and followed by the same constructs is not pronounced.

Before we briefly examine the *translation* computational kernel, we will describe some of the RT-11 Syslib string manipulation routines which are the nucleus of the software.

Character strings are represented under RT-11 as a block of contiguous bytes, each byte containing the ASCII representation of the relevant character. The length of a string is defined implicitly in that the byte following the last character contains zero, the *null* character. Note that the *blank* or *space* character is ASCII 40(8). The RT-11 system library (Syslib) contains efficient FORTRAN callable subprograms for string manipulation. For example, GETSTR reads a string from a specified logical unit into a given LOGICAL*1 array while PUTSTR does the reverse. GETSTR removes trailing blanks and terminates the string with the null character. LEN computes the length of a given string while CONCAT creates string *c* from strings *a* (left string) and *b* (right string). *a* (but not *b*) and *c* can specify the same string. We will list the two routines which form the nucleus of the English text to VOTRAX translator. The very efficient use of autoincrement mode and the condition codes should be noted.

SUBSTR: SUBSTR copies string *a* into string *b*, starting at the *i*'th position of string *a*, and stopping when a specified number of characters *n* have been copied or when a null byte is detected in string *a*, whichever comes first. Thus, if *n* is not specified, all of *a* is copied into *b*.

```
        .TITLE   SUBSTR              ;USE--CALL SUBSTR(ASTRNG,BSTRNG,ISTRT!,N!)
        .GLOBL   SUBSTR
SUBSTR:
        MOV      (R5)+,R3            ;NUMBER OF ARGUMENTS
        MOV      (R5)+,R1            ;a STRING STARTING ADDRESSS
        MOV      (R5)+,R2            ;b STRING STARTING ADDRESSS
        MOV      @(R5)+,R4           ;POSITION OF FIRST CHARACTER TO BE COPIED
        BEQ      NTST                ;ERROR
SKIP:   TSTB     (R1)+               ;SKIP a STRING CHARACTERS NOT TO BE COPIED
        BEQ      ZDST                ;ZERO BYTE ALWAYS MEANS END OF STRING
        SOB      R4,SKIP             ;SYSLIB USES DEC, BNE FOR COMPATIBILTY
        DEC      R1                  ;BACK UP A BYTE
NTST:   CMPB     #4,R3               ;IS n SPECIFIED?  (I.E., 4 ARGUMENTS TO CALL)
        BHI      MOVALL              ;NO. MOVE REST OF a STRING INTO b STRING
        MOV      @(R5)+,R4           ;YES. GET n
        BEQ      ZDST                ;n = 0
MOVN:   MOVB     (R1)+,(R2)+         ;BLOCK BYTE MOVE
        BEQ      EXIT                ;ALWAYS CHECK FOR END OF INPUT STRING
        SOB      R4,MOVN
ZDST:   CLRB     (R2)+               ;NULL BYTE TERMINATES b STRING
EXIT:   RTS      PC
MOVALL: MOVB     (R1)+,(R2)+         ;MOV a INTO b
        BNE      MOVALL              ;UNTIL END OF a DETECTED
        RTS      PC
        .END
```

SCOMP: SCOMP compares strings *a* and *b*, returning zero if they are equal and the position *i* of the first mismatched character if they are not equal. The sign of *i* indicates which string is shorter when they are not equal. ($i < 0$ means $a < b$). SCOMP may be called as a subroutine or used as a function.

```
                .TITLE    SCOMP
                .GLOBL    SCOMP ISCOMP
        SCOMP:
        ISCOMP:
                MOV       (R5)+,R3        ;NUMBER OF ARGUMENTS
                MOV       (R5)+,R1        ;a STRING STARTING ADDRESSS
                MOV       (R5)+,R2        ;b STRING STARTING ADDRESSS
                CLR       R0              ;R0 IS OUTPUT INDICATOR
        NXTCHR: INC       R0              ;R0 ← R0 + 1
                TSTB      (R1)            ;STRING a END?
                BEQ       SAEND           ;YES
                TSTB      (R2)            ;STRING b END?
                BEQ       SBEND           ;YES
                CMPB      (R1)+,(R2)+      ;CHARACTERS THE SAME?
        ENDTST: BEQ       NXTCHR          ;YES. TRY NEXT CHARACTER.
                BGT       BLTA            ;NO. b < a ?
        ALTB:   NEG       R0              ;     a < b .
        BLTA:                             ;     b < a .
                CMPB      #3,R3           ;IS THIS A SUBROUTINE?
                BHI       EXIT            ;NO. FUNCTION, SO i RETURNED IN R0
                MOV       R0,@(R5)+       ;YES. RETURN i AS ARGUMENT
        EXIT:   RTS       PC
        ;
        SAEND:  TSTB      (R2)            ;STRING a ENDED. b ALSO?
                BEQ       EQUAL           ;YES, SO STRINGS ARE EQUAL
                CMPB      #40,(R2)+       ;NO. DOES b have LAGGING BLANKS?
                BR        ENDTST          ;BACK TO MAINSTREAM TO FIND OUT
        ;
        SBEND:  CMPB      (R1)+,#40       ;STRING b ENDED.
                                          ;   DOES a HAVE LAGGING BLANKS?
                BR        ENDTST          ;BACK TO MAINSTREAM TO FIND OUT
        ;
        EQUAL:  CLR       R0              ;EQUALITY
                BR        BLTA
                .END
```

In describing the program kernel, we will refer to the line numbers of the relevant FORTRAN code in parentheses. We assume that the input text, padded with a leading and lagging blank, is in the string L. Tests are performed (not shown) to determine the starting (ISTRT) and stopping (ISTOP) indices of the rule string arrays (A, B, and C) corresponding to the character pointed to by IPOINT, which is initialized to the first non-blank character in the string.

Then starting with I = ISTRT (138), the first rule of the relevant group is tested:

1. BD receives a substring S of the input string L (from the pointer rightwards) such that length of BD = length of rule body being tested, (B(1,I)). AD and CD receive the substrings of L *left* and *right* of S, respectively. Thus, AD&BD&CD = L where "&" is the concatenation operator. (139-142)

2. If BD and the rule body (B(1,I)) are *not* identical, I ← I+1 and go to 1 if I ≤ ISTOP. (143-144)

3. If AD does *not* satisfy the prefix rule (A(1,I)), I ← I+1 and go to 1 if I ≤ ISTOP. (146-155)

4. If CD does *not* satisfy the suffix rule (C(1,I)), I ← I+1 and go to 1 if I ≤ ISTOP. (157-166).

5. SUCCESS! Prefix, body, *and* suffix "match". Output to VOTRAX buffer (168-170), bump IPOINT by length of rule body (171), and start scan of rules relevant to character at new pointer position. New ISTRT, ISTOP are determined by another part of the program.

Steps (3) and (4) are carried out via two subroutines, FNPRE and FNSUF, respectively. For example, for a given body rule match, FNPRE is called repeatedly with successively more left portions of the prefix rule string, A(1,I), and AD as arguments until either no match occurs (failure) *or* the prefix rule string is exhausted (success, since there must have been matches up to that point) *or* AD is exhausted (failure, since there are still portions of the left rule string to be matched). If FNPRE is successful, FNSUF is used to test the suffix rule string, C(1,I), against CD in a similar manner. Again, for any alphabetic character *c* pointed to by IPOINT, the last rule (I = ISTOP) is always [*c*] = VOTRAX pronunciation of that character. Thus, success is always guaranteed for alphabetic characters; at *worst*, the words will be spelled!

Text can be input from a file if desired. Properly interfaced to the operating system, a "talking computer" is possible.

```
      C     ENGLISH TO VOTRAX**********************************************
      C     POINTER POINTS TO FIRST (NON-BLANK) CHARACTER IN INPUT STRING
0122        IPOINT=2
      C     LENGTH OF INPUT STRING
0123        ISTRLN=LEN(L)
              .
            compute ISTRT, ISTOP
              .
      C     CHECK ALL RULES WHOSE 1'ST BODY CHAR MATCHES POINTER CHAR
0138        DO 12030 I= ISTRT,ISTOP
      C     SEGMENT INPUT STRING INTO LEFT, MIDDLE, AND RIGHT STRINGS
      C     LENGTH OF MIDDLE STRING = IB = LENGTH OF BODY OF RULE TESTED
0139        IB=LEN(B(1,I))
0140        CALL SUBSTR(L,AD,1        ,IPOINT-1)
0141        CALL SUBSTR(L,BD,IPOINT   ,IB)
0142        CALL SUBSTR(L,CD,IPOINT+IB,LEN(L)+1-IPOINT-IB)
      C     ***********************************************************
      C     "BODY" OF STRING = BODY OF RULE? IF NOT, FORGET IT!
0143        CALL SCOMP(BD,B(1,I),IFLAG0)
0144        IF(IFLAG0.NE.0) GO TO 12030
      C     ***********************************************************
```

```
         C         CHECK PREFIX RULE FOR RELEVANT BODY
0146               CALL FNPRE(A(1,I),AD)
0147               IF(IX1.LE.0) GO TO 1110
0149               CALL SUBSTR(A(1,I),L1,1)
0150     10001 CALL SUBSTR(L1     ,L1,1,IX-IX1)
0151     10002 CALL SUBSTR(AD     ,AD,1,IY-IY1)
0152     105   CALL FNPRE(L1,AD)
0153               IF(IX1.GT.0) GO TO 10001
         C         NO MATCH (OR NO MORE RULES) FOR PREFIX? FORGET IT!
0155     1110  IF(IX1.NE.-1) GO TO 12030
         C         ************************************************************
         C         CHECK SUFFIX RULE FOR RELEVANT BODY
0157               CALL FNSUF(C(1,I),CD)
0158               IF(IX1.LE.0) GO TO 2220
0160               CALL SUBSTR(C(1,I),L1,1)
0161     20001 CALL SUBSTR(L1     ,L1,IX1+1,IX-IX1)
0162     20002 CALL SUBSTR(CD     ,CD,IY1+1,IY-IY1)
0163     205   CALL FNSUF(L1,CD)
0164               IF(IX1.GT.0) GO TO 20001
         C         NO MATCH (OR NO MORE RULES) FOR SUFFIX? FORGET IT!
0166     2220  IF(IX1.NE.-1) GO TO 12030
         C         ************************************************************
         C         PREFIX, SUFFIX AND BODY ALL MATCH! SUCCESS!!
0168     3330  LIM=E(1,I)
         C         OUTPUT OCTAL EQUIVALENT OF PHONEMES TO VOTRAX
0169               DO 3333 JJ=1,LIM
0170     3333  CALL VSK(E(JJ+1,I))
         C
         C         BUMP POINTER BY LENGTH OF RULE JUST FOUND, AND KEEP GOING
0171               IPOINT=IPOINT+IB
0172               GO TO 5131
0173     12030   CONTINUE
         C
         C         MESSAGE FOR UNKNOWN TEXT
0174               WRITE(7,12031)IPOINT
0175     12031 FORMAT(1X,'NO RULE FOUND AT CHAR' I7)
         C         SKIP REST OF STRING WHEN UNKNOWN TEXT ENCOUNTERED
0176               IPOINT=ISTRLN
0177               GO TO 5131
0178               END
```

10.5.3 Real-Time Software Speech Synthesis

VOTRAX is essentially an analog formant synthesizer. Hence, a cascade of analog filter circuits, (i.e., a resonator for each of the formants, and two correctional filters to approximate the effect of the vocal folds/mouth) driven by a periodic impulse generator will *approximate* a given vowel if the frequency of each of the variable formants is chosen as per Fig. 10-13.

It is well known that such filters can also be implemented digitally. In fact, one can model the vocal system and derive the following transfer function:

$$H(z) = H_V(z) * H_{s/s}(z)$$

where

$$H_V(z) = \prod_{k=1}^{4} \frac{(1-\exp(-2\pi b_k T)*2\cos(2\pi F_k T) + \exp(-4\pi b_k T))}{(1-\exp(-2\pi b_k T)*2\cos(2\pi F_k T)*z^{-1} + \exp(-4\pi b_k T)*z^{-2})}$$

is the transfer function of the *vocal tract* and

$$H_{s/s}(z) = \frac{(1-\exp(-aT)) * (1+\exp(-bT))}{(1-\exp(-aT)*z^{-1})*(1+\exp(-bT)*z^{-1})}$$

is the correctional factor which approximates the influence of the *vocal cords* and *mouth.* Here, $z = \exp(j2\pi fT)$, T is the sampling rate, and *b* and F are the formant *bandwidths* and *frequencies*, respectively. Then

$$H(z) = C/[1 + \sum_{i=1}^{10} a(i) * z^{-i}]$$

where the *a(i)* are obtained by polynomial expansion (i.e., multiplication of the factors) of the denominator above. C, the numerator, is the value of the denominator when $f = 0$, i.e., $z = 1$; thus, $H(f = 0, z = 1) = 1$.

A sketch of $|H(f)|$ vs. *f* for the vowel */ae/* as in *at* is shown below, with the formants "F" at 660, 1720, 2410 and 3500 Hz. Note the pronounced formant peaks.

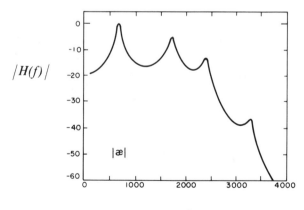

f

The impulse response of the filter with the given transfer function, $H(f)$, is computed as, simply,

$$h(n) = \sum_{i=1}^{10} a(i) * h(n-i), \quad n = 1,2,\ldots,N$$

where $h(0) = C$, and all other $h(n-i)$ are initially zero. This can be computed using fixed-point arithmetic if the $a(i)$ are scaled to ensure maximum accuracy. Since the largest positive integer representable in a 16-bit 2's complement word is $2**15-1$, each $a(i)$ should be multiplied by the same factor $2**(15-m)$, $m > -2$, so that $2**14 \le \max|a(i)| < 2**15-1$.

Thus, the n'th speech sample $h(n)$ is computed as

$$h(n) = \sum_{i=1}^{10} \{[a(i) * 2**(15-m)]*[h(n-i)*2**(m+1)]/2**16\}$$

That is the stored coefficients — $[a(i)*2**(15-m)]$ — are multiplied by the scaled $h(n-i)$, $[h(n-i)*2**(m+1)]$, and the accumulation of the most significant word of the results (i.e., divide 32-bit result by $2**16$) is $h(n)$, since $(15-m) + (m+1) -16 = 0$.

In the following program, polynomial multiplication using the values of Fig. 10-13 was first carried out so as to produce the table COEFF, each row of which contains 10 scaled $a(i)$, a scaled C, and the shift factor corresponding to $(m+1)$ for direct input to an ASH instruction. Eighty samples are produced for each vowel pitch period ($N = 80$), and each vowel is repeated 100 times before proceeding to the next. The output of the D/A must be lowpass filtered sharply above 4 kHz. (A poor loudspeaker approximates a lowpass filter!)

Endless repetition of the first 10 msec of the impulse response synthesizes a sustained vowel for a male speaker. By using speech analysis techniques to derive *tables of coefficients* for spoken words, the computer can be made to speak sentences. In the TI *Speak & Spell* synthesizer, the coefficients used for synthesis are related to the coefficients used here by a well known transformation. This alternate synthesis algorithm requires twice as many multiplications per speech sample output. However, fewer bits per coefficient are required and, because these alternative coefficients may be interpolated, fewer coefficients per second of speech output are required to be stored.

```
.TITLE SPEAK      ;REAL-TIME ON 11/34, 35, 40, 45, 50, 55, 60, 70
.GLOBL SPEAK
.CSECT
DA=170412
CLKV1=344
CLKV2=346
CLKSR=170404
CLKBR=170406
CLK=177546
```

```
;           10
; h(n) = Σ |[a(i)*2**(15-m)]*[h(n-i)*2**(m+1)]/2**16|, n = 0, 1, ..., 79
;          i=1
SPEAK:
        CLR     @#CLK               ;TURN OFF 60 HZ CLOCK
        MOV     #COEFF,R0           ;POINTER TO 10 SETS OF a(i), C, (m+1)
;
        MOV     #SERV,@#CLKV1       ;CLOCK ISR VECTOR
        MOV     #340,@#CLKV2        ;PRIORITY 7
        MOV     #-125.,@#CLKBR      ;125 USEC PER SAMPLE
        MOV     #0503,@#CLKSR       ;REPEAT MODE, 1 USEC PER TICK,
                                    ;GO!
        CLR     FLAG                ;ISR FLAG
;
START:  MOV     #100.,NREP          ;EACH VOWEL OUTPUT 100 TIMES
;
LOOP1:  MOV     #80.,R3             ;PITCH PERIOD IS 80 SAMPLES

        MOV     20.(R0),R2          ;h(0) = C
        MOV     22.(R0),SF          ;SHIFT FACTOR, (m+1)
        MOV     #SAMPL,R1           ;BUFFER POINTER TO h(n-1)
;
LOOP2:                              ;USE IN-LINE CODE FOR SPEED
        .REPT   10.                 ;10'TH ORDER FILTER, i = 1, ..., 10
        MOV     (R1)+,R4            ;GET SAMPLE h(n-i) FROM DELAY LINE
        MUL     (R0)+,R4            ;MULTIPLY BY COEFFICIENT, a(i)
        ADD     R4,R2               ;ACCUMULATE 16 MSB'S OF RESULT
        .ENDR
;
        ADD     #1000,R2            ;CONVERT h(n) FROM 2'S COMP TO OFFSET
        MOV     R2,TEMP             ;PUT IN OUTPUT BUFFER FOR PICKUP BY ISR
        SUB     #1000,R2            ;CONVERT BACK TO 2'S COMP
        ASH     SF,R2               ;SCALE BY CORRECT POWER OF TWO, (m+1)
        SUB     #22.,R1             ;BACK UP SAMPLE POINTER
        MOV     R2,(R1)             ;h(n-1) NEXT TIME IS h(n) SCALED
        SUB     #20.,R0             ;BACK UP COEFFICIENT POINTER
        CLR     R2                  ;ZERO ACCUMULATOR
TST:    TST     FLAG                ;WAIT FOR INTERRUPT
        BEQ     TST
        CLR     FLAG                ;INTERRUPT RECEIVED
        SOB     R3,LOOP2            ;ANOTHER SAMPLE
;
        DEC     NREP                ;REPEAT THE CURRENT VOWEL?
        BNE     LOOP1               ;YES!
        ADD     #24.,R0             ;NEXT VOWEL
        CMP     R0,#FIN             ;END OF VOWEL TABLE?
        BNE     START               ;NO, NEXT VOWEL
        MOV     #COEFF,R0           ;YES, START AGAIN AT FIRST VOWEL
        BR      START
;
        RTS PC
;
SERV:   MOV     TEMP,@#DA           ;OUTPUT SAMPLE TO D/A
        INC     FLAG
        RTI
;
NREP:   0
TEMP:   0
FLAG:   0
SF:     0
```

```
     .BLKW   80.              ;n MAXIMUM = 80
SAMPL:  0,0,0,0,0,0,0,0,0,0        ;h(n-i) = 0, n = 0, i = 1, 2, ..., 10
;EACH ROW IS TEN [a(i)*2**(15-m)] COEFFS, C, AND "ASH" SRC FOR 2**(m+1) FACTOR
COEFF:
 161535,  12236,  41325,  24216,165740,142601,160522,   5607,  12463,  1257,360,3
   4266,  20207,  71570,  43414,154025,115706,145461,162335,  44576,  5275,531,1
  24101,   1466,  36741,  25272,160106,142546,164463,151621,  43226,  5275,662,1
  40067,162271,  13762,  16230,160106,160224,   2466,143434,  42134,  5275,723,1
  50452,165646,165157,176770,175421,  11141,  11322,142571,  16672,  2536,347,2
  47642,170720,161244,171220,   1403,  15066,   7344,142675,  16734,  2535,272,2
  65234,166367,152567,167507,   2527,  24072,  14131,132572,  15555,  2536,120,2
  71664,146744,164214,  12654,164107,  10653,  26611,131334,  15230,  2536,152,2
  40207,102147,107735,   4670,172175,   6337,  15041,152554,   6256,  1257, 57,3
  43141,137417,   3022,  32653,151142,170722,  31234,152514,   6036,  1257,175,3
FIN:    0
     .END SPEAK
```

This program will endlessly cycle through the 10 vowels. Minicomputer simulation of speech-related digital signal processing algorithms has been instrumental in development of such devices as VOTRAX and Speak & Spell.

10.6 COMPUTER MUSIC SYNTHESIS

Computers are also capable of creating musical sounds. In this section, we will present a short example showing how simple table-lookup techniques can be used to synthesize high quality organ music.

10.6.1 Wavetable Manipulation for Four-part Harmony

Just as signals can be analyzed into sinusoidal components, signals can be synthesized from sinusoidal components. In this example, one period of a waveform consisting of a fundamental and first and second harmonics is stored in a 256 byte table, WAVE. If this table is repetitively output, one sample every T seconds, the fundamental frequency of the output will be F = (1/256T). If T = 114 $u$sec, then F = 34.25 Hz with the 1'st and 2'nd harmonics at 2F and 3F respectively. If instead, every n'th sample of the table is output, the fundamental frequency will be nF. For example, for the note C2 = 65.405 Hz, n = 65.405/34.25 = 1.9096. Thus, the table INCR contains values N = 256n for each note C2 to D6 (1174.6 Hz). Each note also has associated with it an ID code corresponding to its location in the INCR table. Thus songs can be specified in terms of ID numbers for the required note.

A simple technique to make the waveform table into a "circular buffer" (so that the waveform is effectively repeated continuously) is to start it at a zero byte boundary and only modify the lower byte of the pointer into the table when addressing it. A 16-bit accumulator, AC, is incremented by N once every sample interval and the *upper* byte of the result used as a byte index or offset into the wavetable. After i increments, assuming AC was initially cleared, AC = iN. The upper byte of AC can be interpreted as AC/256 with the fraction truncated (i.e., iN/256 = $i*$n).

Four part harmony can be achieved by having 4 different increments iN, 4 AC's, and 4 different pointers into the one waveform table. The four referenced samples (i.e., the 4 voices) are simply added before being sent to the D/A converter. The format used for the song definition uses 5 bytes for each note. Byte 1 is the duration of the note (in samples) while bytes 2-5 are the ID numbers of each of the four "voices".

The time crucial "inner loop" requires some explanation. The pointer increment table (VINC) and the pointer table (VPTR) are made contiguous for convenience. With #VPTR and #WAVE in R2 and R3, respectively,

```
ADD VINC-VPTR(R2),(R2)+
```

conventionally updates the i'th wavetable pointer and points to the next. Then

```
MOVB -1(R2),.+8.
```

moves the *upper* byte of the i'th pointer into the *lower* byte of the initially zero SRC offset of

```
MOVB 0(R3),TMP
```

A conventional MOVB SRC,Rn would result in an erroneous sign extended result in Rn. In contrast, the *upper* byte of the initially zeroed memory word TMP remains zero and

```
ADD TMP,R1
```

accumulates the unsigned byte, since there is no ADDB instruction in the PDP-11 repertoire. Still, due to the power and versatility of the PDP-11 address modes, only 4 instructions per voice are required to update pointers *and* accumulate samples. The power of the macro in "compressing" structured information at the source level is vividly illustrated here.

10.6.2 Chord Organ Software for "Take Me Out to the Ballgame"

In this program, the first two voices carry the "melody", while the last two supply the "beat". Since the beat is only required occasionally, the zeroes (i.e., voice silent) are included inside the body of the macro BAR rather than being unnecessarily duplicated for each call. Again, the output of the D/A converter should be sharply attenuated above 4 kHz by a lowpass filter.

```
            .TITLE BALLGAME  ;PROGRAM BY IAN MACRAE, DAVE WEILER AND BOB MORRIS
DAC=170412                   ;D/A CONVERTER
CKSR=170404                  ;PROGRAMMABLE CLOCK
CKBF=CKSR+2
RPT=400+100          ;--- REPEAT, OVERFLOW
USEC=2               ;--- RATE= MICRO-SECS.
START=1              ;--- ENABLE CLOCK
CKINT=344            ;CLOCK INTERRUPT VECTOR
CKPRIO=300           ;PRIORITY (BR7)
NVOX=4               ;# VOICES IN SONG TABLE
            .RADIX  10
;DATA AREA
DUR:    1                            ;TIME LEFT TO PLAY THIS NOTE
NOTE:   BALL                         ;ADDRESS OF NEXT NOTE TO BE PLAYED
VINC:   .BLKW   NVOX                 ;NOTE INCREMENT (UPDATED EACH NOTE)
VPTR:   .BLKW   NVOX                 ;WAVETABLE INDEX (UPDATED EACH SAMPLE)
;
;THIS MACRO IS USED IN THE GENERATION OF THE TEXT OF THE SONG
;
            .MACRO  BAR     A,B,C,D,E
            .BYTE   8,A,0,0 ;DURATION 8, MELODY (A1,A2), NO BEAT (0,0) .
            .BYTE   4,B     ;DURATION 4, MELODY (B1,B2), BEAT (B3,B4)
            .BYTE   4,C,0,0 ;DURATION 4, MELODY (C1,C2), NO BEAT (0,0)
            .BYTE   4,D     ;DURATION 4, MELODY (D1,D2), BEAT (D3,D4)
            .BYTE   4,E,0,0 ;DURATION 4, MELODY (E1,E2), NO BEAT (0,0)
            .ENDM   BAR
            .PAGE
;WAVE SHAPE TABLE.
;       THESE VALUES ARE USED TO SIMULATE THE SOUND OF AN ORGAN
WAVE:
  .BYTE 163,166,169,172,175,178,180,182,184,186,187,189,190,191,192,192
  .BYTE 193,193,194,194,194,193,193,193,192,192,191,191,190,190,189,188
  .BYTE 188,187,187,186,186,185,185,184,184,184,184,184,184,184,184,185
  .BYTE 185,186,186,187,187,188,189,190,191,192,192,193,194,195,196,197
  .BYTE 198,199,200,200,201,202,202,203,203,203,203,203,202,202,202,201
  .BYTE 200,199,198,197,196,194,192,190,188,186,184,181,179,176,173,170
  .BYTE 167,164,161,158,154,151,148,144,141,138,134,131,128,125,122,119
  .BYTE 116,113,111,108,106,104,102,100, 98, 97, 96, 95, 94, 93, 93, 92
  .BYTE  92, 92, 93, 93, 94, 94, 95, 97, 98, 99,101,102,104,106,108,110
  .BYTE 112,114,116,118,120,122,124,126,128,129,131,133,134,135,136,137
  .BYTE 138,138,139,139,139,138,138,137,136,135,133,132,130,128,125,123
  .BYTE 120,117,114,110,107,103, 99, 95, 91, 87, 83, 79, 74, 70, 66, 61
  .BYTE  57, 53, 48, 44, 40, 36, 32, 29, 25, 22, 19, 16, 13, 11,  8,  6
  .BYTE   5,  3,  2,  1,  1,  1,  1,  1,  2,  3,  4,  5,  7,  9, 12, 14
  .BYTE  17, 20, 24, 28, 31, 36, 40, 44, 49, 53, 58, 63, 68, 73, 79, 84
  .BYTE  89, 94, 99,105,110,115,120,125,130,134,139,143,147,152,155,159
;NOTE INCREMENT TABLE.
;       DURATIONS ARE FOR 8.772 KHZ SAMPLE RATE (114. USEC)
; (C2-B2) 65.405 69.295 73.415 77.783 82.408
;  87.308 92.498 97.998 103.83 110.00 116.54 123.47
; (C3-B3) 130.81 138.59 146.83 155.57 164.82
;  174.62 185.00 196.00 207.65 220.00 233.08 246.94
; (C4-B4) 261.62 277.18 293.66 311.13 329.63
;  349.234 369.994 391.995 415.308 440.006 466.162 493.882
; (C5-B5) 523.243 554.364 587.324 622.267 659.266
;  698.467 739.989 783.981 830.607 880.001 932.323 987.763
; (C6-D6) 1046.56 1108.78 1174.68
```

```
INCR:   0                                               ;NOTE 0= SILENCE
        489,518,549,581,616,652,691,732,776,822,871,922
        977,1035,1097,1162,1231,1305,1382,1464,1551,1644,1741,1845
        1955,2071,2194,2325,2463,2609,2764,2929,3103,3287,3483,3690
        3909,4142,4388,4649,4926,5218,5529,5858,6206,6575,6966,7380,8284,8776
;MUSIC TABLE: CONTAINS THE TEXT OF THE SONG "TAKE ME OUT TO THE BALL-GAME"
BALL:   BAR     <26,74>,<50,58,64,0>,<0,0>,<50,58,64,98>,<0,98>
        BAR     <26,92>,<50,58,64,88>,<0,88>,<50,58,64,82>,<0,82>
        BAR     <16,88>,<48,54,64,88>,<0,88>,<48,54,64,88>,<0,88>
        BAR     <30,78>,<48,54,64,78>,<0,78>,<48,54,64,78>,<0,78>
        BAR     <26,74>,<50,58,64,0>,<0,0>,<50,58,64,98>,<0,98>
        BAR     <26,92>,<50,58,64,88>,<0,88>,<50,58,64,82>,<0,82>
        BAR     <16,88>,<48,54,60,88>,<0,88>,<48,54,60,88>,<0,88>
        BAR     <30,88>,<48,54,60,88>,<0,88>,<48,54,60,88>,<0,88>
        BAR     <12,92>,<44,50,60,92>,<0,92>,<44,50,60,92>,<0,92>
        BAR     <16,78>,<48,54,60,82>,<0,82>,<48,54,60,84>,<0,84>
        BAR     <26,88>,<50,58,64,0>,<0,0>,<50,58,64,82>,<0,82>
        BAR     <16,74>,<50,58,64,74>,<0,74>,<50,58,64,74>,<0,74>
        BAR     <30,92>,<54,62,74,92>,<0,92>,<54,62,74,92>,<0,92>
        BAR     <20,92>,<54,62,74,96>,<0,96>,<54,62,74,98>,<0,98>
        BAR     <16,102>,<48,54,60,96>,<0,96>,<48,54,60,92>,<0,92>
        BAR     <16,88>,<20,54,60,82>,<20,82>,<24,54,60,78>,<24,78>
        BAR     <26,74>,<50,58,64,0>,<0,0>,<50,58,64,98>,<0,98>
        BAR     <26,92>,<50,58,64,88>,<0,88>,<50,58,64,82>,<0,82>
        BAR     <16,88>,<48,54,64,88>,<0,88>,<48,54,64,88>,<0,88>
        BAR     <30,78>,<48,54,64,78>,<0,78>,<48,54,64,78>,<0,78>
        BAR     <26,74>,<50,58,74,0>,<0,0>,<50,58,70,78>,<0,78>
        BAR     <16,82>,<50,58,70,84>,<0,84>,<50,58,70,88>,<0,88>
        BAR     <12,92>,<44,50,60,92>,<0,92>,<44,50,60,92>,<0,92>
        BAR     <26,0>,<44,50,60,92>,<0,92>,<44,50,60,96>,<0,96>
        BAR     <12,98>,<44,50,60,0>,<0,0>,<44,50,60,0>,<0,0>
        BAR     <12,98>,<44,50,60,0>,<0,0>,<44,50,60,0>,<0,0>
        BAR     <26,98>,<50,58,64,96>,<0,96>,<50,58,64,92>,<0,92>
        BAR     <16,88>,<50,58,64,86>,<0,86>,<50,58,64,88>,<0,88>
        BAR     <30,92>,<54,62,74,92>,<0,92>,<54,62,74,92>,<0,92>
        BAR     <16,96>,<48,54,60,96>,<0,96>,<48,54,60,96>,<0,96>
        BAR     <26,98>,<50,58,64,98>,<0,98>,<50,58,64,98>,<0,98>
        BAR     <16,98>,<20,58,64,82>,<20,82>,<24,58,64,78>,<24,78>
        .BYTE   0       ;MARKS END OF SONG
        .EVEN
        .RADIX  8
PLAY:   MOV     #ENTRY,@#CKINT  ;LOAD ISR ADDRESS
        MOV     #CKPRIO,@#CKINT+2 ;   AND PRIORITY
        MOV     #-114.,@#CKBF   ;SET UP CLOCK FOR 114 USEC INTERRUPTS
        MOV     #RPT+USEC+START,@#CKSR ;START CLOCK
WTR:    WAIT                    ;PLAY FOREVER!
        BR      WTR
NNOTE:  MOV     NOTE,R0         ;NEXT NOTE
        TSTB    (R0)            ;END?
        BNE     1$
        MOV     #BALL,R0        ;YES, RESTART SONG
1$:     MOVB    (R0)+,DUR+1     ;SET DURATION (HIGH BYTE, LOW=0)
        MOV     #VINC,R2        ;SET INCREMENTS FOR NEW NOTE
        .REPT   NVOX            ;4 VOICES, SO NVOX = 4
        MOVB    (R0)+,R1        ;PULL NOTE FROM TABLE
        CLR     VPTR-VINC(R2)   ;CLEAR ENTRY IN WAVETABLE POINTER TABLE
        MOV     INCR(R1),(R2)+  ;SET INCREMENT TO BE USED IN UPDATING
        .ENDM                   ;   WAVETABLE POINTER TABLE
        MOV     R0,NOTE         ;SAVE FOR LATER USE
```

```
;SYNTHESIZE NEXT OUTPUT SAMPLE
SAMPLE: CLR     R1                ;CLEAR ACCUMULATOR
        MOV     #VPTR,R2          ;POINTER TO BLOCK OF 4 WAVETABLE POINTERS
        MOV     #WAVE,R3          ;START OF WAVE TABLE
;A "MOVB SRC,Rn" SIGN EXTENDS INTO THE UPPER BYTE, AND THERE IS NO "ADDB".
;THEREFORE, MUST USE TECHNIQUES AS SHOWN BELOW.
        .REPT   NVOX              ;FOR i = 1,2,3,4
        ADD VINC-VPTR(R2),(R2)+   ;UPDATE i'th WAVETABLE PTR
        MOVB    -1(R2),.+8.       ;HIGH BYTE OF i'th PTR IS BYTE OFFSET
                                  ;      OF DESIRED SAMPLE IN WAVE TABLE
        MOVB    0(R3),TMP         ;SRC = #WAVE + BYTE OFFSET OF DESIRED SAMPLE
        ADD     TMP,R1            ;ACCUMULATE i'th SAMPLE
        .ENDM
;
        MOV     R1,@#DAC          ;OUTPUT i'TH SAMPLE TO D/A CONVERTER
        RTI
;
TMP:    0                         ;LOW BYTE USED AS MOVB DST,
                                  ;      HIGH BYTE ALWAYS ZERO.
;
ENTRY:  DEC     DUR               ;TIME FOR NEW NOTE?
        BNE     SAMPLE            ;NO, SAME NOTE
        BR      NNOTE             ;YES, START A NEW ONE
;
        .END    PLAY
```

10.7 SPEED ENHANCEMENT OF APPLICATIONS SOFTWARE VIA MICROPROGRAMMING

As suggested in Chapter 6, microprogramming is a systematic and economical method for implementing the control section of a computer. Its flexibility allows the tailoring of a processor, particularly the data flow, to a particular application. In recent years, user microprogramming options, which allow users to do the tailoring, have become available for some minicomputers, including the PDP-11/60. Program activity analysis (Section 9.1) is a crucial first step in determining which code segments to microprogram. However, in the application programs described below, the high activity areas are the computational kernels (*ck*'s) of the DSP programs examined in Chapter 9. Other candidate segments for microprogramming have been eliminated by the *autogen* process.

In this section, we describe the performance enhancements made possible by extending the *autogen* techniques described earlier to microprogramming of *ck*'s. In this way, the central processor can be tailored to implement a particular class of algorithms more efficiently while retaining all the advantages of general purpose computers. It is shown that speed increases ranging from 2 to nearly 10 times that of conventional software can be achieved by the combination of autogen software plus microprogramming of *ck*'s. Moreover, we will attempt to quantify the contributions of the various techniques to the final result. The simple model illustrating the processing of instructions in a computer, introduced in Section 2.5 and extended in Section 3.5.4, is used to aid in analysis of performance improvements. The specific ck's to be accelerated via microprogramming are the PB autocorrelation add/multiply/add, the linear predictive coding multiply/accumulate, and the FFT butterfly.

10.7.1 Review: The Stages of Processing Instructions in a Computer

To show the sources of performance gain via microprogramming, we must first recall the instruction processing steps in a minicomputer, as per Section 2.5:

1. In the I-phase, the instruction is fetched from memory and decoded.

2. In the O-phase, the operand addresses are calculated and the operands are fetched from memory.

3. In the E-phase, an operation is performed upon the operands; the number of steps varies according to the complexity of the operation. For example, addition is usually done in one step, whereas multiplication and division take several. Additional O-phase processing may be necessary if the result is to be stored in memory instead of a register.

The I-cycles and O-cycles can be viewed as overhead. Indeed, computer designers pay careful attention to reducing it by instruction set design, inclusion of registers, abbreviated address forms, and other techniques. The autocorrelation example will show how I- and O-cycles can be reduced by tailoring the data flow. To save E-cycles, however, different algorithms must be used. The next section shows how micro-level control of the machine makes this possible.

10.7.2 The Microprogrammer's Resources and Objectives

Just as the FORTRAN programmer does not generally concern himself with issuing assembly language instructions or with register allocation, the assembly language programmer does not directly control the micro-level elemental units that perform data manipulation. Figure 10-13 shows a simplified version of the PDP-11 data path, described in detail in Section 6.3.

As noted earlier (Section 6.8), some of the units can be operated in parallel. For example, the BA register can be loaded with an address held in the SR at the same time that the D register is being loaded from a register in BSP. Three of the registers in ASP and BSP are dedicated to the user microprogrammer. Moreover, if he does not invoke the integral floating-point microcode, a further 24 registers in BSP and ASP are available.

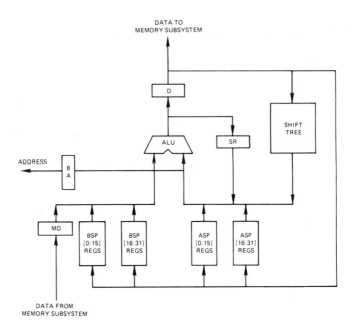

DATA TO
MEMORY SUBSYSTEM

DATA FROM
MEMORY SUBSYSTEM

Fig. 10-13 A very simplified diagram of the 11/60 datapath.

In summary, when the programmer moves down to the microprogramming level, he has

1. more flexibility in the use of the ALU,

2. access and control of processing elements not visible at the macro-level,

3. more registers, and

4. the possibility of some parallelism in operations.

10.7.3 I- and O-Cycle Manipulation

The PB autocorrelation algorithm, because of its small number and small size of computational kernels, will be used to illustrate savings gained by *I*- and *O*-cycle manipulation. For convenience, three computational kernels are defined and targeted for microcoding:

1. **XFCSS1:** Computes the sum of squares of the data, and hence $r(0)$.

2. **XFCSS2:** Computes, for a given k, $[f(m+k)+f(m-k)]*f(m)$.

3. **XFCSS3:** Computes, for a given k, $f(m-k)*f(m)$, *i.e., the terms of XFCSS2 for which* $m + k > N$ *so that* $f(m+k) = 0$.

Since $r(0) > r(k)$, $k > 0$, *XFCSS1* also yields a power-of-2 scale factor later applied to all $r(k)$ so that $2**14 \leq$ the 16 MSB's of $r(0) < 2**15$. Since the three instructions differ essentially in source of operands, we shall examine the most general, *XFCSS2*. The user-defined instruction *XFCSS2* achieves the same result as the following sequence of PDP-11 instructions:

```
MOV  K(R1),R4    ;R4       ← f(m+k)
ADD  MK(R1),R4   ;R4       ← f(m+k)+f(m-k)
MUL  (R1),R4     ;R4,R5    ← [f(m+k)+f(m-k)]*f(m)
ADD  R5,R3       ;R3       ← R3 + R5
ADC  R2          ;R2       ← R2 + carry
ADD  R4,R2       ;R2       ← R2 + R4
MOV  (R0)+,R1    ;FETCH POINTER TO f(m)
```

The microprogrammer first eliminates all *I*-cycles except those necessary to fetch and decode the single instruction *XFCSS2*. Further, since ND and MD are dependent on k only, they are stored within fast registers visible only to the microprogrammer. Thus, the recurrent *O*-cycle overhead involved in ND, MD fetch is eliminated. The multiplication microsubroutine uses a copy of the 11/60 base machine MUL microinstructions without the prologue (decoding) and epilogue (setting micromachine states to conform with general protocol). Fig. 10-14 illustrates the cycle and thus time savings obtained via these basic techniques which are generally applicable to all machine code to microcode conversions.

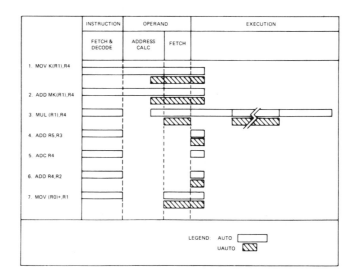

Fig. 10-14 Cycle-by-cycle analysis of an autocorrelation ck.

PDP-11/60 execution times for a 128 point, 12 lag autocorrelation with 16-bit data and 32-bit results were:

```
1. Conventional, base machine:   17.35 msec

2. PB Autogen, base machine  :   11.35 msec    (AUTO, Fig. 10-14)

3. PB Autogen, microcoded    :    7.5 msec     (UAUTO, Fig. 10-14)
```

10.7.4 Recoding of Fundamental Operations for E-Cycle Reduction

It is evident from Fig. 10-14 that the *E*-cycles of the fixed-point multiply (MUL) dominate the *ck* execution overhead. Although this is not the case for all algorithms, it is desirable and, fortunately, sometimes possible to recode the MUL to drastically reduce *E*-cycles. As noted in Section 5.2.4, if fixed-point multiplication is done by shifting over strings of 1's or 0's in the multiplier (MIER), and either adding or subtracting the multiplicand (MAND) from the shifted partial product at each bit transition of the MIER, then the average shift per add/subtract is 3 bits. Each MIER therefore gives rise to a unique sequence of right shift (R), add (A), or subtract (S) operations. Again using the example MIER = 1377(8) = 767(10), the sequence (assuming zero initial partial product) is S, R, R, R, R, R, R, R, R, S, R, R, A, R, R, R, R, R, R. If a hardware unit is available which implements the operation R, ..., R, A *or* S in one cycle, then, on the average, an *n*-bit multiplication may be effected in *n/3* cycles.

As we have seen, this is available in the 11/60 shift tree, or barrel shifter, which, in combination with the ALU and a register (D) is able to effect the operation "D ← [D shiftr *n*] ± B" in a single cycle of 170 nsec. Here, "shiftr *n*" is a signed right shift, $0 < n < 15$, and B is any register in the B scratch pad (BSP), Fig. 10-13. Thus, a microprogrammed 16 x 16 bit multiply/add is possible in, on average, about 5.33 cycles (0.91 *u*sec). This is in contrast to the 16 cycles required by the inner loop of the base machine MUL. Note that MAND magnitude must be less than $2**14$ to guarantee no overflow and that, since the D register is 16 bits, only the 16 MSB (truncated) of the 32-bit product accumulate. Hence, this technique is not suitable for autocorrelation, but is applicable to other DSP algorithms, digital filters and the FFT in particular.

In these applications, the primary restriction is that since each fast multiply microsubroutine (of average length 6 microwords) represents a specific MIER, the number of MIER's is limited by the size of the WCS. Assuming that, at most, about 1/2 the WCS is devoted to multiply microsubroutines, approximately 80 MIER's can be accommodated simultaneously. This limits the FFT size to 256 complex points (i.e., a 64 entry cosine "table"), but easily accommodates various practical digital filters.

Because of the systematic nature of the sequences arising from application of Booth's algorithm, a program can be written to generate the microsubroutines for each MIER.

10.7.5 Alternative Algorithm Selection

In addition to allowing recoding of fundamental operations, the availability of more resources at the microprogramming level allows more flexibility in algorithm selection.

Linear Prediction Coding (LPC) Speech Synthesis: In LPC speech synthesis, the current speech output sample $h(n)$ is computed as per Section 10.5.3. Although the autoincrement mode facilitates time efficient PDP-11 assembler coding, at the 11/60 microcode level only direct addressing is available. This would ordinarily mean MOVing $h(n-9)$ into the position formerly occupied by $h(n-10)$, $h(n-8)$ into $h(n-9)$, and so on until, finally $h(n-1)$ is replaced by $h(n)$ so that a new $h(n)$ can now be computed. However, a "delay line" really need not be implemented. For example, a third order synthesizer can be coded as follows, when direct addressing is necessary:

```
START:  h(n)    = h(n-1)*a(1) + h(n-2)*a(2) + h(n-3)*a(3)
        h(n-3) = h(n)
        h(n)    = h(n-3)*a(1) + h(n-1)*a(2) + h(n-2)*a(3)
        h(n-2) = h(n)
        h(n)    = h(n-2)*a(1) + h(n-3)*a(2) + h(n-1)*a(3)
        h(n-1) = h(n)
        go to START
```

In other words, replace the oldest sample with the newest and reinterpret the indexing of the rest. A counter and test for exit should be included at each step. In general, this saves M−1 store operand operations per speech sample calculation at the expense of an M fold increase in code length. In the 11/60 user microprogramming or writeable control store option (WCS), the relevant extra resources for efficient implementation of the speech synthesizer as above are the 24 extra scratch registers. Using this technique *and* the recoded multiply, a 6'th order "speech synthesizer" was microprogrammed on the 11/60 with the following results (M = 6):

```
11/60       +    WCS: t/sample = (1.8M + 2.4) usec = 13.2 usec,

11/60 BASE MACHINE: t/sample = (8.6M + 10) usec  = 61.6 usec.
```

Thus, 11/60 WCS is about 4.7 times faster than the base machine. It is of interest that this is about 2.5 times faster than conventional software on a bipolar 11/55, currently the fastest PDP-11. In Fig. 10-15, we show "pitch periods" of a 6'th order, 3 formant, digital synthesizer alternately being computed by WCS and base machine code and output to a D/A converter.

371

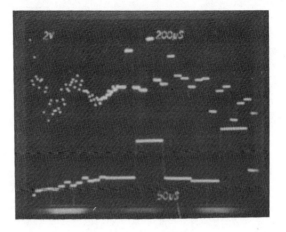

Fig. 10-15 Upper trace: Sixth-order digital filter impulse response computed and output first from WCS and then from base machine. Lower trace: Expanded view of central portion of upper trace.

This dramatically illustrates the relative speedup of WCS. Extrapolation to M = 12, the minimum required for high quality 5 kHz synthesis, gives about 25 $usec$/sample for WCS, about 25% of real-time. Note that the base machine is 26% too slow for real-time implementation of this task.

The Fast Fourier Transform: As noted earlier, FFT's of limited size can be coded using the recoded MUL. However, data points must reside in main memory or the cache. (For 256 complex points, the 512 real data points would automatically migrate to the 11/60 cache during the first of 8 FFT stages so that all data reads on the subsequent 7 stages would be cache hits.) Code examination of the autogen fixed-point radix-2 FFT, yielded a projected microcode execution time of 26 msec vs the benchmarked time of 50 msec for the autogen base machine program. However, the availability to the microprogrammer of extra scratch registers enables an algorithm change. Specifically, as noted earlier, an efficient autogen implementation of a radix-4 FFT requires 4 registers for data access pointers and 8 registers for computation temporaries. Projected execution time for an autogen/ microcode radix-4, 256 point complex FFT is about 13 msec. This gain is not surprising since a radix-4 algorithm requires 1/4 the number of butterflies, 1/2 the data read/writes to/from memory, and 3/4 the multiplications of an equivalent radix-2 program.

Here, FORTRAN programs could use the autogen technique both in generating multiply microsubroutines from 16-bit sine table entries and in generating the thread which drives the butterfly ck's, each a separate microsubroutine. In this case, the thread contains XFC opcodes which invoke the appropriate microcode butterfly (instead of macrocode butterfly module starting addresses), microaddresses of the relevant multiply microsubroutine (instead of pointers to a macro sine table), and the same data pointers as are used in a macro autogen FFT program.

10.7.6 Summary

The availability of microprogramming on a general purpose computer increases the number of resources available to the programmer. Time savings are generally realized through elimination or decrease of *I*- and *O*-cycles. When possible, recoding of fundamental operations will substantially reduce *E*-cycles and alternative algorithm selection may further reduce *I*-, *O*- and *E*-cycle overhead.

It is possible to project, *a priori*, the performance gains realizable from microprogramming a well-understood application. One first identifies the computational kernels and then applies the analysis techniques used for autocorrelation as above. A factor-of-two speedup can be realized in most applications. The next step, not always applicable, is to exploit the capabilities of the micro-level machine. One can eliminate some *O*-phase processing by using the extra registers and reduce some of the *E*-phase processing by using new algorithms. The LPC microcode program illustrates this dramatically.

In Table 10-1, the execution times of various fixed-point arithmetic DSP algorithms on a PDP-11/60 are listed, noting the speedup possible using the various techniques discussed in Chapters 9 and 10.

Table 10-1 PDP-11/60 DSP Algorithm Performance vs. Software, Algorithm

	DIGITAL SIGNAL PROCESSING ALGORITHM		
	Autocorrelation	FFT	12'th order LPC Speech Synthesizer
Software Technique Used	N=128, p=12 16-bit data, 32-bit results	256 complex points, 16-bit data, results	16-bit data, results, and coefficients (including D/A output)
Conventional	17.35 msec <1.5> PB/A	122 msec <2.4> A	124 usec <1.0>
Autogen	11.35 msec <1.5> PB/A/I/O	50 msec <1.3> A/I/O	124 usec <2.0> I/O/RADL
Microcode 1 (W/autogen)	7.50 msec	39 msec <1.5> A/I/O/RM	62 usec <2.4> I/O/RADL/RM
Microcode 2 (W/autogen)		26 msec <2.0> A/I/O/RM/R4	26 usec
Microcode 3 (W/autogen)		13 msec	
Best Time	7.5 msec	13 msec	26 usec
Overall Speedup	<2.3>	<9.4>	<4.8>

Notes: < > shows ratio of preceding and following execution times in a gi column, followed by techniques applied beyond a conventional algorithm us assembly language code: PB = PB autocorrelation algorithm, A = autogen, I-cycle elimination, O = O-cycle reduction/elimination, RM = recoded multip RADL = random access delay line, and R4 = radix-4 FFT (instead of radix-2).

Microprogramming has two serious drawbacks. It is more time-consuming than assembly language programming. Informal studies have shown that it is a factor-of-three worse than writing operating-system code. Secondly, microcode by its very nature is not transportable among computer models. Nevertheless, if the program primitives chosen for microprogramming are useful to a range of applications, as is the case with DSP software, the effort appears to be worthwhile.

REFERENCES

Analog/digital converters are examined in detail in Sheingold (1972), while Newman and Sproull (1973), and Giloi (1978) discuss interactive graphics processor hardware, display data structures, picture transformation algorithms, and graphics languages. The DEC VT-11 manuals describe the VT-11 hardware and extend the programming aspects treated here. Flanagan's book (1972) is the standard reference on speech analysis, synthesis and perception while Flanagan and Rabiner (1973) consists of reprints of classic papers on speech synthesis. Digital processing of speech signals is covered by Rabiner and Schafer (1978); speech analysis/synthesis via linear prediction coding is fully explained by Markel and Gray (1976). Morris (1978) contains the complete spectrogram software while Morris and Mudge (1978) did the 11/60 microcoding experiments of Section 10.7. Morris and Allan (1979) describe a speech synthesizer microprogrammed on a PDP-11/60. Elovitz *et. al.* (1976) derived the technique and rules for English-to-VOTRAX translation; Broihier and Crowley implemented the Elovitz algorithm, originally programmed in SNOBOL, in BASIC-PLUS. This served as the basis for Morris' software (1978). Gagnon (1978), the VOTRAX inventor, describes the device in some detail and references more detailed descriptions, while Wiggins and Brantingham (1978) explain the pipeline multiplier which forms the nucleus of the *Speak & Spell* synthesizer chip set. Moorer (1977) surveys the signal processing aspects of computer music, giving an extensive bibliography. Chamberlin (1977) describes computer music synthesis from a practical viewpoint, the wavetable technique in particular.

11

Operating Systems

Today it is inconceivable that a minicomputer system could exist without an operating system for its users. Indeed, even most microcomputers can have reasonably sophisticated disk or tape operating systems. For this reason, almost all programmers will, at one time or another, come face to face with an operating system environment.

Operating systems, if properly designed, exist for the users' convenience. They serve to bridge the gap between the needs of the user and the characteristics of the hardware. In this capacity, they directly assist the user in solving his problems through simplified programming and more efficient computer operation. However, to a large extent, the user never knows what the operating system is really doing. Instead, the user sees the system in terms of the services it provides: program preparation, translation, execution, debugging, and filing.

In order to understand what a computer system is all about, it is necessary to understand the system components and their organization. These components, computer hardware and software, were discussed in previous chapters. This chapter is thus concerned with the general job of organization as it is performed by the operating system. However, since our concern has been with small computer systems, we shall continue that interest as we take a look at rather specialized operating environments which exist for this class of machines. Because of the limited resources available, operating systems for small machines tend to be more constrained than for their larger computer system counterparts. Nonetheless, the same principles and concepts apply, the chief difference being that of the relative emphasis placed on the various system components.

11.1 VERY BASIC COMPUTER SYSTEMS

Until recently, most computers came with facilities for input/output of paper tape. Although the advent of the "floppy disk" has made paper tape economically obsolete as a "system device", paper tape is still of use for diagnostic purposes, and in the hobbyist environment. In the paper tape environment, very reminiscent of the early days of computing, the input and output of programs and data are performed manually by the user via a paper tape reader and punch. The user communicates with, and receives printed output from, system and user programs through the teletypewriter device connected to the machine.

Even though the loading of programs is performed manually, a paper tape system normally contains a comprehensive software package of commonly used system programs which provide the user with complete facilities for writing, editing, translating, debugging, loading, and running his own programs. Since system programs have already been covered in Chapter 8 and earlier chapters, the reader is familiar with the capabilities of such a paper tape system.

Unless the reader has had the experience of using a paper tape system, he is not likely to realize how unsatisfactory and trying it can be. Operating such a basic system requires the user to take his coded program and manually perform the following operations:

1. Load and execute the editor, which is stored on paper tape.

2. Produce paper tape source programs using the editor.

3. Load and execute the assembler, which is stored on paper tape.

4. Translate the editor-produced source program.

5. Load and execute the assembler-produced binary object program, stored on paper tape.

6. Debug the program, repeating the first five steps as necessary.

Each step presumes that the software bootstrap and absolute loaders remain intact during successive program loads and executions. Unfortunately, this is not usually the case, and more often than not, the beginning programmer will reload both loaders at one time or another.

Manual control of the operating environment is clearly inconvenient. It involves manipulating and maintaining numerous paper tape programming systems, and it results, in general, in the inefficient use of the hardware and the *very* inefficient use of the human operator. Consequently, a more automatic level is desirable, and this level of control is found in the typical general-purpose disk operating system (e.g., RT-11).

11.2 COMPONENTS OF A DISK OPERATING SYSTEM

The addition of a *secondary storage system device* (e.g., a disk) is what makes the *disk operating system* (DOS) a comprehensive operating environment for both the development and execution of user programs. User programs and data, along with system programs, can all reside on the disk and other secondary storage devices, to be loaded into memory under program control. Instead of loading and reloading paper tapes, the DOS user can perform the same functions by issuing *commands* to the system. These commands not only provide user services (such as program loading) but also provide for efficient program and system management. Typical commands and their functions are shown in Table 11-1 for the PDP-11 RT-11 operating system.

Table 11-1 Typical RT-11 System commands.

Command	Function
ASSIGN	Assign device a name
DATE	Enter date, used to tag files
E	Examine specified memory locations
RUN	Load and start a specified program
GET	Load a specified program into memory
START	Begin execution (of a loaded program) at a specified address
TIME	Enter time of day; used for system clock
SUSPEND	Suspend execution of current job
RSUME	Resume execution of the suspended job

Commands, however, are only the outward manifestation of an operating system. To gain an understanding of how its functions and facilities are provided, it is necessary to consider the components of the system and their organization. Since one of the most important functions of an operating system is the effective management of its information structures (e.g., programs and data), it is important to understand the basic informational unit of the system. This unit is called a *file*.

11.2.1 Files — Organization and Access

A file is a collection of *related records* or data items treated as a *unit*. The word "file" is thus used in the general sense of "any collection of information items similar to one another in purpose, form, and content." For example, a program may be a file, just as a data structure (called a dataset) or even some system program such as an editor or assembler, may be. Unfortunately, the same word *file* is also generally applied to external storage media, such as disks and tapes, when what is really meant is *file-oriented* devices.

Each file-oriented peripheral device has a *file structure*, which represents the method of recording, linking, and cataloging data files. The file structure indicates

the organization of the file on the device and the method of file access. This
organizational structuring is important because a file can be effective for a user
application only if it is designed to meet specific user requirements. Such factors as
size, activity, and accessibility must be considered when determining the structure
of a file.

The way in which a file is organized upon a storage medium depends upon
the way in which the user normally expects to create and later process it. Three
methods that have been used are: (1) contiguous allocation, (2) linked list allocation, and (3) indexed allocation. Each of these methods is illustrated in Fig. 11-1.

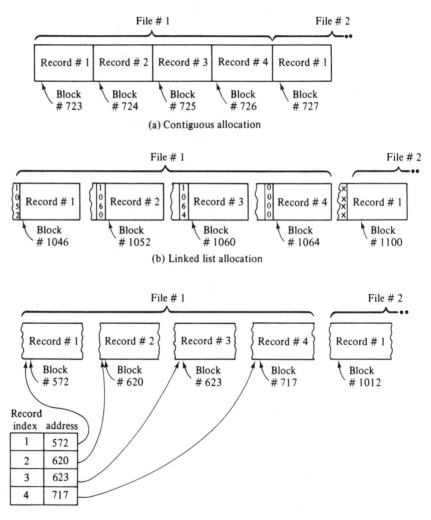

(a) Contiguous allocation

(b) Linked list allocation

(c) Indexed allocation

Fig. 11-1 File organization.

In the small computer system, file structure organization is not usually left up to the user but is predefined for the various peripheral devices. Similarly, the method of access is system defined and is ultimately connected with the file structure. The most usual access technique involves *sequential access* to both the data file and the individual data records. This access method is characteristic of unidirectional devices, such as magnetic tape, although other devices, such as disks, may also be organized so as to permit sequential access.

Sequential access is a storage retrieval technique in which a file and the records within it must be retrieved in the sequence in which they physically occur. Sequential access, when applied to the process of locating the beginning of a file or a data record within the file, means that the time required for such access is dependent on the necessity for waiting while nondesired files or records are processed in turn.

Traditionally, contiguous allocation is used to implement sequentially accessed files on sequentially organized devices such as magnetic tape. After each record is processed, the next record is immediately available, since positioning of the physical medium will leave that record positioned at the read/write head of the device.

As an alternative to the sequential organization, the *linked-list* organization may be used for *direct-access* devices such as disks, where the time to search for and locate the next record is insignificant in processing the file. The linked-list structure has the advantage over the contiguous allocation of allowing files to grow larger with time by simply linking in a new record to the end of the list. This is not generally possible for the contiguous allocation, since the next block may already have been allocated.

Another technique for accessing a file is *random access*. Random access of a file and records within the file means that the time required for such access is independent of the location of the file or record relative to other files or records on the medium. Thus, the order of retrieval of file information is unimportant and can be ignored.

Again, two possibilities exist when file access is random. These are contiguous location and indexed allocation. By knowing where the contiguous file begins, random accessing occurs in much the same fashion as element accessing occurs for a one-dimensional array. The limitation of the contiguous location remains the same, however: files cannot, in general, expand in length with time.

The use of an index into the file allows both random access and growth with time. Thus this method of allocation is preferred over contiguous allocation unless access time is important. Like linked-list allocation, indexed allocation requires that the location of the next record be fetched before the actual record may be accessed.

As a third alternative to the two access methods presented, an intermediate method may be used. This method, normally employed on disk and disk-like devices, allows a file to be accessed randomly while the file's data records may be accessed sequentially. This access method is called *indexed-sequential* and uses the indexed organization with more than one data record per block.

Indexed-sequential organization is well suited to those applications where it is necessary to access sets of records randomly but individual records of the set sequentially. A typical example of such an application would be a personnel records file where, having found the records for a certain employee, it is necessary to update these employee records in a sequential fashion.

11.2.2 Directories

Having provided a file structure, and having specified its access method, the next problem is how the file is located by the system once stored away. One method that could be used is to keep track of the device addresses so that each file can be retrieved directly. The use of absolute addresses is not very acceptable, however, for much the same reasons that absolute addresses are avoided in symbolic programming. Instead, symbolic names must be associated with each file so that the files may be referred to by their *file names.*

To provide a connection between the file names and their device locations, a *file directory* or table of contents for each directoried file device must be part of the system. The file directory will contain not only the unique name of the file and its starting address on the device, but also its file structure, including, if necessary, a pointer to an index table. Figure 11-2 shows a directoried data access for a sequentially organized file that can be randomly accessed.

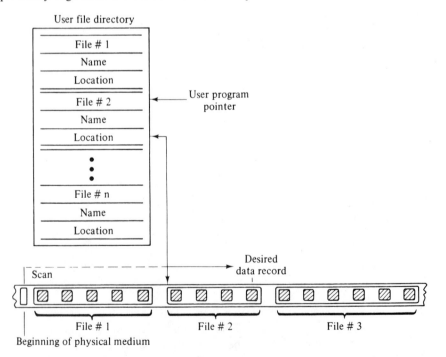

Fig. 11-2 Directoried data access.

Devices such as tape cassettes and DECtapes have this capacity by which the transport may search to a known location before it begins processing the file.

When directoried data files are removable from the system, it is necessary to preserve the directory of files between uses. To do so requires that the directory be stored on the physical medium, in a known location, along with the files it points to. As part of these directories, *bit maps* are often maintained both to indicate which device blocks each file occupies and to show which blocks are occupied.

File structures that employ a directory allow simpler and, in the long run, faster access to a file (i.e., the beginning of a file). This is a distinct advantage over those devices which do not use a directory and must therefore rely on a file's position relative to other files in order to locate it.

11.2.3 Multilevel Directories

When two or more people share the same device (such as the system disk) for storing files, problems may arise because of duplicate file names. Since both will have access to the same set of files, one user may accidently modify or destroy another's file by simply not knowing that the file name used was already assigned. The solution to this dilemma is to establish a separate user file directory for each system user. The separate directory will therefore allow each user to name a file without regard to the names chosen by others.

The basic mechanism for locating user files on a shared device requires a two-level file directory, as shown in Fig. 11-3. Each user has a unique code that must be provided whenever the LOGIN command is used. This code serves to identify a particular entry into the master file directory, which is actually a pointer to the user's file directory.

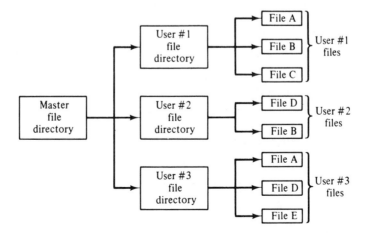

Fig. 11-3 Master and user file directories.

11.2.4 Problems of Control

Now that we have described an elaborate scheme to define the files within the system, it becomes obvious that one of the central functions of an operating system is *control*. For example, the file system represents one large facility that must be controlled in its allocation of peripheral device space and its storage and retrieval of file information on the peripheral devices. Fortunately, the function of the file system is precisely the minimization of the potential problem.

As far as the user is concerned, devices themselves are not of primary interest; the information sets or files that reside on them are. Thus a simple and useful extension may be made by broadening the concept of a file to encompass all information sets, including devices. In this manner it is easy to conceive of a paper tape reader as an information set (and hence a file) of a very special type. By *special type* is meant that the information set must be handled in only a very limited fashion (e.g., output not allowed to an input device). With suitable limitations, there is no reason why all devices cannot be conceived of as being file-like information sets. All that is necessary is to recognize and build into the system the fact that it is not possible to treat all files uniformly (e.g., not all files can be read from, written to, or executed).

Both the system and the user can treat I/O devices uniformly as information sets. Within the system, however, there must be an interface between the system or user-created program and the external world of I/O devices. The purpose of the interface is to minimize I/O programming for the user, as discussed in Chapter 7. There it was pointed out that the IOPS routines served to relieve the RT-11 user of the burden of I/O service, file management, overlapping I/O considerations, and unnecessary device dependence. The last point, device independence, is especially important in a disk operating system, where an I/O service routine for a nonfile-structured device, such as the paper tape reader, must ignore (rather than declare as an error) a command to "seek a file" (which is required for all file-structured devices prior to issuing read commands).

Clearly, the central function of IOPS is to establish the information path between the system and the device. This requirement is met somewhat independently of the user, since one of the goals of IOPS is to minimize the user knowledge required. And since the user is to be spared the task of writing system software to perform I/O, standard system routines (called device handlers) must be a central part of IOPS. These routines perform the functions of

1. Driving the I/O devices.

2. Manipulating files on the devices.

3. Allocating/deallocating storage space on the devices.

4. Maintaining current records about user requests and device status.

5. Coordinating peripheral activities (such as buffering and blocking) as required by the I/O.

As pointed out in Chapter 8, system macros are the means of communication between user programs and I/O device handlers. These I/O commands are also referred to as *programmed requests*. Table 11-2 lists typical requests for the RT-11 system. Not all requests shown in the table actually perform I/O. Some, such as .ENTER and .CLOSE, merely serve to initialize a dataset or file for subsequent I/O processing. Others, such as .DSTATUS and .FETCH perform auxiliary operations on the data, the data file, or the device.

Table 11-2 Typical RT-11 Programmed requests.

```
.CLOSE      Terminates activity on the specified channel
.DELETE     Deletes a named file from an indicated device
.DSTATUS    Obtains information about a specific device
.ENTER      Allocates space for a file on a specified device
.EXIT       Causes the user program to terminate and return to the monitor
.FETCH      Loads specified device handlers into memory
.GTIM       Allows user programs to access the current time of day
.READ/WRITE Allows the user program to read/write files on system devices
.SPND/RSUM  Allows a user to temorarily suspend and then resume his program
.TTYIN      Transfers characters from the console terminal
              to the user's program
.TTYOUT     Transfers characters form the user's program
              to the console terminal
.WAIT       Suspend current program until all I/O requests
              on a specified channel are completed
```

11.2.5 File Management Utility

Although programmed requests for file management provide the basic functions needed to utilize files, it is inconvenient to have to write a program every time one wishes to manipulate files. Thus most operating systems include a system software package for the transfer of data files from one I/O device to another, while performing simple editing and control functions as well. This package, known as PIP (Peripheral Interchange Program) on the PDP-11, handles all data and file formats found in RT-11 so as to

1. Transfer a file or group of files from one device to another.

2. Merge files into a single file.

3. Delete, update, rename, or replace files.

4. Allocate file space and initialize whole devices.

5. Print listings of file directories.

6. Handle file protection.

In effect, the file utility package provides at the user level the same sort of services that systems macros provide at the program level. Users need only enter commands to the PIP program and it will decode the command and perform the desired function. For example, the user might wish to make a backup copy on a floppy disk of an existing main disk file. To do so he might run the PIP program and then, in response to PIP's request for a command (indicated by a * sign), type in

```
DX1:BACKUP.FOR=DK0:MYFILE.FOR
```

The new file, named BACKUP.FOR, would then be a copy of the original file, called MYFILE.FOR. Alternatively, later versions of RT-11 — incorporating the *DEC standard Command Language* (DCL) — use a slightly modified form:

```
COPY DK0:MYFILE.FOR DX1:BACKUP.FOR
```

To examine the directory for a certain device, the command to PIP would be

```
LP:=DK0:/L (or DIR DK0: using DCL)
```

indicating that a *directory* listing of the contents of disk unit zero is to be produced on the line printer. This listing would appear as

```
     1-JUL-78
MONITR.SYS    58 15-MAY-78
TT    .SYS     2 15-MAY-78
DX    .SYS     2 15-MAY-78
PIP   .SAV    14 15-MAY-78
LINK  .SAV    25 15-MAY-78
MACRO .SAV    31 15-MAY-78
FORTRA.SAV    96 15-MAY-78
SYSLIB.OBJ    37 15-MAY-78
RUNOFF.SAV    30 26-JUN-78
TECO  .SAV    27 15-MAY-78
VT52  .TEC     5 15-MAY-78
VEG            4 15-MAY-78
EDIT  .FIL     1  1-JUL-78
EDIT  .SAV    19 15-MAY-78
SYSMAC.SML    20 16-MAY-78
EDIT  .BAK     1 30-JUN-78
16 FILES, 372 BLOCKS
 108 FREE BLOCKS
```

where the fields indicate the file name and extension, file size, and file creation date. *File extensions* serve to designate the use and/or format of the file. For example, "SYS" files contain machine code used by the system whereas "SAV" files are loadable/executable machine code program images; the "OBJ" extension indicates relocatable machine code output from an assembler or compiler in a form suitable for manipulation by a linker or linking loader.

It is important to bear in mind that a file management utility is a system software program in the same sense as were the programs in Chapter 8. The goal of such programs is to provide routines that assist the user in solving his problems. As a consequence, these programs do not themselves produce useful results but rather allow the user to utilize the hardware available to him effectively.

11.2.6 Device Independence

As the reader may recall, system macros are implemented using trap-generating instructions. Ordinarily, a programmer specifies I/O devices as he writes the program. However, there are circumstances when he will want to change the device specifications when his program is run. For example:

1. A device that the user specified when he wrote his program is not in operation at run time, but an alternative device is available.

2. The programmer does not know the configuration of the target system or does not wish to specify it (e.g., he is writing a general-purpose package).

Through the use of the Device Assignment Tables (called User Name Tables internally to RT-11), the ASSIGN command allows the programmer to write programs that are device-independent. This command assigns a user-defined logical name as an alternate name for a physical device. From the user's point of view, such device independence results in very flexible programming.

11.2.7 The Monitor

The user communicates with the system in two ways: (1) through keyboard instructions, which have been referred to as commands, and (2) through programmed requests. In both cases the effect is to initiate a *control program* or routine which loads a file, makes a correspondence between a logical file and a physical device, opens a dataset, writes onto a device, etc.

Clearly, the various control programs must work in mutual harmony if the system is to operate successfully. Although much of the system can be conceived as the sequencing of one program or *task* after the other, it is possible to have two tasks operating in parallel (e.g., an I/O operation and a computation). As used here, a task is a well-defined unit of work that competes for the resources of the system (e.g., memory, files, I/O etc.). Thus a master control program called the *monitor*, which can be responsible for the entire operating system and all of its component parts, is needed.

The monitor must be responsible for the initiation, maintenance, and termination of all other programs. It coordinates program-to-program and task-to-task transitions and processes the communications among the user, the system, and the many control programs. It also must act on monitor calls, validate and transmit I/O calls to device handlers, supervise data and file manipulations, and provide error diagnostics.

There are basically three sections of a monitor: (1) the permanently resident monitor, (2) the nonresident monitor, and (3) the system loader. The resident monitor remains in memory when system or user programs are running and acts as the interface between the program and the system's facilities.

The user/operator may alter the structure of the resident monitor via commands to the nonresident monitor. The nonresident monitor allows the user to alter many key parts of the system, in order to set up the system for the next program. Normally, at the end of a particular program, the computer user or the program itself returns control to the nonresident monitor. At that point the user issues new commands to set up the system for the next program to be run.

The system loader builds the resident monitor according to prior commands to the nonresident monitor. It loads all system programs and all handlers for those system programs from the system disk, and these programs in turn allow the user to edit, assemble, load and link, perform file manipulations on, execute, debug, and so on, his programs. Since the purpose of the system loader is basically to set up the system (e.g., by loading system programs and setting them into execution), it is completely invisible to the user.

Monitor/User Interaction: The console terminal is the primary user-system interface for RT-11 program control. This control is implemented by commands to the monitor which cause system and user programs to be loaded and executed (as described in Section 11.2), by commands that perform special services, and by control character commands that provide system control while running user or system programs.

Most of the monitor commands must be issued prior to loading programs and are interpreted by the nonresident monitor, since it is not, in general, necessary to keep the command recognizer in memory during system or user program execution. However, during program execution, a small set of keyboard commands must be available for general program control. These commands are interpreted by a portion of the terminal's I/O device handler (which is part of the resident portion of the monitor) and are used to control program start and restart, dumping of memory, and reloading of the nonresident monitor.

Since the monitor and any program running under it must share the same console terminal, the user must specify whether the given keyboard input is intended for the monitor or for the executing program. Consequently, the modes of operation are determined by a special character entered. All characters following a special control character (a CTRL/C for RT-11) are interpreted as monitor commands and are passed to the monitor for execution after the running program is suspended. All other characters are assumed to be for the operating program, and the characters will be buffered until required by the program.

Monitor Organization: Figure 11-4 illustrates the data flow and general organization of the monitor. Although most of the functions of the various modules have already been described, several require further comment.

The first modules of interest are the *command processor* and the *monitor command decoder*. Both the user and the monitor share the same control program, called the *command string interpreter*. This routine preprocesses the characters for whatever user or system program it was called by. By having one routine for both the system and the user, a common format for input and output dataset specifications to a program is provided through a single monitor routine.

The next module of interest is the one labeled *device assignment table* (DAT). This table is used to store the data from each ASSIGN entry, since device/file specification by console assignment can occur at any time, even before the program that requires the new assignment is loaded. The DAT resides within the monitor so that its entry may be checked whenever the program under execution calls for dataset initialization.

The use of a device assignment table can be illustrated by the following example. Before being run, a user program wishes to assign a DECtape in place of a floppy disk. The ASSIGN command would be used:

```
ASSIGN DX1:DT0
```

where the colon separates the name of the physical device (DX1 for the floppy) from the new logical replacement(DT0 for the DECtape).

At first, the use of the ASSIGN command and the device assignment table may seem strange. However, the FORTRAN programmer should be able to recognize that these new commands and tables are nothing more than a new solution to an old problem. In FORTRAN, when performing reads and writes, the programmer must write statements of the form

```
READ  (u,f) I/O list
WRITE (u,f) I/O list
```

where u represents a unit number and f a FORMAT statement label. Usually there are default values for u, and reading a data card is performed on unit 5 [e.g., READ (5,10) A,B,C] while printing a line occurs on unit 6 [e.g., WRITE (6,20) A,B,C]. However, when file-oriented devices such as tapes are used, some form of an assign command (or control card) must be used to equate the unit numbers to their particular devices. This, of course, associates all the files on the device media with the unit number, and it is up to the user to separate out the various files.

Monitor Residency Table: An important part of the trap handler is the monitor residency table (MTR), which supplies two types of information for the trap handler:

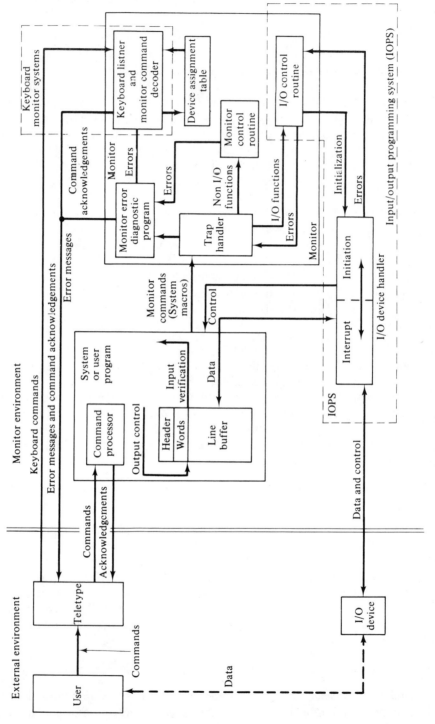

Fig. 11-4 Command, control, and data flow in monitor environment.

388

1. It shows which monitor routines are resident in memory, either permanently or for the duration of a program run, and where they are loaded currently.

2. It acts as a directory to the remaining routines as stored within the monitor library on the system device, to enable immediate access when one of these routines must be brought into memory.

The state of the table depends on which routines must remain within the computer memory at all times, because they control the system generally, and which routines may reside upon the system device, because they perform ephemeral tasks. By using the system loader, nonresident routines may be loaded when required and can later be removed when their purpose is served. In this way, available memory space need not be used by the system (e.g., the monitor) but may be made available to the user. Clearly, this is a necessary requirement for the small computer user who has a machine with somewhat limited memory space.

Monitor Memory Organization: From the previous sections it is clear that certain monitor routines/modules must be resident in memory at all times. These routines determine the minimum allocation of the computer's memory, as shown in Fig. 11-5. The modular structure of the monitor allows the user to determine which modules are to be resident and which modules are to be swapped from the disk. In the latter case, it should be noted that a temporarily loaded routine occupies a reserved area within the monitor [the user service routine (USR) area] and does not require that a part of a program be swapped out first (unless it overlays the USR). This means that no restrictions need be placed upon the activities of a program as might be the case if part of its area were potentially removable.

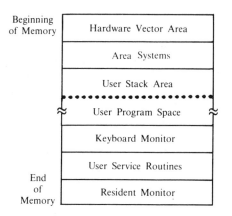

Fig. 11-5 Memory allocation

Despite the fact that swapping can be accomplished fairly quickly from the disk, it still takes a finite time, and the user who has memory to spare may prefer to make use of it. Modularity of the monitor routines again helps, in that

1. If a particular module is required frequently by the user(s) of the system, that module can be added to the list of those already part of the permanently resident monitor.

2. Or, if a module is particularly appropriate to one application, the routine can be loaded with the program concerned so that the routine is resident for the duration of the run.

Dynamic Memory Management: Another feature of the monitor as shown in Fig. 11-4 is its dynamic buffer allocation scheme for free memory management. This scheme postpones the allocation of memory for the purpose of I/O service until a running program actually requires it. Only then are the I/O drivers loaded, and when they are no longer required, their memory space is released. The allocation and deallocation of memory, being dynamic, means that the basic memory map varies with time.

A consequence of dynamic memory allocation is that all the modules that take advantage of this feature must be independent of the positions they occupy. Position-independent coding represents no problems for a computer such as the PDP-11, but allowing independent modules to intercommunicate does. What is needed is a *system vector table* (SVT), which provides a common area for the storage of information on the state of the system at any time. In particular, the SVT must contain pointers to the other parts of the system which provide such information as the address of the last location of the monitor, the start of the monitor residency table, the name of the loaded program, and so on.

11.3 USE OF OPERATING SYSTEMS

Having discovered something about the internals of a typical disk-based operating system, it is worthwhile to examine how an operating system meets the more general needs of its users. As might be expected, the needs tend to be rather diverse, and since it is clearly impossible to write operating systems tailored to each user's application, operating system designers generate systems that meet the needs of particular application areas. These areas and their operating environment may be broadly classified as one of the following:

1. Batch and time-sharing systems.

2. Real-time control systems.

3. Data-base systems.

4. Computer communications systems.

Batch processing and time-sharing systems are familiar operating environments for most computer system users. These general-purpose programming systems are best suited for the programmer who wishes to develop and execute his programs. From the standpoint of the small computer disk operating system, these systems represent add-on capabilities to the basic disk operating system environment.

Real-time control systems are designed for operating environments where many tasks must be maintained and controlled as events occur that are external to the computer. These systems must be capable of scheduling the real-time programs (called tasks) performing the input or output of necessary task information, communicating to the human operator what is happening, and performing such other functions as required for a real-time, multiprogrammed operation. A typical example might be found in a process control application. In these types of operations, asynchronous external events (e.g., alarm switch closure in computer controlled devices) require the operating system to respond quickly by passing control to the proper servicing task.

The distinguishing feature of the data-base system is clearly the enormous amounts of information that must be managed. This information must be readily available to the user who queries the system, and must be well protected against accidental loss or unauthorized intrusion. Like the real-time system, emphasis is placed on program use rather than program development or testing.

Computer communications systems are often likened to electrical power utilities and natural gas networks. In both cases the system presents itself as a vast web of interconnected units capable of almost indefinite growth so that as the customer load increases, the system can be expanded without limit both by adding extra units and by connecting with other utilities to draw on their unused capacity. Such systems require well-defined interfaces and interconnection structures.

What follows in this chapter is an examination in more detail of each of these operating systems. Since the subject of this book is the small computer, emphasis will be on what types of small computer operating systems have been developed, and what function they serve.

11.4 BATCH AND TIME-SHARING SYSTEMS

Given the capabilities of the small computer plus the added flexibility of the disk-base operating system, it is not too difficult to develop a batch processing system. The batch processor is actually an additional control program within the monitor which allows user commands to come from the same device as the user programs. By placing user commands and programs together to form jobs, the system is capable of running many jobs consecutively without requiring operator intervention.

Special monitor commands (in addition to nonbatch commands) are used to

1. Enter batch mode.
2. Define and separate jobs.

3. Indicate that data follow.

4. Indicate the end of the job.

5. Terminate batch mode.

These commands form what is called a *job control language*, and if the batch input device is a card reader, they are punched into job control cards.

Besides the batch system, it is not uncommon to find *time-sharing systems* on small computers. Rather generally defined, a time-sharing system is one that provides many users with simultaneous access to a central computing facility.

A time-sharing system is, in fact, a *multiprogrammed* computer which allows its multiple users to share system resources in such a fashion that each user thinks that he is getting individual attention. The system is multiprogrammed in that several user programs will be simultaneously resident in memory at any given time. Each program receives a quantum of computer time, called a *time slice*, during which it may perform computations. Should it use up its time slice, or reach a point where further computation is not possible (e.g., some I/O information is needed), the CPU will be turned over to another program. This transfer of control is handled rapidly since the next program to gain the CPU will already be in memory.

The time-shared operation of a computer implies sharing the computer's time and space resources on a dynamic, and hence temporary, basis. Several (or all) user programs may be memory resident, while others may be in the process of being loaded from or to auxiliary mass storage. Indeed, if memory is not large enough to hold all the user programs and data, it will be necessary to swap user information in and out from the auxiliary storage upon demand.

The time-sharing operating system (TSOS) requires a sophisticated set of control programs to handle the sharing of system resources, the time slicing, the storage allocation and program relocation, and the basic servicing sequence of users, besides the types of operations normally associated with a disk operating system. One of these control programs, the *scheduler*, has primary responsibility for both the basic servicing of the users and the optimal uses of the system resources. Each time the monitor gains control, it utilizes the scheduler to determine which program is to be put into execution next and what user swapping must occur if it is to keep the system busy and the users satisfied.

Because of heavy demands placed on the computer, it is often necessary to limit the flexibility of the TSOS. The most flexible TSOS is an *open, conversational system* that gives the user direct access to all the facilities (including I/O devices) of the operating system. *Closed, conversational systems* usually limit the user to specific languages and systems. *Remote program entry systems* are the most restricted form of time sharing, in that the user is capable of preparing and submitting programs from remote terminals, but he may not interact with the running program and he must wait for the program to run to completion before accessing the generated results.

The closed, conversation TSOS is the most common form of a small computer time-sharing system. Usually eight to sixty-four users are able to program in a higher-level language, taking advantage of most of the system resources. Generally speaking, it is not the computer power which greatly limits the number of users but the amount of memory that is available to the system.

11.5 REAL-TIME CONTROL SYSTEMS

Real-time control systems are designed for handling data in a time that is consistent with the response time demanded by the process that generated the information. Such systems operate in a multiprogrammed environment with the real-time monitor controlling and supervising a large number of memory- or disk-resident programs and tasks. This control and supervision allows the tasks to share memory and disk space, I/O device handlers, and resource allocation and use.

The execution of the many tasks is determined by software priorities, hardware interrupts, timing algorithms, and requests from other tasks. Additionally, the user of the real-time system can install new tasks on-line, establish their software priority, and request their activation at any time with an automatic reactivation at a periodic interval of time thereafter.

The actual system response time for a task request depends mainly on whether or not another task is running at a higher-priority level. To prevent high-priority tasks from executing too long, a *watchdog timer* is often used to guarantee that all tasks are serviced. This timer is set at the start of each task with the maximum duration that a task may run, at a particular priority level, before being suspended or dropped.

The real-time monitor controls and executes all input and output operations. This is one of the areas of direct concern to the real-time user, since most real-time applications are characterized by a large amount of I/O. Indeed, tasks are initiated or suspended by the occurrence of some I/O operation.

11.5.1 Real-Time Programming

Programming for real-time control is generally performed in either assembly language or a higher-level language, usually FORTRAN, with extensions to allow real-time monitor calls. Program development can be done on-line with the real-time monitor, although the amount of memory available or the sophistication of the system may require off-line development.

Real-time programs rely heavily on system macro calls to schedule, queue, run, suspend, synchronize, and so on, tasks within the system. Often the data that are collected by the task is simply stored to be analyzed later under a general-purpose programming environment.

11.6 DATA-BASE SYSTEMS

Operating as a text-oriented information utility, the data-base system allows a large number of users to access a common data base. A *data-base* is a coordinated collection of information (e.g., files). Problems such as order entry systems, automated medical records, seat reservations, information directories, and catalog searching represent prime candidates for implementation of data-base systems.

The conversational environment in which such systems are designed to operate typically demands little computer processing power, but tends to demand large storage facilities. When data are entered, the system must check its legality, decide where to file it, and select an appropriate response to be given to the user. None of these actions requires large amounts of processing, except for character manipulation applications.

When data are fetched and reports are generated, there will be a manipulation of information and/or the accessing of data from peripheral storage devices, in order to assemble the required data. Still, only a small amount of processing is necessary to actually format and produce the report. As a consequence of the small demand for the central processor, such systems can be time-shared between a large number of users.

Although most of the data within the system may be potentially accessed at any time, large volumes of data need be available only for low-level, low-frequency usage. Thus the important aspect of these systems is the availability of large-capacity peripheral storage devices such as disks, drums, and data cells. Further, an effective data management system must use the storage effectively, minimizing the amount of storage utilized and providing fast and efficient data retrieval.

11.6.1 Effective Data Management

Features and techniques used to provide effective data management include:

1. Storing data in a hierarchical tree structure so that the most frequently accessed material can be optimally located in the structure.

2. Simultaneously updating and retrieving information.

3. Allowing particular collections of data (e.g., an employee record) to be accessed differently by different users. For example, one user sees only names and job titles while another can access employee numbers and salaries.

4. Allowing dynamic (but user transparent) manipulation of a structure.

5. Allocating space within the system as required rather than on a static basis.

6. Optimally mapping a data structure onto a peripheral device and retrieving it or rewriting it only as needed.

7. Making the system device-independent to avoid reprogramming.

8. Operating the system in a reentrant manner so that one copy may be shared by all users.

9. Keeping most of the system and user tasks resident in memory to minimize swapping.

One of the most time-consuming aspects of developing information system programs involves the optimal interfacing of the user and the system within a particular application area. Much attention must be given to human engineering and to the modification and revision of the techniques available to the user for the storage and retrieval of system data. In addition, the protection and security of the information itself must be guaranteed.

11.6.2 Storage, Manipulation, and Access of Data

The complexity, integrity, security, and variety of the data that must be handled in a data-base information system impose a number of requirements on the system. A considerable amount of information will be input in the form of text strings of variable length. In processing this data, the system will often be required to check their syntax and even determine, where possible, their semantic content against some established limits.

When the information is accessed and possibly manipulated, the system must check to see if the user has been given such privileges. Consequently, each system user must have some capability/clearance which can be compared with the list attached to the data he wishes to access and which will prevent unauthorized access or transformation. The security and privacy so gained will often be selective and data-dependent.

One way to aid the system in protecting itself is to make it a closed, conversational time-sharing system. Users may only make responses to predefined system requests, and may not write, test, or debug general-purpose programs. Additionally, the terminals for such systems may be designed to as to require push-button responses to "canned" messages displayed by the system. Alternatively, high-level languages may be used to construct more complex search patterns or data structuring, but such languages should be executed interpretively so that system integrity may be preserved.

11.7 COMPUTER COMMUNICATION SYSTEMS

The computer communication system operates as an interconnected network of independent computer elements which communicate with each other and share resources. As a component of these networks, the small computer generally serves as a dependent system that acts either as a data communicator or a data concentrator.

As a data communicator, the computer serves as one or more of the following:

1. A device for the storing and subsequent forwarding operation of network messages.

2. A message translator and formator.

3. A controller for a large machine which it interfaces to the network.

4. A data entry system for providing remote job entry to a processing facility.

   As a data concentrator, the small computer serves as

1. A multiplexer that processes many low-speed terminals locally, concentrating the data into one medium-speed communications lines to a larger system.

2. A message buffer, communications line control, and character-to-message assembler/disassembler for low-speed devices connected to it.

   In both applications, the small computer offers a powerful, low-cost alternative to hard-wired communications controllers on the front end of large computer systems. And since these small computers are general-purpose machines with character-handling instructions and powerful interrupt structures, they may be programmed to

1. Route messages.

2. Provide code and speed conversions.

3. Handle line and error control.

4. Compress data and format messages.

5. Automatically identify terminals and their characteristics.

6. Provide time and date stamping of messages.

7. Establish communications automatically.

8. Preanalyze messages before transmission.

9. Provide editing, tabulation, and other formating services.

11.7.1 Communications Software

Manufacturer-supplied software comes in two forms: complete systems, often referred to as *turn-key systems*, which may be installed and placed in operation immediately, and *modular systems*, which consist of both hardware (including the computer and special communications hardware) and special-application software, such as device drivers and communication executives. DECnet is an example of the latter.

Turn-key systems do not require the user to program the computer. Indeed, some of these systems are supplied with read-only memories, which cannot be accidentally destroyed and which have been specifically programmed to perform a fixed sequence of instructions. On the other hand, modular systems are used as a base on which the user can build special-purpose systems tailored to his needs.

Within the modular systems there will be interrupt service routines, terminal application programs, and system control/interface packages. Utilizing these routines, the user tailors his system to his specific application, thereby minimizing the amount of hardware and software required.

REFERENCES

Many good books on the subject of operating systems can be found. However, most of them, like Watson (1970), Katzan (1973), Donovan, (1972) and Organick (1972), are concerned with the features and structure of particular systems (e.g., OS/360, Multics, and XDS-940). The notable exceptions are Brinch Hansen (1973), Cohen (1970), Denning and Coffman (1973), and Shaw (1974). Unfortunately, the latter four books tend to be more mathematical and theoretical in nature and may not be as useful as those geared to specific implementations. For a general treatment of modern operating systems, the reader should peruse Denning's (1971) survey article. Finally, Haberman (1976) treats operating system design in detail while Holt (1978) examines aspects of concurrent programming structures.

12

A Multiprogramming Applications Environment

A computing system with the ability to incorporate user-defined programs as one of its tasks is essential in environments for scientific and laboratory experiments, process control, and real-time systems where continuous, long-term monitoring of a number of variables is required. Particular applications might include the monitoring of laboratory animals who have been trained to perform certain tasks, the control of refining plants where the flow of volatile fluids must be accurately regulated, and the processing of messages between one central computer and the multitude of remotely located terminal devices.

Although seemingly diverse, all these applications can be well served by the small computer system. Because of its low cost and yet sophisticated capability, the small computer can be programmed to provide task scheduling, I/O control, operator communication, and other functions as required by the particular application. Indeed, most small-computer manufacturers provide some form of real-time software package that can readily be adapted to the user's environment.

To gain some insight into what these systems do, this chapter is devoted to the development of a Modest Multiprogramming System, MMS, which can be used to execute, concurrently, several tasks on a PDP-11 computer. MMS itself is very unsophisticated, but it performs its function well and utilizes a minimum of memory and processor time to accomplish its task. Of particular importance is the fact that MMS has been set up as an open-ended system, so that once its basic functions have been understood, it can easily be expanded (see Section 12.5 and the Exercises at the end of the chapter).

12.1 OVERALL VIEW OF MMS

Since the cost of an operating system is measured in terms of both the resources it requires (and uses) and the amount of time required to process a user's task (e.g., the *overhead* associated with executing the system's programs), a primary goal of such a system is to use a minimum amount of memory. The minimum amount of memory for MMS is approximately 200 words because of its unsophisticated nature. This small amount of memory required occurs because each user must provide his own I/O routines, and there is no operator communication facility built in.

The purpose of the system is to perform three kinds of operations involving user programs or *tasks*:

1. Upon a call from a task, switch the state of this task from "running" to "pending" and place the task on a queue according to its priority.

2. Examine the queue of tasks that are pending, and, having selected the task with the highest priority, unchain the task from the queue and switch its state from "pending" to "running".

3. Assign the CPU to the task now in the "running" state.

The general nature of such a system means that no special hardware is required, and any user-defined interfaces may be incorporated within it. The user need only define his tasks, written as PDP-11 programs, and integrate them into the base system by

1. Adding them somewhere between the end of one routine and the start of another.

2. Creating the proper entries in the various queues, tables, and PSECTs, as defined in the next section.

12.2 STRUCTURE OF THE QUEUES, TABLES, AND PSECTS

When a user places a task in the system, he must specify one of four levels of priority (0 through 3) for his task. These software or user levels are all below the four system levels of priority that are entered due to an I/O or instruction trap interrupt. However, the three software (user) interrupt levels are true priority levels and set the processor status word accordingly. For instance, if an interrupt occurs, indicating that it is time for a new task to begin, and the new task is of higher priority than the task interrupted, the lower-priority task is suspended and the higher-level task is activated. When the higher-level task gets suspended, the lower-level task is continued until the higher-level task can resume operation.

12.2.1 CPU Queue

The CPU Queue (CPUQ) is the data structure in which the information about which tasks are waiting to gain control of the CPU is kept. The queue is a vector of 8 bytes, divided into four entries, each entry corresponding to one of the four software priority levels allowed for tasks making use of the system. Consequently, each entry is 2 bytes long, with the high-order byte containing the identification (ID) of the first task (of that priority level) on a linked list (Section 12.2.2) waiting to be served, and the lower-order byte containing the ID of the last task (at that priority level) on that list. The 2 bytes thus serve as the head and tail pointers for the set of tasks (which are linked together) with a given priority level.

If no tasks exist at a certain priority level, the corresponding entry in the CPUQ will be zero. This means that no tasks making use of the system are allowed to have an ID equal to zero, because a zero in any entry of the CPUQ means "no tasks waiting at this priority level." Alternatively, if only one task is waiting to be served at a certain priority level, both bytes of the CPUQ for that level will contain the ID of the waiting task, because in this particular case the task is both the "first" and "last" task waiting on the queue. From what has been said it should be obvious that every task must have a unique ID. This ID is assigned by the user when he defines a PSECT (Section 12.2.4) for a task.

The structure of the CPUQ is shown in Fig. 12-1. For this example we have shown that

1. There are no tasks with priorities 0 or 1 waiting to be served.

2. There is a list of tasks waiting to be served at priority level 2. The task with ID = 5 is the first task on the list and the task with ID = 1 is the last.

3. There is only one task waiting to be served at priority level 3. Its ID is 4.

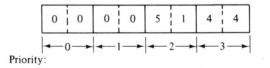

Priority:

Fig. 12-1 Structure of the CPUQ.

The serving of tasks proceeds from highest priority level to lowest. Thus the task with ID = 4 would be served first.

12.2.2 CPU Queue Table

The CPU queue table, CPUQTB, is a vector that will have as many entries (words) as there are tasks in the system. (Actually, it has as many entries as the number of tasks plus one, because entry zero is not used, for reasons which will become clear shortly.) The CPUQTB is a linked list of task ID's such that all tasks at the same priority level will be linked on the same list. Since there are four priority levels, four linked lists may exist on the CPUQTB at a time.

Assuming that there are N tasks within the system (maximum N = 255), the structure of the CPUQTB can be drawn as shown in Fig. 12-2. As stated before, each task has an identification number or ID which was assigned to it when its PSECT was created. These ID numbers run in numerical order from 1 up to the number of tasks that will be using the system, with a maximum of 255. Thus, if three tasks are to be defined, ID's assigned to them would be 1, 2, and 3. (We remember that an ID of zero is illegal because zero is interpreted by the supervisor as the "nonexistence of a pending task" at a given priority level.)

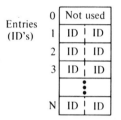

Fig. 12-2 Structure of the CPU queue table.

As shown, each entry in the CPUQTB corresponds to the ID of a task waiting to be served. For example, entry 1 corresponds to the task with ID = 1, entry 2 corresponds to the task with ID = 2, and so on. (Of course, entry 0 is wasted because no valid task can have ID = 0.) Looking at the contents of each entry, we see that the words are divided into two bytes with each byte storing a forward or backward pointer for the linked list. These pointers are not addresses, however. They are the ID's of the tasks in the linked list.

To clarify this last point, let us give an example. Suppose that there are four tasks with ID's 5, 2, 3, and 1, all with priority 2 waiting in the CPUQTB to be served. Further, there is a task with ID = 4 at level 3, also waiting to be served. Figure 12-1 shows the CPUQ for these five tasks and Fig. 12-3 shows the CPUQTB. As shown in Fig. 12-1, the first task at priority level 2 is the task with ID = 5; the last task in the list is the task with ID = 1.

ID:

0	Not used
1	0 ¦ 3
2	3 ¦ 5
3	1 ¦ 2
4	0 ¦ 0
5	2 ¦ 0

Fig. 12-3 Example of the entries in the CPUQTB.

As shown in Fig. 12-3, the entry for task with ID = 5 is divided into two bytes. The high-order byte contains an ID = 2 meaning: "task with ID = 2 follows task with ID = 5 on this linked list." The low-order byte contains a zero, meaning: "no task precedes this task with ID = 5," or "the task with ID = 5 is the head of the list." Going on, entry 2 of the CPUQTB corresponds to the task with ID = 2, and the following information is found in this entry: high-order byte = 3, low-order byte = 5, meaning: "task with ID = 5 precedes and task with ID = 3 follows this task with ID = 2." Finally, entry 1 of the CPUQTB is for the task with ID = 1 and it contains a 0 and a 3 in the high- and low-order bytes, meaning "the task with ID = 3 precedes and no tasks follow this task with ID = 1", so the task with ID = 1 is the last task on the list.

Reexamining the CPUQTB for the task with ID = 4, the reader will find both bytes zero for this entry. The entry contains zeros because the task with ID = 4 is not preceded or followed by any other on the queue (i.e., this task is the only task waiting for the CPU at priority 3).

12.2.3 PSECT Table

A PSECT (for "Process Section", where *process* is synonomous with *task*; see Section 12.2.4) is a vector, 11 words long, which is created for each task by the user. Information found in the PSECT of each task is used by the *supervisor* in task-switching operations. Before describing the PSECT, however, we shall examine the structure of the PSECT Table, PSECTB.

The PSECTB is a table that contains one entry for each PSECT. As each task must necessarily have one PSECT, the PSECTB will have as many entries as there are tasks. However, entry 0 of the PSECTB is not used, so in reality the PSECTB, like the CPUQTB, will have as many entries as the number of tasks plus one.

Each entry in the PSECTB corresponds to the ID of the task for which that entry will store information. The information stored in these entries is the address for the PSECT of the corresponding task. An example of the structure of this table is given in Fig. 12-4. As shown, entry 0 contains no information because there cannot exist a task with ID = 0. The remaining five entries correspond to tasks with ID's 1 through 5 for which the addresses of the PSECTs are defined symbolically as PSECT 1 through PSECT 5, respectively.

ID:

0	Not used
1	Psect 1
2	Psect 2
3	Psect 3
4	Psect 4
5	Psect 5

Fig. 12-4 Example of the entries in the PSECTB.

At this point the reader should recognize the value of the PSECT table and the use of ID's instead of actual addresses for the many tasks within the system. By not using address but rather indices (or ID's) for the various tables, less space is consumed (e.g., a byte rather than a word) for the various entries, thereby compressing the amount of memory required by the system. At the same time, processing of these tables is simplified because only linear lists in the form of one-dimensional tables or vectors are used, and accessing an entry requires only two steps: (1) shifting the index value left once to convert a byte offset into a word offset, and (2) adding in the base address of the table to produce the actual table entry in the PSECTB, as in:

```
ASL    R0            ;CONVERT INDEX TO WORD OFFSET
ADD    #PSECTB,R0    ;ADD IN TABLE BASE ADDRESS
```

12.2.4 PSECT Vector

The 11 words in a PSECT vector are reserved by the user at assembly time, one PSECT for each task. The vector is identified by the address of its first word, and this address is placed in the appropriate entry of the PSECTB. The PSECT contains information unique to the task, including a private stack where the contents of the task's registers will be saved while the task is waiting on a queue.

The structure of the PSECT is shown in Fig. 12-5. The first word of the PSECT is split into 2 bytes. The low-order byte contains the ID number assigned to the task. The high-order byte contains the task state. A task can be in one of two states: a "running" state, in which it has control of the CPU, and a "pending" state, in which the task is waiting on a queue. Other states could be defined, either by utilizing the individual bits to represent different states (up to 8), or by coding the state as a numerical value (up to 256), but for this simple system the two states are: running = 1 and pending = 2.

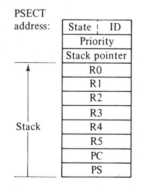

Fig. 12-5 Structure of a PSECT.

The second word of the PSECT will contain the priority level of the task. As stated earlier, a task can be in any one of four priority levels (0, 1, 2, and 3). The priority bits are set according to the structure of the processor status word, that is, bits 5, 6, and 7 form the priority, so if a task is to run at priority level 2, the second word of its PSECT should be set to 100 octal.

The third word of the PSECT will be used to save the stack pointer for that task. The rest of the PSECT (8 words) is then used as a private stack where the contents of the registers PC and PS will be saved when the task is switched from the running to the pending state. The code to define a PSECT, therefore, appears as

```
PSECT1: .BYTE    1,1       ;STATE AND ID BYTES
        .WORD    100       ;PRIORITY WORD, LEVEL 2
        .WORD    0         ;STACK POINTER SAVED HERE
        .BLKW    6         ;STACK AREA FOR R0-R5
        .WORD    TASK1     ;PC FOR TASK 1
        .WORD    0         ;PS FOR TASK 1
```

Since the user's stack is defined to be in the PSECT area, there are certain restrictions on its use. First, if the user wishes to use his stack while running, no more than nine entries may be pushed onto the stack. Second, at the time the task relinquishes the processor, the stack pointer, register 6, must be restored to its original value of #PSECT+26 (i.e., the top of the stack value), and no entries may be left on the stack during the time that the task is in a pending state. Of course, these restrictions can be removed, but this is left as an exercise for the reader (see Exercise 2 at the end of the chapter).

12.3 MMS SUPERVISOR

The heart of the MMS system is the supervisor, which may be called by any running task upon issue of a QUEUE supervisor call. *QUEUE* is an emulator trap instruction (QUEUE = 104000) which will trap to a two-word vector starting at location 30 octal. The first word of this vector contains the address of the first of a series of supervisor routines that will be executed in order to carry on the queue request. The second word of this vector contains the priority at which the supervisor routines will be executed.

The five routines that make up the supervisor are, in order of execution:

1. *SCHEDL:*   the scheduling routine.

2. *SAVE:*   the register save routine.

3. *INSLAS:*   the insert last in queue routine.

4. *DISPCH:*   the dispatch and register restore routine.

5. *UNCHN:*   the unqueue routine.

Each of these routines is described in the following sections.

12.3.1 Schedule Routine

Control passes to the schedule routine, SCHEDL, as the result of a QUEUE supervisor call (i.e., an SVC). This call on the supervisor requires that the first word of the two-word trap vector contain the address of SCHEDL. As a result of the execution of a QUEUE SVC, the processor status and the program counter are "automatically" pushed onto the private stack for the task issuing the SVC. Then, the first action of SCHEDL is to save (upon a call to the SAVE routine) the contents of all registers, that is, to push them also onto the user's private stack.

Next, using the PSECT for the task issuing the SVC, SCHEDL gets the priority for the task and finds the correct entry to the CPUQ. The task is then inserted (upon a call to the INSLAS routine) at the end of the queue (CPUQTB), its state is switched from running to pending, and a new task is selected to be given control of the CPU (upon a call to the DISPCH routine).

12.3.2 Register Save Routine

The SAVE subroutine is called from SCHEDL. Since R5 is already pushed onto the stack by the JSR instruction, only the remaining registers R4 through R1 need be saved. At this point the user's stack pointer is saved, and the address of the active PSECT is placed in register 5. Finally, the system is switched to supervisor state, by making SUPSTK the new available stack, and control is given back to the calling routine.

In returning from this subroutine, the program must not execute an RTS instruction, since the new stack pointed to does not contain the return address. Instead, a jump instruction is used, utilizing the return address held in register 5. The jump instruction has the added advantage of not popping the stack, since this would contravene one of the purposes of the SAVE subroutine.

12.3.3 Insert Routine

SCHEDL calls the INSLAS routine after it calculates the entry address in the CPUQ of the calling task. INSLAS's purpose is to take the task that issued a SVC and place it in its appropriate waiting list. The steps that INSLAS goes through are explained as follows.

First, INSLAS gets the task ID from the task's PSECT, and with this ID it finds the appropriate entry in the CPUQTB. Since this task is going to be the most recent task placed in the queue, it means that the high-order byte of the CPUQTB entry is going to be zero (i.e., no other task follows this one on the waiting list). INSLAS knows the priority of this task, so it checks the appropriate entry of the CPUQ to see whether the queue is empty or not. If the queue is empty (i.e., the entry contains zeros), it means that this is going to be the only task in the queue, and INSLAS clears (zeros) the CPUQTB entry. It then goes on to store the ID for this task in both bytes of the CPUQ entry.

If the queue is not empty (i.e., the entry in the CPUQ is not zero), it means that there is a task (or several tasks) already waiting at that priority level, and INSLAS must insert this new task into the various queues. In this case INSLAS performs the following steps:

1. Get the contents of the low-order byte of CPUQ entry. This byte stores the ID of the last task, at that priority, waiting in the queue.

2. Get the entry for this ID in the CPUQTB. The high-order byte of this entry is zero, because this is the last task waiting in the queue.

3. Place the ID of the task being inserted in the queue into the high-order byte of the CPUQTB entry.

4. Place the old contents of the low-order byte of the CPUQ entry in the low-order byte of the CPUQTB entry for the newly inserted task.

5. Place the ID of the inserted task in the low-order byte of the CPUQ entry.

Figure 12-6 illustrates the action of the insert routine for a task whose ID is 4 and whose priority level is 2. In the first case [Fig. 12-6(a) and (b)], we assume that no other task with priority 2 is waiting in the queue. In the second case [Fig. 12-6(c) and (d)], we assume there are four tasks at priority level 2 waiting in the queue. These tasks, in order, have ID's of 3, 6, 1, and 5.

12.3.4 Dispatch Routine

After a task is inserted into a waiting queue, its status is set to pending, and a new task is selected as a candidate for execution. The routine that selects this new task is the DISPCH routine called from SCHEDL. DISPCH performs its function by searching the CPUQ, from highest priority level to lowest, for any tasks that can be activated. If DISPCH finds such a task, it calls the unchain routine, UNCHN, in order to delink the selected task from its queue.

After the waiting task is delinked from the queue, the ACTIVE pointer is updated to point to the PSECT for the newly selected task, the task's PSECT is set to indicate that it is in the running state, and the stack pointer for this task is loaded into the SP register. Finally, the contents of the task's registers are restored, and, as its final action, DISPCH issues an RTI (return from interrupt), which restores the contents of the PC and PS for this task. At this point the task takes control of the CPU.

12.3.5 Unchain Routine

When called by DISPCH, the unchain subroutine, UNCHN, takes the first waiting task out of the appropriate queue and updates the entries in both the CPUQ and the CPUQTB. In effect, the action of UNCHN is just the reverse of the

INSLAS routine in that it performs a "remove first" rather than an "insert last" on the queue. The reader should recall that a queue is *first in, first out* data structure.

Besides updating entries, UNCHN also gets the address of the PSECT for the unchained task from the PSECTB. It then returns control to the DISPCH routine.

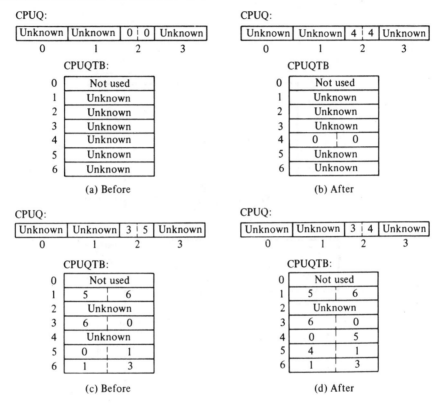

Fig. 12-6 Structure of the CPUQ and the CPUQTB before and after an INSLAS operation.

12.4 WRITING PROGRAMS TO RUN UNDER MMS

Although there is no constraint on the form programs may take while running under MMS, initializing this system properly is vital to get it to work correctly. Specifically, this means that the user must establish the correct entries in the CPU queue, the CPU queue table, and the PSECT table, and also define a new PSECT for each task to be run (see Section 12.2.4). Having done so, the user can then set the system in motion by setting up the processor status and the user's stack pointer, by defining the PSECT pointer to the active task, and then jumping to the first task to be executed.

A listing of MMS is included at the end of this chapter to show the code for implementing a running system. There are two example tasks, "TASK1" and

"TASK2", included to show how MMS might be used. The tasks are nearly identical and have a logical structure, as shown in Fig. 12-7. The tasks perform their own I/O but do so without using the interrupts. Thus, each task tests the status of a device, and if it is not ready, the task queues itself, thereby relinquishing the CPU.

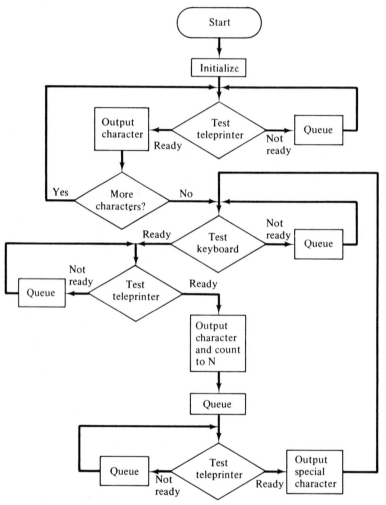

Fig. 12-7 Logical structure of example tasks in MMS system.

12.5 EXPANDED SYSTEM

As shown, the system has the ability to interpret only one type of command, a QUEUE supervisor call, which places the task issuing the SVC at the end of a pending list and removes the task at the head of this list, assigning the CPU to it.

Other supervisor calls could be implemented with little extra work, and an obvious candidate would be a "WAIT" SVC, which would place the task issuing it at the end of a "waiting state" list. Tasks on this list would not be placed on the pending list (e.g., made eligible for use of the CPU) until an external event, such as receipt of an interrupt signal, occurred.

The implementation of the WAIT SVC would speed up operations utilizing I/O devices, because a task requesting input or output would not regain control of the CPU until the I/O was actually ready or available. In the present system, any task at the head of the pending state list will gain control of the CPU and will have to test and possibly re-queue if the I/O device is not ready. In those cases where a mix of I/O- and CPU-bound tasks were being executed, taking control away from the CPU-bound task before the I/O-bound task can proceed is clearly wasteful.

Three other features commonly found in small multiprogrammed operating systems are an I/O Programming System (IOPS), a command language interpreter, and an error processor. The ideas behind an IOPS have already been discussed in Chapter 7, and these could be readily incorporated into MMS. A small and efficient command language interpreter would be useful in allowing the user to load and run tasks from a terminal device rather than by "programming them into" the system itself. Particularly useful might be commands that allow the terminal user to examine and change the contents of memory. Finally, error-diagnosis routines are necessary if the system is to be able to continue either after an error has occurred and some system (or user) action is required, or because an unexpected or unanticipated condition requires immediate attention.

12.6 LISTING OF MMS

```
        .TITLE MMS
;       M M S - - A MODEST MULTIPROGRAMMING SYSTEM
;       WRITTEN BY ED MACHADO AND MODIFIED BY R. ECKHOUSE AND R. MORRIS
;
        .CSECT
;
;       D A T A    D E F I N I T I O N S
;
        QUEUE=104000      ;SUPERVISOR CALL TRAP
        RUNBIT=1          ;RUN STATE BIT
        PENBIT=2          ;PENDING STATE BIT
        TKSTAT=1          ;TASK STATE OFFSET
        PRIO=2            ;PRIORITY OFFSET
        TKSP=4            ;STACK POINTER OFFSET
        STATMK=17         ;STATE MASK
        IOF=340           ;TO TURN OFF INTERRUPT
        HBM=177400        ;HIGH BIT MASK
        PSW=177776        ;PROCESSOR STATUS WORD
        USERST=TASK1      ;STARTING ADDRESS OF USER TASK
```

```
;
;          D E V I C E     D E F I N I T I O N S
;
          TKS1=177560      ;KEYBOARD 1 STATUS REG
          TKB1=TKS1+2      ;KEYBOARD 1 BUFFER
          TPS1=TKS1+4      ;TELEPRINTER 1 STATUS REG
          TPB1=TKS1+6      ;TELEPRINTER 1 BUFFER
          TKS2=175610      ;KEYBOARD 2 STATUS REG
          TKB2=TKS2+2      ;KEYBOARD 2 BUFFER
          TPS2=TKS2+4      ;TELEPRINTER 2 STATUS REG
          TPB2=TKS2+6      ;TELEPRINTER 2 BUFFER
;
;          C P U    Q U E U E     D E F I N I T I O N
;
;        THERE ARE FOUR ENTRIES (EIGHT BYTES) IN
;        WHICH ENTRY 2 (PRIORITY 2) HAS THE ID
;        FOR THE ONLY TASK (TASK2) WAITING ON THE QUEUE
;
;        NOTE THAT .BYTES ARE OFFSET TO VISUALLY SUGGEST HIGH, LOW BYTES
;
CPUQ:
               .BYTE    0        ;ID OF LAST TASK AT LEVEL 0
          .BYTE    0             ;ID OF 1'ST TASK AT LEVEL 0
               .BYTE    0        ;ID OF LAST TASK AT LEVEL 1
          .BYTE    0             ;ID OF 1'ST TASK AT LEVEL 1
               .BYTE    2        ;ID OF LAST TASK AT LEVEL 2
          .BYTE    2             ;ID OF 1'ST TASK AT LEVEL 2
               .BYTE    0        ;ID OF LAST TASK AT LEVEL 3
          .BYTE    0             ;ID OF 1'ST TASK AT LEVEL 3
;
;          C P U    Q U E U E     T A B L E    D E F I N I T I O N
;
;        ENTRY 2 IS THE ONLY ENTRY STORING RELEVANT
;        INFORMATION.  IT CONTAINS ZEROS BECAUSE THE
;        TASK WITH ID=2 (TASK2) IS NOT PRECEDED OR
;        FOLLOWED BY ANY OTHER TASK ON THE QUEUE, E.G.
;        TASK WITH ID=2 IS THE ONLY TASK WAITING FOR THE CPU
;
;        NOTE THAT .BYTES ARE OFFSET TO VISUALLY SUGGEST HIGH, LOW BYTES
;
CPUQTB: .BYTE     0,0
;
               .BYTE    0        ;ID OF TASK BEFORE TASK1
          .BYTE    0             ;ID OF TASK AFTER TASK 1
;
               .BYTE    0        ;ID OF TASK BEFORE TASK2
          .BYTE    0             ;ID OF TASK AFTER TASK2
;
               .BYTE    0        ;ID OF TASK BEFORE TASK3
          .BYTE    0             ;ID OF TASK AFTER TASK3
;
               .BYTE    0        ;ID OF TASK BEFORE TASK4
          .BYTE    0             ;ID OF TASK AFTER TASK4
```

```
;               P S E C T     T A B L E     D E F I N I T I O N
;
;      THE PSECTB IS INITIALIZED WITH THE ADDRESS OF
;      THE PSECT'S (PSECT1 AND PSECT2) DEFINED FOR
;      THE TASKS WITHIN THE SYSTEM (TASK1 AND TASK2)
;
PSECTB: .WORD    0
        .WORD    PSECT1              ;ADDRESS OF PSECT FOR TASK1
        .WORD    PSECT2              ;ADDRESS OF PSECT FOR TASK2
        .WORD    0                   ;ADDRESS OF PSECT FOR TASK3
        .WORD    0                   ;ADDRESS OF PSECT FOR TASK4

;         P O I N T E R S     A N D     T E M P O R A R I E S
;
;      ACTIVE HAS (IS INITIALIZED WITH) THE ADDRESS OF
;      THE PSECT FOR THE FIRST TASK TO GAIN CONTROL OF THE CPU
;
ACTIVE: .WORD    PSECT1
;
;      SUPSTK IS THE STACK USED BY THE SUPERVISOR WHILE IN CONTROL
;
        .BLKW    20.
SUPSTK: .WORD    0        ;STACK'S TOP CELL
;
;         P S E C T     D E F I N I T I O N S
;
;      NOTE THAT .BYTES ARE OFFSET TO VISUALLY SUGGEST HIGH, LOW BYTES
;
PSECT1:          .BYTE 1  ;ID FOR TASK1
        .BYTE    1        ;STATE FOR TASK1
        .WORD    100      ;PRIORITY OF 2
        .WORD    0        ;STACK POINTER WILL BE SAVED HERE
        .BLKW    6        ;STACK AREA FOR R0-R5
        .WORD    TASK1    ;PC FOR TASK1
        .WORD    0        ;PSW FOR TASK1 WILL BE SAVED HERE
;
PSECT2:          .BYTE 2  ;ID FOR TASK2
        .BYTE    2        ;STATE FOR TASK2
        .WORD    100      ;PRIORITY OF 2
        .WORD    0        ;STACK POINTER WILL BE SAVED HERE
        .BLKW    6        ;STACK AREA FOR R0-R5
        .WORD    TASK2    ;PC FOR TASK2
        .WORD    0        ;PSW FOR TASK2 WILL BE SAVED HERE
;
;      INITIALIZE THE SYSTEM
;
START:  CLR      @#177546            ;TURN OFF LINE CLOCK
        BIC      #100,@#TKS1         ;DISABLE INTERRUPTS FOR DEVICE 1
        BIC      #100,@#TKS2         ;DISABLE INTERRUPTS FOR DEVICE 2
;
        CLR      R0
ST1:    INC      R0                  ;INITIALIZE
        INC      R0                  ;ALL
        MOV      R0,-2(R0)           ;INTERRUPT VECTORS
        CLR      (R0)+               ;TO HAVE THE PC
        CMP      #400,R0             ;POINT TO THE NEXT LOCATION
        BNE      ST1                 ;WHICH IS A HALT INSTRUCTION
```

```
;
;          SET UP THE TRAP VECTOR
;
           MOV      #SCHEDL,@#30      ;FOR SVC TRAP
           MOV      #IOF,@#32         ;WITH PRIORITY 7
;
;          SET UP PSW AND STACK, THEN BEGIN
;
           CLR      PSW               ;SET UP PROCESSOR STATUS
           MOV      #PSECT1+26,SP     ;SET UP STACK POINTER
           MOV      #PSECT1,ACTIVE    ;DEFINE THE ACTIVE TASK
           JMP      USERST            ;USER'S STARTING ADDRESS

;
;          T H E    S C H E D U L E    R O U T I N E
;
;                        "S C H E D L"
;
;          THIS IS THE SUPERVISOR ROUTINE CALLED BY A
;          TRAP THROUGH LOCATION 30 (OCTAL), IN RESPONSE
;          TO AN SVC OR QUEUE CALL.
;
SCHEDL: JSR      R5,SAVE           ;SAVE ALL REGISTERS, INCL. TSK SP
        MOV      PRIO(R5),R0       ;GET PRIORITY OF TASK TO BE QUEUED
                                   ;R5 CONTAINS ADDRESS OF PSECT FOR THAT TASK
        ASR      R0                ;SHIFT
        ASR      R0                ; RIGHT TO
        ASR      R0                ;  GET CORRECT
        ASR      R0                ;    ENTRY IN CPUQ (I.E., 2*ACTUAL PRIORITY)
        ADD      #CPUQ,R0          ;ADD IN ADDRESS OF BASE OF QUEUE TO GET
                                   ;POINTER TO CPUQ ENTRY FOR PRIORITY "N"
        JSR      PC,INSLAS         ;INSERT TASK IN QUEUE
        BICB     #STATMK,TKSTAT(R5) ;CLEAR TASK STATE OF NEWLY QUEUED ITEM
        BISB     #PENBIT,TKSTAT(R5) ;SET IT TO PENDING STATE
        JMP      DISPCH            ;HEAD OF WAITING LIST
;
;          T H E    S A V E    R O U T I N E
;
;                    "S A V E"
;
;          SUPERVISOR SUBROUTINE CALLED FROM SCHEDL WHICH
;          PUSHES THE CONTENTS OF THE USER'S REGISTERS INTO
;          THE PSECT STACK AND SWITCHES THE SYSTEM TO
;          SUPERVISOR STATE (THE SYSTEM IS IN THE SUPERVISOR
;          STATE WHEN IT IS USING THE SUPERVISOR STACK).
;
SAVE:   MOV      R4,-(SP)          ;PUSH
        MOV      R3,-(SP)          ; REMAINING
        MOV      R2,-(SP)          ;  REGISTERS
        MOV      R1,-(SP)          ;   ONTO
        MOV      R0,-(SP)          ;    STACK
        MOV      R5,RETADR         ;SET UP RETURN ADDR
        MOV      ACTIVE,R5         ;ADDRESS OF ACTIVE PSECT
        MOV      SP,TKSP(R5)       ;SAVE STACK PTR
        MOV      #SUPSTK,SP        ;SUPERVISOR STATE/STACK
        JMP      @#0               ;RETURN
        RETADR=.-2                 ;2ND WORD OF JMP INSTR
```

```
;
;          T H E     I N S E R T     R O U T I N E
;
;                    "I N S L A S"
;
;          SUPERVISOR SUBROUTINE CALLED FROM SCHEDL TO
;          INSERT THE TASK THAT ISSUED AN SVC AT
;          THE END OF A WAITING LIST ("CPUQTB")
;
INSLAS: MOVB    @R5,R2              ;ID OF NEW LAST TASK AT LEVEL "N", NLT(N)
        BIC     #HBM,R2            ;CLEAR THE HIGH BYTE OF REGISTER
        ASL     R2                 ;MULTIPLY BY TWO
        ADD     #CPUQTB,R2         ;ADDRESS OF BACKWARD PNTR BYTE FOR NLT(N)
        CLRB    1(R2)              ;CLEAR FORWARD POINTER OF CPUQTB FOR NLT(N)
        MOVB    @R0,R1             ;GET ID FOR PREVIOUS LAST TASK, PLT(N)
        BEQ     EMPTYQ             ;IS IT ZERO?
        BIC     #HBM,R1            ;NO, CLEAR HIGH BYTE OF ID WORD
        ASL     R1                 ;MULTIPLY BY TWO
        ADD     #CPUQTB,R1         ;ADDRESS OF BACKWARD POINTER FOR PLT(N)
        MOVB    @R5,1(R1)          ;ID OF NLT(N) INTO FORWARD POINTER OF PLT(N)
        MOVB    @R0,@R2            ;OLD LAST TASK IS PRECEDING TASK
        MOVB    @R5,@R0            ;NEW TASK IS LAST TASK
        RTS     PC                 ;RETURN
EMPTYQ: MOVB    @R5,@R0            ;TASK ID INTO LOW BYTE
        MOVB    @R5,1(R0)          ;AND HIGH BYTE OF CPUQ ENTRY
        RTS     PC                 ;RETURN
;
;          T H E     D I S P A T C H     R O U T I N E
;
;                    "D I S P C H"
;
;          SUPERVISOR ROUTINE TO UNCHAIN A TASK FROM THE
;          WAITING LIST AND ASSIGN THE CPU TO IT
;
DISPCH: MOV     #CPUQ+10,R0        ;TRY HIGHEST PRIORITY
LOOP:   TST     -(R0)              ;ANYTHING TO DO?
        BEQ     LOOP               ;NO, TRY THE NEXT LEVEL
        JSR     PC,UNCHN           ;YES, UNCHAIN
        MOV     R5,ACTIVE          ;MAKE NEW TASK ACTIVE
        BICB    #STATMK,TKSTAT(R5)    ;CLEAR TASK STATE
        BISB    #RUNBIT,TKSTAT(R5)    ;SET STATE TO RUN
        MOV     TKSP(R5),SP        ;GET TASK'S STACK POINTER
        MOV     (SP)+,R0           ;RESTORE
        MOV     (SP)+,R1           ;  CONTENTS
        MOV     (SP)+,R2           ;    OF
        MOV     (SP)+,R3           ;     REGISTERS
        MOV     (SP)+,R4           ;      PREVIOUSLY
        MOV     (SP)+,R5           ;       SAVED
        RTI                        ;RETURN FROM INTERRUPT
```

```
;
;           T H E    U N C H A I N    R O U T I N E
;
;                      "U N C H N"
;
;       SUPERVISOR SUBROUTINE CALLED FROM THE DISPCH ROUTINE
;       WHOSE ACTION IS TO TAKE THE FIRST TASK OUT OF A
;       WAITING LIST AND UPDATE THE ENTRIES BOTH IN CPUQ AND
;       CPUQTB.
UNCHN:  MOV     @R0,R1              ;ID OF FIRST TASK ON QUEUE
        SWAB    R1                  ;SWAP ID'S
        BIC     #HBM,R1             ;CLEAR HIGH BYTE
        ASL     R1                  ;MULTIPLY BY TWO
        MOVB    CPUQTB+1(R1),1(R0)  ;NEW FIRST TASK
        BNE     ANTKS               ;THERE IS ANOTHER TASK
        CLR     @R0                 ;NO MORE TASKS-ZERO OUT ENTRY
        BR      ARND                ;SKIP NEXT INSRTS
ANTKS:  MOVB    1(R0),R0            ;NEW "FIRST TASK" ON QUEUE
        BIC     #HBM,R0             ;CLEAR HIGH BYTE
        ASL     R0                  ;MULTIPLY BY TWO
        CLRB    CPUQTB(R0)          ;NO TASK PROCEEDS
ARND:   CLR     CPUQTB(R1)          ;CLEAR THIS ENTRY
        MOV     PSECTB(R1),R5       ;GET PSECT'S ADDRESS
        RTS     PC                  ;RETURN


;
;           "T A S K 1"
;
;       SIMPLE LITTLE TASK TO READ AND TYPE A CHARACTER,
;       COUNT TO 100 (OCTAL), AND THEN INSERT A SPACE.
;       AFTER EACH STEP, A QUEUE IS PERFORMED
;
TASK1:  MOV     BLANK,R5            ;PUT A BLANK IN R5
        MOV     #6,R1              ;LETTER COUNT
        MOV     #RDY,R2            ;BUFR POINTER
TA1:    TSTB    TPS1               ;TIME TO PRINT?
        BMI     PR1                ;YES
        QUEUE                      ;NO, GIVE UP CPU
        BR      TA1                ;TRY AGAIN
PR1:    MOVB    (R2)+,TPB1         ;PUT OUT CHARACTER
        DEC     R1                 ;DECR LETTER COUNT
        BNE     TA1                ;MORE TO DO
AGN1:   TSTB    TKS1               ;ANYTHING THERE?
        BMI     YES1               ;YES, DON'T QUEUE
        QUEUE                      ;GIVE UP CPU
        BR      AGN1               ;TRY AGAINNAT
YES1:   TSTB    TPS1               ;CAN WE PRINT?
        BMI     YES2               ;YES, DON'T QUEUE
        QUEUE                      ;GIVE UP CPU
        BR      YES1               ;TRY AGAIN
YES2:   MOVB    TKB1,TPB1          ;PUT OUT CHARACTER
        MOV     #100,R0            ;LOOP COUNT
T2:     DEC     R0                 ;DECR COUNT
        BNE     T2                 ;LOOP UNTIL ZERO
        QUEUE                      ;TIME TO GIVE UP CPU
T3:     TSTB    TPS1               ;CAN WE SPACE?
        BMI     YES3               ;YES, GO AHEAD
        QUEUE                      ;GIVE UP CPU
        BR      T3                 ;TRY AGAIN
```

414

```
YES3:    MOVB    R5,TPB1         ;MOVE SPACE TO BUFFER
         QUEUE                   ;GIVE UP CPU
         BR      AGN1            ;REPEAT THE WHOLE THING
BLANK:   .ASCII  / /             ;SOME BLANKS
RDY:     .ASCII  /READY!/        ;READY MESSAGE

;
;        "T A S K  2"
;
;        THIS IS THE SAME AS TASK 1 WHICH SHOWS THAT
;        THE TWO TASKS CAN RUN CONCURRENTLY WITHOUT
;        USING INTERRUPTS AND WITHOUT THE LOSS OF INFORMATION.
;
TASK2:   MOV     DASH,R5         ;DIFFERENT SEPARATOR
         MOV     #7,R1           ;CHARACTER COUNT
         MOV     #PRO,R2         ;BUFR POINTER
TA2:     TSTB    TPS2            ;TIME TO PRINT?
         BMI     PR2             ;YES
         QUEUE                   ;NO
         BR      TA2             ;TRY AGAIN
PR2:     MOVB    (R2)+,TPB2      ;PUT OUT CHARACTER
         DEC     R1              ;DECR CHAR COUNT
         BNE     TA2             ;KEEP GOING
AGN2:    TSTB    TKS2            ;ANYTHING THERE?
         BMI     YES4            ;YES, DON'T QUEUE
         QUEUE                   ;GIVE UP CPU
         BR      AGN2            ;TRY AGAIN
YES4:    TSTB    TPS2            ;CAN WE PRINT?
         BMI     YES5            ;YES, DON'T QUEUE
         QUEUE                   ;GIVE UP CPU
         BR      YES4            ;TRY AGAIN
YES5:    MOVB    TKB2,TPB2       ;PUT OUT CHARACTER
         MOV     #200,R1         ;LOOP COUNT
T4:      DEC     R1              ;DECR COUNT
         BNE     T4              ;LOOP UNTIL ZERO
         QUEUE                   ;GIVE UP CPU
T5:      TSTB    TPS2            ;CAN WE DASH?
         BMI     YES6            ;YES, GO AHEAD
         QUEUE                   ;GIVE UP CPU
         BR      T5              ;TRY AGAIN
YES6:    MOVB    R5,TPB2         ;MOVE DASH TO BUFFER
         QUEUE                   ;GIVE UP CPU
         BR      AGN2    ;REPEAT
DASH:    .ASCII  /--/            ;SOME DASHES
PRO:     .ASCII  /PROCEED/       ;DIFF MESSAGE
         .END    START           ;END OF ASSEMBLY
```

EXERCISES

1. One of the problems with MMS is that there are insufficient states to handle tasks at various priority levels properly. Thus, if one job is at level 3 and one at level 7, the level 3 program can never pass the CPU to the level 7 program because the level 3 program is always chosen from the CPU queue of pending tasks. How could MMS be changed to overcome this limitation?

2. Instead of requiring the user to restore his stack, suggest an alternative whereby the system maintains the PSECT stack within the "system area."

3. If a system such as MMS can be written to operate without interrupts, what advantage do interrupts provide over polling or "scout's honor" programming (i.e., programming where each program guarantees to relinquish the CPU via an SVC within a given time interval).

4. How could an interrupting clock be added to MMS so that tasks would be forced to relinquish the CPU after a given time interval? Would such time slicing help or hinder the user? Would he need to know that it existed?

5. As suggested in Section 12.5, a WAIT SVC would be quite useful. How could it be integrated into MMS? What other SVCs could be added?

6. Design an IOPS for MMS. What type of SVCs would have to be added to MMS? How would the user call IOPS?

7. What type of commands would you implement in MMS? What new systems, besides IOPS, could be integrated into MMS (e.g., a loader, a text editor) requiring some form of command language interpretation?

8. MMS has no way to perform memory management. One technique is to form a chain of all unallocated words of memory into a chain of "free blocks." The first word of each block contains the size of the block; the link is maintained in the second word. When a request for memory is made, the chain is followed until a block, large enough to satisfy the request, if found. If such a block cannot be found, the system fails. When the block is found, the amount requested is removed from the end of the block and the block size is adjusted. Note that at least two words are necessary to maintain a block on the chain. If the block to be split exactly equals the requested size + 1, the entire block is allocated. Deallocation operations are combined with maintenance operations. Each time a block is relinquished to the deallocator, the chain is searched for block contiguities. This is done in two steps. In the first, the chain is scanned to find a block that immediately follows the block being returned (tail contiguity). If such a block is found, it is unlinked from the chain and concatenated with the block being returned. This new block is then the subject of a head contiguity scan. If contiguity is detected, the block being returned is appended to the block on the chain and the size of the block is adjusted correspondingly. Integrate this memory management system into MMS.

9. What type of error-diagnosis routines should be implemented in MMS? Must these routines reside in memory.

10. Design and implement a file system for MMS.

Appendix A:
Primer of Number Systems

The concept of writing numbers, counting, and performing the basic operations of addition, subtraction, multiplication, and division has been directly developed by man. Every person is introduced to these concepts during his formal education. One of the most important facts in scientific development was the invention of the decimal numbering system. The system of counting in units of tens probably developed because man has 10 fingers. The use of the number 10 as the base of our number system is not of prime importance; any standard unit would do as well. The main use of a number system in early times was for measuring quantities and keeping records, not performing mathematical calculations. As the sciences developed, old numbering systems became more and more outdated. The lack of an adequate numerical system greatly hampered the scientific development of early civilizations.

Two basic concepts simplified the operations needed to manipulate numbers; the concept of position, and the numeral zero. The concept of position consists of assigning to a number a value that depends both on the symbol and on its position in the whole number. For example, the digit 5 has a different value in each of the three numbers 135, 152, and 504. In the first number, the digit 5 has its original value 5; in the second, it has the value of 50; and in the last number, it has the value of 500, or 5 times 10 times 10.

Sometimes a position in a number does not have a value between 1 and 9. If this position were simply left out, there would be no difference in notation between 709 and 79. This is where the numeral zero fills the gap. In the number 709, there are 7 hundreds, 0 tens, and 9 units. Thus by using the concept of position and the numeral 0, arithmetic becomes quite easy.

A few basic definitions are needed before we proceed to see how these concepts apply to digital computers.

1. *Unit:*   the standard utilized in counting separate items is the unit.

2. *Quantity:*   the absolute or physical amounts of units.

3. *Number:*   a number is a symbol used to represent a quantity.

4. *Number system:*   A number system is a means of representing quantities using a set of numbers. All modern number systems use the zero to indicate no units, and other symbols to indicate quantitities. The base or radix of a number system is the number of symbols it contains, including zero. For example, the decimal number system is base or radix 10, because it contains 10 different symbols (0, 1, 2, 3, 4, 5, 6, 7, 8, and 9).

A.1 BINARY NUMBER SYSTEMS

The fundamental requirement of a computer is the ability to represent numbers physically and to perform operations on the numbers thus represented. Although computers that are based on other number systems have been built, modern digital computers are all based on the binary (base 2) system. To represent 10 different numbers (0, 1, 2, ..., 9) the computer must possess 10 different states with which to associate a digit value. However, most physical quantities have only two states: a light bulb is on or off; switches are on or off; holes in paper tape or cards are punched or not punched; current is positive or negative; material is magnetized or demagnetized; and so on. Because it can be represented by only two such physical states, the binary number system is used in computers.

To understand the binary number system upon which the digital computer operates, an analysis of the concepts underlying the decimal number system is beneficial.

A.1.1 Positional Coefficient

Although the decimal number system is familiar to us all, what we read and write as decimal numbers are not true mathematical quantities, but *symbolic representations*. These representations are sufficient for our use because they imply a *positional notation* which is well accepted. For example, 347 is the symbolic representation of

$$3 * 10^2 + 4 * 10^1 + 7 * 10^0$$

Each numeral has a value that depends upon its position. The value of a position is called the *positional coefficient*, the *digit-position weighting value*, or simply the *weight*. The weights for each position are

$$\ldots \quad 10^3 \quad 10^2 \quad 10^1 \quad 10^0 \quad 10^{-1} \quad \ldots$$

Weighting values appear to serve no useful purpose in our familiar decimal numbering system, but their purpose becomes apparent when we consider the binary or base 2 numbering system. In binary we have only two digits, 0 and 1. In order to represent the numbers 1 to 10, we must utilize a count-and-carry principle familiar to us from the decimal system (so familiar that we are not always aware that we use it). To count from 0 to 10 in decimal, we count as follows:

```
0
1
2
3
4
5
6
7
8
9
10   with a carry in the 10**1 column
```

Continuing the counting, when we reach 0 in the units column again, we carry another 1 to the tens column. This process is continued unitl the tens column becomes 0 and a 1 is carried into the hundreds column:

```
0                10               90
1                11               91
2                12               92
3                13               93
4                14               94
5                15               95
6                16               96
7                17               97
8                18               98
9                19               99
10 one carry     20 one carry     100 two carries
```

A.1.2 Counting in Binary Numbers

In the binary number system, the carry principle is used with only two digit symbols, 0 and 1. Thus the numbers used in the binary number system to count up to a decimal value of 10 are the following:

```
Binary:  0000 0001 0010 0011 0100 0101 0110 0111 1000 1001 1010

Decimal:    0    1    2    3    4    5    6    7    8    9   10
```

When using more than one number system, it is customary to subscript numbers with the applicable base (e.g., 101(2) = 5(10)).

A weighting table is used to convert binary numbers to the more familiar decimal system:

```
4         3         2         1         0
2         2         2         2         2 (Weight Table)
1         0         1         0         1 (Binary Number)

|         |         |         |         |              Position
|         |         |         |         |        Digit  Coefficient
|         |         |         |         |        -----  -----------
|         |         |         |         --- → = 1  *  1       = 1
|         |         |         ----------- → = 0  *  2       = 0
|         |         -------------------- → = 1  *  4       = 4
|         ---------------------------- → = 0  *  8       = 0
---------------------------------------- → = 1  * 16       = 16
                                                                  --
                                            Decimal Number   21
```

It should be obvious that the binary weighting table can be extended, like the decimal table, as far as desired. In general, to find the value of a binary number, multiply each digit by its positional coefficient and then add all the products.

A.1.3 Arrangement of Values

By convention, weighting values are always arranged in the same manner, the highest on the extreme left and the lowest on the extreme right. Therefore, the position coefficient begins at 1 and increases from right to left. This convention has two very practical advantages. The first advantage is that it allows the elimination of the weighting table, as such. It is not necessary to label each binary number with weighting values, as the digit on the extreme right is always multiplied by 1, the digit to its left is always multiplied by 2, the next by 4, and so on. The second advantage is the elimination of some of the 0's. Whether a 0 is to the right or left, it will never add to the value of a binary number. Some 0's are required, however, as any 0's to the right of the highest-valued 1 are utilized as spaces or place keepers, to keep the 1's in their correct positions. The 0's to the left, however, provide no information about the number and may be discarded; thus the number 0001010111 = 1010111.

A.1.4 Significant Digits

The "leftmost" 1 in a binary number is called the most significant digit (MSD). It is called the "most significant" in that it is multiplied by the highest positional coefficient. The least significant digit (LSD) is the extreme right digit. It may be a 1 or 0 and has the lowest weighting value, 1. The terms LSD and MSD have the same meaning in the decimal system as in the binary system:

A.1.5 Conversion of Decimal to Binary

There are two commonly used methods for converting decimal numbers to binary equivalents. The reader may choose whichever method he finds easier to use.

Subtraction-of-powers method: To convert any decimal number to its binary equivalent by the subtraction-of-powers method, proceed as follows: Subtract the highest possible power of 2 from the decimal number and place a 1 in the appropriate weighting position of the partially completed binary number. Continue this procedure until the decimal number is reduced to 0. If, after the first subtraction, the next lower power of 2 cannot be subtracted, place a 0 in the appropriate weighting position.

Example:

```
              42 (10)   = ? binary

              42         10          2
             -32         -8         -2
             --          --         --
              10          2          0
```

5	4	3	2	1	0	
2	2	2	2	2	2	Power
32	16	8	4	2	1	Value
1	0	1	0	1	0	Binary

Therefore, 42 (10) = 101010 (2).

Division method: To convert a decimal number to binary by the synthetic division method, proceed as follows. Divide the decimal number by 2. If there is a remainder, put a 1 in the LSD of the partially formed binary number; if there is no remainder, put a 0 in the LSD of the binary number. Divide the quotient from the first division by 2, and repeat the process. If there is a remainder record a 1; if there is no remainder, record a 0. Continue until the quotient has been reduced to 0.

Example:

```
47 (10) = ? binary
```

```
                    Quotient Remainder
                    --------  ---------
    47/2    =        23    +   1 --------------------------------|
                                                                 |
    23/2    =        11    +   1 ----------------------------|   |
                                                             |   |
    11/2    =         5    +   1 ------------------------|   |   |
                                                         |   |   |
     5/2    =         2    +   1 -----------------|      |   |   |
                                                  |      |   |   |
     2/2    =         1    +   0 ------------|    |      |   |   |
                                            |    |      |   |   |
     1/2    -         0    +   1 -|         |    |      |   |   |
                                 |         |    |      |   |   |
                                 v    v    v    v      v   v   v
                                 1    0    1    1      1   1
```

Therefore, 47 (10) = 101111 (2).

A.2 GROUPED-BIT NUMBER SYSTEMS

A.2.1 Octal

It is probably quite evident at this time that the binary number system, although quite nice for computers, is a little cumbersome for human usage. It is very easy for humans to make errors in reading and writing quantities of large binary numbers. The octal or base 8 numbering system helps to alleviate this problem. The base 8 or octal number system utilizes the digits 0 through 7 in forming numbers. The count-and-carry method mentioned earlier applies here also. Table A-1 shows the octal numbers with their binary equivalents.

Table A-1 Decimal/octal/binary equivalents

Decimal	Octal	Binary	Decimal	Octal	Binary
0	0	0	7	7	111
1	1	1	8	10	1000
2	2	10	9	11	1001
3	3	11	10	12	1010
4	4	100	11	13	1011
5	5	101	12	14	1100
6	6	110	13	15	1101

The octal number system eliminates many of the problems involved in handling the binary number system used by a computer. To convert from binary numbers to octal numbers, the binary digits are separated into 3-bit groups. These

3-bit groups can be represented by one octal digit using the previous table of equivalents. A binary number,

11010111101

is separated into 3-bit groups by starting with the LSD end of the number and supplying leading zeros if necessary:

011 010 111 101

The binary groups are then replaced by their octal equivalents:

$$
\begin{array}{rcl}
011\ (2) & = & 3\ (8) \\
010\ (2) & = & 2\ (8) \\
111\ (2) & = & 7\ (8) \\
101\ (2) & = & 5\ (8)
\end{array}
$$

and the binary number is converted to its octal equivalent, 3275. Conversely, an octal number can be expanded to a binary number using the same table of equivalents:

5307(8) = 101 011 000 111 (2)

A.2.2 Hexadecimal

Another convenient number system is the hexadecimal or base 16 number system. Like octal, hexadecimal is used to represent binary numbers in a more convenient fashion. Since it is base 16, there are 16 characters needed to represent the 16 digits in this number system. The decimal-hexadecimal-binary equivalents are shown in Table A-2.

Table A-2 Decimal / Hexadecimal / Binary Equivalents

Dec	Hex	Bin	Dec	Hex	Bin	Dec	Hex	Bin	Dec	Hex	Bin
0	0	0000	4	4	0100	8	8	1000	12	C	1100
1	1	0001	5	5	0101	9	9	1001	13	D	1101
2	2	0010	6	6	0110	10	A	1010	14	E	1110
3	3	0011	7	7	0111	11	B	1011	15	F	1111

In a fashion similar to the method for converting binary to octal, binary may be converted to hexadecimal by separating the binary digits into 4-bit groups. These 4-bit groups may be represented by one hexadecimal digit using Table A-2 as follows. The binary number

11010111101

is separated into 4-bit groups (supply leading zeros, if necessary):

$$0110 \quad 1011 \quad 1101$$

and then the groups are replaced by their hexadecimal equivalents, 6 B D. That is,

$$6BD \ (16) \ = \ 0110 \ 1011 \ 1101 \ (2)$$

A.2.2 Octal-to-Decimal Conversion

Octal numbers may be converted to decimal by multiplying each digit by its weight or position coefficient and then adding the resulting products. The position coefficients in this case are powers of 8, which is the base of the octal number system.

Example:

$$2167 \ (8) \ = \ ? \ \text{decimal}$$

$$2167 \ (8) \ =$$

$$
\begin{aligned}
&+\ 7\ *\ 8**0 &= 7\ *\ \ \ 1\ &=\ \ \ \ \ \ 7 \\
&+\ 6\ *\ 8**1 &= 6\ *\ \ \ 8\ &=\ \ \ \ \ 48 \\
&+\ 1\ *\ 8**2 &= 1\ *\ \ 64\ &=\ \ \ \ \ 64 \\
&+\ 2\ *\ 8**3 &= 2\ *\ 512\ &=\ \ 1024
\end{aligned}
$$

Therefore, 2167 (8) = 1143 (10).

A.2.3 Decimal-to-Octal Conversion

There are two commonly used methods for converting decimal numbers to their octal equivalents. The reader may choose the method that he prefers.

Subtraction-of-powers method: The following procedure is followed to convert a decimal number to its octal equivalent. Subtract from the decimal number the highest possible value of the form $a*8**n$, where a is a number between 1 and 7 and n is an integer. Record the value of a. Continue to subtract decreasing powers of 8 (recording the value of a each time) until the decimal number is reduced to zero. Record a value of $a = 0$ for all powers of 8 that could not be subtracted. Table A-3 may be used to convert any number that can be represented by 12-bits (4095 or less).

Example:

$$2591 \ (10) \ = \ ? \ \text{octal}$$

```
   2591                                    5   0   3   7
  -2560 = 5 * 8**3 = 5 * 512 -----^       ^   ^   ^
  -----                                   |   |   |
     31                                   |   |   |
  -   0 = 0 * 8**2 = 0 *  64 ---------|   |   |   |
  -----                                   |   |   |
     31                                       |   |
  -  24 = 3 * 8**1 = 3 *   8 -------------|   |   |
  -----                                       |
      7                                       |
  -   7 = 7 * 8**0 = 7 *   1 -----------------|
  -----
      0
```

Therefore, 2591 (10) = 5037 (8).

Table A-3 Octal-decimal conversion.

Octal-Digit Position	Positional Coefficients (Multipliers)							
8**n	0	1	2	3	4	5	6	7
1st (8**0)	0	1	2	3	4	5	6	7
2nd (8**1)	0	8	16	24	32	40	48	56
3rd (8**2)	0	64	128	192	256	320	384	448
4th (8**3)	0	512	1024	1536	2048	2560	3072	3584

Division method: A second method for converting a decimal number to its octal equivalent is by successive division by 8. Divide the decimal number by 8 and record the remainder as the least significant digit of the octal equivalent. Continue dividing by 8, recording the remainders as the successively higher significant digits until the quotient is reduced to zero.

Example:

```
            1376 (10) = ? octal

            Quotient  Remainder
            --------  ---------
  1376/8 =     172   +   0 ------------------------------|
                                                         |
   172/8 =      21   +   4 --------------------------|   |
                                                     |   |
    21/8 =       2   +   5 ----------------------|   |   |
                                                 |   |   |
     2/8 =       0   +   2 ----------------|     |   |   |
                                           |     |   |   |
                                           |     |   |   |
                                           v     v   v   v
                                           2     5   4   0
```

Therefore, 1376 (10) = 2540 (8).

Using the division method to convert from one base to another is fine as long as one remembers that the arithmetic used must be in the base that one is converting from. Thus if we wish to convert 2540 in base 8 to its decimal equivalent, the example would appear as

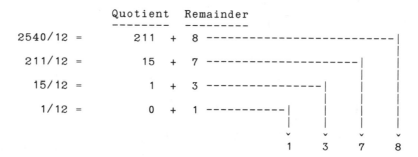

```
                    Quotient   Remainder
                    --------    ---------
    2540/12  =         211   +    8  --------------------------------|
                                                                     |
     211/12  =          15   +    7  ----------------------|         |
                                                           |         |
      15/12  =           1   +    3  ----------------|     |         |
                                                     |     |         |
       1/12  =           0   +    1  -----------|    |     |         |
                                                |    |     |         |
                                                v    v     v         v
                                                1    3     7         8
```

Therefore, 2540 (8) = 1378 (10). Here 12 (8) = 10 (10) so that all arithmetic is in octal!

A.3 ARITHMETIC OPERATIONS WITH BINARY AND OCTAL NUMBERS

Now that the reader understands the conversion techniques between the familiar decimal number system and the binary and octal number systems, arithmetic operations with binary and octal numbers will be described. The reader should remember that the binary numbers are used in the computer and that the octal numbers are used as a means of *representing* the binary numbers conveniently.

A.3.1 Binary Addition

Addition of binary numbers follows the same rules as decimal or other bases. In adding decimal 1 + 8, we obtain the sum of 9. This is the highest-value digit. Adding one more requires the least significant digit to become a 0 with a carry of 1 to the next place in the number. Similarly, adding binary 0 + 1 we reach the highest value a single digit can have in the binary system, and adding one more (1 + 1) requires a carry to the next higher power (1 + 1 = 10). Take the binary numbers 101 + 10 (i.e., 5 + 2):

```
 101 = 5 (10)
+010 = 2 (10)
 ---   -
 111 = 7 (10)
```

0 + 1 = 1, 1 + 0 = 1, and 0 + 1 = 1 with no carries required. The answer is 111, which is 7. Suppose that we add 111 to 101:

```
11  ← carries

 111 =  7 (10)
+101 =  5 (10)
 ---    --
1100 =12 (10)
```

Now $1 + 1 = 0$ plus a carry of 1. In the second column, 1 plus the carry $1 = 0$, plus another carry. The third column is $1 + 1 = 0$ with a carry, plus the previous carry, or $1 + 1 + 1 = 11$. Our answer, 1100, is equal to $1 * 2**3 + 1 * 2**2$ or $8 + 4 = 12$, which is the correct solution for $7 + 5$.

A.3.2 Octal Addition

Addition for octal numbers should be no problem if we keep in mind the following basic rules for addition.

1. If the sum of any column is equal to or greater than the base of the system being used, the base must be subtracted from the sum to obtain the final result of the column.

2. If the sum of any column is equal to or greater than the base, there will be a carry to the next column equal to the number of times the base was subtracted.

3. If the result of any column is less than the base, the base is not subtracted and no carry will be generated. Examples:

```
                               1          ← carries
 5 (8) = 5 (10)         3 5 (8) = 29 (10)
+3 (8) = 3 (10)         6 3 (8) = 51 (10)
 -                      ---
 8                      10 8
-8                      -8-8
10 (8) = 8 (10)        1 2 0 (8) = 80 (10)
```

A.4 NEGATIVE NUMBERS AND SUBTRACTION

Up to this point only positive numbers have been considered. Negative numbers and subtraction can be handled in the binary system in either of three ways: direct binary subtraction, by the two's complement method, or by the one's-complement method.

A.4.1 Binary Subtraction (direct)

Binary numbers may be directly subtracted in a manner similar to decimal subtraction. The essential difference is that if a borrow is required, it is equal to the base of the system, 2:

```
                        110 = 6 (10)
                       -101 = 5 (10)
                        ---
                        001 = 1 (10)
```

To subtract 1 from 0 in the first column, a borrow of 1 was made from the second column which effectively added 2 to the first column. After the borrow, $2 - 1 = 1$ in the first column; in the second column $0 - 0 = 0$; and in the third column $1 - 1 = 0$.

The method of representation for direct binary subtraction is to show both the *sign* and the *magnitude* of the numbers being subtracted (the lack of a sign being taken to mean that the number is positive). In the example above, a smaller number was subtracted from a larger number so that the result was positive. If the problem had been stated as

```
                        101 =  5 (10)
                       -110 =  6 (10)
                        ---    -
                       -001 =-1 (10)
```

then the technique given for subtraction would not have worked. The technique requires us to always subtract the smaller number from the larger one and adjust the sign of the result if necessary.

As stated, the technique for subtracting binary *sign-magnitude* numbers on a computer is just too complicated. What is needed is a better, more uniform method which does not specify side conditions. What is used is *two's-complement arithmetic* because of its inherent simplicity for the computer.

A.4.2 Two's-Complement Arithmetic

To see how negative numbers are handled in the computer, consider a mechanical register, such as a car mileage indicator, being rotated backward. A five-digit register approaching and passing through zero would read the following:

```
                        00005
                        00004
                        00003
                        00002
                        00001
                        00000
                        99999
                        99998
                         etc.
```

It should be clear that the number 99998 corresponds to -2. Further, if we add

```
                        00005
                        99998
                        -----
carry out of MSB 1      00003
```

and ignore the carry to the left, we have effectively performed the operation of subtracting

$$5 - 2 = 3$$

The number 99998 in this example is described as the *ten's-complement* of 2. Thus in the decimal number system, subtraction may be performed by *adding* the ten's complement of the number to be subtracted.

If a system of complements were to be used for representing negative numbers, the minus sign could be omitted in negative numbers. Thus all numbers could be represented with five digits; 2 represented as 00002 and -2 represented as 99998. Using such a system requires that a convention be established as to what is and is not a negative number. For example, if the mileage indicator is turned back to 48732, is it a negative 51268, or a positive 48732? With an ability to represent a total of 100,000 different numbers (0 to 99999), it would seem reasonable to use half for positive numbers and half for negative numbers. In this situation, 0 to 49999 would be regarded as positive, and 50000 to 99999 would be regarded as negative.

In this same manner, the two's complement of binary numbers are used to represent negative numbers and to carry out binary subtraction. In 12-bit octal notation, numbers from 0000 to 3777 are regarded as positive and the numbers from 4000 to 7777 are regarded as negative.

The two's-complement of a number is defined as that number which when added to the original number will result in a sum of zero. The binary number 110110110110 has a two's-complement equal to 001001001010, as shown in the following addition:

```
                   110 110 110 110
                   001 001 001 010
Carry from         ---------------
MSB            1   000 000 000 000
```

The easiest method of finding a two's-complement is first to obtain the one's-complement, which is formed by setting each bit to the opposite value:

```
        101 000 110 111    number
        010 111 001 000    one's-complement of the number
```

The two's-complement of the number is then obtained by adding 1 to the one's-complement:

```
        110 001 110 010    number
        001 110 001 101    one's-complement of the number
                    +1     add 1
        ---------------
        001 110 001 110    two's-complement of the number
```

Subtraction may be performed using the two's-complement method. That is, to subtract A from B, A must be expressed as its two's-complement, and then the value of B is added to it. Example:

```
        010 010 010 111     A

        101 101 101 001     two's-complement of A
        011 001 100 010     B
        ---------------
1       000 111 001 011     B - A
(carry is ignored)
```

A.4.3 One's-Complement Arithmetic

In generating the two's-complement form of a binary number, we first obtain the one's-complement form. This form may also be used to perform subtraction, as follows:

```
        010 010 010 111     A

        101 101 101 000     one's-complement of A
        011 001 100 010     B
        ---------------
1       000 111 001 010     B - A
|------------- → 1          carry is added in
        ---------------
        000 111 001 011     true result
```

The difference between one's- and two's-complement arithmetic is that in the first case the carry is not ignored (e.g., it is added back in), whereas in the second case it is.

A.4.4 Octal Subtraction

Octal subtraction can be performed directly as illustrated in the following examples:

```
3567 - 2533 = ?     2022 - 1234 = ?

      3567                2022
    - 2533              - 1234
      -----               -----
      1034                0566
```

Whenever a borrow is needed in octal subtraction, an 8 is borrowed, as in the second example above. In the first column, an 8 is borrowed which is added to the 2 already in the first column and the 4 is subtracted from the resulting 10. In the second column, an 8 is borrowed and added to the 1 which is already in the column (after the previous borrow) and the 3 is subtracted from the resulting 9. In the third column the 2 is subtracted from a borrowed 1 (originally a borrowed 8), and in the last column 1 – 1 = 0.

Octal subtraction may be performed by adding the eight's-complement of the subtrahend to the minuhend. The eight's complement is formed by generating the seven's-complement (the difference between 777...777 and the number) and adding in one.

EXERCISES

1. ***Decimal-to-binary conversion:*** Convert the following decimal numbers to their binary equivalents:

1.	15	11.	4095
2.	18	12.	1502
3.	42	13.	377
4.	100	14.	501
5.	235	15.	828
6.	1	16.	907
7.	294	17.	4000
8.	117·	18.	3456
9.	86	19.	2278
10.	4090	20.	1967

2. ***Binary-to-decimal conversion:*** Convert the following binary numbers to their decimal equivalents:

1.	110	9.	11011011101
2.	101	10.	1110001110001
3.	1110110	11.	111010110100
4.	1011110	12.	111111111111
5.	0110110	13.	101011010101
6.	11111	14.	111111
7.	1010	15.	000101001
8.	110111	16.	111111111111

3. ***Binary-to-octal conversion:*** Convert the following binary numbers to their octal equivalents:

1.	1110	9.	10111111
2.	0110	10.	11111111111
3.	111	11.	010110101011
4.	101111101	12.	111110110100
5.	110111110	13.	010100001011
6.	100000	14.	000010101101
7.	11000111	15.	110100100100
8.	011000	16.	010011111010

4. *Octal-to-binary conversion:*   Convert the following octal numbers to their binary equivalents:

1.	354	9.	70
2.	736	10.	64
3.	15	11.	7777
4.	10	12.	7765
5.	7	13.	3214
6.	5424	14.	4532
7.	307	15.	7033
8.	1101	16.	1243

5. *Decimal-to-octal conversion:*   Convert the following decimal numbers to their octal equivalents:

1.	796	7.	1080
2.	32	8.	1344
3.	4037	9.	1512
4.	580	10.	3077
5.	1000	11.	4056
6.	3	12.	4095

6. *Decimal-to-hexadecimal conversion:*   Convert the decimal numbers in (5) to their hexadecimal equivalents.

7. *Octal-to-decimal conversion:*   Convert the following octal numbers to their decimal equivalents:

1.	17	7.	7773
2.	37	8.	7777
3.	734	9.	3257
4.	1000	10.	4577
5.	1200	11.	0012
6.	742	12.	0256

8. Perform the following binary additions:

```
1.    10110        2.    100         3.    11011
    +  101             + `10             + 0010
    -----             ----             ------

4.    10110111      5.    1110        6.    100111
    +        1           100              111001
    --------           + 11             +101101
                       ----             -------

7.    1101          8.    1111        9.    11011001
       101                 101              10010011
    +  11               +1000             +11100011
    ----                -----             ---------
```

```
10.   101          11.  110111      12.   11011011
        1               100100            10111011
     +110             +110001            00101011
     ----             -------            01010111
                                       +01111101
                                       ---------
```

9. Find the one's-complement and the two's-complement of the following numbers:

```
1.  011 100 110 010      7.   000 000 000 111
2.  010 111 011 111      8.   100 000 000 000
3.  011 110 000 000      9.   100 000 010 010
4.  000 000 000 000     10.   100 001 100 110
5.  000 000 000 001     11.   111 111 111 110
6.  000 100 100 100     12.   111 111 111 111
```

10. Subtract the following binary numbers directly:

```
1.    101000001         3.    101011010111
    - 010111101            - 011111111101
    -----------            --------------

2.   1010111010         4.    101111100111
    - 0101110101           - 010101110010
    -----------            --------------
```

11. Perform the following subtractions by the two's-complement method. Check your work by direct subtraction. Show all work.

```
1.  011 011 011 011 - 001 111 010 110
2.  000 111 111 111 - 000 001 001 101
3.  011 111 111 101 - 010 101 100 011
4.  001 101 111 110 - 001 100 101 011
5.  011 111 111 111 - 010 101 101 101
```

Appendix B:
Primer of Logic Operations

Computers use logic operations in addition to arithmetic operations to solve problems. The logic operations have a direct relationship with the algebraic system and allow for the presentation of logic statements in a special algebra of logic. In logic, three basic connectives are used to express the relationship between two statements. These are the AND, the OR, and the exclusive-OR.

B.1 THE AND OPERATION

The following simple circuit with two switches illustrates the AND operation. If current is allowed to flow through a switch, the switch is said to have a value of 1. If the switch is open and current cannot flow, the switch has a value of 0. If the whole circuit is considered, it will have a value of 1 (i.e., current may flow through it) whenever both A and B are 1. This is the AND operation.

The AND operation is often stated A ∧ B = F. The inverted ∨ symbol (∧) is used to represent the AND connective. The relationship between the variables and the resulting value of F is summarized in the following table.

A	B	F
0	0	0
0	1	0
1	0	0
1	1	1

When the AND operation is applied to binary numbers, a binary 1 will appear in the result if a binary 1 appeared in the corresponding position of the two numbers. The AND operation can be used to mask out a portion of a 12-bit number:

```
-----------------------------------------
To be          To be Retained
Masked         for Subsequent
Out            Operation
-----------------------------------------
010 101        010 101           (12 bit number)
000 000        111 111           (mask)
000 000        010 101           (result)
-----------------------------------------
```

B.2 THE OR OPERATION

A second logic operation is the OR (sometimes called the inclusive-OR). Statements that are combined using the OR connective are illustrated by the following circuit diagram:

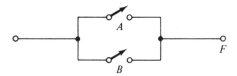

In this diagram current may flow whenever either A or B (or both) is closed (F = 1 if A = 1, or B = 1, or A = 1 and B = 1). This operation is expressed by a " ∨ "; thus A ∨ B = F. The following table shows the resulting value of F for changing values of A and B:

```
--------------------
A      B      F
--------------------
0      0      0
0      1      1
1      0      1
1      1      1
--------------------
```

Thus, if A and B are the 12-bit numbers given here, A ∨ B is evaluated as follows:

```
    A   = 011 010 011 111
    B   = 100 110 010 011
A ∨ B   = 111 110 011 111
```

B.3 THE EXCLUSIVE-OR OPERATION

A third logic operation is the exclusive-OR. The exclusive-OR is similar to the inclusive-OR with the exception that one set of conditions for A and B are excluded. This exclusion can be symbolized in the circuit diagram by connecting the two switches together mechanically. This connection makes it impossible for the switches to be closed simultaneously, although they may be open simultaneously or individually.

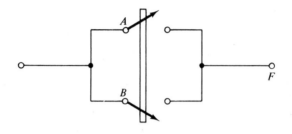

Thus the circuit is completed with A = 1 and B = 0, and when A = 0 and B = 1. This operation is expressed by the ⊻; thus A ⊻ B = F. The results of the exclusive-OR operation are summarized in a table:

A	B	F
0	0	0
0	1	1
1	0	1
1	1	0

The exclusive-OR of two 12-bit numbers is evaluated and labeled F in the following operation:

$$A = 011\ 010\ 011\ 111$$
$$B = 100\ 110\ 010\ 011$$
$$F = 111\ 100\ 001\ 100$$

B.4 BOOLEAN ALGEBRA

Although we have considered only the three logical functions ∧, ∨ , and ⊻, there are others that we could have presented. These functions may be developed by considering all possible resulting values of F for changing values of A and B. The table of A's, B's, and F's is as follows:

A	B	F 0	F 1	F 2	F 3	F 4	F 5	F 6	F 7	F 8	F 9	F 10	F 11	F 12	F 13	F 14	F 15
0	0	0	0	0	0	0	0	0	0	1	1	1	1	1	1	1	1
0	1	0	0	0	0	1	1	1	1	0	0	0	0	1	1	1	1
1	0	0	0	1	1	0	0	1	1	0	0	1	1	0	0	1	1
1	1	0	1	0	1	0	1	0	1	0	1	0	1	0	1	0	1

There are 16 different F's corresponding to two things (A and B) with two states (0 and 1) taken two at a time (16 = [(2**2)**2]).

We may recognize that F(1) is the AND operation, F(7) the OR operation, and F(6) the exclusive-OR operation. In fact, all F's have been named and represent such operations as A[F(3)], NOT B[F(10)], and A AND NOT B[F(2)]. From this set of 16 functions it is possible to form an algebra, called *Boolean algebra*, by choosing a set of functions (AND, OR, and NOT) different from the first three functions considered (e.g., AND, OR, and exclusive-OR), from which all other functions may be generated.

The term "algebra" refers to a mathematical system in which certain rules (called postulates) are defined and which relate how quantities in a certain domain may be manipulated. Boolean algebra is the product of George Boole, a nineteenth-century English mathematician, who wished to devise a mathematical formalism in which to express the concepts of symbolic logic. By developing a new algebra he hoped to be able to use the deductive properties of the system to deduce (prove) theorems from the given postulates.

The basic postulates in Boolean algebra are:

1. *Commutativity:*

```
A V B = B V A
A ∧ B = B ∧ A
```

2. *Associativity:*

```
A V (B V C) = (A V B) V C
A ∧ (B ∧ C) = (A ∧ B) ∧ C
```

3. *Distributivity:*

```
A ∧ (B V C) = (A ∧ B) V (A ∧ C)
A V B ∧ C = (A V B) ∧ (A V C)
```

4. *Idempotence:*

```
A V A = A
A ∧ A = A
```

5. *Operation on 0 and 1:*

```
0 V A = A
1 V A = 1
0 ∧ A = 0
1 ∧ A = A
```

6. *Complementarity:*

```
A ∧ ~A = 0
A V ~A = 1 where ~A = NOT A
```

plus the laws of dualization, referred to as DeMorgan's laws:

7.
$$\sim (A \land B) = \sim A \lor \sim B$$
$$\sim (A \lor B) = \sim A \land \sim B$$

These postulates are actually more than sufficient, and it is easy to demonstrate that one postulate may be proved by utilizing the others.

For example, to prove

$$(A \lor B) \land (A \lor C) = A \lor B \land C$$

we show the following steps:

$$(A \lor B) \land (A \lor C) = (A \land A) \lor (A \land B) \lor (A \land C) \lor (B \land C)$$

But

$$(A \land A) = A = (A \land 1)$$
$$(A \land B) \lor (A \land C) = A \land (B \lor C)$$

so

$$(A \lor B) \land (A \lor C) = (A \land 1) \lor A \land (B \lor C) \lor (B \land C)$$

Now by applying the steps

$$(A \land 1) \lor A \land (B \lor C) = A \land (1 \lor B \lor C)$$
$$(1 \lor B \lor C) = 1 \lor (B \lor C) = 1$$

the result is

$$(A \lor B) \land (A \lor C) = A \land 1 \lor (B \land C)$$
$$= A \lor (B \land C)$$

Another means of proving such a deduction is through the use of a truth table. A truth table is nothing more than the table used show the results of $A \lor B = F$ or $A \land B = F$, and so on. Each vertical column in the table represents a step toward the generation of the final desired result, which is equality of the functions on the right- and left-hand sides of the given equation. If the column result for the right-hand side agrees with the column result for the left-hand side, then equality is assumed to have been demonstrated.

For example, we may show that the equation

$$A \land B = \sim (\sim A \lor \sim B)$$

is true by constructing a truth table:

A	B	~A	~B	(~A V ~B)	~(~A V ~B)	A ∧ B
0	0	1	1	1	0	0
0	1	1	0	1	0	0
1	0	0	1	1	0	0
1	1	0	0	0	1	1

Since the last two columns are equal, the truth of the equation has been demonstrated.

Besides demonstrating the truth-table method, this example also points out that it is possible to construct the Boolean functions from each other. Thus given OR and NOT, AND can be constructed along with the other 13 Boolean functions. Interestingly enough, two of the functions (labelled $F(8)$ and $F(14)$ and called NOR and NAND, respectively), are universal functions in that from just the one function all other functions may be constructed.

EXERCISES

1. Prove that $A \wedge B = \sim(\sim A \vee \sim B)$ by use of the postulates of Boolean algebra.

2. Prove that $(A \vee B) \wedge (A \vee C) = A \vee B \wedge C$ by use of the truth-table method.

Appendix C:
ASCII and Radix-50
Character Sets

C.1 ASCII CHARACTER SET

Even-Parity Bit	7-Bit Octal Code	Character	Remarks
0	000	NUL	Null, tape feed, control/shift/P.
1	001	SOH	Start of heading: also SOM, start of message, control/A.
1	002	STX	Start of text; also EOA, End of address, control/B.
0	003	ETX	End of text; also EOM, end of message, control/C.
1	004	EOT	End of transmission (end); shuts off TWX machines, control/D.
0	005	ENQ	Enquiry (enqry); also WRU, control/E.
0	006	ACK	Acknowledge; also RU, control/F.
1	007	BEL	Rings the bell. Control/G.
1	010	BS	Backspace; also FEO, format effector. Backspaces some machines, control/H.
0	011	HT	Horizontal tab. Control/I.
0	012	LF	Line feed or line space. (new line); advances paper to next line, duplicated by control/J.
1	013	VT	Vertical tab (VTAB). Control/K.
0	014	FF	Form feed to top of next page (page). Control/L.
1	015	CR	Carriage return to beginning of line. Duplicated by Control/M.
1	016	SO	Shift out; changes ribbon color to red. Control/N.

Even-Parity Bit	7-Bit Octal Code	Character	Remarks
0	017	SI	Shift in; changes ribbon color to black. Control/O.
1	020	DLE	Data line escape. Control/P (DC0).
0	021	DC1	Device control 1, turns transmitter (reader) on, control/Q(X on).
0	022	DC2	Device control 2, turns punch or auxiliary on. Control/R (tape, aux on).
1	023	DC3	Device control 3, turns transmitter (reader) off, control/S (X off).
0	024	DC4	Device control 4, turns punch or auxilliary off. Control/T (aux off).
1	025	NAK	Negative acknowledge; also ERR, error. Control/U.
1	026	SYN	Synchronous file (SYNC). Control/V.
0	027	ETB	End of transmission block; also LEM, Logical end of medium. Control/W.
0	030	CAN	Cancel (Cancl). Control/X.
1	031	EM	End of medium. Control/Y.
1	032	SUB	Substitute. Control/Z.
0	033	ESC	Escape. Control/shift/K.
1	034	FS	File separator. Control/shift/L.
0	035	GS	Group separator. Control/shift/M.
0	036	RS	Record separator. Control/shift/N.
1	037	US	Unit separator. Control/shift/O.
1	040	SP	Space.
0	041	!	
0	042	"	
1	043	#	
0	044	$	
1	045	%	
1	046	&	
0	047	'	Accent acute or apostrophe.
0	050	(	
1	051	)	
1	052	*	
0	053	+	
1	054	,	
0	055	−	Hyphen
0	056	.	
1	057	/	
0	060	0	
1	061	1	
1	062	2	
0	063	3	
1	064	4	
0	065	5	
0	066	6	
1	067	7	
1	070	8	
0	071	9	
0	072	:	
1	073	;	
0	074	<	
1	075	=	
1	076	>	
0	077	?	
1	100	@	

Even-Parity Bit	7-Bit Octal Code	Character	Remarks
0	101	A	
0	102	B	
1	103	C	
0	104	D	
1	105	E	
1	106	F	
0	107	G	
0	110	H	
1	111	I	
1	112	J	
0	113	K	
1	114	L	
0	115	M	
0	116	N	
1	117	O	
0	120	P	
1	121	Q	
1	122	R	
0	123	S	
1	124	T	
0	125	U	
0	126	V	
1	127	W	
1	130	X	
0	131	Y	
0	132	Z	
1	133	[	Shift/K.
0	134	\	Shift/L.
1	135	]	Shift/M.
1	136	^	Up arrow on some machines.
0	137	_	Underline, back arrow (←) on some machines.
0	140	`	Accent grave.
1	141	a	
1	142	b	
0	143	c	
1	144	d	
0	145	e	
0	146	f	
1	147	g	
1	150	h	
0	151	i	
0	152	j	
1	153	k	
0	154	l	
1	155	m	
1	156	n	
0	157	o	
1	160	p	
0	161	q	
0	162	r	
1	163	s	
0	164	t	
1	165	u	
1	166	v	
0	167	w	
0	170	x	
1	171	y	
1	172	z	

Even-Parity Bit	7-Bit Octal Code	Character	Remarks
0	173	⁝	
1	174	|	
0	175	⁝	This code generated by alt mode.
0	176	~	This code generated by prefix key,
1	177	DEL	Delete, rub out.

C.2 RADIX-50 CHARACTER SET

Character	ASCII Octal Equivalent	Radix-50 Equivalent
Space	40	0
A-Z	101-132	1-32
$	44	33
.	56	34
Unused		35
0-9	60-71	36-47

The maximum Radix-50 value is, thus,

$$47 * 50^2 + 47 * 50^1 + 47 = 174777$$

The following table provides a convenient means of translating between the ASCII character set and its Radix-50 equivalents. For example, given the ASCII string X2B, the Radix-50 equivalent is (arithmetic is performed in octal):

```
        X = 113000
        2 = 002400
        B = 000002
        -----------
      X2B = 115402
```

Single Character or First Character		Second Character		Third Character	
A	003100	A	000050	A	000001
B	006200	B	000120	B	000002
C	011300	C	000170	C	000003
D	014400	D	000240	D	000004
E	017500	E	000310	E	000005
F	022600	F	000360	F	000006
G	025700	G	000430	G	000007
H	031000	H	000500	H	000010
I	034100	I	000550	I	000011
J	037200	J	000620	J	000012
K	042300	K	000670	K	000013
L	045400	L	000740	L	000014
M	050500	M	001010	M	000015
N	053600	N	001060	N	000016
O	056700	O	001130	O	000017
P	062000	P	001200	P	000020
Q	065100	Q	001250	Q	000021

443

Single Character or First Character		Second Character		Third Character	
R	070200	R	001320	R	000022
S	073300	S	001370	S	000023
T	076400	T	001440	T	000024
U	101500	U	001510	U	000025
V	104600	V	001560	V	000026
W	107700	W	001630	W	000027
X	113000	X	001700	X	000030
Y	116100	Y	001750	Y	000031
Z	121200	Z	002020	Z	000032
$	124300	$	002070	$	000033
.	127400	.	002140	.	000034
unused	132500	unused	002210	unused	000035
0	135600	0	002260	0	000036
1	140700	1	002330	1	000037
2	144000	2	002400	2	000040
3	147100	3	002450	3	000041
4	152200	4	002520	4	000042
5	155300	5	002570	5	000043
6	160400	6	002640	6	000044
7	163500	7	002710	7	000045
8	166600	8	002760	8	000046
9	171700	9	003030	9	000047

Appendix D:
Instruction Repertoire
of the PDP-11

```
-------------------------------------------------------------------------
Notation:
-------------------------------------------------------------------------
```

1. For order codes:

.	word/byte bit; set for byte instruction, cleared for word instruction
SS	source field (Mode, Register)
DD	destination field (Mode, Register)
XX	offset (8-bit)
R	a general purpose register

2. For operations:

( )	contents of
~	not
∧	and
V	or
∀	exclusive or
-(SP) ←	"is pushed onto the processor stack"
← (SP)+	"the contents of the top of the processor stack is popped and becomes"

3. For condition codes:

?	set conditionally
—	not affected
0	cleared
1	set

```
==============================================================================
Mnemonic              Instruction              Op Code           Condition
                      Operation                                  Codes
                                                                 ZNCV
==============================================================================
------------------------------------------------------------------------------
Double Operand Group (general): OPR src,dst
------------------------------------------------------------------------------

MOV(B)                MOVe (Byte)              .1SSDD            ??-0
                      (dst) ← (src)

CMP(B)                CoMPare (Byte)           .2SSDD            ????
                      compute (src) - (dst),
                      set condition codes.

BIT(B)                Bit Test (Byte)          .3SSDD            ??-0
                      compute (src) ∧ (dst),
                      set condition codes.

BIC(B)                Bit Clear (Byte)         .4SSDD            ??-0
                      (dst) ← ~(src) ∧ (dst)

BIS(B)                Bit Set (Byte)           .5SSDD            ??-0
                      (dst) ← (src) V (dst)

ADD                   ADD                      06SSDD            ????
                      (dst) ← (src) + (dst)

SUB                   SUBtract                 16SSDD            ????
                      (dst) ← (dst) - (src)

------------------------------------------------------------------------------
Double Operand Group (register): OPR src,reg or OPR reg,dst     ZNCV
------------------------------------------------------------------------------

MUL                   MULtiply                 070RSS            ???0
                      (R, R V 1) ← (R) * (src)

DIV                   DIVide                   071RSS            ????
                      (R)     ← quotient of (R,R V 1)/(src)
                      (R V 1) ← remainder of (R,R V 1)/(src), R even

ASH                   Arithmetic SHift         072RSS            ????
                      (R) ← (R) * 2**(src)

ASHC                  Arithmetic SHift Combined  073RSS          ????
                      (R,R V 1) ← (R,R V 1) * 2**(src),
                      R even

RMR                   Rotate Multiple Right    073RSS            ????
                      (R) ← (R) rotated right |(src)|,
                      R odd and -16 ≤ (src) ≤ 0

XOR                   eXclusive OR             074RDD            ??-0
                      (dst) ← (R) ∀ (dst)
```

```
============================================================================
Mnemonic               Instruction           Op Code        Condition
                       Operation                             Codes
                                                             ZNCV
============================================================================
----------------------------------------------------------------------------
Single Operand Group:  OPR dst                               ZNCV
----------------------------------------------------------------------------

CLR(B)             CLeaR (Byte)              .050DD          1000
                   (dst) ← 0

COM(B)             COMplement (Byte)         .051DD          ??10
                   (dst) ← ~(dst)

INC(B)             INCrement (Byte)          .052DD          ??-?
                   (dst) ← (dst) + 1

DEC(B)             DECrement (Byte)          .053DD          ??-?
                   (dst) ← (dst) - 1

NEG(B)             NEGate (Byte)             .054DD          ????
                   (dst) ←  -(dst)

ADC(B)             ADd Carry (Byte)          .055DD          ????
                   (dst) ← (dst) + (C)

SBC(B)             SuBtract Carry (Byte)     .056DD          ????
                   (dst) ← (dst) - (C)

TST(B)             TeST (Byte)               .057DD          ??00
                   (dst) ← (dst) - 0

ROR(B)             ROtate Right (Byte)       .060DD          ????
                   rotate right 1 place with C

ROL(B)             ROtate Left (Byte)        .061DD          ????
                   rotate left 1 place with C

ASR(B)             Arithmetic Shift Right (Byte)  .062DD     ????
                   (dst) ← (dst) / 2, result truncated
                   (shift right with sign extension)

ASL(B)             Arithmetic Shift Left (Byte)  .063DD      ????
                   (dst) ← 2 * (dst)
                   (shift left with low-order bit zeroed)

SWAB               SWAp Bytes                0003DD          ??00
                   bytes of a word are exchanged

SXT                Sign eXTend               0067DD          ?--0
                   (dst) ←  -1 * (N)

----------------------------------------------------------------------------
Unconditional Branches:  BR loc and JMP dst                 ZNCV
----------------------------------------------------------------------------

BR                 BRanch (unconditionally)  0004XX          ----
                   (PC) ← loc

JMP                JuMP                      0001DD          ----
                   (PC) ← dst
```

Mnemonic	Instruction Operation	Op Code	Condition Codes ZNCV

Conditional Branches: Bxx loc   ZNCV

Mnemonic	Instruction Operation	Op Code	Condition Codes ZNCV
BNE	Branch if Not Equal (Zero) $(PC) \leftarrow$ loc if $Z = 0$	0010XX	----
BEQ	Branch if EQual (Zero) $(PC) \leftarrow$ loc if $Z = 1$	0014XX	----
BGE	Branch if Greater or Equal (zero) $(PC) \leftarrow$ loc if $N \,\forall\, V = 0$	0020XX	----
BLT	Branch if Less Than (Zero) $(PC) \leftarrow$ loc if $N \,\forall\, V = 1$	0024XX	----
BGT	Branch if Greater Than (Zero) $(PC) \leftarrow$ loc if $Z \,V\, (N \,\forall\, V) = 0$	0030XX	----
BLE	Branch if Less than or Equal (zero) $(PC) \leftarrow$ loc if $Z \,V\, (N \,\forall\, V) = 1$	0034XX	----
BPL	Branch if PLus $(PC) \leftarrow$ loc if $N = 0$	1000XX	----
BMI	Branch if MInus $(PC) \leftarrow$ loc if $N = 1$	1004XX	----
BHI	Branch if HIgher $(PC) \leftarrow$ loc if $C = 0$ and $Z = 0$	1010XX	----
BHIS	Branch if HIgher or Same $(PC) \leftarrow$ loc if $C = 0$	1030XX	----
BLO	Branch if LOwer $(PC) \leftarrow$ loc if $C = 1$	1034XX	----
BLOS	Branch if LOwer or Same $(PC) \leftarrow$ loc if $C \,V\, Z = 1$	1014XX	----
BVC	Branch if oVerflow Clear $(PC) \leftarrow$ loc if $V = 0$	1020XX	----
BVS	Branch if oVerflow Set $(PC) \leftarrow$ loc if $V = 1$	1024XX	----
BCC (or BHIS)	Branch if Carry Clear) $(PC) \leftarrow$ loc if $C = 0$	1030XX	----
BCS (or BLO)	Branch if Carry Set $(PC) \leftarrow$ loc if $C = 1$	1034XX	----
SOB	Subtract One from register, Branch if not zero $(R) \leftarrow (R) - 1$ $(PC) \leftarrow$ loc if $(R) \neq 0$	077RXX	----

```
================================================================================
Mnemonic                  Instruction              Op Code            Condition
                          Operation                                     Codes
                                                                         ZNCV
================================================================================


--------------------------------------------------------------------------------
Subroutine Call and Return: JSR reg, dst and RTS reg                     ZNCV
--------------------------------------------------------------------------------


JSR                    Jump to SubRoutine            004RDD              ----
                         (tmp) ← (dst)
                         -(SP) ← (R)
                          (R) ← (PC) = return address
                         (PC) ← (tmp)


RTS                    ReTurn from Subroutine        00020R              ----
                         (PC) ← (R)
                         (R) ← (SP)+



--------------------------------------------------------------------------------
Zero Address Group: FLOP R [PDP-11/03,35,40, PDT-11, LSI-11]             ZNCV
--------------------------------------------------------------------------------


FADD                   Floating-point ADD            07500R              ??00
                         [((R)+4),((R)+6)] ←
                         [((R)+4),((R)+6)] + [(R),((R)+2)]
                         if result ≥ 2**(-128)
                         else [((R)+4),((R)+6)] ← 0

FSUB                   Floating-point SUBtract       07501R              ??00
                         [((R)+4),((R)+6)] ←
                         [((R)+4),((R)+6)] - [(R),((R)+2)]
                         if result ≥ 2**(-128)
                         else [((R)+4),((R)+6)] ← 0

FMUL                   Floating-point MULtiply       07502R              ??00
                         [((R)+4),((R)+6)] ←
                         [((R)+4),((R)+6)] * [(R),((R)+2)]
                         if result ≥ 2**(-128)
                         else [((R)+4),((R)+6)] ← 0

FDIV                   Floating-point DIVide         07503R              ??00
                         [((R)+4),((R)+6)] ←
                         [((R)+4),((R)+6)] / [(R),((R)+2)]
                         if result ≥ 2**(-128)
                         else [((R)+4),((R)+6)] ← 0

--------------------------------------------------------------------------------
Condition Code Operators: OPR
--------------------------------------------------------------------------------
```

Condition code operators set or clear combinations of condition code bits. Selected bits are set if S = 1 and cleared otherwise. Condition code bits corresponding to bits set as marked in the following word are set or cleared:

condition code operators:

```
    0 000 000 020 4SN ZVC
```

Thus SEC = 000261 sets the C-bit and has no effect on the other condition code bits (CLC = 000241 clears the C-bit).

```
====================================================================
Mnemonic              Instruction              Op Code              Condition
                      Operátion                                     Codes
                                                                    ZNCV
====================================================================
--------------------------------------------------------------------
Operate Group OPR
--------------------------------------------------------------------

HALT          HALT                            000000               ----
              processor stops; (R0) and the HALT address in lights

WAIT          WAIT                            000001               ----
              processor releases bus, waits for interrupt

RTI           ReTurn from Interrupt           000002        loaded from (SP)
              (PC) ← (SP)+
              (PS) ← (SP)+,
              T-bit trap enabled.

RTT           ReTurn from Trap                000006        loaded from (SP)
              (PC) ← (SP)+
              (PS) ← (SP)+,
              T-bit trap disabled.

IOT           Input/Output Trap               000004        loaded from (22)
              -(SP) ← (PS)
              -(SP) ← (PC)
              (PC) ← (20)
              (PS) ← (22)

RESET         RESET                           000005               ----
              an INIT pulse is issued by the CPU

EMT           EMulator Trap          104000-104377 loaded from (32)
              -(SP) ← (PS)
              -(SP) ← (PC)
              (PC) ← (30)
              (PS) ← (32)

TRAP          TRAP                   104400-104777 loaded from (36)
              -(SP) ← (PS)
              -(SP) ← (PC)
              (PC) ← (34)
              (PS) ← (36)

BPT           Break Point Trap                000003        loaded from (16)
              -(SP) ← (PS)
              -(SP) ← (PC)
              (PC) ← (14)
              (PS) ← (16)

NOP           No OPeration                    000240
              Used to "delete" unwanted
              instructions during debugging
```

Appendix E:
Operator's Console

The *PDP-11 Operator's Console* allows the operator to achieve convenient control of the system. Through switches and keys on the console, programs or information can be manually inserted or modified. Moreover, indicator lamps on the console face display the status of the machine, the contents of the Bus Address Register, and the data at the output of the data paths. Although there are differences in the console among the members of the PDP-11 family, these differences can be ignored in this appendix and the 11/40's console can be explained as a fairly representative Operator's Console. The console is shown in Figure E-1. The 11/34 and 11/60 have keypad consoles whose function is described in the relevant manual; the 11/03 (LSI-11) console functions are embedded in a terminal dialog or mini-ODT. Thus, the console we discuss is representative of the 11/05, 10, 15, 20, 35, 40, 45, 50, 55, and 70.

Fig. E-1 PDP-11 Operator's Console.

E.1 CONSOLE ELEMENTS

The console has the following indicators and switches:

1. A bank of six indicators, indicating the following conditions or operations: Run, Processor, Bus, Console, User, and Virtual.

2. An 18-bit Address Register display.

3. A 16-bit Data display.

4. An 18-bit Switch Register.

5. Control switches:

```
a.   LOAD ADRS (Load Address)
b.   EXAM (Examine)
c.   CONT (Continue)
d.   ENABLE/HALT
e.   START
f.   DEP (Deposit)
```

E.1.1 Indicator Lights

The indicators signify specific machine functions, operations, or states. Each is defined below:

1. **Run:** lights when the processor clock is running. It is off when the processor is waiting for an asynchronous peripheral data response, or during a RESET instruction. It is on during a WAIT or HALT instruction.

2. **Processor:** lights when the processor has control of the bus.

3. **Bus:** lights when the UNIBUS is being used.

4. **Console:** lights when in console mode (manual operation). Machine is stopped and is not executing the stored program.

5. **User:** lights when the CPU is executing program instructions in User mode.

6. **Virtual:** lights when the ADDRESS Register display shows the 16-bit Virtual Address.

E.1.2 Register Displays

The Operator's Console has an 18-bit Address Register display and a 16-bit Data display. The Address Register display is tied directly to the output of an 18-bit flip-flop register called the Bus Address Register. This register displays the address of data examined or deposited.

The 16-bit data register is divided on the face of the console, by a line, into two 8-bit bytes. This register is tied to the output of the processor data paths and will reflect the output of the processor adder. After execution of a HALT instruction, the Data display will show the content of the R0 register. It also will show data either examined or deposited when doing these control functions.

E.1.3 Switch Register

The PDP-11/10 and the PDP-11/20 can reference $2**16$ byte addresses, while the PDP-11/40 and PDP-11/45 can, using the memory management unit, reference $2**18$ byte addresses. Thus, the UNIBUS was designed with an expansion capability for full 18-bit addressing. In order that the console can access the entire 18-bit address space, the switch register is 18 bits wide. These bits are assigned as 0 through 17. The highest two are used only as addresses. A switch in the "up" position is considered to have a "1" value and in the "down" position to have a "0" value. The condition of the 18 switches can be loaded into the Bus Address Register or any memory location by using the appropriate control switches which are described below. Similarly, the PDP-11/70, which can address $2**22$ bytes has a 22 bit switch register console.

E.1.4 Control Switches

The switches listed in item 5 of the "Console Elements" have these specified control functions:

1. LOAD ADRS: transfers the contents of the 18-bit switch register into the bus address register.

2. EXAM: displays the contents of the location specified by the bus address register.

3. CONT: allows the machine to continue without initialization from whatever state it was in when halted, provided no other key operations have been performed.

4. ENABLE/HALT: allows or prevents running of programs. For a program to run, the switch must be in the ENABLE position (up). Placing the switch in the HALT position (down) will halt the system.

5. START: starts executing a program when the ENABLE/HALT switch is in the ENABLE position. When the START switch is depressed, it asserts a system initialization signal; the system actually starts when the switch is released. The processor will start executing at the address which was last loaded by the LOAD ADRS key, provided no other key operations have been performed. In HALT mode, depressing START effectively resets the entire system, thus acting as a manual I/O reset.

6. DEP: deposits the contents of the low 16 bits of the switch register into the address then display in the address register. (This switch is actuated by raising it).

When the system is running a program, the LOAD ADRS, EXAM, and DEPOSIT functions are disabled to prevent disrupting the program. When the machine is to be halted, the ENABLE/HALT switch is thrown to the halt position. The machine will halt at the end of the current instruction.

E.2 OPERATING THE CONTROL SWITCHES

When the PDP-11 has been halted, it is possible to examine and update bus locations. To examine a specific location, the operator sets the switches of the switch register to correspond to the location's address. The operator then presses LOAD ADDRS, which will transfer the contents of the switch register into the bus address register. The location of the address to be examined is then displayed in the address register display. The operator then depresses EXAM. The data in that location will appear in the data register display.

If the operator then depresses EXAM again, the bus address register will be incremented by 2 to the next word address and the new location will be examined. In the PDP-11, the bus address register will always be pointing to the data currently displayed in the data register. The incrementation occurs when the EXAM switch is depressed, and then the location is examined.

The examine function has been designed so that if LOAD ADDR and then EXAM are depressed, the address register will not be incremented. In this case, the location reflected in the address register display is examined directly. However, on the second (and successive) depressings of EXAM, the bus address register is incremented. This will continue for successive depressings as long as another control switch is not depressed.

If the operator finds an incorrect entry in the data register, he can enter new data by putting it in the switch register and raising the DEP key. The address register will not increment when this data is deposited. Therefore, when the operator presses the EXAM key, he can examine the data he just deposited. However, when he presses EXAM again, the address will increment.

If the operator attempts to examine data from, or deposit data into, a non-existent memory location, the "time out" feature will cause an error flag. The data register will then reflect location 4, the trap location, for references to nonexistent locations. To verify this condition, the operator should try to deposit some number other than four in the location causing the error; if four is still indicated, this would imply that either nothing is assigned to that location, or that whatever is assigned to that location is not working properly.

When doing consecutive examines or consecutive deposits, the address will increment by 2, to successive word locations. However, if the programmer is examining the general-purpose registers, the system only increments by 1. The reason for this is that once the switch register is set properly, the programmer can then use the four least significant bits of the switch register in examining the *gp* registers from the front panel.

To start a PDP-11 program, the programmer loads the starting address of the program in the switch register, depresses LOAD ADDR, and after ensuring that the ENABLE/HALT switch is in the ENABLE position, depresses START. The program will start to run as soon as the START switch is released.

The Run indicator lamp is driven off the flip-flop that controls the clock. Normally, when the system is running, not only will this light be on, but the other lights (RUN, PROCESSOR, BUS, CONSOLE, USER, the Address lights, and the Address and Data registers) will be flickering. If the run light is on, and none of the other indicators are flickering, the system could be executing a "wait" instruction which waits for an interrupt. In this case, a "1" will appear in the data display.

While in the halt mode, if the operator wishes to do a single instruction, he simply depresses CONT. When CONT is depressed, the console momentarily passes control to the processor, allowing the machine to execute one instruction before regaining control. Each time the CONT switch is depressed, the machine will execute one instruction. The Bus Address Register will then show the last address referenced by the instruction (not necessarily the address of the instruction itself) and the Data display will reflect the data acted upon at that address.

To start the machine running its program again, the operator places the ENABLE/HALT switch in the ENABLE position, and depresses the CONT switch.

Appendix F:
EIS Autogen FFT
Thread Generator

The user should compile FTMULF.BLD (which follows below) using RT-11 FORTRAN to get FTMULF.SAV. When run, FTMULF asks for an input integer. Respond with one of 4, 5, 6, 7, 8, 9, 0 and a driver program FTMUF*m*.MAC will be generated on DK0, where *m* is the number you entered. These are drivers for complex fixed-point FFT's of 2**4, 2**5,....., 2**10 points. Note that FTMUF0.MAC requires 385 blocks on disk so that twice that number must be present during generation, or a "READ/WRITE PAST END OF FILE" error is generated. Run time storage for FTMUF*m*.MAC is about 0.75*m*∗n + 5.5∗*n* words, where *n* = 2**m. The general structure of a FORTRAN program using FTMUF*m* is:

```
        INTEGER X(2n), Y(2n),IREAL(n), IIMAG(n)
        COMMON /XX/X,Y
        N = 2**m
        DO 1 J = 1,N
        X(2*J-1) = IREAL(J)
1       X(2*J) = IIMAG(J)
        CALL FTMUFn
        DO 2 J = 1,N
        IREAL(J) = Y(2*J-1)
2       IIMAG(J) = Y(2*J)
        STOP
        END
```

Here, 2*n*, *n*, and *m* are *constants* equal to 2**(M + 1), 2**M, and M, respectively, for a transform of N = 2**M complex points. See the digital oscilloscope program (Section 10.3) for an example.

```
C
C        FILE NAME:   F T M U L F . B L D
C
C        OPERATING INSTRUCTIONS:
C                             RU FORTRN
C                             FTMULF=FTMULF.BLD
C
C                             RU LINK
C                             FTMULF=FTMULF/F
C
C                             RU FTMULF
C
C
C        SUBROUTINES CALLED:
C              ASSIGN
C
         DIMENSION NA(1000)
         DIMENSION NSCRAM(1024),INAME(7),NTRIG(2000),NUM(7),NNAME(7)
         DATA INAME(1),INAME(2),INAME(3),INAME(4),INAME(5),
       + INAME(6),INAME(7)/2HDK,2H0:,2HFT,2HMU,2H  ,2H.M,2HAC/
         DATA NNAME(1),NNAME(2),NNAME(3),NNAME(4),NNAME(5),NNAME(6),
       + NNAME(7)/2HF4,2HF5,2HF6,2HF7,2HF8,2HF9,2HF0/
         DATA NUM(1),NUM(2),NUM(3),NUM(4),NUM(5),NUM(6),NUM(7)/
       + 1H4,1H5,1H6,1H7,1H8,1H9,1H0/
         CALL ASSIGN(6,'TT:')
790      WRITE(6,800)
800      FORMAT(1X,'ENTER THE DESIRED POWER OF TWO  (4,5,..9,0[0=10])',/)
         READ(6,810) NPOWER
810      FORMAT(A1)
         DO 820 I=1,7
         IF (NUM(I).EQ.NPOWER) GOTO 830
820      CONTINUE
         WRITE(6,825)
825      FORMAT(1X,'NUMBER WAS OUT OF RANGE')
         GOTO 790
830      INAME(5)=NNAME(I)
         M=I+3
         IUNIT=5
         CALL ASSIGN(IUNIT,INAME(1),14)
         WRITE(5,1000) (INAME(I),I=3,5)
1000     FORMAT(9X,'.TITLE ',3A2)
         WRITE(5,1005) (INAME(I),I=3,5)
1005     FORMAT(9X,'.GLOBL ',3A2,' BUTTOV BUTT BUT225 BUT270 BUT315',
       +       /9X,'.GLOBL LE1,BUT0,OFFSET')
         N=2**M
         NADDR=4*N
         WRITE(5,1006) NADDR,(INAME(I),I=3,5)
1006     FORMAT(9X,'.CSECT XX',/9X,'A=.',/9X,'B=.+',O5,/9X,'.CSECT',
       + /9X,'.IRPC X,0123456',/9X,'R''X=%''X',/9X,'AC''X=%''X',
       + /9X,'.ENDM',
       + /9X,'SP=%6',/9X,'PC=%7',/1X,3A2,':',/9X,'MOV R5,-(SP)',
       + /9X,'MOV #ARRAY,R5',/9X,'MOV LE1,-(R6)',
       + /9X,'JMP @(R5)+',/'ARRAY:')
         NV2=N/2
         NSIZE=N+NV2+4
         NM1=N-1
         J=1
```

```
          DO 1 JK=1,N
1         NSCRAM(JK)=4*JK-2
          DO 7 I=1,NM1
          IF (I.GE.J) GO TO 5
          NSCRAM(I)=4*J-2
          NSCRAM(J)=4*I-2
5         K=NV2
6         IF (K.GE.J) GO TO 7
          J=J-K
          K=K/2
          GO TO 6
7         J=J+K
          NWRITE=0
          NCOUNT=0
          NTYPE=0
          NTYPL=5
          WRITE (5,2466)
          WRITE(5,1466)
C
          DO 20 L=1,M
          LE=2**L
          LE1=LE/2
          IOFF=6*N/LE
          DO 2020 J=1,LE1
          JM1=J-1
          J1=JM1*IOFF+4
          IFLAG=1
          IF (JM1.NE.0) GO TO 50
          IFLAG=5
          GO TO 80
50        IF (LE1.LT.2) GO TO 80
          IF (JM1.NE.LE1/2) GO TO 52
          IFLAG=2
          GO TO 80
52        IF (LE1.LT.4) GO TO 80
          IF (JM1.NE.LE1/4) GO TO 54
          IFLAG=3
          GO TO 80
54        IF (JM1.NE.3*LE1/4) GO TO 80
          IFLAG=4

80        DO 10 I=J,N,LE
          IP=I+LE1
          GO TO (100,110,120,130,140),IFLAG
C
100       NTYPE=1
          IF(NTYPE.EQ.NTYPL) GO TO 107
          IF(J1.GE.NSIZE) WRITE(5,106)
          IF(J1.LE.NSIZE) WRITE(5,1066)
106       FORMAT(3X,'0',/6X,'BUTT')
1066      FORMAT(3X,'0',/6X,'BUTTOV')
          WRITE(5,105) NSCRAM(IP),J1
105       FORMAT(8X,'A+',O5,',COSTBL+',O5)
          NTYPL=NTYPE
          GO TO 10
107       WRITE(5,105) NSCRAM(IP),J1
          GO TO 10
110       NTYPE=2
          IF(NTYPE.EQ.NTYPL) GO TO 117
```

```
              WRITE(5,116)
116           FORMAT(3X,'0',/6X,'BUT270')
              WRITE(5,115) NSCRAM(I)
115           FORMAT(8X,'A+',O5)
              NTYPL=NTYPE
              GO TO 10
117           WRITE(5,115) NSCRAM(I)
              GO TO 10
120           NTYPE=3
              IF(NTYPE.EQ.NTYPL) GO TO 127
              WRITE(5,126)
126           FORMAT(3X,'0',/6X,'BUT315')
              WRITE(5,125) NSCRAM(IP)
125           FORMAT(8X,'A+',O5)
              NTYPL=NTYPE
              GO TO 10
127           WRITE(5,125) NSCRAM(IP)
              GO TO 10
130           NTYPE=4
              IF(NTYPE.EQ.NTYPL) GO TO 137
              WRITE(5,136)
136           FORMAT(3X,'0',/6X,'BUT225')
              WRITE(5,135) NSCRAM(IP)
135           FORMAT(8X,'A+',O5)
              NTYPL=NTYPE
              GO TO 10
137           WRITE(5,135) NSCRAM(IP)
              GO TO 10
140           NTYPE=5
              IF(NTYPE.EQ.NTYPL) GO TO 147
              WRITE(5,146)
146           FORMAT(3X,'0',/6X,'BUT0')
1466          FORMAT(6X,'BUT0')
              WRITE(5,145) NSCRAM(I)
145           FORMAT(8X,'A+',O5)
              NTYPL=NTYPE
              GO TO 10
147           WRITE(5,145) NSCRAM(I)
10            CONTINUE
2020          CONTINUE
              WRITE(5,246)
246           FORMAT(3X,'0',/4X,'OFFSET')
2466          FORMAT(4X,'OFFSET',/3X,'0')
              NTYPL=6
20            CONTINUE
C
              WRITE(5,155)
155           FORMAT(3X,'0',/9X,'BITREV',/'BITREV:')
              WRITE(5,900)
900           FORMAT(9X,'MOV #A,R1')
              DO 30 I=1,N
              NSC=NSCRAM(I)-2
              WRITE(5,910) NSC,NSCRAM(I)
910           FORMAT(9X,'MOV (R1)+,B+',O4,/9X,'MOV (R1)+,B+',O4)
30            CONTINUE
              WRITE(5,1010)
1010          FORMAT(9X,'TST (SP)+',/9X,'MOV (SP)+,R5',/9X,'RTS PC')
```

```
          RMAX=2.**15-1.
          RMAX1=2.**14-1.
          PI=3.141592
          NV4=N/4
          NV4P1=NV4+1
          NSIZE=N+NV2
          XN=N
          WRITE(5,200)
200       FORMAT(1X,'COSTBL:')
          DO 210 I=1,NV4
          XI=1-I
          ARG=2.*PI*XI/XN
          SINE=SIN(ARG)
          COSINE=COS(ARG)
          NTRIG(3*I-2)=RMAX1*(COSINE-SINE)+.5
          NTRIG(3*I-1)=RMAX*SINE+.5
          NTRIG(3*I)=RMAX*COSINE+.5
210       CONTINUE
          DO 220 I=NV4P1,NV2
          XI=1-I
          ARG=2.*PI*XI/XN
          SINE=SIN(ARG)
          COSINE=COS(ARG)
          NTRIG(3*I-2)=RMAX*(COSINE-SINE)+.5
          NTRIG(3*I-1)=RMAX*SINE+.5
          NTRIG(3*I)=RMAX*COSINE+.5
220       CONTINUE
          WRITE(5,230) (NTRIG(I),I=1,NSIZE)
230       FORMAT((9X,O6,7(',',O6))))
          LE1W=(NSCRAM(2)-NSCRAM(1))*2
          WRITE(5,240) LE1W
240       FORMAT('LE1:',2X,O5,/9X,'.END',/)
          END FILE 5
          STOP
```

Appendix G:
The Interactive Graphics
"Towers of Hanoi" Program

Figure 10-7 (p. 325) shows an interactive graphics implementation of the classical "Towers of Hanoi" problem. The object of the problem is to transfer N disks, initially stacked on a peg, to one of the other two pegs. Only one disk may be transferred at a time and at no time may a larger disk rest on a smaller one. The problem can be couched in recursive terms, as explained by Tannenbaum (1976).

The solution of moving N disks from peg 1 to peg 3, for example, consists first of moving N-1 disks from peg 1 to peg 2, then moving one disk from peg 1 to peg 3, and then moving N-1 disks from peg 2 to peg 3. Thus a recursive routine is needed, containing three calls to itself embedded within the routine. The program below implements the solution using Tannenbaum's stack frame structure: source, destination, and "other" peg number for any call are stored on the stack.

The output of the "Towers" program causes the required disk to move up the source peg, across, and down onto the required destination peg. In Fig. 10-7, a blurred disk is seen moving from peg 1 to peg 3, as per the message printed on the screen. The speed of disk movement is controlled by a light pen potentiometer, at upper right of the screen. The user is first prompted to supply the number of disks desired, from 1 to 10.

The use of macro's to define the disks should be noted. Finally, the implementation of the *light pen potentiometer* for disk speed control is of interest as it utilizes the light pen interrupt and employs a check routine which limits the minimum slider position change to 5 raster units. This prevents the light pen ISR from tying up the CPU.

```
                .TITLE   HANOI - TOWERS OF HANOI/VT-11 DISPLAY
;
;    -RECURSIVE ALGOL W PROCEDURE FOR SOLVING THE TOWERS OF HANOI:
;         PROCEDURE TOWERS(INTEGER VALUE N,I,J);
;            IF N=1 THEN WRITE ("MOVE A DISK FROM",I,"TO",J);
;                         ELSE BEGIN
;                            TOWERS(N-1,I,6-I-J);
;                            TOWERS(1,I,J);
;                            TOWERS(N-1,6-I-J,J);
;                         END;
;         END TOWERS;

          GTPC=172000
          GTY=172006
          LPOFPT=114100
          LPONPT=114140
;
          XMENU = 1000.
          YMENU = 750.
          LINLGT = 200.
          XSHFT = 5.
          XARROW = 1022.
          ARWLGT = 40.
;
          Y1 = YMENU - <LINLGT/2>
          END1=YMENU-LINLGT
          BACKUP=LINLGT
          DASH=LONGV+INT5+LINE2
          LINE=LONGV+INT7+LINE0
          I=INTX                    ;INTENSIFY
          M=MINUSX                  ;MINUS DIRECTION
;
          H=60.                     ;DISK HEIGHT
          PH=10.*H+30.              ;PEG HEIGHT
          TOP=11.*H
          INS=2*H+PH
;
HANOI:    MOV      #1000,SP         ;INITIALIZE STACK POINTER
          BIC      #100,KBS         ;DISABLE KEYBOARD
          BIC      #100,PRS         ;DISABLE PRINTER
;
          MOV      #<LINLGT/2>,IY1  ;INITIALIZE LIGHT PEN POT CURSOR VALUE
          MOV      #Y1,YPOS1        ;INITIALIZE LIGHT PEN POT CURSOR POSITION
          MOV      #LPINT,@#324     ;SET LP SERVICE ROUTINE ADDRESS
          MOV      #200,@#326       ;AND PSW
;
START:    MOV      #PROMPT,R0       ;PRINT PROMPT MESSAGE
PRINT:    TSTB     PRS              ;PRINTER READY?
          BPL      PRINT
          MOVB     (R0)+,PRB        ;PRINT A CHARACTER
          TSTB     (R0)             ;NULL CHARACTER?
          BNE      PRINT
WAIT:     TSTB     KBS              ;KEYBOARD READY?
          BPL      WAIT
          MOVB     KBB,R1           ;READ IN NUMBER OF DISKS
          BIC      #177600,R1       ;MASK OUT 7-BIT ASCII
ECHO:     TSTB     PRS              ;PRINTER READY?
          BPL      ECHO
          MOVB     R1,PRB           ;PRINT NUMBER OF DISKS
          SUB      #'0,R1
          BLE      START            ;LESS THAN ASCII 1?
          CMP      #10.,R1
```

462

```
        BLT     START           ;GREATER THAN 10.?
        BIS     #100,KBS        ;ENABLE KEYBOARD
        BIS     #100,PRS        ;ENABLE PRINTER
;
;       SETUP FOR CALL TO TOWERS, START DISPLAY PROCESSOR
;
        MOV     R1,-(SP)        ;PUSH INITIAL N, 0 < N < 11
        MOV     #1,-(SP)        ;PUSH I=1
        MOV     #3,-(SP)        ;PUSH J=3
        ASL     R1              ;MULTIPLY NUMBER BY 2
        ADD     R1,TOPPNT       ;SET PEG 1 TOP POINTER
        MOV     @TOPPNT,R2
        MOV     #DJMP,(R2)+     ;INSERT JUMP COMMAND
        MOV     #DFILE,(R2)+    ;  IN DISPLAY FILE
        MOV     (R2),TOPADR     ;SET PEG 1 TOP ADDRESS
;
        MOV     #DFILE,DPC      ;START DISPLAY PROCESSOR
        JSR     PC,TOWERS       ;INITIAL CALL TO TOWERS
        .EXIT                   ;RETURN TO RT-11
;
;       RECURSIVE TOWERS SUBROUTINE
;
TOWERS: MOV     6(SP),-(SP)     ;PUSH N
        DEC     (SP)            ;DECREMENT TO N-1
        BEQ     MOVE            ;N=1?
        MOV     6(SP),-(SP)     ;PUSH I
        MOV     #6,R2
        SUB     (SP),R2         ;SUBTRACT I
        SUB     6(SP),R2        ;SUBTRACT J
        MOV     R2,-(SP)        ;PUSH 6-I-J
        JSR     PC,TOWERS       ;RECURSIVE CALL TO TOWERS
;
        MOV     #1,-(SP)        ;PUSH N=1
        MOV     6(SP),-(SP)     ;PUSH I
        MOV     6(SP),-(SP)     ;PUSH J
        JSR     PC,TOWERS       ;RECURSIVE CALL TO TOWERS
;
        MOV     6(SP),-(SP)     ;PUSH N
        DEC     (SP)            ;DECREMENT TO N-1
        MOV     #6,R2
        SUB     6(SP),R2        ;SUBTRACT I
        SUB     4(SP),R2        ;SUBTRACT J
        MOV     R2,-(SP)        ;PUSH 6-I-J
        MOV     6(SP),-(SP)     ;PUSH J
        JSR     PC,TOWERS       ;RECURSIVE CALL TO TOWERS
;
        MOV     (SP),6(SP)      ;REALIGN RETURN ADDRESS
        ADD     #6,SP           ;POP J,I & N
        RTS     PC              ;RETURN
;       ROUTINE TO MODIFY DISPLAY FILE TO MOVE A DISK
MOVE:   MOV     6(SP),R1        ;GET I
        MOV     4(SP),R2        ;GET J
        BICB    #3,MOVINS+17.   ;UPDATE MOVE INSTRUCTION
        BISB    R1,MOVINS+17.   ;SET SOURCE PEG
        BICB    #3,MOVINS+22.
        BISB    R2,MOVINS+22.   ;SET DESTINATION PEG
        ASL     R1              ;MULTIPLY I BY 2
        ASL     R2              ;MULTIPLY J BY 2
        MOV     2(SP),8.(SP)    ;REALIGN RETURN ADDRESS
        ADD     #8.,SP          ;POP N,J,I & N
        SUB     #2,TOPPNT-2(R1) ;UPDATE SOURCE PEG TOP POINTER
        MOV     @TOPPNT-2(R1),R3 ;GET TOP DISK
```

```
            MOV       R3,@TOPPNT-2(R2)  ;STORE DISK ON DESTINATION PEG
            ADD       #2,TOPPNT-2(R2)   ;UPDATE DEST. PEG TOP POINTER
            SUB       #H,TOPADR-2(R1)   ;UPDATE SOURCE PEG TOP ADDRESS
;
UP:         INC       4(R3)             ;MOVE DISK UP OVER SOURCE
            JSR       PC,DELAY          ;  PEG ALONG Y-AXIS
            CMP       #TOP,4(R3)        ;STOP AT TOP
            BNE       UP
;
ACROSS:     MOV       #1,R4             ;SET LATERAL INCREMENT (TO RIGHT)
            MOV       #345.,R5          ;SET NUMBER OF LATERAL MOVES
            CMP       R1,R2             ;DETERMINE DIRECTION
            BEQ       DOWN              ;DESTINATION PEG REACHED?
            BLT       OVER
            NEG       R4                ;CHANGE INCREMENT TO LEFT
OVER:       ADD       R4,2(R3)          ;MOVE DISK FROM ONE PEG TO
            JSR       PC,DELAY          ;  ANOTHER ALONG X-AXIS
            DEC       R5
            BNE       OVER
            ASL       R4                ;MULTIPLY INCREMENT BY 2
            ADD       R4,R1             ;UPDATE SOURCE PEG
            BR        ACROSS
;
DOWN:       DEC       4(R3)             ;MOVE DISK DOWN ON DEST.
            JSR       PC,DELAY          ;  PEG ALONG Y-AXIS
            CMP       TOPADR-2(R2),4(R3) ;STOP AT PEG TOP ADDRESS
            BNE       DOWN
;
            ADD       #H,TOPADR-2(R2)   ;UPDATE DEST. PEG TOP ADDRESS
            RTS       PC                ;RETURN
;
;           DELAY ROUTINE DETERMINES SPEED OF DISK MOVEMENT
;
DELAY:      MOV       IY1,R0            ;GET VALUE OF LIGHT PEN POT
            ASL       R0                ;*2
            ASL       R0                ;*2
            BEQ       RET               ;IF ZERO, THEN RETURN
LOOP:       DEC       R0                ;DECREMENT VALUE UNTIL ZERO
            BNE       LOOP              ;PROVIDES DELAY IN DISK MOVEMENT
RET:        RTS       PC                ;RETURN AFTER APPROPRIATE DELAY
;
;           POINTERS
;
TOPPNT:  PEG1,PEG2,PEG3                 ;TOP POINTER FOR PEGS
TOPADR:  0,0,0                          ;TOP ADDRESS FOR PEGS
;           INITIALLY, ALL DISKS ON PEG1
PEG1: DISK1,DISK2,DISK3,DISK4,DISK5,DISK6,DISK7,DISK8,DISK9,DISK10,DISK11
PEG2: 0,0,0,0,0,0,0,0,0,0
PEG3: 0,0,0,0,0,0,0,0,0,0
;           DISPLAY FILE
;
DFILE:   113124                         ;LP OFF,BK OFF,SOL.LINES,LONGV
         170240                         ;INTENS ON LP HIT
LPBUF:   LPONPT                         ;**DRAW THE VERTICAL LINES, LP ON
         XMENU
         YMENU
         LONGV
         INTX,<LINLGT + MINUSY>,0,0,XSHFT,BACKUP,INTX,<LINLGT + MINUSY>
         LPOFPT                         ;**DRAW THE CURSOR, LP OFF
         XARROW
```

```
YPOS1:  Y1
        LONGV
        <ARWLGT+MINUSX+INTX>,0
        POINT,0,0                   ;**DRAW THE PEGS
        DASH                        ;SHORT DASH LINE FOR PEGS
        150.+I,0,0+I,PH,20+I,0,0+I,PH+M
        330.+I,0,0+I,PH,20+I,0,0+I,PH+M
        330.+I,0,0+I,PH,20+I,0,0+I,PH+M,153.+I,0
        POINT,345.,INS
        CHAR                        ;**DRAW THE "MOVE" MESSAGE
MOVINS: .ASCII  /MOVE A DISK FROM 0 TO 0:/
;
        .MACRO DISK DISK1,X,Y,N1;N1=WIDTH OF DISK, H=HEIGHT
DISK1:  POINT,X,Y                   ;**DRAW THE DISKS--LS,TOP,RS,BOTTOM
        LINE,0+I,H,N1+I,0,0+I,H+M,N1+I+M,0
        .ENDM
;
        DISK    DISK1,20.,0*H,280.
        DISK    DISK2,30.,1*H,260.
        DISK    DISK3,40.,2*H,240.
        DISK    DISK4,50.,3*H,220.
        DISK    DISK5,60.,4*H,200.
        DISK    DISK6,70.,5*H,180.
        DISK    DISK7,80.,6*H,160.
        DISK    DISK8,90.,7*H,140.
        DISK    DISK9,100.,8.*H,120.
        DISK    DISK10.,110.,9.*H,100.
DISK11: DJMP,DFILE,10.*H
;
PROMPT: .BYTE   12,15
        .ASCIZ  /INPUT NUMBER OF DISKS (1 TO 9 & ':' FOR 10) - /
;
        .EVEN
LPINT:  MOV     R0,-(SP)            ;SAVE R0
        MOV     R1,-(SP)            ;SAVE R1
        MOV     R2,-(SP)            ;SAVE R2
        MOV     GTY,YCOORD          ;GET  NEW Y CO-ORDINATE
        BIC     #176000,YCOORD      ;MASK TO TEN BITS
POT1:   MOV     YPOS1,R1            ;POT 1
        JSR     PC,CHKSEN           ;CHECK INCREMENT
        TST     R0                  ;TOO CLOSE?
        BNE     QUIT                ;SKIP UPDATE IF TOO CLOSE
        MOV     YCOORD,YPOS1        ;UPDATE ARROW POSITION
        SUB     #END1,YCOORD        ;GET IT RELATIVE TO POT MIN
        MOV     YCOORD,IY1          ;SAVE IT
QUIT:   MOV     #1,GTPC             ;RESUME DISPLAY
        MOV     (SP)+,R2            ;RESTORE R2
        MOV     (SP)+,R1            ;RESTORE R1
        MOV     (SP)+,R0            ;RESTORE R0
        RTI                         ;RETURN
CHKSEN: CLR     R0                  ;CLEAR FLAG
        MOV     YCOORD,R2           ;SAVE THE NEW Y-COORD
        SUB     R1,R2               ;GET THE DIFFERENCE
        BPL     .+4                 ;OK IF PLUS
        NEG     R2                  ;NEGATE IF REQUIRED
        CMP     #5,R2               ;NOT ENOUGH CHANGE?
        BLT     .+4                 ;LEAVE FLAG ALONE
        INC     R0                  ;TOO SMALL
        RTS     PC                  ;RETURN
YCOORD: .WORD   0
IY1:    .WORD   LINLGT/2
;
        .END HANOI
```

Appendix H:
Radix-4 FPP Autogen FFT

H.1 INTRODUCTION

The *Autogen* radix-4 FFT described in Section 9.6.2 is listed and documented here for convenience. The software consists of three modules:

1. A FORTRAN thread generator, RAD4.BLD.

2. A set of five assembler code radix-4 FFT butterflies. These modules use the FPP instructions and floating-point registers present on the PDP/11-23, 24, 34, 45, 50, 55, 60 and 70 to efficiently compute floating-point, complex FFT's.

3. A test program

The program RAD4.BLD, when compiled and run, produces a radix-4 program, driver array, and trig coefficient table for an $N = 4**M$ point transform, $M = 2, 3, 4,$ or 5. The resultant program requires $0.6MN + 5.2N$ words of storage and uses RX4BUT.MAC (445 words of storage) to compute the DFT as per Section 9.3.2 in the execution times noted in Section 9.6.2.

H.2 PROGRAM GENERATION

The driver program generator is compiled using FORTRAN (i.e., RAD4 = RAD4.BLD), and linked (i.e., RAD4 = RAD4/F).

```
C       RAD4.BLD
        DIMENSION ARRAY(6000),IN(7),NX(5)
        DIMENSION NFAC(11),NP(209)
        DIMENSION AT(23),CK(23),BT(23),SK(23)
        DIMENSION NA(100)
        DATA IN(1),IN(2),IN(3),IN(4),IN(5),IN(6),IN(7)/
     +  2HDK,2H0:,2HRD,2HX4,2H  ,2H.M,2HAC/
        DATA NX(1),NX(2),NX(3),NX(4),NX(5)/
     +  2H01,2H02,2H03,2H04,2H05/
        EQUIVALENCE (I,II)
C
        WRITE(7,8000)
8000    FORMAT(1X,'ENTER M FOR 4**M POINTS, 1 < M < 6')
        READ(7,8001)MX
8001    FORMAT(I1)
        N=4**MX
        NTOT=N
        NSPAN=N
        N1TEST=N/16
        N2TEST=N/8
        N3TEST=(3*N)/16
        NSPAN4=NSPAN/4
        IBASE=0
        ISN=1
        MAXF=23
        MAXP=209
        IF(N.LT.2) STOP
        INC=ISN
        RAD=8.0*ATAN(1.0)
        S72=RAD/5.0
        C72=COS(S72)
        S72=SIN(S72)
        S120=SQRT(0.75)
        IF(ISN.GE.0) GO TO 10
        S72=-S72
        S120=-S120
        RAD=-RAD
        INC=-INC
10      NT=INC*NTOT
        KS=INC*NSPAN
        KSPAN=KS
        KSBYTE=8*KSPAN
        NN=NT-INC
        JC=KS/N
        RADF=RAD*FLOAT(JC)*.5
        I=0
        JF=0
C       DETERMINE THE FACTORS OF N
C       ALL FACTORS MUST BE 4 FOR THIS VERSION
        M=0
        K=N
        GO TO 20
```

```
15        M=M+1
          NFAC(M)=4
          K=K/16
20        IF(K-(K/16)*16.EQ.0) GO TO 15
          J=3
          JJ=9
          GO TO 30
25        M=M+1
          NFAC(M)=J
          K=K/JJ
30        IF(MOD(K,JJ).EQ.0) GO TO 25
          J=J+2
          JJ=J**2
          IF(JJ.LE.K) GO TO 30
          IF(K.GT.4) GO TO 40
          KT=M
          NFAC(M+1)=K
          IF(K.NE.1) M=M+1
          GO TO 80
40        IF(K-(K/4)*4.NE.0)GO TO 50
          M=M+1
          NFAC(M)=2
          K=K/4
50        KT=M
          J=2
60        IF(MOD(K,J).NE.0) GO TO 70
          M=M+1
          NFAC(M)=J
          K=K/J
70        J=((J+1)/2)*2+1
          IF(J.LT.K) GO TO 60
80        IF(KT.EQ.0) GO TO 100
          J=KT
90        M=M+1
          NFAC(M)=NFAC(J)
          J=J-1
          IF(J.NE.0)GO TO 90
          KSPAN0=KSPAN
          NTYPL=0
          NCOUNT=1
          NWRITE=0
C
          IUNIT=5
          IN(5)=NX(M)
          CALL ASSIGN (IUNIT,IN(1),14)
          WRITE(5,7000) (IN(IV), IV=3,5)
7000      FORMAT(9X,'.TITLE ',3A2)
          WRITE(5,7001) (IN(IV), IV=3,5)
7001      FORMAT(9X,'.GLOBL ',3A2,' ABE S924 S707 S383 ABC',
         +        /9X,'.GLOBL OFFSET ')
          WRITE(5,7002) (IN(IV), IV=3,5),KSBYTE
7002      FORMAT(9X,'.CSECT XX',/9X,'A=.',/9X,'.CSECT',
         +        /9X,'.IRPC X,012345',/9X,'R''X=%''X',
         +        /9X,'AC''X=%''X',/9X,'.ENDM',
         +        /9X,'SP=%6',/9X,'PC=%7',/1X,3A2,':',
         +        /9X,'MOV #',06,',R4',/9X,'SETF',
         +        /9X,'MOV #ARRAY,R5',/9X,'JMP @(R5)+',
         +        /1X,'ARRAY:')
100       NDELTA=KSPAN0/KSPAN
          INDEX=0
          SD=RADF/FLOAT(KSPAN)
          CD=2.0*SIN(SD)**2
```

468

```
          SD=SIN(SD+SD)
          KK=1
          I=I+1
C         TRANSFORM FOR A FACTOR OF 4
400       IF(NFAC(I).NE.4) GO TO 600
          KSPNN=KSPAN
          KSPAN=KSPAN/4
          WRITE(5,5020)
5020      FORMAT(1X,3X,'OFFSET')
410       C1=1.0
          S1=0.0
420       K1=KK+KSPAN
          K2=K1+KSPAN
          K3=K2+KSPAN
          IF(ISN.LT.0) GO TO 450
          IF(S1.EQ.0.0) GO TO 460
430       CONTINUE
          IF(KSPAN.NE.NSPAN4) GO TO 431
          ARRAY(IBASE+5)=S1+C1
          ARRAY(IBASE+6)=C1
          ARRAY(IBASE+4)=S1-C1
          ARRAY(IBASE+8)=S2+C2
          ARRAY(IBASE+9)=C2
          ARRAY(IBASE+7)=S2-C2
          ARRAY(IBASE+2)=S3+C3
          ARRAY(IBASE+3)=C3
          ARRAY(IBASE+1)=S3-C3
          IBASE=IBASE+9
431       CONTINUE
C
          KKP=(KK-1)*8
          IF(INDEX.NE.N1TEST) GO TO 150
          NTYPE=1
          IF(NTYPE.EQ.NTYPL) GO TO 145
          NOFF=NWRITE*2
          WRITE(5,4031) NOFF
4031      FORMAT(6X,'S924,LOOPB+',O4)
          WRITE(5,6031) KKP
6031      FORMAT(25X,'A+',O6)
          NWRITE=NWRITE+1
          NA(NWRITE)=NCOUNT
          NCOUNT=1
          NTYPL=NTYPE
          GO TO 5035
145       NCOUNT=NCOUNT+1
          WRITE(5,6031) KKP
          GO TO 5035
C
150       IF(INDEX.NE.N2TEST) GO TO 160
          NTYPE=2
          IF(NTYPE.EQ.NTYPL) GO TO 155
          NOFF=NWRITE*2
          WRITE(5,4032) NOFF
4032      FORMAT(6X,'S707,LOOPB+',O4)
          WRITE(5,6031) KKP
          NWRITE=NWRITE+1
          NA(NWRITE)=NCOUNT
          NCOUNT=1
          NTYPL=NTYPE
          GO TO 5035
155       NCOUNT=NCOUNT+1
          WRITE(5,6031) KKP
          GO TO 5035
```

```
160       IF(INDEX.NE.N3TEST) GO TO 170
          NTYPE=3
          IF(NTYPE.EQ.NTYPL) GO TO 165
          NOFF=NWRITE*2
          WRITE(5,4033) NOFF
4033      FORMAT(6X,'S383,LOOPB+',O4)
          WRITE(5,6031) KKP

          NWRITE=NWRITE+1
          NA(NWRITE)=NCOUNT
          NCOUNT=1
          NTYPL=NTYPE
          GO TO 5035
165       NCOUNT=NCOUNT+1
          WRITE(5,6031) KKP
          GO TO 5035
C
170       NTYPE=4
          IF(NTYPE.EQ.NTYPL) GO TO 175
          NOFF=NWRITE*2
          WRITE(5,4034) NOFF
4034      FORMAT(6X,' ABC,LOOPB+',O4)
          INDEXP=(INDEX-1)*36
          WRITE(5,6032) KKP,INDEXP
6032      FORMAT(25X,'A+',O6,',TRIG+',I6,'.')
          NWRITE=NWRITE+1
          NA(NWRITE)=NCOUNT
          NCOUNT=1
          NTYPL=NTYPE
          GO TO 5035
175       NCOUNT=NCOUNT+1
          INDEXP=(INDEX-1)*36
          WRITE(5,6032) KKP,INDEXP
5035      KK=K3+KSPAN
          IF(KK.LE.NT) GO TO 420
440       CONTINUE
          INDEX=INDEX+NDELTA
          C2=C1-(CD*C1+SD*S1)
          S1=(SD*C1-CD*S1)+S1
          C1=C2
          C2=C1*C1-S1*S1
          S2=C1*S1+C1*S1
          C3=C2*C1-S2*S1
          S3=C2*S1+S2*C1
          KK=KK-NT+JC
          IF(KK.LE.KSPAN) GO TO 420
          KK=KK-KSPAN+INC
          IF(KK.LE.JC) GO TO 410
          IF(KSPAN.EQ.JC) GO TO 800
          GO TO 100
450       WRITE(5,5040)
5040      FORMAT('AT 450, ERROR')
          IF(S1.NE.0.0) GO TO 430
460       CONTINUE
          NTYPE=5
          KKP=(KK-1)*8
          IF(NTYPE.EQ.NTYPL) GO TO 185
          NOFF=NWRITE*2
          WRITE(5,4035) NOFF
4035      FORMAT(6X,' ABE,LOOPB+',O4)
          WRITE(5,6031) KKP
          NWRITE=NWRITE+1
          NA(NWRITE)=NCOUNT
          NCOUNT=1
```

470

```
            NTYPL=NTYPE
            GO TO 5050
185         NCOUNT=NCOUNT+1
            WRITE(5,6031) KKP
5050        KK=K3+KSPAN
            IF(KK.LE.NT) GO TO 420
            GO TO 440
C
800         NA(NWRITE+1)=NCOUNT
            DO 6500 JX=1,NWRITE
6500        NA(JX)=NA(JX+1)
C           PERMUTE THE RESULTS TO NORMAL ORDER
C           DONE IN TWO STEPS
C           PERMUTATION FOR SQUARE FACTORS OF N
            NP(1)=KS
            IF(KT.EQ.0) GO TO 890
            K=KT+KT+1
            IF(M.LT.K) K=K-1
            J=1
            NP(K+1)=JC
810         NP(J+1)=NP(J)/NFAC(J)
            NP(K)=NP(K+1)*NFAC(J)
            J=J+1
            K=K-1
            IF(J.LT.K) GO TO 810
            K3=NP(K+1)
            KSPAN=NP(2)
            KK=JC+1
            K2=KSPAN+1
            J=1
C           PERMUTATION FOR SINGLE VARIATE TRANSFORM
            WRITE(5,818)
818         FORMAT(4X,'BITREV',/1X,'BITREV:',
     +             /9X,'MOV #BITAB,R0',/9X,'MOV NLOOP,R3',
     +             /1X,'LOOPC:',
     +             /9X,'MOV (R0)+,R1',/9X,'MOV (R0)+,R2',
     +             /9X,'LDF (R1),AC0',/9X,'LDF (R2),AC1',
     +             /9X,'STF AC0,(R2)+',/9X,'STF AC1,(R1)+',
     +             /9X,'LDF (R1),AC0',/9X,'LDF (R2),AC1',
     +             /9X,'STF AC0,(R2)',/9X,'STF AC1,(R1)',
     +             /9X,'SOB R3,LOOPC',/9X,'RTS PC')
            NLOOP=0
            WRITE(5,819)
819         FORMAT(1X,'BITAB:')
820         CONTINUE
            KKP=(KK-1)*8
            K2P=(K2-1)*8
            WRITE(5,822) KKP,K2P
822         FORMAT(9X,'A+',O6,',','A+',O6)
            NLOOP=NLOOP+1
            KK=KK+INC
            K2=KSPAN+K2
            IF(K2.LT.KS) GO TO 820
830         K2=K2-NP(J)
            J=J+1
            K2=NP(J+1)+K2
            IF(K2.GT.NP(J)) GO TO 830
            J=1
840         IF(KK.LT.K2) GO TO 820
            KK=KK+INC
            K2=KSPAN+K2
            IF(K2.LT.KS) GO TO 840
            IF(KK.LT.KS) GO TO 830
            JC=K3
            GO TO 890
```

```
890        IF(2*KT+1.GE.M) GO TO 2000
600        WRITE(5,1000)
1000       FORMAT(1H ,'SOMETHING IS WRONG')
2000       CONTINUE
           WRITE(5,824) NLOOP
824        FORMAT(1X,'NLOOP:',2X,O6)
           NTIMES=N/4-1
           WRITE(5,4000)
4000       FORMAT(1X,'TRIG:')
           DO 4001 J=1,NTIMES
           IBASE=(J-1)*9
           WRITE(5,4002) (ARRAY(IBASE+KK), KK=1,9)
4002       FORMAT(1X,'.FLT2',E17.9,2('.',E17.9)/,
          +           1X,'.FLT2',E17.9,2('.',E17.9)/,
          +           1X,'.FLT2',E17.9,2('.',E17.9))
4001       CONTINUE
           WRITE(5,4100)
4100       FORMAT(1X,'LOOPB:')
           NTIMES=NWRITE/5
           NREM=NWRITE-5*NTIMES
           DO 4102 I=1,NTIMES
           IBASE=(I-1)*5
           WRITE(5,4101) (NA(J+IBASE), J=1,5)
4101       FORMAT(1X,O6,4('.',O6))
4102       CONTINUE
           IF(NREM.EQ.0) GO TO 4104
           IBASE=NTIMES*5
           WRITE(5,4103) (NA(J+IBASE), J=1,NREM)
4103       FORMAT(1X,4(O6,'.'))
4104       CONTINUE
           WRITE(5,4003)
4003       FORMAT(1X,7X,'.END',/)
           END FILE 5
           STOP
           END
```

When run, RAD4 asks the user for the desired power of 4 ($m = 2, 3, 4,$ or 5) and then generates a file RDX40m.MAC on DK0.

Warning: RDX405.MAC, the 1K transform driver routine, requires 226 blocks of storage so that twice this number of free blocks must be available on DK0 during the generation phase.

H.3 TEST PROGRAM

The following program, RX3.FOR, tests and times RDX403.MAC, the 64 complex point transform. After compilation (R FORTRA, RX3 = RX3), modules are linked using RX3 = RX3, SYSLIB, FORLIB, RDX403, RX4BUT. Note that SYSLIB is always mentioned before FORLIB when system routines (the timer in this case) are to be used:

```
C          RX3.FOR: TEST AND TIME 64 POINT COMPLEX TRANSFORM
C          DIMENSION 128 BECOMES 2*N FOR AN N-POINT TRANSFORM
           DIMENSION B(128),A(128)
           COMMON /XX/A
           XN=64.
           PI=3.1415926
C          COMPUTE COS - j SIN
```

472

```
        DO 110 J=1,64
        XJ=J-1
        B(2*J-1)= COS(2.*PI*XJ/XN)
110     B(2*J)=  -SIN(2.*PI*XJ/XN)
C       ************************
        T0=SECNDS(0.0)
C       LOAD ARRAY 1000 TIMES
        DO 100 L=1,1000
        DO 100 J=1,64
        A(2*J-1)=B(2*J-1)
100     A(2*J)=B(2*J)
        T1=SECNDS(T0)
C       ************************
        T0=SECNDS(0.0)
C       LOAD ARRAY AND DO FFT 1000 TIMES
        DO 400 L=1,1000
        DO 640 J=1,64
        A(2*J-1)=B(2*J-1)
640     A(2*J)=B(2*J)
400     CALL RDX403
        TT1=SECNDS(T0)
        TD=(TT1-T1)/1.
C       ************************
C       DIFFERENCE IS FFT TIME IN MSEC.
        WRITE(7,250)TD
250     FORMAT(1X,'TIME = ',F14.5, ' MILLISECONDS')
        WRITE(7,260) A
260     FORMAT(1X,E15.8,5X,E15.8)
        STOP
        END
```

H.4 RADIX-4 FFT BUTTERFLY FPP MODULES

Note that in those PDP-11's where FPP and CPU may overlap in operation (i.e., 11/45, 50, 55, 60, and 70), time may be saved in the sections so denoted:

```
        .TITLE  RX4BUT
        .GLOBL  ABC ABE S924 S707 S383 OFFSET
        .IRPC X, 012345
R'X=%'X                         ;gp REGS ARE R0, R1, ..., R5
AC'X=%'X                        ;fp REGS ARE AC0, AC1, ..., AC5
                                ;AC6, AC7 ARE MEMORY LOCATIONS
        .ENDM
SP=%6
PC=%7
;
        .MACRO  PROLOG A1,A2,A3,A4
        MOV     @(R5)+,COUNT    ;SET UP COUNTER (+ EXP)
        MOV     (R5)+,R0        ;R0=KK
        MOV     R0,R1
        LDF     (R0),AC0
        ADD     R4,R1           ;K1 (OVERLAP)
        MOV     R1,R2
        LDF     AC0,AC1         ;AC0,AC1 ← A(KK)
        ADD     R4,R2           ;K2 (OVERLAP)
        ADDF    (R2),AC0        ;AC0 ← AKP=A(KK)+A(K2)
        MOV     R2,R3           ;OVERLAP
        SUBF    A1,AC1          ;AC1 ← AKM=A(KK)-A(K2)
        ADD     R4,R3           ;K3 (OVERLAP)
```

473

```
          LDF       (R1)+,AC2
          LDF       AC2,AC3           ;AC2,AC3 ← A(K1)
          ADDF      (R3),AC2          ;AC2 ← AJP=A(K1)+A(K3)
          STF       AC2,AC5           ;AC5 ← AJP
          SUBF      (R3)+,AC3         ;AC3 ← AJM=A(K1)-A(K3)
          ADDF      AC0,AC2           ;AC2 ← AKP+AJP
          STF       AC2,(R0)+         ;A(KK) ← AKP+AJP
          SUBF      AC5,AC0           ;AC0 ← AJP=AKP-AJP
          STF       AC0,A2            ;AC7 ← AJP
          LDF       (R0),AC0
          LDF       AC0,AC2           ;AC0,AC2 ← B(KK)
          SUBF      (R2),AC0          ;AC0 ← BKM=B(KK)-B(K2)
          STF       AC0,AC5           ;AC5 ← BKM
          ADDF      (R2),AC2          ;AC2 ← BKP=B(KK)+B(K2)
          LDF       (R1),AC0          ;AC0 ← B(K1)
          SUBF      (R3),AC0          ;AC0 ← BJM=B(K1)-B(K3)
          STF       AC0,AC4           ;AC4 ← BJM
          LDF       (R1),AC0          ;AC0 ← B(K1)
          ADDF      (R3),AC0          ;AC0 ← BJP=B(K1)+B(K3)
          STF       AC0,AC6           ;AC6 ← BJP
          ADDF      AC2,AC0           ;AC0 ← BJP=BJP+BKP
          STF       AC0,(R0)          ;B(KK) ← BJP
          SUBF      AC6,AC2           ;AC2 ← BJP=BKP-BJP
          STF       AC2,A3            ;AC6 ← BJP
          LDF       AC5,AC0           ;AC0 ← BKM
          SUBF      AC3,AC0           ;AC0 ← BKM=BKM-AJM
          STF       AC0,A4            ;AC2 ← BKM
          .ENDM
;
ABC:
          PROLOG (R2)+,AC7,AC6,AC2
          ADDF      AC5,AC3           ;AC3 ← BKP=BKM+AJM
          LDF       AC1,AC0           ;AC0 ← AKM
          ADDF      AC4,AC0           ;AC0 ← AKM=AKM+BJM
          SUBF      AC4,AC1           ;AC1 ← AKP=AKM-BJM
          STF       AC2,AC5           ;AC5 ← BKM
          STF       AC1,AC4           ;AC4 ← AKP
          LDF       AC0,AC1           ;AKM
          MULF      @(R5)+,AC0        ;AC0 ← AKM*(SIN3-COS3)
          MOV       R5,-(SP)          ;SAVE TABLE POINTER ON STACK
          MOV       -2(R5),R5         ;MOVE TRIG TBLE POINTER INTO R5
          ADD       #4,R5             ;SKIP OVER ENTRY ALREADY DONE
          MULF      (R5)+,AC2         ;AC2 ← BKM*(SIN3+COS3)
          ADDF      AC5,AC1           ;AC1 ← AKM+BKM
          MULF      (R5)+,AC1         ;AC1 ← (AKM+BKM)*COS3
          ADDF      AC1,AC0           ;AC0 ← AKM*SIN3+BKM*COS3
          SUBF      AC2,AC1           ;AC1 ← AKM*COS3-BKM*SIN3
          STF       AC0,(R3)          ;B(K3)
          STF       AC1,-(R3)         ;A(K3)
          LDF       AC3,AC2           ;AC2 ← BKP
          LDF       AC4,AC1           ;AC1 ← AKP
          MULF      (R5)+,AC1         ;AC1 ← AKP*(SIN1-COS1)
          MULF      (R5)+,AC3         ;AC3 ← BKP*(COS1+SIN1)
          ADDF      AC4,AC2           ;AC2 ← AKP+BKP
          MULF      (R5)+,AC2         ;AC2 ← (AKP+BKP)*COS1
          ADDF      AC2,AC1           ;AC1 ← AKP*SIN1+BKP*COS1
          SUBF      AC3,AC2           ;AC2 ← AKP*COS1-BKP*SIN1
          STF       AC1,(R1)          ;B(K1)
          STF       AC2,-(R1)         ;A(K1)
          LDF       AC7,AC1           ;AC1 ← AJP
          LDF       AC6,AC3           ;AC3 ← BJP
          LDF       AC3,AC0           ;AC0 ← BJP
          ADDF      AC1,AC0           ;AC0 ← AJP+BJP
          474
```

```
        MULF      (R5)+,AC1         ;AC1 ← AJP*(SIN2-COS2)
        MULF      (R5)+,AC3         ;AC3 ← BJP*(COS2+SIN2)
        MULF      (R5)+,AC0         ;AC0 ← COS2*(AJP+BJP)
        MOV       (SP)+,R5          ;GET TABLE POINTER BACK INTO R5
        ADDF      AC0,AC1           ;AC1 ← BJP*COS2+AJP*SIN2
        SUBF      AC3,AC0           ;AC0 ← AJP*COS2-BJP*SIN2
        STF       AC1,(R2)          ;B(K2)
        STF       AC0,-(R2)         ;A(K2)
        DEC       COUNT
        BNE       ABC+4
        JMP       @(R5)+
;
ABE:
        PROLOG (R2),(R2)+,(R2),(R3)
;
        ADDF      AC5,AC3           ;AC3 ← BKP=BKM+AJM
        STF       AC3,(R1)          ;B(K1) ← BKP
        LDF       AC1,AC0           ;AC0 ← AKM
        ADDF      AC4,AC0           ;AC0 ← AKM=AKM+BJM
        STF       AC0,-(R3)         ;A(K3) ← AKM
        SUBF      AC4,AC1           ;AC1 ← AKP=AKM-BJM
        STF       AC1,-(R1)         ;A(K1) ← AKP
        DEC       COUNT
        BNE       ABE+4
        JMP       @(R5)+
;
S707:
        PROLOG (R2)+,AC7,AC6,AC2
;
        ADDF      AC5,AC3           ;AC3 ← BKP=BKM+AJM
        LDF       AC1,AC0           ;AC0 ← AKM
        ADDF      AC4,AC0           ;AC0 ← AKM=AKM+BJM
        SUBF      AC4,AC1           ;AC1 ← AKP=AKM-BJM
        SUBF      AC0,AC2           ;AC2 ← BKM-AKM
        MULF      MP7,AC2           ;AC2 ← -.707*(BKM-AKM)=.707(AKM-BKM)
        STF       AC2,(R3)          ;B(K3)
        MULF      MP72,AC0          ;AC0 ← AKM*-1.414
        ADDF      AC0,AC2           ;AC2 ← -.707*(AKM+BKM)
        STF       AC2,-(R3)         ;A(K3)
        ADDF      AC3,AC1           ;AC1 ← AKP+BKP
        MULF      P7,AC1            ;AC1 ← .707*(AKP+BKP)
        STF       AC1,(R1)          ;B(K1)
        MULF      P72,AC3           ;AC3 ← BKP*1.141
        SUBF      AC3,AC1           ;AC1 ← (AKP-BKP)*.707
        STF       AC1,-(R1)         ;A(K1)
        LDF       AC7,AC1           ;AC1 ← AJP
        STF       AC1,(R2)          ;B(K2)
        LDF       AC6,AC1           ;AC1 ← BJP
        NEGF      AC1               ;AC1 ← -BJP
        STF       AC1,-(R2)         ;A(K2)
        DEC       COUNT
        BNE       S707+4
        JMP       @(R5)+
;
        .MACRO MUL8 S383,K9M3,K9P3,COS3,K3M9,K3P9,COS1,0PF,ACX,MP72
S383:
        PROLOG (R2)+,AC7,AC6,AC2
;
        ADDF      AC5,AC3           ;AC3 ← BKP=BKM+AJM
        LDF       AC1,AC0           ;AC0 ← AKM
        ADDF      AC4,AC0           ;AC0 ← AKM=AKM+BJM
        SUBF      AC4,AC1           ;AC1 ← AKP=AKM-BJM
        STF       AC2,AC5           ;AC5 ← BKM
```

```
            STF     AC1,AC4         ;AC4 ← AKP
            LDF     AC0,AC1         ;AKM
            MULF    K9M3,AC0        ;AC0 ← AKM*(SIN3-COS3)
            MULF    K9P3,AC2        ;AC2 ← BKM*(COS3+SIN3)
            ADDF    AC5,AC1         ;AC1 ← AKM+BKM
            MULF    COS3,AC1        ;AC1 ← (AKM+BKM)*COS3
            ADDF    AC1,AC0         ;AC0 ← AKM*SIN3+BKM*COS3
            SUBF    AC2,AC1         ;AC1 ← AKM*COS3-BKM*SIN3
            STF     AC0,(R3)        ;B(K3)
            STF     AC1,-(R3)       ;A(K3)
            LDF     AC3,AC2         ;AC2 ← BKP
            LDF     AC4,AC1         ;AC1 ← AKP
            MULF    K3M9,AC1        ;AC1 ← AKP*(SIN1-COS1)
            MULF    K3P9,AC3        ;AC3 ← BKP*(COS1+SIN1)
            ADDF    AC4,AC2         ;AC2 ← AKP+BKP
            MULF    COS1,AC2        ;AC2 ← (AKP+BKP)*COS1
            ADDF    AC2,AC1         ;AC1 ← AKP*SIN1+BKP*COS1
            SUBF    AC3,AC2         ;AC2 ← AKP*COS1-BKP*SIN1
            STF     AC1,(R1)        ;B(K1)
            STF     AC2,-(R1)       ;A(K1)
            LDF     AC7,AC3         ;AC3 ← AJP
            OPF     AC6,AC3         ;AC3 ← AJP-/+BJP
            MULF    P7,AC3          ;AC3 ← (AJP-/+BJP)*.707
            STF     AC3,(R2)        ;B(K2)
            LDF     ACX,AC1         ;AC1 ← AJP/BJP
            MULF    MP72,AC1        ;AC1 ← AJP*-1.41/BJP*-1.41
            ADDF    AC1,AC3         ;AC3 ← (AJP+BJP)*-.707/(AJP-BJP)*.707
            STF     AC3,-(R2)       ;A(K2)
            DEC     COUNT
            BNE     S383+4
            JMP     @(R5)+
            .ENDM
;
            MUL8    S383,K9M3,K9P3,COS3,K3M9,K3P9,COS1,SUBF,AC7,MP72
            MUL8    S924,J9M3,J9P3,JCOS3,J3M9,J3P9,JCOS1,ADDF,AC6,MP72
;
OFFSET:     ASR     R4
            ASR     R4
            JMP     @(R5)+
;
MP7:        .FLT2   -.7071067812
P7:         .FLT2    .7071067812
MP72:       .FLT2   -1.4142135624
P72:        .FLT2    1.4142135624
K9M3:       .FLT2   .541196100
K9P3:       .FLT2   -1.306562965
K3M9:       .FLT2   .541196100
K3P9:       .FLT2   1.306562965
COS1:       .FLT2   .382683432
COS3:       .FLT2   -.923879533
J9M3:       .FLT2   .541196100
J9P3:       .FLT2   1.306562965
J3M9:       .FLT2   -.541196100
J3P9:       .FLT2   1.306562965
JCOS3:      .FLT2   .382683432
JCOS1:      .FLT2   .923879533
M72:        .FLT2   1.414213563
AC6:        .FLT2   0.0
AC7:        .FLT2   0.0
COUNT:      0
            .END
```

476

Bibliography

Abrams, M. D., and Stein, P. G., *Computer Hardware and Software: An Interdisciplinary Introduction*, Addison-Wesley, Reading, Massachusetts, 1973.

Aho, A. V., Hopcroft, J. E., and Ullman, J. D., *The Design and Analysis of Computer Algorithms*, Addison-Wesley, Massachusetts, 1976.

Baase, S., *Computer Algorithms: Introduction to Design and Analysis*, Addison-Wesly, Massachusetts, 1978.

Barron, D. W., *Recursive Techniques in Programming*, American Elsevier, New York, 1968.

Bell, C. G., and A. Newell, *Computer Structures: Readings and Examples*, McGraw-Hill, New York, 1971.

Bell, C. G., Mudge, J. C., and McNamara, J., *Computer Engineering*, Digital Press, Maynard, Ma., 1978.

Bell, J., "Threaded code,", *Communications of the ACM*, Vol. 16, pp. 370-372, June 1973.

Berztiss, A. T., *Data Structures - Theory and Practice*, Academic Press, New York, 1971.

Blankinship, W. A., "Note on computing autocorrelations," *IEEE Trans. Acoustics, Speech, Signal Processing*, vol. ASSP-22, pp. 76-77, February 1974.

Brender, R. F.,"Turning cousins into sisters: an example of software smoothing of hardware differences," in *Computer Engineering*, ibid Bell *et. al.*

Brillinger, P. C., and D. J. Cohen, *Introduction to Data Structures and Nonnumeric Computations*, Prentice-Hall, Englewood Cliffs, N.J., 1972.

Brinch Hansen, P., *Operating System Principles*, Prentice-Hall, Englewood Cliffs, N.J., 1973.

Broihier, J. C., and Crowley, M. J., "A RSTS/E audio response application," pp. 1355-1375, *DECUS Proceedings*, Boston, May 1977.

Burr, W. E., and Smith, W. R., "Comparing computer architectures," *Datamation*, vol. 23, pp. 48-52, February 1977.

Chamberlin, H., "A sampling of techniques for computer performance of music," *BYTE*, vol. 2, pp. 62-83, September 1977.

Cohen, L. J., *Operating Systems Analysis and Design*, Spartan Books, New York, 1970.

Denning, P. J., "Third Generation Computer Systems," *Computing Surveys*, Vol. 3, No. 4, 1971.

Donovan, J. J., *Systems Programming*, McGraw-Hill, New York, 1972.

Elovitz, H. S., Johnson, R. W., McHugh, A., and Shore, J. E., "Automatic translation of English text to phonetics by means of letter-to-sound rules," *NRL Report 7948*, January 21, 1976.

Flanagan, J. L., *Speech Analysis, Synthesis and Perception*, Springer-Verlag, New York, 1972.

Flanagan, J. L., and Rabiner, L. R., *Speech Synthesis*, Dowden, Hutchison, and Ross, Pennsylvania, 1973.

Flores, I., *Computer Organization*, Prentice-Hall, Englewood Cliffs, N.J., 1969.

Flores, I., *Data Structure and Management*, Prentice-Hall, Englewood Cliffs, N.J., 1970.

Foster, C. C., *Computer Architecture*, Van Nostrand Reinhold, New York, 1970.

Gagnon, R. T., "VOTRAX real time hardware for phoneme synthesis of speech," *Conf. Rec.*, 1978 IEEE International Conf. on Acoustics, Speech, and Signal Processing, pp. 175-178, Tulsa, Oklahoma.

Gear, C. W., *Computer Organization and Programming*, 2nd ed., McGraw-Hill, New York, 1974.

Giloi, W. K., *Interactive Computer Graphics: data structures, algorithms, languages*, Prentice-Hall, Englewood Cliffs, N.J., 1978.

Haberman, A. N., *Introduction to Operating Systems Design*, Science Research Associates, Chicago, 1976.

Hayes, J. P., *Computer Architecture and Organization*, McGraw-Hill, New York, 1978.

Hellerman, H., *Digital Computer System Principles*, 2nd ed., McGraw-Hill, New York, 1973.

Holt, R. C., *Structured Concurrent Programming with Operating Systems*, Addison-Wesley, Reading, Massachusetts, 1978.

Husson, S. S., *Microprogramming: Principles and Practices*, McGraw-Hill, New York, 1970.

Jackson, T. L., *PDP-11/60 Microprogramming Specification*, Digital Equipment Corporation, Massachusetts, 1977.

Johnson, L. R., *System Structure in Data, Programs, and Computers*, Prentice-Hall, Englewood Cliffs, N.J., 1970.

Katzan, H., *Computer Organization and the System/370*, Van Nostrand Reinhold, New York, 1971.

Katzan, H., Jr., *Operating Systems - A Pragmatic Approach*, Van Nostrand Reinhold, New York, 1973.

Kent, W., "Assembler-Language Macroprogramming", *Computing Surveys*, Vol. 1, No. 4, 1969.

Knuth, D. E., *The Art of Computer Programming, Vol. 1: Fundamental Algorithms*, Addison-Wesley, Reading, Massachusetts, 1968.

Lewis, T. G., and Smith, M. Z., *Applying Data Structures*, Houghton Mifflin, Boston, 1976.

Lowry, E. S., and Medlock, C. W., "Object code optimization", *Communications of the ACM*, vol. 12, pp. 13-22, Jan. 1969.

Markel, J. D., and Gray, A. H., *Linear Prediction of Speech*, Springer-Verlag, New York, 1976.

Mauer, W. D., *Programming: An Introduction to Computer Languages and Techniques*, Holden-Day, San Francisco, 1968.

Maurer, H. H., *Data Structures and Programming Techniques*, Prentice-Hall, Englewood Cliffs, N.J., 1977.

McNamara, J. E., *Technical Aspects of Data Communication*, Digital Press, Massachusetts, 1977.

Moorer, J. A., "Signal processing aspects of computer music," *Proceedings of the IEEE*, vol. 65, pp. 1108-1137, August 1977.

Morris, L. R., "Fast speech spectrogram reduction and display on minicomputer/ graphics processors", *IEEE Trans. Acoustics, Speech, Signal Processing*, vol. ASSP-23, pp. 297-300, June 1975.

Morris, L. R., "Fast digital signal processing software package for the PDP-11," *DECUS Program Library*, no. 11-296, Nov. 1976.

Morris, L. R., "Automatic generation of time efficient digital signal processing software," *IEEE Trans. Acoustics, Speech, Signal Processing*, vol. ASSP-25, pp. 74-79, February 1977.

Morris, L. R. and Mudge, J. C., "Speed enhancement of digital signal processing software via microprogramming a general purpose computer", *IEEE Trans. Acoustics, Speech, Signal Processing*, vol. ASSP-26, pp. 135-139, April 1978.

Morris, L. R., "A comparative study of time efficient FFT and WFTA programs for general purpose computers," *IEEE Trans. Acoustics, Speech, Signal Processing*, vol. ASSP-26, pp. 141-150, April 1978.

Morris, L. R. and Pearlman, M., "A software package for fast speech spectrogram generation and display on PDP-11 computer/graphics processors," *DECUS Program Library*, no. 11-361, July 1978.

Morris, L. R., "Fast FORTRAN/RT-11 Syslib software for implementing the Naval Research Laboratory 'English text to VOTRAX parameters' algorithm," *DECUS Program Library*, no. 11-375, November 1978.

Morris, L. R. and Allan, D. I., "An LPC k-parameter software speech synthesizer via dynamic microprogramming a general purpose computer," *Conf. Record*, IEEE International Conference on Acoustics, Speech and Signal Processing, Washington, D. C., April 1979.

Mudge, J. C., "Design decisions achieve price/performance balance in mid-range computers," *Computer Design*, pp. 87-95, August 1977.

Newman, W. and Sproull, R., *Principles of Interactive Computer Graphics*, McGraw-Hill, New York, 1973.

Oppenheim, A. V., and Schafer, R. W., *Digital Signal Processing*, Prentice-Hall, Englewood Cliffs, N.J., 1975.

Organick, E. I., *The Multics System: An Examination of Its Structure*, MIT Press, Cambridge, Mass., 1972.

Pfeifer, L. L., "Multiplication reduction in short-term autocorrelation," *IEEE Trans. Audio and Electroacoustics*, vol. AU-21, pp. 556-558, December 1973.

Phister, M., *Logical Design of Digital Computers*, Wiley, New York, 1959.

Presser, L., and J. R. White, "Linkers and Loaders", *Computing Surveys*, Vol. 4, No. 3, 1972.

Rabiner, L. R., and Gold, B., *Theory and Application of Digital Signal Processing*, Prentice-Hall, Englewood Cliffs, N.J., 1975.

Rabiner, L. R., and Schafer, R. W., *Digital Processing of Speech Signals*, Prentice-Hall, Englewood Cliffs, N. J., 1978.

Ralston, A., *Introduction to Programming and Computer Science*, McGraw-Hill, New York, 1971.

Rosin, R. F., "Contemporary Concepts of Microprogramming and Emulation", *Computing Surveys*, Vol. 1, No.4, 1969.

Rubinfeld, L. P., "A proof of the modiified Booth's algorithm for multiplication," *IEEE Trans. on Computers*, vol. C-24, pp. 1014-1015, October 1975.

Shaw, A. C., *Logical Design of Operating Systems*, Prentice-Hall, Englewood Cliffs, N.J., 1974.

Sheingold, D. H., *Analog-digital Conversion Handbook*, Analog Devices, Norwood, Massachusetts.

Singleton, R. C., "An algorithm for computing the mixed radix fast Fourier transform," *IEEE Trans. Audio and Electroacoustics*, vol. AU-17, pp. 93-103, June 1969.

Snyder, D. C., "Computer performance improvement by measurement and micro-programming," *Hewlett-Packard Journal*, pp. 17-24, February 1975.

Steiglitz, K., *An Introduction to Discrete Systems*, John Wiley, New York, 1974.

Stone, H. S., and Siewiork, D., *Introduction to Computer Organization* and Data Structures, McGraw-Hill, New York, 1975.

Stone, H. S., *Introduction to Computer Architecture*, SRA, Chicago, 1975.

Strecker, W. D., "Cache memories for PDP-11 family computers," *Proc. 3rd Annual Symposium on Computer Architecture*, pp. 155-158, 1976.

Szymanski, T. G., "Assembling code for machines with span dependent instructions," *Comm. ACM*, vol. 21, pp. 300-308, April 1978.

Tannenbaum, A. S., *Structured Computer Organization*, Prentice-Hall, Englewood Cliffs, N.J., 1976.

T-Thong, and Liu, B., "Fixed-point fast Fourier transform error analysis", *IEEE Trans. Acoustics, Speech, Signal Processing*, vol. ASSP-24, pp. 563-573, December 1976.

Van Dam, A., and D. E. Rice, "On-Line Text Editing: A Survey", *Computing Surveys*, Vol. 3, No. 3, 1971.

Wald, B. et. al, *Military Computer Architectures*, special issue of *Computer*, IEEE, October 1977.

Walker, T. M., *Introduction to Computer Science: An Interdisciplinary Approach*, Allyn and Bacon, Boston, 1972.

Watson, R. W., *Timesharing System Design Concepts*, McGraw-Hill, New York, 1970.

Wegner, P., *Programming Languages, Information Structures, and Machine Organization*, McGraw-Hill, New York, 1968.

Wiggins, R., and Brantingham, L., "Three-chip system synthesizes human speech", *Electronics*, vol. 51, pp. 109-116, August 31, 1978.

Wirth, N., *Algorithms + Data Structures = Programs*, Prentice-Hall, Englewood Cliffs, N.J., 1976.

PDP-11 Peripherals Handbook, Digital Equipment Corp., Maynard, Mass., 1978.

PDP-11/04/34/45/55/60 Processor Handbook, Digital Equipment Corp., Maynard, Mass., 1978.

Index

Absolute loader, 226
Absolute vs. relative symbolic addressing, 248
Accumulator, 22-24
Activity analysis, 278
Address specification (general), 26-35
  address modification, 28-29
  autoindexing, 32-33
  basic addressing, 26-28
  deferred addressing, 33-35
  general registers, 30-31
  immediate mode, 31-32
ALGOL, 157
Algorithms, 280-290
  data-dependent, 280-281
  data-independent, 282-283
Analog information, 3
Analog-to-digital converters, 316-320
  structure, 318-319
AND, 67, 145, 434-435
Architectures for operand addressing, 19-26
  general register machines, 23-24
  one address machines, 22-23
  three address machines, 19-21
  three-plus-one address machines, 19-21
  two address machines, 21-22
  zero address machines, 24-26
Arithmetic, 47-48
Arithmetic and logical unit (ALU), 8, 47
Argument transmission, 98-101

Arrays, 155-160
  address calculation, 156-160
  manipulation, 155-160
ASCII character set, 129, 440-443
ASCII-to-octal conversion, 153
Assembler, 38-41, 76-79, 171-177
  alphabetic symbols, 40
  hashing of symbol table, 172-173
  numeric symbols, 40
  packed entries, 174-177
  radix-50 symbols, 175
  symbol table, 38, 171
  two-pass flowchart, 172
Assembly language statements
  control, 39, 41
  declarative, 39
  imperative, 39
Autocorrelation, 283-285, 291-298
  conventional implementation, 283-284
  definition, 283
  P/B algorithm, 285
  time/space/hardware results, 296-298
  via microcoding, 368-370
Autogen software, 290-291
  characteristics, 290
  generation, 291

Balanced operation, 249
BASIC, 2

Basic computer systems, 7-11, 376
Batch systems, 391-392
Binary
  addition, 426-427
  coding, 17
  numbers, 418-422
  subtraction, 427-430
Bit, 10
  least significant, 53, 420-421
  map, 381
  most significant, 420-421
Block structured language, 157
Block transfers, 211-212
Boolean algebra, 436-439
Booth's algorithm (signed multiplication), 136-139
Bootstrap,
  disk, 236
  paper tape, 224-226
Branch instructions
  offset calculation, 68-69
  signed, 144
  simple, 67-69
  unsigned, 143-145
  use of condition codes, 49
Branch microtests (BUT's), 203-204
Buffer, 212, 248-249, 262
  circular buffer, 162-166
  double buffer, 255, 337-338
Bus, 46
Bytes
  .BYTE directive, 129
  character representation, 129, 440-443
  .EVEN directive, 129
  manipulation, 128, 353-358
  integer range, 54

Cache memory, 81, 84-86
Call, 94
  by address, 99-100
  by value, 99-100
Carry, 129-131
CDC-6600, 21
Central processor modes, 255-259
Characters, 10
  ASCII, 129, 440-443
  packed, 174-177
  Radix-50, 174-176, 443-444
Circular buffer, 162-166
Circular shift, 135
Commands
  Dynamic debugger, 274-275
  Editor, 262-266
  RT-11 program requests, 383

RT-11 system, 377
Computational kernel (ck), 282
Computer
  applications, 3
  architecture, 4
  capabilities, 4
  communications, 395-397
  hardware elements, 7-11, 186-190
  implementation, 4
  limitations, 4
  organization, 4
Concurrent I/O, computation, 211
Condition codes, 49
  manipulation, 133
Control and status registers
  AR-11 A/D, 321
  AR-11 clock, 321
  DECdisk (RK05), 235
  DECtape, 229
  high-speed paper-tape punch, 222
  high-speed paper-tape reader, 222
  terminal/keyboard 215
  printer/punch, 216
Control unit, 8
Coroutines, 110-112
  concept, 110-112
  PDP-11 implementation, 111
  sample program, 254-255
Created symbol, 114
Cycle stealing, 212
Cylinder, 233

Data
  management, 394
  storage, manipulation, and access, 395
Data-base systems, 394-395
Data structures
  arrays, 155-160
  binary tree, 125-126
  circular buffer, 162-166
  deques, 160-162
  in practice, 177-178
  lists, 166-171
  queues, 162-166
  stacks, 95-96, 160
Debugging session, 274-275
Decimal-to-octal conversion, 424-426
Decision table, 16-17
DECdisk operation, 234-236
DECtape operation, 226-232
Deferred address, 33-35, 63-66
DeMorgan's laws, 438
Density, 234

Deposit mechanism, 223
Deques, 160-162
Destination address, 21
Device independent I/O, 385
Digital information, 3
Digital oscilloscope, 337-347
Digital signal processing (DSP) algorithms, 282-290
Digital-to-analog converters, 317-318
  characteristics, 318
  structure, 317
  use in drawing pictures, 321-324
Digit position weighting value, 52
Direct memory access (DMA), 211
Directories, 380-381
Discrete Fourier transform, 285-286, 336-337
  definition, 285
  properties, 336-337
Disk operating system components, 377-390
Disk operation; 233-236
Display file, 325
Division
  algorithm, 141-142
  DIV (EIS) syntax, 142
Documentation, 12-17
Double buffering, 255, 337-338
Dump, 217-220
Dynamic debugging techniques, 272-275

Editor, 261-266
  general attributes, 261-262
  RT-11 EDIT, 262-264
  sample EDIT session, 264
  window editors, 264-266
Effective address, 30
Emulator trap (EMT), 253
Entry point, 269
Errors, 12, 214
Exclusive-OR, 145, 435-436
Execute cycle, 37, 209
Exponent, 55-57, 146-147
Extended arithmetic element (EAE), 81
Extended instruction set (EIS), 81
External symbol, 269

Family concept, 80
Fastbus, 81, 84
Fast Fourier transform (FFT), 286-290, 298-306
  bit reversal phase, 287
  butterfly modules (EIS), 299-305
  ck (FORTRAN), 298
  derivation, 286-290
  EIS autogen thread generator, 456-460
  FORTRAN program, 289

  flow diagram, 287
  in-place characteristic, 288
  real signal analysis, 337
  time-efficient EIS implementation, 298-305
  time/space/hardware results, 305-306
  use for DFT evaluation, 286-290
  via microcoding, 372
Fetch cycle 37, 207-208
FIFO, 162
Fields, 40-41
  comments, 40-41
  label, 40-41
  operand, 40
  operator/operation, 40
File directory, 384
File management utility, 383-385
Files--organization and access, 377-380
Fixed-head disk, 233
Fixed-point arithmetic, 129-145
  carry, 129-131
  condition code manipulation, 133-134
  division, 141-143
  integer representation, 54
  multiple precision addition/subtraction, 131-133
  multiplication, 136-141
  overflow, 130-131
  shifting, 134-135
Flip-flop, 185
Floating-point arithmetic, 146-147
  multiplication/division, 146
  addition/subtraction, 147
Floating-point instruction set (FIS), 81, 147-150
  instructions, 147-148
  sample programs, 148-150
Floating-point numbers, 55-58
  normalized form, 56-57
  range, 55, 57
  representation (general), 55-57
  PDP-11, 57-58
Floating-point processor (FPP), 81, 150-153
  architecture, 150
  instructions, 151-152
  sample programs, 152-153
Flowcharts, 13-15
FORTRAN, 2
Fraction, 55-57, 146-147
Free list, 169

Garbage collection, 169
Gate, 181-182
General purpose registers, 23, 30
Global, 269
Grouped-bit number systems, 422-426

Hashing, 172-174
Head of list, 166
Hexadecimal numbers, 53, 423-424
High level language output code, 306-315
  in-line code (EIS/FIS), 308-310
  in-line code (EIS/FPP), 310-312
  in-line code (VAX-11), 312-313
  threaded code, 306-308
High level language vs. assembler, 314-315
Hybrid computers, 3

IBM 370, 22
IBM 650, 21
IBM 1130, 23
IBM 1620, 22
IBM 7090, 23
I-fetch, 37, 207-208
Immediate operand, 31-32, 70, 75
Indexed address, 32-33, 62-63, 75
Indexed-sequential file, 378-379
Index register, 30-31
Indirect address, 33-35, 63-66
Initial load problem, 223-226
In-line code, 282, 308-313
Input/output page, 50
Input/output programming, 211-259
  basic I/O, 9, 212-213
  disc bootstrap, 236
  octal dump, 217-220
  paper tape bootstrap, 223-226
Input/output programming systems, 250-255
Instruction organization, 19-26
Instruction processing phases, 35-37, 82-84, 207-209
  E-phase, 37, 83, 209 (11/60)
  general, 35-37
  I-phase, 37, 82, 207-208 (11/60)
  O-phase, 37, 83, 208 (11/60)
  PDP-11, 82-84
  PDP-11/60, 207-209
Instruction register (IR), 36, 196, 202, 208
Instruction timing, 84-85
Instruction trace program, 278-279
Instruction types, 18
  arithmetic/logical, 18
  input/output, 18
  internal data transmission, 18
  program control, 18
Interactive graphics processors, 324-335
  characteristics, 324-326
  data formats, 328-330
  display file manipulation, 331-332
  instruction set, 326-328

light pen interaction, 333-335
  subroutines/subpictures, 332-333
Interlocked I/O, computation, 211
Internal and external data forms, 153-154
Interpreter, (command string), 387
Interrupts, 236-247
  automatic priority interrupts, 239-240
  linkages, 237
  machine state during interrupt, 237
  priority levels and masking, 241-247
  service routines (ISR), 236
  stacking of interrupts, 238-239

Jump instruction, 92
Jump table construct, 93

Keyboard/reader, 213-215

Label, 39-41
Latency, 234
Least significant digit, (LSD), 53
Library, 269
Light pen, 333-335
Linking of programs, 269-272
Lists, 166-171
Loader, 266-272
  linking loader, 271-272
  program linking, 269-272
  program relocation, 267-269
  transfer vectors, 271
Local symbol, 114
Location counter, 38, 76
Logical circuits, 181-186
Logical operations, 145-146, 434-439
Longwords, 54
Loop, 28-30, 49

Machine and memory hierarchies, 80-88
Machine language, 17
MACRO-11, 76-79, 112-123
  direct assignment, 76
  location counter, 76
  WORD directive, 77
Macros, 112-123
  concatenation, 118-119
  conditional assembly, 116-117
  defining PDP-11 macros, 112-113
  location and created symbols, 113-114
  macros calling macros, 115-116
  nesting, 114-115
  numeric arguments, 119
  recursive macro calls, 116-117

repeat blocks, 118
  use in code translation (VAX-11 example), 119-122
Masking, 241-242
Massbus, 81
MC68000, 22
Memory address register (MAR), 36, 82-83, 190-191, 202
Memory data register (MDR), 36, 82-83, 190-191, 202
Memory management, 86-88, 255-259
Memory organization, 10-11, 50-51
Memory protection, 86-88
Memory unit, 9, 50-51
Microbranching, 203-204
Microcycle (11/60), 198-200
Microinstructions, 190-191, 198-199
  sequencing, 203-204
Microprogrammed machines, 190-192
Microprogramming, 190-209, 366-374
  applications software speed enhancement, 366-374
  fundamentals, 190-209
Minicomputer system (typical configuration), 5-6
Mnemonic, 37
Modular software, 337-338
Monitor, 385-390
  characteristics, 385-386
  memory management, 390
  memory organization, 389-390
  organization, 387
  residency table, 387-389
  user interaction, 386
Most significant bit, 53, 420-431
Moving head disk, 234
Multiple precision addition/subtraction, 131-133
Multiplication
  array multiplication, 140
  Booth's algorithm, 136-139
  fixed-point, 136-141
  MUL (EIS syntax), 139-140
  MUL (microcoded on PDP-11/60), 205-207
Multiprogramming, 398-416
Multilevel directories, 381
Music synthesis, 362-366

Negative numbers, 53-54, 427-431
Newton-Raphson algorithm, 280-281
Nibble, 10
Normalized form, 56-57
NOT, 61, 145
Number representation, 53-58
Number systems, 51-53, 417-431

Object program, 39

Octal
  addition, 427
  numbers, 53, 422-423
  subtraction, 430-431
Octal-to-ASCII conversion, 153-154
Octal-to-decimal conversion, 424-426
One's complement arithmetic, 430
Operating systems, 375-397
  batch and time-sharing, 391-393
  characteristics, 390-391
  computer communications, 391
  control, 382-383
  real-time control, 391
Operator's console, 451-455
Optimizing compilers, 308-315
OR, 67, 145, 435
Overflow, 130-131
Overlap of computation, I/O programming, 249-250, 254-255

Parallelism in microcoding, 205-207
Parameterization of labels, 114
PDP-11
  alphanumeric character representation, 58, 440-443
  arithmetic and logical unit (ALU), 47
  compatibility, 81-82
  condition codes (N, Z, C, V), 46, 48
  control unit, 48-50
  data representation, 51-58
  fast arithmetic processors, 47-48
  flow diagrams of addressing modes, 74-76
  general register address modes
    autodecrement, 62, 74
    autodecrement deferred, 65, 75
    autoincrement, 62, 74
    autoincrement deferred, 64, 74
    index, 63, 75
    index deferred, 65, 75
    register, 61, 74
    register deferred, 64, 74
  implementations, 80-81
  instruction implementation on PDP-11/60, 198-209
  instruction formats
    branch instructions, 67-69
    double operand instructions, 66-67
    EIS (MUL, DIV, ASH, ASHC), 135-143
    expanded branches, 143-145
    FIS (FADD, FSUB, FMUL, FDIV), 147-150
    FPP, 150-153
    Jump (JMP), 92
    Jump-to-Subroutine (JSR), 94-96
    logical instructions, 145-146

operate instructions, 59-60
Return-from-Subroutine (RTS), 95-97
rotates, 135
shifts, 134
simple conditional branches, 67-69
single operand instruction, 60-66
subtract one and branch (SOB), 49
instruction processing phases, 82-84
instruction repertoire, 445-450
optional enhancements, 81
program counter (PC), 48
PC address modes
  absolute, 71, 75
  immediate, 70, 75
  relative, 72-75
  relative deferred, 72, 76
processor status register (PSW), 48
relative mode offset computation, 73-74
structure, 46-51
word and byte numbering, 51
  Unibus concept, 46
PDP-11/60 Micromachine, 191-209
  A and B scratch pads (ASP, BSP), 193-197
  ALU input/output, 197-198
  ALU functions, 192-193
  CIN, 197
  C scratch pad (CSP), 197
  datapaths, 192, 194-195
  datapath I/O, 202
  D(C), 197
  D register, 197
  guard register, 201
  microcycle, 198-200
  microword fields, 194-195
  organization, 191, 194-195, 368
  RES bits, 201
  residual control, 202-203
  shift register, 197, 201-202
  shift tree, 198, 200-201
  X multiplexer, 197
Peripheral device, 212
Platter, 233
Pointer, 23, 33, 95, 99, 106, 166, 262
Polling, 236
Position coefficient, 52
Position independent programming (PIC), 102-107
  automatic PIC, 105
  nonautomatic PIC, 105-107
  PIC address modes, 102-104
  relocating pointers, 106-107
  setting up fixed core locations, 105-106
Primary storage, 9
Printer/punch, 215-217

Priority interrupt, 238-247
Program analysis programs, 278-279
Program coding, 17
Program definition and documentation, 12-17
Program execution speeds (PDP-11), 84-86
Programming A/D, D/A, clock,
  320-324, 339-340, 361, 364-366
Programming phases, 11
Program structures for computational kernels (ck's)
  in-line code, 292
  subroutines, 293
  threaded code, 293-294
  knotted code, 295-296
PROGRAMS
  add (11/60 microprogram), 199
  add byte (macro), 113
  amplitude spectrum of DFT, 344-345
  array
    address calculation, 156-160
    exchange, 115
    multiplication, 140
    summing elements (general), 29, 31-33
    summing elements (PDP-11), 78-79
    zeroing, 34, 49
  ASCII-to-octal conversion, 153
  autocorrelation
    conventional, 283-284
    in-line, 292
    subroutines, 293
    threaded code, 294
    knotted code, 295-296
  block move
    (looped), 113
    (in-line), 118
  bootstrap
    DECdisk, 236
    paper tape, 224
  complex multiplication (FPP), 152-153
  coroutines using RT-11 system macros, 255
  DECdisk
    bootstrap, 236
    read, 235
  DECtape
    read, 232
    search, 232
  deque operations, 161
  digital oscilloscope, 338-347
  division, 142
  drawing square, VT-11, 331
  drawing triangle via D/A, 322-323
  English-to-VOTRAX, control, 357-358
  factorial
    integer, recursive EIS, 110

floating-point, non-recursive FIS, 148-149
fast Fourier transform (FFT)
  ck (FORTRAN EIS/FIS code), 309-310
  ck (FORTRAN EIS/FPP code), 311-312
  ck (FORTRAN threaded code), 307-308
  ck (FORTRAN VAX-11 code), 313
  EIS Autogen thread generator, 456-460
  EIS butterflies, 298-306
  FORTRAN, 289
  FPP Autogen thread generator, 467-472
  FPP butterflies, 473-476
  two real from one complex, 341-342
  2N-point real from N-point complex, 342-343
graphic display of waveform, DFT, 344-347
graphics subroutines via DSTOP, 332-333
hashing of byte strings, 173
instruction trace, 278-279
I-phase (11/60 microprogram), 207
jump table, 93
keyboard echo, 217
light pen follow (VT-11), 334
list manipulation, 168
longword
  addition, 133
  negation, 134
Modest Multiprogramming System, 409-415
multiplication
  microprogrammed inner loop, 206
  signed, 138-139
  unsigned, 136
music synthesis, 364-366
Newton-Raphson root finding, 281
octal dump (PIC), 219-220
octal-to ASCII conversion, 153-154
O-phase of 11/60 instruction (microprogram), 208
paper tape
  bootstrap, 224
  reader (interrupts, PIC), 242
polynomial evaluation (Horner's technique)
  FIS, 149-150
  FPP, 152
program tracing (T-bit), 278-279
queue, de-queue, 165
queue manipulation, 163
radix-50 packing, 176
RT-11 console I/O via programmed request, 252
RT-11 programmed request, 251
SOBC (macro), 118
speech synthesis, 360-362
string comparison, 356
substring extraction, 355
sum of squares of complex data, 140

time teller, 245-246
translation of text to speech, 357-358
tree traversal, 125
triggered A/D sampler, 339-340
VAX-11 index modes on PDP-11 (macro), 120-122
windowing an array, 340-341
Program tracing, 278-279
Processor status word (PSW), 46, 256
Pseudo-op, 41
Pure code, 108

Queues, 162-166

Radix, 52
Radix-50
  character set, 443-444
  use in symbol table, 174-176
Random access file, 379
Random access memory, 50
Real-time control systems, 393
Real-time programming, 393
Records and buffering, 248-250
Recursive programs
  factorial calculation (EIS), 110
  tree traversal, 125
Reentrancy, 107-109
Register, 60-61
Relocation of programs, 267-269
Repeat block, 118
Rotational delay, 234
RT-11 programmed request, 250-253
  example of use, 252
  expansion, 251
  role of EMT, 253

Sampling of data, 319-320
Second gp register set, 256
Scheduler, 405
Secondary storage, 9, 377
Sector, 233
Seek time, 234
Self intializing program, 30
Self modifying program, 30, 108, 120, 225, 284
Sequential access, 9, 226, 379
Shifting, 134-135
SNOBOL4, 123
Software bootstraps, 223-226, 236
  disk, 236
  paper tape, 223-226
Source address, 21
Source language, 38
Source program, 39

Stacks, 95-96, 160
  concept, 95
  data structure, 160
  stack pointer, 95
  use, 95-97
Status bits, 213
Stored program concept, 18
String manipulation, 353-358
Structure of a file, 377-380
Spectral analysis via FFT, 335-347
Speech analysis/synthesis, 351-362
  characteristics, 351-352
  Speak & Spell, 352
  via software, 358-362
  via microcoding, 371
  VOTRAX, 352-358
Speech spectrogram, 347-350
  conventional production, 347
  fast, software production and display, 348
  software package, 349
Subroutines/Subprograms, 94-101
  argument transmission, 94, 98-101
  PDP-11 subroutine call, 94, 96
  PDP-11 subroutine return, 95-97
  recursion, 109-110
  reentrancy, 109-110
  register usage, 101
  transfer of control, 94
  utility, 94
Supervisor, 404-407
Symbolic assembler, 38-41, 76-79, 171-177
  assembly process, 38
  directives, 77
  flow chart, 172
  hashing, 172-174
  label, 39
  location counter, 38, 76
  packed entries, 174-177
  symbolic addresses, 39
  symbol table, 39, 171

Tables (MMS), 400-403
Tail of list, 166
Tape and disk units, 226-236

Task, 107-108, 391
T-bit trap, 278
Temporary storage, 97-98
Terminal programming, 213-223
Threaded code, 293-294, 306-308
Time-sharing systems, 391-393
Time/space tradeoffs, 279-283, 291-298
Time teller routine, 242-247
Towers of Hanoi, 325, 461
Trace, 278
Track, 233
Transfer rate, 234
Transfer vector, 271
Translation of text to speech, 353-358
Translation process, 38
Traps, 253-254, 278
  occurence, 253
  system handling, 254
  T-bit, 278
Two's complement arithmetic, 428-430

UNIBUS, 46-47
UNIVAC 1105, 22

Variable length instruction processor, 59
VAX-11, 22, 119-122, 149, 312-315
Vectored interrupts, 239-247
VOTRAX, 352-358
VTECO, 265
VT-11, 324-350
  data format, 328-330
  instruction set, 326-328
VT-52, 265
VT-100, 265

Window editors, 264-266
Words, 54

XOR, 145, 435-436

Zero address machine,
  24-26, 147-150, 308-310
Z8000, 22